CERTIFICATE IN ESG INVESTING CURRICULUM 2024

COPYRIGHT

© 2023 CFA Institute. All rights reserved.

No part of this publication may be reproduced or transmitted in any form or by any means, electronic or mechanical, including photocopy, recording, or any information storage and retrieval system, without permission of the copyright holder.

To view a list of CFA Institute trademarks and the Guide for the Use of CFA Institute Marks, please visit our website at www.cfainstitute.org.

ISBN: 978-1-953337-91-7 (paper)
ISBN: 978-1-953337-90-0 (ebook)

Authors

Chapters 1 and 2

Clarisse Simonek, CFA, WeESG
Thomas Verhagen, WeESG

Chapter 3

Shuen Chan, Legal & General Investment Management (LGIM), Real Assets
Iancu Daramus, Fulcrum Asset Management

Chapter 4

Vincent van Bijleveld, Finance Ideas Sustainable Investment Consultants
Rudy Verstappen, Altera Vastgoed

Chapters 5, 6 and 9

Paul Lee, Redington

Chapter 7

Ben Yeoh, CFA, RBC Global Asset Management

Chapter 8

J. Jason Mitchell, Man Group plc

CFA Institute would also like to sincerely thank the following contributors:

Sylvia Solomon, ASIP
Brishni Mukhopadhyay, CFA
Monica Filkova, CFA
Claudia Gollmeier, CFA, CIPM
Matyas Horak, CFA, FRM
Vincent Piscaer
Maxine Wille, CFA
Christopher Merker, CFA
Priyanka Shukla, CFA, CIPM
Peter Wilmshurst, CFA

CONTENTS

	Copyright	ii
	Authors	ii
	Introduction	xi
	ESG Update	xi
	Foreword by Marg Franklin	xii

Chapter 1 — Introduction to ESG Investing — 13

- Introduction — 13
- What Is ESG Investing? — 14
  - Long-Termism and ESG Investing — 14
  - ESG Definition and Scope — 15
- Types of Responsible Investment — 16
  - Responsible Investment — 17
- Macro-Level Debate on ESG Incorporation — 22
  - Macro-Level Debate on Integrating ESG Considerations — 22
- Financial Materiality of ESG Integration — 30
  - Efficiency and Productivity — 31
  - Reduced Risk of Fines and State Intervention — 32
  - Improved Ability to Benefit from Sustainability Megatrends — 36
- Challenges in Integrating ESG Factors — 39
- ESG Factors' Influence on Financial Performance — 41
- Putting ESG Investing into Practice — 43
  - Investment Decisions — 43
  - Shareholder Engagement — 44
  - Policy Engagement — 44
- Key Initiatives — 45
  - United Nations Initiatives — 45
  - Reporting Initiatives — 50
- Key Facts — 53
- Further Reading — 55
- *References* — 56
- *Practice Problems* — 60
- *Solutions* — 64

Chapter 2 — The ESG Market — 67

- Introduction — 67
- ESG Investing in Numbers — 68
- Market Drivers of ESG and Challenges in ESG Integration — 72
- Asset Owners — 74
  - Pension Funds — 76
  - Insurance — 80
  - Sovereign Wealth — 80
  - Individual (Retail) Investors and Wealth Management — 81
- Asset Managers, Fund Promoters, and Financial Services — 82
  - Asset Managers — 82
  - Fund Promoters — 83

	The Role of the PRI for Consultants and Retail Financial Advisers	84
	Investment Platforms	84
	Fund Labelers	85
	Financial Services	85
Policymakers, Regulators, Investees, Governments, Civil Society, and Academia		86
	Examples of Policy and Regulatory Developments across the Globe	88
	Investees	97
	Governments	97
	Civil Society	97
	Academia	98
Key Facts		98
Further Reading		100
References		*101*
Practice Problems		*104*
Solutions		*108*

Chapter 3   Environmental Factors   111

Introduction	112
Key Environmental Issues—Climate Change	113
Tipping Elements	124
The Cost of Climate Change	125
Pressures on Natural Resources	132
Depletion of Natural Resources	133
Pollution, Waste, and a Circular Economy	139
Systemic Relationships between Business Activities and Environmental Issues	142
Systemic Risks to the Financial System: Physical and Transitional Risks	142
The Relationship between Natural Resources and Business	145
Supply, Operational, and Resource Management Issues	146
Supply Chain Transparency and Traceability	147
Key "Megatrends" and Drivers Influencing Environmental Change in Terms of Potential Impact on Companies and Their Environmental Practices	151
Growth of Environmental and Climate Policies	151
International Climate and Environmental Agreements and Conventions	151
Carbon Pricing	165
Assessment of Materiality of Environmental Issues	168
Corporate and Project Finance	169
Public Finance Initiatives	170
Asset Management	172
Approaches to Account for Material Environmental Analysis and Risk Management Strategies	174
Levels of Environmental Analysis	175
Analyzing Environmental Risks	177
Nature Assessment and TNFD Framework	185
Nature and Biodiversity	186
Assessing Nature	187

	Applying Material Environmental Factors to Financial Modeling, Ratio Analysis, and Risk Assessment	191
	Opportunities Relating to Climate Change and Environmental Issues	195
	Circular Economy	196
	Clean and Technological Innovation	197
	Green and ESG-Related Products	203
	Blue Economy	209
	Key Facts	210
	Appendix	212
	The TNFD Disclosure Framework Approach	214
	Further Reading	217
	References	*218*
	Practice Problems	*235*
	Solutions	*240*

Chapter 4   Social Factors   243

Introduction	244
Social and Environmental Megatrends	244
What Are Social Megatrends?	244
Globalization	245
Automation and Artificial Intelligence (AI)	245
Inequality and Wealth Creation	246
Digital Disruption, Social Media, and Access to Electronic Devices	246
Changes to Work, Leisure Time, and Education	247
Changes to Individual Rights and Responsibilities and Family Structures	248
Changing Demographics, Including Health and Longevity	248
Investor Initiatives: Equitable Circulation of COVID-19 Vaccines	249
Urbanization	249
Religion	250
Environmental Megatrends with Social Impact	250
Key Social Issues and Business Activities	251
Internal Social Factors	252
Human Capital Development	252
Working Conditions, Health, and Safety	253
Human Rights	254
Labor Rights	257
External Social Factors	259
Stakeholder Opposition and Controversial Sourcing	259
Product Liability and Consumer Protection	260
Social Opportunities	261
Animal Welfare and Antimicrobial Resistance	261
Identifying Material Social Factors for Investors	261
Country	262
Sector	263
Company Level	264
Application of Social Factors in Investments	264
Materiality or Risk Assessment	264
Quality of Management	267

	Ratio Analysis and Financial Modeling	268
Key Facts		269
	Megatrends	269
Further Reading		270
References		*272*
Practice Problems		*274*
Solutions		*279*

Chapter 5 — Governance Factors — 283

Corporate Governance: Accountability and Alignment	284
What Is Governance? Why Does It Matter?	284
Formalized Corporate Governance Frameworks	288
Corporate Governance Codes	288
Major Corporate Scandals: Governance Failures and Lessons Learned	290
Shareholder Engagement and Alignment	301
Characteristics of Effective Corporate Governance: Board Structure and Executive Remuneration	303
Board Structure, Diversity, Effectiveness, and Independence	304
Executive Remuneration	309
Characteristics of Effective Corporate Governance: Transparency, Capital Allocation, and Business Ethics	311
Reporting and Transparency	311
Financial Integrity and Capital Allocation	313
Business Ethics	314
Structural Corporate Governance Differences in Several Major World Markets	315
Examples from Developed Markets	316
Examples from Emerging Markets	323
Corporate Governance and the Independent Audit Function	328
Reviewing Financial Statements, Annual Reports, and Wider Reporting (including Sustainability Reports)	328
The Independence of Audit Firms and Conflicts of Interest	330
Auditor Rotation	330
Sampling and Audit Work	330
Enhanced Auditor Reports	331
Auditor Liability	332
Internal Audit	332
Corporate Governance and the Investment Decision-Making Process	333
Integrating Governance into Investment and Stewardship Processes	337
Key Facts	338
Further Reading	339
References	*340*
Practice Problems	*342*
Solutions	*348*

Chapter 6 — Engagement and Stewardship — 353

Introduction	353
Stewardship and Engagement: What's Involved and Why It's Important	354
What Is Stewardship? What Is Engagement?	354

	Why Engagement?	359
	Engagement in practice	361
Codes and Standards		364
	Code Revisions in 2020	366
	Code Provisions	367
Engagement Styles		369
	Styles: Top-Down and Bottom-Up	369
	Styles: Issue-Based and Company-Focused	370
Effective Engagement: Forms, Goal Setting		370
	Forms of Engagement	370
	Success Factor Characteristics of Engagement Approach	371
	Success Factor Characteristics of Investor Collaboration	371
	Strategy and Tactics: Goal Setting and Resources	372
	Strategy and Tactics: Investment Context	373
	Setting Engagement Objectives	376
	Practicalities of Engagement	377
Voting		377
	Escalation of engagement	380
	Collective engagement	382
Engagement across Different Asset Classes		385
	Corporate Fixed Income	386
	Sovereign Debt	387
	Private Equity	388
	Infrastructure	388
	Property	389
	Fund Investments	389
Key Facts		390
Further Reading		391
References		*392*
Practice Problems		*395*
Solutions		*399*

Chapter 7   ESG Analysis, Valuation, and Integration — 403

The Different Approaches to ESG Integration		404
	Qualitative ESG Analysis	404
	Quantitative ESG Analysis	404
	Tools and Elements of ESG Analysis	406
	Challenges in ESG Integration	407
	Criticism of ESG Integration	408
ESG Integration in Listed Equities		409
	Idea Generation	410
	Materiality Assessments and Gathering Information	410
	Managed and Unmanaged Risks	416
	Scorecards to Assess ESG Factors	417
	The Challenges of Company Disclosures of ESG Information	417
ESG Integration in Listed Equities: Valuation Considerations		419
	Discounted Cash Flow Input Adjustments	419
	Adjustments to Valuation Multiples	423
ESG Integration in Other Asset Classes: Fixed Income		423

	ESG Integration in Sovereign and Investment-Grade Fixed Income	425
	ESG Integration in Credit-Sensitive Fixed Income	427
	ESG Integration in Credit Ratings	427
	Potential Bias in Ratings	428
	Green Bonds	428
ESG Integration in Other Asset Classes: Real Estate and Private Markets		429
	ESG Integration in Real Estate Markets	429
	ESG Integration in Private Equity	429
Case Studies in ESG Integration		431
ESG Integration Databases and Software		438
	ESG Assessment and Ratings of Issuers	439
Mutual Fund and Fund Manager ESG Assessment and Other Uses of ESG Data		442
	ESG Index Providers	443
	Primary and Secondary ESG Data Sources	444
	Conclusion	444
Key Facts		445
Further Reading		445
References		*447*
Practice Problems		*449*
Solutions		*454*

Chapter 8 Integrated Portfolio Construction and Management — 459

Introduction	460
ESG Integration: Strategic Asset Allocation Models	460
ESG Integration: Asset Manager Selection	465
Approaches to ESG Integration: Portfolio-Level Framework	468
Approaches to ESG Integration: Role of Analysts, Portfolio Managers, and Internal and External Research	469
Role of Analysts	469
Role of Portfolio Managers	470
Complementing Internal Research with External ESG Resources	471
Measuring Portfolio Carbon Intensity	473
Approaches to ESG Integration: Quantitative Research Developments in ESG Investing	474
The Evolution of ESG Integration: Exclusionary Preferences and Their Application	476
Universal Exclusions	477
Conduct-Related Exclusions	478
Faith-Based Exclusions	478
Idiosyncratic Exclusions	478
Applying Exclusionary Preferences	478
ESG Screening within Portfolios and across Asset Classes: Fixed Income, Corporate Debt, and ESG Bonds	480
Fixed Income (Government, Sovereign, Corporate, and Other)	480
ESG Screening within Portfolios and across Asset Classes: Green Securitization and Sovereign Debt Green Securitization	484
ESG Screening within Portfolios and across Asset Classes: Listed and Private Equity	487

Contents

Long–Short, Hedge Fund Equity Strategies	488
Private Equity	489
ESG Screening within Portfolios and across Asset Classes: Real Assets–Real Estate and Infrastructure	491
Integrating ESG Screens in Portfolios to Manage Risk and Generate Returns	495
ESG Integration to Manage Portfolio Risk	495
ESG Integration to Generate Investment Returns	495
Quantitative Approaches That Embed ESG Factors	496
Applying ESG Screenings to Individual Listed and Unlisted Companies and Collective Investment Funds	498
Listed Companies and Collective Investment Funds	498
Unlisted Companies and Collective Investment Funds	502
Managing the Risk and Return Dynamics of an ESG-Integrated Portfolio	503
Full ESG Integration, Exclusionary Screening, and Positive Alignment	505
Full ESG Integration	506
Exclusionary Screening	507
Positive Alignment or Best in Class	507
ESG Strategies, Objectives, Investment Considerations, and Risks: Thematic and Impact Investing	508
Thematic Investing	508
Impact Investing	509
ESG Integration in Index-Based Portfolios and Established Datasets	512
Relying on Established Datasets	515
Key Facts	517
Further Reading	518
References	*522*
Practice Problems	*526*
Solutions	*531*

Chapter 9 Investment Mandates, Portfolio Analytics, and Client Reporting — 535

Introduction	535
Accountability to Clients and Alignment with Them	536
Clarifying Client Needs: Defining the ESG Investment Strategy	538
Fully Aligning Investment with Client ESG Beliefs	540
Developing Client-Relevant ESG-Aware Investment Mandates	544
Holding Fund Managers Accountable	544
Evaluating Managers' Investment Strategies	545
The RFP Process	546
Assessing Stewardship and Engagement	548
Investment Integration	549
Engagement and Voting	550
Assessing the Quality of Engagement and Voting	551
Greenwashing and Its Consequence	552
Categories of Misrepresentation	552
Reputational Consequences	553
Using Data to Combat Greenwashing	554
Assessing Indirect and Direct Impacts of Greenwashing	555
Addressing Greenwashing	556

Misleading statements	557
Core Greenwashing Characteristics	557
Regulation, Code, Guidelines	558
Tailoring the ESG Investment Approach to Client Expectations	565
Holding Managers to Account: Monitoring Delivery	568
Portfolio-Wide Assessment	573
Holding Managers to Account: Measurement and Reporting	575
Annual Reports	576
Real World Impacts	577
Disclosures	577
Key Facts	579
Appendix: CFA Institute Disclosure Standards and SFDR Disclosures	579
Global ESG Disclosure Standards for Investment Products	579
SFDR Disclosures	580
ESMA Supervisory Briefing on Sustainability	581
Further Reading	582
References	*584*
Practice Problems	*588*
Solutions	*593*

INTRODUCTION

This curriculum provides essential reading for candidates of the Certificate in ESG Investing, including examples, key facts and self-assessment questions.

Content is valid for examinations taken beginning 1 February 2024. Candidates must confirm that the version of the curriculum they are preparing from corresponds to and is valid for the period when they intend to take the examination.

ESG Update

Changes will be made as necessary to keep the curriculum up to date.

Details of the date of the latest change and of any outstanding corrections or amendments can be found at CFAInstitute.org.

Candidates should check the website on a regular basis to ensure their study material is up to date.

Curriculum errata are periodically updated and posted by test date online on the Curriculum Errata webpage (www.cfainstitute.org/en/programs/submit-errata). If you believe you have found an error in the curriculum, you can submit your concerns through our curriculum errata reporting process found at the bottom of the Curriculum Errata webpage.

The exam is made up of one unit, covering the following topic areas:

1. Introduction to ESG Investing
2. The ESG market
3. Environmental factors
4. Social factors
5. Governance factors
6. Engagement and stewardship
7. ESG analysis, valuation and integration
8. Integrated Portfolio Construction and Management
9. Investment mandates, portfolio analytics and client reporting

The curriculum provides broad coverage and excellent preparation for the examinations.

The Certificate in ESG Investing is developed, administered and awarded by CFA Institute.

FOREWORD BY MARG FRANKLIN

At CFA Institute, our long history demonstrates that while many things change in our industry over time, finance will always require highly educated, ethical professionals who pledge to put their clients' interests first. As an organization, we remain committed to providing financial education that investment professionals need from career entry through to career exit.

These efforts speak directly to our mission: to lead the investment profession globally by promoting the highest standards of ethics, education, and professional excellence for the ultimate benefit of society.

Investment professionals play a vital role in understanding, analyzing, and ultimately placing value on plans and intentions around environmental, social, and governance (ESG) factors.

This idea is not new or novel to us. We have been focused on the impact of ESG considerations for years and have remained steadfast in our commitment to arming investment professionals with the information and tools they need to address it head on.

We need to understand the investment implications, both from a risk and opportunity perspective, to ensure we are well prepared to act in the best interest of and at the behest of our clients globally.

Since we first globalized the Certificate in ESG Investing, the consistent demand underscores the very need that the Certificate addresses, closing a critical skills gap that persists throughout the investment industry. We've seen commitment from asset managers, asset owners, and other investors to offer the Certificate to their staffs, and we applaud these employers for their ability to recognize the benefits of continuing education for practitioners at their firms, for the benefit of their clients.

We continue to invest in the curriculum for the Certificate in ESG Investing, applying the same rigorous standards that we apply across our Education portfolio. We are proud of our teams and partners who work tirelessly to interpret, understand, and incorporate the latest concepts into the Certificate in ESG Investing, connecting with practitioners throughout the industry, ensuring that learners are educated on the entire ESG-ecosystem.

Thank you to everyone who has played a role in the continued success of the Certificate in ESG Investing. We remain committed to the creation of educational opportunities and resources that equip investment professionals with the tools necessary to navigate the complex ESG landscape.

Margaret Franklin, CFA
President and CEO, CFA Institute

CHAPTER 1

Introduction to ESG Investing

LEARNING OUTCOMES

Mastery	The candidate should be able to:
☐	**1.1.1** define ESG investment and different approaches to ESG investing: responsible investment, socially responsible investment, sustainable investment, best-in-class investment, ethical/values-driven investment, thematic investment, green investment, social investment, shareholder engagement
☐	**1.1.2** define the following sustainability-based concepts in terms of their strengths and limitations: corporate social responsibility and triple bottom line (TBL) accounting
☐	**1.1.3** describe the benefits and challenges of incorporating ESG in decision making, and the linkages between responsible investment and financial system stability
☐	**1.1.4** explain the concepts of the financial materiality of ESG integration, double materiality, and dynamic materiality and how they relate to ESG analysis, practices, and reporting
☐	**1.1.5** explain different ESG megatrends, their systemic nature, and their potential impact on companies and company practices
☐	**1.1.6** explain the three ways in which investors typically reflect ESG considerations in their investment process
☐	**1.1.7** explain the aims of key supranational ESG initiatives and organizations and the progress achieved to date

INTRODUCTION

There was a time when environmental, social, and governance (ESG) issues were the niche concern of a select group of ethical or socially responsible investors. That time is long gone.

The consideration of ESG factors is becoming an integral part of investment management. Asset owners and investment managers are developing ways to incorporate ESG criteria into investment analysis and decision-making processes. The emergence of responsible investment proponents, such as the **Principles for Responsible Investment (PRI)**, has encouraged a fundamental change in investment practices whereby investors explicitly employ ESG factor analysis to enhance returns and better manage risks. Societal, regulatory, and client pressure and the growing evidence of the direct financial benefits of incorporating ESG analysis have led integration to become more mainstream.

This chapter provides an overview of the concept of ESG investing, as well as the different types of responsible investment approaches and their implications. It highlights the main benefits of integrating ESG factors and identifies ways in which ESG investing is implemented in practice.

ESG investing sits within a broader context of sustainability; this chapter also highlights a number of key initiatives in the business and investment communities that seek to assist all parties to navigate the associated challenges.

2 WHAT IS ESG INVESTING?

> 1.1.1 define ESG investment and different approaches to ESG investing: responsible investment, socially responsible investment, sustainable investment, best-in-class investment, ethical/values-driven investment, thematic investment, green investment, social investment, shareholder engagement

ESG investing is an approach to managing assets where investors explicitly incorporate environmental, social, and governance (ESG) factors in their investment decisions with the long-term return of an investment portfolio in mind.

Long-Termism and ESG Investing

Many investment industry stakeholders, including finance regulators, have recognized the shortfalls of short-termism in investment practice and have sought to increase awareness of the value of long-termism and encourage this approach.

Short-termism covers a wide range of activities. For the purpose of this topic, the two most relevant ones are

- trading practices, where investors trade based on anticipation of short-term price movements rather than long-term value, and
- investors engaging with investee companies in a way that prioritizes maximizing near-term financial results, over long-term value creation.

These short-term strategies might offer rewards but may have adverse long-term consequences. With its disproportionate focus on immediate returns, short-termism may leave companies less willing to take on projects (such as research and development) that may take multiple years—and patient capital—to develop. This was indeed confirmed by a review conducted on the UK equity market and long-term decision making by Professor John Kay (2012) for the UK Government. Instead of productive investment in the real economy, short-termism may promote bubbles, financial instability, and general economic underperformance. Furthermore, short-term investment strategies tend to ignore factors that are generally considered more long term, such as ESG factors. Because of the adverse effects mentioned, regulators are catching up and taking action. For example, the *Shareholder Rights Directive (SRD)* was issued by the European Union (EU) in September 2020, requiring investors to be active owners and to act with a more long-term focus.

What Is ESG Investing?

In other words, ESG investing aims to correctly identify, evaluate, and price social, environmental, and economic risks and opportunities. ESG factors are defined in Exhibit 1.

Exhibit 1: ESG Factors Defined

	Environmental Factors	Social Factors	Governance Factors
Definition	Pertain to the natural world. These include the use of and interaction with renewable and non-renewable resources (e.g., water, minerals, ecosystems, and biodiversity).	Affect the lives of humans. The category includes the management of human capital, non-human animals, local communities, and clients.	Involve issues tied to countries and/or jurisdictions or are common practice in an industry, as well as the interests of broader stakeholder groups.

ESG Definition and Scope

There is currently no universal standard for what factors are included under the "E," "S," and "G" definitions, and they may overlap with one another. For example, animals and animal well-being may be considered in both environmental and social factors. How these factors are split among themselves varies depending on those who are defining them (for example, for an ESG framework) and their stakeholders. Stakeholders are members of groups without whose support an organization would cease to exist (Freeman and Reed 1983), as well as communities impacted by companies and regulators.

Examples of the definition and scope of ESG issues can be illustrated by Exhibit 2.

Exhibit 2: Examples of ESG Topics

Environmental	Social	Governance
• Climate change	• Human rights	• Bribery and corruption
• Resource depletion	• Modern slavery	• Executive pay
• Waste	• Health and safety	• Board diversity and structure
• Pollution	• Working conditions	• Trade association, lobbying, and donations
• Deforestation	• Employee relations	• Tax strategy

Source: PRI (2020).

3. TYPES OF RESPONSIBLE INVESTMENT

☐ **1.1.2** define the following sustainability-based concepts in terms of their strengths and limitations: corporate social responsibility and triple bottom line (TBL) accounting

ESG investing is part of a group of approaches collectively referred to as **responsible investment**. ESG investing is concerned with how ESG issues can impact the long-term return of assets and securities, whereas other responsible investment approaches can also take into account non-financial value creation and reflect stakeholder values in an investment strategy. The main investment approaches are presented in this section to demonstrate the wide spectrum of responsible investment activities.

Responsible investment is an umbrella term for the various ways in which investors can consider ESG factors within security selection and portfolio construction. As such, it may combine financial and non-financial outcomes and complements traditional financial analysis and portfolio construction techniques.

All forms of responsible investment (except for engagement) are ultimately related to portfolio construction (in other words, which securities a fund holds). The exception of engagement (both by equity owners and bond holders) concerns whether and how an investor tries to influence an issuer's behavior on ESG matters. There is no standard classification in the industry; the types of responsible investment overlap and evolve over time.

Exhibit 3 illustrates some of the conceptual differences between these approaches and how they range from strictly "finance-only" investment, with limited or no consideration of ESG factors, to the other end of the spectrum, where the investor may be prepared to accept below-market returns in exchange for the high positive impact the projects and companies in the portfolio can deliver. As investors move toward the left-hand side of the spectrum, they are increasingly interested in aligning their capital with contributing to positive environmental and/or social outcomes.

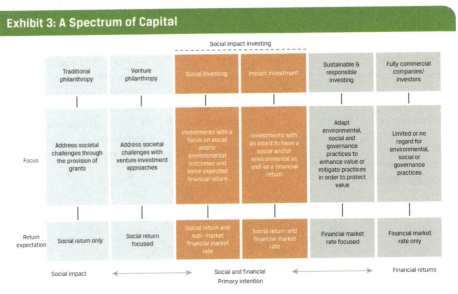

Exhibit 3: A Spectrum of Capital

Note: For illustrative purposes only.

Source: OECD (2019). Used with permission of OECD; permission conveyed through Copyright Clearance Center, Inc.

Responsible Investment

Responsible investment is a strategy and practice to incorporate ESG factors into investment decisions and active ownership (PRI 2020). It is sometimes used as an umbrella term for some (or all) of the investment approaches mentioned in the following subsections.

At a minimum, responsible investment consists of mitigating risky ESG practices in order to protect value. To this end, responsible investment encompasses how ESG factors might influence the risk-adjusted return of an asset and the stability of an economy and how investment in and engagement with assets and investees can impact society and the environment. The key investment approaches falling under responsible investment are discusses next. These approaches are not mutually exclusive, and they can be combined into a single portfolio.

Socially Responsible Investment

Socially responsible investment (SRI) refers to approaches that apply social and environmental criteria in evaluating companies. Investors implementing SRI generally score companies using a chosen set of criteria, usually in conjunction with sector-specific weightings. A hurdle is established for qualification within the investment universe, based either on the full universe or sector by sector. This information serves as a first screen to create a list of SRI-qualified companies.

SRI ranking can be used in combination with best-in-class investment, thematic funds, high-conviction funds, or quantitative investment strategies.

Best-in-Class Investment

Best-in-class investment (also known as "positive screening") involves selecting only the companies that overcome a defined ranking hurdle, established using ESG criteria within each sector or industry.

- Typically, companies are scored on a variety of factors that are weighted according to the sector.
- The portfolio is then assembled from the list of qualified companies.

Bear in mind, though, that not all best-in-class funds are considered "responsible investments."

Due to its all-sector approach, best-in-class investment is commonly used in investment strategies that try to maintain certain characteristics of an index. In these cases, security selection seeks to maintain regional and sectorial diversification along with a similar profile to the benchmark or target market-cap index while targeting companies with higher ESG ratings. As an example, the MSCI World SRI Index, which is designed to represent the performance of companies with high ESG ratings and uses a best-in-class selection approach to target the top 25% companies in each sector, has characteristics similar but not identical to those of the MSCI World Index.

Sustainable Investment

Sustainable investment refers to the selection of assets that contribute in some way to a sustainable economy—that is, an asset that minimizes natural and social resource depletion.

- It is a broad term, with a wide range of interpretations that may be used for the consideration of typical ESG issues.
- It may include best-in-class and/or ESG integration, which considers how ESG issues impact a security's risk and return profile.

- It is further used to describe the prioritization of the selection of companies with positive impact or companies that will benefit from sustainable macro-trends.

The term "**sustainable investment**" can also be used to mean a strategy that screens out activities considered contrary to long-term environmental and social sustainability, such as mining or burning coal or exploring for oil in the Arctic regions.

Thematic Investment

The **thematic investment** approach in an ESG context is often based on needs arising from environmental or social challenges. Two common investment themes focus on (1) access to low-carbon energy and (2) access to and efficient use of water. Global economic development has raised the demand for energy at the same time as increasing greenhouse gas emissions are negatively affecting the Earth's climate. Similarly, rising global living standards and industrial needs have created greater demand for water and electricity and the need to prevent drought or increase access to clean drinking water in certain regions of the world. While these themes are based on trends related to environmental issues (refer to the following subsection), social issues—such as access to affordable health care and nutrition, especially in the poorest countries in the world—are also of great interest to thematic investors (refer to the subsequent "Social Investment" subsection.

Bear in mind, though, that not all thematic funds are considered to be responsible investments or best-in-class. Becoming such a fund depends not only on the theme of the fund but also on the ESG characteristics of the investee companies.

Green Investment

Green investment refers to allocating capital to assets that mitigate

- climate change,
- biodiversity loss,
- resource inefficiency, and
- other environmental challenges.

These can include

- low-carbon power generation and vehicles,
- smart grids,
- energy efficiency,
- pollution control,
- recycling,
- waste management and waste of energy, and
- other technologies and processes that contribute to solving particular environmental problems.

Green investment can thus be considered a broad subcategory of thematic investing and/or impact investing. Green bonds, a type of fixed-income instrument that is specifically earmarked to raise money for climate and environmental projects, are commonly used in green investing.

Further details on green investing and green bonds can be found in Chapter 3.

Social Investment

Social investment refers to allocating capital to assets that address social challenges. These can be products that address the bottom of the pyramid (BOP). "BOP" refers to the poorest two-thirds of the economic human pyramid, a group of more than four billion people living in poverty. More broadly, BOP refers to a market-based model of economic development that seeks to simultaneously alleviate poverty while providing growth and profits for businesses serving these communities. Examples include

- micro-finance and micro-insurance,
- access to basic telecommunication,
- access to improved nutrition and health care, and
- access to (clean) energy.

Social investing can also include social impact bonds, which are a mechanism to contract with the public sector. This sector pays for better social outcomes in certain services and passes on part of the savings achieved to investors.

Impact Investment

Impact investing refers to investments made with the specific intent of generating positive, measurable social or environmental impact alongside a financial return (which differentiates it from philanthropy). It is a relatively smaller segment of the broader responsible investing market. Impact investing is usually associated with direct investments, such as in private debt, private equity, and real estate. However, in recent years, there is increasing demand from investors on impact investing products in public markets.

Impact investments can be made in both emerging and developed markets. They provide capital to address the world's most pressing challenges. An example is investing in products or services that help achieve one (or more) of the 17 Sustainable Development Goals (SDGs) launched by the United Nations in 2015, such as the following:

- "SDG 6: Clean Water and Sanitation—Ensure availability and sustainable management of water and sanitation for all"
- "SDG 11: Sustainable Cities and Communities—Make cities and human settlements inclusive, safe, resilient and sustainable"[1]

Measurement and tracking of the agreed-upon impact generally lie at the heart of the investment proposition.

Impact investors have diverse financial return expectations. Some intentionally invest for below-market-rate returns in line with their strategic objectives. Others pursue market-competitive and market-beating returns, sometimes required by fiduciary responsibility. The Global Impact Investing Network (GIIN) estimated the size of the global impact investing market to be US$502 billion; its 2019 annual survey indicated that 66% of investors in impact investing pursue competitive, market-rate returns (Mudaliar, Bass, Dithrich, and Nova 2019).

Ethical (or Values-Driven) and Faith-Based Investment

Ethical and faith-based investment refers to investing in line with certain principles, often using negative screening to avoid investing in companies whose products and services are deemed morally objectionable by the investor or certain religions, international declarations, conventions, or voluntary agreements. Typical exclusions include:

- tobacco,
- alcohol,
- pornography,
- weapons, and

- significant breach of agreements, such as the *Universal Declaration of Human Rights* or the *International Labour Organization's Declaration on Fundamental Principles and Rights at Work*.

From religious individuals to large religious organizations, faith-based investors have a history of shareholder activism to improve the conduct of investee companies. Another popular strategy is portfolio building with a focus on screening out the negative; in other words, avoiding "sin stocks" or other assets at odds with their beliefs.

Next, we cover a few examples of faith-based negative screening.

Christian

Investors wishing to put their money to work in a manner consistent with Christian values seek to avoid, in addition to the activities listed previously, investing in firms that

- facilitate abortion, contraceptives, or embryonic stem-cell research or
- are involved in the production and sale of weapons.

They often favor firms that support human rights, environmental responsibility, and fair employment practices via the support of labor unions.

Shari'a

In general terms, investors seeking to follow Islamic religious principles have restrictions around the following:

- investment in firms that profit from alcohol, pornography, or gambling;
- investment in companies that pay interest;
- investments that pay interest;
- liaisons with firms that earn a substantial part of their revenue from interest; or
- investment in pork-related businesses.

Exhibit 4 shows negative screening strategies for various types of funds.

Exhibit 4: Negative Screening Strategies

Negative Screening	Christian Funds	Islamic Funds	SRI Funds
Alcohol	X	X	X
Gambling	X	X	X
Tobacco	X		X
Pornography	X	X	
Pork products		X	
Interest-based financial services		X	
High leverage companies		X	
Anti-family entertainment	X		
Marriage lifestyle	X		
Abortion	X		
Human rights	X		X
Workers' rights	X		X
Bioethics	X		

Negative Screening	Christian Funds	Islamic Funds	SRI Funds
Weapons	X	X	X

Source: Adapted from Inspire Investing (2019).

Shareholder Engagement

Shareholder engagement reflects active ownership by investors in which the investor seeks to influence a corporation's decisions on ESG matters, either through dialogue with corporate officers or votes at a shareholder assembly (in the case of equity). It is seen as complementary to the previously mentioned approaches to responsible investment to encourage companies to act in the best interest of stakeholders. Its efficacy usually depends on

- the scale of ownership (of the individual investor or the collective initiative),
- the quality of the engagement dialogue and method used, and
- whether the company has been informed by the investor that divestment is a possible sanction.

For further details on the process of engagement, see Chapter 6.

ESG investing also recognizes that the generation of long-term sustainable returns is dependent on stable, well-functioning and well-governed social, environmental and economic systems. This is the so-called **triple bottom line** coined by business writer John Elkington. However, since its inception, the concept of TBL evolved from a holistic approach to sustainability and further into an accounting tool to narrowly manage trade-offs. Therefore, Elkington (2018) "recalled" the term in a *Harvard Business Review* article.

Ultimately, ESG investing recognizes the dynamic interrelationship between social, environmental, and governance issues and investment. It acknowledges that

- social, environmental, and governance issues may impact the risk, volatility, and long-term return of securities (as well as markets) and
- investments can have both a positive and a negative impact on society and the environment.

Corporate Social Responsibility

The concept of ESG investing is closely related to the concept of *corporate sustainability*. Corporate sustainability is an approach aiming to create long-term stakeholder value through the implementation of a business strategy that focuses on the ethical, social, environmental, cultural, and economic dimensions of doing business (Ashrafi, Acciaro, Walker, Magnan, and Adams 2019. Related to this approach, *corporate social responsibility (CSR)* is a broad business concept that describes a company's commitment to conducting its business in an ethical way. Throughout the 20th century and until recently, many companies implemented CSR by contributing to society through philanthropy. While such philanthropy may indeed have a positive impact on communities, modern understanding of CSR recognizes that a principles-based behavior approach can play a strategic role in a firm's business model, which led to the theory of TBL.

The TBL accounting theory expands the traditional accounting framework focused only on profit to include two other performance areas: the social and environmental impacts of a company. These three bottom lines are often referred to as the three Ps:

1. people,
2. planet, and
3. profit.

While the term and concept are useful to know, including for historical reasons, they have been replaced in the industry with a broader framework of sustainability that is not restricted to accounting.

Effective management of the company's sustainability can

- reaffirm the company's license to operate in the eyes of governments and civil society,
- increase efficiency,
- attend to increasing regulatory requirements,
- reduce the probability of fines,
- improve employee satisfaction and productivity, and
- drive innovation and introduce new product lines.

ESG investing recognizes these benefits and aims to consider them in the context of security/asset selection and portfolio construction.

There are many organizations and institutions contributing to the further exploration of interactions between society, environment, governance, and investment. This curriculum focuses on how professionals in the investment industry can better understand, assess, and integrate ESG issues when conducting stock selection, carrying out portfolio construction, and engaging with companies.

4 MACRO-LEVEL DEBATE ON ESG INCORPORATION

1.1.3 describe the benefits and challenges of incorporating ESG in decision making, and the linkages between responsible investment and financial system stability

There is a range of beliefs about the purpose and value, both to investors and to society more broadly, of integrating ESG considerations into investment decisions. Some of the main reasons for integrating ESG factors are detailed in this section. It starts with an overview of some important perspectives in the debate on integrating ESG considerations, financial materiality, and challenges in integrating ESG issues and finishes with integration and financial performance.

Macro-Level Debate on Integrating ESG Considerations

This subsection describes various perspectives from which, over the years, the debate on the purpose and value of integrating ESG factors has been held. These include perspectives of risk, fiduciary duty, economics, impact and ethics, client demand, and regulation.

Risk Perspective

Evidence of the risks current megatrends carry is illustrated by "The Global Risks Report 2020" (World Economic Forum 2020), which for many years has highlighted the growing likelihood and impact of extreme weather events and the failure to address climate change. Note that Exhibit 5 highlights how risks related to the environment have been significantly increasing in importance in recent years while classic economic risks have disappeared from the top five risks.. Among all global risks, climate now tops the agenda.

Macro-Level Debate on ESG Incorporation

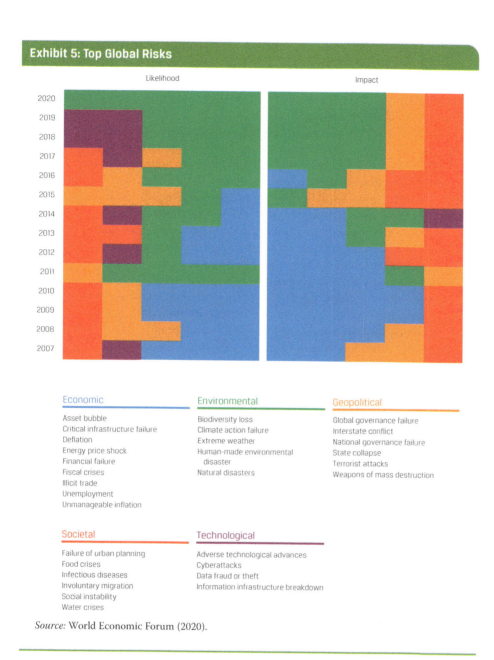

Exhibit 5: Top Global Risks

Source: World Economic Forum (2020).

Recognizing the change in profile of key risks to the economy, in 2015, Mark Carney, then governor of the Bank of England and chairman of the Financial Stability Board (the international body set up by the G20 to monitor risks to the financial system), referred to this challenge in a speech that became a cornerstone for the integration of climate change to financial regulators:

> *Climate change is the tragedy of the horizon. We don't need an army of actuaries to tell us that the catastrophic impacts of climate change will be felt beyond the traditional horizons of most actors—imposing a cost on future generations that the current generation has no direct incentive to fix. . . . The horizon for monetary policy extends out to two to three years. For financial stability it is a bit longer, but typically only to the outer boundaries of the credit cycle—about a decade. In other words, once climate change becomes a defining issue for financial stability, it may already be too late. (Carney 2015)*

In line with Carney, in his annual letter to chief executives in 2020, Larry Fink, the CEO of BlackRock, stated that the investment firm would step up its consideration of climate change in its investment considerations because it was reshaping the world's financial system (Fink 2020). Concretely, in a parallel letter to its clients, BlackRock (2020) committed to divesting from companies that generate more than 25% of their revenues from coal production for its actively managed portfolios and required reporting from investee companies on their climate-related risks and plans for operating under the goals of the Paris Agreement to limit global warming to less than 2°C (3.6°F). Blackrock's implementation of the commitment has been questioned: In January 2021 it still held US$85 billion in coal equities, and in 2022, it told a British parliamentary committee that it will not stop investing in coal, oil, and gas. Nonetheless, as the largest asset manager in the world, were BlackRock to deliver on its commitment, it would represent a new paradigm in the investment industry in the mainstream integration of material ESG factors.

Prudent investors are engaging with companies to ask them to disclose not only what they are emitting today but also how they plan to achieve their transition to the net-zero world of the future. There is value in being able to spot winners and losers in a rapidly changing risk landscape. Investors that are attempting to take advantage of this usually operate with a longer time frame than the quarterly or one-year time horizon typical for many investors, with the objective of understanding emerging risks and new demands so that they can convert these into above-market performance. While more than one-third (34%) of the world's largest companies are now committed to being aligned with the Paris Agreement (i.e., committing to being "net-zero" emitters), a study estimated that nearly all (93%) will fail to achieve their goals if they do not at least double the pace of emission reduction by 2030 (Accenture 2022). Lack of ambition and leadership, challenges to secure quality data, and the need to balance carbon reduction with business and social impacts of the transition are all key challenges to companies delivering on their climate-related commitments. According to the report, growing energy price inflation and supply insecurity is pushing commitments even further out of reach. For more details on the benefits and challenges of companies aligning to net zero, refer to Chapter 3.

CASE STUDIES

Water Depletion Due to Climate Change

Companies are already experiencing risks in their manufacturing due to water depletion, which has been aggravated by acute impacts of climate change. Water has largely been considered a free raw material and therefore is used inefficiently, but many companies are now experiencing the higher costs of using the resource, as well as suffering an increasing frequency of extreme weather events.

Pacific Gas and Electric Company (PG&E), a listed US utility, was driven to bankruptcy proceedings due to wildfire liabilities (McFall-Johnsen 2019). The company's equipment led to more than 1,500 fires between 2014 and 2017. As low humidity and strong winds worsen due to climate change, the fire hazard increases. In 2018, a problem with PG&E equipment was deemed to have led to fires that killed at least 85 people, forced about 180,000 to evacuate from their homes, and razed more than 18,800 structures.

The Brazilian Aluminium Company (CBA) estimated that the water crisis in the second half of 2021 caused a reduction in its EBITDA of between US$27 million and US$33 million. Hydropower accounts for around 55% of electricity generation in Brazil. Water scarcity in the country resulted in shortfalls in hydropower generation, leading to energy shortages and price increases.

> Although CBA generally has the capacity to generate 100% of electricity from its own hydroelectric plants, its reservoirs were also low, requiring it to purchase electricity from the grid at high prices (CBA 2022).
>
> In extreme cases, assets can become stranded—in other words, obsolete due to regulatory, environmental, or market constraints. In Peru, for example, social conflict related to disruptions to water supplies has resulted in the indefinite suspension of US$21.5 billion in mining projects since 2010 (Energy and Mines 2015).

There are many ways in which ESG factors can impact a company's financial results. Nonetheless, identifying those issues that are genuinely material to a sector and company is one of the most active challenges in ESG investment. Each company is unique and faces its own challenges related to its culture, business model, supply chain, and so on. So not only are there substantial differences between sectors, but there are also differences between what is material to individual companies in a single sector. There are also other factors to consider, such as the growth stage of the company and the geographic location of the operations.

For further details on how to assess materiality and what tools are available, refer to Chapters 7 and 8.

Fiduciary Duty Perspective

For many years, fiduciary duty was considered a barrier to considering ESG factors in investments. In the modern investment system, financial institutions or individuals, known as fiduciaries, manage money or other assets on behalf of beneficiaries and investors and have a duty to ensure that they act in their beneficiaries' interests, rather than serving their own. These best interests are typically defined exclusively in financial terms. The misconception that ESG factors are not financially material has led some investors and regulators to use the concept of fiduciary duty as a reason not to incorporate ESG issues.

In 2005, the **United Nations Environment Programme Finance Initiative (UNEP FI)** commissioned the law firm Freshfields Bruckhaus Deringer to publish a report titled "A Legal Framework for the Integration of Environmental, Social and Governance Issues into Institutional Investment" (commonly referred to as the *Freshfields report*). The authors argued that "integrating ESG considerations into an investment analysis so as to more reliably predict financial performance is clearly permissible and is arguably required in all jurisdictions" (Freshfields Bruckhaus Deringer 2005, p. 13). Despite the conclusions of the report, many investors continue to point to their fiduciary duties and the need to deliver financial returns to their beneficiaries as reasons why they cannot do more in terms of responsible investment.

However, an increasing number of academic studies, along with work undertaken on the topic by progressive investment associations, including the UNEP FI and the PRI, have clarified that financially material ESG factors must be incorporated into investment decision making. The Freshfields report (Freshfields Bruckhaus Deringer 2005) and a more recent report published by the PRI (2019) both argue that failing to consider long-term investment value drivers—which include ESG issues—in investment practice is a failure of fiduciary duty. The PRI report concluded that modern fiduciary duties require investors to do the following:

- Incorporate financially material ESG factors into their investment decision making, consistent with the time frame of the obligation.
- Understand and incorporate into their decision making the sustainability preferences of beneficiaries or clients, regardless of whether these preferences are financially material.

- Be active owners, encouraging high standards of ESG performance in the companies or other entities in which they are invested.
- Support the stability and resilience of the financial system.
- Disclose their investment approach in a clear and understandable manner, including how preferences are incorporated into the scheme's investment approach.

For further details on fiduciary duty, see Chapter 2.

Economic Perspective

Another reason for considering ESG issues stems from the recognition that negative megatrends will, over time, create a drag on economic prosperity as basic inputs (such as water, energy, and land) become increasingly scarce and expensive and that the prevalence of health and income inequalities increase instability both within countries and between the "global north and south." There is an understanding that unless these trends are reversed, economies will be weakened. While this may not have a significant impact on asset managers whose performance is judged by their ability to provide above-market returns, it may considerably affect asset owners, who depend on market returns to pay out pensions and meet their liabilities.

As mentioned previously, the Financial Stability Board (FSB) has already identified climate change as a potential systemic risk, which may also be the case for other environmental megatrends The economic implications of these environmental issues (such as climate change, resource scarcity, biodiversity loss, and deforestation) and social challenges (such as poverty, income inequality, and human rights) are increasingly being recognized.

In fact, the Stockholm Resilience Centre (2015) has identified nine "planetary boundaries" (see Exhibit 6) within which humanity can continue to develop and thrive for generations to come and found that four of them—climate change, loss of biosphere integrity, land-system change, and altered biogeochemical cycles (phosphorus and nitrogen)—have been crossed. Two of these—climate change and biosphere integrity—are deemed "core boundaries," for which significant alteration would "drive the Earth system into a new state."

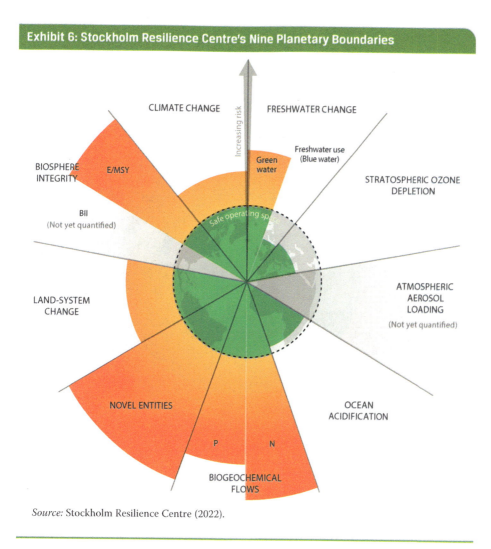

Source: Stockholm Resilience Centre (2022).

A popular framework that builds on that of planetary boundaries is *doughnut economics*, as shown in Exhibit 7. The diagram, developed by economist Kate Raworth, combines planetary boundaries with the complementary concept of social boundaries.

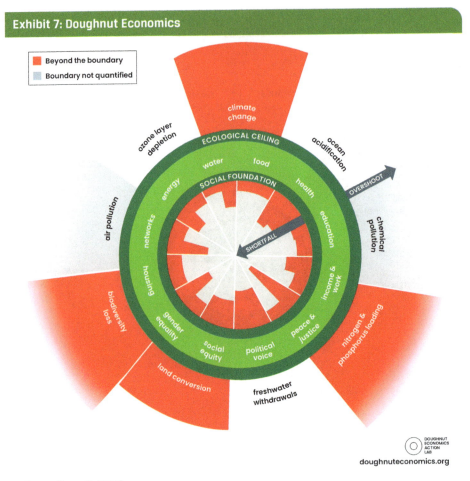

Exhibit 7: Doughnut Economics

Source: Raworth (2017).

Social issues are also having a significant impact on the wider economy. Income inequality in OECD countries is at its highest level in 30 years, and Oxfam estimated that as of January 2022, the wealth of the 10 richest billionaires had doubled since the beginning of the COVID-19 pandemic; together, they have the same wealth as the 3.8 billion people who make up the poorest half of the planet's population (Ratcliff 2019). This level of income inequality is creating social stresses, including security-related issues (PRI 2017). The World Economic Forum estimates that conflict and violence cost the world more than US$14 trillion a year. Undernutrition is still common in developing economies and has severe economic consequences: The economic cost of undernutrition in Ethiopia alone is just under US$70 million a year. While the number of undernourished people in the world has declined sharply, one out of eight people suffers from chronic malnutrition.

Large institutional investors have holdings that, due to their size, are highly diversified across all asset classes, sectors, and regions. As a result, the portfolios of *universal owners*, as they are known, are sufficiently representative of global capital markets that they effectively hold a slice of the overall market. Their investment returns are thus dependent on the continuing good health of the overall economy. Inefficiently allocating capital to companies with high negative **externalities** can damage the profitability of other portfolio companies and the overall market return. It is in their interests to act to reduce the economic risk presented by sustainability challenges to improve their total, long-term financial performance. There is therefore a growing school of thought that investors should integrate the price of externalities into the investment process and take into account the wider effects of investments by considering the impact on society, the environment, and, ultimately, the economy as a whole.

For that reason, investors increasingly call for governments to set policies in line with the fundamental challenges to our future. The UN's Sustainable Development Goals (SDGs), an agreed framework for all UN member state governments to work toward in aligning with global priorities (such as the transition to a low-carbon economy and the elimination of human rights abuses in corporate supply chains), were welcomed by the investment community.

Impact and Ethics Perspective

Yet another reason for practicing responsible investment is some investors' belief that investments can or should serve society alongside providing financial return. This belief translates into focusing on investments with a positive impact and/or avoiding those with a negative impact.

- Those investing for *positive impact* see investment as a means of tackling the world's social and environmental problems through effective deployment of capital and/or stewardship activities. The aim is to put beneficiaries' money to good use rather than to invest it in any activity that could be construed as doing harm—essentially a moral argument. This idea is giving rise to the growing area of impact investment, itself a response to the limits of philanthropy and a recognition of the potential to align returns with positive impacts.

- Those avoiding *negative impact*, at times for religious reasons, usually do not invest (negative screening) in securities from controversial sectors (such as arms, gambling, alcohol, tobacco, and pornography). Negative screening can also consider other factors—for example, environmental factors, such as avoiding fossil fuel companies, or governance factors, such as avoiding companies that are in breach of certain business practices.

Client Demand Perspective

Clients are increasingly calling for greater transparency about how and where their money is invested. This effort is driven by the following:

- Growing awareness that ESG factors influence
  - company value,
  - returns, and
  - reputation
- Increasing focus on the environmental and social impacts of the companies they are invested in

Asset owners, such as pension funds and insurers (as defined in Chapter 2), are instrumental for responsible investment because they make the decisions about how their assets, representing on average around 34% of GDP in OECD countries, are managed (Sievänen, Rita, and Scholtens 2012). The number of them that are integrating ESG considerations continues to grow. In 2020–2021, 88 asset owners signed on to the PRI for the first time. In 2020, a group of asset owners launched the Net-Zero Asset Owner Alliance (now part of the Glasgow Financial Alliance for Net Zero) under the auspices of the UN, committing to transition their investment portfolios to net-zero greenhouse gas (GHG) emissions by 2050.

Further details on the demand for, and supply of, responsible investment, as well as the market more broadly, are discussed in Chapter 2.

Regulatory Perspective

Finally, regardless of their views or beliefs, some investors are being required to increasingly consider ESG matters. Since the mid-1990s, responsible investment regulation has increased significantly, with a particular surge in policy interventions since the 2008 financial crisis. Regulatory change has also been driven by a realization among regulators that the financial sector can play an important role in meeting global challenges, such as combating climate change, modern slavery, and tax avoidance.

Among the world's 50 largest economies, the PRI found that 48 have some form of policy designed to help investors consider sustainability risks, opportunities, or outcomes. In fact, among these economies, there have been over 730 hard and soft law policy revisions that encourage or require investors to consider long-term value drivers, including ESG factors (see Exhibit 8). Hard laws are actual binding legal instruments and laws. Soft laws are quasi-legal instruments that do not have legally binding force or whose binding force is somewhat weaker than the binding force of traditional law. Soft law over time may become hard law.

For further details on how regulation has played a key role in increased demand for responsible investment, refer to Chapter 2.

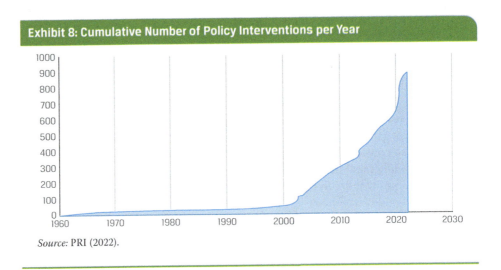

Source: PRI (2022).

5 FINANCIAL MATERIALITY OF ESG INTEGRATION

- [ ] 1.1.4 explain the concepts of the financial materiality of ESG integration, double materiality, and dynamic materiality and how they relate to ESG analysis, practices, and reporting
- [ ] 1.1.5 explain different ESG megatrends, their systemic nature, and their potential impact on companies and company practices

One of the main reasons for **ESG integration** is recognizing that considering ESG factors can reduce risk and enhance returns because it considers additional risks and injects new and forward-looking insights into the investment process. ESG integration may therefore lead to

1. reduced cost and increased efficiency,

Financial Materiality of ESG Integration

2. reduced risk of fines and state intervention,
3. reduced negative externalities, and
4. improved ability to benefit from sustainability megatrends.

Each of these outcomes is described in greater detail in the following subsections.

Efficiency and Productivity

Sustainable business practices build efficiencies by

- conserving resources,
- reducing costs, and
- enhancing productivity.

Sustainability was once perceived by businesses and investors as requiring sacrifices, but the perception today is very different. Significant cost reductions can result from improving operational efficiency through better management of natural resources, such as water and energy, as well as from minimizing waste.

Research conducted by McKinsey & Company found that resource efficiency can affect operating profits by as much as 60% and that more broadly, resource efficiency of companies across various sectors is significantly correlated with the companies' financial performance (Henisz, Koller, and Nuttall 2019).

A strong ESG proposition can help companies attract and retain quality employees and enhance employee motivation and productivity overall. Employee satisfaction is positively correlated with shareholder returns. The London Business School's Alex Edmans found that the companies that made Fortune's 100 Best Companies to Work For list generated 2.3%–3.8% higher stock returns a year than their peers over a horizon of longer than 25 years (Edmans 2011).

CASE STUDIES

Savings from Efficiency Measures

The Dow Chemical Company

The Dow Chemical Company's long-established focus on cost reductions through resource efficiency enabled it to achieve savings of US$31 million on its raw materials alone, compared to a net income of approximately US$4 billion, in 2018 (Dow 2018).

General Electric

In 2013, General Electric reduced its GHG emissions by 32% and water use by 45% compared to the 2004 and 2006 baselines, respectively. This resulted in savings of around US$300 million (GE 2014).

Aeon Group

Between 2015 and 2018, the Japanese retail group Aeon achieved a decrease of 9.7% in food waste emissions, which was equal to approximately 32 kg per US$9,100 in net sales (Aeon 2019).

Nike

Almost half (40%) of Nike's footwear manufacturing waste is generated by cutting scraps from materials such as textiles, leather, synthetic leather, and foams. In 2018, modern cutting equipment, which can achieve smaller gaps between cut parts than traditional die-cutting can, was deployed to various factories. The

> estimated value of savings was US$12 million, compared to its net income of US$1.1 billion, and nearly 1.2 million kilograms of material for that fiscal year (Parker 2018).

Reduced Risk of Fines and State Intervention

With all the discussion regarding climate change, dwindling energy resources, and environmental impact, it is no surprise that state and federal government agencies are enacting regulations to protect the environment. Integrating sustainability into a business will position it to anticipate changing regulations in a timely manner. For example, a UN Environment Programme (2019) report found that there has been a 38-fold increase in environmental laws put in place since 1972. It found that while enforcement remains weak today, significant events indeed result in large fines. It also concluded that the level of enforcement could quickly change with little notice to investors.

Analysis conducted by McKinsey & Company showed that, typically, one-third of corporate profits are at risk from state intervention (not only fines; Henisz et al. 2019). For pharmaceuticals, the profits at stake are about 25%–30%, and for the automotive, banking, and technology sectors, where government subsidies (among other forms of intervention) are prevalent, the value at stake can reach 60% (see Exhibit 9).

Exhibit 9: Estimated Share of EBITDA at Stake

Estimated Share of EBITDA at Stake		Examples
Automotive, aerospace and defense, technology	50%–60%	Government subsidies, renewable regulation, and carbon-emissions regulation
Transport, logistics, infrastructure	45%–55%	Pricing regulation and liberalization of sector
Telecom and media	40%–50%	Tariff regulation, interconnection, fiber deployment, spectrum and data privacy
Energy and materials	35%–45%	Tariff regulation, renewables subsidies, interconnection, and access rights
Resources	30%–40%	Resource nationalism, mineral taxes, land-access rights, community reach and reputation
Consumer goods	25%–30%	Obesity, sustainability, food safety, health and wellness, and labeling
Pharmaceuticals and health care	25%–30%	Market access, regulation of generic drugs, pricing, innovation funding, and clinical trials

Source: W. Henisz, T. Koller, and R. Nuttall, "Five Ways That ESG Creates Value," *McKinsey Quarterly* (November 2019). www.mckinsey.com/business-functions/strategy-and-corporate-finance/our-insights/five-ways-that-esg-creates-value?cid=soc-web. Copyright (c) 2021 McKinsey & Company. All rights reserved. Reprinted by permission.

> ## CASE STUDIES
>
> ### Three of the Highest ESG-Related Fines in History
>
> #### BP and Deepwater Horizon
>
> The biggest corporate fine to date was levied against BP in the wake of the 2010 Deepwater Horizon oil spill in the Gulf of Mexico, the largest in history. BP settled with the US Department of Justice for US$20.8 billion in 2016 (Rushe 2015); total compensation ultimately paid out by the company reportedly exceeded US$65 billion.
>
> #### Financial Crisis and the Bank of America
>
> Several of the largest fines have hit the financial services industry, a direct result of the scrutiny facing banks in the wake of the financial crisis. These include the second highest fine (US$16.65 billion), which was paid by Bank of America in 2014 for its role in the subprime loan crisis ("Bank of America and the Financial Crisis" 2014). Just two years before that, the bank agreed to a US$11.8 billion settlement with the US federal government over mortgage foreclosure abuses.
>
> #### Volkswagen's Emission Scandal
>
> The third largest fine was paid by Volkswagen, which in 2016 faced US$14.7 billion in civil and criminal penalties from the United States in the wake of its scandal over emissions cheating ("VW in $14.7bn US Deal over Rigged Cars" 2016). The scandal dampened the hype of diesel as a fuel for environmental efficiency. Today, most major automotive companies are directing their current investments toward electric vehicles while striving to meet increasingly aggressive emission targets.
>
> ### Reduced Negative Externalities
>
> The term *externalities* refers to situations where the production or consumption of goods and services creates costs or benefits for others that are not reflected in the prices charged for them. In other words, externalities affect people not directly involved in the transactions. Externalities can be either negative or positive.
>
> The concept of externality, though central to the concept of sustainability and responsible investment, dates back to 1920, having been introduced by Cambridge professor Arthur Pigou in his book *The Economics of Welfare*. Externalities often occur when the production or consumption of a product's or service's private price equilibrium cannot reflect the true costs or benefits of that product or service for society as a whole.
>
> In the case of pollution, a polluter makes decisions based only on the direct cost and profit opportunity associated with production and does not consider the indirect costs to those harmed by the pollution. These indirect costs—which are not borne by the producer or user—may include decreased quality of life, higher health care costs, and forgone production opportunities (for example, when pollution harms activities, such as tourism).

Professor William Nordhaus, who was recently awarded the Nobel Prize for his work on the externality of climate change, developed a model to measure the impact of environmental degradation on economic growth and thus created a price for carbon pollution. However, externalities can also be due to social factors—for example, when companies fail to pay a living wage or submit their employees to poor working conditions or from the health impacts of smoking or junk food.

In short, when externalities are *negative*, private costs are lower than societal costs, resulting in market outcomes that may not be efficient or, in other words, leading to "market failures" through excessive production of the good or service.

For that reason, externalities are among the main reasons why governments intervene in markets (Helbling 2010). As far back as the 1920s, Pigou suggested that governments should tax polluters an amount equivalent to the cost of the harm incurred by others. Such a tax would yield the market outcome that would have prevailed with adequate internalization of all costs by polluters. Internalization refers to all measures (public or private) to ensure that externalities become reflected in the prices of commercial goods and services (Ding, He, and Deng 2014). As environmental and social regulation and taxation become more common, an increasing proportion of this cost might be forced into companies' accounts.

In the social sphere, recent developments in the interpretation of the OECD (2018) Guidelines for Multinational Enterprises and the UN Guiding Principles for Business and Human Rights (UNGC 2011)—clarifying that these instruments apply to investors and give rise to responsibility for conducting human rights due diligence on investments—are in effect paving the way for more formal internalization of social costs in hard law (see, e.g., Marotta 2013; Norwegian National Contact Point for the OECD Guidelines for Multinational Enterprises 2013).

Internalization can happen in various ways. In the transportation industry, for example, internalization can happen through

- market-based instruments (e.g., charges, taxes, and tradable permits),
- regulation (e.g., vehicle emission and safety standards, traffic restrictions), or
- voluntary agreements (e.g., agreements with the car industry to reduce CO_2 emissions from new passenger cars).

Understanding the risks posed by "externalized" environmental and social costs in the real economy is central to the practice of investment, because the internalization of these externalities could significantly impact the costs and profits of companies' products and services. The uncertainty surrounding the timing and extent of internalization is a critical component of the overall risk landscape facing investors.

Beyond affecting companies' financial performance, these externalities can also have a drag on the wider economy, potentially affecting the total return investors may achieve in the long term. A study by an environmental consulting company found that the top 3,000 publicly traded companies were responsible for US$2.15 trillion worth of environmental damage in 2008 and that global environmental damage would cost an estimated US$28 trillion by 2050 (Wainwright 2010). Environmental harm was found to be a material risk that could significantly affect the value of capital markets and global economic growth.

CASE STUDIES

Air Travel and Carbon Emissions

Before the COVID-19 pandemic, air travel was the source of around 2.5% of global CO_2 emissions, but it is estimated to grow by 300% by 2050. For that reason, the European Commission (EC) has for many years been assessing and advocating for the internalization of externalities associated with transportation.

In 2010, the EU expanded the scope of its Emissions Trading System (ETS) to include aviation (European Commission 2019). The ETS for aviation requires all non-commercial operators who travel into, out of, and between EU and European Economic Area (EEA) member states to monitor their CO_2 flight emissions and purchase carbon allowances equal to the emissions on intra-EU flights when emitting more than 1,000 tonnes of CO_2 under the full scope (in, out of, and within the EU).

In 2019, the ministers of finance of the Netherlands, Germany, France, Sweden, Italy, Belgium, Luxembourg, Denmark, and Bulgaria asked the EC to introduce a measure to offset the CO_2 emissions of planes.

A report from the independent research and consultancy organization CE Delft showed that tax exemptions for the aviation sector lead to a greater number of flights and that a tax could result in a 10% increase in average ticket price and an 11% decline in passenger demand, leading to an 11% reduction in CO_2 emissions (CE Delft and Directorate-General for Mobility and Transport 2019). See Exhibit 10.

Exhibit 10: Impact of Taxes in Aviation

Impacts in the aviation sector	Current Situation Value	Abolition of Ticket Tax Value	Change	Introducing VAT on All Tickets (19%) Value	Change	Introducing Fuel Excise Duty Value	Change
Passenger demand (millions)	691.5	718.5	+4%	570.4	−18%	616.0	−11%
Average ticket price (€)	304	293	−4%	358	+17%	333	+10%
Number of flights and connectivity			+4%		−18%		−11%
Employment (1,000 FTE)	362	376	+4%	296	−18%	321	−11%
Value added (€ billions)	43.4	45.1	+4%	35.6	−18%	38.5	−11%
CO_2 emissions (metric ton)	149.5	155.3	+4%	123.3	−18%	133.1	−11%
People affected by noise (thousands)	2,851.5	2,919.8	+2%	2,495.9	−12%	2,637.1	−8%
Aviation-related fiscal revenue (€ billions)	10.0	2.6	−74%	39.9	+297%	26.9	+168%

Source: CE Delft and Directorate-General for Mobility and Transport (2019).

Sweden and France have acted unilaterally (Stokel-Walker 2019): Sweden introduced a US$6–US$35 carbon tax for all airline passengers in April 2018. In France, the tax rate depends on the class of travel and the passenger's final destination. Passengers traveling in the lowest class of travel pay the lower rate, whereas all other airline passengers pay the higher rate. Passengers traveling to destinations in the EEA and Switzerland are currently charged US$3.25 (lower rate) or US$25.00 (higher rate) per passenger. Passengers traveling to all other destinations pay US$9.30 (lower rate) or US$76.50 (higher rate) per passenger. The French government estimated that the "eco-tax" will raise US$220 million a year from flights, which will be invested in other, more environmentally friendly forms of transport, such as trains, according to the transport ministry.

> Air France expects the eco-tax to cost the company an extra €60 million a year, which is believed to have encouraged it to buy more efficient planes in order to negotiate with the government (Stokel-Walker 2019). Price sensitivity for passengers is relatively low, however, and the tax is deemed more of a symbolic first step. In the past, governments often started environment-related taxes low to get people used to the idea before increasing them. For example, the United Kingdom's landfill tax, introduced in 1996, started at £7 per tonne of waste deposited but later increased 12-fold (Stokel-Walker 2019).
>
> In 2021, French lawmakers voted in favor of a bill to end flights where the same journey could be made by train in under two and a half hours. In December 2022, the move was officially approved by the European Commission. France is not the first country to replace flights with train rides. In 2020, Austrian Airlines replaced a flight route between Vienna and Salzburg with an increased train service, after receiving a government bailout with a requirement to cut its carbon footprint.

Improved Ability to Benefit from Sustainability Megatrends

There is a multitude of implications from the so-called sustainability megatrends. Being able to integrate a response to these trends into business operations can be a success factor for an investee firm. From the investor perspective, these megatrends can be part of a successful portfolio construction strategy.

For this reason, business leaders, investors, economists, and governments are increasingly recognizing the economic implications of

- social challenges (such as increasing income inequality, poverty, and human and labor rights abuses) and
- environmental issues (such as climate change, biodiversity loss, and resource scarcity).

These factors have interacted with

- the aftermath of the 2007–08 financial crisis,
- aging populations,
- the rise of emerging economies, and
- rapid technological changes.

This interaction increases the complexity and the impact that social and environmental challenges have on the growth and profitability of sectors and businesses.

Global Megatrends

Four widely recognized megatrends that affect everyone are emerging markets and urbanization, technological innovation, demographic changes and wealth inequality, and climate change and resource scarcity.

Emerging Markets and Urbanization

The locus of economic activity and dynamism is shifting to emerging markets and to cities within those markets, which are going through industrial and urban revolutions simultaneously; 97% of the Fortune Global 500 were once headquartered in developed economies, but nearly half of the world's large companies are expected to be headquartered in emerging markets by 2025. Nearly half of global GDP growth between 2010 and 2025 will come from 440 cities in emerging markets—95% of them small and medium-size cities (McKinsey & Company 2017). This change will impact not only where company headquarters are located but also supply chains, workforces, and the expectation of the local communities, as well as where new consumers come from.

Technological Innovation

Technology has always had the power to change behavior and expectations. What is new is the speed of change. It took 76 years for the telephone to penetrate half of all US households. The smartphone has achieved the same in less than a decade (PWC 2020). Accelerated adoption invites accelerated innovation. By 2014, seven years after the iPhone's launch, the number of applications created had hit 1.2 million and users had downloaded more than 75 billion apps in total, more than 10 for every person on the planet (McKinsey & Company 2017). Speed of adoption keeps increasing, with ChatGPT recently achieving 100 million users in two months.

Social media is the new zeitgeist and acts as a platform for both crowd intelligence and influence. Its influence stretches far beyond its initial use as a means to stay connected with family and friends and now reaches into corporate risk management and geopolitics. Its capacity both to mobilize online crowds and to lead people into narrow filter bubbles has had major repercussions in recent years, including civil strife. Furthermore, issues around human rights, including free speech, and tensions between big social media companies and sovereign nation states have led to headlines and point in the direction of a possible new ordering of societal power, the outcome of which remains to be seen.

Artificial intelligence—namely, computer systems able to perform tasks normally requiring human intelligence—is poised to change and grow at an exponential speed. It is being used by the health industry to track patients' data and medication intake, by businesses to automate customer service and manufacturing, by energy companies' smart grids to forecast and manage energy supply and demand, and by self-driving cars to optimize routes. Gartner (an IT research firm) estimated that one-third of jobs will be replaced by smart machines and robots, and Google estimated that robots will attain the level of human intelligence by 2029.

Demographic Changes and Wealth Inequality

By 2030, the world's population is projected to rise by more than 1 billion. At the same time, the population is getting older. Germany's population is expected to shrink by one-fifth, and the number of people of working age could fall from 54 million in 2010 to 36 million in 2060. China's labor force peaked in 2012. Today, about 60% of the world's population lives in countries with fertility rates below the replacement rate (McKinsey & Company 2017).

A smaller, older workforce in some countries will place a greater onus on productivity for driving growth and may cause economists to rethink an economy's potential. Caring for large numbers of elderly people has already started to reshape industries and put severe pressure on government finances. At the same time, the rise in population overall will only increase the demand for and stress on scarce resources. A growing global population is expected to demand about 3.5% more food annually until 2030.

Finally, increasing wealth concentration and rising inequality have already led to growing social strains. This increase in inequality has happened both across and within countries, contributing to depressed economic growth, criminal behavior, and undermined educational opportunities (Lawson et al 2020).

Climate Change and Resource Scarcity

As the world becomes more populous, urbanized, and prosperous, the demand for energy, food, and water will rise. But the Earth has a finite amount of natural resources to satisfy this demand. At the current pace of global action, average temperatures are predicted to increase by more than 1.5°C (2.7°F), a threshold at which scientists believe significant and potentially irreversible environmental changes will occur. The interconnectivity between trends in climate change and resource scarcity is amplifying the impact: climate change could reduce agricultural productivity by up to a third across large parts of Africa over the next 60 years. Globally, demand for water will increase by 40% and demand for energy by 50%.

In short, the world's current economic model is pushing beyond the limits of the planet's ability to cope.

Evolution of Materiality: From Static to Dynamic

Movements (such as #MeToo and Black Lives Matter), events (such as the COVID-19 pandemic), and their implications, including regulation, highlight that priority issues can suddenly present new, previously unaccounted for risks for corporations and their investors. These require agile responses not only from corporations but also from capital providers to mitigate the risks that can impact a business's financials . This concept—that what is financially material to a company not only can but most likely will change—has been defined as *dynamic materiality*. For investors, it means that the understanding of what is financially material for a company must be constantly reviewed to reflect the quickly evolving nature of ESG factors.

Double Materiality

Double materiality is an extension of the accounting concept of financial materiality. Information of a company is material and should therefore be disclosed if a reasonable person would consider the information important. As illustrated in the previous section, because ESG factors, especially climate, can be material for a company, they have now been widely accepted in financial markets as potentially financially material, therefore requiring disclosure.

The concept of double materiality takes this notion one step further: It is not just climate-related impacts on the company that can be material but also impacts of a company on the climate—or any other ESG factor. For further detail, see Exhibit 11. In 2019, the European Commission was the first to formally describe the concept of double materiality in the context of sustainability reporting and the need to get a full picture of a company's impacts. This means in practice that both companies and investors are increasingly identifying, monitoring, and managing the most significant impact that companies and investment portfolios have on society and the environment.

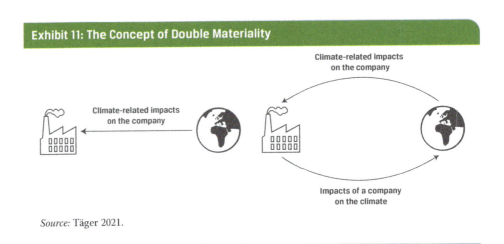

Exhibit 11: The Concept of Double Materiality

Source: Täger 2021.

CHALLENGES IN INTEGRATING ESG FACTORS

ESG investing has seen rapid development in recent years, but challenges to its further growth remain. Challenges to taking a more proactive approach to ESG investing exist across the whole of the investment decision-making process.

The following challenges are common prior to wishing to implement ESG investing:

- The perception that implementing ESG investing may have a negative impact on investment performance
- The interpretation that fiduciary duty prevents investors from integrating ESG factors
- The advice given by investment consultants and retail financial advisers many times not having been supportive of products that integrate ESG factors

Once the decision has been made to implement ESG investing, the following challenges are typical:

- A lack of understanding of how to build an investment mandate that effectively promotes ESG investing or a lack of understanding of what are the needs of asset owners regarding ESG investing
- The impression that significant resources, which may be lacking in the market or may be expensive, are needed—including human resources, technical capability, data, and tools
- A gap between marketing, commitment, and delivery of funds regarding their ESG performance

Some investors still question whether considering ESG issues can add value to investment decision making despite wide dissemination of research that demonstrates that ESG integration can help limit volatility and enhance returns. Interviews conducted by the PRI (2016) show that investment professionals place a greater weight on experience from their own careers than they do on third-party evidence. It can thus be helpful for an internal evidence base to be built or to engage with direct peers on ESG processes and investment benefits.

Interpretations of fiduciary duty are partially related to perception of the impact on ESG investing on risk-adjusted returns. Despite regulators in various jurisdictions clarifying a modern interpretation of fiduciary duty, contrasting views remain as to how ESG integration fits with institutional investors' duties. Some institutional investors remain reluctant to adapt their governance processes because they see a conflict between their responsibility to protect the financial interests of their beneficiaries and the consideration of ESG factors.

The challenge pertains not only to the impact of ESG investing on portfolio returns. Screening, divestment, and thematic investment strategies can involve "tilting" the portfolio toward desired ESG characteristics by over- or underweighting sectors or companies that perform either well or poorly in those areas. Institutional investors may feel that this conflicts with their obligation to invest prudently, because it involves straying from established market benchmarks. This increases tracking error, a key measure of active risk widely used in the industry, that arises from active investment decisions versus the benchmark made by the portfolio manager.

For further details on the challenges of portfolio construction, refer to Chapter 8.

The barriers mentioned earlier, together with other reasons, may explain why investment consultants and retail financial advisers have offered advice that is not seen as supportive of ESG investing. Consultants and advisers often base their advice on a very narrow interpretation of investment objectives. What they perceive as a lack of interest by asset owners in responsible investment has also contributed to them being less willing to integrate ESG investing into their mainstream offerings. Asset owners and individual retail investors can ensure ESG factors are standing items in meetings and ask how consultants and advisers integrate ESG factors into their advice. Investor-led initiatives can also increase engagement with these actors to enhance their understanding of ESG investing and address barriers to its consideration in investment advice.

Even once an investor has decided to consider ESG factors in investment decision making, various barriers remain. Some asset owners believe they do not have the scale or capacity to influence the products offered by fund managers. Others are unsure of how to integrate ESG factors in requests for proposals or mandates. The absence of clear signals from asset owners that they are interested in ESG investing means that investment managers have limited understanding of what asset owners expect on such matters and reduced incentive to develop such products. As a result, asset owners have fewer options for ESG investing products in the market to choose from. There are investor-led initiatives that hope to address this problem. The International Corporate Governance Network (ICGN) established a Model Mandate Initiative, the University of Cambridge Institute for Sustainability Leadership developed a toolkit for establishing long-term, sustainable mandates, and the PRI published numerous guidance documents to support asset owners in incorporating ESG investing into manager selection and investment mandates.

For further details on mandates, refer to Chapter 9.

The challenge of resources is especially prominent for asset owners who have funding constraints or investors who see ESG investing as separate from the core investment process (e.g., as a marketing or compliance, rather than investment, issue). In addition to the costs of building or buying expertise in ESG investing, investors may face other costs for items, such as research, data, monitoring, and reporting. A recent study showed that corporate issuers are currently spending an average of more than US$675,000 per year on climate-related disclosures, and institutional investors are spending nearly US$1.4 million on average to collect, analyze, and report climate data (Lee, Brock, and MacNair 2022).

Even when financial resources are available, investors still have difficulty identifying or creating technical resources, such as high-quality, standardized datasets, modelling capability, and valuation techniques. Without such resources, it is not always straightforward to understand the effects of ESG risks and opportunities at the investee company level. These risks and opportunities will be incorporated into the investee's overall financial performance and, therefore, before their materialization, will be invisible in the investor's (non-ESG) financial models. Some common risks and opportunities include the following:

- ▶ Data availability: Although ESG data from investees are increasingly available from specialized providers, disclosure and data quality are still significant challenges, especially in asset classes other than listed equities. Investment analysis thus remains limited by corporate disclosure, which varies in quality and scope. It is also limited by investors' understanding of those data and which metrics are financially material. There is considerable effort by the private sector and policymakers to reach a consensus on what degree and type of corporate disclosure is needed, but no single standard is universally implemented.

- ▶ Modeling: It can be challenging to integrate ESG factors into traditional financial models, because they do not always have a short-term financial impact. ESG factors are not implemented consistently among managers, and hence the impact on market security price is inconsistent. Furthermore, most financial analysts' models extrapolate from historical data, which may be less relevant for forecasting future ESG-related outcomes. For example, measuring a company's past and current carbon footprint does not give as much information about its future valuation as understanding its strategy for reducing its carbon intensity or the impact of evolving carbon legislation/markets. Similarly, it is hard to estimate the viability or impact of a breakthrough technological innovation based on historical patterns. Notably, a lot of modeling of ESG factors focuses on risks, and there are fewer tools for assessing positive ESG impacts.

▶ Valuation techniques: Equity investors can adjust corporate valuations for ESG factors in a number of ways. Investors could vary the discount rate applied to corporate cash flows, which raises the question of how much of a valuation discount should be applied for various ESG risks. Alternatively, they could apply higher or lower multiples to valuation ratios (such as price-to-earnings or book value), which might lead to double-counting if ESG factors are already partially priced by the market. Revenues or costs could also be forecast to include the impact of ESG factors.

As a result of these difficulties, ESG analysis often takes the form of a qualitative input that is used alongside traditional quantitative models. The portfolio manager might use the quality score just for information or might set a hurdle for a stock to be included in the portfolio. These types of risk metrics are less respected by portfolio managers than financial analysis because quantifying the input and its impact is generally a challenge.

For further details on financial materiality, data suppliers, and integrating ESG factors in valuation techniques, refer to Chapter 7.

A growing challenge for the industry is greenwashing. Greenwashing originally described misleading claims about environmental practices, performance, or products but has been used more widely to also consider social or governance factors. The phenomenon is not restricted to the investment industry, but with the rise of a plethora of new ESG-type funds, including impact funds, the challenge of how to spot and avoid greenwashing has become more prevalent.

The EU has recently launched various initiatives to standardize claims around the green and ESG credential of funds and indexes, which will contribute to a clampdown on greenwashing. Further advancements from the governments of other jurisdictions, as well as voluntary action and initiatives of investors themselves, would contribute to maintaining and enhancing the implementation and credibility of responsible investment.

ESG FACTORS' INFLUENCE ON FINANCIAL PERFORMANCE 7

There is growing recognition in the financial industry and in academia that ESG factors indeed influence financial performance. An analysis of over 2,000 academic studies on how ESG factors affect corporate financial performance found "an overwhelming share of positive results," with just 1 in 10 showing a negative relationship (Global Research Institute 2018). Various studies also indicate that engaging with companies on ESG issues can create value for both investors and companies, by encouraging better ESG risk management and more sustainable business practices (PRI 2018; Dimson, Karakaş, and Li 2017). These studies provide evidence that ESG issues can be financially material to companies' performance and potentially to investment performance.

Mounting evidence shows that sustainable business practices deliver better financial performance. The topic has not only been the focus of various individual studies but also the subject of meta-analysis.

In summary, these meta-studies suggest that in most research papers, there was a positive correlation between ESG performance and corporate financial performance, including stock prices. These findings provide academic evidence for the financial materiality of ESG factors. This correlation, however, does not hold for fund performance, suggesting that the asset management industry in general has not been consistently able to translate ESG analysis into alpha.

> **CASE STUDIES**
>
> ### Meta-Data Studies
>
> One of the first meta-data studies, in 2012, was conducted by Deutsche Bank (Fulton, Kahn, and Sharples 2012), assessing over 100 individual studies. The vast majority (89%) showed that companies highly rated for ESG factors outperformed the market, while 85% demonstrated outperformance in terms of business performance. These results were strongest over the medium to long term. Deutsche Bank found weaker results with respect to the influence of ESG factors on investment funds. They concluded that companies with good ESG factors outperform but that investors were not always good at capturing that outperformance.
>
> The University of Oxford and asset manager Arabesque in 2014 reviewed the academic literature on sustainability and corporate performance and found that out of the 200 studies analyzed,
>
> - 90% concluded that good ESG standards lower the cost of capital,
> - 88% showed that good ESG practices result in better operational performance, and
> - 80% showed that stock price performance is positively correlated with good sustainability practices (Clark, Feiner, and Viehs 2015).
>
> Another study combined the findings of around 2,200 individual studies (35 times larger than the average sample of previous meta-analyses) and thus claimed to be the most exhaustive overview of the academic evidence on ESG factors and performance (Friede, Busch, and Bassen 2015). In this case, about 90% of studies demonstrated a relationship between ESG factors and financial performance that was not negative (i.e., positive or neutral performance), with the large majority showing positive correlation between ESG factors and performance across equity, fixed income, and property, as well as in aggregate.
>
> The meta-study showed a significant difference between the impact of ESG factors on corporate financial performance, at the asset-class level, and on investment fund performance:
>
> - 15% of the studies on portfolio-level impact were positive and
> - 11% were negative.
>
> Friede et al. (2015) suggested three reasons why the results differ:
>
> 1. The alpha from ESG factors might be captured elsewhere in factor studies (and thus is "drowned out by noise").
> 2. The impacts of different ESG approaches in the various studies might cancel each other out.
> 3. The costs of implementation consume the available alpha.

Finally, a meta-study conducted by researchers at the NYU Stern Center for Sustainable Business and Rockefeller Asset Management examined the relationship between ESG factors and financial performance in more than 1,000 research papers from 2015 to 2020 (Whelan, Atz, Van Holt, and Clark 2021). They conducted the research differently from previous meta-studies. They divided the articles into those focused on corporate financial performance (e.g., operating metrics, such as ROE, ROA, or stock performance for a company or group of companies) and those focused on investment performance (from the perspective of an investor, generally measures of alpha or such metrics as the Sharpe ratio on a portfolio of stocks).

They found a positive relationship between ESG and financial performance for 58% of the "corporate" studies focused on operational metrics, such as ROE, ROA, or stock price, with 13% showing neutral impact, 21% with mixed results (the same study finding a positive, neutral, or negative results), and only 8% showing a negative relationship. For investment studies typically focused on risk-adjusted attributes, such as alpha or the Sharpe ratio of a portfolio of stocks, 59% showed similar or better performance relative to conventional investment approaches, while only 14% found negative results. They also found positive results when they reviewed 59 climate change or low-carbon studies related to financial performance. On the corporate side, 57% arrived at a positive conclusion, 29% found a neutral impact, 9% had mixed results, and 6% were negative. Looking at investor studies, 65% showed positive or neutral performance compared to conventional investments, with only 13% indicating negative findings.

PUTTING ESG INVESTING INTO PRACTICE

1.1.6 explain the three ways in which investors typically reflect ESG considerations in their investment process

ESG investing is a strategy and practice related to incorporating ESG factors in investment decisions and active ownership. Institutional investors typically reflect ESG considerations in three ways:

1. incorporating ESG factors into investment decision-making,
2. through corporate engagement, and
3. through policy engagement.

Different institutions take different approaches and blend these elements differently, reflecting their culture and investment style.

Investment Decisions

Incorporating ESG factors into investment decision making can happen throughout the investment value chain:

- Asset owners
- can include ESG factors in their requests for proposal and consider them in their appointment process,

- are often supported by investment consultants, who can factor in asset managers' ESG policy, implementation, and outcomes in their selection process, and
- can reassure themselves that their views on ESG issues are implemented by integrating them into investment mandates and monitoring processes.

▶ Asset owners and some asset managers can embed ESG considerations into **strategic asset allocation (SAA)**. SAA is the process in which an investor chooses to allocate capital across asset classes, sectors, and regions based on their need for return and income and their risk appetite.

▶ Asset managers and asset owners who invest directly can incorporate ESG issues into their security selection and portfolio management process. This can be done by

- using ratings to apply a filter or threshold, which rules potential investments in or out of the investment universe,
- integrating ESG issues in their financial and risk analysis, or
- using ESG criteria to identify investment opportunities through a thematic approach (e.g., a water fund, impact investing).

For further details on this process, see Chapters 7 and 8.

Shareholder Engagement

Investors can encourage investees to improve their ESG practices via a company's annual general meeting (AGM) by formally expressing their views through voting on resolutions. Engagement can also happen outside this process (with an investment firm, individually, or through a collective initiative), discussing ESG issues with an investee company's board or management.

For further details on this process, see Chapter 6.

Policy Engagement

The proper functioning of the market and thus public policy, such as the EU's taxonomy for sustainable activities, critically affects the ability of institutional investors to generate sustainable returns and create value. Policy engagement by institutional investors is therefore a natural extension of an investor's responsibilities and fiduciary duties to the interests of beneficiaries.

Investors can work with regulators, standard setters, and other parties (e.g., consultants and stock exchanges) to design a financial system that

▶ is more sound and stable,
▶ levels the playing field, and
▶ brings ESG factors more effectively into financial decision making.

Investors can

▶ respond to policy consultations,
▶ participate in collective initiatives, and
▶ make recommendations to policymakers.

Further details on this process are discussed in Chapter 6.

KEY INITIATIVES

1.1.7 explain the aims of key supranational ESG initiatives and organizations and the progress achieved to date

Various initiatives have contributed to increasing the investment industry's awareness of ESG issues, as well as enhancing its ability and capacity to integrate ESG factors into the investment process.

United Nations Initiatives

The United Nations (UN) has played a critical role in the advancement of sustainability and specifically responsible investment in the past 30 years. Three of its initiatives are of particular interest to investors.

United Nations Global Compact

Chief among the supranational initiatives, the **United Nations Global Compact (UNGC)** was launched in 2000 as a collaboration between leading companies and the UN. It has since gained remarkable traction and now claims to be the largest corporate sustainability initiative in the world, with over 8,000 corporate signatories spanning the globe. These signatories agree to adhere to the 10 principles, derived from broader global standards, such as the Universal Declaration of Human Rights and the International Labour Organization's Declaration on Fundamental Principles and Rights at Work. The 10 principles of the UNGC cover the areas of human rights, labor, environment, and anti-corruption. It has provided investors with a helpful set of principles to assess and engage with companies, as well as directly aided companies in becoming more sustainable.

United Nations Environment Programme Finance Initiative

UNEP FI is a partnership between UNEP and the global financial sector to mobilize private sector finance for sustainable development.

UNEP FI started in 1992 with a few banking institutions, and today it works with over 300 members—banks, insurers, and investors—to catalyze integration of sustainability into financial market practice. The frameworks UNEP FI has established or cocreated include the following:

- The Principles for Responsible Investment, established in 2006 by UNEP FI and the UN Global Compact, now applied by more than half the world's institutional investors (US$103.4 trillion)
- The Principles for Sustainable Insurance (PSI), established in 2012 by UNEP FI and today applied by more than one-quarter of the world's insurers (more than 25% of world premium volume)
- The Principles for Responsible Banking (PRB): As of April 2021, more than 220 banks have signed up to the PRB, representing US$57 trillion in total assets, or more than one-third of the global banking sector.

Principles for Responsible Investment

The PRI comprises a UN-supported international network of investors—signatories working together toward a common goal to understand the implications of ESG factors for investment and ownership decisions and ownership practices.

The PRI provides support in four main areas:

1. The PRI provides a broad range of tools and reports on best practices for asset owners, asset managers, consultants, and data suppliers, supporting the implementation of the principles across all asset classes and providing insights into ESG issues.
2. It hosts a collaborative engagement platform, by which it leads engagements and also enables like-minded institutions to coordinate and take forward engagement with individual companies and sectors.
3. The PRI reviews, analyzes, and responds to responsible investment-related policies and consultations. It also provides a policy map to investors and facilitates communication between investors and their regulators on the topic of responsible investment.
4. The PRI Academy develops, aggregates, and disseminates academic studies on responsible investment-related themes.

The PRI developed six voluntary principles that provide overarching guidance on actions members can take to incorporate ESG issues into investment practice. The six principles are as follows:

1. We will incorporate ESG issues into investment analysis and decision-making processes.
2. We will be active owners and incorporate ESG issues into our ownership policies and practices.
3. We will seek appropriate disclosure on ESG issues by the entities in which we invest.
4. We will promote acceptance and implementation of the principles within the investment industry.
5. We will work together to enhance our effectiveness in implementing the principles.
6. We will each report on our activities and progress towards implementing the principles.[1]

The PRI also leads or establishes partnerships with other organizations to develop initiatives, such as a review of fiduciary duty around the world and the establishment and implementation of the Sustainable Stock Exchanges Initiative. Many of its workstreams and initiatives are supported by committees made of members, which is a key way for investors to gain further insight and contribute to the development of knowledge and the further implementation of responsible investment across the industry.

For some in the investment industry, membership in the PRI has become a badge for being a responsible investor. The PRI requires members to report annually on their responsible investment practices, which are assessed by the PRI. The report is made available to the public, while the assessment is private to the member, which can then decide whether and with whom it shares the assessment (e.g., asset managers share the report with an existing or prospective client asset owner). Amid criticism that despite the assessment, there were no minimum requirements to become a member beyond payment of the membership fees, the PRI implemented minimum requirements in 2018. The three requirements are as follows:

1. Investment policy that covers the firm's responsible investment approach, covering >50% of assets under management (AUM)

---

[1] Source: www.unpri.org/about-us/what-are-the-principles-for-responsible-investment.

Key Initiatives

2. Internal or external staff responsibility for implementing responsible investment policy
3. Senior-level commitment and accountability mechanisms for responsible investment implementation

In recent years, the growth of the ESG market and the increased use of the term "ESG" has been highly correlated to the growth in PRI membership. This relationship may be linked to the fact that the principles are designed to be compatible with a wide range of investment styles that operate within a traditional fiduciary framework. PRI signatories have grown about 30% a year since 2006. This growth rate demonstrates the overall market opportunity for ESG investing.

Exhibit 12 shows the number of new PRI signatories through the period April 2006 to March 2022, inclusive. Exhibit 13 shows the number of signatories worldwide by region in 2022.

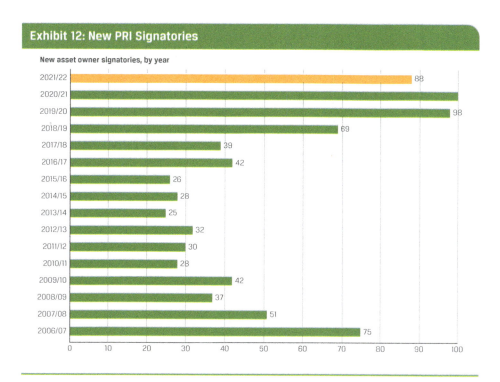

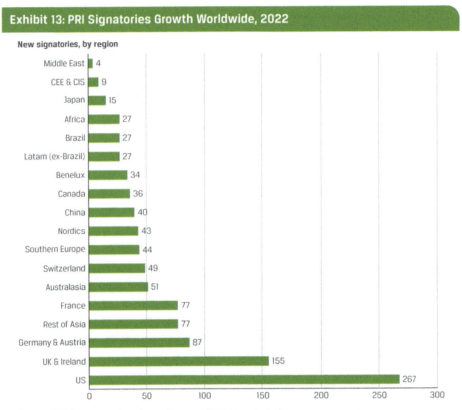

Source: PRI (www.unpri.org/annual-report-2022/signatories).

Growth in signatory numbers increased 28% year over year to 4,902 signatories (4,395 investors and 507 service providers) by March 2022. Investor signatories' AUM are estimated at US$121.3 trillion.

United Nations Framework Convention on Climate Change

Climate change has been a focus of the UN and, more recently, of investors as well. The **United Nations Framework Convention on Climate Change (UNFCCC)**, launched at the Rio de Janeiro Earth Summit in 1992, aims to stabilize GHG emissions to limit man-made climate change.

The UNFCCC hosts annual Conference of the Parties (COP) meetings, which seek to advance member states' voluntary agreements on limiting climate change.

The following are the two COPs of particular importance:

1. The COP3 meeting in Kyoto in 1997, which created the *Kyoto Protocol*. This commits industrialized countries to limit and reduce their GHG emissions in accordance with agreed individual targets.

2. The COP21 meeting in Paris in 2015, which led to the *Paris Agreement*. This commits developed and emerging economies to strengthen the response to the threat of climate change by keeping a global temperature rise this century well below 2°C (3.6°F) above pre-industrial levels.

The Paris Agreement had a significant impact on investors, including government and civil societies' expectations of them. This has led to investor-led initiatives to understand how to become aligned with the Paris Agreement, as well as various organizations engaging with investors on the topic.

Key Initiatives

UN Sustainable Development Goals

The **Sustainable Development Goals (SDGs)**, agreed to by all UN members in 2015 in replacement of the *UN Millennial Goals*, are the UN's blueprint to address key global challenges, including those related to poverty, inequality, climate change, environmental degradation, peace, and justice. The 17 goals are interconnected and particularly aimed at governments. The Paris Agreement, though negotiated in parallel to the SDGs, became one of its goals.

Despite the goals and subsequent targets not being directly applicable to businesses and investors, the SDGs have become a powerful framework for these groups, with some investors already reporting against their impact on the SDGs and allocating capital to contribute to their achievement. Exhibit 14 provides an illustration of the SDGs.

Exhibit 14: UN Sustainable Development Goals

Note from UN: The content of this publication has not been approved by the United Nations and does not reflect the views of the United Nations or its officials or Member States.
Source: UN (2020).

Glasgow Financial Alliance for Net Zero (GFANZ)

GFANZ brings together existing and new net-zero finance initiatives across banking, insurance, and asset management in one sector-wide coalition. It provides a forum for its 550 members to accelerate the transition to a net-zero global economy. GFANZ was launched in 2021 by Mark Carney, UN Special Envoy for Climate Action and Finance and UK Prime Minister Johnson's Finance Adviser for COP26, and the COP26 Private Finance Hub in partnership with the UNFCCC Climate Action Champions, the Race to Zero campaign, and the COP26 Presidency.

Race to Zero is the UN-backed global campaign rallying non-state actors—including companies, cities, regions, and financial and educational institutions—to take rigorous and immediate action to halve global GHG emissions by 2030. All members are committed to the same overarching goal: reducing GHG emissions across all scopes swiftly and fairly in line with the Paris Agreement, with transparent action plans and robust near-term targets.

Reporting Initiatives

Currently, there is a lack of standardization in sustainability reporting because there are multiple competing frameworks and methodologies. This situation has repercussions for the integrity of ESG data.

ESG-Related Initiatives

Global Reporting Initiative
The **Global Reporting Initiative (GRI)** publishes the GRI Standards, which provide guidance on disclosure across environmental, social, and economic factors for all stakeholders, including investors, whereas the other major frameworks are primarily investor focused. Several thousand organizations worldwide use the GRI framework, which is among the most well known and is the standard for the United Nations Global Compact. The framework covers the most categories of sustainability activity and encourages anecdotes and further prose to help contextualization.

Value Reporting Foundation
The Value Reporting Foundation (VRF) was formed upon the merger of the **International Integrated Reporting Council (IIRC)** and the **Sustainability Accounting Standards Board (SASB)**, two well-known global reporting initiatives. The objective of the VRF is to provide investors and corporations with a comprehensive corporate reporting framework across the full range of enterprise value drivers and standards. Before the merger, the IIRC developed the **Integrated Reporting Framework (IRF)** and the SASB issued the SASB Standards. IRF encouraged companies to integrate sustainability into their strategy and risk assessment by integrating it into the traditional annual report. The aim of the integrated report was to make it easier for investors to review such information as part of normal research processes and thus increase the likelihood that sustainability information is material to investment decisions. The SASB Standards were focused on key material sustainability issues, which affect 70-plus industry categories and were developed along with the SASB materiality maps. The SASB products were particularly helpful for investors determining what is material for reporting, and they aid more standardized benchmarking. The product suites of the two merging organizations are expected to be combined into one portfolio of offerings.

International Business Council ESG Disclosure Framework
The *ESG Disclosure Framework (EDF)* of the *International Business Council (IBC)* aims to bring greater consistency and comparability to sustainability reporting by establishing common metrics for company disclosure. The framework encourages disclosure on a "comply or explain" basis, with materiality, confidentiality, and legal constraints listed as acceptable reasons for not disclosing to a particular disclosure metric. Reporting is encouraged via annual reports or proxy statements to help ensure board oversight and participation of sustainability disclosure.

International Sustainability Standards Board (ISSB)
In 2021, the IFRS Foundation Trustees announced the creation of a new standard-setting board—the ISSB. The intention is for the ISSB to deliver a comprehensive global baseline of sustainability-related disclosure standards that provide capital market participants with information about companies' sustainability-related risks and opportunities to help them make informed decisions. The ISSB's proposals build on the work of the Climate Disclosure Standards Board, the International Accounting Standards Board, the Value Reporting Foundation (which houses Integrated Reporting and SASB Standards), the TCFD, and the World Economic Forum. ISSB plans to issue its first

Key Initiatives

reporting standards by the end of June 2023, with the ambition to have them effective for annual reporting periods beginning January 2024. This means a business would report its first sustainability-related disclosures in 2025.

Corporate Sustainability Reporting Directive (CSRD)

Due to go live in 2023, the CSRD will replace the Non-Financial Reporting Directive (NFRD), the previous regulation that required many EU corporations to report against the ESG metrics. The CSRD will cover nearly five times more corporations (50,000) and will be more prescriptive in terms of the format and standards.

Climate-Related Initiatives

Task Force on Climate-Related Financial Disclosures

The Financial Stability Board **Task Force on Climate-Related Financial Disclosures (TCFD)** takes the Paris Agreement's target of staying well under 2°C (3.6°F), with the ambition of staying under 1.5°C (2.7°F), and tries to operationalize it for the business world. Its June 2017 final report urges companies to disclose against the following:

- *Governance*—the organization's governance around climate-related risks and opportunities
- *Strategy*—the actual and potential impacts of climate-related risks and opportunities on the organization's businesses, strategy, and financial planning
- *Risk management*—the processes used by the organization to identify, assess, and manage climate-related risks
- *Metrics and targets*—the metrics and targets used to assess and manage relevant climate-related risks and opportunities

The TCFD recommends that these disclosures are provided as part of mainstream financial filings. For many, the emphasis that the TCFD puts on climate change as a board-level issue is its greatest contribution, both in terms of enhancing disclosure and in helping to ensure that this crucial issue is actively considered at the top of organizations. It should also drive a substantial advance in disclosures by seeking transparency about realistic scenario planning, particularly around the physical impacts of climate change.

CDP (Formerly, the Carbon Disclosure Project)

CDP is a non-governmental organization (NGO) that supports companies, financial institutions, and cities to disclose and manage their environmental impact. It runs a global environmental disclosure system in which nearly 10,000 companies, cities, states, and regions report on their risks and opportunities on climate change, water security, and deforestation.

Climate Disclosure Standards Board

The **Climate Disclosure Standards Board (CDSB)** is an international consortium of business and environmental NGOs with the mission to create the enabling conditions for material climate change and natural capital information to be integrated into mainstream reporting.

Other Initiatives

Asia Investor Group on Climate Change

The *Asia Investor Group on Climate Change (AIGCC)* is an initiative to create awareness among Asia's asset owners and financial institutions about the risks and opportunities associated with climate change and low-carbon investing. AIGCC provides capacity for investors to share best practices and to collaborate on investment activity, credit analysis, risk management, engagement, and policy.

Global Impact Investing Network

The **Global Impact Investing Network (GIIN)** focuses on reducing barriers to impact investment by building critical infrastructure and developing activities, education, and research that help accelerate the development of a coherent impact investing industry. It does the following:

- facilitates knowledge exchange,
- highlights innovative investment approaches,
- builds the evidence base for impact investing, and
- produces tools and resources.

Of note are its databases IRIS+ (of metrics for measuring and managing impact) and ImpactBase (of impact investing funds).

Global Sustainable Investment Alliance

Many countries have a national forum for responsible investment. The **Global Sustainable Investment Alliance (GSIA)** is an international collaboration of these membership-based sustainable investment organizations. It is a forum itself for advancing ESG investing across all regions and asset classes.

Core members of the GSIA include representatives from the regional responsible investment forums of Europe, the United States, Canada, Japan, Australia, and New Zealand. The GSIA reports draw on in-depth regional and national reports and work from GSIA members.

International Corporate Governance Network

The **International Corporate Governance Network (ICGN)** is an investor-led organization established in 1995 to promote effective standards of corporate governance and investor stewardship to advance efficient markets. Of note, the ICGN developed two key guidance documents for investors: one on stewardship and another on investment mandates.

The EU's Sustainable Finance Disclosure Regulation

In 2021, the European Union's Sustainable Finance Disclosure Regulation (SFDR) came into force. The SFDR is designed to support institutional asset owners and retail clients to compare, select, and monitor the sustainability characteristics of investment funds by standardizing sustainability disclosures. The disclosures are about the integration of sustainability risks, the consideration of adverse sustainability impacts, the promotion of environmental or social factors, and sustainable investment objectives. The SFDR is one of the building blocks of the EU's Sustainable Finance Action Plan. It applies to all financial advisers and financial market participants that construct financial products and/or provide investment advice or insurance advice in the European Economic Area (the EU member states plus Iceland, Liechtenstein, and Norway). The SFDR stipulates areas of mandatory disclosure at two levels: that of the investment firm and that of the product. Further, it introduces a new concept into the EU's regulatory environment: Principal Adverse Impacts (PAIs). PAIs are the negative effects from an investment on sustainability factors. These PAIs go into great detail and consist of 18 indicators for which disclosure is obligatory and 46 voluntary disclosure indicators. Further, the SFDR defines two categories of sustainable financial products: Article 8 products that *promote sustainability characteristics* and the more strictly defined Article 9 products that have stringent primary objectives for positive sustainability outcomes.

CFA Institute Global ESG Disclosure Standards for Investment Products

In 2021, CFA Institute published the Global ESG Disclosure Standards for Investment Products, the first global voluntary standards for disclosing how an investment product considers ESG issues in its objectives, investment process, and stewardship activities.

KEY FACTS

1. ESG investing is an approach to managing assets where investors explicitly acknowledge the relevance of environmental, social, and governance (ESG) factors in their investment decisions, as well as their own role as owners and creditors. ESG investing also recognizes that the generation of long-term sustainable returns is dependent on stable, well-functioning and well-governed social, environmental, and economic systems.

2. The concept of ESG investing is closely related to the concept of investees' corporate sustainability. Related to this, corporate social responsibility (CSR) is a broad business concept that describes a company's commitment to conducting its business in an ethical way. In the past few years, environmental, social, and governance considerations have evolved to go beyond a moral prism and have become increasingly strategic for companies.

3. All forms of responsible investment, except for engagement, are ultimately related to portfolio construction (in other words, which securities a fund holds). Some focus more on improving financial returns using financially material ESG factors, while others combine robust returns with optimizing the impact the investment has on society and the environment. Engagement, both by equity owners and bond holders, concerns whether and how a fund tries to encourage and influence an issuer's behavior on ESG matters.

4. One of the main reasons for ESG integration is that responsible investment can reduce risk and enhance returns. Financial materiality can be due to
    a. reduced cost and increased efficiency,
    b. reduced risk of fines,
    c. reduced externalities, and
    d. improved adaptability to sustainability megatrends.

5. Evidence of the risks that ESG megatrends carry is illustrated by the World Economic Forum's annual Global Risks Report, which for many years now has highlighted the growing likelihood and impact of extreme weather events and the failure to address climate change.

6. For many years, fiduciary duty was considered a barrier to considering ESG factors in investments. However, the modern interpretation of fiduciary duty, put forward in the Freshfields report, recognizes that failing to consider long-term investment value drivers—which include ESG issues—in investment practice is a failure of fiduciary duty.

7. Large institutional investors, known as universal owners, have holdings that are highly diversified across all asset classes, sectors, and regions. Their investment returns are thus mostly dependent on the overall economy. A

reason for implementing ESG stems from the recognition that negative megatrends will, over time, create a drag on economic prosperity and may increase instability both within and between countries.

8. A reason for practicing responsible investment is the belief that some investors have that investments can or even should serve society alongside providing financial return. The UN Sustainable Development Goals (SDGs), a framework agreed by all UN member state governments to work toward aligning with global priorities, has been adapted by some of the investment community to manage and improve the impact of their investments.

9. Client demand is instrumental for responsible investment because clients make the decisions about how their assets, representing on average 34% of GDP in OECD countries, are managed. The number of them that are integrating ESG considerations continues to grow.

10. Institutional investors typically reflect ESG considerations by such processes as
    a. including them in investment mandates,
    b. factoring them in their strategic asset allocation process,
    c. applying a filter based on ratings,
    d. integrating ESG issues into financial models, or
    e. using ESG factors to identify investment opportunities.

11. The financial materiality of ESG factors is driven by their ability to reduce risk and enhance returns, because they consider additional risks and inject new and forward-looking insights into the investment process.

12. The ability to integrate a response to sustainability megatrends into business operations can be a success factor for an investee firm, such as helping them anticipate growth opportunities or finding alternatives for rising costs of raw material.

13. ESG investing has seen rapid development in recent years, but challenges to its further growth remain. These challenges manifest themselves both prior to a firm wishing to implement ESG investing (perceptions about performance, old interpretations around fiduciary duty, or non-supportive advice) and once the decision has been made to implement ESG investing (a lack of understanding, resource intensity, access to good quality data, or a gap between marketing, commitment, or delivery).

14. There is a growing recognition in the financial industry and in academia that ESG factors influence financial performance. Various studies indicate that engaging with companies on ESG issues can create value for both investors and companies by encouraging better ESG risk management and more sustainable business practices. There are also meta-studies that demonstrate a relationship between ESG integration and improved financial performance at a corporate level.

15. The UN hosts or sponsors various initiatives that drive sustainability and ESG investing. Of note is the Principles for Responsible Investment (PRI), which comprises an international network of investors working together to understand the implications of ESG factors for investment and ownership decisions, and ownership practices. The PRI provides a broad range of tools

and reports on best practice for the various actors in the investment value chain. Recently, the growth of the ESG market and the increased use of the term "ESG" has been highly correlated with the growth in PRI membership.

16. The Financial Stability Board Task Force on Climate-Related Financial Disclosures (TCFD) has developed a framework to help public companies and other organizations disclose climate-related risks and opportunities. It should drive a substantial advance in disclosures by seeking transparency about realistic scenario planning, particularly around the physical impacts of climate change, including for investors. While this is a voluntary set of recommendations, various jurisdictions have started translating them into disclosure-related laws.

FURTHER READING

- Eccles, R., I. Ioannou, and G. Serafeim. 2012. "The Impact of Corporate Sustainability on Organizational Processes and Performance." National Bureau of Economic Research Working Paper 17950.
- International Corporate Governance Network. 2012. "ICGN Global Stewardship Principles—ICGN Global Stewardship Principles & Endorsers."
- International Corporate Governance Network. 2016. "ICGN Global Stewardship Principles."
- International Corporate Governance Network. 2017. "ICGN Global Governance Principles."
- Law Commission. 2013. "Fiduciary Duties of Investment Intermediaries." www.lawcom.gov.uk/project/fiduciary-duties-of-investment-intermediaries.
- PRI. 2016. "From Principles to Performance." http://10.unpri.org/wp-content/uploads/2016/04/PRI-final-report_-single-pages.pdf.

REFERENCES

Freeman, R. Edward, David L. Reed. 1983. "Stockholders and Stakeholders: A New Perspective on Corporate Governance." California Management Review 25 (April): 88–106. www.researchgate.net/publication/238325277_Stockholders_and_Stakeholders_A_New_Perspective_on_Corporate_Governance10.2307/41165018.

Kay, John. 2012. "The Kay Review of UK Equity Markets and Long-Term Decision Making: Final Report" (July).

PRI 2020. "What Is Responsible Investment?" www.unpri.org/an-introduction-to-responsible-investment/what-is-responsible-investment/4780.article.

Ashrafi, M., M. Acciaro, T. R. Walker, G. M. Magnan, M. Adams. 2019. "Corporate Sustainability in Canadian and US Maritime Ports." *Journal of Cleaner Production* 220 (20 May): 386–97. .10.1016/j.jclepro.2019.02.098.

Elkington, J. 2018. "25 Years Ago I Coined the Phrase 'Triple Bottom Line.' Here's Why It's Time to Rethink It." *Harvard Business Review* (25 June). https://hbr.org/2018/06/25-years-ago-i-coined-the-phrase-triple-bottom-line-heres-why-im-giving-up-on-it.

Investing, Inspire. 2019. "Faith-Based Investment and Sustainability." www.inspireinvesting.com/2019/03/26/faith-based-investment-and-sustainability/.

Mudaliar, A., R. Bass, H. Dithrich, N. Nova. 2019. "2019 Annual Impact Investor Survey". Global Impact Investing Network (19 June). https://thegiin.org/research/publication/impinv-survey-2019.

OECD 2019. Social Impact Investment 2019: The Impact Imperative for Sustainable Development. Paris: OECD Publishing.

PRI 2020. "What Is Responsible Investment?" (2020). www.unpri.org/an-introduction-to-responsible-investment/what-is-responsible-investment/4780.article.

Accenture 2022. "Nearly All Companies Will Miss Net Zero Goals Without At Least Doubling Rate of Carbon Emissions Reductions by 2030, Accenture Report Finds." Accenture *Newsroom* (1 November). https://newsroom.accenture.com/news/nearly-all-companies-will-miss-net-zero-goals-without-at-least-doubling-rate-of-carbon-emissions-reductions-by-2030-accenture-report-finds.htm.

BlackRock 2020. "Sustainability as BlackRock's New Standard for Investing." www.blackrock.com/au/individual/blackrock-client-letter.

Carney, M. 2015. "Breaking the Tragedy of the Horizon—Climate Change and Financial Stability." Bank of England, speech given at Lloyd's of London (29 September). www.bankofengland.co.uk/speech/2015/breaking-the-tragedy-of-the-horizon-climate-change-and-financial-stability.

CBA 2022. "4Q21 Earnings Release." https://www.cba.com.br/en/media.

Energy and Mines 2015. "Social Conflicts in Peru Have Delayed $21billion Worth of Mining Projects." energyandmines.com/2015/10/social-conflicts-in-peru-have-delayed-21billion-worth-of-mining-projects.

Fink, L. 2020. "A Fundamental Reshaping of Finance." BlackRock. www.blackrock.com/corporate/investor-relations/2020-larry-fink-ceo-letter.

Freshfields Bruckhaus Deringer 2005. "A Legal Framework for the Integration of Environmental, Social and Governance Issues into Institutional Investment." UNEP Finance Initiative (October). www.unepfi.org/publications/investment-publications/a-legal-framework-for-the-integration-of-environmental-social-and-governance-issues-into-institutional-investment.

McFall-Johnsen, M. 2019. "Over 1,500 California Fires in the Past 6 Years—Including the Deadliest Ever—Were Caused by One Company: PG&E. Here's What It Could Have Done but Didn't." *Business Insider* (3 November). www.businessinsider.com/pge-caused-california-wildfires-safety-measures-2019-10?r=US&IR=T.

References

PRI 2017. "The SDG Investment Case—Macro Risks: Universal Ownership" (12 October). www.unpri.org/sdgs/the-sdgs-are-an-unavoidable-consideration-for-universal-owners/306.article.

PRI 2019. "Fiduciary Duty in the 21st Century: Executive Summary." www.unpri.org/fiduciary-duty/fiduciary-duty-in-the-21st-century/244.article.

PRI 2022. "Regulation Database" (updated in April). www.unpri.org/sustainable-markets/regulation-map.

Ratcliff, A. 2019. "Billionaire Fortunes Grew by $2.5 Billion a Day Last Year As Poorest Saw Their Wealth Fall." Oxfam International (21 January). www.oxfam.org/en/press-releases/billionaire-fortunes-grew-25-billion-day-last-year-poorest-saw-their-wealth-fall.

Raworth, K. 2017. Doughnut Economics: Seven Ways to Think Like a 21st Century Economist. White River Junction, VT: Chelsea Green Publishing.

Sievänen, R., H. Rita, B. Scholtens. 2012. "The Drivers of Responsible Investment: The Case of European Pension Funds." Journal of Business Ethics 117 (September): 137–51. www.researchgate.net/publication/236667333_The_Drivers_of_Responsible_Investment_The_Case_of_European_Pension_Funds.

Stockholm Resilience Centre 2015. "The Nine Planetary Boundaries." www.stockholmresilience.org/research/planetary-boundaries/planetary-boundaries/about-the-research/the-nine-planetary-boundaries.html.

Stockholm Resilience Centre 2022. "New Assessment Reveals Dramatic Changes to the Global Water Cycle, with Parts of the Amazon Drying Out." www.stockholmresilience.org/research/research-news/2022-04-26-freshwater-boundary-exceeds-safe-limits.html.

World Economic Forum 2020. "The Global Risks Report 2020" (15 January). www.weforum.org/reports/the-global-risks-report-2020.

Aeon. 2019. "Aeon Sustainability Data Book 2019." www.aeon.info/export/sites/default/common/images/en/environment/report/e_2019pdf/19_data_en_a4.pdf.

"Bank of America and the Financial Crisis." 2014. *New York Times* (21 August). www.nytimes.com/interactive/2014/06/10/business/dealbook/11bank-timelime.html.

CE Delft and Directorate-General for Mobility and Transport. 2019. "Taxes in the Field of Aviation and Their Impact: Final Report." https://op.europa.eu/s/oarR.

Ding, H., M. He, C. Deng. 2014. "Lifecycle Approach to Assessing Environmental Friendly Product Project with Internalizing Environmental Externality." *Journal of Cleaner Production* 66 (1 March): 128–38. www.sciencedirect.com/science/article/abs/pii/S0959652613006811. .10.1016/j.jclepro.2013.10.018.

Dow. 2018. *2018 Sustainability Report*. https://corporate.dow.com/content/dam/corp/documents/science-sustainability/910-00008-01-dow-2018-annual-sustainability-report.pdf.

Edmans, A. 2011. "Does the Stock Market Fully Value Intangibles? Employee Satisfaction and Equity Prices." Journal of Financial Economics 101 (September): 621–40. www.sciencedirect.com/science/article/abs/pii/S0304405X11000869.10.1016/j.jfineco.2011.03.021.

European Commission 2019. "Aircraft Operators and Their Administering Countries." https://ec.europa.eu/clima/policies/ets/monitoring/operators_en.

GE 2014. "GE Works: 2013 Annual Report." Letter to shareowners. www.ge.com/jp/sites/www.ge.com.jp/files/GE_AR13.pdf.

Helbling, T. 2010. "What Are Externalities?" Finance & Development 47 (4). www.imf.org/external/pubs/ft/fandd/2010/12/basics.htm.

Henisz, W., T. Koller, R. Nuttall. 2019. "Five Ways That ESG Creates Value." *McKinsey Quarterly* (November). www.mckinsey.com/business-functions/strategy-and-corporate-finance/our-insights/five-ways-that-esg-creates-value?cid=soc-web.

Lawson, Max, Anam Parvez Butt, Rowan Harvey, Diana Sarosi, Clare Coffey, Kim Piaget, Julie Thekkudan. 2020. "Time to Care: Unpaid and Underpaid Care Work and the Global Inequality Crisis." Oxfam International (20 January). www.oxfam.org/en/research/time-care.

Marotta, F. 2013. "Subject: Request from the Chair of the OECD Working Party on Responsible Business Conduct" (27 November). www.ohchr.org/Documents/Issues/Business/LetterOECD.pdf.

McKinsey & Company 2017. "McKinsey Special Collections: Trends and Global Forces" (April). www.mckinsey.com/~/media/McKinsey/Business%20Functions/Strategy%20and%20Corporate%20Finance/Our%20Insights/Strategy%20and%20corporate%20finance%20special%20collection/Final%20PDFs/McKinsey-Special-Collections_Trends-and-global-forces.ashx.

Norwegian National Contact Point for the OECD Guidelines for Multinational Enterprises 2013. "Final Statement: Complaint from Lok Shakti Abhiyan, Korean Transnational Corporations Watch, Fair Green and Global Alliance and Forum for Environment and Development vs. Posco (South Korea), ABP/ APG (Netherlands) and NBIM (Norway)" (27 May). https://vdocuments.mx/final-statement-nettsteder-for-final-statement-complaint-from-lok-shakti-abhiyan.html?page=1.

OECD 2018. "OECD Guidelines for Multinational Enterprises." www.oecd.org/corporate/mne/.

Parker, M. 2018. "Letter to Shareholders." NIKE, Inc. (24 July). https://s1.q4cdn.com/806093406/files/doc_financials/2018/ar/docs/nike-shareholders-letter-2018.pdf.

PWC 2020. "Technological Breakthroughs." www.pwc.co.uk/issues/megatrends/technological-breakthroughs.html.

Rushe, D. 2015. "BP Set to Pay Largest Environmental Fine in US History for Gulf Oil Spill." *Guardian* (2 July). www.theguardian.com/environment/2015/jul/02/bp-will-pay-largest-environmental-fine-in-us-history-for-gulf-oil-spill.

Stokel-Walker, C. 2019. "Only Extreme Eco-Taxes on Flights Will Change Our Flying Habits." *Wired* (12 July). www.wired.co.uk/article/plane-tax-eco-france-sweden.

Täger, Matthias. 2021. "'Double Materiality': What Is It and Why Does It Matter?" www.lse.ac.uk/granthaminstitute/news/double-materiality-what-is-it-and-why-does-it-matter.

UN Environment Programme 2019. "Environmental Rule of Law: First Global Report" (24 January). www.unenvironment.org/resources/assessment/environmental-rule-law-first-global-report.

UNGC 2011. "Guiding Principles Business on Human Rights: Implementing the United Nations 'Protect, Respect and Remedy' Framework." www.unglobalcompact.org/library/2.

"VW in $14.7bn US Deal over Rigged Cars." 2016. *Financial Times* (27 June).

Wainwright, S. 2010. "Putting a Price on Global Environmental Damage." *Trucost News* (5 October).

Whelan, T., C. Fink. 2016. "The Comprehensive Business Case for Sustainability." *Harvard Business Review* (21 October). https://hbr.org/2016/10/the-comprehensive-business-case-for-sustainability.

Lee, Mark, Emily K. Brock, Doug MacNair. 2022. "Costs and Benefits of Climate-Related Disclosure Activities by Corporate Issuers and Institutional Investors." The SustainAbility Institute by ERM. www.sustainability.com/thinking/costs-and-benefits-of-climate-related-disclosure-activities-by-corporate-issuers-and-institutional-investors.

PRI 2016. "How Asset Owners Can Drive Responsible Investment: Beliefs, Strategies and Mandates." www.unpri.org/download?ac=1398.

Clark, G. L., A. Feiner, M. Viehs. 2015. "From the Stockholder to the Stakeholder: How Sustainability Can Drive Financial Outperformance." https://ssrn.com/abstract=2508281.

Dimson, Elroy, Oğuzhan Karakaş, Xi Li. 2017. "Local Leads, Backed by Global Scale: The Drivers of Successful Engagement." *RI Quarterly Vol. 12: Highlights from the Academic Network Conference and PRI in Person 2017* (19 September). www.unpri.org/academic-research/local-leads-backed-by-global-scale-the-drivers-of-successful-engagement/537.article.

References

Friede, G., T. Busch, A. Bassen. 2015. "ESG and Financial Performance: Aggregated Evidence from More Than 2000 Empirical Studies." *Journal of Sustainable Finance & Investment* 5 (15 December): 210–33. .10.1080/20430795.2015.1118917

Fulton, M., B. Kahn, C. Sharples. 2012. "Sustainable Investing: Establishing Long-Term Value and Performance." DB Climate Change Advisors (June). .10.2139/ssrn.2222740

Global Research Institute 2018. "Digging Deeper into the ESG-Corporate Financial-Performance-Relationship" (September). https://download.dws.com/download?elib-assetguid=714aed4c2e83471787d1ca0f1b559006.

PRI 2018. "How ESG Engagement Creates Value for Investors and Companies: Executive Summary" (26 April). www.unpri.org/academic-research/how-esg-engagement-creates-value-for-investors-and-companies/3054.article.

Whelan, Tensie, Ulrich Atz, Tracy Van Holt, Casey Clark. 2021. "ESG and Financial Performance: Uncovering the Relationship by Aggregating Evidence from 1,000 Plus Studies Published between 2015–2020" (10 February). https://rcm.rockco.com/insights_item/esg-and-financial-performance.

UN 2020. "Take Action for the Sustainable Development Goals." www.un.org/sustainabledevelopment/sustainable-development-goals/.

PRACTICE PROBLEMS

1. Which of the following investment approaches is *most likely* to be at risk of short-termism?
   a. ESG investing
   b. Impact investing
   c. Conventional investing

2. Which of the following types of responsible investment is focused on the bottom of the pyramid (BOP)?
   a. Green bonds
   b. Microfinance bonds
   c. Funds investing in smart grid technology

3. According to the Stockholm Resilience Centre, the two core boundaries of the nine planetary boundaries are:
   a. biosphere integrity and climate change.
   b. climate change and land-system change.
   c. biosphere integrity and land-system change.

4. ESG integration can have a material financial impact on a company leading to:
   a. reduced risk of fines.
   b. increased negative externalities.
   c. increased risk of state intervention.

5. Which of the following statements regarding externalities is *most* accurate?
   a. Externalities occur due to environmental or social factors.
   b. When externalities are positive, private costs are lower than societal costs.
   c. Internalization of externalities improves companies' financial performance.

6. In addition to the payment of dues and reporting annually on their responsible investment practices, which of the following is a minimum requirement for signatories to the Principles of Responsible Investment (PRI)? Members must:
   a. be active owners in the companies in which they are invested.
   b. seek appropriate disclosure on ESG issues by the investee companies.
   c. have senior-level commitment for responsible investment implementation.

7. Which of the following organizations developed the Model Mandate Initiative?
   a. Principles for Responsible Investment (PRI)
   b. International Corporate Governance Network (ICGN)
   c. University of Cambridge Institute for Sustainability Leadership

8. Which of the following statements is *most* accurate? The majority of studies suggest that:
   a. a company with high ESG standards increases its cost of capital.
   b. ESG performance and investment fund performance are positively correlated.
   c. ESG performance and corporate financial performance are positively correlated.

Practice Problems

9. Greenwashing *most likely* refers to:
   a. countries exporting hazardous waste to other countries.
   b. companies making misleading claims about their environmental practices.
   c. companies introducing substances into the environment that are harmful.

10. The standard for the UN Global Compact is overseen by the:
    a. Global Reporting Initiative (GRI).
    b. Value Reporting Foundation (VRF).
    c. International Business Council (IBC).

11. Which of the following requires investors to act with a more long-term focus?
    a. Stockholm Resilience Centre
    b. Financial Stability Board (FSB)
    c. UN Shareholder Rights Directive (SRD)

12. Which of the following types of responsible investing is not related to portfolio construction?
    a. Thematic investing
    b. Shareholder engagement
    c. Socially responsible investing (SRI)

13. Which of the following responsible investment approaches *most likely* incorporates positive screening?
    a. Faith-based investment
    b. Values-driven investment
    c. Best-in-class investment

14. Double materiality is *best* described as:
    a. an extension of financial materiality that considers the impacts of a company on the climate or any other ESG factor.
    b. an accounting framework with three parts: social, environmental (or ecological), and financial (people, planet, and profit).
    c. investments made with the specific intent of generating positive, measurable social and environmental impact alongside a financial return.

15. Universal owners are *best* described as:
    a. large institutional investors that have diversified holdings.
    b. retail investors that diversify through index funds or ETFs.
    c. stakeholders impacted by externalized environmental and social costs.

16. Which of the following statements about the internalization of externalities is *most* accurate?
    a. Internalization of negative externalities can be achieved only by regulatory means.
    b. Internalization through taxation is an innovative, new idea to address externalized pollution costs.
    c. Internalization refers to all measures to ensure externalities are reflected in the prices of commercial goods and services.

17. The Shareholder Rights Directive (SRD) is a regulatory initiative to:

  a. counter short-termism.

  b. reduce the use of proxies by management.

  c. protect minority shareholders' interests.

18. The Freshfields report was seminal in understanding that:

  a. corporate profits are materially at risk from state intervention.

  b. ESG issues are relevant for financial valuation and fiduciary duty.

  c. humanity's ability to thrive is contingent on respecting planetary boundaries.

19. The proportion of Fortune Global 500 companies headquartered in emerging markets is expected to:

  a. decrease.

  b. remain approximately the same.

  c. increase.

20. Which of the following statements about population is *most* accurate?

  a. China's labor force has already peaked.

  b. The global population is getting younger.

  c. The world's population is expected to shrink by 2030.

21. Investors demonstrate short-termism by:

  a. engaging with investee companies to maximize long-term value.

  b. encouraging the development of a long-term ESG implementation plan.

  c. trading based on short-term price movements rather than long-term value.

22. Which of the following is not an example of a social factor?

  a. Biodiversity

  b. Labor standards

  c. Health and safety

23. ESG considerations are difficult to value precisely and difficult to time because ESG data:

  a. are not always available.

  b. can only be measured quantitatively.

  c. have no impact on financial statements.

24. Institutional investors generate sustainable returns from their investments by:

  a. not engaging actively with companies on ESG matters.

  b. disclosing their corporate social responsibility activities.

  c. integrating ESG factors into their portfolio construction decisions.

25. What are the four broad groupings of issues covered by the UN Global Compact?

  a. Environmental, social, governance, and impact

  b. Poverty, diversity, sustainability, and transparency

  c. Human rights, labor, environment, and anti-corruption

26. Which of the following is *not* one of the three Ps in the triple bottom line con-

Practice Problems

cept?

   a. People
   b. Planet
   c. Principles

27. Best-in-class investment:

   a. uses negative screening to exclude companies.
   b. refers to selecting companies that fall under a sustainability-related theme.
   c. involves selecting only the companies that overcome a defined ranking hurdle.

28. Which of the following sectors is *least likely* to be excluded by ethical and faith-based investments?

   a. Alcohol
   b. Weapons
   c. Technology

29. The efficiency of shareholder engagement depends on:

   a. the amount of security in free float.
   b. the length of ownership of shareholders.
   c. whether divestment is known to be a possible sanction.

30. In which way can ESG matters reduce risk and enhance return?

   a. Increased likelihood of fines
   b. Increased cost and reduced efficiency
   c. Increased adaptability to sustainability megatrends

31. Which of the following situations *best* illustrates the term "negative externality"?

   a. The stress that workers take home with them
   b. An unexpected cost increase in an input of production
   c. A product's price not reflecting the true costs of that product for society as a whole

32. Which of the following megatrends is *most* closely related to Oxfam's report that "the richest 1% in the world have more than double the wealth of 6.9 billion people"?

   a. Emerging markets and urbanization
   b. Demographic changes and inequality
   c. Climate change and resource scarcity

33. Institutional investors are *most likely* to engage with policymakers on ESG issues because:

   a. asset owners need regulators to level the playing field.
   b. considering ESG-related matters can contribute to the proper functioning of the financial markets.
   c. policy consultations on ESG investing are mandatory to ensure that all perspectives are taken into consideration.

SOLUTIONS

1. **C is correct**. Conventional financial investing is subject to short-termism, where investors trade based on anticipation of short-term price movements rather than long-term value and make investments in companies that prioritize maximizing near-term financial results over long-term value creation.

2. **B is correct**. Social investments allocate capital to investments that address the bottom of the pyramid—that is, the poorest two-thirds of the economic human pyramid. Microfinance is an example of such social investment.

3. **A is correct**. The Stockholm Resilience Centre has identified nine planetary boundaries within which humanity can continue to develop and thrive. Two of these—climate change and biosphere integrity—are deemed core boundaries, for which significant alteration would "drive the Earth system into a new state."

4. **A is correct**. ESG investing can reduce risk and enhance returns, because it considers additional risks and injects new and forward-looking insights into the investment process. ESG integration may therefore lead to reduced cost and increased efficiency, reduced risk of fines and state intervention, reduced negative externalities, and improved ability to benefit from sustainability megatrends.

5. **A is correct**. Externalities can occur due to environmental factors, such as pollution, or social factors—for example, when companies fail to pay a minimum wage. When externalities are positive, private costs are higher than societal costs. When externalities are negative, private costs are lower than societal costs. Internalization of these externalities could significantly impact the costs and profits of companies' products and services, affecting their bottom line.

6. **C is correct**. Amid criticism that despite the assessment, there were no minimum requirements to become a member beyond payment of the membership fees, the PRI implemented minimum requirements in 2018, one of which is the senior-level commitment and accountability mechanisms for responsible investment implementation. The PRI requires members to report annually on their responsible investment practices, which are assessed by the PRI.

7. **B is correct**. The ICGN established the Model Mandate Initiative. The University of Cambridge Institute for Sustainability Leadership developed a toolkit for establishing long-term, sustainable mandates, and the PRI published numerous guidance documents to support asset owners in incorporating ESG investing into manager selection and investment mandates.

8. **C is correct**. Most studies suggest that there is a positive correlation between ESG performance and corporate financial performance. Studies are mixed on the correlation of ESG performance and investment fund performance. Most studies indicate good ESG standards lower the cost of capital.

9. **B is correct**. Greenwashing is the overrepresentation or misrepresentation—either intentionally or unintentionally—of the qualifications and credibility of an investment portfolio or company that promotes itself as green, sustainable, responsible, or ESG friendly.

10. **A is correct**. The GRI publishes the GRI Standards, which provide guidance on disclosure across environmental, social, and economic factors for all stakeholders, including investors, whereas the other major frameworks are primarily investor focused. Several thousand organizations worldwide use the GRI framework, which

Solutions

is among the most well known and is the standard for the UN Global Compact.

11. **C is correct**. The SRD was issued by the European Union in September 2020, requiring investors to be active owners and to act with a more long-term focus.

12. **B is correct**. All forms of responsible investment are ultimately related to portfolio construction with the exception of engagement. Engagement is the attempt to influence a company's behavior on ESG matters and is not related to portfolio construction. Both thematic investing and SRI screen securities to select a pool of investments that match the investor's investing preferences.

13. **C is correct**. Best-in-class investment is also known as "positive screening" and involves selecting only those companies that overcome a defined ranking hurdle, established using ESG criteria in each sector or industry. Both ethical (also known as values-driven) and faith-based investment use negative screening to avoid investing in companies whose products and services are deemed morally objectionable by the investor.

14. **A is correct**. Double materiality is an extension of the accounting concept of financial materiality. Double materiality considers the impacts of a company on the climate—or any other ESG factor. An accounting framework with three parts is known as the triple bottom line. Impact investing refers to investments made with the specific intent of generating positive, measurable social and environmental impact alongside a financial return.

15. **A is correct**. Large institutional investors, due to their size, have holdings that are highly diversified across all sectors, asset classes, and regions. As a result, their portfolios are sufficiently representative of global capital markets that they effectively hold a slice of the overall market. Their investment returns are thus dependent on the continuing good health of the overall economy—hence, the term *universal owners*. While stakeholders are impacted by negative externalities and retail investors with broad equity exposure are also somewhat geographically diverse, they lack the diversity achievable only through scale.

16. **C is correct**. Internalization refers to all measures (public or private) to ensure that externalities become reflected in the prices of commercial goods and services. It is not limited to regulatory means. Using taxation to force internalization of pollution costs was first suggested in the 1920s.

17. **A is correct**. The SRD was issued by the EU in September 2020, requiring investors to be active owners and to act with a more long-term focus. The SRD is not related to proxies or protecting minority shareholders.

18. **B is correct**. The Freshfields report argued that "the modern interpretation of fiduciary duty recognizes that failing to consider long-term investment value drivers—which include ESG issues—in investment practice is a failure of fiduciary duty." The planetary boundaries were identified by the Stockholm Resilience Centre, and it was analysis conducted by McKinsey that addressed corporate profits being at risk from state intervention.

19. **C is correct**. 97% of the Fortune Global 500 were once headquartered in developed economies, and nearly half of the world's large companies are expected to be headquartered in emerging markets by 2025. The locus of economic activity and dynamism is shifting to emerging markets and to cities in those markets.

20. **A is correct**. China's labor force peaked in 2012. By 2030, the world's population is projected to rise by more than 1 billion. At the same time, the population is getting older.

21. **C is correct**. Short-termism covers a wide range of activities; for the purpose of this topic, the most relevant activities are trading practices where investors trade based on short-term momentum and price movements rather than long-term value.

22. **A is correct**. Biodiversity pertains to the natural world and is classified as an environmental factor. Labor standards and health and safety are social factors because they directly affect the lives of humans.

23. **A is correct**. ESG considerations are difficult to value precisely and difficult to time because ESG data are not always available and do not always have a short-term impact. As such, ESG considerations are often—but not always—measured qualitatively. In the longer run, ESG considerations will have an impact on financial statements.

24. **C is correct**. Disclosing their own corporate social responsibility activities doesn't directly incorporate ESG factors in institutional investors' investment approaches. Instead, institutional investors integrate ESG factors into their portfolio construction decisions and use corporate and policy engagement to further their ability to generate sustainable returns from their investments.

25. **C is correct**. The 10 principles of the UN Global Compact cover the areas of human rights, labor, environment, and anti-corruption.

26. **C is correct**. The triple bottom line concept expands the traditional, accounting-based focus on profit to also incorporate social impacts ("people") and environmental impacts ("planet"). As such, the "three Ps" include people, planet, and profit, not principles.

27. **C is correct**. The best-in-class approach involves selecting only the companies that overcome a defined ranking hurdle, thereby allowing portfolios to be constructed in a way that maintains desired index characteristics. Selecting companies according to a particular theme is referred to as thematic investment.

28. **C is correct**. Ethical and faith-based investment portfolios often avoid investments whose products or services are considered morally objectionable by the investors. Companies that sell alcohol or weapons, but not technology, are commonly targeted for exclusion.

29. **C is correct**. Shareholder engagement is used by investors to influence a corporation's decisions on ESG matters. Its efficiency depends on such factors as ownership levels and the threat of divestment, not the amount of security in free float.

30. **C is correct**. ESG matters can become financially material in all the ways listed, but only through increased adaptability to sustainability megatrends will they contribute to reduced risk and enhanced return.

31. **C is correct**. Negative externalities arise when the private price equilibrium for goods or services does not reflect their true cost. In these situations, the externalized costs are borne by those not involved in the production or consumption of the goods or services or by society as a whole.

32. **B is correct**. The Oxfam statement refers to the increasing concentration of wealth and resulting inequality that can lead to social strain. The most relevant megatrend is demographic changes and inequality.

33. **B is correct**. The proper functioning of the financial markets critically affects institutional investors' ability to generate sustainable returns. As such, they have an obligation to work with policymakers to achieve and protect functioning financial markets.

CHAPTER 2

The ESG Market

LEARNING OUTCOMES

Mastery	The candidate should be able to:
☐	2.1.1 explain the size and scope of ESG investing in relation to geography, strategy, investor type, and asset class
☐	2.1.2 explain key market drivers of ESG integration: investor demand/intergenerational wealth transfer, regulation and policy, public awareness, and data sourcing and processing improvements
☐	2.1.3 explain the key drivers and challenges for ESG integration among key stakeholders: asset owners, asset managers, fund promoters, financial services, policymakers and regulators, investees, government, civil society, and academia

INTRODUCTION

The environmental, social, and governance (ESG) investing market has become mainstream. A growing number of institutions assert that they integrate ESG considerations into their investment decisions and into their ownership activity. ESG investing commands a sizable share of professionally managed assets across all regions and across global financial markets.

There are multiple drivers for the growth in assets managed under an ESG approach in recent years. There is growing demand from institutional asset owners and individual retail **investors**, providing direct commercial incentives for asset managers to engage. In addition, there has been an increase in government policy and regulation relevant to ESG investing across various regions, including pressure from non-governmental organizations (NGOs) and other members of civil society, which has also stimulated the market's growth.

This chapter highlights the size and scope of the ESG investing market, identifies some key characteristics, and discusses the challenges to further growth and enhanced quality of ESG investing, as well as some of the ways these barriers can be overcome.

2 ESG INVESTING IN NUMBERS

2.1.1 explain the size and scope of ESG investing in relation to geography, strategy, investor type, and asset class

Given the many definitions of responsible investment, there is a range of data regarding the responsible investment market. One of the most comprehensive market reviews is conducted by the Global Sustainable Investment Alliance. The GSIA conducts research in the five major markets for responsible investment (Europe, the United States, Japan, Canada, and Australia/New Zealand) every two years, with the most recent edition covering 2020 data (GSIA 2021). This most recent report showed sustainable investing assets in the five major markets stood at USD35.3 trillion at the start of 2020, a 15% increase in two years (GSIA 2021). In all the regions except Europe, the market share of ESG investing has grown, as seen in Exhibit 1. In terms of where sustainable and responsible investing assets are domiciled globally, the United States (48%) and Europe (34%) continue to manage the highest proportions.

Exhibit 1: Growth of ESG Assets by Region

Region	2012 (USD bn)	2014 (USD bn)	2016 (USD bn)	2018 (USD bn)	2020 (USD bn)
Europe	8,758	10,775	12,040	14,075	12,017
United States	3,740	6,572	8,723	11,995	17,081
Japan		7	474	2,180	2,974
Asia excl. Japan		45	52		
Asia incl. Japan	40				
Canada	589	729	1,086	1,699	2,423
Australia/New Zealand	134	148	516	734	906
Total	13,261	18,276	22,891	30,683	35,301

Notes: Asia excluding Japan 2014 assets are represented in US dollars based on the exchange rates at year-end 2013. All other 2014 assets, as well as all 2016 assets, were converted to US dollars based on exchange rates at year-end 2015. All 2018 assets were converted to US dollars at the exchange rates at the time of reporting. Assets for 2020 were reported as of 31 December 2019 for all regions except Japan, which reported as of 31 March 2020.
Source: GSIA (2021, 2019, 2013).

Responsible investment directs a sizable share of managed assets in each region, as can be seen in Exhibit 2. This share of assets ranges from 24% in Japan to 62% in Canada. Clearly, sustainable investing constitutes a major force across global financial markets. The proportion of sustainable investing relative to total managed assets grew in most regions, and in Canada, responsible investing assets now make up most of the total assets under professional management. The exceptions to this trend are Europe and Australia/New Zealand, where sustainable investing assets have declined relative to total managed assets since 2018. At least part of the market share decline in Europe and Australia/New Zealand stems from a shift to stricter standards and definitions for sustainable investing in those markets.

ESG Investing in Numbers

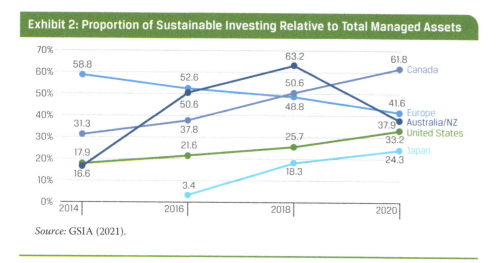

Exhibit 2: Proportion of Sustainable Investing Relative to Total Managed Assets

Source: GSIA (2021).

As of 2020, the largest sustainable investment strategy globally was ESG integration, as shown in Exhibit 3, with a combined USD25.1 trillion in assets under management (AUM). This is followed by negative, or exclusionary, screening, which had remained roughly stable in terms of AUM over the prior four years at USD15.0 trillion in assets.

- Norms-based and negative/exclusionary screening is the largest strategy in Europe.
- Sustainability thematic investing, impact/community investing, positive/best-in-class investing, and ESG integration command most assets in the United States.
- ESG integration along with corporate engagement and shareholder action constitutes the predominant strategy in Japan.

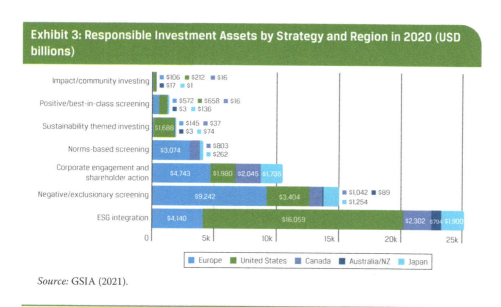

Exhibit 3: Responsible Investment Assets by Strategy and Region in 2020 (USD billions)

Source: GSIA (2021).

Over the 2016–20 period, as shown in Exhibit 4, the ESG integration strategy had the largest growth, which was mostly driven by the US market. Anecdotally, this growth is attributable to "relabeling" or "recycling" of already-existing funds by fund managers, with an open debate as to what extent such relabelings lead to increased greenwashing.

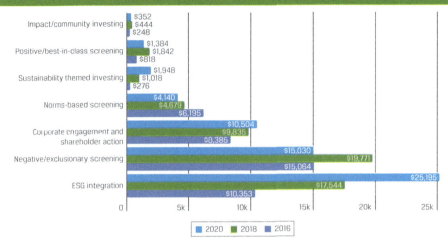

Source: GSIA (2021).

Investments managed by professional asset managers are often classified as either

- retail (investment by individuals) or
- institutional (investment firms).

Although institutional investors tend to dominate the financial market, interest by retail investors in responsible investing has been steadily growing:

- In 2012, institutional investors held 89% of assets, compared with 11% held by retail investors.
- In 2018, the retail portion had grown to one quarter, as seen in Exhibit 5.

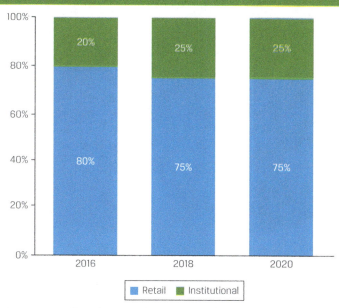

Exhibit 5: Global Shares of Institutional and Retail Sustainable Investing Assets, 2016–2020

Note: This data was not collected in Australasia or Europe for 2020.
Source: GSIA (2021).

Responsible investment extends across the range of asset classes commonly found in diversified investment portfolios; Exhibit 6 shows the asset class allocation reported by the GSIA in Europe, the United States, Japan, and Canada in the *Global Sustainable Investment Review 2018* (GSIA 2019). In that year, collectively in these regions,

- most assets were allocated to public equities (51% at the start of 2018), whereas
- the next largest asset allocation was in fixed income (36%).

In 2018, real estate/property and private equity/venture capital each held 3% of global sustainable investing assets. Sustainable investments could also be found in hedge funds, cash or depository vehicles, commodities, and infrastructure. These assets are reflected in the "other" assets category; for further details, see Exhibit 6.

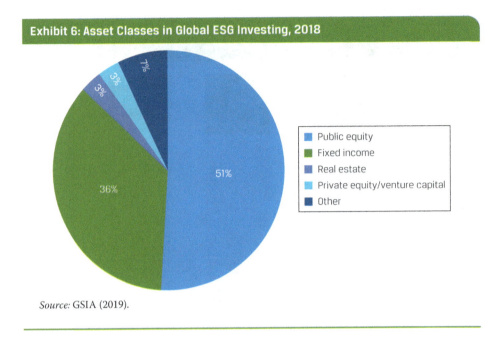

Exhibit 6: Asset Classes in Global ESG Investing, 2018

- Public equity: 51%
- Fixed income: 36%
- Real estate: 3%
- Private equity/venture capital: 3%
- Other: 7%

Source: GSIA (2019).

3 MARKET DRIVERS OF ESG AND CHALLENGES IN ESG INTEGRATION

☐ 2.1.2 explain key market drivers of ESG integration: investor demand/intergenerational wealth transfer, regulation and policy, public awareness, and data sourcing and processing improvements

Various stakeholders shape the push and pull for responsible investment, steering its demand and supply. There are a significant number of actors involved. This section presents the main stakeholders, focusing on the actors that influence investment decisions more directly, either by

- the choices they make or
- the services and/or information they provide.

The main stakeholders are as follows:

A. Asset owners (pension funds, insurers, sovereign wealth funds, endowment funds and foundations, and individual (retail investors)
B. Asset managers
C. Fund promoters (investment consultants and retail investment advisers, investment platform, and fund labelers)
D. Financial services (investment banks, investment research and advisory firms, stock exchanges, financial and ESG rating agencies)
E. Policymakers and regulators
F. Investees
G. Government

Market Drivers of ESG and Challenges in ESG Integration

H. Civil society and academia

All these stakeholders are covered in detail later in this chapter.

There is no standard way of dividing up the investment value chain; the main actors were aggregated in this manner for the purpose of discussing their role within responsible investment. Exhibit 7 provides an example of the investment value chain for listed equities. The value chain for other asset classes may differ slightly, with more or fewer intermediaries between the assets and the final owner of capital.

Exhibit 7: Investment Management Value Chain

1. Asset Owners	2. Investment Consultants	3. Investment Managers	4. Investment Brokers	5. Stock Exchanges	6. Policy Makers
Advanced sustainability commitments are widely implemented throughout the asset owners, including board, trustees, CIO, portfolio managers, research analysts, and legal counsel, and across asset classes and investment strategies. Sustainability factors are integrated in the selection process for investment consults, investment managers, and embedded in investment mandates	As asset owners signal their commitment to sustainability consideration, investment consultants will be incentivized to better assess investment managers on ESG performance, and make recommendations accordingly. Investment consults will offer a wide range of ESG investment products and services to markets, in line with trustees' needs, including explanations of how these products align with fiduciary duties.	As market signals grow, investment managers will offer advanced ESG investment products, in order to maintain their market share. This will include meaningful shareholder engagement, consistent with the investment beliefs of their clients, with advanced reporting to asset owners on implementation and the outcomes that have resulted.	Investment brokers and independent research providers will integrate research on ESG performance in company buy, hold, and sell recommendations, requiring companies to provide robust, credible, and detailed accounts of their management of ESG issues, and of the financial significance of these issues. Investment brokers and independent research providers with engage ratings agencies, data providers, and policy makers on issues relevant to responsible investment.	Sitting at the heart of the investment chain, stock exchanges will strengthen listing requirement for companies and offer advanced sustainability indices on a range of ESG metrics.	With sustainability embedded through the investment chain, policy makers will be more inclined to support regulator initiatives which reinforce responsible investment practice, engaging pension funds on issues beyond capital allocation, such as climate change, including policy formulation and policy implementations.

Source: PRI (2016).

It is, however, worthwhile to generally clarify the roles of **shareholders**, investors, and **investment managers**.

4. ASSET OWNERS

- **2.1.2** explain key market drivers of ESG integration: investor demand/intergencrational wealth transfer, regulation and policy, public awareness, and data sourcing and processing improvements
- **2.1.3** explain the key drivers and challenges for ESG integration among key stakeholders: asset owners, asset managers, fund promoters, financial services, policymakers and regulators, investees, government, civil society, and academia

Asset owners include pension funds, insurance companies, sovereign wealth funds, family offices, foundations, and endowments. They generally invest their assets in an investment vehicle with the goal of getting returns from the invested capital. They seek to maximize returns at a given level of risk, and some derive utility from non-financial return drivers as well. In practice, asset owners have legal ownership of their assets and make asset allocation decisions. Many asset owners manage their money directly, while others outsource the management of all or a portion of their assets to external managers. Exhibit 8 presents the differences between asset owners, asset managers, and intermediaries. In 2019, institutional asset owners accounted for USD54 trillion, of which 35%—around USD19 trillion—was concentrated in the 100 largest asset owners (Willis Towers Watson 2019).

Asset Owners

Source: BlackRock (2014).

Asset owners set the tone for the investment value chain. Their understanding of how ESG factors influence financial returns and how their capital affects the real economy can significantly drive the amount and quality of ESG investing from the investment value chain.

The approach that owners take to ESG investing and how meaningful they are in steering the investment value chain are influenced by the type of investor they are. This includes, in particular, whether they are investing

- ▶ directly or via external asset managers or
- ▶ out of their own account or acting on behalf of (or in trust for) beneficiaries.

The effectiveness of asset owners in steering the investment value chain toward an increased integration of ESG and its impact on the ESG investment market as a whole depends on

- ▶ the number of asset owners implementing responsible investment,
- ▶ the total AUM of these assets, and
- ▶ the quality of implementation across the different asset classes.

This situation creates a multiplier effect throughout the investment market. Effective implementation of responsible investment by individual asset owners signifies to the market that responsible investment is a priority for asset owners. In turn, this influences the willingness of investment consultants and investment managers to focus on responsible investment and ESG issues in their products and advice. By implementing their commitments to responsible investment with enough scale and depth, asset owners can accelerate the development of responsible investment through the investment chain.

Institutional asset owners establish contracts, known as *investment mandates*, with asset managers. These are important because they define the expectations around the investment product and, at times, even aspects around the manager's processes and resources more broadly.

Morningstar surveyed 500 institutional asset owners in 2022 and found that 85% of them state that ESG is 'fairly material' to 'very material' to their total portfolio and 70% indicate that ESG has become 'more material' or 'much more material' in the past 5 years. However, only 29% of them indicate that this applies to more than half of their organization's AUM, indicating that ESG considerations are not taken into account for many assets under management. As an organization's AUM increases, so too does its consideration of ESG concerns (Morningstar 2022).

One of the challenges asset owners occasionally face in integrating ESG considerations is the hesitancy of retail financial advisers to integrate ESG investing into their offerings or to assess the ESG characteristics of funds, leading to fewer options for the asset owners to choose from in the market. Related to this issue is that some asset owners also believe they do not have the scale or capacity to influence the products offered by fund managers or these managers' interpretation of fiduciary duty. Other asset owners are unsure of how to integrate ESG considerations within requests for proposals or mandates. Finally, there can be challenges for smaller asset owners who have limited resources to conduct their own ESG assessment of managers and their funds.

Pension Funds

Of the 100 largest asset owners, 56% are pension funds (Thinking Ahead Institute 2022). For their size, as well as the long-term nature of their investment, pension funds play a key role in influencing the investment market.

Pension funds are responsible for the management of pension savings and payouts to beneficiaries upon retirement. Given the long-term nature of their liabilities, ESG risks—often more long term in nature—are particularly relevant to their investments.

Pension funds as institutions are driven by three internal players:

1. *Executives*, who manage the fund's day-to-day functioning
2. *Trustees*, who hold the ultimate fiduciary responsibility, act separately from the employer, and hold the assets in the trust for the beneficiaries of the scheme
3. *Beneficiaries* (or *members*), who pay into the fund or are pensioners benefiting from the assets

Similar to the board of a company, the board of trustees is responsible for ensuring that the pension scheme is run properly and that members' benefits are secure. The level of delegation between trustees and executives (on such matters as policy and asset manager selection) varies depending on the governance of the pension fund. The level of alignment between them also varies significantly across pension funds.

Beneficiaries are generally not aware of the details of investment decisions but may inquire why their pension funds are invested in, say, a company that is violating human rights or, for example, engage with their pensions to divest from nuclear weapons. As a result, these actors have different roles and, at times, different interests but may all help advance pensions' fund policy and implementation of responsible investment.

National and local governments are also often among the largest institutional investors—typically through pension schemes or sovereign wealth funds. When governments align their policy intent with their own direct investment influence, there is scope for significant impetus to be added toward ESG integration. Some governments and investment funds have recognized this fact.

In theory, asset owners with long-term liabilities (such as pension funds) are well aligned with long-term investing and are due to benefit from it. In practice, they at times help create the problem by rewarding managers and companies for short-term behavior.

Pension funds can, however, integrate long-termism into their investment belief statements. They can, for example, set up investment mandates that place value on long-termism and demand long-term metrics from asset managers and underlying assets. The requirement to consider ESG factors within investment mandates also reinforces the asset owners' appreciation for the link between ESG factors and long-term risk-adjusted returns.

CASE STUDIES

ABP Pension Fund

In September 2021, ABP, the Dutch pension fund for educational workers and civil servants, announced that it will divest its entire USD17 billion worth of investments in fossil fuel producers by 2023. ABP is the fifth largest pension fund in the world and stated that "radical change" is needed because global temperatures are projected to rise beyond 1.5°C in the next seven years.

At the time of the statement, the holdings in about 80 companies accounted for almost 3% of ABP's total assets (Flood and Cumbo 2021). The fund stated that it did not expect the divestment to have a negative effect on its long-term returns.

"We [will exit] our investments in fossil fuel producers because we see insufficient opportunity for us as a shareholder to push for the necessary significant acceleration of the energy transition at these companies," said Corien Wortmann-Kool, ABP's chair.

Moreover, in January 2023, ABP issued a warning to banks that it may start divesting from the banking sector unless ABP starts to see proof that claims of bank portfolio decarbonization are matched by real action (Schwarzkopf 2023).

ABP was facing the risk of legal action in the Netherlands over its earlier refusal to divest from fossil fuels.

CASE STUDIES

HSBC Bank UK Pension Scheme

In 2016, the HSBC Bank UK pension schemes transitioned the equity component of its defined contribution (DC) default investment strategy to a passive smart beta fund that integrates ESG factors by embedding climate tilts (Johansson 2016).

An HSBC comment piece on the product noted, "Investment performance does not need to be negatively impacted. This is critical, because although investors are increasingly demanding that funds are allocated responsibly, they are not necessarily prepared to compromise on performance."

In fact, the scheme aims to provide a better risk-adjusted return than is available from a conventional market cap–weighted index. The inclusion of the climate tilts gives scheme members greater relative exposure to firms less at risk from climate change.

In a follow-up move in November 2021, the pension scheme announced that it set an emissions reduction target of 50% across all of its GBP36 billion in assets as part of its efforts to achieve net zero greenhouse gas emissions in its portfolio by 2050 (HSBC 2021).

CASE STUDIES

Government Pension Investment Fund

Between 2017 and 2022, the Government Pension Investment Fund (GPIF), an influential universal owner from Japan with investments worldwide, invested in ten different ESG-themed indexes. GPIF promotes ESG investment for the purpose of improving the long-term return of the whole asset by reducing the negative externality to the environment and society.

GPIF holds the view that among important ESG issues, environmental concerns, such as climate change, represent a cross-border, global challenge. Therefore, it has embarked on investment that incorporates all elements of ESG investing in both its domestic and foreign portfolios. In choosing the ESG indexes, GPIF emphasized the following:

1. "positive screening" that determines constituent companies based on their ESG evaluation should be adopted;
2. the evaluation should be based on public information, and its method and results should be publicly disclosed; and
3. ESG evaluators and index providers should be properly governed, and their conflicts of interest should be properly managed (GPIF 2017)."

CASE STUDIES

UK Environment Agency Pension Fund

In 2014, the GBP2.4 billion UK Environment Agency Pension Fund (EAPF) launched a formal search for investment managers to manage a portfolio of sustainable, global listed equities, with a specific focus on the long-term contract with the appointed manager. Candidates were expected to

- have a long-term strategic approach to sustainability,
- integrate ESG considerations broadly, and
- have a strong commitment to non-financial research, which should go beyond short-term considerations of ESG risk factors and "standard" corporate governance.

The request for proposal (RFP), known at the time as the "RFP for a long-term mandate," sent a strong signal to the market of the link between long-termism, with regard to both the contract itself and the investment horizon, and ESG investing.

In 2018, the EAPF investment pool became a part of Brunel Pension Partnership and published the Asset Management Accord, which sets out expectations for long-term manager relationships (Brunel Pension Partnership 2018). Of note, the accord highlights long-term value creation and stewardship and clarifies that frequent communication should not lead to short-term pressure.

Pension Fund Trustees

Pension fund trustees, as fiduciaries of the pension fund members, have a responsibility to act in the best interests of the beneficiaries. Regulation regarding fiduciary duty defines a significant part of their role and responsibilities, and thus, its interpretation can have a significant impact on whether trustees believe they can, must, or must not integrate ESG considerations into their fund policies and processes.

Asset Owners

Litigation

Pension fund trustees may face fiduciary legal risks from financial losses caused by climate change. Lawyers have been commissioned in Australia and the United Kingdom to assess the matter. They have found that pension fund trustees may be failing to take sufficient steps to address climate risk and, therefore, may be failing to manage the scheme's investments in a manner consistent with members' best interests. This situation could result in trustees exposing themselves to the possibility of legal challenges for breach of their fiduciary duties.

The risk of legal action is highlighted by a 2018 case filed in Australia where a member of the Retail Employees Superannuation Trust (Rest) took his pension fund to court for failing to disclose information on the impact of climate change on his investments and how they were addressing the issue (Thompson 2018). Rest settled the case in 2020, pledging to reach net zero emissions by 2050. In the media release, the superannuation trustee "acknowledges that climate change could lead to catastrophic economic and social consequences" and thus will "continue to develop its management processes for dealing with the financial risks of climate change on behalf of its members" (Rest 2020).

Also in 2018, 14 of the United Kingdom's biggest pension funds were warned by lawyers that they risk legal action if they fail to consider the effects of climate change on their portfolios (Thompson 2018). As a result, in some jurisdictions, fiduciary duty is a driver for trustees and their pensions to act on ESG issues. In a survey that was conducted among more than 300 global institutional investors, 46% of respondents cited the need to meet fiduciary duty and regulations as a key driver for adopting ESG principles (Comtois 2019).

Pension Fund Members

Although pension fund members are not investment professionals, they can influence pension fund decisions because they represent the ultimate beneficiaries. Interpretation of fiduciary duty in some jurisdictions recognizes that "acting in the interest" of pension fund beneficiaries is not necessarily restricted to financial outcomes and may incorporate their other interests, such as ethical preferences. Though still rare in the industry, some pension funds have started to use feedback from members to fine-tune their sustainable investment policies.

CASE STUDIES

Surveys by Dutch Pension Funds

The EUR26.2 billion Dutch multi-sector pension fund PGB conducts an annual survey on responsible investment among its participants (Van Alfen 2018). In order to make decisions based on its members' input, the fund conducted a mandatory survey on members' risk appetite and included an additional questionnaire that related to ESG issues.

Of the 3,500 respondents, 90% indicated a preference for investments in sustainable energy, whereas just 14% supported investments in arms and only 17% supported investments in tobacco. As a result of the input from the respondents, PGB excluded tobacco firms and companies selling firearms to civilians from its investment universe. In 2020, PGB transitioned to a fully integrated ESG strategy, with all of its EUR36.9 billion AUM falling in the scope of a new ESG policy (Pensioenfonds PGB 2023).

The EUR9.9 billion Dutch hospitality pension fund Horeca & Catering conducted its most recent survey at the end of 2017, generating a response from 9,500 members and 526 employers. Its participants indicated that labor conditions, environment, fraud, and corruption mattered the most to them. As

> a result of the consultation, the scheme excluded companies that violate the UN's Global Compact Principles and aimed to reduce carbon emissions from its investment portfolio by 20% in the next two years (Pensionenfonds Horeca & Catering 2018).

Insurance

Insurance is divided into the following categories:

- *Property and casualty (P&C)*. This category includes insurance from liabilities and damages to property (due to calamities or from legal liabilities in the home, vehicle, etc.).
- *Life*. This category covers financial losses resulting from loss of life of the insured, as well as offering retirement solutions, such as annuities.
- *Re-insurance*. A reinsurer provides insurance to an insurer, sharing a portion of an insurer's risk against payment of some premium.

Many insurers have an (internal) asset management business that invests the insurance premiums. The interactions between the insurance business and the internal asset management business within insurance companies led to these asset managers advancing rapidly in their understanding of ESG issues.

Insurers are by nature sensitive to certain ESG issues due to factors affecting insurance products, such as

- the frequency and strength of extreme weather events (P&C, reinsurance),
- the impact of climate change on long-term asset values (life insurance), and
- demographic changes (life insurance).

This sensitivity has contributed to insurers having developed a very advanced understanding of these issues. Regulator expectations for insurers to manage systemic risks – including climate change – have also been supportive in building analytical capacity across insurance and investment.

Importantly, in terms of climate risks, insurers are double exposed because both sides of their balance sheet can be hit by climate risks: On the liability side, property and casualty insurers face climate physical risks; on the asset side, climate risks affect insurers' portfolios as the assets are repriced. Another aspect is the rise of climate litigation and how climate change might impact liability and business insurance.

Sovereign Wealth

Sovereign wealth is wealth managed through a state-owned investment fund—a *sovereign wealth fund (SWF)*. The amount of investment capital is usually large and is held by a sovereign state. The global volume of assets under management by sovereign wealth funds was estimated to be USD11.4 trillion in 2022 (Global SWF 2023). Often, the wealth comes from a sovereign state's capital surpluses.

Sovereign wealth funds are often mandated in line with the mid- to long-term objectives of their state, which might go beyond optimizing financial return and include broader policy objectives, such as

- economic stabilization,
- securing wealth for future generations, and
- strategic development of the state's territory.

These objectives can but don't necessarily have to align with ESG concerns. There is some evidence that SWFs take ESG issues into account in asset selection and investor engagement in listed equities, but this evidence is mainly driven by observation of the practices of some of the more transparent SWFs (Liang and Renneboog 2020).

Endowment Funds

Endowment funds are funds set up in a foundation by institutions (universities or hospitals, for example) that wish to fund their ongoing operations through withdrawals from the fund. Given the often societal purpose of endowments, there is an active debate on how to align the ongoing operational funding with such topics as divestment. Examples of this debate can be found in the United Kingdom, where universities are pressured by their students to have more sustainable investments in their endowments (Mooney and Riding 2020). In October 2022, student pressure led to 100 UK universities, including the Universities of Cambridge, Oxford, and Edinburgh, to pledge to divest from fossil fuels, making their endowments worth GBP18 billion unavailable for fossil fuel investments (Horton 2022).

Foundations and Public Charities

In such countries as the United States, private foundations and public charities are charitable organizations that invest their capital to fund charitable causes. Usually for both, the legal form of organization (LFO) is a "foundation," but the difference between the two is that

- private foundations originate their capital through one funder (typically a family or a business), whereas
- public charities originate their capital through publicly collected funds.

Foundations can have ESG exposures through their investment, as well as ESG objectives through their charitable work.

Individual (Retail) Investors and Wealth Management

The adoption of ESG investing by retail investors has been generally slower than for institutional investors.

At the end of 2018 in the United States, only USD161 billion of the total USD22.1 trillion in assets have gone to those referencing ESG considerations. This percentage is much smaller than for institutional investors (GSIA 2019).

Inflows in open-ended and exchange-traded funds (ETFs) in the United States reached an all-time high of USD21.5 billion in Q1 2021. In 2022, the net annual inflow of ESG funds sank to USD3.1 billion, the lowest level in seven years. Much of that decline was driven by the broader market environment, with the 2022 net negative flows out of non-ESG funds in the United States being the largest on record (Stankiewicz 2023).

5. ASSET MANAGERS, FUND PROMOTERS, AND FINANCIAL SERVICES

☐ 2.1.2 explain key market drivers of ESG integration: investor demand/intergenerational wealth transfer, regulation and policy, public awareness, and data sourcing and processing improvements

☐ 2.1.3 explain the key drivers and challenges for ESG integration among key stakeholders: asset owners, asset managers, fund promoters, financial services, policymakers and regulators, investees, government, civil society, and academia

The process of ESG integration is unique for all industry participants. Special considerations for key stakeholders in the market are discussed below.

Asset Managers

Asset managers select securities and offer a portfolio consisting of those securities to asset owners. They influence the ESG characteristics of the portfolio through selection, as well as engaging with investee companies to improve their ESG performance. While they react to asset owners' interest in ESG issues, they can also play a key role in proposing new products and approaches to considering ESG factors.

ESG offerings by asset managers began with active funds invested in listed equities but have evolved to other asset classes and in passive investing. The knowledge gained by integrating ESG considerations in the equity valuation of companies was, to a certain extent, transferred to that of corporate bonds. Because fixed-income funds also include non-corporate issuers (such as supranationals, governments, and municipalities), methodologies to integrate ESG considerations expanded to enable the ESG analysis to incorporate all types of issuers.

Over the past 10 years, the rise of green bonds has further propelled fixed-income as an asset class of interest to responsible investors. Funds of infrastructure, real estate, private equity, and private credit have been slower to systematically and explicitly conduct ESG integration because it is difficult to get consistent ESG data from portfolio holdings. Nonetheless, real estate, private equity, and private credit have been instrumental in the structuring of impact investing funds, for example.

The offering of indexes and passive funds with ESG integration by asset managers started 20 years after that of active investments. The use of indexes is nonetheless critical for the investment industry: They are performance benchmarks and serve as the basis for passive investment funds, such as ETFs. The first ESG index, the Domini 400 Social Index (now called MSCI KLD 400 Social Index), was launched by KLD Research & Analytics in 1990. In recent years, the trend toward passive investment and, particularly, investors' preferences for ETFs, together with the increased availability of ESG data and research, have spurred the market's development of ESG indexes (see Exhibit 9 for further detail).

According to the Index Industry Association (IIA), as of 2022 there were over 55,000 ESG indexes of the more than 3 million indexes that were globally available (IIA 2022)—reflecting the growing appetite of investors for ESG products and the need for measurement tools that accurately represent the objectives of sustainable investors. ESG factors have also been successfully integrated into factor investing, smart beta funds, and derivatives, reflecting the penetration of ESG within a much

Asset Managers, Fund Promoters, and Financial Services

more complex product offering by asset managers. The IIA also reported in the 2022 edition of its annual survey that the number of ESG-themed indexes grew by 55%, surpassing the 2021 growth figure of 43% (IIA 2022).

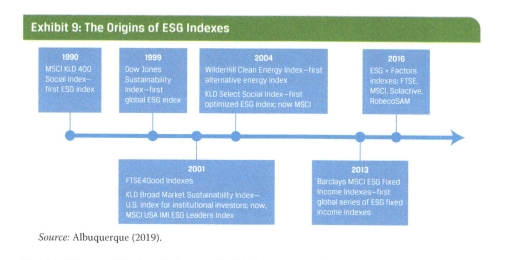

Source: Albuquerque (2019).

Asset managers who wish to differentiate themselves have been investing significantly in ESG-related resources. Some have merged with or acquired asset managers specializing in ESG or impact investing; others have invested significant amounts in technology, using data science to develop their in-house scoring systems and dashboards. One global investor, for example, has built a proprietary system to measure the progress of fixed-income issuers against specific ESG-related objectives. Asset managers have also expanded their human resources, with some responsible investment teams increasing to over 20 people.

Some of the challenges faced by asset managers in integrating ESG issues include

- a lack of clear signals from asset owners that they are interested in ESG investing;
- a very narrow interpretation of investment objectives on which consultants and advisers base their advice for owners;
- resource challenges, especially for investors who see ESG investing as separate from the core investment process (e.g., engagement, marketing, or compliance), and
- an increasing amount of ESG/sustainability regulation, which varies depending on the jurisdictions. This regulation has resulted in the need to add additional resources to meet the new ESG regulatory disclosure and reporting requirements.

Fund Promoters

For this purpose, the *fund promoter* is defined as including:

- investment consultants and retail financial advisers,
- investment platforms, and
- fund labelers.

Investment consultants and retail financial advisers are investment professionals who help institutions and individuals, respectively, set and meet long-term financial goals, usually through the proposal of investment funds. They can consider ESG characteristics of the funds in their screening and short-listing of funds to clients. Fund labelers can set standards to award labels to investment vehicles after the assessment of their ESG processes and performance.

The Role of the PRI for Consultants and Retail Financial Advisers

Ensuring that *investment consultants* and *retail financial advisers* incorporate ESG factors into their core service provision is crucial for the next wave of responsible investment. These two groups are considered the gatekeepers for the growth of ESG investing, since they advise asset owners and individual investors, respectively. As a trusted source of knowledge to trustees (particularly for small and medium-sized asset owners) and retail investors, the PRI's aim is for consultants and advisers to understand the investment implications of ESG issues and turn them into investment recommendations because their advice is often accepted with little hesitation.

This focus of the PRI was prompted by its review in 2017 concluding that most consultants were failing to consider ESG issues in investment practice (PRI 2017). The PRI found that often the advice it gives to investors did not support products that integrate ESG factors. To address this issue, the PRI published guidance in 2019 for asset owners to request ESG information from consultants (PRI 2019a). Further challenges could emerge because consultants and financial advisers often base their advice on a narrow interpretation of investment objectives. What investment consultants and retail financial advisers perceive as a lack of appetite by asset owners in responsible investment has also led historically to them being less keen to integrate ESG investing into their mainstream offerings.

Some jurisdictions, such as the EU, are sidestepping this conundrum by introducing mandatory regulation for investment funds and rating agencies to explicitly disclose sustainability issues (Sustainable Finance Disclosure Regulation, or SFDR, and EU Credit Rating Guidelines) and for financial service providers to explicitly take stock of investors' ESG preferences across various investor categories and asset classes (Markets in Financial Instruments Directive, or MiFID, Undertakings for the Collective Investment of Transferable Securities, or UCITS; Alternative Investment Fund Managers Directive, or AIFMD).

There is much that consultants can do. With regard to investment strategy, they can

- aid trustees in understanding their fiduciary obligations,
- formulate a strategy inclusive of ESG considerations, and
- draft investment principles and policies in line with the strategy and fiduciary obligations.

Within their manager selection role, consultants can help asset owners design a proposal and formulate a mandate that integrates their investment beliefs on ESG issues and expectations on implementation.

Finally, consultants can include asset managers' capabilities and processes related to ESG investing within their research, screening, selection, and appointment processes. Advisers can play a similar role with individual investors, proactively providing relevant ESG information and including ESG investments in their offerings and advice.

Investment Platforms

The research and recommendations of *investment platforms* can be highly influential in the asset management industry and can be a positive or negative recommendation driving a significant amount of capital into or away from any given fund.

Morningstar, one of the main investment platforms, offers a service that rates asset managers and their funds. In 2016, the platform started integrating ESG ratings in its offerings. Investment platforms can integrate the extent and depth that funds integrate ESG investing to

- increase awareness of ESG funds for both retail and institutional investors and
- enable easier identification of and information on these funds.

In February 2022, Morningstar reclassified almost 1,700 funds, worth USD1.2 trillion, away from its list of sustainable funds. It cited its own research analyzing additional criteria provided by funds following the implementation of the previously mentioned new EU disclosure rules called SFDR.

Fund Labelers

Labels provide benchmarks and quality guarantees for both practitioners and clients. In just over a decade, sustainable finance has led to the creation of eight specialized labels in Europe alone. Labels are usually either general, looking at ESG investing as a whole, or thematic, usually focused on environment or climate. Few labels have been applied to multiple countries, creating challenges for global investors seeking to offer certified ESG funds across multiple jurisdictions. Certifications labels have been perceived as a marketing tool by some actors. Nonetheless, in practice, it is not necessarily associated with a marketing strategy in line with the fund's promises. A quarter of the funds certified on ESG criteria in Europe do not have a name reflecting a sustainable approach, and around 30 are thematic environmental funds (Novethic 2019).

Financial Services

Financial services are defined as including

- investment banks,
- custodian banks,
- investment research and advisory firms,
- stock exchanges, and
- financial and ESG rating agencies.

Financial service companies are important enablers of responsible investment because they make significant contributions to the availability of securities with higher ESG quality and increase the quality of information about ESG characteristics of securities and assets in general. For example:

- Investment banks can support a company issuing a green bond (a bond where proceeds are specifically earmarked to be used for climate and environmental projects).
- Sell-side analysts and credit rating agencies can consider ESG factors within their analysis, recommendations, and ratings.
- Stock exchanges can increase disclosure requirements on ESG data by listed companies (as encouraged by the Sustainable Stock Exchange Initiative).
- Proxy voting service providers—those who vote on behalf of shareholders at companies' annual general meetings—can integrate ESG considerations in their voting and voting recommendations.

Improvements in ESG data sourcing, analysis, and disclosure have contributed to the growth of the ESG market. Analysis and ratings of investees from an ESG perspective have been dominated by traditional credit rating companies, as well as a handful of specialist firms. Consultants, such as those specializing in helping investors understand and quantify the risk posed by climate change to their portfolios, are also well established, though many new ones continue to enter the market. The growth of the industry and its consolidation (through partnerships, mergers, and acquisitions) have increased investors' ability to further implement ESG investing. This further supports efforts by policymakers and regulators to improve transparency, disclosure, and reporting of ESG-related risks and opportunities.

Further details on ESG rating agencies and suppliers can be found in Chapter 7.

6. POLICYMAKERS, REGULATORS, INVESTEES, GOVERNMENTS, CIVIL SOCIETY, AND ACADEMIA

- 2.1.2 explain key market drivers of ESG integration: investor demand/intergenerational wealth transfer, regulation and policy, public awareness, and data sourcing and processing improvements
- 2.1.3 explain the key drivers and challenges for ESG integration among key stakeholders: asset owners, asset managers, fund promoters, financial services, policymakers and regulators, investees, government, civil society, and academia

Financial regulation is downstream from policy choices. Financial supervision is downstream from financial regulation. This section highlights the various roles of policymakers and regulators and provides some examples of sustainable finance regulation from across the globe.

Policymakers are responding to the growing urgency of sustainability risks and opportunities. Some issues can have a profound impact on:

- the stability of the financial system (for example, climate change and emerging issues, such as biodiversity and resource scarcity) and
- the risks to an individual investor's portfolio.

The objectives of *financial regulators* are to:

- maintain orderly financial markets,
- safeguard investments in financial instruments, savings/pensions, and investment vehicles, and
- bring about an orderly expansion of activities of the financial sector.

Financial regulators consider how ESG factors might impact the stability of economies and the financial markets and how these factors might influence the long-term risk–return profile of financial instruments. They also encourage and enable the growth of certain ESG products, such as green bonds, and require disclosure on ESG characteristics or sustainability objectives.

Other regulators can influence the ESG characteristics of companies by strengthening matters regarding environment, labor, communities, and governance and can require further disclosure on those issues.

Sustainability-related financial regulations that are relevant to investment generally involve four themes:

1. *Corporate disclosure.* Guidelines on corporate disclosure typically come from government or stock exchanges to encourage or require investee companies to disclose information on material ESG risks. This improves investors' ability to consider these risks in their investment decisions. Examples of corporate disclosure are reporting in line with the recommendations of the **Task Force on Climate-Related Financial Disclosures (TCFD)** or the Global Reporting Initiative (GRI). TCFD has become a regulatory requirement in the United Kingdom, for example, while in the EU companies are required to report under the Corporate Sustainability Reporting Directive (CSRD).

2. *Stewardship.* Regulation on stewardship governs the interactions between investors and investee companies and seeks to protect shareholders and beneficiaries as well as the health and stability of the market. In most jurisdictions, stewardship codes remain voluntary, though mandatory regulation has been approved in Europe.

3. *Asset owners.* Regulation on asset owners typically focuses on pension funds, requiring them to integrate ESG factors and disclose their process and outcome. Some regulators, such as those in the United Kingdom, Australia, and Singapore, are also beginning to consider climate risk for the insurance market and the financial industry more widely.

4. *Investor protection.* Investor protection regulations aim to protect investors by improving transparency and efficiency in markets. Examples of investor protection regulations that take sustainability into account are the EU's MiFID regulation, which includes an obligation to integrate sustainability preferences of investors, the EU's SFDR regulation, which entails a mandatory sustainability classification of investment products, and the EU's green label regulation, which regulates sustainability claims including in investment products.

Exhibit 10 illustrates how policymakers and regulators tie together various sustainability policy objectives with regulatory interventions.

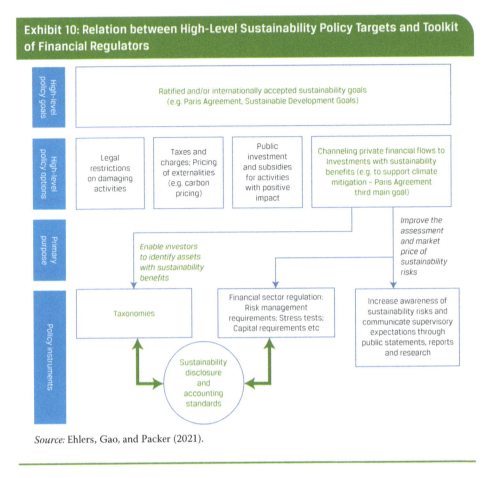

Exhibit 10: Relation between High-Level Sustainability Policy Targets and Toolkit of Financial Regulators

Source: Ehlers, Gao, and Packer (2021).

Examples of Policy and Regulatory Developments across the Globe

In a review conducted by the PRI on sustainable finance policy in 2019, 97% of the new or revised policies were developed after 2000 (PRI 2019b). The continued acceleration has been driven by the rapid development in Europe (with many initiatives being developed under the EU Action Plan on Financing Sustainable Growth) and Asia (where markets have seen significant updates to reporting requirements and corporate governance expectations). Another significant factor has been periodic revisions of stewardship and corporate governance codes, with national authorities introducing or periodically strengthening ESG expectations. Stewardship is closely linked to shareholder engagement. Further details can be found in Chapter 6.

What follows is a high-level overview of policy, regulatory, and supervisory initiatives for a select set of jurisdictions. This is only a snapshot of the most important regulatory initiatives covering the largest markets; there are many more regulations across the globe and for a range of policy objectives. Typically, these policies and regulatory initiatives are subject to periodic review in order to keep pace with global sustainability goals and technological advancements, thereby allowing the measures to stay relevant and effective.

Global—Task Force on Climate-Related Financial Disclosures

In 2017, the Task Force on Climate-Related Financial Disclosures (TCFD) released climate-related financial disclosure recommendations to help firms voluntarily disclose information to support capital allocation. Since its launch, the TCFD recommendations have been made mandatory in various jurisdictions, including New Zealand, Switzerland, Hong Kong SAR, Japan, Singapore, and the United Kingdom. In the EU, SFDR, which has a broader scope than TCFD in terms of sustainability topics, effectively made TCFD mandatory. In the near future, wider TCFD implementation is expected, with all of the G–7 countries backing mandatory reporting.

The TCFD recommendations center on four key areas:

1. Governance
2. Strategy
3. Risk management
4. Metrics and targets

In late 2021, TCFD released guidance disclosing metrics, targets, and transition plans. It also updated its implementation guidance. These updates are shaping evolving disclosure regulations (TCFD 2021).

The International Sustainability Standards Board (ISSB) released two new International Financial Reporting Standards (IFRS) on sustainability disclosures in June 2023. The first standard, IFRS S1 General Requirements for Disclosure of Sustainability-Related Financial Information, sets out overall requirements for entities to disclose sustainability-related financial information about their sustainability-related risks and opportunities. The second standard, IFRS S2 Climate-Related Disclosures, requires entities to disclose information about their climate-related risks and opportunities (IFRS Foundation 2023).

Europe—CSRD, EU Taxonomy, SFDR, Ecolabel Regulation

With the adoption of an EU Sustainable Finance Strategy in 2018 and the sustainability-focused industrial strategy called the EU Green Deal in 2020, the EU has installed a sweeping set of strategies and regulations aimed at both the real economy as well as the financial economy. For the latter, the EU devised five interlocking regulations, that overlap to cover the majority of the investment value chain.

These regulations are listed in the chronological order of the investment value chain:

1. CSRD for corporate sustainability reporting
2. The EU Taxonomy for defining sustainable (corporate) activities
3. SFDR to standardize sustainability reporting for financial products
4. The EU Ecolabel for financial products' sustainability claims (see earlier)

MiFID for retail investor protection through identifying sustainability investment preferences. The *EU Corporate Sustainability Reporting Directive (CSRD)* is EU legislation that aims to ensure that consumers and investors know the sustainability impact of businesses. Adopted in 2021 and coming into force in the fiscal year 2024, CSRD was created as a replacement of the EU's existing sustainability disclosure legislation (named Non-Financial Reporting Directive or NFRD) since the latter was deemed insufficiently fit to support the EU Green Deal and the EU Sustainable Finance Strategy.

To fall in scope of mandatory compliance with CSRD companies would need to meet two of the following three conditions:

1. EUR40 million in net turnover
2. EUR20 million in assets
3. 250 or more employees

In addition, CSRD also applies to companies based abroad that have a presence in the EU, with non-EU companies that have a turnover of above EUR150 million in the EU having to comply.

CSRD more than quadruples the number of companies required to report on sustainability, from the 11,000 covered by its predecessor, the NFRD, to nearly 50,000 that will be covered as of the introduction of CSRD in FY2024. CSRD will require that companies report in accordance with new European Sustainability Reporting Standards (ESRS), which cover environmental, social, and governance standards (Wajon and Farbstein 2023).

The *EU Taxonomy Regulation*, published in June 2020, established a framework that states conditions for an economic activity to be considered environmentally sustainable. These include

- contributing substantially to at least one of the six environmental objectives listed in the next paragraph,
- "doing no significant harm" to any of the other environmental objectives, and
- complying with minimum, EU-specified social and governance safeguards.

The Taxonomy Regulation establishes six environmental objectives:

1. Climate change mitigation
2. Climate change adaptation
3. The sustainable use and protection of water and marine resources
4. The transition to a circular economy
5. Pollution prevention and control
6. The protection and restoration of biodiversity and ecosystems

The *EU Sustainable Finance Disclosure Regulation (SFDR)*, published in December 2019, created requirements for the disclosure about the extent to which investment products consider or promote environmental and social factors. These disclosures aim to enhance transparency of sustainably invested products to prevent green washing. It identifies so-called *principal adverse impacts* that have a negative impact on the environmental and social issues stemming from investment decisions (Deloitte 2023).

United Kingdom

The UK adopted the Climate Change Act in 2008 and was the first country to enshrine its net zero commitment into law in 2019.

The Prudential Regulation Authority (PRA) issued climate-related *supervisory expectations* for regulated firms in 2019, with a deadline for firms to have embedded them as far as possible by end-2021. In doing so, the Bank of England became the first central bank and supervisor to set supervisory expectations for banks and insurers on the management of climate-related financial risks, identifying current risks and those that can plausibly arise in the future, and appropriate actions to mitigate those risks.

The UK's Ten Point Plan for a Green Industrial Revolution (HM Government 2020) outlines key sectors and activities that will be prioritized and provides examples of planned policy developments, policy instruments, and the financing commitment from the UK Government. Specifically, the *UK Green Finance Strategy* identifies three key areas where policy levers can be used:

- Greening finance – ensuring that the financial sector systematically considers environmental and climate factors in its lending and investment activities
- Financing green – directing private sector financial flows to economic activities that support an environmentally sustainable and resilient growth
- Capturing the opportunity – strengthening the role of the UK financial sector in driving green finance

A key aspect of implementation is improving disclosures. As part of the Green Finance Strategy, HM Treasury and the five financial regulators produced a roadmap to making *TCFD-aligned disclosures* mandatory across the economy by 2025. Implementation started from January 2021 with the largest listed companies and pension funds and has been rolled out further. The Financial Conduct Authority (FCA) introduced specific requirements for asset managers, life insurers, and FCA-regulated pension providers applicable from January 2022. In 2022, the UK Department of Work and Pensions (DWP) announced it will amend *occupational pension scheme regulations* to require pension trustees "to measure - as far as they are able - and report on their investment portfolios' Paris alignment"; in other words, "to calculate and disclose a portfolio alignment metric describing the extent to which their investments are aligned with the goal of limiting the increase in the global average temperature to 1.5 degrees Celsius above pre-industrial levels (UK DWP 2022)."

The *Sustainability Disclosure Requirements (SDR)* aim to improve alignment of the financial sector with climate objectives and are mandatory. In late 2022, the FCA sought input on extending SDR to require considering double materiality and looking at other sustainability issues, not just climate change. It also ran a consultation on sustainability fund product labeling aimed at increasing clarity, protecting retail investors, and tackling greenwashing, with the results to be published in Q3 2023 (FCA 2023).

In 2022, HM Treasury launched the *Transition Plan Taskforce*, tasking it with developing a standard for climate transition plans for UK companies. Transition plans, as recommended by the TCFD, are also embedded in the proposed IFRS S1 and IFRS S2 (see above) and the proposed SEC disclosure rule (see below).

In early 2023, The Pensions Regulator (TPR) launched a campaign to ensure trustees meet their ESG and climate change reporting duties (TPR 2023).

China—Guidelines for Green Financial System, Green Asset Taxonomy, and PBOC 2021-25 Strategy

In 2016, the People's Bank of China (PBoC), in collaboration with six other government agencies, issued guidelines establishing the green financial system. These guidelines marked a turning point for China's sustainable finance policy. Previous policy reforms tended to be reactive to financial crises. The new generation of policy recognizes that to be effective, reforms need to tackle multiple aspects of interconnected and complex capital markets. In addition, in 2021the PBOC announced a new, five-year strategy with strong support for the origination of green loans, bonds, insurance, and derivatives.

At the end of 2021, the *Common Ground Taxonomy (CGT)* was published by China's central bank (PBoC) and the EU Commission. The CGT builds on the EU taxonomy (see below) and China's Green Bond Endorsed Projects Catalogue (see below) and establishes a framework that states conditions for an economic activity to be considered environmentally sustainable. The objective of aligning with the CGT is to simplify cross-border green capital flows, which can be achieved by minimizing transaction costs and eliminating redundant verification processes. Furthermore, it aims to enhance market confidence and decrease market fragmentation, thereby facilitating more streamlined and efficient operations.

To determine the eligibility criteria for each activity, the CGT either adopts criteria present in both sets of taxonomies or adopts whichever taxonomy criteria is more stringent.

The sectors covered by the Common Ground Taxonomy are as follows:

- Agriculture, forestry, and fishing
- Manufacturing
- Electricity, gas, steam, and air conditioning supply
- Water supply, sewage, waste management, and remediation activities

- Construction
- Transportation and storage

> ## CASE STUDIES
>
> ### China
>
> In 2018, the Asset Management Association of China (AMAC) released the Guidelines for Green Investment. These guidelines state that "ESG is an emerging investment strategy in the asset management industry and an important initiative for the investment fund industry to implement the green development concept and establish a green financial system" (AMAC 2018).
>
> It is anticipated that the AMAC will make great efforts to facilitate the implementation of the guidelines.
>
> In June 2021, the China Securities Regulatory Commission issued a set of ESG disclosure guidelines. The guidelines entail mostly voluntary reporting on climate risks; biodiversity risks; pollution of air, water, and soil; and waste management.

Singapore–GFIT Taxonomy and Regulatory and Supervisory Measures

The regulator Monetary Authority of Singapore (MAS) developed its *Green Finance Action Plan* in 2019. It contains strategies to support a sustainable Singapore and facilitate Asia's transition to a low carbon economy. The main regulatory tenets of this plan are the development of sustainable finance taxonomies and regulatory and supervisory measures. MAS has two strands of work on sustainable finance taxonomies: one in Singapore, and one on a multilateral collaboration basis with the other member countries of the Association of Southeast Asian Nations (ASEAN).

MAS convened the *Green Finance Industry Taskforce* in Singapore, which from 2021 to 2023 published three public consultations on what a Singapore sustainable finance taxonomy should look like. This taxonomy is under development with the Association of Banks in Singapore (ABS) and focuses on Singapore-based financial institutions, with particular relevance to those active across ASEAN (ABS 2023). The third consultation was closed as of March 2023, and next steps can be expected in the future.

MAS also published regulatory and supervisory guidance for three areas of sustainable investment:

- *Environmental risk management,* via the "Guidelines on Environmental Risk Management for Asset Managers" (MAS 2020) and an "Information Paper on Environmental Risk Management for Asset Managers" (MAS 2022c)
- *Sustainability-related disclosures* in the form of:
- 'Comply or explain'- based climate reporting applying to all companies that are listed on the Singapore Stock Exchange as of 1 January 2022 (SGX 2023)
- Disclosure and Reporting Guidelines for Retail ESG Funds having come into force as of 1 January 2023 (MAS 2022a)
- *Sustainability stress tests* of regulated insurers in 2018, as well as financial industry-wide in 2022 (MAS 2022b)

ASEAN – ASEAN Taxonomy for Sustainable Finance

ASEAN has 10 member states, including Indonesia, Malaysia, the Philippines, Singapore, and Thailand. ASEAN published its *ASEAN Taxonomy for Sustainable Finance* at the end of 2021. The ASEAN Taxonomy seeks to create an umbrella framework that will harmonize other frameworks within scope in the region. An important difference between the ASEAN Taxonomy and the EU Taxonomy is that the former takes a multi-tiered approach in classifying whether activities are sustainable and the latter uses a binary approach. The ASEAN Taxonomy consists of two main elements (ASEAN 2021):

- A principles-based Foundation Framework, which is applicable to all ASEAN member states and allows a qualitative assessment of the sustainability of activities
- The Plus Standard, with metrics and thresholds to further qualify and benchmark eligible green activities and investments

Australia–CFR Measures

In Australia, sustainable finance regulation focuses on climate change and is coordinated by the Council of Financial Regulators (CFR). CFR's climate change activity so far has consisted of the following:

- Climate Vulnerability Assessment (CVA), which is an exercise in climate stress testing large banks, that was executed by the Australian Prudential Regulation Authority (APRA) in 2022
- Contributing to developing a global standard for climate disclosures, with the Australian Securities and Investments Commission (ASIC) coordinating a joint CFR submission responding to the ISSB draft standards

The CFR agencies are supportive of the industry-led initiatives in Australia to develop an Australian Sustainable Finance Taxonomy, a draft of which was published by the Australian Sustainable Finance Institute (ASFI) in December 2022 (ASFI 2022).

New Zealand – Financial Sector (Climate-Related Disclosures and Other Matters) Amendment Bill

In New Zealand, sustainable finance legislation focuses on climate-related disclosures that became mandatory on a comply-or-explain basis for in-scope companies as of January 2023. Businesses covered by the requirements have to make annual disclosures covering governance arrangements, risk management, and strategies for mitigating any climate change impacts. If businesses are unable to disclose, they must explain why. New Zealand's Financial Markets Authority, Te Mana Tātai Hokohoko (FMA), was made responsible for independent monitoring and enforcement of the regime, providing guidance about compliance expectations, and reporting on monitoring activities and findings. The Financial Sector (Climate-Related Disclosures and Other Matters) Amendment Bill (CRD Bill) applies to the following (FMA 2021):

- All registered banks, credit unions, and building societies with total assets of more than NZD1 billion (USD621,382).
- All managers of registered investment schemes with greater than NZD1 billion (USD621,382) in total assets under management
- All licensed insurers with greater than NZD1 billion (USD621,382) in total assets under management or annual premium income greater than NZD250 million (USD155,346)
- All equity and debt issuers listed on the NZX

- Crown financial institutions with greater than NZD1 billion (USD621,382) in total assets under management, such as ACC and the NZ Super Fund

The United States—2022 SEC Proposal

In the United States, policies have long remained voluntary or based on a "comply or explain" expectation, which has led some investors to continue to challenge the assertion that ESG integration is a requirement. However, in April 2022, the US SEC proposed far-ranging disclosure requirements for climate risks. This proposal was open to a 60-day consultation process, but in its initial version, it governs how a regulated firm is to report on the following (US SEC 2022):

- How climate-related risks are governed by a firm's board and management
- The firm's climate-related impacts, goals, targets, and transition plans
- The firm's Scope 1 (direct operational emissions) and Scope 2 (emissions from energy used by the firm) greenhouse gas emissions
- The firm's Scope 3 emissions, if material—that is, the emissions in its upstream and downstream supply chains

The proposal drew intense opposition from many US industry groups, centering on the mandatory scope 3 emission disclosures. While some business groups have balked at the cost and complexity of complying with a scope 3 mandate, others pushed by groups that include sustainability-focused shareholders and eco-conscious consumers, intend to comply with rule whether it becomes final or not (Vanderford 2023).

Combined Effect of Global, Regional, and National Strategies

Combined, these global, regional, and national strategies have been a significant driver in the overall policy growth in in this space—in particular, the EU Action Plan on Financing Sustainable Growth. Moreover, it is anticipated that as policies on ESG issues and financial regulation reach maturity, an increasing number of governments will recognize the importance of moving to stronger requirements in the following ways:

- moving away from "comply or explain" regulation and to "comply and explain" regulation,
- changing from voluntary to mandatory disclosures, and
- moving from policy to implementation and reporting.

For example, the Network for Greening the Financial System, a group of 140 central banks and supervisors established in 2017, explicitly recognizes climate risks as relevant to a supervisory mandate. It also has challenged policymakers, other central banks, and supervisors to act to limit the catastrophic impacts of runaway climate change.

Challenges to ESG investing can emerge if regulators hold a narrow interpretation of fiduciary duty, such as with the US Department of Labor's (DOL's) 2020 ruling on fiduciary duty and non-financial objectives (see the following case studies).

CASE STUDIES

The United States

In the United States, private sector retirement plans are subject to the provisions of the *Employee Retirement Income Security Act (ERISA)*. ERISA sets standards for fiduciaries based on the principle of a prudent-person standard.

While only pension plans in the private sector are under the jurisdiction of the US DOL, the public sector often looks to ERISA principles as a benchmark for best practice in meeting common law fiduciary standards in their governance.

Under ERISA, plan sponsors and other fiduciaries generally must do the following:

1. Act solely in the interest of plan participants and beneficiaries.
2. Invest with the care, skill, and diligence of a prudent person with knowledge of such matters.
3. Diversify plan investments to minimize the risk of large losses.

Plan sponsors that breach any of these fiduciary duties may be held personally liable.

To some extent, the DOL started addressing ESG matters within ERISA in the 1990s (US DOL 2015). Its Interpretive Bulletin (IB) 1994-1 it established that economically targeted investments (ETIs), which generate societal benefits in addition to financial return, are compatible with ERISA's fiduciary obligations as long as their expected rate of return is commensurate with the rates of return offered by alternative investments with similar risk characteristics. This was referred to as the "all things being equal" test.

In 2008, the DOL stated that the fiduciary consideration of collateral, non-economic factors in selecting plan investments should be rare and, when considered, documented in a manner that demonstrates compliance with ERISA's rigorous fiduciary standards.

Thus, the responsible investment community welcomed the DOL's IB 2015-01confirmed "that plan fiduciaries may invest in ETIs based, in part, on their collateral benefits so long as the investment is appropriate for the plan and economically and financially equivalent with respect to the plan's investment objectives, return, risk, and other financial attributes as competing investment choices," ... and "also acknowledges that in some cases ESG factors may have a direct relationship to the economic and financial value of the plan's investment" (US DOL 2015).

Yet in 2020, the pendulum swung back when the DOL issued the so-called final rule, 85 FR 72846. This ruling removed all mention of ESG concepts and replaced it with the words "non-financial objectives" on the basis that the term "ESG" lacks uniform usage and a precise definition. This rule included the following ideas:

- The DOL believed that "tie-breaker" scenarios permitting investment decisions based on non-financial factors are extremely rare, and therefore, as a practical matter, ERISA fiduciaries should continue to refrain from making investment decisions based on non-financial factors.
- Fiduciaries must evaluate investments based solely on financial factors that have a material effect on the return and risk of an investment, and ESG factors may be considered as financial factors in evaluating an investment only if they present material economic risks or opportunities.
- Specific obligations were further imposed, such as documentation requirements, on ERISA plan fiduciaries considering ESG-oriented investing.

In March 2021, the DOL released a statement of non-enforcement, and in October 2021, it issued a new rule to allow consideration of ESG criteria and proxy voting in private sector retirement plans (White House 2021).

The latest status is that in December 2022, the DOL released another final rule on Prudence and Loyalty in Selecting Plan Investments and Exercising Shareholder Rights under ERISA: "This rule clarifies that retirement plan fiduciaries may consider climate change and other environmental, social, and governance factors in selecting retirement investments decisions and exercising shareholder rights, when those factors are relevant to the risk and return analysis" (Office of Management and Budget 2023).

> **CASE STUDIES**
>
> ### The United Kingdom
>
> There has been an extensive discussion in the United Kingdom about the fiduciary duties of institutional investors. In the wake of the 2008 global financial crisis, Professor John Kay was commissioned by the UK government to conduct a review of the structure and operation of UK equity markets. His report, "The Kay Review of UK Equity Markets and Long-Term Decision Making: Final Report," published in July 2012, emphasized the need for a culture of long-term decision making, trust, and stewardship to protect savers' interests (Kay 2012). The report recognized the essential role that fiduciary duties play in the promotion of such a culture but highlighted the damage being done by misinterpretations and misapplications of fiduciary duty in practice.
>
> In response, the government asked the Law Commission to investigate the subject of fiduciary duty in more detail. In 2014, the Law Commission published its report, "Fiduciary Duties of Investment Intermediaries." On financial factors, the report concluded that "whilst it is clear that trustees may take into account environmental, social and governance factors in making investment decisions where they are financially material, we think the law goes further: Trustees should take into account financially material factors" (Law Commission 2014).
>
> On non-financial factors, the Law Commission's term for ESG factors, the report concluded:
>
> "By 'non-financial' factors we mean factors which might influence investment decisions motivated by other (non-financial) concerns, such as improving members' quality of life or showing disapproval of certain industries. In broad terms, trustees should take into account financially relevant factors. However, the circumstances in which trustees may make non-financially related decisions are more limited. In general, non-financial factors may only be taken into account if two tests are met:
>
> 1. trustees should have good reason to think that scheme members would share the concern; and
> 2. the decision should not involve a risk of significant financial detriment to the fund" (Law Commission 2014).

> **CASE STUDIES**
>
> ### The EU
>
> The EU's **Shareholder Rights Directive** II, which came into force in 2019, seeks to improve the level and quality of investors with their investee companies, better aligning executive pay with corporate performance and increasing disclosure on

how an asset manager's investment decisions contribute to the medium- and long-term performance of investee companies. In order to achieve that, it requires investors to have an engagement policy and annually report on the following:

- how this is integrated into their investment strategy,
- how the dialogue is carried out,
- how voting rights and shareholder rights are being executed,
- how the manager collaborates with other shareholders, and
- how potential conflicts of interest are dealt with.

Investees

Investees include all entities in which investments can be made. These include

- companies,
- projects (such as infrastructure projects and joint ventures),
- agencies (including the World Bank and International Finance Corporation), and
- jurisdictions (for instance, countries/regions, provinces, and cities).

Decision makers in these entities can influence how they manage ESG risks and the impact they have on the environment and society. Furthermore, they decide on the level of disclosure of ESG factors to provide to existing and potential investors. In fact, one of the most pressing issues for ESG investing is a lack of access to reliable and consistent ESG data. Various reporting initiatives exist to try to address this issue.

Governments

Governments in general have recognized three main ways in which the investment industry and, more specifically, responsible investment play a significant role in achieving positive outcomes for society.

1. Social security systems and public pensions are in a predicament in many countries, and their citizens are thus turning to corporate or private pension plans for financial stability later in life.
2. Many countries, developed or developing, need to build or restore public infrastructure (such as water systems, transportation means, and energy distribution), which is usually costly for government treasuries.
3. Many governments have recognized that a transition to a low-carbon economy will require significant shifts in capital. These are all areas where governments can encourage the consideration of the financial materiality of ESG issues and the social and environmental impact of investments to advance national priorities.

Civil Society

Civil society, including non-governmental organizations (NGOs), has played a major role in pushing for increased sustainability at the company level and, more recently, in demanding increased transparency and consideration around the impact that investment has on society and the environment. Some partner with investment firms and regulators to help improve their understanding of specific ESG matters, while others bring to light actions that are deemed insufficient to address global challenges.

Academia

Academic research has been influential in validating the business case for integrating ESG factors into the investment process. Academia can continue to conduct studies focusing on the various aspects of ESG factors and their integration into investment decisions, as well as their impact on investment returns and the financial markets more broadly.

7 KEY FACTS

1. The Global Sustainable Investment Alliance's 2021 report, shows ESG investing assets in the five major markets stood at USD35.3 trillion at the end of 2020. The proportion of ESG investing relative to total managed assets grew in almost every region, and in Canada and Australia/New Zealand, ESG investing assets now make up most of the total assets under professional management.

2. Although institutional investors tend to dominate the financial market, interest by retail investors in responsible investing has been steadily growing, reaching a quarter of total ESG assets in 2018. The adoption of ESG investing by retail investors has been generally slower than that of institutional investors. Surveys have generally found that millennials are interested in ESG investing, which may increase ESG assets in retail investing in the near future.

3. Most ESG assets are allocated to public equities (over 50% at the start of 2018). The next largest asset allocation is in fixed income (36%).

4. Asset owners set the direction of the investment value chain. Asset owners' understanding of how ESG factors influence financial returns and how their capital impacts the real economy can significantly drive the amount and quality of ESG investing from the investment value chain.

5. Institutional asset owners establish contracts, known as investment mandates, with asset managers to define the expectations around the investment product and at times even aspects about the manager's processes and resources more broadly. The large majority (over 90%) of asset owner signatories of the PRI require in their investment mandate that asset managers act in accordance with the asset owner's responsible investment policy, and over half of the asset owners (65%) also require reporting.

6. Many actors in the investment value chain have recognized the shortfalls of short-termism in investment practice and have sought to increase awareness of the value of long-termism and encourage it. Short-termism may leave companies less willing to take on projects (such as research and development) that may take multiple years—and patient capital—to develop. Furthermore, short-term investment strategies tend to ignore factors that are considered more long term, such as ESG factors.

Key Facts

7. In theory, asset owners with long-term liabilities (such as pension funds and life insurers) are well aligned with long-term investing. However, in practice, they may at times reward managers and companies for short-term behavior, entrenching short-termism.

8. Insurers are by nature sensitive to certain ESG aspects due to factors impacting insurance products, such as the frequency and strength of extreme weather events (property and casualty, reinsurance), climate change impacts on long-term asset value, and demographic changes (life insurance).

9. Asset managers influence the ESG characteristics of the portfolio through selection, as well as by engaging with investee companies to improve their ESG performance. While they react to asset owners' interest in ESG issues, they can also play a key role in proposing new products and approaches to considering ESG factors.

10. ESG offerings by asset managers generally began with active-listed equities but recently evolved to other asset classes, especially fixed income. The offering of indexes and passive funds with ESG integration by asset managers started 20 years after that of active investments. The use of indexes is nonetheless critical for the investment industry: They are performance benchmarks and the basis for passive investment funds, such as ETFs.

11. Investment consultants and retail financial advisers can consider the ESG characteristics of the funds in their screening and short-listing of funds for institutional and individual (retail) clients. However, the advice given by investment consultants and retail financial advisers has often not been supportive of products that integrate ESG factors. Investor-led initiatives that engage with these actors have contributed to this situation gradually changing.

12. Financial regulators consider how ESG factors might impact the stability of economies and the financial markets and how these factors might influence the long-term risk–return profile of financial instruments. They also encourage and enable the growth of certain ESG products, such as green bonds, and require disclosure on ESG characteristics.

13. Over 95% of new or revised policies were developed after 2000. These policies were driven by rapid development in Europe and Asia as well as by the rise of stewardship and corporate governance codes, with national authorities introducing or periodically strengthening ESG expectations.

14. Companies and other investees can contribute to the growth of ESG investing by how they manage ESG risks, the impact they have on the environment and society, and the level of disclosure they provide on these matters.

15. Governments have recognized that responsible investment can play a role in funding both public infrastructure and the transition to a low-carbon society. They also recognize that responsible investment can play a role in the transition of pension systems, whereby citizens rely more heavily on private pension plans.

16. Civil society and NGOs can help increase the awareness of companies on their ESG risk. They can also help with improving disclosure. The outcomes of academic research can increase focus on various aspects of ESG factors and investment decision making.

17. Some investors still question whether considering ESG issues can add value to investment decision making despite wide dissemination of research that demonstrates that ESG integration can help limit volatility and enhance returns.

18. Some investors also still question whether their fiduciary duty allows them to implement ESG investing. Internal evidence on the impact of considering ESG factors and engaging with direct peers can help overcome these barriers.
19. A lack of understanding on how to implement ESG factors in the various phases of the investment process, as well as perceptions around the cost and availability of data and tools, can limit the growth of ESG investing.
20. The rise of ESG-labeled funds also increased the risk of "greenwashing." Further work by regulators combined with the development of voluntary market standards would make it easier for investors to understand the characteristics of responsible investments and the differences between various types of responsible investment, helping build trust in the market.

8. FURTHER READING

- Amel-Zadeh, A., and G. Serafeim. 2018. "Why and How Investors Use ESG Information: Evidence from a Global Survey." Financial Analysts Journal 74 (3): 87–103. doi:10.2469/faj.v74.n3.2www.cfainstitute.org/research/financial-analysts-journal/2018/faj-v74-n3-2
- Bassen, A., T. Busch, and G. Friede. 2015. "ESG and Financial Performance: Aggregated Evidence from More than 2,000 Empirical Studies." Journal of Sustainable Finance & Investment 5 (4): 210–33. doi:10.1080/20430795.2015.1118917
- Forum pour l'Investissement Responsable, Forum. 2016. "Understanding the French Regulation on Investor Climate Reporting." Article 173-VI. www.frenchsif.org/isr-esg/wp-content/uploads/Understanding_article173-French_SIF_Handbook.pdf.
- Fulton, M., B. Kahn, and C. Sharples. 2012. "Sustainable Investing: Establishing Long-Term Value and Performance." Working paper 12 (June).
- International Corporate Governance Network. 2012. "ICGN Global Stewardship Principles."
- National Association Pension Funds. 2014. "What Do Pension Scheme Members Expect of How Their Savings Are Invested?"

REFERENCES

GSIA 2013. Global Sustainable Investment Review 2012. http://gsiareview2012.gsi-alliance.org/.

GSIA 2019. Global Sustainable Investment Review 2018. www.gsi-alliance.org/wp-content/uploads/2019/06/GSIR_Review2018F.pdf.

GSIA 2021. Global Sustainable Investment Review 2020. www.gsi-alliance.org/wp-content/uploads/2021/08/GSIR-20201.pdf.

Principles for Responsible Investment (PRI) 2016. "How Asset Owners Can Drive Responsible Investment: Beliefs, Strategies and Mandates." www.unpri.org/download?ac=1398.

BlackRock 2014. "Who Owns the Assets? Developing a Better Understanding of the Flow of Assets and the Implications for Financial Regulation" (May). www.blackrock.com/corporate/literature/whitepaper/viewpoint-who-owns-the-assets-may-2014.pdf.

Brunel Pension Partnership 2018. "Brunel Launches Pioneering Asset Management Accord." Press release (29 November). \www.brunelpensionpartnership.org/2018/11/29/brunel-launches-pioneering-asset-management-accord.

Comtois, James. 2019. "Institutional Investors See ESG as Part of Their Fiduciary Duty – Survey." Pensions & Investments (12 November). www.pionline.com/esg/institutional-investors-see-esg-part-their-fiduciary-duty-survey.

Flood, Chris, Josephine Cumbo. 2021. "Dutch Pension Giant ABP to Dump €15bn in Fossil Fuel Holdings." Financial Times (26 October).

Schwarzkopf, Frances. 2023. "Europe's Biggest Pension Fund Issues ESG Warning to Banks." Bloomberg (23 January). www.bloomberg.com/news/articles/2023-01-23/europe-s-biggest-pension-fund-issues-warning-to-banks-over-co2#xj4y7vzkg.

Global SWF 2023. "Executive Summary." 2023 Annual Report: SOIs in a Multipolar World (1 January). https://globalswf.com/reports/2023annual#executive-summary-1.

GPIF (Government Pension Investment Fund) 2017. "GPIF Selected ESG Indices" (3 July). www.gpif.go.jp/en/investment/esg/.

GSIA 2019. Global Sustainable Investment Review 2018. www.gsi-alliance.org/wp-content/uploads/2019/06/GSIR_Review2018F.pdf.

Horton, Helena. 2022. "100 UK Universities Pledge to Divest from fossil Fuels." The Guardian (27 October). www.theguardian.com/education/2022/oct/27/uk-universities-divest-fossil-fuels.

HSBC 2021. "HSBC Bank (UK) Pension Scheme Sets Out Plans to Achieve Net Zero by 2050 or Sooner." (8 October). https://futurefocus.staff.hsbc.co.uk/active-hybrid/information-centre/announcements/net-zero.

Johansson, Elena K. 2016. "HSBC's £1.85bn UK Scheme Takes New LGIM Climate Tilted Fund as DC Default." Responsible Investor (7 November). www.responsible-investor.com/hs-dc/.

Liang, H., L. Renneboog. 2020. "The Global Sustainability Footprint of Sovereign Wealth Funds." Oxford Review of Economic Policy36 (2): 380–426. 10.1093/oxrep/graa010

Mooney, A., S. Riding. 2020. "Students Call on UK University Endowments to Invest Responsibly." Financial Times (3 October). www.ft.com/content/aa92fcfa-ca0d-4e18-a249-93d11403c2bd.

Morningstar 2022. Voice of the Asset Owner Survey (September). https://indexes.morningstar.com/page/voice-of-asset-owner-survey.

Pensioenfonds PGB 2023. "Socially Responsible Investing." www.pensioenfondspgb.nl/en/about-pensioenfonds-pgb/investing/SRI/.

Pensionenfonds Horeca & Catering 2018. "Pensioenfonds Horeca & Catering stapt uit fossiel." www.phenc.nl/over-ons/nieuws/PensioenfondsHoreca&Catering-stapt-uit-fossiel.

PRI 2016. "How Asset Owners Can Drive Responsible Investment: Beliefs, Strategies and Mandates." www.unpri.org/download?ac=1398.

Rest 2020. "Rest Reaches Settlement with Mark McVeigh." Media release (2 November). https://rest.com.au/why-rest/about-rest/news/rest-reaches-settlement-with-mark-mcveigh.

Stankiewicz, Alyssa. 2023. "The 2022 U.S. Sustainable Funds Landscape in 5 Charts." Morningstar (17 February). www.morningstar.com/articles/1138540/the-2022-us-sustainable-funds-landscape-in-5-charts.

Thinking Ahead Institute 2022. Asset Owner 100 (November). www.thinkingaheadinstitute.org/research-papers/the-asset-owner-100-2022/.

Thompson, Jennifer. 2018. "Pension Funds Warned of Legal Action over Climate Risk." Financial Times (12 August).

Van Alfen, Sameer. 2018. "Dutch Schemes Fine-Tune ESG Investments Following Member Feedback." IPE (7 November). www.ipe.com/dutch-schemes-fine-tune-esg-investments-following-member-feedback/10027711.article.

Willis Towers Watson 2019. "Largest Asset Owners Are Critical to Aiding Society's Biggest Issues." Press release (14 November). www.willistowerswatson.com/en-SG/News/2019/11/largest-asset-owners-are-critical-to-aiding-societys-biggest-issues.

Albuquerque, Filipe. 2019. "A Short History: A Journey from ESG Ratings to Sustainable Indices." https://nordsip.com/2019/04/12/a-short-history.

IIA 2022. "Sixth Annual Index Industry Association Benchmark Survey Reveals Continuing Record Breaking ESG Growth, Multi-Asset Expansion by Index Providers Globally" (1 November). www.indexindustry.org/sixth-annual-index-industry-association-benchmark-survey-reveals-continuing-record-breaking-esg-growth-multi-asset-expansion-by-index-providers-globally%EF%BF%BC/.

Novethic 2019. "Overview of European Sustainable Finance Labels." www.novethic.com/sustainable-finance-trends/detail/overview-of-european-sustainable-finance-labels.html.

PRI 2017. "Investment Consultants Services Review." www.unpri.org/sustainable-financial-system/investment-consultants-services-review/571.article.

PRI 2019a. "Investment Consultants and ESG: An Asset Owner Guide." www.unpri.org/asset-owner-resources/investment-consultants-and-esg-an-asset-owner-guide/4577.article.

ABS 2023. "Green Finance Industry Taskforce (GFIT) Taxonomy Public Consultation." https://abs.org.sg/industry-guidelines/gfit-taxonomy-public-consultation.

AMAC 2018. "Green Investment Guidelines (for Trial Implementation)" (10 November). www.amac.org.cn/industrydynamics/guoNeiJiaoLiuDongTai/jjhywhjs/esg/202001/P020200120447423886721.pdf.

ASEAN 2021. "Taxonomy for Sustainable Finance—Version 1" (November). https://asean.org/wp-content/uploads/2021/11/ASEAN-Taxonomy.pdf.

ASFI 2022. "Australian Framing Paper: Designing Australia's Sustainable Finance Taxonomy" (December). www.asfi.org.au/research-and-recommendations.

Deloitte 2023. "Principal Adverse Impact (PAI) Disclosures under the SFDR." www2.deloitte.com/nl/nl/pages/legal/articles/pai-disclosures-under-the-sfdr.html.

Ehlers, Torsten, Diwen (Nicole) Gao, Frank Packer. 2021. "A Taxonomy of Sustainable Finance Taxonomies." Bank for International Settlements, BIS Papers No. 118 (October). www.bis.org/publ/bppdf/bispap118.pdf.

FCA 2023. "CP22/20: Sustainability Disclosure Requirements (SDR) and Investment Labels." www.fca.org.uk/publications/consultation-papers/cp22-20-sustainability-disclosure-requirements-sdr-investment-labels.

FMA 2021. "Climate-Related Disclosures Regime: Implementation Approach" (November). www.fma.govt.nz/assets/Guidance/Climate-related-disclosures-implementation-approach.pdf.

HM Government 2020. *The Ten Point Plan for a Green Industrial Revolution*. https://assets.publishing.service.gov.uk/government/uploads/system/uploads/attachment_data/file/936567/10_POINT_PLAN_BOOKLET.pdf.

IFRS Foundation 2023. "ISSB Issues Inaugural Global Sustainability Disclosure Standards" (26 June). www.ifrs.org/news-and-events/news/2023/06/issb-issues-ifrs-s1-ifrs-s2/.

References

Kay, John. 2012. "The Kay Review of UK Equity Markets and Long-Term Decision Making: Final Report" (July). https://assets.publishing.service.gov.uk/government/uploads/system/uploads/attachment_data/file/253454/bis-12-917-kay-review-of-equity-markets-final-report.pdf.

Law Commission 2014. "Fiduciary Duties of Investment Intermediaries." www.lawcom.gov.uk/app/uploads/2015/03/lc350_fiduciary_duties.pdf.

MAS 2020. "Guidelines on Environmental Risk Management for Asset Managers" (8 December). www.mas.gov.sg/regulation/guidelines/guidelines-on-environmental-risk-management-for-asset-managers.

MAS 2022a. "CFC 02/2022 Disclosure and Reporting Guidelines for Retail ESG Funds." www.mas.gov.sg/regulation/circulars/cfc-02-2022---disclosure-and-reporting-guidelines-for-retail-esg-funds.

MAS 2022b. "Climate Stress Testing and Scenario Analysis." www.mas.gov.sg/development/sustainable-finance/regulatory-and-supervisory-approach.

MAS 2022c. "Information Paper on Environmental Risk Management (Asset Managers)" (May). www.mas.gov.sg/-/media/mas-media-library/publications/monographs-or-information-paper/bd/2022/information-paper-on-environmental-risk-management-asset-managers.pdf.

Office of Management and Budget 2023. "Statement of Administration Policy." Executive Office of the President (27 February). www.whitehouse.gov/wp-content/uploads/2023/02/SAP-H.J.-Res.-30.pdf.

PRI 2019b. "Taking Stock: Sustainable Finance Policy Engagement and Policy Influence." www.unpri.org/Uploads/c/j/u/pripolicywhitepapertakingstockfinal_335442.pdf.

SGX 2023. "Sustainability Reporting." www.sgx.com/sustainable-finance/sustainability-reporting.

TCFD 2021. "Task Force on Climate-Related Financial Disclosures: Guidance on Metrics, Targets, and Transition Plans" (October). www.fsb.org/wp-content/uploads/P141021-2.pdf.

TPR 2023. "The Pensions Regulator Increases Its Focus on Climate and ESG Non-Compliance" (22 February). www.thepensionsregulator.gov.uk/en/media-hub/press-releases/2023-press-releases/the-pensions-regulator-increases-its-focus-on-climate-and-esg-non-compliance.

UK DWP 2022. "Climate and Investment Reporting: Setting Expectations and Empowering Savers – Consultation on Policy, Regulations and Guidance" (17 June). www.gov.uk/government/consultations/climate-and-investment-reporting-setting-expectations-and-empowering-savers/climate-and-investment-reporting-setting-expectations-and-empowering-savers-consultation-on-policy-regulations-and-guidance.

US DOL 2015. "Economically Targeted Investments (ETIs) and Investment Strategies That Consider Environmental, Social and Governance (ESG) Factors" (22 October). www.dol.gov/sites/dolgov/files/ebsa/about-ebsa/our-activities/resource-center/fact-sheets/etis-and-investment-strategies-that-consider-esg-factors.pdf.

US SEC 2022. "Fact Sheet: Enhancement and Standardization of Climate-Related Disclosures." www.sec.gov/files/33-11042-fact-sheet.pdf.

Vanderford, Richard. 2023. "SEC's Climate-Disclosure Rule Isn't Here, But It May as Well Be, Many Businesses Say." *Wall Street Journal* (25 April). www.wsj.com/articles/secs-climate-disclosure-rule-isnt-here-but-it-may-as-well-be-many-businesses-say-854789bd.

Wajon, Eline, Evan Farbstein. 2023. "Corporate Sustainability Reporting Directive (CSRD), Explained." https://normative.io/insight/csrd-explained.

White House 2021. "Fact Sheet: List of Agency Actions for Review" (20 January). www.whitehouse.gov/briefing-room/statements-releases/2021/01/20/fact-sheet-list-of-agency-actions-for-review.

PRACTICE PROBLEMS

1. Which of the following asset classes has the *highest* allocation of global ESG integrated investment strategies?
   a. Real estate
   b. Listed equity
   c. Fixed income

2. Which of the following parties holds the ultimate fiduciary responsibility for a pension fund?
   a. Trustees
   b. Auditors
   c. Senior executives

3. Which of the following established a framework that lays out the conditions for economic activities to be considered environmentally sustainable?
   a. EU Taxonomy Regulation
   b. Climate Disclosure Standards Board
   c. Task Force on Climate-Related Financial Disclosures

4. Insurance companies are *best* categorized as:
   a. asset owners.
   b. savings funds.
   c. intermediaries.

5. An ESG government policy with a "comply and explain" approach suggests that:
   a. ESG integration for supervised entities is voluntary.
   b. ESG integration at a country level is at a mature stage.
   c. the country is applying less stringent ESG requirements than countries that apply a "comply or explain" approach.

6. Which of the following required investors to be active owners and act with a long-term focus?
   a. EU Taxonomy Regulation
   b. EU Shareholder Rights Directive (SRD)
   c. EU Sustainable Finance Disclosure Regulation

7. Individual investors:
   a. are often referred to as "universal owners."
   b. have been faster in adopting ESG investing than institutional investors.
   c. are more likely to review the ESG impact of their investment holdings the younger they are.

8. With regards to ESG investing, financial regulators:
   a. act as fiduciaries.
   b. participate in collective engagements on behalf of beneficiaries.
   c. consider how ESG factors might influence the long-term risk–return profile of financial instruments.

Practice Problems

9. Which of the following stakeholders directly influences investment decisions through the choices they make or the services/information they provide in the context of responsible investment?
   a. Retail customers
   b. Local community leaders
   c. Government

10. What significantly drives the amount and quality of ESG investing in the investment value chain?
    a. The choices of external asset managers
    b. The approach and understanding of ESG factors by asset owners
    c. The regulations set by government bodies

11. What does the 2022 Morningstar survey indicate about the significance of ESG to institutional asset owners?
    a. ESG is 'fairly material' to 'very material' to their total portfolio.
    b. ESG is 'not material' to their total portfolio.
    c. ESG is 'slightly material' to their total portfolio.

12. What creates a multiplier effect throughout the investment market in terms of ESG investing?
    a. The level of ESG training provided to asset managers
    b. The total AUM of asset managers
    c. The effective implementation of responsible investment by individual asset owners

13. Which of the following has the *highest* reported proportion of sustainable investing relative to total managed assets?
    a. Japan
    b. Europe
    c. Canada

14. In contrast to the European market, which sustainable investing strategy is the US market *more likely* to follow?
    a. ESG integration
    b. Shareholder action
    c. Negative/exclusionary screening

15. Relative to institutional investors, retail investors' share of sustainable investing assets has:
    a. decreased.
    b. remained the same.
    c. increased.

16. Which of the following statements about ESG indexes is *most* accurate?
    a. There are fewer than 20 ESG indexes globally.
    b. The first ESG index was the MSCI KLD 400 Social Index.
    c. ESG indexes launched around the same time as actively managed ESG funds.

17. The demographic group *most likely* to incorporate ESG into their investment decisions is:
    a. retirees.
    b. millennials.
    c. Generation X.

18. Regulations requiring financial service providers to explicitly take stock of investors' ESG preferences:
    a. are limited to public equities.
    b. have been introduced in the EU.
    c. are widely implemented globally.

19. Which of the following investment strategies is *most* popular globally?
    a. ESG integration
    b. Impact investing
    c. Best-in-class screening

20. How are insurers double exposed to climate risks?
    a. Increased insurance premiums and decreased investment returns
    b. Liability from property and casualty insurance and re-pricing of assets
    c. Decreased life insurance premiums and increased re-insurance premiums

21. Investment mandates are important for ESG investing because they:
    a. define the requirements of asset owners with regard to ESG issues.
    b. require asset managers to report on the ESG ratings of their funds.
    c. require asset managers to report on the impact of ESG issues on financial performance.

22. How are pension fund beneficiaries *most likely* to influence responsible investment?
    a. They act in the interest of sustainable companies.
    b. Their investment direction to pension fund executives must be implemented.
    c. Their ethical preferences may be taken into account within investment policies.

23. Which of the following challenges is the greatest limiter in the development of ESG investing?
    a. Lack of ESG indexes for benchmarking
    b. Lack of clear signals from asset owners that they are interested in ESG investing
    c. Slower adoption of ESG investing by institutional investors compared to retail investors

24. The "comply or explain" approach to ESG investment policies:
    a. requires mandatory disclosures.
    b. allows challenges to the assertion that ESG integration is required.
    c. is considered a more stringent requirement than "comply and explain."

25. The EU Taxonomy states conditions for an economic activity to be considered

environmentally sustainable. These include:
- a. complying with the highest social and governance standards.
- b. "doing no significant harm" to any of the environmental objectives.
- c. contributing substantially to at least three environmental objectives.

26. Stock exchanges can *best* support the advancement of ESG investing by:
    - a. assessing the ESG characteristics of a listed security.
    - b. increasing ESG disclosure requirements for listed securities.
    - c. integrating ESG considerations within their voting recommendations.

27. How has the adoption of ESG investing by retail investors compared to institutional investors?
    - a. It has been slower.
    - b. It has been faster.
    - c. It has been at the same pace.

28. How has the ESG offering by asset managers evolved over time?
    - a. It started with active funds invested in listed equities and evolved to other asset classes and passive investing.
    - b. It started with passive investing and evolved to active funds invested in listed equities.
    - c. It has remained constant and focused on listed equities.

29. Why have funds of infrastructure, real estate, private equity, and private credit been slower in conducting ESG integration?
    - a. Because they have no interest in ESG considerations
    - b. Because it is difficult to get consistent ESG data from portfolio holdings
    - c. Because they prioritize active investment over passive investment

30. What is the aim of investor protection regulations that consider sustainability?
    - a. To protect investors by improving transparency and efficiency in markets
    - b. To restrict the information available to investors regarding the sustainability practices of investee companies
    - c. To prevent investors from incorporating sustainability preferences into their investment decisions

31. Which of the following is not a key area of focus in the TCFD recommendations?
    - a. Governance
    - b. Risk management
    - c. Credit ratings

32. The Common Ground Taxonomy (CGT) established by the EU and China aims to:
    - a. increase the level of transparency for investors.
    - b. establish a shared understanding of what constitutes a green economic activity.
    - c. reduce the carbon footprint of both regions.

SOLUTIONS

1. **B is correct**. Listed equity has the highest allocation of asset classes, followed by fixed income. Real estate has the lowest allocation of global ESG investments.

2. **A is correct**. Pension fund trustees hold the ultimate fiduciary responsibility. They act separately from the employer and hold the assets in trust for the beneficiaries.

3. **A is correct**. The EU Taxonomy Regulation established a framework that states conditions for an economic activity to be considered environmentally sustainable.

4. **A is correct**. Insurance companies are asset owners; they have legal ownership of their assets and make asset allocation decisions.

5. **B is correct**. An ESG policy with a "comply and explain" approach suggests that the policy is mandatory, and stronger ESG requirements apply to supervised entities. Hence, ESG integration is at a mature stage.

6. **B is correct**. The SRD was issued by the EU and requires investors to be active owners and act with a more long-term focus.

7. **C is correct**. Studies and surveys have generally found that younger high-net-worth investors are most likely to review the ESG impact of their investment holdings, including 88% of millennials and 70% of Generation X.

8. **C is correct**. Financial regulators consider how ESG factors might impact the stability of economies and the financial markets and how these factors might influence the long-term risk–return profile of financial instruments.

9. **C is correct**. In the context of responsible investment, the government is a key stakeholder that directly influences investment decisions. It can do so through the choices it makes, such as formulating policies and regulations that guide responsible investment. Additionally, the government can also influence through the services and information it provides, such as data on environmental impact or sustainability metrics, which investors may use to guide their investment decisions.

10. **B is correct**. Asset owners set the tone for the investment value chain. Their understanding of how ESG factors influence financial returns and how their capital affects the real economy significantly drives the amount and quality of ESG investing. The approach they take to ESG investing can meaningfully steer the investment value chain.

11. **A is correct**. The Morningstar survey of 500 institutional asset owners in 2022 found that 85% of them state that ESG is 'fairly material' to 'very material' to their total portfolio. This shows a significant acknowledgment of the importance of ESG factors in their investment decision-making.

12. **C is correct**. When individual asset owners effectively implement responsible investment, it signifies to the market that responsible investment is a priority for them. This situation creates a multiplier effect throughout the investment market as it influences the willingness of investment consultants and investment managers to focus on responsible investment and ESG issues in their products and advice. This can accelerate the development of responsible investment through the investment chain.

Solutions

13. **C is correct.** Responsible investment directs a sizable share of managed assets in each region, which ranges from 24% in Japan to 62% in Canada. "The proportion of sustainable investing relative to total managed assets grew in most regions, and in Canada, responsible investing assets now make up most total assets under professional management. The exceptions to this trend are Europe and Australia/New Zealand, where sustainable investing assets have declined relative to total managed assets since 2018."

14. **A is correct.** As of 2020, the largest sustainable investment strategy globally was ESG integration. The US market comprises most of the assets managed under this strategy. Norms based and negative/exclusionary screening is the largest strategy in Europe. Corporate engagement and shareholder action constitute the predominant strategy in Japan.

15. **C is correct.** Although institutional investors tend to dominate the financial market, interest by retail investors in responsible investing has been steadily growing: In 2012, institutional investors held 89% of assets compared with 11% held by retail investors. In 2018, the retail portion had grown to one quarter.

16. **B is correct.** "The first ESG index, the Domini 400 Social Index (now called MSCI KLD 400 Social Index), was launched by KLD Research & Analytics in 1990."
As of 2021, there are over 1,000 ESG indexes (roughly 1% of the 3.3m indexes that are globally available according to the Index Industry Association IIA). The offering of indexes and passive funds with ESG integration by asset managers started 20 years after that of active investments.

17. **B is correct.** 75% of individual investors in the United States were interested in sustainable investment; the percentage of millennials was higher, at 86%. Further, "younger high-net-worth investors are most likely to review the ESG impact of their investment holdings, including 88% of millennials and 70% of Generation X."

18. **B is correct.** A review by the PRI in 2017 concluded that most consultants were failing to consider ESG issues in investment practice. Jurisdictions like the EU are addressing this issue by introducing mandatory regulation for financial service providers to explicitly take stock of investors' ESG preferences across various investor categories and asset classes. Such regulations are not otherwise widely implemented, nor are they opposed by the UN.

19. **A is correct.** ESG integration is used to manage over USD25 trillion of assets and is particularly prominent in US markets. Much smaller volumes are managed using impact investing and best-in-class screening strategies (less than USD5 trillion combined).

20. **B is correct.** Insurers are double exposed to climate risks because both sides of their balance sheet can be affected by these risks. On the liability side, property and casualty insurers face physical climate risks such as increased frequency and severity of natural disasters. On the asset side, climate risks affect insurers' portfolios as the assets are repriced.

21. **A is correct.** Investment mandates define the asset owners' requirements with regards to ESG issues. These requirements may, but do not necessarily include reporting on the ESG rating of the funds or the impact of ESG issues on financial performance.

22. **C is correct.** Members may help advance pension funds' adoption of responsible

investment practices simply by expressing their ethical preferences and questioning investments in companies that produce controversial products or engage in human rights violations.

23. **B is correct**. The perceived lack of ESG investing appetite on behalf of asset owners has historically led asset managers to be less keen to integrate ESG.

24. **B is correct**. The policy directive to "comply or explain" provides an opening for investors to challenge the assertion that ESG integration is required.

25. **B is correct.** The EU Taxonomy Regulation, published in June 2020, established a framework that states conditions for an economic activity to be considered environmentally sustainable. These include: contributing substantially to at least one of the six environmental objectives; "doing no significant harm" to any of the other environmental objectives; and complying with minimum, EU-specified, social and governance safeguards.

26. **B is correct.** Stock exchanges can support ESG investing by imposing ESG disclosure requirements on listed entities. This information can then be used by rating organizations to assess listed securities.

27. **A is correct**. The adoption of ESG investing by retail investors has generally been slower than for institutional investors. In the United States, only a small fraction of total assets invested had gone to those referencing ESG considerations.

28. **A is correct**. The ESG offerings by asset managers began with active funds invested in listed equities. Over time, this has evolved to include other asset classes and methodologies, such as passive investing and ESG considerations in the valuation of corporate bonds and non-corporate issuers.

29. **B is correct**. Funds of infrastructure, real estate, private equity, and private credit have been slower to systematically and explicitly conduct ESG integration primarily due to the difficulty of obtaining consistent ESG data from their portfolio holdings. Despite this, they have played a role in structuring impact investing funds.

30. **A is Correct.** Investor protection regulations that consider sustainability aim to protect investors by improving transparency and efficiency in markets. This may involve obligating financial service providers to integrate the sustainability preferences of investors or requiring mandatory sustainability classification of investment products.

31. **C is correct.** The TCFD recommendations center on four key areas: Governance, Strategy, Risk Management, and Metrics and Targets. Credit ratings are not among these four key areas.

32. **B is correct**. The EU and China's Common Ground Taxonomy (CGT) aims to establish a shared understanding of what constitutes a green economic activity to help orient investments towards sustainable solutions.

CHAPTER 3

Environmental Factors

LEARNING OUTCOMES

Mastery	The candidate should be able to:
☐	**3.1.1** explain key concepts relating to climate change, including climate change mitigation, climate change adaptation, and resilience measures.
☐	**3.1.2** explain key concepts related to other environmental issues, including pressures on natural resources, including depletion of natural resources, water, biodiversity loss, land use and marine resources, pollution, waste, and a circular economy
☐	**3.1.3** explain the systemic relationships between business activities and environmental issues, including systemic impact of climate risks on the financial system; climate-related physical and transition risks; the relationship between natural resources and business; supply, operational, and resource management issues; and supply chain transparency and traceability
☐	**3.1.4** assess how megatrends influence environmental factors; environmental and climate policies; international climate and environmental agreements and conventions; international, regional, and country-level policy and initiatives; and carbon pricing
☐	**3.1.5** assess material impacts of environmental issues on potential investment opportunities, corporate and project finance, public finance initiatives, and asset management
☐	**3.1.6** identify approaches to environmental analysis, including company-, project-, sector-, country-, and market-level analysis; environmental risks, including carbon footprinting and other carbon metrics; the natural capital approach; and climate scenario analysis

LEARNING OUTCOMES	
Mastery	The candidate should be able to:
☐	3.1.7 describe and explain key methodologies that apply to biodiversity and its valuation, risk management, and interconnectedness with environmental factors and nature-related risks
☐	3.1.8 apply material environmental factors to financial modeling, ratio analysis, and risk assessment
☐	3.1.9 explain how companies and the investment industry can benefit from opportunities relating to climate change and environmental issues: the circular economy, clean and technological innovation, green and ESG-related products, and the blue economy

1
INTRODUCTION

The range of environmental factors that have a material financial impact on investments—the *E* in "ESG"—is broad and far reaching. Environmental risks have continued to gain prominence, generating heightened concern worldwide. The increased understanding of the mechanisms through which human actions impact the planet has led to growing public acceptance of the need to reduce pollution and global emissions of greenhouse gases, to preserve and improve biodiversity, and to use natural resources more efficiently. In addition to measures aimed at the *mitigation* of environmental impact, there is a growing need for *adaptation* to a changing environment, as advances in climate science have also cast light on processes that are already or may soon become irreversible: "The cumulative scientific evidence is unequivocal: Climate change is a threat to human well-being and planetary health. Any further delay in concerted anticipatory global action on adaptation and mitigation will miss a brief and rapidly closing window of opportunity to secure a livable and sustainable future for all" (IPCC 2022a).

Environmental decision making requires navigating both *factual* considerations (about what is likely to happen) and *normative* considerations (about what conditions of the world are desirable or acceptable). For investors, gaining an appreciation of the evolving policies, technologies, and consumer preferences regarding sustainability can support the pursuit of profitable investments and help prevent losses in investment value. Whether it is governments planning industrial policy, regulators deciding emission accounting rules and securities regulation, executives setting out corporate strategy, or consumers weighing purchase options, we will illustrate in what follows how environmental factors are already affecting a wide and expanding share of behaviors, sectors, and institutions.

Other investors may see the support of projects and activities with a positive environmental impact as a standalone end, regardless of financial impact. More broadly, the nature of investment mandates, time horizons, ultimate beneficiaries, or personal values can all play a role in defining the preferences of investors in terms of risk, return, and impact. Growing awareness of environmental and climate impacts is reflected in the increasing levels and scope of corporate disclosure (e.g., the adoption of the recommendations of the Task Force on Climate-Related Financial Disclosures, or TCFD) and the introduction of policies (e.g., the European Green Deal) to accelerate sustainable finance.

This chapter identifies and describes some of the key environmental factors and major external drivers to help analysts, portfolio managers, and asset owners define investor beliefs and assess material environmental risks and opportunities in their portfolios.

The environmental issues covered in this chapter include

A. climate change,
B. pressures on natural resources and systems (including water, biodiversity, land use and forestry, and marine resources), and
C. pollution, waste, and a circular economy.

It is important to note that these issues are linked and have systemic consequences for business activities and vice versa, as we will further explain.

KEY ENVIRONMENTAL ISSUES—CLIMATE CHANGE

3.1.1 explain key concepts relating to climate change, including climate change mitigation, climate change adaptation, and resilience measures.

Economics and the environment are inextricably linked. Consider the similarities between one widely used definition of economics—the study of "the relationship between ends and scarce means which have alternative uses" (Robbins 1932, p. 15)—and a widely used definition of environmental sustainability: seeking "to meet the needs and aspirations of the present without compromising the ability to meet those of the future" (United Nations 1987). The use and depletion of natural resources and the trade-offs between present costs and future benefits are topics that have been central to economics since its inception as a discipline.

Less appreciated, historically, has been the dependency of the successful conduct of economic activity on a stable, habitable planetary system. In recent decades, however, the scientific community (most notably, the reports from the Intergovernmental Panel on Climate Change, or IPCC, an intergovernmental body of the United Nations) has issued increasingly stark warnings that the consequences of economic activities—notably the burning of fossil fuels for energy, the conversion and degradation of ecosystems from resource extraction and land development, and other forms of pollution and environmental degradation—are jeopardizing the stability of what for over 10,000 years has been a relatively stable climate system, supportive of human society. This instability could lead to dangerous, potentially catastrophic consequences for all life on earth.

The differing time horizons for the consequences of the range of human actions present a major challenge for policymakers and investors in this area. First, the *impacts* of environmental change unfold over different scales in time and space, from short-term, acute manifestations to longer-term, chronic patterns (e.g., the failure of a farmer's annual crop due to a flash flood compared to long-term reduced food productivity in an entire region due to the cumulative effects of erosion of fertile topsoil, drought, and a changing climate). Second, the *causes* of change also exhibit different dynamics. In some cases, the removal of a stressor removes the associated harm (e.g., if logging stops, a forest may regrow), but in other cases, the harm persists (e.g., if a factory stops emitting greenhouse gases, its past emissions continue to warm the atmosphere in the future).

The notion of *planetary boundaries* has been introduced as a way to highlight certain classes of risks and stressors. They describe boundaries to processes (such as global temperature and nitrogen limits, continued protection from damaging ultra-violet radiation provided by the stratospheric ozone layer, and biodiversity loss) that regulate the stability and resilience of the Earth's operating system, with concerns that we have pushed beyond the safe limits for life. For example, it is estimated that human activities "now convert more atmospheric nitrogen into reactive forms than all of the Earth's terrestrial processes combined" (Stockholm Resilience Centre 2022).

According to an update by the Stockholm Resilience Centre from 2022, six of nine planetary boundaries (see Exhibit 1) have already been crossed as a result of human activity:

- climate change,
- loss of biosphere integrity,
- land-system change,
- freshwater (green water boundary),
- novel entities (including plastic pollution), and
- altered biogeochemical cycles (phosphorus and nitrogen loading).

Key Environmental Issues—Climate Change

Exhibit 1: Planetary Boundaries

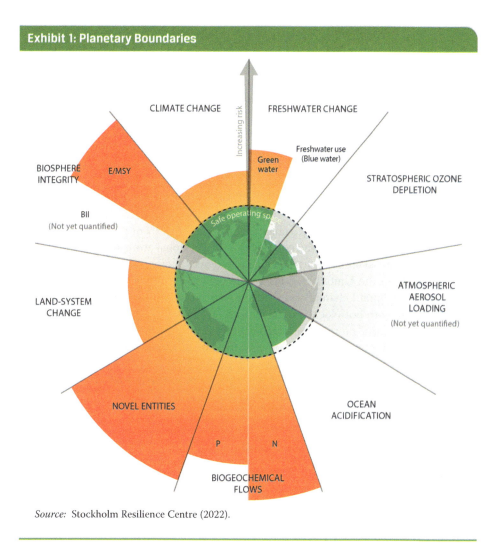

Source: Stockholm Resilience Centre (2022).

Climate change is interrelated to all boundaries either because they contribute to climate change (for example, land-system use change or excessive use of fertilizers) or because it contributes to the problem (e.g., ocean acidification). The crossing of the boundary in terms of climate change, 350 ppm (parts per million) of atmospheric carbon concentration (we are now at about 420 ppm), and the rapid rate of change—both of which are unprecedented—are creating extreme weather patterns.

Beyond these boundaries lie domains of increased risk or uncertainty. Yet, despite the growing sophistication and power of climate modeling, an element of uncertainty remains, stemming from the undetermined consequences of actions and policy measures not yet taken. On the one hand, investment techniques and practices developed to help investors navigate uncertainty (such as the assignment of probability to the costs and benefits of future scenarios, appropriately discounted) can be extended to certain areas of environmental decision making. On the other hand, the possibility of systematic, undiversifiable, and potentially catastrophic risks highlights the importance of precautionary judgments that must be made in the absence of full evidence and perfect information.

Conversely, it has been suggested that bringing investment and economic activities back in line with planetary boundaries can not only help address environmental risks but also—through a more judicious and equitable use of natural resources—protect and enhance important socioeconomic factors, such as employment and access to health (Raworth 2017). Reconciling traditional notions of financial value with a more nuanced understanding of broader positive and negative impacts ("environmental externalities") that are not easily quantifiable in monetary terms represents an area of ongoing innovation—not just in finance but also in policy and law. To choose a few examples that will be discussed in this chapter, the trade in such securities as carbon allowances uses market mechanisms as an incentive for companies to reduce their *future* pollution, the development of natural capital approaches aims to recognize the *present* value of ecosystems as a guide to policymaking, and a growing wave of lawsuits seeks compensation for *past* contributions to environmental damages.

While it may be seen as a good in itself, the pursuit of environmental sustainability can also be justified because it carries financial benefits. Conversely, as societal preferences, regulation, and technology change, ongoing investments in environmentally damaging activities may carry unrewarded risks, which can lead to losses in revenues and falling asset values.

Climate change is defined as a change of climate, directly or indirectly attributed "to human activity, that alters the composition of the global atmosphere and which is in addition to natural climate variability observed over comparable time periods" (this definition is from the United Nations Framework Convention on Climate Change, or UNFCCC). Climate change and nature loss are two of the most complex issues facing us today, with both local manifestations (e.g., extreme weather events, such as more frequent and/or more intense tropical cyclones) and global impacts (e.g., rising global average temperatures and sea levels, food insecurity), which are estimated to increase in severity over time. Because the planet does not warm uniformly—the Arctic is warming more than three times faster than the global average (Arctic Monitoring and Assessment Programme 2021) and the land is warming faster than the sea—atmospheric and ocean circulation patterns are being altered in complex and not fully understood ways.

The main man-made driver of the warming of the planet is rising emissions of heat-trapping **greenhouse gases (GHGs)** in the atmosphere. Somewhat similarly to the tinted windows through which one can see without being seen, GHGs allow *visible* light from the Sun to pass through and reach the Earth's surface but prevent some of the *infrared* radiation reflected by the Earth from escaping into space, redirecting it back toward the Earth.[1] This situation creates a warming effect that, on geological scales, is responsible for the habitability of the Earth: without any water vapor or carbon dioxide in the atmosphere (both of which are GHGs), it is estimated that global temperatures would be about 25°C lower, likely resulting in the entire planet being covered by ice (Saravanan 2022, p. 50).

Carbon dioxide (CO_2) is a significant contributor to the warming effect, because of its higher concentration in the atmosphere, which is now at levels not seen since long before Homo sapiens first appeared (National Ocean Service 2021; see Exhibit 2). (Recent data show that in May 2023, the global average was around 424 ppm.)

---

1 Technically, the "'greenhouse effect" is a misnomer, because the main mechanism warming greenhouses (or a car with closed windows) is convection (i.e., a lack of air circulation), rather than the blockage of infrared radiation.

Exhibit 2: CO₂ Levels in the Atmosphere for the Past 800,000 Years

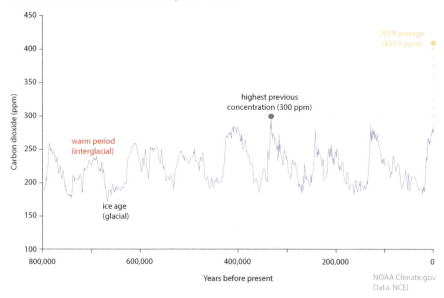

Source: National Ocean Service (2021).

Much of this increase has occurred with the accelerated burning of fossil fuels since the beginning of the Industrial Revolution, with more than half the CO_2 emissions from the late 17th century onward occurring in the last 30 years (Institute for European Environmental Policy 2020). Just as abruptly pressing the accelerator will have a different effect on the passengers in a car compared to a gradual increase in speed, concerns have been raised around the potentially destabilizing effect of such an unprecedented *rate* of emissions: "High quantities of any pollutant put us at a rapidly increasing risk of destabilizing the climate, a system that is integral to the biosphere. Ergo, we should build down CO_2 emissions, even regardless of what climate models tell us" (Norman, Read, Bar-Yam, and Taleb 2015).

Two important related concepts are climate sensitivity and the transient climate response. *Climate sensitivity* attempts to describe what would happen to global temperatures if CO_2 concentrations in the atmosphere were to *double* relative to the pre-industrial average. "The *likely* range of equilibrium climate sensitivity has been narrowed to 2.5°C–4.0°C (with a best estimate of 3.0°C)" (IPCC 2023b, p. 33). Note that the uncertainty is around the *higher end* of temperatures; multiple lines of evidence suggest low-end climate temperatures can be "ruled out" because the world has already reached CO_2 concentrations around 50% higher compared to the pre-industrial average (Forster, Hausfather, Hegerl, Sherwood, and Armour 2020). Thus, climate sensitivity can play the role of a "speed limit" in identifying potential danger zones.

However, just as pressing the accelerator does not immediately change the speed of a car, the *stock* of emissions in the overall atmosphere changes more slowly than the *flows* (Forster et al. 2020). The concept of *transient climate response* aims to capture the changes in temperature that would result from a more gradual doubling of concentrations, occurring over about 70 years (Saravanan 2022, p. 53). Thus, the transient response can be compared to a speedometer aiming to describe how fast we are going. Such modeling has been used to derive estimates of the temperature impact of adding or removing a given ton of carbon from the atmosphere, which is then used to calculate the "implied temperature" of announced changes in government or corporate policies. For example, the International Energy Agency (2022b) estimates that "renewed policy momentum and technology gains made since 2015 have shaved around 1°C off the long-term temperature rise, assuming that countries meet their commitments."

Other important GHGs include methane, nitrous oxide, and other fluorinated gases. Although the average lifetime in the atmosphere of such gases is shorter than that of carbon dioxide, they have a much higher "global warming potential"—30 times stronger in the case of methane and over 23,000 times stronger for sulphur hexafluoride—when compared to the effects of carbon dioxide over a century (this is usually expressed as tons of CO_2 equivalent, or CO_2e; US Environmental Protection Agency 2021). This interplay between impact and lifetime creates both risks and opportunities. Sudden releases of methane—for example, from the melting permafrost or from damage to natural gas infrastructure—can have a significant shorter-term impact on the global climate; it is estimated that methane is responsible for about 30% of the observed rise in temperatures since the Industrial Revolution (International Energy Agency 2022a). However, "unlike CO_2, methane has a short atmospheric lifetime, such that emissions released today will mostly disappear from the atmosphere after 12 years. This is the main reason why the world would cool notably by 2100 if all GHG emissions fell to zero. This would result in around 0.5°C of cooling compared to a scenario where only CO_2 falls to zero" (Hausfather 2021).

Emissions of GHGs primarily come from energy, industry, transport, agriculture, and changes in land use (such as deforestation and the degradation of forests, grasslands, wetlands, and agricultural soils), with manmade CO_2 emissions resulting primarily from the burning of fossil fuels (e.g., in power plants, gas boilers, and vehicles) representing the highest share—around two-thirds—of all GHGs (see Exhibit 3; UNEP 2019).[2] While not all emissions have an exclusively warming effect (both water vapor and certain aerosols, for example, can also prevent sunlight from reaching earth in the first place), the IPCC notes that "human activities, principally through emissions of greenhouse gases, have unequivocally caused global warming, with global surface temperature reaching 1.1°C above 1850–1900 in 2011–2020" (IPCC 2023b, p. 6).

---

2 For more information, go to the SASB's "Exploring Materiality" webpage: https://materiality.sasb.org.

Key Environmental Issues—Climate Change

Exhibit 3: Sources and Influence of GHG Emissions

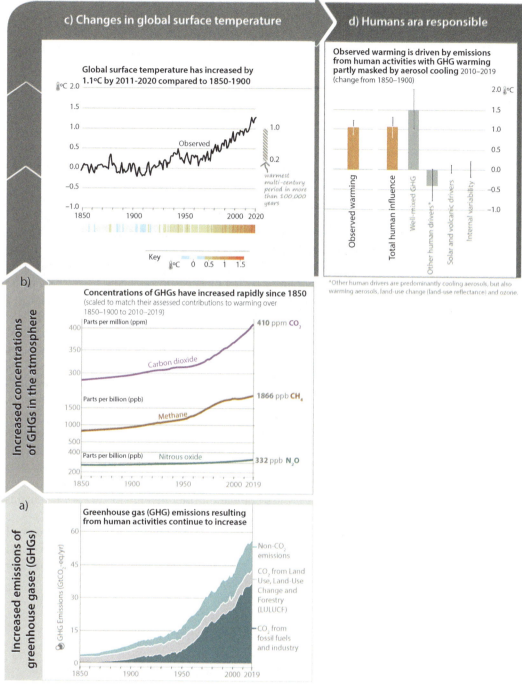

Source: IPCC (2023b).

Limiting global warming has been compared with avoiding overfilling a bathtub by simultaneously turning off the faucets and opening the drain—in other words, reducing both the flow of new emissions and removing the stock of existing GHGs in the atmosphere. It is only after additions and removals are equal (i.e., once emissions reach "net zero") that temperatures can begin to stabilize. One way to quantify this idea is via the concept of a *carbon budget*—the amount of CO_2 emissions that can be emitted while maintaining a chance of temperatures not exceeding a given level: "For every 1,000 GtCO$_2$ [gigatons of carbon dioxide] emitted by human activity, global surface temperature rises by 0.45°C (best estimate, with a likely range from 0.27 to 0.63°C). The best estimates of the remaining carbon budgets from the beginning of 2020 are 500 GtCO$_2$ for a 50% likelihood of limiting global warming to 1.5°C and 1,150 GtCO$_2$ for a 67% likelihood of limiting warming to 2°C" (IPCC 2023a).

It is important to note, first, that carbon budgets are *probabilistic*. Temperature scenarios usually (including the aforementioned ones) refer to expected warming *by 2100*; by definition, therefore, we cannot have full certainty over an outcome that has not yet happened. One way to tackle this problem is to model climate scenarios and pathways with different technologies, levels of emissions, and other socioeconomic variables (e.g., GDP growth and economic development). By aiming to identify common outcomes among different models, the aim is to develop some probabilistic assessment of the emission pathways that are compatible or incompatible with certain temperature thresholds.

Second, carbon budgets and climate scenarios are *path dependent*. To make the bathtub analogy more realistic, we should imagine a wide range of separate taps, all flowing into the same bathtub. Turning one tap off may allow more time until the *other ones* cause an overflow. Similarly, how much CO$_2$ can be emitted partly depends on the levels of other GHGs, such as methane, and vice versa. The same is true of different industries: Faster-than-expected progress in replacing fossil fuels with low-carbon alternatives to generate electricity, for example, can increase the budget available for "harder-to-abate" sectors, such as cement, where the alternatives are less developed. Moreover, the availability of technologies for carbon capture—akin to adding another drain to the tub—can also affect the carbon budget. As such, the modeling of climate pathways will necessarily involve some assumptions about the costs, maturity, and deployment of certain technologies (see the following case study on "business as usual"), about the nature and levels of economic development in different countries, and about the resulting balance between CO$_2$ and other GHGs. For example, one as-of-yet undetermined key variable is the extent to which the economic development of countries in the Global South will be dependent on fossil fuel usage. The explosive growth of China since 1990 has been to a significant degree fueled by reliance on coal power. But with renewable energy now being the cheapest source of new power for two-thirds of the world's population (BloombergNEF 2022a), it remains to be seen whether development can "leapfrog" to lower-carbon alternatives.

The upshot of this is that there are multiple ways to meet a given carbon budget. As illustrated in Exhibit 4, the IPCC considers a variety of scenarios with different assumptions, aiming to identify both commonalities and variation ranges for key variables, such as emissions levels.

Key Environmental Issues—Climate Change

Exhibit 4: Emissions Reductions Needed to Limit Global Warming to Various Temperatures

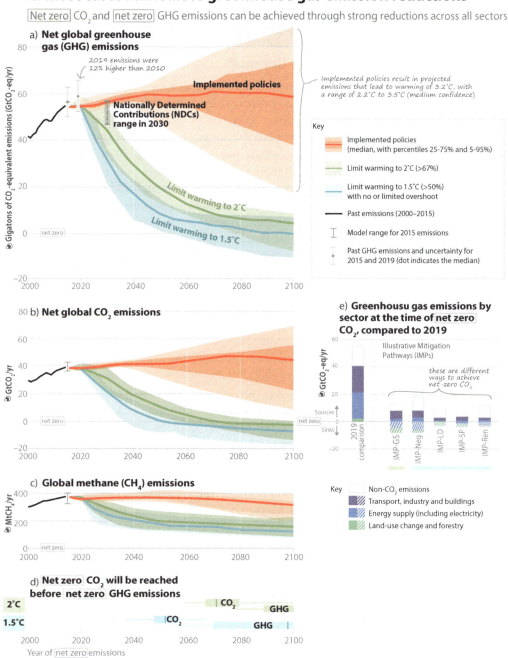

Note: The bold line describes median emission pathways, while the shaded areas highlight the 5th–95th percentile ranges falling within a given class of scenarios.

Source: IPCC (2023a).

As you can see, one commonality is that scenarios that achieve the target of the Paris Agreement to keep global temperatures in the 1.5°C–2°C range require rapid and sustained reductions in CO_2 emissions, followed by other GHGs. In particular, reaching net zero CO_2 emissions by around 2050 has emerged as a key milestone, which is increasingly being adopted by governments worldwide as a policy objective.

Another important conclusion is that the window for action is shrinking fast. At current rates of GHGs—of about 40–60 $GtCO_2e$ every year—there may be less than a decade before we exhaust the previously mentioned carbon budgets (which only had at best a two-in-three chance of meeting their temperature targets in the first place).

CASE STUDIES

Business as Unusual

Climate scenarios are developed and used for different purposes. Some are explicitly based on normative elements: Impose an outcome or constraint (e.g., achieving net zero emissions by 2050), and then reverse-engineer it to see what *needs to happen* in the interim period to achieve the goal.

Other scenarios have predictive elements, aiming to capture what is *likely* to happen. And others may lie somewhere in between, as "what if" exercises that do not claim to represent forecasts. For example, what if the governments of the world do not introduce any new policies? What if emissions keep rising? Such "business-as-usual" scenarios can play a useful analytical role, by investigating the climate response to a stronger signal that at lower levels might be lost in "noisier" processes (somewhat like testing headphones by playing music loud). However, caution must be exercised in understanding the assumptions, particularly if scenarios are to inform policymaking.

One scenario that is often referred to as "business as usual" is the IPCC's RCP8.5 scenario (RCP stands for "representative concentration pathways," with the numbers describing the amount of heat trapped by the atmosphere by 2100). It represents a high-emission scenario, leading to 4°C–5°C of warming by 2100 and severely damaging climate impacts as a result.

First developed at the time of China's rapid coal-powered industrialization, when the costs of solar panels, wind turbines, and battery storage were much higher than today, this scenario assumes, for example, that due to population growth and economic development, global coal use grows more than four-fold by 2100 compared to today's levels (Hausfather 2019). Given the falling costs of alternatives and the shrinking global pipeline of coal plants, such assumptions seem increasingly unrealistic. And while the IPCC does not assign explicit probabilities to its various scenarios, it notes that "the likelihood of high-emissions scenarios such as RCP8.5 . . . is considered low in light of recent developments in the energy sector" (IPCC 2021, pp. 238–39).

As shown in Panel a of Exhibit 4, already implemented policies are estimated to put the world on track for a central case of 3.2°C, while announced but not yet implemented national policies (so-called nationally determined contributions, or NDCs) could bring that temperature even lower, closer to the 2°C range.

While small differences in degree may sound insignificant, they are associated with highly consequential outcomes, as illustrated in the next sections.

The levels of climate change already experienced by the world have increased the likelihood of certain hazards with significant socioeconomic impacts. Exhibit 5 illustrates some of the socioeconomic impacts resulting from climate change.

Exhibit 5: Select Socioeconomic Impacts of Climate Change

Impacted Economic System	Area of Direct Risk	Socioeconomic Impact	How Climate Change Exacerbated Hazard
Liveability and workability	2003 European heat wave	US$15 billion in losses	2× more likely
	2010 Russian heat wave	≈55,000 deaths attributable	3× more likely
	2013–2014 Australian heat wave	≈US$6 bn in productivity loss	Up to 3× more likely
	2017 East African drought	≈800,000 people displaced in Somalia	2× more likely
	2019 European heat wave	≈1,500 deaths in France	≈10× more likely
Food systems	2015 Southern African drought	Agriculture outputs declined by 15%	3× more likely
	Ocean warming	Up to 35% decline in North Atlantic fish yields	Ocean surface temperatures have risen by 0.7°C (1.3°F) globally
Physical assets	2012 Hurricane Sandy	US$62 bn in damage	3× more likely
	2016 Fort McMurray fire, Canada	US$10 bn in damage, 1.5 million acres of forest burned	1.5×–6× more likely
	2017 Hurricane Harvey	US$125 bn in damage	8%–20% more intense
Infrastructure services	2017 flooding in China	US$3.55 bn of direct economic loss, including severe infrastructure damage	2× more likely
Natural capital	30-year record low Arctic sea ice in 2012	Reduced albedo effect, amplifying warming	70%–95% attributable to human-induced climate change
	Decline of Himalayan glaciers	Potential reduction in water supply for more than 240 million people	70% of global glacier mass lost in past 20 years is due to human-induced climate change

Sources: Woods Hole Research Center (now Woodwell Climate Research Center); analysis by Woetzel, Pinner, Samandari, Engel, Krishnan, Boland, and Powis (2020).

While such attribution retains some probabilistic value (since there are usually more *proximate* causes and we do not, strictly speaking, have a "control" Earth against which to test), it can be useful to think of climate change like an important *background condition.* To use an analogy, if the strength of gravity on Earth went up by 10%, it would significantly increase the chance of people falling to the ground, even if any person's particular fall may have something more immediate—an untied shoelace or a sidewalk—as a trigger.

The more pressing question is which impacts are likely to get worse—and by how much—in the absence of further action. Much of the discussion so far has highlighted average temperature outcomes that differ by only a few degrees: 1.5, 2, and so on.

These differences may seem small but are highly consequential. Note, first, that warming numbers are usually global averages and may mask important differences between regions (warming over land has been twice that observed over oceans, for example; Byrne 2020) and for different seasons (with average summer temperatures potentially increasing by much more than global averages).

The IPCC (2018) estimates that limiting warming to 1.5°C (2.7°F) instead of 2°C (3.6°F) by the end of this century could reduce "climate-related risks to health, livelihoods, food security, water supply, human security, and economic growth": around 400 million fewer people frequently exposed to extreme heat waves and around 10 million fewer people exposed to rising sea levels, in addition to reduced impacts on vulnerable ecosystems, such as the Arctic and warm water coral reefs (which "mostly disappear" at 2°C [3.6°F]).

Whereas much of the discussion focuses on *global* emissions and *global* temperatures, there is a growing body of literature focused on more specific, potentially highly consequential dynamics of the climate system. For example, as the world warms from direct GHG additions, amplifying feedbacks cause additional warming from nature. A warming ocean adds more water vapor, and thawing permafrost releases more methane, thus melting sea ice, ice caps in Greenland and Antarctica, and glaciers everywhere. And less snow and ice cover reduces the amount of sunlight that is reflected back into space (the so-called "albedo" effect, which is also why houses painted white are cooler in the summer than those with darker coats of paint). Hence, the warming Earth causes natural processes to create additional warming.

Tipping Elements

One concerning possibility is that either directly as a result of emissions or indirectly as a result of self-reinforcing feedbacks, the world might cross thresholds for "tipping elements." Like a sand pile toppling when just a few more grains are added, this notion is used to describe components of the Earth system that exhibit phase shifts, which is to say large-scale, long-term, and/or potentially irreversible changes upon reaching critical levels of global warming, greenhouse gases, or other thresholds. A recent literature review (Wang et al. 2023) aims to summarize the main candidates for tipping elements,[3] illustrated in Exhibit 6.

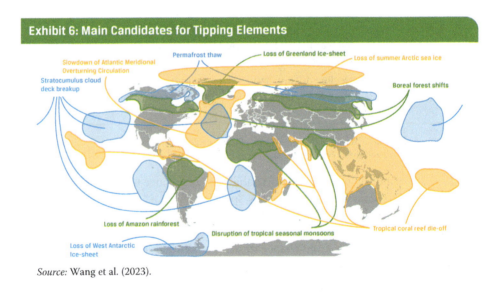

Source: Wang et al. (2023).

The authors make a distinction between the potential magnitude of tipping element impacts, the timelines over which they manifest, and their likely irreversibility. Wang et al. (2023) make the following conclusions:

> *"Many tipping elements have uncertain thresholds, which could be crossed this century if human emissions and impacts remain unabated.*

---

[3] Wang et al. (2023) prefer the term "tipping elements" over the more commonly used "tipping points," noting that there is inconsistency in the literature as to "whether tipping behaviour is necessarily irreversible, fast-acting once activated, or triggered at a precise threshold. Inconsistency in terminology can produce confusion, particularly regarding the timescales over which climate mechanisms act." They explain that the use of "tipping point" in contexts outside climate usually describes *fast-acting* processes that may not appropriately describe climate phenomena.

> *Many tipping elements significant to global climate may exhibit slower onset behavior, responding to climate forcing over a century or more.*
>
> *Emissions pathways and climate model uncertainties may dominate over tipping elements in determining overall multi-century warming."*

The Cost of Climate Change

A study by the World Bank (2018) estimated that the cost of climate change could reach $20 trillion by 2100. This estimate includes the cost of damage to infrastructure, agriculture, and human health.

The cost of climate change will be felt disproportionately by the poorest and most vulnerable people in the world. These people are already experiencing the effects of climate change, such as more extreme weather events and rising sea levels. They are also less able to adapt to these changes. The cost of climate change will also have a significant impact on the global economy. It is estimated that climate change could reduce global GDP by up to 20% by 2100.

There are, however, important caveats when considering such results, which are highly dependent on assumptions and scenarios. First, under the standard economic practice of discounting, cash flows far into the future have very little present value. This perspective, however, may be under-representing the risks of potentially catastrophic outcomes that could severely affect economies and countless human lives. This argument has been put forth by climate economist Martin Weitzman, with his so-called *dismal theorem*, which suggests that standard cost–benefit analysis is inadequate to deal with the potential downside losses from climate change. However small their probability, as long as we cannot completely rule out scenarios of climate-induced civilizational collapse, their expected value must be properly understood as being equivalent to negative infinity, Weitzman (2011) has argued (for a critical reply, see Nordhaus 2011).

Second, many economic models used to calculate future climate damages usually share the limitation of assuming negative impacts that ramp up only gradually and usually do not model sharp discontinuities and "tipping points." In other words, they model a society that "keeps warm and carries on," even though some of these scenarios approach the limits of adaptability and habitability.

Almost inevitably, models are calibrated using past economic outcomes, but this situation presents a potential tension when dealing with what may be radically different future outcomes.

Responding to climate change is usually presented in terms of two main approaches:

1. reducing and stabilizing the levels of heat-trapping GHGs in the atmosphere (**climate change mitigation**) or
2. adapting to the climate change already taking place (**climate change adaptation**) and increasing climate change resilience.

However, this is not a binary option: Climate change adaptation will always be required because we are already experiencing the effects of climate change, and some of the most effective climate policies pursue both objectives simultaneously. We will look at climate change mitigation and adaptation in the following subsections.

Climate Change Mitigation

Climate change mitigation is a human intervention that involves reducing the sources of GHG emissions (for example, the burning of fossil fuels and wood for electricity, heat, or transport) and simultaneously enhancing the sinks that store these gases (such as forests, oceans, and soil) in an attempt to slow down the process of climate change. The goal of mitigation is to

- "prevent dangerous . . . interference with the climate system" (UNFCCC 1992)
- stabilize GHG levels in a time frame sufficient to allow ecosystems to adapt naturally to climate change,
- ensure that food production is not threatened, and
- enable economic development to proceed in a sustainable manner.

While discussions of climate change policy usually call for adaptation to the warming that is irreversible, the overarching framing is usually that of mitigation—that is, trying to prevent what is not inevitable.

Examples of mitigation strategies include greater adoption of policies to promote sustainability in different areas, such as the following:

- *Energy:* Deploying renewable energy sources (such as wind, solar, geothermal, hydro, and some biofuels that are shown to be low carbon and produced sustainably). Unfortunately, not all biofuels are better than petroleum alternatives when life-cycle emissions, including nitrous oxide from fertilizing crops, and other production emissions are considered (Jeswani, Chilvers, and Azapagic 2020). Burning wood to generate electricity or commercial-scale heat releases more CO_2 at the time of combustion and forgoes accumulation of carbon had the trees been allowed to continue growing (Sterman, Moomaw, Rooney-Varga, and Siegel 2022).
- *Buildings:* Retrofitting buildings to become more energy efficient and using building materials and equipment that reduce buildings' operational and embodied carbon.
- *Transport:* Adopting more sustainable, low-carbon transportation and infrastructure (such as electric vehicles, rail and metro, and bus rapid transit), particularly in cities, but also decarbonizing shipping, road, and air transport.
- *Land use and forestry:* Improving forest management, reducing deforestation, and growing more of our existing forests to achieve their potential for biodiversity and carbon accumulation—a management process known as *proforestation* (Moomaw, Masino, and Faison 2019).
- *Agriculture:* Improving crop and grazing land management to increase soil carbon storage.
- *Carbon pricing and other economic measures:* Implementing carbon reduction policies that penalize heavy emitters and promote GHG emission reductions in the form of either a carbon tax or a cap-and-trade mechanism and direct payment for carbon accumulation by forests and soils.
- *Industry and manufacturing:* Developing more energy-efficient processes and less carbon-intensive products; reducing process emissions from cement and steel making and other greenhouse gases, including methane leaks from the fossil fuel industry and agriculture; and developing equipment and processes to facilitate carbon capture, energy storage (e.g., batteries, pump systems), recycling efficiency, and so on.

Key Environmental Issues—Climate Change

Industry, materials, and manufacturing present particular challenges. Although deindustrialization or a reduction in consumption could, in theory, have mitigation effects (consider the significant drop in GHG emissions and in economic output accompanying the COVID-19 pandemic), due consideration must also be given to the associated negative societal impacts (e.g., recessions and unemployment).

The IPCC outlined a number of opportunities for scaling up climate action, noting their potential contribution in reducing emissions and potential synergies between mitigation and adaptation, illustrated in Exhibit 7.

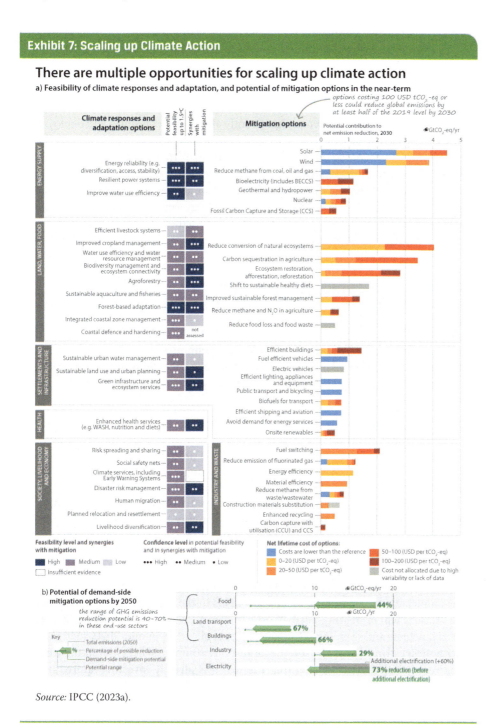

Source: IPCC (2023a).

While multiple options exist, the IPCC (2022b, p. 38) has noted the relatively uneven state of play with regard to technological innovation in several relevant areas:

> *For almost all basic materials—primary metals, building materials, and chemicals—many low- to zero-GHG intensity production processes are at the pilot to near-commercial and in some cases commercial stage but not yet established industrial practice. Introducing new sustainable basic materials production processes could increase production costs but, given the small fraction of consumer cost based on materials, [such processes] are expected to translate into minimal cost increases for final consumers.... [For example,] light industry, mining, and manufacturing have the potential to be decarbonised through available abatement technologies (e.g., material efficiency, circularity), electrification (e.g., electrothermal heating, heat pumps), and low- or zero-GHG emitting fuels (e.g., hydrogen, ammonia, and bio-based and other synthetic fuels).*

The level of policy support can significantly affect the economics and deployment of key technologies, by enabling new markets and encouraging economies of scale and learning effects, particularly if private sector investments are "crowded in." The passage of the Inflation Reduction Act in the United States in 2022, for example, has led to a significant increase in domestic corporate capital expenditures for key low-carbon areas (such as green hydrogen), while triggering, at the international level, a series of policy responses that are likely to spur further international competition between countries vying to attract low-carbon investment and spur the development (or "reshoring") of relevant industries.

CASE STUDIES

The Race to Net Zero

As of April 2022, 88% of global emissions of greenhouse gases, 92% of GDP, and 85% of the world's population were in jurisdictions covered by net-zero targets.[4]

Moreover, over 200 cities and over 850 (mostly listed) companies had similarly set net-zero targets.

While there are significant details, on the corporate front, regarding the details of these targets (the role of offsets, the precise timelines, etc.), the momentum across public and private actors is indicative of a direction of travel with significant investment opportunities, as well as growing regulatory risk.

The higher the ambition of mitigation policies, the higher the required upfront investment. The IPCC has estimated that in the energy sector alone, between US$1 trillion and US$4 trillion of additional annual investment in energy supply and around US$1 trillion in energy demand will be needed by 2050 to limit warming to 1.5°C (2.7°F; IPCC 2018). However, even scenarios without climate mitigation require investments, and it is unclear how those costs may evolve alongside temperatures. For example, around half of the oil and gas fields in the Russian Arctic are estimated to be in areas where melting permafrost can cause severe damage to infrastructure, such as pipelines and shipping terminals (Hjort et al. 2018); in mid-2020, such melting under a diesel storage tank caused the largest environmental accident in the Russian Arctic region (BBC 2020). Given that the world is already investing approximately US$1 trillion yearly in the energy sector (International Energy Agency 2020b), the

---

[4] Source: Net Zero Tracker (https://zerotracker.net/)

important question is, What kind of energy system is being financed for new and expired capital replacement, and what is the extent to which today's investments risk locking in future emissions?

Despite a suite of policies introduced to foster a "green recovery" after the COVID-19 pandemic, the UN has noted that given the global rebound in emissions, "the opportunity to use pandemic recovery spending to reduce emissions has been largely missed" (UNEP 2021). Nevertheless, as another geopolitical shock unfolds–the Russo–Ukrainian War and the associated energy price spikes–policymakers worldwide are increasingly attuned to the benefits that low-carbon energy and infrastructure can provide in terms of energy security and independence.

As illustrated in Exhibit 8, a significant gap still remains between the shorter-term policy commitments of governments (known as nationally determined contributions, which are submitted to the UN and cover measures up to 2030) and the magnitude of emission cuts still needed to meet different scenarios.

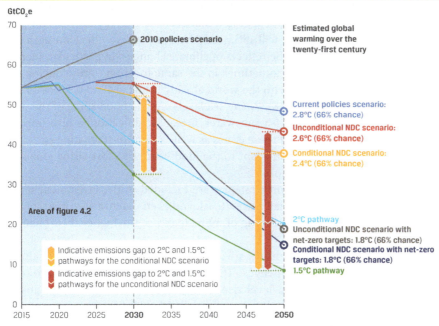

Exhibit 8: Projections of GHG Emissions under Various Scenarios Up to 2050 and Indications of Emissions Gap and Global Warming Implications over This Century (medians only)

Note, first, that certain policy commitments are "conditional" (e.g., they depend on the availability of financing, aid, and technology transfer from the Global North to emerging economies). Second, note that there is a gap between shorter-term pledges up to 2030 (which are compatible with approximately 2.5°C of warming) and longer-term measures (including the various net-zero commitments of governments) that may, if implemented in full and on time (a big "if"!), bring the world to a below-2°C pathway.

Source: UNEP (2022b).

Regardless of the precise outcome achieved, one upshot is that some element of further warming is likely unavoidable. This brings us to the actions needed in response to warming that cannot be averted—in other words, to climate adaptation.

Climate Change Adaptation and Resilience Measures

Adapting to a changing climate involves adjusting to actual or expected future climate events, thereby increasing society's resilience to climate change and reducing vulnerabilities to its harmful effects. The faster and the more the climate changes, the more challenging it will be to adapt. The World Bank (2019) has aptly described adaptation and resilience as "two sides of the same coin."

Most adaptation focuses on anticipating the adverse effects of climate change and taking appropriate action to prevent or minimize the damage they can cause, but there may also be opportunities such as polar melting opening new maritime trade routes across the Arctic or the growth of viticulture in areas that are currently too cold for it.

In light of humankind's ability to survive—and even thrive—in hostile climates, it is tempting to assume that adaptation is a less costly option than mitigation, but this assumption is far from certain and adaptation requires thousands, not tens, of years—that is, longer time frames than the rate of change. Consider one example: air conditioning (AC), the use of which is becoming increasingly common as incomes and populations rise, particularly in the world's warmer regions. AC units are power intensive and use powerful GHGs as refrigerants. It is anticipated that by 2050, air conditioning alone may result in GHG emissions equivalent to those of India, the world's third-largest emitter today, which would create a vicious circle of more global overheating, which requires more AC, and so on (Kalanki and Sachar 2018).

Alternatively, it is sometimes suggested that because CO_2 is a nutrient for plants, more CO_2 in the atmosphere will ultimately have a positive effect on agriculture around the world. However, other effects of climate change—in particular, increased droughts and stronger floods, sometimes in the same location—are reducing yields and accelerating soil erosion, with the world already losing around 0.5% of its arable land every year (Grantham 2018). Rising sea levels already flood some of the world's major rice-producing deltas with salt water. Ocean acidification is also impacting marine food sources. In light of these issues as well as signs of stagnating agricultural productivity, how the world will adapt to the food needs of a fast-rising global population is a crucial open question.

The more climate adaptation strategies are included in the investment plans of the finance sector; the industrial, agricultural, and even defense sector strategies of governments; and the urban planning of municipalities, the higher their chances of success.

Adaptation strategies encompass a wide range of developmental plans aimed at addressing environmental challenges. These include such measures as protecting coastlines and adapting to sea-level rise, building flood defenses, managing land use and forestry practices, and planning more efficiently for scarce water resources. They also involve developing drought-resilient crops, protecting energy and public infrastructure, and creating clean cooling systems.

As mentioned earlier, researchers have observed that some of the most effective climate policies (such as the protection of coastal and freshwater wetlands (Moomaw et al. 2018) and the promotion of sustainable agroforestry) contribute to both adaptation and mitigation simultaneously (Suarez 2020).

Not just an issue of government policy, adaptation is also increasingly being factored into corporate business plans. For example, water risks are proving to be an issue of increased importance in the mining sector, which requires sufficient water to convey or help separate the desired ores. It is estimated that up to 50% of global production of copper, gold, iron ore, and zinc—metals with a key contribution to low-carbon energy technologies—is located in areas where water stress is already high (Delevingne, Glazener, Grégoir, and Henderson 2020).

Too much water can also be a problem, because floods can shut down mines and cause significant local pollution. Close to half of the global production of iron ore and zinc is estimated to be in areas facing high flood risk (Delevingne et al. 2020).

CASE STUDIES

Escondida Copper Mine

Located in one of the most arid places on earth, the Atacama Desert in Chile, Escondida is the world's largest copper mine by production. BHP, the mining company operating it, has been planning a transition away from using fresh groundwater.

In early 2020, BHP announced it was able to operate the mine using only desalinated water from the ocean. BHP already uses more than 50% of the water it needs from the ocean in an effort to reduce pressure on freshwater resources, which are often also used by local communities (Jamasmie 2020; BHP 2020).

States, provinces, cities, and municipalities are at the frontline of adaptation and resilience due to their high concentration of people, assets, and economic activities.[5] Representing 80% of global gross domestic product, cities are heavily exposed to climate change risks in the forms of

- sea level rise,
- extreme weather events, such as flooding and drought, and
- an increase in the spread of tropical diseases.

All of these will have an economic and social cost to cities' inhabitants, infrastructure, and businesses and the built environment. At the same time, cities are a major contributor of GHG emissions, mainly from transport and buildings. Useful best practices of various cities' climate adaptation strategies include

- incorporating flood risk into building designs (in New York City) and planning for enhanced water absorption rates in city infrastructure ("sponge cities," such as Wuhan, China; Jing 2019),
- modeling the impact of natural disasters on energy supply (in Yokohama, Japan), and
- analyzing the resiliency to disruption of food supply systems (in Los Angeles and Paris; C40 Cities and AXA 2019).

Estimates of the relative costs of adaptation to climate change vary. In the "Adaptation Gap Report 2022," the UN Environment Programme (UNEP) estimated that adaptation costs in developing countries alone were estimated to be in the range of US$160 billion and US$340 billion by 2030 and between US$315 billion and US$565 billion by 2050.

These costs are expected to increase even further if greenhouse gas emissions continue to rise. The benefits of adaptation can be significant, including reduced economic losses, improved human health, and increased resilience to climate change. However, there is a significant gap between the costs of adaptation and the amount of funding that is available.

In 2020, international adaptation finance flows to developing countries totaled only US$20 billion. This is far below the estimated needs, which is leading to a growing adaptation gap. The "Adaptation Gap Report 2022" calls for urgent action to close the adaptation gap, which will require increased investment in adaptation measures, as well as a more equitable distribution of resources. It is also important to integrate adaptation into all aspects of development planning, so that countries can build resilience to climate change and reduce the risks of future disasters (Global Commission on Adaptation 2019).

---

5 See, for example, the websites of the Under2 Coalition (www.theclimategroup.org/under2-coalition) and Climate Mayors (https://climatemayors.org/).

In late 2019, the Climate Bonds Initiative published the first Climate Resilience Principles, which provide a framework for developing location-specific climate resilience measures and financing them in the green bond market (Climate Bonds Initiative 2019). In addition, a group of multilateral development banks have put forward "A Framework and Principles for Climate Resilience Metrics in Financing Operations," which provides guidance on how to create effective climate resilience projects and how to measure direct outcomes and wider system impacts (African Development Bank, Asian Development Bank, Asian Infrastructure Investment Bank, European Bank for Reconstruction and Development, European Investment Bank, Inter American Development Bank, International Development Finance Club, and Islamic Development Bank 2019).

It is important to recognize that there can be trade-offs between adaptation/resilience and mitigation. For example, the decision to invest in a desalination plant that helps prevent a potential water shortage in a crisis may be warranted, despite its high associated emissions. Understanding and assessing such potential conflicts is critical to building resilience with limited impact on mitigation efforts.

3 PRESSURES ON NATURAL RESOURCES

> 3.1.2 explain key concepts related to other environmental issues, including pressures on natural resources, including depletion of natural resources, water, biodiversity loss, land use and marine resources, pollution, waste, and a circular economy

The relationship between businesses and natural resources is becoming increasingly important due to dramatically accelerating biodiversity loss and less secure access to natural resources. For the purposes of this section, natural resources cover

- fresh water,
- biodiversity loss,
- land use, and
- forestry and marine resources.

Natural resources also include non-renewable resources (such as fossil fuels, minerals, and metals), which cannot be replenished quickly enough to keep up with their consumption.

NATURAL CAPITAL

Natural capital is defined as "the world's stocks of natural assets, which include geology, soil, air, water, and all living things. It is from this natural capital that humans derive a wide range of services, often called ecosystem services, which make human life possible" (World Forum on Natural Capital 2021).

The importance of taking a natural capital approach is explained in more detail in the section titled "Assessment of Materiality of Environmental Issues," which discusses investment opportunities.

Pressures on Natural Resources

It is estimated that the annual monetary value of ecosystem services is around US$125 trillion to US$140 trillion, more than 1.5 times the global GDP (OECD 2019). Biodiversity also has intrinsic value: The ideas that the beauty of nature is worth preserving and that mankind and other species should strive for a harmonious coexistence have been a mainstay of many cultures, religions, and belief systems (see, for example, the Convention on Biological Diversity, signed by a majority of governments worldwide).

Governments and businesses are having to deal with increased pressure on natural resources, caused by

- population growth,
- health improvements leading to people living longer,
- economic growth, and
- the accompanying increased consumption in developed and emerging economies.

Simultaneously, these drivers are leading to the risk of resource scarcity. These developments are therefore compelling companies to become more efficient in the way that they use natural resources if they are to remain competitive and become more sustainable. This increased efficiency can help drive better financial management of resources but also spur technological innovations that can have a beneficial impact on the bottom line in support of a more sustainable and resilient economy and society.

Depletion of Natural Resources

According to the UN, the current world population of 7.6 billion is expected to reach 8.6 billion in 2030, 9.8 billion in 2050, and 11.2 billion in 2100. The rising population can put increased strain on the world's natural resources, most notably in terms of access to food, which presents a number of related challenges:

1. "Modern agriculture is dependent on phosphorus derived from phosphate rock, which is a non-renewable resource, and current global reserves may be depleted in 50–100 years. While phosphorus demand is projected to increase, the expected global peak in phosphorus production is predicted to occur around 2030," with the quality of remaining reserves expected to fall while costs—and the global population—continue to rise (Cordell, Drangerta, and White 2009).

2. The world is already using half its vegetated land for agriculture. Avoiding worsening climate change, which itself would reduce agricultural productivity, requires feeding a rapidly growing population without further deforestation (Ranganathan, Waite, Searchinger, and Hanson 2018).

3. The issue is compounded by changes in lifestyle: "While population growth was the leading cause of increasing consumption from 1970 to 2000, the emergence of a global affluent middle class has been the stronger driver since the turn of the century" (Oberle, Bringezu, Hatfield-Dodds, and Hellweg 2019; see also Wiedmann, Lenzen, Keyßer, and Steinberger 2020; European Environment Agency 2021). From the rare earths and other metals that go into smartphones and computers to the rising emissions associated with a higher standard of living (for example, bigger homes with higher heating and cooling needs, increased travel, and increased meat and dairy consumption), these dynamics are also set to increase the pressure on natural resources.

To a certain degree, technological innovation and moving from a linear to a circular economy has the potential to reduce the need for virgin resources. The decoupling of economic activities from resource usage has been observed; for example, between 2010 and 2020, global GDP per capita has risen by over 15% while carbon emissions per capita have fallen by about 2% (see Exhibit 9).

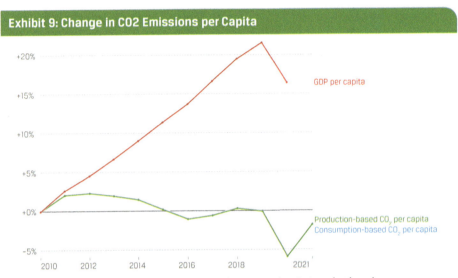

Exhibit 9: Change in CO2 Emissions per Capita

Note: Consumption-based emissions are national or regional emissions that have been adjusted for trade. They are calculated as domestic (or "production-based" emissions) minus the emissions generated in the production of goods and services that are exported to other countries or regions, plus emission from the production of goods and services that are imported. Consumption based emissions = Production-based − Exported + Imported emissions

This measures fossil fuel and industry emissions. Fossil emissions measure the quantity of carbon dioxide (CO_2) emitted from the burning of fossil fuels, and directly from industrial processes such as cement and steel production. Fossil CO_2 includes emissions from coal, oil, gas, flaring, cement, steel, and other industrial processes. Fossil emissions do not include land use change, deforestation, soils, or vegetation.

Land use change is not included.

Note: GDP figures are adjusted for inflation.

Source: Ritchie (2021).

The same dataset shows that in the United Kingdom, GDP per capita has grown by more than one-third since 1990, with carbon emissions per capita falling by 40%–50% (this includes adjustments to reflect the offshoring of production abroad). More broadly, the IPCC's latest report finds that "at least 18 countries have sustained absolute production-based GHG and consumption-based CO_2 reductions" (IPCC 2023a, p. 10). However, looking at wider material use, beyond CO_2, a literature review of decoupling found a mixed picture: "Relative decoupling is frequent for material use as well as GHG and CO_2 emissions, [but] examples of absolute long-term decoupling are rare" (Haberl et al. 2020).

One reason is that relative improvements in efficiency (using fewer resources per unit of production) may be offset by increased consumption of a given product—an effect known as the *Jevons paradox*.[6] The issue of resource usage will remain crucial for investors and policymakers, who will have to navigate trade-offs and consider not

---

[6] Source: https://en.wikipedia.org/wiki/Jevons_paradox.

just use efficiency but also how to facilitate changing the whole model (moving from linear to circular in products, processes, and ultimately, the economy) to reduce the strain on natural resources.

Another idea that is gaining ground is decoupling the definition of development and progress from GDP growth to a measurement of asset wealth and assigning economic value not just to produced capital and human capital but also to natural capital, as proposed in the Dasgupta Review (HM Treasury 2021). Historically, growth in produced capital has been at the expense of natural capital, which has been ignored, and at the expense of countries rich in natural resources, many of which have been left behind in the distribution of benefits in the form of human capital development and left with the impact of natural capital depletion and increasing social inequities. Valuing "ecosystem services" and their loss as the benefits and costs if they were supplied by the market is another alternative means of including natural inputs in the traditional GDP accounting (Costanza et al. 2014). There are also examples of individuals and governments paying someone for maintaining a beneficial ecosystem service (Jack, Kousky, and Sims 2008).

Water

Nearly 70% of the planet is covered by water, but only 2.5% of it is freshwater. Water is a vital natural resource, not only for human consumption but also for a range of agricultural, industrial, and household energy generation, as well as for recreational and environmental activities. It is critical to many industrial processes, including mineral extraction and cooling for industrial plants. Water demand is set to increase in all sectors (UNESCO World Water Assessment Programme 2018).

According to the World Economic Forum (2019), water also connects these sectors to a broader economic system that must balance social development and environmental interests. As the world continues to face multiple water challenges, a decision to allocate more water to any one sector implies that less water will be available for other economic uses, for public water supply and other social services, or for environmental protection (World Economic Forum 2019).

Water scarcity is the lack of freshwater resources to meet water demand. Water scarcity is present on every continent and is one of the largest global risks in terms of potential impact over the next decade. UN-Water (2019) reported that over 2 billion people experience high water stress in various countries, and about 4 billion people experience severe water scarcity at least one month of the year.

The UN's Sustainable Development Goal (SDG) 6 is the need "to ensure availability and sustainable management of water and sanitation to all" by 2030 (United Nations Department of Economic and Social Affairs 2021). Water scarcity—caused either by economic factors, such as lack of investment, or by physical impacts related to climate change—continues to cause major concern, especially among developing and emerging economies.

Biodiversity

Biodiversity, land use, and associated ecosystems provide a range of invaluable services to society that underpin human health, well-being, and economic growth. Ecosystem services are the benefits that people and businesses derive from ecosystems. Biodiversity, as defined by the Convention on Biological Diversity, is the "variability among living organisms from all sources including, among other things, terrestrial, marine, and other aquatic ecosystems and the ecological complexes of which they are part; this includes diversity within species, between species, and of ecosystems" (United Nations 1992).

As noted by the IPCC (2022a, Sections D.4 and D.4.1):

> *Safeguarding biodiversity and ecosystems is fundamental to climate resilient development, in light of the threats climate change poses to them and their roles in adaptation and mitigation (very high confidence). Recent analyses, drawing on a range of lines of evidence, suggest that maintaining the resilience of biodiversity and ecosystem services at a global scale depends on effective and equitable conservation of approximately 30% to 50% of Earth's land, freshwater, and ocean areas, including currently near-natural ecosystems (high confidence). . . .*
>
> *Building the resilience of biodiversity and supporting ecosystem integrity can maintain benefits for people, including livelihoods, human health and well-being, and the provision of food, fiber, and water, as well as contributing to disaster risk reduction and climate change adaptation and mitigation.*

The World Wildlife Fund (WWF 2022) noted that the world's wildlife populations have plummeted by 69% since 1970, with this trajectory likely to be further exacerbated by global warming. A major driver of this decline is loss of habitat linked to overexploitation, agriculture, and urbanization

Already, biodiversity loss is presenting challenges to such industries as fishery and agriculture. Around 75% of global food crop types directly rely on animal pollination; given the decline in natural pollinators due to pollution and pesticides, US farmers paid approximately US$300 million for artificial (sometimes manual) pollination in 2017. Another area of concern is medicine and health, with an estimated 70% of cancer drugs being organic or derived from organic substances (Paun 2020). WWF (2020) estimated that inaction on biodiversity may result in cumulative costs of approximately US$10 trillion by 2050, through changes to crop yields and fish catches, economic damages from flooding and other disasters, and the loss of potential new sources of medicine.

Biodiversity underpins ecosystem services, provides natural resources, and constitutes our "natural capital." Some of these ecosystem services are

- food,
- clean water,
- genetic resources,
- flood protection,
- nutrient cycling, and
- climate regulation (Juffe-Bignoli 2014).

The Dasgupta Review (HM Treasury 2021) argued for assigning economic asset value to biodiversity to reverse its treatment as a free resource and attempt to halt depletion. In the same vein, PBL Netherlands Environmental Assessment Agency (2020) published an important report titled "Indebted to Nature," exploring the biodiversity risks for the Dutch financial sector, effectively identifying nature and biodiversity as a systemic risk.

It is important to emphasize the potentially large *unrecognized value*. There are myriad interactions between different species, playing highly complex roles in cycling nutrients, regulating the numbers of (potentially invasive) plant and animal species, and even altering the formation of landscapes.

The Organisation for Economic Co-Operation and Development (OECD 2019) has noted it is difficult to predict where biodiversity thresholds lie, "when they will be crossed, and what will be the scale of impact. Given this uncertainty and the potential impact of regime shifts, it is prudent to take a precautionary approach." There is evidence that conservation can be effective: A study from 2009 found that conservation investments over more than a decade reduced extinction risk by almost a third for mammals and birds in 109 countries (Waldron et al. 2017). Without existing conservation efforts, the extinction risk of mammals, birds, and amphibians would have been at least 20% higher, according to the IPBES (2019). This is not just a conservation issue; the OECD (2020) noted the link between safeguarding biodiversity and human health: "Land-use change resulting from agricultural expansion, logging, infrastructure development and other human activities is the most common driver of infectious disease emergence."

In summary, conserving nature and improving the sustainable use of natural resources are possible but can be achieved only through transformative changes across economic, social, political, and technological factors.

Land Use and Forestry

Land use management practices and forestry—also known as agriculture, forestry, and other land use (AFOLU)—have a major impact on natural resources, including water, soil, nutrients, plants, and animals.

Covering approximately 30% of the world's land area, or just under 4 billion hectares, forests are a vital part of the carbon cycle (Nunez 2019). They convert the CO_2 in the air to oxygen, through the process of photosynthesis, and are a natural regulator of CO_2, with the world's tropical forests playing a particularly important role in accumulating and storing carbon. The more mature and old growth trees in our forests, the less atmospheric CO_2 and the more oxygen there is in the atmosphere (Law et al. 2022).

Unfortunately, deforestation is accelerating: From 2001 to 2019, there was a total of 386 million hectares of tree cover loss globally, equivalent to a 9.7% decrease in tree cover since 2000 and 105 gigatons of CO_2 emissions, according to Global Forest Watch (2020).

The production of commodities (particularly relating to agriculture) is a key driver of deforestation—responsible for up to two-thirds of deforestation by some estimates (Global Canopy 2021). As a result, there is increased investor focus on investee companies' contribution to deforestation. According to the CDP (previously the Carbon Disclosure Project), approximately US$1 trillion of turnover in publicly listed companies is dependent on commodities linked to deforestation, including soy, palm oil, cattle, and timber. The risks from these soft commodities can be transmitted across supply chains to affect companies' revenues, asset valuation, or costs, which can impact the creditworthiness or market value of the debt or equity of investee companies (CDP and Global Canopy 2017).

Companies with exposure to deforestation in their supply chains may face material financial risks, such as

- supply disruption,
- cost volatility, and
- reputational damage.

In contrast, shifting business practices to adopt more sustainable land management approaches contributes to

- agricultural and economic development, both locally and globally,
- the health and stability of forests and ecosystems and the continued provision of ecosystem services at an increasing scale, and
- the reduction of GHG emissions from deforestation and degradation.

Sustainable agriculture will remain an issue of growing focus for policymakers and companies. Citi GPS (2021) has noted that conventional agricultural practices often contribute to biodiversity loss, exacerbating the vulnerability of food systems to climate change–induced weather extremes. Citi GPS warned that the stability of the global food supply is projected to decrease as the magnitude and frequency of extreme weather events that disrupt food chains increases.

In summary, the protection and management of land resources play a vital role in ensuring the balance of nature and the health of the ecosystem. Unsustainable management will negatively affect biodiversity, ecosystems, and all the natural resources that underpin economic growth and human flourishing.

Marine Resources

Storing 43 times more CO_2 than the atmosphere, the ocean is the planet's largest carbon reservoir. It is also the second largest sink in terms of removing CO_2 from the atmosphere (Global Carbon Project 2022). Photosynthetic microorganisms on its surface layer also produce over half of the world's oxygen (National Ocean Service 2021). It is one of the earth's most valuable natural resources.

The OECD has estimated that ocean-based industries contribute roughly US$1.3 trillion to global gross value added. Oceans provide seafood and are widely used for transportation (shipping). They are also mined for minerals (salt, sand, and gravel, as well as some manganese, copper, nickel, iron, and cobalt, which can be found in the deep sea) and drilled for crude oil. The oceans' resources are a source of economic growth and are also known as the *blue economy*. According to the World Bank (2017), the blue economy is the "sustainable use of ocean resources for economic growth, improved livelihoods, and jobs while preserving the health of ocean ecosystem." The blue economy as an investment opportunity is discussed in the section in this chapter titled "Applying Material Environmental Factors to Financial Modeling, Ratio Analysis, and Risk Assessment."

Communities in close connection with coastal environments, small islands (including Small Island Developing States), polar areas, and high mountains are particularly exposed to ocean change, such as sea level rise. Low-lying coastal zones are currently home to around 680 million people (nearly 10% of the 2010 global population), projected to reach more than 1 billion by 2050 (IPCC 2019).

Due to the increase in the human population, the oceans have been overfished, with a resulting decline of fish critical to the economy. In 2015,

- ▶ 33% of marine fish stocks were being harvested at unsustainable levels,
- ▶ 60% were fished to maximum capacity, and
- ▶ only 7% were harvested at levels lower than what can be sustainably fished (IPBES 2019).

Although there are 66 international agreements governing regional fisheries management organizations, just 7 of them have a secretariat, a scientific body, and enforcement powers. In most cases, fishing quotas are politically agreed on and overrule the recommendation for maximum sustained yield recommended by the scientific body. This "legal overfishing" is in addition to the illegal, unreported, and unregulated catch. In addition, almost all fishing nations subsidize fishing fleets to be much larger than the fishery can sustain (Moomaw and Blankenship 2014). The control of the world's fisheries is a controversial subject, because production is unable to satisfy the demand, especially when there are not enough fish left to breed in healthy ecosystems. Environmental finance think tank Planet Tracker (2020b) estimated that "if historic trends continue and coastal ecological health continues declining, total production forecasts for coastal farmed Atlantic salmon to 2025 may be 6% to 8% lower than predicted, equivalent to US$4.1 billion". However, there are options to address this problem: By improvements in traceability and sustainability certifications, which have lower impacts on biodiversity, Planet Tracker estimated that "the typical seafood processor can double its EBIT [earnings before interest and tax] margin, which is currently at a low 3%, mainly due to lower recall, product waste, and legal costs" (Planet Tracker 2020b; see also Planet Tracker 2020c).

Pollution, Waste, and a Circular Economy

Air Pollution

Clean air is essential to health, the environment, and economic prosperity. Increased air pollution

- adversely affects the environment,
- has a negative impact on human health,
- destroys ecosystems,
- impoverishes biodiversity, and
- reduces crop harvests as a result of soil acidification.

Indoor and outdoor air pollution are together responsible for over 7 million deaths globally each year, according to the World Health Organization (WHO 2020). Research by the WHO further shows that in 2019, 99% of the world's population was living in places where the WHO air quality guideline levels were not met (WHO 2020). Urban air pollution is predicted to worsen, as migration and demographic trends drive the creation of more megacities.

Pollution is the largest environmental cause of disease and premature death in the world today. According to findings published in October 2017 by the Lancet Commission on Pollution and Health, diseases caused by pollution were responsible for an estimated 9 million premature deaths in 2015—16% of all deaths worldwide—which is three times more deaths than from AIDS, tuberculosis, and malaria combined and 15 times more than from all wars and other forms of violence (Landrigan et al. 2018).

Research published in 2021 in the journal *Environmental Research* focused on isolating the impact of fossil fuel combustion and concluded that "the burning of fossil fuels—especially coal, petrol, and diesel—is a major source of airborne fine particulate matter ($PM_{2.5}$) and a key contributor to the global burden of mortality and disease. . . . The greatest mortality impact is estimated over regions with substantial fossil fuel related $PM_{2.5}$" (Vohra et al. 2021).

Using new modeling, the scientists estimated that parts of China, India, Europe, and the northeastern United States are among the hardest-hit areas, suffering a disproportionately high share of the 8.7 million annual deaths attributed to fossil fuels, compared to a 2017 study, which had put the annual number of deaths from all outdoor airborne particulate matter—including dust and smoke from agricultural burns and wildfires—at 4.2 million (Green 2021). These findings lend further support to the focus on reducing fossil fuel emissions.

Water Pollution

Water is essential to all living organisms. Yet water pollution is one of the most serious environmental threats faced. Water pollution occurs when contaminants (such as harmful chemicals or microorganisms) are introduced into the natural environment through the ocean, rivers, streams, lakes, or groundwater. Water pollution can be caused by spills and leaks from untreated sewage or sanitation systems and industrial waste discharge. Plastic waste also appears in waterways.

> **CASE STUDIES**
>
> **Water-Related Fines**
>
> Partially due to increased public interest litigation, fines for water pollution are increasing around the world. In 2014, Chinese media reported what was at the time the largest ever fine levied in the country—whereby six companies were fined a total of 160 million yuan (US$ 22.4 million) for chemical discharges into rivers (BBC 2014).
>
> In 2020, the US Environmental Protection Agency announced its largest ever fine relating to the Clean Water Act. Almost US$3 million was charged to a horseracing facility for repeated discharge of animal waste into New Orleans waterways (US Attorney's Office 2020).

Waste and Waste Management

In view of the concerns about growing pressures on natural resources—combined with opposition to all types of pollution—waste and waste management has, in recent decades, become a bigger priority for policymakers, businesses, and citizens. Increasing consumption and waste levels are putting more pressure on space for landfill waste, which, in turn, is causing landfill taxes to rise. Alongside tougher regulation on how waste is handled and managed, businesses are becoming increasingly incentivized to help economies, notably through recycling and by adopting a circular economy business model.

A recent striking example of the public's concern over excessive waste is the campaign against plastics, especially in relation to the serious damage that they are doing to the oceans. This campaign has led to actions by national and local authorities on waste management and greater responsibility conferred on businesses to manage their waste responsibly.

In most developed countries, domestic waste disposal is funded from national or local taxes, which may be related to income or property values. Commercial and industrial waste disposal is typically charged for as a commercial service, often as an integrated charge that includes disposal costs. This practice may encourage disposal contractors to opt for the cheapest disposal option, such as using landfills and incineration—which generate GHG emissions and contribute to local pollution—rather than opting for such solutions as reuse and recycling.

Although many consumer products (such as metal cans and glass bottles) are recyclable, recycling practices are very uneven among (and sometimes even within) countries. However, there has been growing public concern with excessive waste, particularly for single-use plastics and the serious damage that they are doing to the oceans and marine wildlife. This has led to actions by national and local authorities on waste management and greater responsibility conferred on businesses to manage their waste responsibly. Coupled with a slowdown in the ability to export hazardous waste, including plastics, to a rising number of Asian jurisdictions (most notably China), this puts further pressure on those in Australia, Europe, and North America, in particular, to develop their own recycling and waste management solutions onshore.

In 2022 at the UN Environment Assembly, heads of state and government representatives from around the world committed to develop by 2024 an international legally binding agreement to end plastic pollution (UNEP 2022c).

A financial mechanism that is growing in popularity in the consumer space is the use of fees and taxes, including a charge on plastic bags, designed to discourage waste and promote recycled usage. The European Strategy for Plastics in a Circular Economy, agreed on in January 2018, requires that all plastic packaging must be reusable or recyclable by 2030. This trend has material implications for investors. As the use of oil for transportation declines amid a shift to electric vehicles, numerous companies in the oil industry are looking toward petrochemicals—and plastics in particular—as an alternative source of growth. Yet, think tank Carbon Tracker has estimated that if policymakers implement stricter recycling measures in response to ongoing public pressure, up to US$400 billion of investments in new petrochemical facilities might become "stranded," unprofitable assets (Bond 2020).

Conversely, there are opportunities in better waste management, from the reuse or transformation of recovered waste (for example, using old tires to create road surfacing and expanded recycling programs under the TerraCycle [2021] initiative) to finding new ways to break down waste into useful or less harmful materials (such as graphene; Snowden 2020).

A global commitment by companies led by the Ellen MacArthur Foundation and UNEP has set a benchmark for best practices to address the plastic waste and pollution system (New Plastics Economy 2017). In a sign of the times, the International Criminal Police Organization has also started tracking criminal trends in the global plastic waste market (INTERPOL 2020).

Circular Economy

The **circular economy** is an economic model that aims to avoid waste and to preserve the value of resources (raw materials, energy, and water) for as long as possible. It is an effective model for companies to assess and manage their operations and resource management (see Exhibit 10); it is an alternative approach to the use-make-dispose economy. The circular economy is based on three principles:

1. design out waste and pollution,
2. keep products and materials in use, and
3. regenerate natural systems (Ellen MacArthur Foundation 2019b).

The Netherlands has developed a program for a circular economy, aimed at "preventing waste by making products and materials more efficiently and reusing them. If new raw materials are needed, they must be obtained sustainably so that the natural and human environment is not damaged"(Government of the Netherlands 2017).

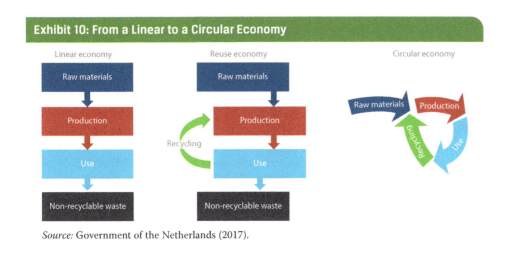

Exhibit 10: From a Linear to a Circular Economy

Source: Government of the Netherlands (2017).

A report from the Ellen MacArthur Foundation (2019a) stresses the importance of a circular economy as a fundamental step toward achieving climate targets. To illustrate this potential, the paper argues that changes in the sources and use of energy could help halve the emissions associated with the production of goods; however, the other half of emissions comes from the use of materials, not energy. Applying circular economy strategies in just five key areas (cement, aluminum, steel, plastics, and food) can eliminate almost half of these remaining emissions. By 2050, the cumulative impact of these strategies would be equivalent to eliminating all current emissions from transport (Ellen MacArthur Foundation 2019a).

The circular economy will also be covered in the section titled "Applying Material Environmental Factors to Financial Modeling, Ratio Analysis, and Risk Assessment."

4 SYSTEMIC RELATIONSHIPS BETWEEN BUSINESS ACTIVITIES AND ENVIRONMENTAL ISSUES

3.1.3 explain the systemic relationships between business activities and environmental issues, including systemic impact of climate risks on the financial system; climate-related physical and transition risks; the relationship between natural resources and business; supply, operational, and resource management issues; and supply chain transparency and traceability

Much of the understanding of key environmental factors with respect to business and investment centers on specific issues, such as climate change and unsustainable natural resource consumption and production, and on the negative impacts that businesses, consumption habits, and investment demand are having on the health of natural capital stocks. There is, however, less of an understanding of how businesses and financial activities depend on natural resources and properly functioning ecosystem services. Due to the difficulty in valuing and measuring natural resources, these detrimental impacts have not been fully priced into the costs of doing business (also known as pricing "negative externalities"). If such costs were to be fully internalized by businesses or their investors, there could be significant market disruptions.

Systemic Risks to the Financial System: Physical and Transitional Risks

Over the last 20 years, environmental themes have become an increasingly important consideration of the business agenda. Of note is the growing appreciation of the *physical risks* of climate change, stemming from more frequent or severe weather events, such as flooding, droughts, and storms. The associated costs are rising: Inflation-adjusted losses from extreme weather events have increased fivefold in recent decades (Breeden 2019). Munich RE (2020) has estimated such losses to be over US$200 billion, with both overall losses and insured losses significantly higher than in previous years. Losses from the historic wildfires in the western United States alone were estimated to be around US$16 billion, with a similar loss figure due to floods in China.

A Swiss Re report (Banerjee, Bevere, Corti, and Lechner 2023) estimated that global economic losses from natural disasters in 2022 amounted to US$275 billion, with insured losses covering 45% of the damage, marking the fourth highest single-year total on record; Hurricane Ian resulted in estimated insured losses of US$50 billion–US$65 billion (see Exhibit 11).

Exhibit 11: Total Economic and Insured Losses from Natural Catastrophes (US$ billion, 2022 prices)

	2022	2021	Annual change
Total losses	275	270	2%
Insured losses	125	111	13%

Source: Banerjee et al. (2023).

Insurers and reinsurers are particularly exposed to these effects, on both sides of their balance sheet. Their investment assets can be impacted if, for example, storms and floods affect real estate in their portfolio. Their liabilities can be affected if extreme weather leads to increases in property insurance claims or extreme-weather-induced diseases and mortality lead to increases in life insurance claims.

As the Bank of England (2021) has noted, physical risks can have significant macroeconomic effects: "For instance, if weather-related damage leads to a fall in house prices (and so reduces the wealth of homeowners), then there could be a knock-on effect on overall spending in the economy."

There are also company- and sector-level implications, given the supply chains of a globalized economy.

CASE STUDIES

Thai Floods

In 2011, Thailand experienced its worst flooding in five decades, with US$45 billion of economic damages, resulting in US$12 billion in insurance claims. Although flooding is not uncommon in the region, the effects of the floods were felt across the globe: Over 10,000 factories for consumer goods, textiles, and automotive products had to close, disrupting the supply chain for such businesses as Sony, Nikon, and Honda, resulting in either reduced or delayed production. Many of these international businesses lodged contingent business interruption claims with their insurers and reinsurers, which cost Lloyd's of London US$2.2 billion (Prudential Regulation Authority 2015).

Occasionally, extreme weather events may lead not just to a hit to a company's finances but to full-scale bankruptcy.

CASE STUDIES

PG&E

In what has been described as "the first climate-change bankruptcy, probably not the last" (Gold 2019), in January 2019, the US power supplier PG&E filed for voluntary Chapter 11 bankruptcy protection, as a result of liabilities stemming from wildfires in northern California in 2017 and 2018. It claimed that it faced an estimated US$30 billion liability for damages from wildfires during those two years, a sum that would exceed its insurance and assets.

Whereas physical risks stem primarily from inaction on climate change, there are also climate risks and trade-offs associated with action—the so-called *transition risks*—as the world shifts toward a low-carbon economy. As the Bank of England (2021) has explained:

Such transitions could mean that some sectors of the economy face big shifts in asset values or higher costs of doing business. It's not that policies stemming from deals like the Paris Climate Agreement are bad for our economy—in fact, the risk of delaying action altogether would be far worse. Rather, it's about the speed of transition to a greener economy—and how this affects certain sectors and financial stability.

One example is energy companies. If government policies were to change in line with the Paris Agreement, then two thirds of the world's known fossil fuel reserves could not be burned. This could lead to changes in the value of investments held by banks and insurance companies in sectors like coal, oil, and gas. The move towards a greener economy could also impact companies that produce cars, ships, and planes or use a lot of energy to make raw materials like steel and cement.

Transition risks are multiple in nature and include the following:

- policy risks, such as increased emission regulation and environmental standards,
- legal risks, such as lawsuits claiming damages from entities (corporations or sovereign states) believed to be liable for their contribution to climate change, and
- technology risks, such as low-carbon innovations disrupting established industries.

These risks are interlocking in nature and potentially have far-reaching impacts, which underscore their systemic relationship to business and financial activities. For example, a study from the Grantham Research Institute (Matikainen, Campiglio, and Zenghelis 2017) found that more than half of corporate bond purchases by the Bank of England and the European Central Bank (ECB) went to carbon-intensive sectors. Such dependencies are increasingly being scrutinized by regulators, with the Bank for International Settlements—the "bank for central banks"—warning that climate change could "be the cause of the next systemic financial crisis" (Bolton et al. 2020).

Exhibit 12 summarizes the main physical and transitional risks.

Exhibit 12: Risks to Financial Stability Due to Climate-Related Physical and Transition Risks

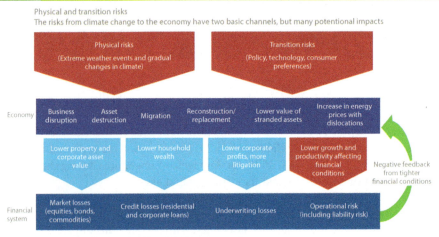

Source: International Monetary Fund (2019, chapter 6).

The Relationship between Natural Resources and Business

In general, businesses and investment activities impact and depend on natural resources and ecosystem services in both direct and indirect ways.

The Global Reporting Initiative (2007), which is a global sustainability reporting framework, explains the causes of direct and indirect impacts and dependencies of businesses on biodiversity resources:

- A direct impact: "An organization's activities directly affecting biodiversity—for example, when
    - degraded land is converted for the benefit of production activities,
    - surface water is used for irrigation purposes,
    - toxic materials are released, or
    - local species are disturbed through the noise and light produced at a processing site."
- An indirect impact: "The impact is caused by parties in an organization's supply chain(s)—for example, when an organization imports fruits and vegetables, produces cotton shirts, sells construction materials, or publishes books, the production of the input for these goods will have indirect impacts on biodiversity."
- Indirect impacts can also include impacts from activities that have been triggered by the operations of the organization. "For example, a road constructed to transport products from a forestry operation can have the indirect effect of stimulating the migration of workers to an unsettled region and encouraging new commercial development alongside the road."
- "Indirect impacts may be relatively difficult to predict and manage, but they can be as significant as direct impacts and can easily affect an organization. Impacts on biodiversity can be either
    - negative (degrading the quality of quantity of biodiversity) or
    - positive (creating a net contribution to the quality or quantity of biodiversity)."

Examples of sectors that rely significantly on natural resources and ecosystem services, with the potential to negatively affect biodiversity, include

- agriculture, aquaculture, fisheries, and food production,
- extractives, infrastructure, and activities or projects involving large-scale construction work,
- fast-moving consumer goods (FMCG) companies, primarily through the sourcing of raw materials in products,
- forestry (wood products, paper, fiber, and energy),
- pharmaceuticals
- tourism and hospitality, and
- utilities, including those involved in hydropower or open-cycle power plants generating significant thermal discharges.

Supply, Operational, and Resource Management Issues

Companies need to measure, manage, and disclose the environmental impact (both positive and negative) from their direct operations. Investors need to assess the extent to which companies understand the impact of their operations and manage resources that are material to their business.

Environmental impacts from direct operations can include toxic waste generation, water pollution, loss of biodiversity, deforestation, long-term damage to ecosystems, water scarcity, hazardous air, and high greenhouse gas emissions, as well as significant energy use.

Failure to address these challenges will expose businesses to additional risks, whereas working on solutions presents a business opportunity to develop climate-resilient business strategies. The previously described circular economy is a useful model for companies to assess and manage their operations and resource management.

The UK government updated its environmental reporting guidelines in March 2019, providing guidelines for businesses to measure and report their environmental impacts, including GHG emissions (HM Government 2019). The guidelines emphasize the use of environmental key performance indicators (KPIs) to capture the link between environmental and financial performance.

The European Commission (2019b) has adopted the ambitious Circular Economy Action Plan to address the challenges of climate change and pressures on natural resources and ecosystems. This was followed by European Commission (2019a) guidelines under the Non-Financial Reporting Directive that introduced the concept of "double materiality"—in other words, asking companies to report both the impact of climate change on their activities and, conversely, the impact of a company's activities on climate change and the environment, stipulating that "companies should consider their whole value chain, both upstream in the supply chain and downstream."

> **CASE STUDIES**
>
> ### Global Mining and Metals Sector
>
> The global mining and metals sector has a considerable impact on the environment and the community in which it operates. In January 2019, Brazil's iron ore producer, Vale, experienced a deadly dam disaster, which resulted in the deaths of more than 250 people. The share price fell, wiping out BRL71.34 billion (US$14.6 billion) in market value (Laier 2019).
>
> The disaster followed a similar incident in 2015, with the industry's use of a particular structure for the storage of waste—tailings dams—being thrown into the spotlight. Credit (and ESG) rating agencies downgraded Vale, with a number of funds selling out of the company, including from the world's largest sovereign wealth fund (Freitas and Andrade 2020).
>
> Recognizing the lack of transparency over the location and safety of such dams, a coalition of investors now representing over US$13 trillion in assets has written to over 700 extractive companies to call for investigations and reporting into this issue, with a view to the development of a global safety standard.
>
> Environmental (and social) scrutiny of the mining and metals sector has been increasing; many of the world's largest mining companies "have some of the worst scores on sustainability ratings compiled by fund managers, . . . as well as external consultants" (Hume and Sanderson 2019). This reinforces the role of adequate management of supply chain and operational impact.

Supply Chain Transparency and Traceability

Supply chain sustainability is the management of ESG impacts and practices beyond the factory gates, looking at the broader life cycle of goods and services, particularly with regard to the sourcing of raw materials and components (UN Global Compact 2015). Supply chains are complex to understand due to the fact that they are heavily interdependent. As such, the relationships between products and services and environmental risk factors are intertwined across sectors and throughout every level of the supply chain. Companies are increasingly expected to understand, manage, and disclose their exposure to supply chain ESG risks or be left exposed to reputational, operational, and financial risks. As such, it is becoming increasingly important for investors to factor into their due diligence and active stewardship a stronger understanding of the supply chain management of their portfolio companies.

Addressing emissions in industry and the food system presents a particularly complex challenge. In industry, a growing demand for materials, coupled with a slow adoption rate of renewable electricity and incremental process improvements, makes it especially difficult to bring emissions down to net zero by 2050. In the food system, significantly reducing emissions will also be challenging and will require changing the consumption habits of billions of people, changing the production habits of hundreds of millions of producers, and decarbonizing long and complex food supply chains.

Traceability is a useful practice to identify and trace the history, distribution, location, and application of products, parts, and materials. This ensures the reliability of sustainability claims in the areas of human rights, labor (including health and safety), the environment, and anti-corruption (UN Global Compact and BSR 2014).

In the context of environmental factors, GHG emissions in supply chains are estimated to be, on average, over five times as high as those from direct operations (CDP 2020b). Examples of sectors with notably intricate or high-risk supply chains are oil and gas, mining, agriculture, and forestry (including such products as beef, cocoa, cotton, and palm oil), as well as fisheries and leather production.

It is, therefore, important for investors to understand key areas of environmental risks as a result of supply chain factors. Some of the main environmental risks in the supply chain are

- material toxicity and chemicals,
- raw material use,
- recyclability and end-of-life products,
- GHG emissions,
- energy use,
- water use and wastewater treatment,
- air pollution,
- biodiversity, and
- deforestation.

CASE STUDIES

Forest-Risk Commodities

Forests annually remove nearly one-third of emitted carbon dioxide (Friedlingstein et al. 2022) and are essential for meeting net-zero goals. Commodity production—mostly that of beef, palm oil, soy, and timber or pulp—is the leading cause of deforestation around the world, with significant amounts of financing devoted to these "forest-risk commodities." Trase Finance estimated in 2021 that approximately US$6 trillion of investments are linked to deforestation, which are facing increased scrutiny from governments and civil society, bolstered by new data and tools (such as satellite monitoring). In 2020, the UK government announced that companies may face fines if they cannot demonstrate that their supply chains are free from illegal deforestation.

Investors have increased their engagement with relevant actors and begun to take action to address these risks. The Norwegian sovereign wealth fund has divested from over 30 palm oil companies, and a coalition of over 30 investors with over US$4 trillion in assets under management has threatened divestment from commodity producers—and even government bonds—due to their impact in accelerating deforestation in the Amazon (Fitch Ratings 2020; Trase Finance 2021; McGrath 2020; Kirakosian 2020).

Yet, much remains to be done. The results from Global Canopy's latest Forest 500 annual survey of the 500 most influential companies and financial institutions in forest supply chains shows that 40% do not have deforestation commitments for any of the forest-risk commodities they are exposed to (Forest 500 2021). The think tank Planet Tracker (2020a) has estimated that deforestation risks are rising in exchange-traded funds (ETFs).

Measurement, frameworks, and investor expectations around supply chains keep evolving. For example, in terms of GHG emissions, the initial focus has been on direct emissions from core operations (Scope 1 emissions) and purchased energy (Scope 2 emissions). However, there is increasing focus on how to measure and incorporate indirect emissions from the whole value chain, including those produced by suppliers and customers (Scope 3 emissions).

CASE STUDIES

Scope 3 in the Spotlight

For companies in certain industries, the greatest contribution to their overall **carbon footprint** comes from outside "the factory gates." In the case of the fossil fuel industry, for example, most emissions come not from the extraction and processing of coal, oil, and gas but from the use of such products by consumers in vehicles, power plants, and steel mills around the world. Although to some degree, the emissions associated with suppliers or consumers (Scope 3) are not under a company's complete control, they nonetheless represent a source of potential business risk: A low-cost oil producer that captured all the emissions from its operations may nevertheless find the market for its main product shrinking or even vanishing as consumers shift to electric vehicles, for example. To address this issue, there has been growing investor pressure for companies to tackle emissions along the value chain that may lie outside "the factory gates."

A growing number of companies are now setting targets to also reduce Scope 3 emissions—associated with the burning of fossil fuels by customers (for miners, such as BHP, Glencore, and Vale), with the production of parts and raw materials by suppliers (in the case of Volkswagen), or with indirect emissions associated with food production, including land-use changes (in the case of Danone).

For more information on classification of corporate emissions, see the section on carbon footprinting titled "Assessment of Materiality of Environmental Issues."

Investors should assess whether a company in their portfolio has policies and systems in place that

1. clearly explain the environmental (and social) requirements that suppliers are expected to meet via a procurement policy (such as a supplier code of conduct) and
2. enable it to assess environmental (and social) risks throughout its supply chain and discuss whether it has a mechanism in place to improve poor practices.

Achieving full transparency and traceability across all stages in a supply chain in order to undertake a complete assessment of a company's environmental risks is often complex. This is a result of multiple actors involved with different systems and requirements in a supply chain that are required to produce an end product, often across international borders.

Despite these challenges, attempting to conduct this full value chain analysis is important for investors to obtain an accurate picture of investee companies and for companies to ensure that their own policies are not undermined by actions taken elsewhere in their supply chain. For example, CDP (2020a) has estimated that while 71% of its partner companies have zero-deforestation targets, only 27% of their suppliers had policies to match this ambition. Conversely, corporate buyers polled by CDP (2020a) stated that suppliers showing environmental leadership were more competitive over the long term. As such, investors should continue to collaborate with and demand greater transparency from both companies and governments.

> **CASE STUDIES**
>
> ### Measurement Frameworks and Tools
>
> Not-for-profit organizations offer measurement frameworks and tools that can help trace critical sustainability issues in company supply chains. These include the following:
>
> - The Sustainability Consortium, which has built a set of performance indicators and a reporting system that highlight sustainability hotspots for more than 110 consumer product categories, covering 80%–90% of the impact of consumer products.
> - WWF offers more than 50 performance indicators for measuring the supply chain risks associated with the production of a range of commodities, as well as the probability and severity of those risks.
> - CDP and the Global Reporting Initiative have created standards and metrics for comparing different types of sustainability impact.
> - The Sustainability Accounting Standards Board (SASB), now part of the International Sustainability Standards Board, has developed standards that help public companies in 11 sectors, including consumer goods, to give investors material information about corporate sustainability performance along the value chain.
> - The EU Taxonomy and the Climate Bonds Sector Criteria provide sector-specific metrics and indicators to assess whether assets, projects, and activities in energy, transport, buildings, industry, agriculture and forestry, water and waste management, and so on, are compliant with the goals of the Paris Agreement.
> - Transparency for Sustainable Economies (Trase) is a partnership between the Stockholm Environment Institute and Global Canopy.
> - The Exploring Natural Capital Opportunities, Risks and Exposure (ENCORE) tool is an initiative of the UNEP World Conservation Monitoring Centre (WCMC), UNEP Finance Initiative, and Global Canopy.
> - The Terra Carta, an initiative under the patronage of the prince of Wales, provides a roadmap for business action on climate change and biodiversity.
>
> Companies and stakeholders in industries with complex supply chains, such as the agricultural and retail industries, have joined forces to build global multi-stakeholder initiatives in order to trace commodities collaboratively. Examples of global traceability schemes include the following:
>
> - the **Forest Stewardship Council (FSC)**,
> - the Marine Stewardship Council,
> - **Roundtable on Sustainable Palm Oil (RSPO)**, and
> - the Fairtrade Labelling Organizations International.

KEY "MEGATRENDS" AND DRIVERS INFLUENCING ENVIRONMENTAL CHANGE IN TERMS OF POTENTIAL IMPACT ON COMPANIES AND THEIR ENVIRONMENTAL PRACTICES

3.1.4 assess how megatrends influence environmental factors; environmental and climate policies; international climate and environmental agreements and conventions; international, regional, and country-level policy and initiatives; and carbon pricing

Growth of Environmental and Climate Policies

There has been a considerable number of environmental and climate policies adopted in the last decade, with the majority coming from Europe. The Grantham Research Institute at the London School of Economics undertook a global review and found that in 2017 there were approximately 1,400 laws related to climate change globally, a 20-fold increase over 20 years (Nachmany, Fankhauser, Setzer, and Averchenkova 2017). Since then, their number has only continued to increase: In January 2023, the Grantham Research Institute's Climate Change Laws of the World database counted a total of 2,092 climate laws and policies in countries across the globe (the database is available at www.lse.ac.uk/granthaminstitute/climate-change-laws-of-the-world-database/).

International Climate and Environmental Agreements and Conventions

International climate and environmental policy is particularly important in times of increasing globalization because many environmental problems, particularly climate change and loss of biodiversity, extend beyond national borders and can be solved only through international cooperation.

UN Framework Convention on Climate Change (1992)

The UNFCCC is the overarching international treaty relating to climate change. It set a general goal "to avoid dangerous anthropogenic interference with the climate system" and established the principle of "common but differentiated responsibilities" that distinguished responsibilities and obligations of developed and developing countries. All agreements including the legally binding Kyoto Protocol are protocols to this treaty. The UNFCCC secretariat is responsible for the annual Conference of the Parties established by the UNFCCC that are held each year so that national governments can evaluate progress and establish new goals, including the nonbinding temperature limits established in 2015 in Paris at COP21.

Kyoto Protocol (2005)

The Kyoto Protocol was adopted in 1997 and became effective in 2005 without US participation. It was the first international convention to set targets for emissions of the main GHGs:

1. CO_2,
2. methane (CH_4),

3. nitrous oxide (N_2O),
4. hydrofluorocarbons (HFCs),
5. perfluorocarbons (PFCs),
6. sulphur hexafluoride (SF_6), and
7. nitrogen trifluoride (NF_3).[7]

It established top-down, binding targets, but only for developed nations, recognizing the historical links between industrialization, economic development, and GHG emissions. The protocol's first commitment period began in 2008 and ended in 2012 but was subsequently extended to 2020. Negotiations on the measures to be taken after the second commitment period ended in 2020 resulted in the adoption of the Paris Agreement.

Paris Agreement (2015)

At the 21st Conference of the Parties to the UNFCCC in Paris in 2015 (COP21), a landmark agreement was reached to mobilize a global response to the threat of climate change in the form of the Paris Agreement.

The agreement's long-term goal is to keep the increase in global average temperature to well below 2°C (3.6°F) above pre-industrial levels and to limit the increase to 1.5°C (2.7°F), since this would substantially reduce the risks and effects of climate change (United Nations 2015).

Although the Paris Agreement does not set any legally binding targets under international law, it serves as a significant landmark in tackling climate change on a global scale.

Nationally determined contributions are at the heart of the agreement.[8] Instead of top-down imposed contributions, they capture voluntary efforts by each country to reduce national emissions and adapt to the impacts of climate change, and they require every signatory (both developed and developing nations) to determine, plan, and report on its NDCs, with updates to commitments every five years.

The deal has been formally endorsed by 191 nations, with only six parties to the UNFCCC that were not signatories to the agreement by February 2021 (Apparicio and Sauer 2020). However, the implementation of certain elements of the agreement—such as the development of global carbon markets and the delivery of a proposed yearly US$100 billion in climate finance—remains the subject of further negotiations under the UNFCCC.

Glasgow Climate Pact (2021)

The Glasgow Climate Pact captures key outcomes of COP26 in Glasgow in 2021, marking the first time governments around the world were expected to announce their updated climate policies since the Paris Agreement (UNFCCC 2021).

As a diplomatic document, the pact is notable for a commitment to phase down the use of unabated coal power and for the recognition of shorter-term emissions pathways (50% reduction in CO_2 emissions by 2030, net zero around mid-century) needed to reach the goal of limiting global warming to 1.5°C. The Glasgow Climate Pact has also seen progress made around carbon markets and other forms of international climate cooperation, including more stringent use around carbon offsetting

---

7 Source: Wikipedia "Kyoto Protocol" webpage (https://en.wikipedia.org/wiki/Kyoto_Protocol).
8 Source: UN "Nationally Determined Contributions (NDCs)" webpage (https://unfccc.int/process-and-meetings/the-paris-agreement/nationally-determined-contributions-ndcs/nationally-determined-contributions-ndcs).

and strengthened pledges from developed countries to increase the financing available for climate adaptation in emerging markets and to reduce the use of non-CO_2 GHGs—notably, methane.

In terms of aggregate impact, it is difficult to assess the outcomes of the Glasgow Climate Pact, because they involve a combination of individual NDCs submitted by countries via the formal UN process (pledges that cover only 5- or 10-year time frames, some of which are also conditional on access to development finance), as well as a swath of longer-term unilateral and multilateral commitments, such as India's pledge to reach net zero by 2070 and the Global Methane Pledge made by over 100 countries (Forster, Smith, and Rogelj 2021).

Analysis suggests that median projected levels of warming by 2100 would fall to around 2.4°C if all Glasgow NDCs were met, with the potential to reach 1.8°C if all other longer-term pledges were implemented on time (Hausfather and Forster 2021). Although compared to the policy trajectories before 2015, the Glasgow Climate Pact has potentially brought the Paris "well below 2°C" temperature goals in closer reach, the significant gaps and uncertainties surrounding the implementation and financing of policies still create the risk of missing the goals, potentially by a wide mark.

Other International Agreements

The following are other international agreements and frameworks that have impacted companies' environmental practices:

- The *UN Sustainable Development Goals (SDGs)* are a set of 17 global goals set in 2015 by the UN General Assembly seeking to address key global challenges, such as poverty, inequality, and climate change. Although primarily intended as a framework for government action, the SDGs are now regularly cited by corporate and investment actors as material to their business planning and operations. SDG 7 (affordable and clean energy), SDG 11 (sustainable cities and communities), SDG 12 (responsible consumption and production), SDG 13 (climate action), SDG 14 (life below water), and SDG 15 (life on land) are some of the most directly relevant to the environmental debate.

- The Kigali Amendment to the Montreal Protocol of 2016 is a global agreement to phase out the manufacture of hydrofluorocarbons. These gases were used in an attempt to replace ozone-depleting chemicals but have the downside of causing a potent warming effect on the planet (UNEP 2016).

- The International Maritime Organization's IMO 2020 regulation caps the maximum sulphur content in the fuel oil used by ships. Limiting sulphur oxide emissions, which contribute to air pollution and acid rain, is estimated to have a very positive impact on human health and the environment (International Maritime Organization 2020).

- CORSIA (Carbon Offsetting and Reduction Scheme for International Aviation) is a UN mechanism designed by the UN International Civil Aviation Organization (ICAO) to help the aviation industry reach its aspirational goal to make all growth in international flights after 2020 carbon neutral, with airlines required to offset their emissions. The scheme is important because domestic aviation emissions are covered by the Paris Agreement, but international flights—which are responsible for around two-thirds of the CO_2 emissions from aviation—are governed by ICAO (note that, due to the impact of the pandemic, the emissions baseline was adjusted to 2019, not 2020; see Timperley 2019).

- The Kunming–Montreal Global Biodiversity Framework was adopted in late 2022 at the United Nations Biodiversity Conference in Montreal (COP 15) by representatives from 188 nations. It aims to address biodiversity loss, restore ecosystems, and protect indigenous rights. "The plan includes concrete measures to halt and reverse nature loss, including putting 30 percent of the planet and 30 percent of degraded ecosystems under protection by 2030. It also contains proposals to increase finance to developing countries—a major sticking point during talks" (UNEP 2022a).

International, Regional, and Country-Level Climate Policy and Initiatives

Over the last five years, there has been an acceleration in environmental and climate initiatives targeting the financial and business sector. The 2015 Paris Agreement has no doubt been the most instrumental driver in terms of bringing together all nations for a common cause to undertake ambitious efforts to combat climate change and adapt to its effects. It has also helped regulators and policymakers at national levels take action.

Sustainable Finance in the EU

In December 2019, the EU announced the *European Green Deal*, a plan to make the EU economy climate neutral by 2050 by boosting the efficient use of resources, restoring biodiversity, and cutting pollution. As part of this program, the EU has renewed its strategy focused on sustainable finance, whose main ambitions are as follows:

- To reorient capital flows by
  - establishing
    - a classification system (taxonomy) for sustainable activities and
    - standards and labels for green bonds, benchmarks, and other financial products
  - increasing EU funding for sustainable projects
- To mainstream sustainability into risk management by efforts to incorporate sustainability into financial advice, credit ratings, and market research, as well as more technical proposals on the treatment of "green" assets in the capital requirements of banks and insurers (the so-called green supporting factor)
- To foster transparency and long-term thinking by strengthening the disclosure requirements relating to sustainability (on both the financial industry and companies more broadly; European Commission 2020).

These developments are intended to embed sustainability across the entire investment chain—from the owners of capital (such as pension funds and insurance companies) to the beneficiaries of capital (such as investee companies), as well as key intermediaries (banks, asset managers, financial advisers, consultants, and credit rating agencies).

Net-Zero Industry Act and the Green Deal Industrial Plan

In 2023, the European Commission unveiled a *Green Deal Industrial Plan*, structured around four key pillars:

- "a predictable and simplified regulatory environment,
- faster access to sufficient funding,
- skills, and
- open trade for resilient supply chain" (European Commission 2023a).

There are multiple components to the plan. Arguably the most high-profile is the Net-Zero Industry Act, aimed at boosting European green industries. It was adopted partly as a result of the conflict in Ukraine—which brought to the forefront the issue of European dependence on fossil fuel—and also in response to the United States unveiling a significant support package for green industries (the Inflation Reduction Act).

The proposal notes,

> *The global market for key mass-manufactured net-zero technologies are set to triple by 2030 with an annual worth of around EUR600 billion. Our partners and competitors have grasped this opportunity and are deploying ambitious measures to secure significant parts of this new market. These developments are also driven by security of supply considerations. The resilience of future energy systems will be measured notably by a secure access to the technologies that will power those systems—wind turbines, hydrogen electrolysers, batteries, solar PV, heat pumps, and other. In turn, a secure supply of energy will be essential for ensuring sustainable economic growth, and ultimately public order and security (European Commission 2023b).*

It suggests such measures as slashing permitting times for "strategic projects," with a view to meeting a growing share of cleantech demand by local production (Di Sario 2023). (This objective is also supported by a separate policy measure focused on diversifying the supply of critical raw materials and increasing their recycling—the Critical Raw Materials Act.)

The act seeks to relax competition rules around state aid, such that EU member states may be able to match the aid offered by a third country for given low-carbon technologies; in theory, this could open the doors to uncapped amounts of state aid.

The EU plans aim to unlock substantial amounts of funding: EU states already had access to about €250 billion in funding to decarbonize industry (via the Recovery and Resilience Facility); an additional €140 billion is available via Horizon Europe and other programs, such as the Just Transition Fund.

CASE STUDIES

The "Just Transition"—Sustainability in Society

The success of the energy transition partly depends on the extent to which it secures and maintains broad social and political support. This has given rise to the notion of the "just transition," defined as "greening the economy in a way that is as fair and inclusive as possible to everyone concerned, creating decent work opportunities and leaving no one behind."[9]

As demonstrated by the "yellow vests" (*gilets jaunes*) protests in France—weekly demonstrations beginning in 2018 and still ongoing as of April 2023a against a proposed increase in fuel tax (partly intended to discourage fossil fuel consumption)—the existing or perceived social implications of decarbonization measures can lead to social unrest. Thus, they deserve careful considerations in the design of climate policies.

The EU's emission targets, for example, have different implications for member states; for some states in Eastern Europe, coal will be responsible for a higher share of power generation and employment, and they may also face higher hurdles when updating their vehicle fleet and industrial stock to meet

---

[9] Source: International Labour Organisation "Frequently Asked Questions on Just Transition" webpage (www.ilo.org/global/topics/green-jobs/WCMS_824102/lang--en/index.htm).

new standards. As such, the Just Transition Fund (and the broader EU Cohesion Policy) aims to help EU states support the territories most negatively affected by decarbonization and to reduce the imbalances between countries and regions.

While any attempts to quantify the number of the "jobs of the future" are unavoidably speculative, multiple estimates suggest that the transition both creates employment opportunities (e.g., building low-carbon infrastructure) and threatens some existing livelihoods (notably in the fossil fuel sector). McKinsey estimated that by 2050, some 200 million jobs could be created, while 185 million would be displaced, leading to a net potential gain of 15 million jobs; the International Labour Organisation has suggested that carefully designed policies—including better, "circular" linkages between sectors—could lead to a net increase in jobs from the transition (You and Chiweshenga 2022).

Individual companies, such as the utility company SSE, have also started to disclose "just transition" plans as part of their net-zero strategies, outlining measures for retraining their workforce.

However, significant uncertainties remain, not least since elements of a decarbonized system are "capex-heavy, opex-light": they require upfront capital and specialized labor (e.g., to install heat pumps or solar panels) but have fewer maintenance requirements afterward (compared to the *ongoing* work and supervision required in fossil fuel extraction, for example). Electric vehicles, similarly, with fewer moving parts, require less servicing—potentially an issue for auto mechanics.

EU Taxonomy Sustainability Disclosures

Two further significant EU developments include the *Sustainable Finance Disclosure Regulation (SFDR)* and the *Corporate Sustainability Reporting Directive (CSRD)*.

Under SFDR, investors are required to provide more transparency around

- how the impacts of sustainability risks on their financial products are being systematically assessed (e.g., integrated into due diligence and research processes),
- how asset managers consider—and seek to address—the potentially negative implications of investment activities on sustainability factors, and
- products labeled with an explicit ESG focus (European Commission 2019b).
- The SFDR introduces a categorization of the depth of ESG integration between so-called
- Article 6 products (which are not promoted as incorporating any ESG factors or objectives),
- Article 8 products (products claimed to promote environmental and social characteristics), and
- Article 9 products (products that have sustainable investment as an objective).

In October 2021, the final draft rules harmonizing disclosure requirements for financial products under SFDR and the Taxonomy Regulation were published by the Joint Committee of the European Supervisory Authorities (2021), covering both precontractual and periodic disclosures.

One challenge common to investors in meeting their obligations is the requirement for Article 8 and 9 funds, as of January 2022, to report the proportion of investments contributing to the first two objectives of the EU taxonomy. However, the companies (which in many cases represent a majority of the underlying holdings of these funds) are not required to report the alignment of their activities to the taxonomy until the following year.

The proposed Corporate Sustainability Reporting Directive would replace and strengthen the existing EU requirements around nonfinancial reporting, covering all large companies and all listed companies on EU-regulated markets (except for "micro-enterprises"). The companies in scope would have to report in line with upcoming EU sustainability reporting standards and have the resulting information audited and made available in a digital format to be incorporable into a "European Single Access Point" that aims to serve as a "one-stop shop" for sustainability-related information regarding EU companies and investment products (European Commission 2021).

One notable concept gaining prominence in EU nonfinancial reporting rules is that of "double materiality"—that is, the two-way impacts between companies and climate change, the environment, and society (see Exhibit 13). This extends the historical focus on the micro, company level (for example, understanding a company's energy usage as a proxy for future production costs) to a broader discussion of a company's role in the macroeconomic environment. At the same time, it renders more explicit the challenge of navigating multiple dimensions of sustainability (e.g., selecting among energy producers for lower-cost sources of energy may inadvertently favor companies in countries with a problematic record on human rights).

Exhibit 13: The Double Materiality Perspective in the Context of Reporting Climate-Related Information

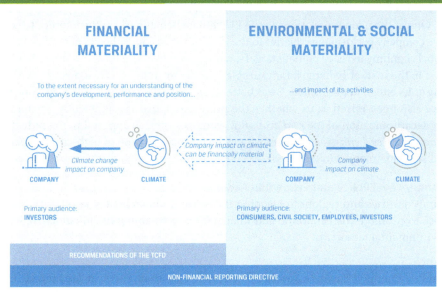

* Financial materiality is used here in the broad sense of affecting the value of the company, not just in the sense of affecting financial measures recognised in the financial statements.

Note: TCFD recommendations are explained in the following section.

Source: European Commission (2019a).

Climate Benchmarks

Another area of EU activity is the creation of *climate benchmarks.* Benchmarks play an important role in investments, serving—as their name suggests—as a comparator to measure the performance of investments (in the case of actively managed funds) or as a target for the construction of investment solutions, which aim to replicate (or "track") the composition of certain widely used benchmarks (e.g., stock market indexes, such as the FTSE 100 Index and S&P 500 Index, in the case of so-called passive, tracker, or index funds).

However, the most widely used benchmarks are primarily based on company size (at least for equities) and thus do not directly reflect low-carbon considerations in their methodologies. This raises the possibility that a significant and, given the rising share of assets managed under index strategies, growing portion of the investment universe might be pursuing environmentally unsustainable investment strategies.

Therefore, the EU has developed two types of climate benchmarks for equities and corporate bonds that aim to start with lower associated carbon emission intensity relative to their investable universe and then continually cut emission thresholds each year by at least 7% (year over year), in line with IPCC estimates for annual reductions necessary for a 1.5°C (2.7°F) temperature scenario.

The following are the two main categories of benchmarks:

1. EU Paris-Aligned Benchmarks (EU PABs), which must
   - reduce carbon emission intensity by at least 50% in their starting year,
   - have a four-to-one ratio of "green" to "brown" investments relative to the investable universe, and
   - not invest in fossil fuels

2. EU Climate Transition Benchmarks (EU CTBs), which require a 30% intensity reduction in the starting year and at least an equal green-to-brown ratio but permit fossil fuel investments as part of a transition process (EU Technical Expert Group on Sustainable Finance 2019)

One of the main innovations in the EU climate benchmarks is the attempt to compare company performance relative to the absolute emission pathways necessary for the global economy to reach climate targets, rather than the more relative approaches that exist in the market (whereby, for example, a company may receive a positive score as long as its emission performance was better than its sector average). However, concerns have also been raised as to whether the proposed approach sufficiently encourages the decarbonization of the *real economy*, across sectors, as opposed to the reduction of *portfolio-level emissions* by overly focusing on the exclusion of high-carbon sectors and stocks (Amenc, Goltz, Liu 2021).

Country-Level Policy and Prudential Actions

Some countries and regions are leading the way in influencing the regulatory framework to promote the economic and financial mainstreaming of climate change and environmental factors.

France

France's Energy Transition for Green Growth Law took effect in January 2016. It requires mandatory disclosures from major institutional investors around their exposure to climate risks and efforts to mitigate climate change. Because the law explicitly targets institutional investors but not banks, it provided a control group for a kind of natural experiment; a 2021 report by the Banque de France found "evidence of a sharp relative decrease in holdings of fossil energy securities in the portfolios" of the investors affected by the law (Méssonier and Nguyen 2021).

United Kingdom

As noted in Chapter 2, in 2020, the UK government announced a 10-point plan for a green industrial revolution that aims to

- scale up low-carbon technologies and infrastructure,
- increase protections for biodiversity, and
- further the green finance agenda (HM Government 2020).

An important element of the plan is a roadmap toward mandatory climate-related disclosures, specifically following the recommendations of the TCFD, for UK companies, starting with large financial institutions and premium listed companies and then gradually widening the scope to other UK-registered companies and financial actors (HM Treasury 2020).

The Prudential Regulation Authority (PRA) and the Financial Conduct Authority published separate consultations on climate change in 2018, which resulted in increased requirements for UK banks and insurers—notably, the introduction of a climate change *stress test* for their liabilities and investments to investigate the resilience of the financial system by testing the implications of high-impact climate change scenarios (Financial Conduct Authority 2018; see also PRA 2019).

This has elements of a precautionary approach, which focuses not on forecasts of plausibility but on avoidance of worst-case outcomes.

THE PRECAUTIONARY PRINCIPLE

The precautionary principle states that "if an action or policy has a suspected risk of causing severe harm to the public domain (affecting general health or the environment globally), the action should not be taken in the absence of scientific near-certainty about its safety"; it is intended to provide a safeguard "in cases where the absence of evidence and the incompleteness of scientific knowledge carry profound implications and in the presence of risks of 'black swans,' unforeseen and unforeseeable events of extreme consequence" (Taleb et al. 2014; see also Norman et al. 2015).

It is impossible to predict with full certainty the future evolution of the global climate system. But this does not mean it is impossible to state whether certain interventions are likely to increase, rather than decrease, climate risks. Moreover, by the time climate damages are confirmed, it may be too late—hence the importance of precaution.

Environmental standards in certain jurisdictions, such as the EU, already embody elements of the precautionary principle. However, some have argued that financial authorities also "need to move towards precautionary approaches to maintaining the safety and soundness of the financial system. Precautionary policy prioritizes preventative action and a qualitative approach to managing risk above quantitative measurement and information disclosure. It aims to steer away from tipping points and build system resilience as a superior means of managing radical uncertainty" (Kedward, Ryan-Collins, and Chenet 2020).

One notable area where precaution is a legal requirement concerns the duties of pension fund trustees (Daramus 2017). Bound to act in the best interest of their beneficiaries, trustees in a number of jurisdictions are expected to act "as a prudent person acting in a like capacity would . . . in the conduct of an enterprise of like character and aims" (Galer 2021). The implications of these duties with regard to, for example, the fossil fuel investments of pension funds have been the subject of significant debate in recent years.

Regulation is also increasing for pension funds, with successive clarifications from the United Kingdom's policymakers that ESG and climate considerations can have material financial impacts and therefore are not "to do with personal ethics, or optional extras," but are risks that must be monitored and addressed by pension trustees as part of their investment duties (Department of Work and Pension 2018).

The Pensions Regulator (TPR) in the United Kingdom has issued guidance to pension funds relating to ESG issues and climate change along similar lines. Since 1 October 2020, trustees of defined contribution (DC) pension schemes will be required to produce an implementation report setting out how they acted on the principles set out in the statement of investment principles. In February 2021, amendments to the Pensions Schemes Act required UK pension schemes, among increased climate requirements, to consider "the steps that might be taken for the purpose of achieving the Paris Agreement goal" (UK Government 2021).

United States

The United States has historically had a more conservative stance on this issue compared to the United Kingdom and the EU. Notably, there has been ongoing debate (and successive policy shifts) as to whether trustees may, may not, or should consider ESG and climate factors in the management of their investments. Under the different administrations since 2015, the US Department of Labor's (DOL's) guidance on the issue has varied, and it is currently once more subject to review. Much of the discussion focuses on the extent to which the incorporation of ESG issues can be interpreted as prioritizing nonfinancial objectives (such as the pursuit of social and policy goals) over the long-term financial security of retirees. Recognizing the evolution of ESG investing, feedback from market participants in response to a DOL consultation in 2019 overwhelmingly stressed the financial materiality of ESG factors (Quinson 2021).

In 2021, the Federal Reserve launched the Financial Stability Climate Committee and the Supervision Climate Committee to investigate the micro- and macro-prudential implications of climate change, respectively (Brainard 2021), including the possibility of "climate stress testing" (see also the subsequent section on NGFS).

In 2022, the Securities and Exchange Commission (SEC) unveiled proposals (SEC 2022) to require companies to report on

- the governance and impacts of climate-related risks,
- GHG emissions (Scope 1, Scope 2, and, where material, Scope 3 emissions) and other climate-related financial statement metrics, some of which would need to be subject to audit/assurance, and
- climate-related targets and goals and transition plans, if any.

Two significant US policy measures are the Inflation Reduction Act of 2022 (IRA) and the Bipartisan Infrastructure Bill enacted in 2021.

The infrastructure bill includes increased funding for public and electrified transit and charging, as well as over US$65 billion in clean energy transmission and grids (White House 2021). It also provides around US$8 billion in funding for clean hydrogen research via local regional hydrogen hubs (Moeller et al. 2021).

Marking a step-change in federal climate action in the United States, the IRA has unveiled a series of investments in clean energy and climate measures, including tax credits, production subsidies and other incentives, estimated around US$370 billion (see Exhibit 14).

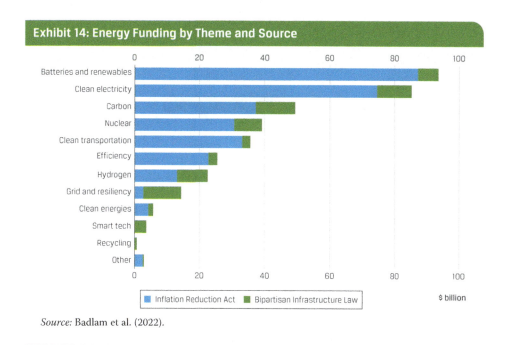

Exhibit 14: Energy Funding by Theme and Source

Source: Badlam et al. (2022).

While the figures are in themselves significant, they represent a potential underestimate—partly, since certain provisions in the act are potentially uncapped (meaning the total financing will depend on the extent to which households and firms make use of the provisions). Moreover, the IRA aims to mobilize private investment, with emerging evidence suggesting that this is already having an effect.

For example, in just five months after the passage of the IRA, total announced US electric vehicle and battery manufacturing investments have increased four-fold (from US$13 billion in October 2022 to $52 billion in March 2023; Bullard 2023).

China

Reckoning with the climate costs associated with decades of explosive economic growth, China's policymakers have begun combining its global leadership position on renewable energy with a greater desire for its financial system to address environmental issues. China is the world's largest manufacturer of solar cells, lithium-ion batteries, and electric vehicles, and these are areas of clear policy priority (BloombergNEF 2020a). In 2020 alone, China doubled its construction of new wind and solar power plants compared to the previous year (Murtaugh 2021). It remains the country both with the highest levels of investment in the low-carbon energy transition and the highest absolute GHG emissions (see Exhibit 15).

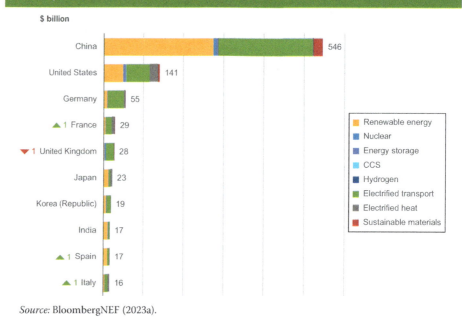

Exhibit 15: Global Investment in Energy Transition by Top 10 Countries (2022, US$ billions)

Source: BloombergNEF (2023a).

At the UN General Assembly in 2020, China's policymakers committed to have the country's CO_2 emissions peak before the year 2030, and in 2021 China published its roadmap to net-zero carbon by 2060. This was followed by an action plan for peak emissions (State Council 2021). More efforts to further embed environmental considerations into the economy are underway, with the rollout of a national carbon market and China's seven ministerial agencies, including the central bank, having previously indicated their support for institutional investors to perform environmental stress tests and for mandatory environmental disclosures for issuers of public debt and equity (Ma 2017).

The country's policymakers are increasingly engaging with international counterparts on issues pertaining to green finance and the green taxonomy. The country's green bond market is now the world's largest, but it has faced barriers regarding investor access and lack of international harmonization. Regulators announced they will exclude fossil fuel projects from their green bond taxonomy, bringing the country closer to international practice (Fatin 2020).

India

The growing focus of financial regulators on environmental risks is reverberating in other Asian countries, too. In 2021, the Securities and Exchange Board of India (SEBI) strengthened and extended disclosure requirements, now covering the 1,000 largest listed companies, which are to report on certain social and sustainability aspects of their businesses (SEBI 2021). India's central bank also published a study in 2020 arguing that climate change can exacerbate food price inflation, and the country also is host to one of the largest green bond markets among emerging markets (Tandon 2020).

Japan

Japan has now committed to net-zero GHG emissions by 2050 (Lies 2020), with multiple policy workstreams, including a new clean energy strategy expected in 2022, the development of a Sustainability Standards Board of Japan to systematize corporate disclosure in this area (Financial Accounting Standards Foundation 2021), and the introduction of climate "stress testing" in the banking sector (Milburn 2020).

Australia

The Australian Securities and Investments Commission (ASIC) is consulting on proposals to develop mandatory climate reporting rules and will investigate potential "greenwashing" with regard to ESG- or green-labeled financial products (ASIC 2022).

As the science on climate change and its impact on the environment continues to improve and become more sophisticated, it would be reasonable to expect these issues to expand the agenda of financial regulators and policymakers. These are likely to have important implications for economic, financial, and business policies.

Task Force on Climate-Related Financial Disclosures

The most influential international framework for disclosure of climate change risks and opportunities affecting companies and financial institutions is the framework from the **Task Force on Climate-Related Financial Disclosures (TCFD)**.[10]

The TCFD was launched in 2015 following a request from the G20 members' finance ministers and central bank governors for the Financial Stability Board—the organization that coordinates the work of national financial supervisors and international standard-setting bodies—to investigate the risks of climate change for the stability of the financial system and the appropriate response.

The TCFD set out to provide a set of recommendations and a framework for companies and financial institutions to provide better information to support investors, lenders, insurers, and other financial stakeholders to identify, build, and quantify climate-related risks and opportunities in their decisions. The TCFD also took the view that better information will help investors engage with companies on the resilience of their strategies and capital spending, including more efficient allocation of capital, which should help promote a smooth transition to a more sustainable, low-carbon economy.

In July 2017, the TCFD published its final recommendations for how companies should report, structured around four thematic areas (see Exhibit 16):

1. governance,
2. strategy,
3. risk management, and
4. metrics and targets.

---

10 For more information, see the organization's website: www.fsb-tcfd.org.

Exhibit 16: TCFD Core Elements of Climate-Related Financial Disclosures

Governance
The organization's governance around climate-related risks and opportunities.

Strategy
The actual and potential impacts of climate-related risks and opportunities on the organization's business, strategy and financial planning.

Risk Management
The processes used by the organisation to identify, assess, and manage climate-related risks.

Metrics and Targets
The metrics and targets used to assess and mange relevant climate-related risks and opportunities.

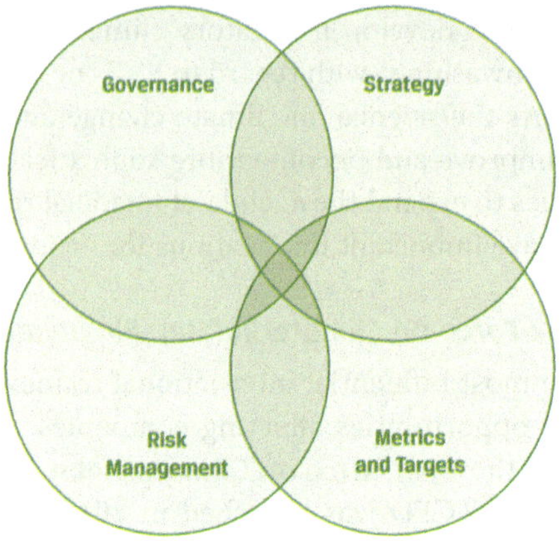

Source: TCFD (2017a).

A growing number of public and private sector organizations are showing their support for the TCFD recommendations, including over 3,800 companies with a total market capitalization of US$26 trillion and financial institutions responsible for assets of US$217 trillion. As noted in Chapter 2, although initially intended as guidelines for voluntary reporting, some jurisdictions, including the United Kingdom, Brazil, the EU, and New Zealand, have announced policies requiring TCFD-aligned disclosures (Financial Stability Board 2022).

The work of the TCFD introduced the influential classification of climate-related risks into physical and transition risks, recommending that companies report on both of these dimensions. One notable recommendation was the use of climate scenario analysis (which will be considered in more detail in the section titled "Assessment of Materiality of Environmental Issues."

Exhibit 17 illustrates climate-related risks, opportunities, and financial impact.

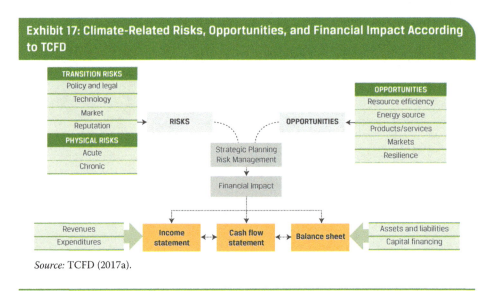

Exhibit 17: Climate-Related Risks, Opportunities, and Financial Impact According to TCFD

Source: TCFD (2017a).

Network for Greening the Financial System

As noted in Chapter 2, a notable related initiative is the *Network for Greening the Financial System (NGFS)*, comprising over 70 central banks and financial supervisors. It was set up to strengthen the global response required to meet the goals of the Paris Agreement and to enhance the role of the financial system to manage risks and to mobilize capital for green and low-carbon investments in the broader context of environmentally sustainable development. The NGFS has developed technical guidance—including publishing a set of climate scenarios—for the regulatory supervision of climate risks (NGFS 2022a). Elements of NGFS guidance for supervisors are increasingly being transposed into national or supranational regulation—most notably, the introduction of "climate stress tests" for banks and other financial institutions by the likes of the European Central Bank (ECB 2022), the Bank of England, the French Treasury, the Hong Kong Monetary Authority, the Brazilian central bank, and other regulators (NGFS 2022b).

Carbon Pricing

There is a growing consensus among governments, the financial community, and businesses on the fundamental role of carbon pricing in the transition to a decarbonized economy. Putting a price on carbon emissions is viewed as one of the most effective methods of tackling climate change; it is often called the *polluter pays principle*.

There are many types of carbon pricing; the most common are emission trading systems (ETSs) and carbon taxes, roughly corresponding to quotas and tariffs in international trade.

Emission Trading System

An ETS is a system based on the exchange of permits for emission units, where actors that exceed their emission limits are required to buy permits from those that have emitted less. The overall quantity of emissions is fixed, and market mechanisms are used to set their price.

In theory, this system creates an economic incentive for emission reductions to occur at the point of least cost; rather than mandating similar levels of reductions for all actors, price discovery helps reward those that can afford to reduce more.

The effectiveness in practice, however, depends crucially on the design of the ETS. If the scheme is too restrictive, it may encourage the offshoring of industries to jurisdictions with fewer constraints (a phenomenon known as "carbon leakage") and thus fail to reduce emissions. As a result, free allocation of allowances (to give industry an initial "buffer") has been a widely used feature of ETSs (International Energy Agency 2020a), although in some cases, overallocation resulted in the price of an emission unit being too low to properly incentivize decarbonization. In contrast, introducing and then raising a minimum price ("floor") for the UK emission trading scheme is considered to have made important contributions to accelerating the United Kingdom's exit from coal (IEA 2020b).

Carbon Taxation

Carbon taxation takes a different approach by directly setting an explicit price for GHG emissions (e.g., per ton of CO_2). This has the advantage of predictability, although the carbon tax rate, alongside the elasticity of demand for different products and the extent to which companies can pass on the carbon costs to their end consumers, will be a key determinant of effectiveness. It has been estimated that an explicit global carbon price of US$40 to US$80 per tCO_2 in the 2020s that more than doubles to US$50 to

US$100 per tCO$_2$ by 2030 is required to meet the goals of the Paris Agreement (Carbon Pricing Leadership Coalition 2017). This price is substantially higher than the current global average price, which is US$4.5 per tCO$_2$ (World Bank 2023).

Carbon pricing and the trading of emission trading certificates began trial use in the United Kingdom in the early 2000s, a process that contributed substantially to the swift displacement of coal in the United Kingdom's electricity mix, which provided less than 1% of electricity in 2020 (Department for Business, Energy & Industrial Strategy 2020), compared to 40% as recently as 2012 (Evans 2016). The EU subsequently adopted emission trading as one of its flagship climate policies with the establishment of the EU ETS in 2005. It covers the main energy and carbon-intensive industries, regulating about half the European economy with a carbon price. Carbon prices in multiple jurisdictions have generally been rising (see Exhibit 18), with the EU price notably reaching a record high of over US$100 per tCO$_2$ in March 2023.[11]

Exhibit 18: Price Evolution in Selected ETSs

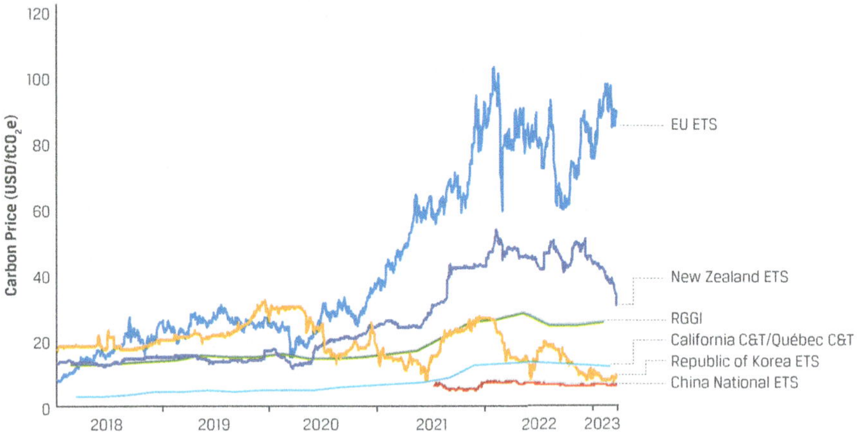

Note: Based on data from ICAP Allowance Price Explorer. Prices for the RGGI Initiative and for California and Quebec CaT come from the primary market, whereas for the other systems the prices reflect the secondary market.

Source: World Bank (2023).

The EU ETS is undergoing significant developments—including a "carbon border adjustment mechanism" that aims to level the playing field with imported goods that do not face similar carbon costs in the country of origin (European Council 2022), an increase in the number of industries to be covered (with newly introduced provisions around aviation, shipping, road transport and buildings), and a phase-out of the number of free carbon allowances (Bond, Fustes, De Catelle, and Solomon 2022).

The growth of national and international carbon markets since then has been steady but sporadic, with growth in such regions as the East Coast and West Coast of the United States, New Zealand, South Korea, and some Canadian provinces. In early 2021, China launched its national ETS, becoming the world's largest carbon market, superseding the EU ETS.

Overall, as of 2023, there were 77 carbon pricing initiatives implemented or scheduled—split roughly equally between carbon taxation and ETS mechanisms. They cover approximately 23% of global GHG emissions and are responsible for raising

---

11 Source: Trading Economics "EU Carbon Permits" webpage: https://tradingeconomics.com/commodity/carbon.

approximately US$100 billion in revenues, half of which is earmarked for financing green projects or compensating households or businesses (World Bank 2023). Exhibit 19 provides an overview of carbon markets around the world.

Exhibit 19: Carbon Markets around the World

Note: Instruments are considered "scheduled for implementation" once they have been formally adopted through legislation and have an official, planned start date. Instruments are considered "under consideration" if the government has announced its intention to work toward the implementation of a carbon pricing initiative and this has been formally confirmed by official government sources. Some countries that have mechanisms implemented also have additional instruments under consideration. For subnational jurisdictions only the subnational instrument is reflected.

Source: World Bank (2023).

Over the last 10 years, many companies—especially in energy-intensive sectors—have used the practice of shadow carbon pricing to guide their decision-making process. An internal or shadow price on carbon creates a theoretical or assumed cost per ton of carbon emissions. For example, the large oil company BP (2020) uses a price assumption of a US$100/tCO$_2$e by 2030 to better understand the potential impact of future climate regulation on the profitability of a project, a new business model, or an investment. Its use reveals hidden risks and enables businesses to build this factor into future valuations and estimates of capital expenditure. In addition, when emissions bear a cost in profit-and-loss statements, it helps uncover inefficiencies and incentivize low-carbon innovation within departments, cutting a company's energy use and carbon pollution.

Some governments are using internal carbon pricing as a tool in their procurement process, policy design, and project assessments in relation to climate change impacts. More recently, financial institutions have also begun using internal carbon pricing to assess their project portfolio. In 2020, more than 2,000 companies—including nearly half of the world's biggest companies by market capitalization—reported that they are currently using an internal price on carbon or plan to do so.[12]

---

12 Source: CDP's "Carbon Pricing" webpage: www.cdp.net/en/climate/carbon-pricing.

Carbon Offsetting

A concept that runs through different aspects of carbon markets is that of offsetting—the extent to which an activity providing an emission reduction in one part of the economy may be seen as compensating for the emission of greenhouse gases elsewhere.

The need for offsetting can be justified by the fact that in a majority of scenarios compliant with the goals of the Paris Agreement, the world does not reach zero *absolute* GHG emissions in the next few decades—with some residual emissions being balanced out by natural or artificial "carbon sinks" (e.g., tree planting).[13] As such, companies or countries that are unable to reduce their emissions organically may require some accounting mechanism through which they can compensate those actors that are contributing *negative* emissions, in order for the global system to reach *net* zero.

However, there are substantial challenges around offsetting, because this market comprises both voluntary and regulated aspects, with uneven levels of transparency and scientific rigor. Part of the challenge stems from the *counterfactual* nature of offsetting and the risk of claiming credits for emission reductions that would have happened anyway, even if a given offset was not purchased (e.g., compensating a farmer to maintain a forest when the farmer had no intention of cutting it down in the first place), or that have not happened yet (e.g., netting present emissions against the *future* carbon sequestered by a newly planted tree over its lifetime). Additional complexities stem from how to account for carbon credits across jurisdictions and over time (e.g., should overachievement *in the past* allow actors to reduce their emission targets in the future?).

One of the positive outcomes of COP26 has been progress around carbon markets and international cooperation (Article 6 of the Paris Agreement), by the introduction of more stringent rules around the use of past credits, adjustments to avoid double counting of reductions, and restrictions around what projects are eligible to count as a genuine offset (Evans et al. 2021).

6 ASSESSMENT OF MATERIALITY OF ENVIRONMENTAL ISSUES

☐ 3.1.5 assess material impacts of environmental issues on potential investment opportunities, corporate and project finance, public finance initiatives, and asset management

Material environmental issues are factors that could have a significant impact—both positive and negative—on a company's business model and value drivers, such as operating and capital expenditure, revenue growth, margins, and risk. Materiality is not static, and it evolves in line with changes in the market, policies, and consumer attitudes. For example, the surge in public concern over plastic pollution seen in recent years—and the subsequent regulatory clampdowns on single-use plastics—has been quoted by the oil company BP as having the potential to have a "material impact" on the future oil demand (Gosden 2019).

As such, efforts by investors to assess the material financial impacts caused by environmental risks have begun to increase in terms of their analytical scope and sophistication. This includes, for example, considering a wider range of environmental factors, such as those from policy and technology responses (transition risks), as well as the impacts of environmental events and physical risks.

---

13 Projected median GHG emissions across 1.5°C scenarios, both with and without "overshoot," range between 9 and 14 in scenarios in IPCC (2022b, p. 63).

Assessment of Materiality of Environmental Issues

Investors need to undertake relevant research and materiality analysis to determine the environmental impact—both positive and negative. The type of analysis and approach will mostly depend on the type of assets being assessed—company, sector, and geographic location and on a portfolio level. Based on both quantitative and qualitative data, environmental analysis will potentially determine adjustments to forecasted financials and ratios, valuation model variables, valuation multiples, credit assessments, and portfolio allocation weightings.

Without sufficient consideration of materiality, investors may be exposed to changes in policy, technology, and consumer sentiment or forgo investment opportunities. However, the challenge is that environmental issues unfold in complex ways over time and across regions and sectors, and there is significant variation in the definitions, classifications, and measurement of these risks and opportunities.

Corporate and Project Finance

At a company or project level, investors looking to identify and measure a company's environmental impact or materiality would need to analyze both quantitative and qualitative environmental factors in order to make an informed evaluation of the environmental risks embedded within. A judgment is then made on how material the risks are and whether those risks are priced in or not. A scoring system is also typically used to benchmark the company against its peers. Materiality is also highly influenced by the industry or sector of the company, as well as its country and jurisdictions where projects are located. This is particularly relevant in the financing and investments of infrastructure projects.

A useful starting point is analyzing how a company or project uses energy, water, and waste:

- *Energy consumption* can be measured by the level of absolute emissions of GHGs from fossil fuel combustion and industrial processes and is estimated by the amount of CO_2e. This could also include savings in energy and performance relative to a benchmark year and can be provided on an annualized or lifetime basis, based on estimates (particularly relevant for projects) or actual measurement (relevant to operational assets).

- *Water utilization* can be calculated as the costs generated by water usage efficiency in operations taken directly from the ground, taken from surface water, or purchased. Water and wastewater treatment can be assessed against indicators tracking reductions in pollutants and harmful substances in supply areas, as well as incident reports and sanctions.

- *Waste utilization* is measured as the costs generated from the disposal of waste in operations, such as through landfills, incinerated waste, or recycled or hazardous waste. Aspects that may need to be factored into the analysis include carbon capture and storage (e.g., for closed landfill and industrial operations), pollution control (soil, air, water), waste-to-energy facilities, and waste-to-biofuel facilities.

At a project finance level, when assessing project infrastructure initiatives, the Equator Principles, which are based on IFC's Performance Standards, have become a globally recognized risk management framework and are adopted by financial institutions for determining, assessing, and managing environmental and social risk in project finance. They set out performance standards that address environmental factors (such as resource efficiency, biodiversity, and land resettlement), as well as other social-oriented standards. Examples of potential risks to be considered are presented in Exhibit 20.

Exhibit 20: Identification of Environmental Risks and Impacts at the Company or Project Level

Risks		Potential Impacts
Release of air pollutants (air emissions)	→	Pollution of air, land, and surface water
Release of liquid effluents or contaminated wastewater into local water bodies or improper wastewater treatment	→	Surface water pollution
Generation of large amounts of solid waste and improper waste management	→	Pollution of land and groundwater and surface water
Improper management of hazardous substances	→	Contamination of adjacent land and water
Excessive energy use	→	Depletion of local energy sources and release of combustion residuals leading to air pollution
Excessive water use	→	Depletion of water resources
High or excessive noise levels	→	Negative effects on human health and disruption of local wildlife
Improper or excessive land use	→	Soil degradation and biodiversity loss

Source: IFC (2015).

While considering the potential negative impacts of investments can illuminate important sources of material risk, considering potential positive impacts (for example, whether a given investment contributes to nature conservation or emission reductions) can highlight opportunities.

Public Finance Initiatives

As governments continue to raise their climate targets in line with the Paris Agreement, resources are being allocated and investments from the public sector are being mobilized to implement these plans—including in partnership with private investors. For example, the *Helsinki Principles*, signed by a number of finance ministers around the world, encourage signatories to "take climate change into account in macroeconomic policy, fiscal planning, budgeting, public investment management, and procurement practices" (Rydge 2020).

Public finance is a key policy instrument to both incentivize and enable the transition to green growth. Domestically, governments are a significant economic actor—commissioning new buildings, roads, and other forms of infrastructure, for example—highlighting the importance of aligning public procurement and sustainability. Governments also contribute to international development, with public sector financing often blended with funding from multilateral development finance institutions in developing countries and disbursed through investment vehicles, such as

- green infrastructure funds (e.g., the Association of Southeast Asian Nations [ASEAN] Catalytic Green Finance Facility under the ASEAN Infrastructure Fund),
- specialized banks (e.g., Asian Infrastructure Investment Bank), and
- funding platforms (e.g., the Tropical Landscapes Finance Facility; Climate Bonds Initiative 2019a).

Assessment of Materiality of Environmental Issues

A variety of financing initiatives leveraging public sector and development finance for sustainable agriculture, biodiversity conservation, and the blue economy are also emerging, particularly targeting more vulnerable and developing economies (Climate Bonds Initiative 2019b).

The Climate Policy Initiative reported that the average annual public climate finance was around US$321 billion in 2019–2020 (Naran et al. 2022; see Exhibit 21), out of a total of US$632 billion of climate finance, with the highest proportion dedicated to energy systems. Other areas of spending include adaptation and resilience, low-carbon transport, land use, and infrastructure projects with cross-sectoral impacts (Macquarie et al. 2020). Direct finance flows (domestic and international) from governments accounting for 12% of public flows (US$38 billion) were driven by low-carbon transport and delivered primarily through grants.

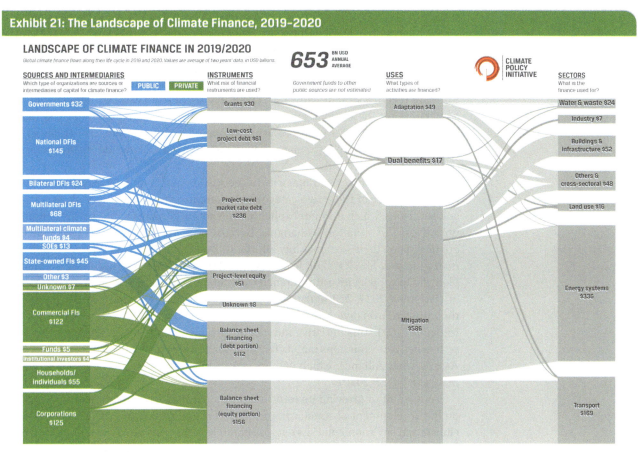

Exhibit 21: The Landscape of Climate Finance, 2019-2020

Source: Naran et al. (2022).

Examples of the types of *public finance* include

- export credit,
- development banks,
- concessionary lending to small and medium-sized enterprises (SMEs),
- guarantees,
- research and development (R&D), and
- investment in infrastructure.

Initiatives that typically require *public and private sector funding* with high environmental impacts are

- energy,
- water and waste,
- transport, and
- flood defenses.

Asset Management

As stewards of capital, asset managers play a key role in helping steer capital toward sustainability. Whether directly (e.g., by deciding to finance a particular green infrastructure project or to buy the debt of a high-carbon company) or indirectly (e.g., by using investor rights to appoint and reward company directors and through the related engagement with investee companies), the decisions made by asset managers can make positive or negative contributions to ESG factors, such as the global emission trajectory.

The environmental profiles of asset managers' portfolios have come under increased scrutiny from the media and civil society in recent years, often relating to campaigns for fossil fuel divestment. However, client mandates from asset owners may impose constraints on the options available to asset managers (particularly in the case of index-tracking funds). Exclusions are only one of a range of potential strategies that asset managers can deploy to manage environmental risks, alongside positive screening or impact investing funds.

Historically, however, a majority of the world's assets under management do not fall under either of these two categories but are invested in a variety of asset classes and strategies, which may not explicitly incorporate climate change or environmental objectives. This situation is changing, because both asset owners and asset managers are increasing their sustainability efforts. In December 2020, over 30 asset managers managing over US$9 trillion in assets joined the Net Zero Asset Managers initiative, pledging to support investing aligned with net-zero emissions by 2050 or sooner.[14] As of December 2021, 220 signatories representing US$57 trillion in AUM have joined the initiative over five waves of public announcements (Net Zero Asset Managers Initiative 2021). This initiative mirrors the growing number of asset owners who are setting net-zero emissions targets for their portfolios (e.g., the UN-convened Net-Zero Asset Owner Alliance, which gathers institutional investors with over US$5 trillion in assets; UNEP 2020).

As a result of growing investor interest, asset managers are increasingly focused on the development of standardized frameworks and data points to be able to assess climate and environmental risks across multiple sectors, down to the level of individual companies or their securities. This recognizes that

1. companies in the same sector may face different levels of risk and
2. these risks are likely to be complex and interlocking and affect all sectors, not just those with high carbon emissions.

Such a framework, used by companies for reporting and disclosure and by investors in assessing the environmental, social, and governance risks of companies, comes from SASB, which was established in 2011 to develop and disseminate sustainability accounting standards. The standards identify financially material issues that are reasonably likely to impact the financial condition or operating performance of a company and

---

14 Source: Net Zero Asset Managers initiative website: www.netzeroassetmanagers.org.

Assessment of Materiality of Environmental Issues

therefore are most important to investors. SASB provides an interactive proprietary tool that identifies and compares disclosure topics across different industries and sectors, described as the "Materiality Map.[15] Environmental factors cover

- GHG emissions,
- air quality,
- energy management,
- water and wastewater management,
- waste and hazardous materials management, and
- ecological impacts.

SASB's analysis reflects the varied nature of different sectors. GHG emissions are assessed to be material for more than 50% of industries in such sectors as extractives and minerals processing and transportation—where the management of energy, waste, and hazardous materials features more prominently—but for less than 50% of industries in such sectors as health care and technology/communications.

One initiative aims to identify "ESG upside" for large, listed companies if they were to bring ESG performance in line with that of top-rated peers. Controlling for industry, size, and sector, improving performance on carbon emissions is found to be the most material variable for over 2,000 large, listed companies. On average, companies could unlock up to a 3% share price increase across all sectors, with the potential for double-digit increases in high-emitting sectors, such as energy (see Exhibit 22; ESG for Investors 2022).

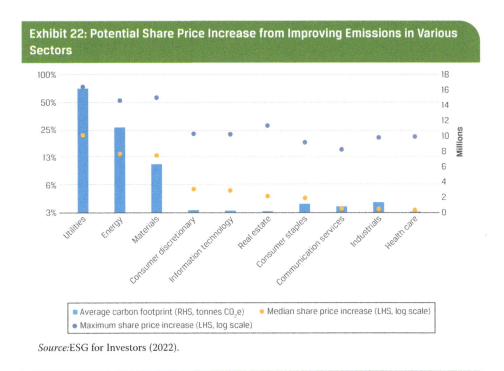

Exhibit 22: Potential Share Price Increase from Improving Emissions in Various Sectors

- Average carbon footprint (RHS, tonnes CO_2e)
- Median share price increase (LHS, log scale)
- Maximum share price increase (LHS, log scale)

Source: ESG for Investors (2022).

However, there are different definitions of materiality and related reporting metrics under the multiple standards and frameworks used for sustainability reporting, including the GRI, the Climate Disclosure Standards Board (CDSB), Integrated Reporting, and CDP. In 2021, the IFRS Foundation, which works on the development of accounting

---

15 For more information, go to the SASB's "Exploring Materiality" webpage: https://materiality.sasb.org.

standards, announced the consolidation of CDSB, SASB, and Integrated Reporting into a single organization, the International Sustainability Standards Board (ISSB), which aims to develop a "comprehensive global baseline of high-quality sustainability disclosure standards to meet investors' information needs" (IFRS Foundation 2021)

At the same time, many investors are incorporating these increasingly available climate and environmental data into their own proprietary investment frameworks, which reflect their house views on the climate and energy transition.

While some environmental risks can be addressed quantitatively, others require a more qualitative approach—for example, through engagement with companies to align management incentives with sustainability goals. Asset managers have stepped up individual engagement efforts but are also collaborating to achieve this.

> **CASE STUDIES**
>
> ### Investor Collaboration on Climate
>
> Launched in 2017, Climate Action 100+ is an investor network with over 700 investors engaging the world's largest corporate emitters of GHGs.[16] Its members conduct joint company engagements and collaborate on shareholder proposals, and the initiative has been developing tools and benchmarks to be able to track company progress toward net-zero emissions.

7. APPROACHES TO ACCOUNT FOR MATERIAL ENVIRONMENTAL ANALYSIS AND RISK MANAGEMENT STRATEGIES

> **3.1.6** identify approaches to environmental analysis, including company-, project-, sector-, country-, and market-level analysis; environmental risks, including carbon footprinting and other carbon metrics; the natural capital approach; and climate scenario analysis

Environmental risks can be effectively integrated into company analysis and investment decision-making processes using various financial tools and models. According to a G20 green finance study, financial institutions need to combine two types of approaches to assess environmental risks:

1. understanding environmental factors that may pose risks to financial assets and liabilities (for example, the wrong pricing of a pollution liability or natural disaster insurance policy could be a risk to liability if the event probability is underestimated) and how such risks may evolve over time and

2. translating environmental risk factors into quantitative measures of financial risk that can, in turn, inform firms' risk management and investment decisions (UNEP 2017).

---

16 Source: "About Climate Action 100+" webpage (www.climateaction100.org/about/).

The types of risk analysis tools and associated metrics primarily depend on the asset classes and risk types financial institutions are exposed to (for instance, a fixed-income analyst may be most interested in credit risk). Similarly, the choice of approach depends on the type of direct or indirect exposure to an environmental risk factor. For example, the probability of physical risks from flooding will have to be incorporated differently than transition risks stemming from the transition to a low-carbon economy due to policy change. Depending on the investment strategy and objectives, different levels of analysis will likely be performed: at the individual asset level, portfolio level, and macroeconomic or systemic level.

It is important to analyze the extent to which environmental and climate-related impacts could affect a company's value chain—supply chain, operation and assets, logistics, and market—which, in turn, would have an impact on financial performance.

Levels of Environmental Analysis

It is important to note that environmental risk assessments are conducted along with social and governance assessments at the

- **A.** company or project level,
- **B.** sector level,
- **C.** country level, or
- **D.** market level.

We will look at each of these in the following subsections.

Company or Project Level

At a company or project level, an assessment of material environmental risk factors will inform key financial metrics as monitored and disclosed in financial statements (such as the profit and loss statement and the balance sheet). For example, companies operating in water-scarce areas are exposed to higher risk than are those operating in areas where water availability is high. Therefore, it is important to undertake an analysis of how well the company is managing these risks (e.g., improvement in water efficiency over time).

Often, analysts and portfolio managers will have their own internal environmental (social and governance) scoring system that uses a combination of external third-party data providers and internal analysis. Qualitative and quantitative assessments are then made to determine the materiality of environmental risks for a particular company and how they will affect key efficiency or profitability ratios that might be used to value and compare across different companies. This could include a decision being made to adjust the target price-to-earnings ratio (P/E), which reflects a company's competitiveness in comparison to its peers with higher or lower environmental standards. Cost assumptions can also be adjusted according to future capital expenditure in environmental (mitigation or adaptation) spending.

> **THE "CARBON RISK PREMIUM"**
>
> A *carbon risk premium* is said to exist when investors require a higher compensation for the perceived risk from investing in high-carbon companies. Several studies have argued that companies with higher (absolute levels of or relative increases in) CO_2 emissions are associated with higher returns; however, studies have also found evidence for the converse—a positive link between reductions in

carbon footprint and improvements returns (see, e.g., Bolton and M. Kakperczyk 2021; Görgen et al. 2020; Andersson, Bolton, and Samama 2016; Garvey, Iyer, and Nash 2018).

These results illustrate the importance of defining investment beliefs, given that risk and return can be seen as two sides of the same coin. For some, remaining invested in sectors or stocks that may be shunned by a growing proportion of "climate-conscious" investors can create an opportunity for excess returns; others may see companies lagging on environmental metrics as being at risk of having permanently depressed future cash flows from changes in consumer preferences, technology, and regulation.

Given the complex nature of the technologies, sectors, and commodities involved, the liquidity of underlying markets, and the availability of alternatives, conclusions around the existence of a carbon risk premium in one sector or industry may not be readily applicable in other sectors.

For example, a study from the University of Oxford found an increase of 54% in loan spreads for coal mining (a perceived measure of the risk of corporate debt relative to government bonds) between 2017 and 2020 compared to the previous decade but that loan spreads for oil and gas had remained relatively stable, reflecting a more "ambivalent" attitude from lenders (Zhou, Wilson, and Caldecott 2021).

Sector Level

Environmental and climate-related factors exert different levels of impact on various sectors. Some sectors, due to their high carbon intensity or the geographical positioning of their assets, are more exposed to environmental risks and physical risks from natural disasters. Sectors such as chemicals, energy, steel and cement, extractives, food and beverages, and transportation tend to be more vulnerable to environmental risks. In contrast, such assets as buildings, production facilities, agricultural land, and urban infrastructure are more susceptible to physical risks arising from natural disasters.

Companies in these sectors tend to be influenced by an environmental risk premium, which may affect the discount rate used. Hence, alongside the previous company-level analysis, these sector-wide considerations need to be considered, and they should be overlaid on the company analysis. Adjustments are made to remove any regional or sector biases that align with the manager's investment strategy and process.

Country Level

A country's environmental regulations, emission targets, and enforcement may vary in emphasis across different jurisdictions. Often, investments may be multi-jurisdictional, and hence, several country-specific considerations and regulations will need to be factored into the valuation of a company based on the country in which it is located or where its operations lie. Disclosure and transparency of environmental data will also vary by region; for example, companies in emerging markets tend to have fewer comprehensive disclosures.

Country analysis is relevant not just to corporate securities but also to government bonds. Climate change, air quality, water stress, vulnerability to natural hazards, and food security can have an immediate and direct impact on a sovereign's ability or willingness to pay (credit risk) or its ESG profile. For example, the consistent deterioration in a country's rating scores on food security and high vulnerability to climate change could lead an asset manager to reduce its position despite the bond's scarcity and attractive relative value. Conversely, the asset manager could also hold an overweight position based on a view that starting with a relatively low environmental score is acceptable when reforms and a green economy push from the government are expected to lead to ESG score improvements (Agha and Singla 2020).

Market Level

Recognizing the cross-cutting impacts of environmental risks, central banks and the Bank for International Settlements have warned of the potential systemic effects of both physical and transitional risks: "In the worst-case scenario, central banks may have to confront a situation where they are called upon by their local constituencies to intervene as climate rescuers of last resort" (Bolton et al. 2020).

Consideration of such market-wide impacts can influence investors' strategic asset allocation and long-term investment strategy, although research has sounded a note of caution with regard to the limits of some traditional risk mitigation strategies, such as diversification and hedging. In a report titled "Unhedgeable Risk," the Cambridge Institute for Sustainability Leadership (2015) warned that in a scenario where investor sentiment turns away from high-carbon sectors, there may not be sufficient available assets—including low-carbon assets—for investors to successfully reallocate capital. It found that around half of the potential decline in the modeled equity and fixed-income portfolios is "unhedgeable," meaning investors and asset owners would be exposed unless some system-wide action is taken to address the risks.

This finding reaffirms the need for predictable policy measures, which prioritize real-world emission reductions and an orderly transition to the low-carbon economy. A growing number of investors (such as those under the Climate Action 100+ initiative) are advocating for this.

Analyzing Environmental Risks

It is not possible to outline all the available approaches for investors to assess environmental risks, because there is no one common standard. However, based on a combination of independent third-party research and data along with useful frameworks, practitioners are able to map out and analyze the environmental risks and costs for different types of asset classes by company and sector in order to make their own quantitative and qualitative risk assessments. The following outlines some of the approaches that are used by investors to assess material environmental risks (and opportunities):

A. carbon footprinting and emission accounting,

B. natural capital approach, and

C. climate scenario analysis.

We will look at each of these approaches in further detail in the following subsections.

Carbon Footprinting and Emission Accounting

Measuring (or "footprinting") emissions of carbon and/or other GHGs is one of the most common approaches used by companies and investors. By footprinting the operations (and/or value chain) of the issuers in a portfolio, investors can

- make comparisons with global benchmarks,
- identify priority areas and actions for reducing emissions, and
- track progress in making those reductions.

When deciding what kinds of emissions to include in the measurement, it is common to refer to the "scope" classifications developed by the GHG Protocol Standards. Scope 1 emissions are direct greenhouse emissions that occur from sources that are controlled or owned by an organization (e.g., emissions associated with fuel combustion in furnaces or company vehicles). Scope 2 emissions are indirect GHG emissions associated with, for example, the purchase of electricity. Scope 3 emissions cover all indirect emissions arising from the activities of an organization; these include emissions from both suppliers and consumers, as shown in Exhibit 23.

Exhibit 23: GHG Protocol Standards: Examples of Direct and Indirect Emissions

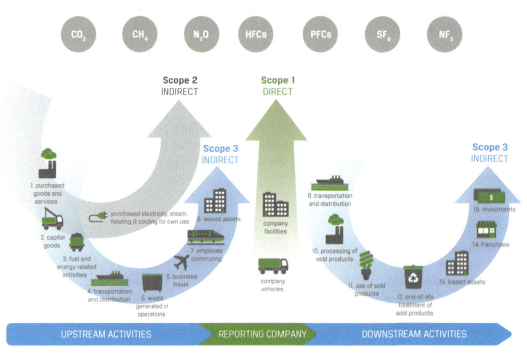

Source: Greenhouse Gas Protocol (2019).

The benefits of carbon footprinting include the potential to aggregate emissions across industries and value chains (for countries and portfolios, enabling comparisons between companies or portfolios) and across sectors and geographies, as well as to focus the analysis on emission intensity. However, the analysis has its limitations and challenges as a risk measure and is increasingly seen as too backward looking or static.

Some of the main challenges of carbon footprinting are

- the lack of disclosure for unlisted or private assets,
- Scope 3 emissions rarely being included, thus failing to capture companies' full value chain,
- double counting (e.g., a metallurgical coal miner's Scope 3 emissions can be a steel maker's Scope 1 emissions),
- the use of different estimation methodologies, and
- ignoring potential investment risks related to the physical impacts of climate change.

Depending on objectives, carbon footprinting can be an absolute or relative metric. It can be used to assess, for example, the total absolute emissions associated with a given investee company or portfolio. This recognizes that investments that are viewed as having a disproportionately high contribution to global emissions may have a higher exposure to future policy interventions on carbon emissions. Conversely, one may argue that, other things being equal, policymakers may want to reduce *global* emissions without necessarily shrinking aggregate economic output. As such, issuers able to provide similar goods and services with lower carbon inputs may be less exposed to regulatory risks. This provides an argument for the use of a relative metric, where emissions are scaled relative to some other measure (e.g. revenues), to provide a measure of comparability between issuers of different sizes.

TOTAL CARBON EMISSIONS

Total carbon emissions
$$= \sum_{n}^{i} \frac{\text{Current value of investment}_i}{\text{Issuer's market capitalization}_i} \times \text{Issuer's Scope 1 and 2 GHG emissions}_i.$$

Source: TCFD (2017b).

Alternatively, investors may wish to track carbon emission *intensity* (e.g., emissions scaled in relation to a particular metric, such as a company's revenues). The TCFD recommends that asset owners and managers report the weighted average carbon intensity associated with their investments (TCFD 2021).

WEIGHTED CARBON EMISSIONS

Weighted average carbon intensity
$$= \sum_{n}^{i} \frac{\text{Current value of investment}_i}{\text{Current portfolio value}} \times \frac{\text{Issuer's Scope 1 and 2 GHG emissions}_i}{\text{Issuer's US\$m of revenue}_i}.$$

Source: TCFD (2017b).

This can provide a measure of how carbon efficient companies are, allowing for an element of comparability between companies of different sizes. The question of comparability (between both companies and different portfolios, which potentially harbor multiple asset classes) remains a complex one, and there is currently variation among different voluntary and mandatory frameworks in terms of the choice of denominator. Alternative methods of calculation include scaling emissions by companies' market capitalization or enterprise value (which takes into account companies' issuance of both equity and debt, as well as in some cases, the companies' cash reserves).

More broadly, high levels of carbon emissions are not a perfect proxy for high climate risks. A coal-burning power plant and a coal-burning steel plant may have very similar levels of emissions. But renewable energy can much more easily—and for two-thirds of the world's population, more cheaply (BloombergNEF 2020b)—replace the use of coal for generating electricity, whereas cleaner and economic alternatives to coal for steel production are not as widespread. As such, the policy focus and future profitability profile of the two plants may look radically different. A useful starting point is to consider companies' announced emission targets and related environmental ambitions, potentially in relation to carbon pricing in different climate scenarios.

Net-Zero/Science-Based Targets

As mentioned previously, companies are increasingly adopting net-zero targets. However, there is significant variation among these targets, because they can

- be absolute or relative targets,
- cover different scopes of emissions (just operational, or Scope 1 and 2) or include some or all of the value chain (Scope 3) and different types of emissions (just carbon dioxide or all GHGs),
- focus on differing or multiple time frames, or
- rely on offsets.

This can make it difficult for investors to accurately measure and benchmark their carbon emission reduction objectives.

One element of standardization comes from the *Science Based Target initiative (SBTi)*, a partnership between several environmental institutions that provides independent certifications of the strength of companies' targets. As of May 2023, over 5,000 companies have committed to set targets via the SBTi, about 2,000 of which have been verified.[17] Of note are also the different methodologies developed by the SBTi for the financial industry, as we will discuss further.

Public companies' and their commitments are only one—albeit important—part of investors' portfolios. Methodologies to assess the environmental profile of private companies, sub- and supra-national debt, or other asset classes are still evolving. The UN Principles for Responsible Investment (PRI), the UNEP Finance Initiative, and the **Institutional Investors Group on Climate Change (IIGCC)** are developing frameworks to help benchmark investors' transition to net zero (see, e.g., UNEP and PRI 2023; IIGCC 2021). The Partnership for Carbon Accounting Financials has also developed guidance for financial institutions to assess the GHG emissions of their loans and investments.[18]

Emission Trajectories

Emission trajectories can be used to assess the required reductions to reach a stated goal (for example, net-zero carbon by 2050) and compare the pathways implied by corporate commitments, policies, or individual assets (for example, proposed refurbishments to a building to improve its energy efficiency). The Transition Pathway Initiative is an asset owner–led collaboration that has developed a publicly available tool that aims to assess companies' preparedness for the low-carbon transition.[19] The SBTi has also developed a sectoral decarbonization approach, which looks at the necessary emission pathways in key sectors, including power, apparel and footwear, information and communication technology, and finance.

Temperature Alignment

Whereas emission pathways are usually expressed in relative or absolute reductions in emissions, another approach comes from measures of *temperature alignment*. It seeks to compare the climate profiles of companies, sectors, or portfolios against a benchmark of global temperature. Because global carbon budgets impose constraints on the amount of emissions that are compatible with maintaining a reasonable chance of global temperatures not exceeding certain levels, it allows a degree of quantification of the implied future temperature levels associated with a company or portfolio: Roughly speaking, if the *world* reduced its emissions at the same rate as a given issuer or portfolio, what would the outcome be? For example, Japan's Government Pension

---

17 Source: SBTi's "Target Dashboard" (https://sciencebasedtargets.org/target-dashboard).
18 For more information, go to https://carbonaccountingfinancials.com/.
19 For more information, go to www.transitionpathwayinitiative.org/.

Investment Fund (GPIF), the world's largest pension fund, estimates its portfolio of equities and bonds are aligned with a warming trajectory of around 3°C (5.4°F; GPIF 2020).

As an illustration, Legal & General Investment Management analyzed the emission intensity trajectory of approximately 2,000 companies against various climate change scenarios and found that the majority were not aligned with the goals of the Paris Agreement. This raised "concerns that some institutional portfolios may be aligned with temperature outcomes of greater than three degrees (3°C)," leaving them exposed to tightening climate policies (Legal & General 2020).

While it is intuitively easy to understand the aim of these measures and seemingly easy to compare temperatures, there is significant variation in the market around such metrics. They

- include implied temperature rise, global warming potential, and temperature alignment,
- use different inputs for climate performance, including carbon footprint, share of investments in "green" technologies, and proportion of investee companies with (science-based) emission targets, which can themselves be derived from a single or multiple scenarios, and
- result in a different quantification of output—a binary statement (aligned or not), a score, a percentage of misalignment, or a temperature number.

Lastly but importantly, different methodologies can offer significantly different alignment results, as illustrated by the choices of different "design judgments" (Glasgow Financial Alliance for Net Zero 2022; see Exhibit 24).

Exhibit 24: Key Design Judgments in Alignment Methodologies

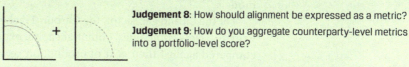

Step 3: Assessing portfolio-level alignment

Judgement 8: How should alignment be expressed as a metric?
Judgement 9: How do you aggregate counterparty-level metrics into a portfolio-level score?

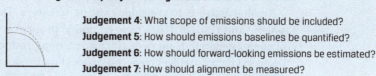

Step 2: Assessing counterparty-level alignment

Judgement 4: What scope of emissions should be included?
Judgement 5: How should emissions baselines be quantified?
Judgement 6: How should forward-looking emissions be estimated?
Judgement 7: How should alignment be measured?

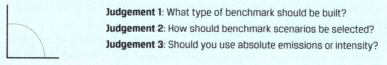

Step 1: Translating scenaro-based carbon budgets into benchmarks

Judgement 1: What type of benchmark should be built?
Judgement 2: How should benchmark scenarios be selected?
Judgement 3: Should you use absolute emissions or intensity?

Note: When measuring alignment, practitioners can follow nine Key Design Judgements across three steps. Step 1 is about building the benchmark; step 2 is about comparing company-level alignment against the benchmark, and step 3 is about aggregating alignment at the portfolio level.

Source: Glasgow Financial Alliance for Net Zero (2022)

> **TEMPERATURE ALIGNMENT TOOLS**
>
> There are several analytical products, both commercial and freely available. In line with changes in investor demand, the major providers of environmental data (which had historically been backward looking) have expanded their toolkit to develop more forward-looking approaches, with temperature ratings emerging as a major area of focus.
>
> Free-to-use tools include the following:
>
> ▶ The WWF-CDP temperature rating methodology, which is recognized by the SBTi as one method for target setting by financial institutions[20]
> ▶ The Paris Agreement Capital Transition Assessment (PACTA), developed by the 2° Investing Initiative with backing from the UN PRI, which provides tools to model publicly listed securities (equity and fixed income) and an open-source data and modeling suite for private portfolios (such as bank loan books)[21]
> ▶ The climate portfolio optimizer from ESG for Investors, which models temperature as part of a "3D" framework, covering risk, return, and climate impact[22]
>
> There is also a wide range of analytical products available in the market. The Glasgow Financial Alliance for Net Zero (2022) report on measuring portfolio alignment provides a useful summary of temperature alignment data providers and methods, in Appendix.

Green Capital Expenditures, Revenues, and Research and Development

A different approach looks in more detail at companies' level of green capital expenditures, revenue streams, and R&D to gauge the direction of travel for their business models.

For the oil and gas sector, the Carbon Tracker Initiative (2020) has created a framework to assess companies' potential capital expenditures on new oil and gas projects, compared against their cost of production, associated emissions, and demand levels in different climate scenarios. There are, however, issues with the analysis; it does not take into account policy responses, energy security, and consumer demand.

An alternative is to consider existing revenues. Data providers, including FTSE Russell[23] and HSBC (2020), have compiled proprietary databases to assess the sales companies generate from over 100 low-carbon products and services.

Several data providers have constructed methodologies to analyze the patents for low-carbon technologies filed by companies. R&D is a potentially useful indicator; however, the mere accumulation of patents need not imply strategic commitment. For example, Kodak engineers invented and patented the digital camera that would eventually render its company's main business obsolete (Gann 2016).

The EU Taxonomy also includes green capex, which is a good proxy for understanding how a company is transitioning. Because it is reported on companies' annual reports, it is a dataset that can be used to hold companies accountable.

---

20 For more information, go to the SBTi "Financial Institutions Tool" webpage: https://sciencebasedtargets.org/finance-tool.
21 For more information, go to the 2° Investing Initiative's "PACTA/Climate Scenario Analysis Program" webpage: https://2degrees-investing.org/resource/pacta/.
22 For more information, go to the ESG for Investors "3D Climate Optimiser" webpage: https://esgforinvestors.com/climate_optimiser/.
23 See the FTSE Russell "Green Revenues 2.0 Data Model" webpage: www.ftserussell.com/data/sustainability-and-esg-data/green-revenues-data-model.

Natural Capital Approach

A term often used to describe the relationship between nature and measuring/valuing nature's role in decision making is *natural capital*. Natural capital helps businesses identify, measure, value, and prioritize their impacts and dependencies on biodiversity and the ecosystem, which ultimately gives businesses new insight into their risks and opportunities (Nature Capital Coalition 2016; see Exhibit 25). Understanding the value of both natural capital impacts and dependencies helps business and financial decision makers assess the significance of these issues for their institution and therefore make more informed decisions.

Exhibit 25: The Natural Capital Approach Explains the Complex Ways in Which Natural, Social, and Economic Systems Interact, Affect, and Depend on One Another

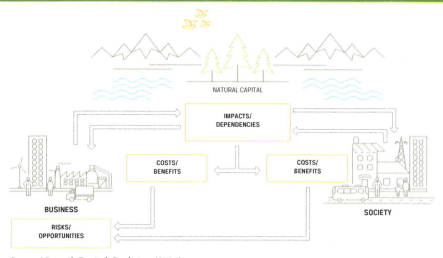

Source: Natural Capital Coalition (2016).

Assessing environmental factors using the Natural Capital Protocol, a decision-making framework, enables organizations to identify, measure, and value the direct and indirect impacts and dependencies of companies on natural capital. It currently provides guidance for the apparel, food and beverage, and forest products sectors. The protocol aims to allow companies to measure, value, and integrate natural capital impacts and dependencies into existing business processes, such as risk mitigation, sourcing, supply chain management, and product design (Natural Capital Coalition 2016).

Recognizing the need for increased consideration of natural capital issues by financial decision makers, an initiative to establish the *Task Force on Nature-Related Financial Disclosures (TNFD)* was announced in mid-2020. It is a collaboration between Global Canopy and WWF, supported by financial institutions and governments. TNFD is covered in the next section.

NATURAL RESOURCE RISK ASSESSMENT TOOLS FOR INVESTORS AND POLICYMAKERS

The Integrated Biodiversity Assessment Tool (IBAT), developed by the International Union for Conservation of Nature, is a central global biodiversity database that includes key biodiversity areas and legally protected areas.

Through an interactive mapping tool, decision makers can easily access and use this up-to-date information to identify biodiversity risks and opportunities within a project boundary.[24]

Enabling a Natural Capital Approach (ENCA) is a policy tool and guidance developed by the UK Department for Environment, Food & Rural Affairs (2020).

CERES and WWF have developed water risk assessment tools, targeted at investors, lenders, and policymakers:

- The CERES Aqua Gauge, developed by CERES and CDP (Ceres 2011)
- The WWF Water Risk Filter[25]
- The World Resources Institute water tool, Aqueduct[26]

Climate Scenario Analysis

Scenario analysis is an approach for the forward-looking assessment of risks and opportunities. Scenario analysis is a process of evaluating how an organization, sector, country, or portfolio might perform in various future states, in order to understand its key drivers and possible outcomes.

Climate-related risk has been identified as one of the most complex macro-existential risks; it is not well understood and is hard to quantify. The TCFD (2022) recommends that companies and financial institutions "describe the resilience of the organization's strategy, taking into consideration different climate-related scenarios, including a 2°C (3.6°F) or lower scenario and, where relevant to the organization, scenarios consistent with increased physical climate-related risks."

In the current landscape, there is no common set of scenario analysis methodology used by investors. Instead, the types of approaches and models will depend largely on the objectives and scope of the work.

The IIGCC (2019) published a practical investor guide, which provides a useful framework with which to approach climate-related scenario analysis. The guide sets out two objectives of undertaking scenario analysis:

1. Financial impact: The use of scenario analysis enables the assessment and pricing of climate-related risks and opportunities.
2. Alignment: Aligning the portfolio(s) with a 2°C (3.6°F) or lower future, which is typically driven by a set of investment beliefs

At the overarching level, however, there is no one-size-fits-all methodology that investors can use to determine materiality, and they consequently use financial modeling and concepts, such as financial ratio analysis. The EU's Non-Financial Reporting Directive, which helps analysts and investors evaluate the nonfinancial performance of large companies, sums up the most effective and recommended approach. It involves

- taking a set of transparent and credible data sources and assumptions, which can be quantitative or qualitative,
- applying recognizable, accepted methodologies, which will probably have the backing of an industry body, government department, or multilateral institution,
- focusing on materiality (looking in particular at business models, operations, and financial performance), and

---

24 For more information, go to the IBAT website: www.ibat-alliance.org/.
25 For more information, go to https://waterriskfilter.org/.
26 For more information, go to www.wri.org/aqueduct.

- generating a set of outputs that can be measured in terms of key performance indicators (European Commission 2014).

In order for the financial system to achieve a better appreciation of climate change risks (and opportunities), there is a need for more data, greater disclosure, better analytical toolkits, advanced scenario analysis, and new risk management techniques (Breeden 2019).

NATURE ASSESSMENT AND TNFD FRAMEWORK

3.1.7 describe and explain key methodologies that apply to biodiversity and its valuation, risk management, and interconnectedness with environmental factors and nature-related risks

An often-cited statistic is that half of the world's GDP is moderately or highly dependent on nature (World Economic Forum and PwC 2020). And yet we rely on nature for the water we drink, the food we eat, the clothes we wear, the climate we live in, the medicines we need, the green spaces we enjoy, and the air we breathe. Viewed holistically, we depend on nature 100%.

Unfortunately, we have been poor guardians of nature; economic growth has come at the expense of nature. WWF (2022) stresses that wildlife populations have plummeted 69% on average since 1970, with a 94% decline in Latin America and 66% in Africa. Instead of biodiversity, healthy soils, resilience in variety, and protecting spaces for wildlife, agriculture has coalesced around soil-degrading monoculture land use and artificial fertilizers, including deforestation (up 40%) for animal feed and meat production (up 244%; WWF 2022). Consequently, we've now crossed six of nine planetary boundaries, including land system change (due to urbanization and agriculture), biodiversity loss, biochemical flows (due to fertilizer use), and green water (in plants and soils; Kotzé 2022).

This is echoed in the Dasgupta Review. It directly links the steep decline of natural capital to the use of resources at an unsustainable rate, without giving nature the time and space to replenish. It notes that "we have collectively failed to engage with nature sustainably, to the extent that our demands far exceed its capacity to supply us with the goods and services we all rely on" (HM Treasury 2021). The report estimates that between 1992 and 2014, produced capital per person doubled, human capital per person increased by about 13% globally, and the stock of natural capital per person declined by nearly 40%.

Deforestation, in particular, exacerbates biodiversity loss, increases water stress and the risk of drought, reduces carbon sequestration and the ability to withstand floods, and increases the risk of zoonotic disease spread and the risk of food insecurity. Encouragingly, "effective conservation and management of at least 30% of the world's lands, inland waters, coastal areas, and oceans, with emphasis on areas of particular importance for biodiversity and ecosystem functioning and services," by 2030 is at the top of the list of 30 targets under *the Global Biodiversity Framework (GBF)*, to which over 190 governments committed in December 2022 (Convention of Biological Diversity 2022).

In 2020, the World Bank presented the economic case and challenges for financing biodiversity and ecosystem services (World Bank 2020). Biodiversity loss is now recognized by the world's central banks as a source of systemic risk alongside climate change (NGFS 2021), and nature policy is now included in the UN PRI's Inevitable Policy Response scenario analysis (UN PRI 2023). Climate and nature are intertwined and need to be addressed holistically as a combined systemic risk.

The Taskforce on Nature-Related Financial Disclosure was set up in 2021 with a mandate to develop a proposal for assessing and disclosing data on nature. The approach to the assessment of impacts, dependencies, risks, and opportunities and the proposed disclosure framework were released in four installments between March 2022 and March 2023 for consultation with a wide range of stakeholders, including nature and biodiversity organizations, standard-setting bodies, the knowledge and data provider community, regional consultation groups, companies, banks, and investors. Version 1 of the TNFD framework is due to be released in September 2023.

Nature and Biodiversity

TNFD builds on existing and evolving nature and biodiversity frameworks. To facilitate integration, it has adopted the following:

- The definition of *nature* used by the Intergovernmental Science-Policy Platform on Biodiversity and Ecosystem Services (IPBES): "The natural world, with an emphasis on the diversity of living organisms (including people) and their interactions among themselves and with their environment" (Díaz et al. 2015)

- The Capitals Coalition (2016) definition of *natural capital*: "The stock of renewable and non-renewable natural resources (e.g., plants, animals, air, water, soils, minerals) that combine to yield a flow of benefits to people."

- The *ecosystem assets* definition of the UN (2021) System of Environmental-Economic Accounting (SEEA): "A form of environmental assets that relate to diverse ecosystems. These are contiguous spaces of a specific ecosystem type characterised by a distinct set of biotic and abiotic components and their interactions."

The reference to biodiversity in the *nature* definition, however, does not limit the scope to species biodiversity; rather, it stresses the interconnections, including with nonliving nature, and how ecosystem assets interact to provide ecosystem services (e.g., pest control, pollination services, soil quality), which, in turn, deliver value (e.g., through increased quality and quantity of crop yields). The key point is that the ability of environmental assets to deliver is underpinned by biodiversity and the resilience afforded by variety.

In common with other biodiversity frameworks, TNFD includes land, freshwater, and oceans as realms, extending to living nature, natural features, natural capital, resources, and ecosystem services (see Exhibit 26). Atmosphere reflects the close association between climate- and nature-related risks and opportunities, while also acknowledging that links with climate mitigation and adaptation occur across all realms. The four realms provide an entry point for understanding how organizations and people depend on and have impacts on the natural capital that provides the resources and services from which business and societies benefit.

Nature Assessment and TNFD Framework

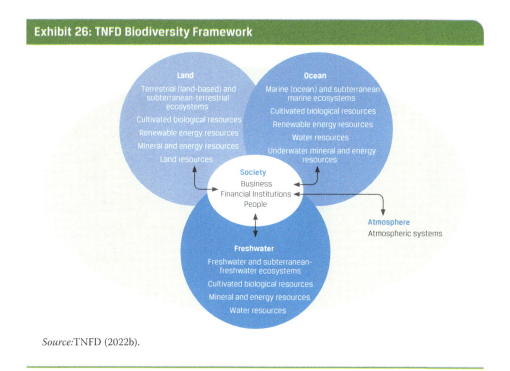

Exhibit 26: TNFD Biodiversity Framework

Source: TNFD (2022b).

Assessing Nature

Nature is complex, with interdependencies and feedback loops between realms and ecosystems, as well as the interplay with climate risks. Nature-related dependencies and impacts can result in earnings and cash-flow vulnerability from the company to the systemic level (see Exhibit 27). Financial risk transmission channels include both micro-channels (e.g., supply chain uncertainty due to disruptions to production, changes in profitability and asset values) and macro-channels (e.g., changing demand patterns, commodity price volatility). Therein lies the opportunity to take action to mitigate risks (e.g., build supply chain resilience, clean up pollution) and reverse nature loss (e.g., afforestation, improve marine reserves) to achieve nature positive results.

For example, a beverage company depends on the availability of clean water. Water provision is an ecosystem service that relies on water resources (an environmental asset) and healthy terrestrial and aquatic ecosystems to purify and replenish the water. The pollution or degradation of waterways can lead to water sedimentation and deterioration of water quality, both of which can have a negative—maybe existential—impact on the company. Restoration of habitats and preservation of biodiversity could reduce water quality deterioration, reducing the operational costs of water treatment and securing the company's license to operate in the community with which it shares the water resources. Many risks and opportunities, however, are not easy to quantify financially.

Exhibit 27: Sources of Nature-Related Financial Risk and Opportunity

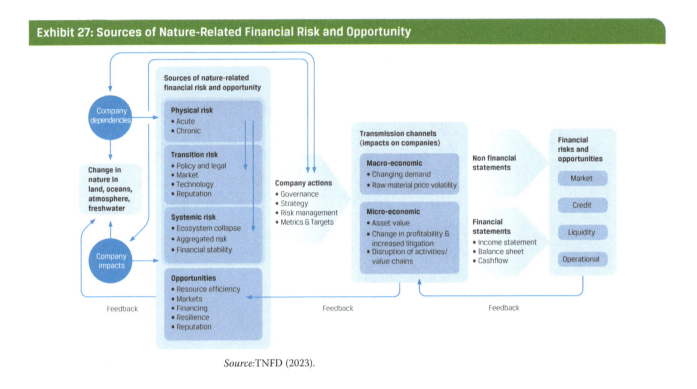

Source: TNFD (2023).

The TNFD considers five main drivers of nature change: climate change; resource exploitation; land and sea use change; pollution; and invasive alien species. While nature-related *dependencies* stem from the reliance on ecosystem assets and services, it is these five drivers that can translate into positive or negative *impacts* (see Exhibit 28). Evaluating dependencies and impacts *on nature* is the first step in assessing the risks and opportunities to a company, city, region, and so on.

Nature Assessment and TNFD Framework

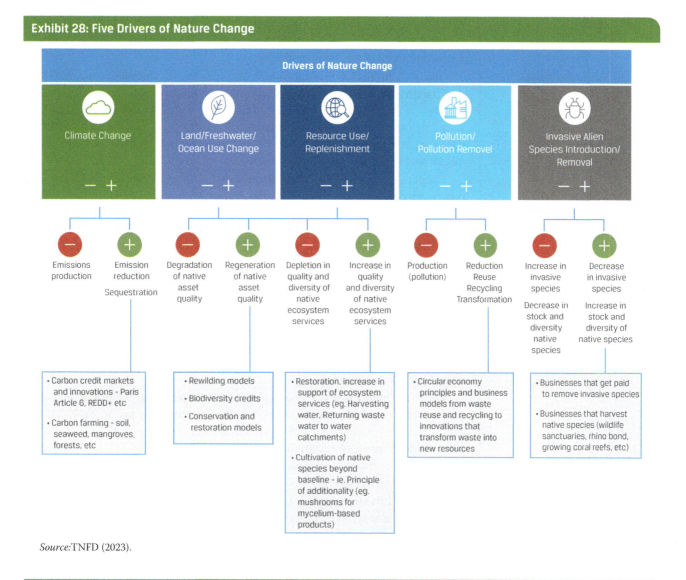

Exhibit 28: Five Drivers of Nature Change

Source: TNFD (2023).

CASE STUDIES

Aviva Deforestation Risk Assessment

Aviva based its approach on the UNEP WCMC ENCORE database.[27] This provides a sector and sub-industry list of impacts and dependencies on ecosystem use, GHG emissions, and soil pollution, among others. Because ENCORE does not give sub-sectors an overall impact score, Aviva developed a sector classification and scoring approach by supplementing ENCORE with the Science Based Targets Network Sectoral Materiality Tool to identify impacts and dependencies upstream and downstream along a sector's supply chain and four datasets to capture the sectors most material to biodiversity—Vigeo Eiris (Moody's) high-biodiversity-impact sectors, World Benchmarking Alliance sectors,[28] the

---

27 For more information, go to https://encore.naturalcapital.finance/en/data-and-methodology/data.
28 For more information, go to www.worldbenchmarkingalliance.org/.

> EU B@B Platform Priority Sectors,[29] and UNEP Finance Initiative's High-Priority Sectors. The resulting sector classification is used in Aviva's Natural Capital Transition Fund assessment model.
>
> The 2022 (initial) deforestation risk assessment of Aviva's investments prioritized direct commodity-driven deforestation. The first step was to carry out a review of available data and tools. In the absence of accurate data reflecting actual deforestation linked to companies, Aviva chose to use datasets, which use proxy indicators on how strong a company's policy is on deforestation. The assessment approach varied by investment asset class.
>
> Corporate investments. Aviva determined an overall score for whether a company's deforestation policy is strong, medium or weak by using a number of indicators across three datasets—CDP Forests, Forest 500 and SPOTT—which identify the companies and financial institutions that are most exposed to deforestation globally. Aviva found that 26% of its corporate holdings by value are included in these datasets. Over half of these are financial institutions. The other half have exposure to deforestation via their supply chains, and the largest holdings are in the pharmaceutical, household and personal products, and retail sectors. Initial results showed that overall, 38% of Aviva's corporate holdings exposed to deforestation risk are judged to be weak on managing this risk, while 43% are medium, and 19% are strong. The assessment showed that the financial and retail sectors have weak deforestation management scores compared to other sectors.
>
> Sovereign investments. Using Global Forest Watch data,[30] Aviva identified the sovereign debt issuers with the greatest average tree cover loss in 2019–2021 as Brazil, the United States, and Canada and found that the main exposure to commodity-driven deforestation is in Brazil, Indonesia, and Malaysia. Based on this work, Aviva determined that it has minimal exposure to the direct or indirect funding of commodity-driven deforestation through sovereign debt.
>
> Real asset investments. Aviva assessed its real estate assets, including developments and assets in construction. Because the assets are located in Europe, the conclusion was that there is no exposure to commodity-driven tree loss in these asset locations, according to Global Forest Watch data.
>
> Loans to companies and infrastructure. The assessment was conducted by sector and country, because more granular data were not available. By taking a sector view, the potential exposure to commodity-driven deforestation was assessed to be in a conglomerate, chemical, and infrastructure companies. Overlaying this information with the geographic locations of these companies, the exposure to forest risk commodities was determined to be low.
>
> *Source:* Aviva (2022).

TNFD has developed the LEAP (locate, evaluate, assess, prepare) assessment framework to help companies and financial institutions locate their interface with nature, understand and evaluate their dependence and impacts on nature, assess material risks and opportunities for their operations, and prepare responses (e.g., business strategy, monitoring metrics, risk management approach, resource allocation) and nature-related disclosures. The TNFD disclosure framework builds on TCFD recommendations and guidance. The LEAP assessment framework and TNFD disclosure framework are covered in the Appendix.

---

29 For more information, go to https://green-business.ec.europa.eu/business-biodiversity_en.
30 For more information, go to www.globalforestwatch.org/ and www.globalforestwatch.org/map/?menu=eyJkYXRhc2V0Q2F0ZWdvcnkiOiJmb3Jlc3RDaGFuZ2UiLCJtZW51U2VjdGlvbiI6ImRhGFzZXRzIn0%3D.

APPLYING MATERIAL ENVIRONMENTAL FACTORS TO FINANCIAL MODELING, RATIO ANALYSIS, AND RISK ASSESSMENT

3.1.8 apply material environmental factors to financial modeling, ratio analysis, and risk assessment

The following case study is based on a WWF Switzerland and Cadmus Group (2019) survey of more than 20 infrastructure investors and related stakeholders. It examines how investors evaluate the sustainability of infrastructure assets. It can, however, be adapted for evaluating individual companies.

It demonstrates how and where to integrate the results of a comprehensive ESG assessment as input into the key financial ratios and variables of a financial model, such as the forecasting of revenues, operating costs, and capital expenditures, which form the basis of discounted cash flow analysis.

Note that this example focuses only on the environmental impacts. In reality, the social and governance factors need to be considered in parallel for a full ESG materiality assessment.

CASE STUDIES

ESG Review—Environmental Factors and Materiality

Over the lifetime of an infrastructure project—from development to construction, to operation, and all the way through to the decommissioning phase—infrastructure assets face all kinds of ESG issues. These vary depending on asset type, sector, size, geographic location, and stage in the life cycle.

Some of the environmental issues may originate outside the asset but could impact its technical ability to operate or impact its profitability (for instance, temperature rise and increased water scarcity). Other issues may be caused by the asset itself and impact its surrounding environment and communities (such as water effluence and the quality of life of the communities around it). In this latter case, these are called externalities, which can (and will) increasingly impact the asset's financial performance via various feedback loops (including protests of the surrounding community). It is thus important to realize that both directions of potential environmental impact (impact *on* the asset and impact *from* the asset) may have financial consequences for the investors.

For the purpose of arriving at a shortlist of environmental factors for which the potential impact of environmental risk on infrastructure financials can be demonstrated, a two-step process was followed:

1. A longlist of widely recognized environmental factors was derived. The longlist was reduced to a shortlist of environmental factors that are typically among those considered key to an environmental assessment in the context of infrastructure.

2. Whether and the extent to which any of the selected environmental factors have a material impact on the infrastructure asset will be revealed by the asset-specific ESG due diligence process (see Exhibit 29).

Exhibit 29: Environmental Factors Material to Infrastructure Projects

Typical Environmental Factors	Material Environment Factors for Infrastructure
Degradation and pollution · Air (climate)—GHG emissions · Air (health)—other pollution · Water · Ground or contamination · Noise and light · Biodiversity	(A) Quantifiable: *degradation and pollution* 1. Air (health) and water pollution 2. Air (climate)—GHG emissions: *Resource efficiency—sourcing, use, or treatment* 3. Energy (E) 4. Water (E) 5. Solid waste (E) 6. (Raw) materials and supply chain (E/S)
Resource efficiency—sourcing, use, or treatment: · (Raw) materials including supply chain · Energy · Water · Waste	(B) Difficult to quantify 1. Biodiversity and habitat (E) 2. Physical climate change impacts (E)
Physical risk—impact on asset, such as flooding	

Approach to Assess the Implications of Environmental Risk on Financial Ratios and Models

The approach used in this case study, which uses survey input across a range of infrastructure projects, simplifies the TCFD classification of risks introduced previously, while broadening it to ESG, not just climate, themes.

Exhibit 30 helps show how the selected environmental factors may impact the financial performance of infrastructure organizations. It elaborates on the potential impact pathways from the selected environmental factors to specific financial ratios or inputs into financial models.

Exhibit 30: Environmental Factor Impacts

Environmental Factor	Risks Considered	Financial Ratio or Factor Impact	Impact of the Risk
Air pollution or water pollution	Tightening regulations	Asset write-off/capital expenditure (CapEx)	Write-offs, asset impairment, or early retirement of existing assets may result from the tightening of regulation.

Applying Material Environmental Factors to Financial Modeling, Ratio Analysis, and Risk Assessment

Environmental Factor	Risks Considered	Financial Ratio or Factor Impact	Impact of the Risk
		Provisions	Provisions may be needed to cover potential fines in case of noncompliance with new regulations. They may also need to be made for potential lawsuits or other legal proceedings.
	Increased costs for obtaining relevant permit	Operating expenditure (OpEx)	The overall production cost will increase due to an additional discharge cost.
	Imposition of new environmental tax	Tax	Taxes will increase.
	Enhanced disclosure requirements	OpEx	Monitoring, reporting, and auditing costs will increase.
	Reputational	Provisions	Reputational damage may lead to loss of revenues.
		Financing costs	Additional interest paid due to higher interest rate or lower credit rating
GHG emissions	Client demand for lower-carbon products and services (e.g., cleaner electricity in the case of a utility company)	Revenues	Decrease in revenues from high-carbon activities.
	Introduction or increase of price for GHG emissions, implementation of a carbon tax, loss of subsidies for high-GHG-intensity energy sources	OpEx/tax/CapEx	Production cost increases (OpEx, tax). Preventive investment (CapEx) in measures of technology to reduce GHG emissions per unit of output or to reduce energy intensity of processes
Greenhouse gas emissions	In a utility example: Clients switch to electricity generated with lower GHG intensity than traditional electricity.	Revenues	Decrease in revenues due to lower demand for conventional fossil fuels
	Introduction or increase of price for greenhouse gas emissions, implementation of a carbon tax, loss of subsidies for high-GHG-intensity energy sources	OpEx/tax/Capex	Production cost increases (OpEx, tax). Preventive investment (CapEx) in measures of technology to reduce GHG emissions per unit of output or to reduce energy intensity of processes

Environmental Factor	Risks Considered	Financial Ratio or Factor Impact	Impact of the Risk
Energy	Physical: rising temperatures	OpEx	Higher temperatures may influence the functioning of equipment and lead to an increase in fuel consumption or lower performance levels (OpEx).
Water	Physical: increased water scarcity	Revenue/OpEx	Insufficient supply for water-reliant assets, such as hydropower plants or district heating networks, leads to loss of revenues due to loss of energy production (hydropower plant) or an increase in operating costs because of the rise in water prices.
	Reputational: conflicts with the surrounding community on water withdrawal	Revenues/provisions/OpEx	Conflicts with community may lead to project delays, which, in turn, may lead to loss of revenues or fines for late completion. Increase in operating expenses due to additional community engagement and marketing measures
	Regulatory: implementation of more stringent regulation regarding water withdrawal	CapEx/OpEx	Investments in water-saving measures may become necessary but may reduce water usage going forward. Implementation of new production processes, which substitute water with more expensive resources, leads to higher OpEx.
Solid waste	Regulatory: tightened regulation on waste disposal and land restoration	Provisions	Potentially stricter regulation for waste disposal, recycling, or land restoration during the decommissioning phase
(Raw) materials supply chain	Reputational: environmental, social, or governance issues may be found in the supply chain	Provisions	Dealing with reputational issues is time consuming and costly, and provisions may need to be made to cover for such cases.

Opportunities Relating to Climate Change and Environmental Issues

Environmental Factor	Risks Considered	Financial Ratio or Factor Impact	Impact of the Risk
Biodiversity and habitat	Regulatory/legal: tightening of regulations or other operating requirements regarding the protection of critical species or habitats	Revenues/CapEx/OpEx	Potential operating restrictions on certain days of the year or on certain times of the day leading to a reduction in sales (revenues) Investments into alterations to existing structures, such as implementation of sound curtains for offshore wind turbines, may be necessary. Adherence to stipulations may lead to increased monitoring and reporting cost.
Climate change impacts (E)	Physical: Extreme weather (storms and floods) can lead to disruptions.	Revenues	Periodic loss of energy production (windfarms) due to shutdown
	Physical: Extreme weather may destroy the asset partially or fully.	Asset book value/revenues/CapEx/OpEx	A write-down or write-off of the assets and a loss of revenues may be the immediate result. Investments will be needed to repair or even rebuild the damaged asset. If the probability of extreme weather increases, the probability of damage or destruction increases; therefore, insurance policies are likely to increase.

Source: Adapted from Weber and Rendlen (2019).

OPPORTUNITIES RELATING TO CLIMATE CHANGE AND ENVIRONMENTAL ISSUES 10

☐ **3.1.9** explain how companies and the investment industry can benefit from opportunities relating to climate change and environmental issues: the circular economy, clean and technological innovation, green and ESG-related products, and the blue economy

Previous sections have covered the risks of neglecting the implications of key environmental factors for companies as a result of direct or indirect business activities. The increased awareness of climate change and environmental impact has resulted in an accelerating search for viable societal and economic solutions to enable a transition to a less carbon-intensive economy. Estimates for this transition reach trillions of dollars, and the magnitude of change required will be pervasive, across all aspects of life as we understand it today.

A 2016 study by the Global Commission on the Economy and Climate found that the world is expected to invest about US$90 trillion in infrastructure over the next 15 years, requiring an urgent shift to ensure that this capital is spent on low-carbon, energy-efficient projects. The report further described that "transformative change is needed now in how we build our cities, produce and use energy, transport people and goods, and manage our landscapes" (New Climate Economy 2016). It is therefore no surprise that there is an increasing number of investment strategies that focus primarily on the opportunities of the low-carbon transition and green finance. Investments in such sectors as technology and resource efficiency, waste management, circular economy, and sustainable agriculture and forestry are just some of the available investment opportunities relating to climate change and environmental issues.

Already, the investment opportunities are becoming visible. FTSE Russell (2022) estimated that the green economy (the total market capitalization of the companies generating revenues from activities providing environmental benefits) in 2022 was "equivalent to 7.1% of the total listed equity market."

This section provides an overview of some of these opportunities as they relate to

A. the circular economy,

B. clean and technological innovation,

C. green and ESG-related products, and

D. the blue economy.

It also highlights how clean technology and innovation will play a critical role and be an investment opportunity in mitigating and adapting to the impacts of climate change and environmental degradation. This section also covers some of the financial products most prevalent in supporting environmental (green) considerations in investments.

Circular Economy

With only a fraction of material inputs being currently recycled (less than 12% in the EU in 2019, for example; European Environment Agency 2021), there are significant investment opportunities from innovations to encourage a shift toward a *circular economy*. This shift is already underway: In September 2020, assets managed through public equity funds with the circular economy as their sole or partial focus were estimated to have increased sixfold compared to the beginning of that year, from US$0.3 billion to US$2 billion, with the number of such funds almost doubling (Ellen MacArthur Foundation 2020).

Companies that factor in circularity in their business model are able to play a major role in safeguarding natural resources, transform the way we currently use natural resources, and support a transition to a low-carbon economy.

In a circular economy, products and materials are repaired, reused, and recycled rather than thrown away, ensuring that waste from one industrial process becomes a valued input into another. The circular economy concept is now a core component of both the EU's 2050 Long-Term Strategy to achieve a climate-neutral Europe and China's five-year plans.

Due to the expanding market of investible opportunities, both in private and public markets, companies are working to bring circularity closer to the heart of their business models.

> **CASE STUDIES**
>
> ### Circular Economics Models in Practice
>
> #### Jurong Island
>
> Singapore's Jurong Island is one of the world's top 10 chemical parks. The close proximity of industries on the island "provides an ecosystem where one company's product can become the feedstock of another. For example, waste from some companies is burned to generate steam for industrial use. Similarly, wastewater is recovered and recycled for industrial use" (Singapore Ministry of the Environment and Water Resources 2019). Industrial developer JTC Corporation is partnering with local companies and regulators to explore further avenues for circularity, by mapping water, energy, and waste flows.
>
> #### Heineken
>
> As part of its Zero Waste Program, 102 of Heineken's 165 production units sent zero waste to landfills in 2018. The waste from these sites was instead recycled into animal feed, material loops, or compost or used for energy recovery (Heineken 2018).
>
> #### Schneider Electric
>
> This company specializes in energy management and automation. It uses recycled content and recyclable materials in its products, prolongs product lifespan through leasing and pay-per-use, and has introduced take-back schemes into its supply chain. Circular activities now account for 12% of its revenues and saved 100,000 metric tons of primary resources between 2018 and 2020 (Schneider Electric 2023).
>
> #### Stora Enso
>
> This company provides renewable solutions in packaging, biomaterials, wooden construction, and paper. Reducing waste operates at the heart of the "bioeconomy and contributes to a circular economy" (Stora Enso 2018).
>
> The European Investment Bank (2019) has launched an investment fund to support the circular bioeconomy.
>
> #### Close the Loop
>
> This Australian company turns old printer cartridges and soft plastics into roads by mixing them with asphalt and recycled glass, resulting in a road surface that is estimated to be up to 65% more durable than traditional asphalt. For a kilometer of road, the equivalent of 530,000 plastic bags, 168,000 glass bottles, and the waste toner from 12,500 printer cartridges is used (World Economic Forum 2019).

Clean and Technological Innovation

Technological innovation and the development of new business ventures associated with the environment have been around for some time. However, the term *cleantech* as an umbrella term "encompassing the investment asset class, technology, and business sectors which include clean energy, environmental, and sustainable or green products and services" became increasingly popular approximately 20 years ago (ISO 2018).

As with many other technological innovations, such as the internet or GPS, state support and a favorable policy and regulatory environment have been instrumental in driving the early growth of technologies, such as wind and solar energy. However, as the technologies have matured, unsubsidized solar and wind have become the cheapest source of new electricity in most regions around the world. Moreover, this dynamic is increasingly undercutting *operational* costs of some existing assets; research has shown that in 2020, on a levelized cost basis, it was cheaper to build new wind and solar capacity than to operate 60% of the existing coal power plants in the world (Lazard 2020; Carbon Tracker Initiative 2020). See Exhibit 31 for data on the costs and adoption rates of several clean energy technologies.

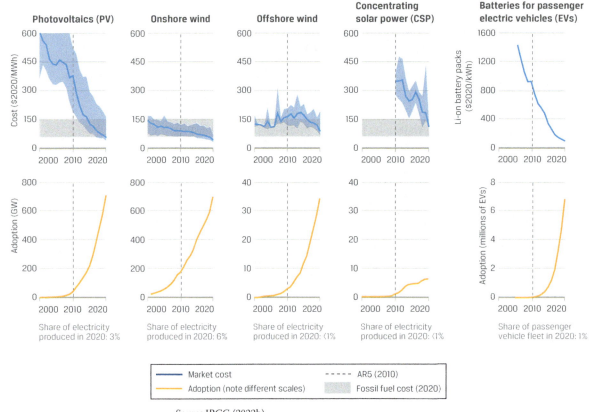

Exhibit 31: Falling Costs (2020 US$/MWh) and Growing Adoption (GW) of Selected Clean Energy Technologies, 2000–2020

Source: IPCC (2022b).

As a result, there is increased interest from private investors in this area. It has been estimated that over the past seven years—a period of intense digitalization and research into automation—venture capital investment into cleantech grew three times faster than similar investments into artificial intelligence (PricewaterhouseCoopers 2020).

Of note, in 2022, investment in key low-carbon energy technologies surged past the $1 trillion mark for the first time (see Exhibit 32); it was also the first year that investments in fossil fuel supply reached parity with low-carbon.

Opportunities Relating to Climate Change and Environmental Issues

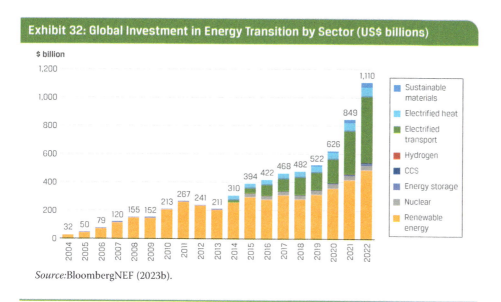

Exhibit 32: Global Investment in Energy Transition by Sector (US$ billions)

Source: BloombergNEF (2023b).

Next, we discuss some of the technologies that can play a role in decarbonizing sectors that contribute substantially to global emissions.

Energy is the "prime mover" of the economy, and reducing the emissions associated with energy production has knock-on effects across all sectors. The production of low-carbon electricity has been at the forefront of these developments, from such sources as solar photovoltaics, onshore and offshore wind, hydroelectricity, nuclear energy, tidal energy, and geothermal energy. Fuels derived from biomass ("biofuels," such as bioethanol) may also be considered a renewable energy source, although this depends on the sustainability of the source, with significant debates around the environmental impacts of large-scale biofuel cultivation (Evans 2018).

A full, global accounting of the agricultural sector shows that it produces about 40% of global emissions when heat, electricity, and transportation are included, so biofuels are seldom the low-GHG source that some claim. Harvesting wood and burning it for electricity is slowly renewable but releases more carbon dioxide than burning coal or other fossil fuels and reduces the amount of CO_2 that can be removed by forests (Sterman et al. 2022). Wood burning also releases large amounts of fine particulates that damage human health, leave sunlight-absorbing black carbon on land, and darken ice and snow, hastening their melting.

Albeit very important, electricity is only one component of energy. The challenge is harder when it comes to decarbonizing heat and cooling. For residential and commercial properties, ground and air source heat pumps, combined heat and power, and district heating are some of the potential heating solutions. More difficult is the decarbonization of high-temperature processes. The use of renewable energy to produce hydrogen—which can burn at high temperatures—is increasingly the focus of governments' and investors' strategies, although the deployment of supportive green hydrogen infrastructure is currently lacking. Other speculative technologies include research into nuclear fusion (very long term) and next-generation battery storage.

The electrification of industrial processes—from clean sources—is an essential lever for the decarbonization of industry. In steel making, which has a substantial carbon footprint, the use of electric arc furnaces coupled with increased steel recycling and alternative reductants (e.g., hydrogen or gas instead of coal) are important avenues. The process CO_2 released from turning iron ore into iron can be captured and stored. In the chemicals industry, the use of green hydrogen, synthetic fuels, new catalysts, and alternative feedstocks (including the use of biogenic materials), as well as the development of lightweight materials and plastic alternatives, can contribute.

The built environment sector contributes up to 40% of total GHGs as a result of the whole life-cycle carbon of the building—the embodied carbon and the carbon associated with construction (building materials) and the operation (energy used to heat, cool, and light). Embodied carbon is associated with the construction materials, major refurbishments, and waste in their production; the building process; and the fixtures and fittings inside, as well as from deconstruction and disposal at the end of a building's lifetime.

In terms of technology drivers in this sector, CO_2 is an inevitable byproduct of the chemical reaction used to create the most widely used form of cement. Developing alternatives to "clinkers" (one of cement's major components) will play a key role, as will capture and storage of the process CO_2 that is released. Several large cement producers have already begun to develop breakthrough technologies in producing cement with lower emissions and higher energy efficiency.

In the transport industry, many of the world's large automobile makers have begun to shift their business models toward battery electric vehicles (BEVs), with global sales of electric cars more than doubling in 2021 and capturing all the net growth in global car demand (Paoli and Gül 2022). Nearly half of the 6.5 million BEVs sold worldwide in 2021 were in China, and just 535,000 were sold in the United States (Canalys 2022). In Norway, 65% of a much smaller but record number of car sales were BEVs; price and other incentives are rapidly transforming the market (Klesty 2022). The extent to which batteries and electrification will play a substantial role in the decarbonization of heavy-duty transport or whether other fuel sources (such as ammonia, hydrogen fuel cells, or biofuels) may be used to power trucks, planes, and ships remains an open question and subject to intense research and investment.

Given the substantial emissions associated with food production, packaging, and consumption, innovation will be needed in the food industry. Protein alternatives (whether plant based, including algae (Moomaw, Berzin, and Tzachor 2017), or laboratory-grown meat, for example) are a fast-growing market. Further innovation in agricultural techniques (e.g., around precision and regenerative agriculture or the development of less toxic pest management and low–nitrous oxide emission nitrogen fertilizers) will also be needed.

CASE STUDIES

But What If Your Electric Vehicle Is Coal Powered?

While the potential for decarbonization *at the point of application* is well understood for many technologies, an often-raised issue is that of a life-cycle assessment. An electric vehicle (EV), for example, has no tailpipe CO_2 emissions (and no tailpipe), but what about the emissions associated with its manufacturing or charging?

As we illustrate in Exhibit 33, when considered on a life-cycle basis, key low-carbon technologies in power, energy, and transport are deserving of their name when compared to fossil-fuel-based alternatives. An EV charged from a high-carbon power grid is roughly half as carbon intensive, for example. And the gap is set to widen further as global electricity supply will decarbonize even more.

Opportunities Relating to Climate Change and Environmental Issues

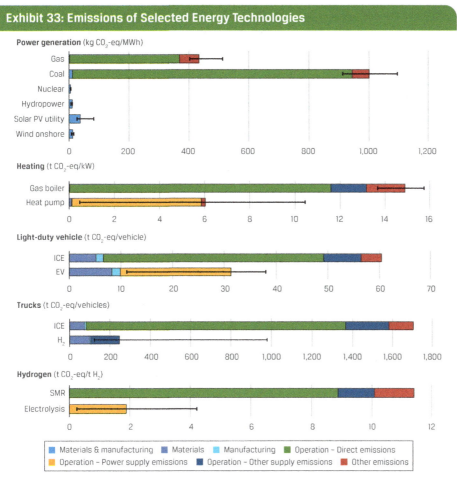

Exhibit 33: Emissions of Selected Energy Technologies

Note: ICE = internal combustion engine; SMR = steam methane reforming (a process to generate hydrogen from natural gas); H_2 = hydrogen (i.e., fuel cell vehicle).

Source: International Energy Agency (2023).

However, it is important to understand that the *technical potential* for a technology to contribute to decarbonization—the list of *possible use cases*—does not guarantee actual deployment, which will also be a function of economics, the availability of alternatives, social preferences, and other factors.

HYDROGEN: HOPE OR HYPE?

The clean-burning qualities of hydrogen, for example, make it a candidate for a variety of applications, including industrial (e.g., in certain high-temperature processes), transport (e.g., long-haul trucking), and domestic (such as replacing gas boilers). As a result, while some governments (notably Japan) have for decades been subsidizing hydrogen research, particularly around fuel cell vehicles, there is renewed policymaker interest in this area, with "hydrogen strategies" and funding commitments announced recently by such governments as those of the United Kingdom, the EU, and China.

However, analysts have highlighted barriers to adoption (e.g., the volumetric density and embrittling effect on steel pipes and the thermodynamic efficiency of transforming electricity into hydrogen and back via a fuel cell). Exhibit 34 shows one energy analyst's ranking of hydrogen use cases in various sectors. Inspired by the energy performance bands now common on electrical appliances, the "hydrogen ladder" aims to situate potential uses cases for clean hydrogen as a function of the availability (or lack thereof) of other, competing cleantech alternatives.

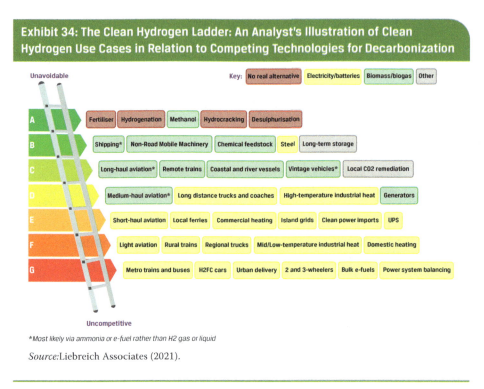

Exhibit 34: The Clean Hydrogen Ladder: An Analyst's Illustration of Clean Hydrogen Use Cases in Relation to Competing Technologies for Decarbonization

*Most likely via ammonia or e-fuel rather than H2 gas or liquid

Source: Liebreich Associates (2021).

The choice of technologies and scenario assumptions remains an area of intense debate in both academia and industry, and the technological realities on the ground are fast evolving. For example, according to BloombergNEF, the rise in gas prices in early 2022 led to the costs of green hydrogen falling below those of "grey" hydrogen (produced from unabated fossil gas) in the Europe, Middle East, and Africa region and China—a point of price parity reached a decade earlier than in some previous estimates (Mathis, Morison, and Dezem 2022; see also the quote from BloombergNEF in Collins 2022). Moreover, in the United States, the tax credits and renewable energy incentives of the Inflation Reduction Act are estimated to reduce the costs of green hydrogen production by almost half.

And as noted earlier, the development of cleantech often works in tandem with standard setting by governments and levels of policy support. One notable example of this is in the case of our built environment.

CASE STUDIES

Environmental Standards in Real Estate

The real estate sector is currently undergoing significant change, with major property developers and managers stepping up their sustainability practices in their role to tackle climate change.

In the United Kingdom, the Better Buildings Partnership (BBP), a coalition of some of the largest commercial property owners, has committed to achieving net-zero carbon by 2050. This is a bold ambition and one that will require significant changes in the current practices throughout the life cycle of a building. The

BBP believes that the UK energy efficiency standard and regulations, which are intended to achieve better energy performance, are actually not "fit for purpose" and will certainly not support the BBP's net-zero carbon goal. These standards are focused on design intent rather than on how a building actually performs in use, hence creating a "performance gap."

As such, the BBP has embarked on an initiative called Design for Performance, which is based on the National Australian Built Environmental Rating System (NABERS), which measures and rates the operational efficiency of commercial offices. NABERS has proven to be very successful as it focuses on target ratings, outcomes, and transparency, so it recently published the "NABERS UK Guide to Design for Performance," aimed at the UK market.

In the near future, we can expect to see other governments that have made commitments to achieve carbon neutrality by 2050 start to strengthen their existing energy performance standards and regulations in the real estate sector and adopt best practice approaches such as this one (BBP 2020).

According to BloombergNEF, in 2021, total investment in the low-carbon energy transition worldwide was US$755 billion, with China as the largest investor, followed by the United States (BloombergNEF 2022b). The largest area of funding in 2021 was renewable energy, followed by electrified transport and heat.

There has also been increasing activity in corporate venturing and investments by incumbent fossil-fuel-based corporations into clean and renewable technologies. These private sector efforts have been complemented by greater supra-national and public sector support—for example, EIT InnoEnergy, which was established to invest in and accelerate sustainable energy innovations. Another initiative, still in the concept phase, is the World Economic Forum's *Sustainable Energy Innovation Fund (SEIF)*, which matches private funding with public investment.

Green and ESG-Related Products

The risks and opportunities associated with environmental sustainability and mitigating climate change necessitate a realignment of financial products and services in order to facilitate the transition to a low-carbon economy. There are three attributes of energy and products: renewability, carbon (or GHG) intensity, and sustainability. For climate, low or zero carbon is the major criterion for determining whether something is "green." Sustainability is a second criterion: Is it "enduring"? Renewability means that the energy or material is replaced in a short time relative to its use. The overall assessment of these three factors determines what is green, but there is no universally agreed-on definition of "green." There have been several developments in this area, along with expectations for rapid expansion of the breadth and depth of these green products and services over the next few years.

Some specific financial products that have emerged are

- a range of green, sustainability, and ESG indexes,
- green bonds and loans, sustainability funds, and ETFs,
- retail and institutional deposit and savings products, and
- crowdfunding investments.

Green Bonds, Loans, and Other Labeled ESG-Related Products

The first green bond issuance was announced in 2007 by the European Investment Bank to raise funding for climate-related projects. Green bonds were created to fund projects that have positive environmental or climate benefits. The majority are green "use-of-proceeds" or asset-linked bonds (see Exhibit 35). Green bond cumulative issuance surpassed US$2.3 trillion in 2022 (Climate Bonds Initiative 2022).

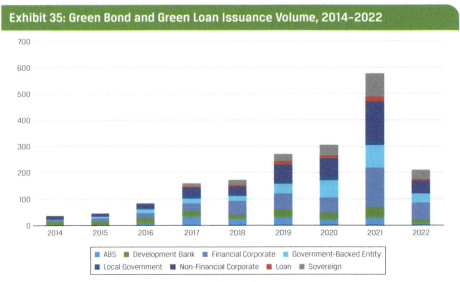

Notes: Data cover up to the end of 2022. All debt instruments have been screened in accordance with the Climate Bonds Initiative Green Bond Database Methodology (Climate Bonds Initiative 2022b) and Social & Sustainability Bond Database Methodology (Climate Bonds Initiative 2022c). Definitions of *green* are derived from the Climate Bonds Taxonomy (Climate Bonds Initiative 2023), and issuer type classification follows Climate Bonds Initiative convention.

Source: Climate Bonds Initiative (2022a).

While clean energy and low-carbon building investment continues to dominate allocations, funding for low-carbon transport has increased dramatically and issuers from the information and communications technology (ICT) and manufacturing sectors have entered the green bond market (see Exhibit 36).

Exhibit 36: Use of Green Bond and Loans Proceeds, 2022

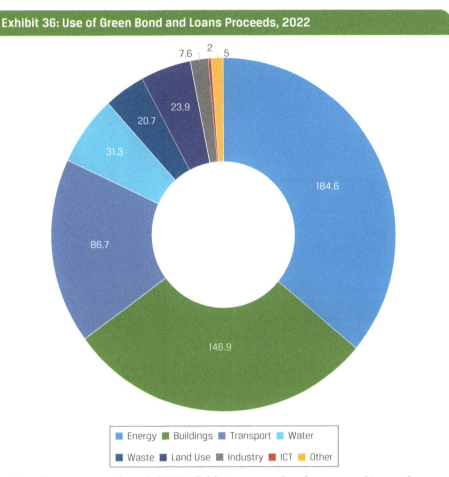

Notes: Data cover up to the end of 2022. All debt instruments have been screened in accordance with the Climate Bonds Initiative Green Bond Database Methodology (Climate Bonds Initiative 2022b) and Social & Sustainability Bond Database Methodology (Climate Bonds Initiative 2022c). Definitions of *green* are derived from the Climate Bonds Taxonomy (Climate Bonds Initiative 2023), and issuer type classification follows Climate Bonds Initiative convention.

Source: Climate Bonds Initiative (2022a).

In addition to green bonds, which focus closely on climate change solutions, there has been increased issuance in other ESG-labeled debt (see Exhibit 37), where the financing terms are linked to environmental, social, or transition performance indicators (for example, investors may receive an increase in the bond's coupon if the company fails to meet certain targets). This category is occasionally also known as "green, social, sustainability+" (or GSS+).

After record issuance of sustainable debt in the previous year, 2022 witnessed a slowdown for the first time on record. This partly reflects higher borrowing costs for issuers overall, but some commentators have also noted increased skepticism around green-labeled instruments, coupled with a broader regulatory clampdown on greenwashing.

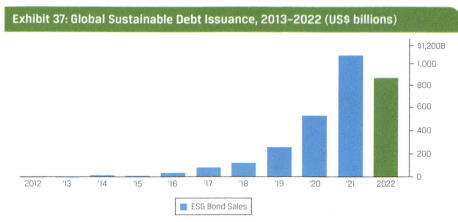

Exhibit 37: Global Sustainable Debt Issuance, 2013–2022 (US$ billions)

Note: Shows full-year issuance of green, social, sustainability, and sustainability-linked bonds across all currencies globally.
Source: Mutua (2023).

Exhibit 38 shows examples of such transactions, ranging from green bonds to sustainability or SDG-linked bonds and loans.

Exhibit 38: Examples of Sustainable Financing Transactions

Issuer and Type	Examples of Use of Proceeds
Green bond issued by Louisiana Local Government Environmental Facilities and Community Development Authority (2018)	Coastal flood defenses
Dutch sovereign green bond (2019)	Flood protection under its Delta Program
First dedicated resilience bond under the Climate Resilience Principles by European Bank for Reconstruction and Development (2019; Bennett 2019)	Climate-resilient infrastructure in Eastern Europe and North Africa
Chile's sovereign green bond (2019 and 2020)	Low-carbon transport (2019 and 2020), low-carbon building upgrades, and water infrastructure (2019)
Rizal Commercial Banking Corporation (RCBC), one of the Philippines' largest banks, issued the first ASEAN sustainability bond (2019; Rizal Commercial Banking Corporation 2019)	Energy, buildings, transport, urban and industrial energy efficiency, waste, water, and land use, affordable basic infrastructure, access to essential services, employment generation, affordable housing, and socioeconomic advancement and empowerment.
First SDG-linked bond, launched by the Italian energy producer Enel (2019)	General purpose proceeds, but with coupon linked to performance on environmental and social indicators
First SDG-linked sovereign bond, launched by the government of Mexico (International Institute for Sustainable Development 2020)	Categories must meet two criteria, prioritizing the location of vulnerable populations and the involvement of a UN organization for oversight.
Seychelles launched the world's first sovereign "blue bond" (World Bank 2018)	Finance the island's transition to sustainable fisheries and marine protection.

Opportunities Relating to Climate Change and Environmental Issues

Issuer and Type	Examples of Use of Proceeds
Starbucks issued a sustainability bond (2019), following its previous issues in 2016 and 2017.	Socioeconomic advancement and empowerment, access to essential services, green buildings
Thames Water became the United Kingdom's first corporation to issue a sustainability-linked revolving credit facility (£1.4 billion, 2018; Thames Water 2019)	Interest payments are linked to its Global Real Estate Sustainability Benchmark (GRESB) infrastructure score.
Solvay, a Belgium chemical company, issued a sustainability-linked loan (Solvay 2019).	Linked to GHG reduction target
Luxembourg was the first European country to launch its own Sustainability Bond Framework, in line with the European taxonomy for green financing (2020; Luxembourg Ministry of Finance 2020)	Combination of EU green projects and sustainability projects

Exhibit 39 shows an example of the "shades of green" methodology developed by the Center for International Climate Research (CICERO) to provide second-party opinions that determine how a green or sustainability bond aligns with a low-carbon resilient future.

Exhibit 39: Example of the "Shades of Green"

Dark Green	is allocated to projects and solutions that correspond to the long-term vision of a low-carbon and climate resilient future
Medium Green	is allocated to projects and solutions that represent significant steps towards the long-term vision but are not quite there yet
Light Green	is allocated to transition activies that do not lock in emissions. These projects reduce emissions or have other environmental benefits in the near term rather than representing low carbon and climate resilient long-term solutions
Yellow	is allocated to projects and solutions that do not explicitly contribute to the transition to a low carbon and climate resilient future. This category also includes activities with too little information to assess.
Red	is allocated to projects and solutions that have no role to play in a low-carbon and climate resilient future. These are the heaviest emitting assets, with the most potential for lock in of emissions and highest risk of stranded assets

Source: CICERO (2015).

There will continue to be a proliferation of green financial products in the marketplace. The important consideration to note is that the quality and transparency of environmental and climate-related data and disclosure will need to improve in order to avoid greenwashing. Efforts by the EU to harmonize and create a common language will be a significant development for green financial products.

> **CASE STUDIES**
>
> ### What Is "Green"?
>
> The Climate Bonds Taxonomy and sector-specific criteria have been scientifically developed to meet the object of the Paris Agreement of keeping global warming under 2°C (3.6°F), and the range of sector criteria keeps expanding, adding transition sectors in 2022. The organization has started focusing on transition and published a framework for delineating green and transition finance (Climate Bonds Initiative 2020). The Climate Bonds Standard v.4 extends the criteria beyond assets and debt to companies (by assessing their transition plans and milestones) and sustainability-linked debt key performance indicators in the context of science-based decarbonization pathways.[31]

In addition to labeled debt, green and sustainable finance includes debt from companies that operate in such sectors. The Climate Bonds Initiative (2018) provides regular information on the scale of the unlabeled climate bond market relative to the green bond market. Defined as entities that generate 75% or more of their revenues from green business lines, climate-aligned issuers had issued US$913 billion in outstanding bonds as of 30 September 2020, up from US$811 billion as of 30 June 2018.[32] LGX, the Luxembourg Green Exchange, launched a climate-aligned issuer segment to complement its existing green bond, sustainability, and social bond segment (Luxembourg Stock Exchange 2021b; the segment is described in Luxembourg Stock Exchange 2021a). From an investment perspective, as the supply of GSS+ products continues to grow, it is important to note that what may be considered green or sustainable for one investor may not be so for another. Therefore, investors need to have a clear framework by which to assess these assets. The following are some of the considerations:

- ▶ the eligibility of assets and criteria to meeting their sustainability-related objectives,
- ▶ the use of proceeds effectively allocated to eligible projects,
- ▶ the transparency and reporting requirements and key measures of impacts, and
- ▶ the existence of a clear firm-wide sustainability strategy for the issuer or borrower.

> **CASE STUDIES**
>
> ### GSS+ Market Transparency and Credibility
>
> The International Capital Markets Association (ICMA 2021) sets out voluntary guidelines called the Green Bond Principles (GBP), which were established in 2014 by a consortium of investment banks to promote the integrity of the green bond market by recommending transparency, disclosure, and reporting. As part of ensuring the integrity of the use of proceeds, external review is obtained through a second-party opinion provider that will track and report on whether proceeds are used as promised.
>
> In 2018, the Green Loan Principles (GLP) were established by the Loan Market Association (LMA) and the Asia Pacific Loan Market Association (APLMA). The four pillars of the GLP are as follows:

---

31 For more information, go to www.climatebonds.net/climate-bonds-standard-v4.
32 Data for 2020 provided by Climate Bonds Initiative in response to a data request by CFA UK.

1. There is clear green use of loan proceeds.
2. The project's sustainability objectives have been clearly evaluated and communicated to lenders.
3. Loan proceeds are strictly managed through project accounts.
4. Detailed and strict reporting is mandated (LMA 2018).

Further to the GLP, in 2019, the LMA, the APLMA, and the Loan Syndications and Trading Association launched the Sustainability-Linked Loan Principles (LMA 2019).

Blue Economy

The World Bank (2017) defines blue economy as the "sustainable use of ocean resources for economic growth, improved livelihoods, and jobs while preserving the health of ocean ecosystems." All other definitions of the term essentially relate to a broader perspective on sustainable economic and social activity associated with the world's oceans and coastal areas.

Examples of ocean-based industries representing the blue economy are shown in Exhibit 40.

Exhibit 40: Examples of Ocean-Based Industries Representing the Blue Economy

Aquaculture	Maritime transport
Fisheries	Desalination
Fish processing industry	Blue bioeconomy and biotechnology
Ports and warehousing	
Ship building and repair	Coastal and environmental protection
Coastal tourism	
Marine extraction	Offshore wind energy
	Ocean energy
	Deep water source cooling

The blue economy has more recently begun to gather more attention and has climbed the policy agenda. As covered previously, it is clear that the ocean is already under stress from overexploitation, pollution, declining biodiversity, and climate change.

Investors and policymakers are now beginning to recognize

- the growth prospects for the ocean economy,
- its capacity for future employment creation and innovation, and
- its role in addressing global challenges (OECD 2016).

There is growing scope for science and technology to manage the economic development of our seas and ocean responsibly. Marine ecosystems lie at the heart of many of the world's global challenges, providing food and medicine, new sources of clean energy and natural cooling systems, climate regulation, job creation, and inclusive growth. But safeguards are required to improve the health of these ecosystems to support an ever-growing use of marine resources. As we have seen in the section on biodiversity, the issue of accounting for natural capital remains a promising but underdeveloped area; this is also true in the case of the blue economy. The World Ocean Initiative has suggested the inclusion of *ocean accounting*—adding ocean-related services and assets—to national balance sheets (World Ocean Initiative 2020).

Based on a study by the OECD, three priority areas for action are presented:

1. approaches that produce win–win outcomes for ocean business and the ocean environment across a range of marine and maritime applications,
2. the creation of ocean-economy innovation networks, and
3. initiatives to improve the measurement of the ocean economy via satellite accounts of national accounting systems.

The OECD suggests that many ocean-based industries have the potential to outperform the growth of the global economy as a whole, both in terms of value added and employment. Projections suggest that the ocean economy could more than double its contribution to global value added, to over US$3 trillion, in addition to huge potential in employment growth by 2030.

CASE STUDIES

Blue Economy Development Framework

The World Bank and the European Commission (2019) have launched the Blue Economy Development Framework (BEDF), which is a new step in the area of international ocean governance. It helps (developing) coastal states transition to diverse and sustainable blue economies while building resilience to climate change.

The BEDF aims to create a roadmap that assists governments in

- preparing policy, fiscal, and administrative reforms,
- identifying value creation opportunities from blue economy sectors, and
- identifying strategic financial investments.

The BEDF intends to help coastal countries and regions develop evidence-based investment and policy reform plans for its coastal and ocean resources.

11 KEY FACTS

1. The range of environmental factors that have a material impact on investments are broad and far reaching. They include but are not limited to:
   a. a rapidly changing climate,
   b. natural resources (including water, biodiversity, land use and forestry, and marine resources), and
   c. pollution, waste, and the circular economy.
2. Driven by the emissions of greenhouse gases (GHGs) into the atmosphere, accelerating climate change carries significant risks to human health, economies, and ecosystems. Effective responses will involve a combination of climate mitigation and adaptation measures.
3. The Paris Agreement of 2015 was reached to mobilize a global response to the threat of climate change, amid growing concern reported by scientific experts. The agreement's long-term goal is to keep the increase in global average temperature well below 2°C (3.6°F) above pre-industrial levels and to limit the increase to 1.5°C (2.7°F).

Key Facts

4. Since the Paris Agreement was signed, a global consensus has begun to emerge that reaching net-zero carbon dioxide emissions around 2050 is required to turn its goals into reality. Governments, companies, and investors are increasingly adopting net-zero targets as a result, which cover 80% of the world's emissions and population, and 90% of the world's GDP is covered by a net-zero target.

5. Putting a price on carbon emissions is seen by many economists as one of the most effective methods of tackling climate change. Carbon markets have steadily grown around the world, but current levels of carbon pricing remain low.

6. Policymakers and investors must navigate both
   - the physical risks of climate change (associated with climate inaction) and
   - the transition risks of climate change (associated with climate action).

7. Environmental degradation, the depletion of natural resources, and the associated losses in biodiversity are presenting multiple, interrelated challenges for governments, the public, and businesses. Such issues as water scarcity, deforestation, degradation of land and oceans, unsustainable agricultural practices, waste, and pollution are increasingly impacting business and investment activities. To help alleviate some of these pressures, the model of the circular economy promotes a more efficient use of raw materials, coupled with increased reuse, recycling, and waste management.

8. Material environmental issues are factors that could have a significant impact—both positive and negative—on a company's business model and value drivers, such as operating and capital expenditure, revenue growth, margins, and risk. The material factors differ from one sector to another.

9. Environmental risks can be effectively integrated into company analysis and investment decision-making processes, using various financial tools and models. The types of risk analysis tools and associated metrics primarily depend on the asset classes and risk types financial institutions are exposed to. Similarly, the choice of approach depends on the type of direct and indirect exposure to an environmental risk factor. Investors have developed a combination of metrics, from carbon footprinting to forward-looking climate scenario analysis. Many solutions for reducing risk bring economic benefits; for example, increasing energy and material productivity (efficiency of use) and such renewables as wind and solar reduce production costs and often have a higher rate of economic return than continuing the use of inefficient technologies and fossil fuels.

10. There is an increasing number of policy initiatives at both the country and regional levels to promote the economic and financial mainstreaming of climate change and environmental factors in jurisdictions around the world. Requirements for climate-related disclosures (both mandatory and voluntary) are increasing in different parts of the entire investment chain, from the owners of capital (pension funds and insurance companies) to the beneficiaries (investee companies).

11. Coupled with regulatory tailwinds, technological innovation is giving rise to increasing investment opportunities from the provision of climate and environmental solutions, in areas including clean energy and mobility,

sustainable buildings, and advanced materials. For a majority of the world's population, unsubsidized clean energy represents the cheapest source of new electricity.
12. There is a growing number of specialized investment products, including low-carbon (active and index) funds and sustainability-linked debt, that aim to capture this opportunity set.

12. APPENDIX

This appendix provides further information on the TNFD LEAP and Disclosure Framework. This content will not be assessed. It is provided to give more insight to how organizations can disclose their nature-related risks and opportunities.

TNFD has developed the LEAP (locate, evaluate, assess, prepare) assessment framework to help companies and financial institutions locate their interface with nature, understand and evaluate their dependence and impacts on nature, assess material risks and opportunities for their operations, and prepare responses (e.g., business strategy, monitoring metrics, risk management approach, resource allocation) and nature-related disclosures (see Exhibit 41).

The assessment approach recognizes that nature issues are specific to the location, sector, and biome—hence the location entry point for corporates. However, it also recognizes that financial institutions will not have the same access to location and biome information. Thus, the analytical entry point for them differs, with greater reliance placed on sectors, geography, and asset classes, at least initially, to facilitate portfolio-level aggregation.

As with climate, the expectation is that direct operations and certain aspects of supply chains will be easier to assess, but the goal is to assess issues along the full value chain and in activities financed by Financial Institutions.

Appendix

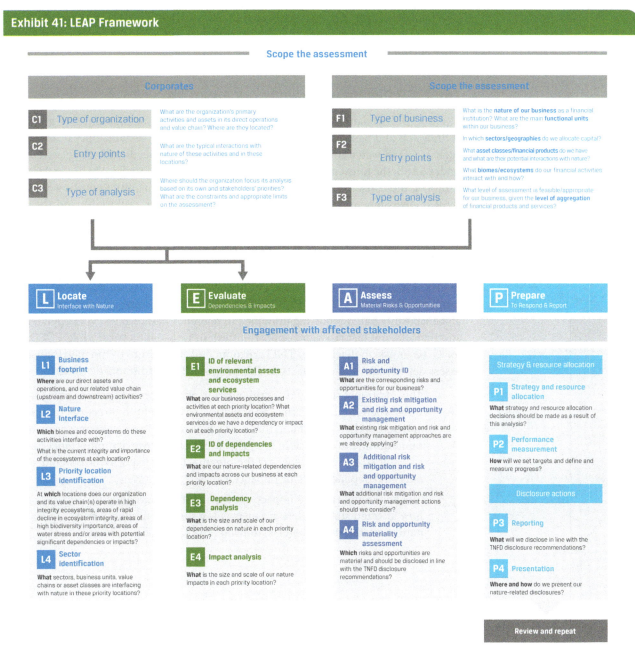

Source: TNFD (2023).

One of the lessons from TCFD implementation has been that data collection and undertaking scenario analysis are challenging, particularly for smaller organizations. So in 2022, TNFD, working with data and analytics providers, launched the Nature-Related Data Catalyst to coordinate data provision and to close knowledge and access gaps. And in 2023, it launched a beta version of an online searchable Tools Catalogue that provides an overview of tools that organizations can use to apply each phase of the LEAP approach.[33] It has also developed a modular approach to the use of scenarios,

---

[33] For more information, go to https://framework.tnfd.global/tools-platforms/.

which includes a set of predefined scenarios as a base to help organizations get started in their use of scenarios and an accompanying set of practical tools, templates, and general guidance.

The TNFD Disclosure Framework Approach

The TNFD disclosure framework builds on TCFD recommendations and guidance. It draws on and feeds into various nature-, climate-, and sustainability frameworks, such as CDSB water and biodiversity guidance, sector-specific nature-related topics under SASB, the forest and water CDP questionnaires, GRI topics, the Natural Capital Protocol, the consultation drafts of the European Sustainability Reporting Standard (ESRS) environmental standards (e.g., biodiversity, water, pollution), and the IFRS sustainability standards released by ISSB, as well as the work of IPBES and other biodiversity-focused organizations.

The consultation draft of the TNFD disclosure framework retains the four pillars of TCFD (governance, strategy, risk management, and metrics and targets), although the third is extended to cover risk and impact management (see Exhibit 42). TNFD proposes to carry over the 11 TCFD-recommended disclosures to provide consistency and enable integrated reporting (modified to reference nature and cover dependencies and impacts, not just risks and opportunities). In terms of metrics, while TCFD asks for GHG emission disclosure, TNFD recommends disclosure of the metrics used to assess dependencies and impacts. It also proposes two additional disclosures:

- ▶ The additional strategy recommendation asks for an assessment of locations where there are assets or activities, covering both direct operation and across the value chain, that are in high-integrity ecosystems; areas of rapid decline in ecosystem integrity; areas of biodiversity importance; areas of water stress; or areas where the organization is likely to have significant potential dependencies or impacts.

- ▶ The additional risk and impact management recommendation focuses on how affected stakeholders are engaged in the assessment of and response to nature-related dependencies, impacts, risks, and opportunities.

Appendix

Exhibit 42: TNFD Disclosure Framework

TCFD-Aligned Disclosure Recommendations

Governance	Strategy	Risk & Impact Management	Metrics & Targets
Disclose the organisation's governance around nature-related dependencies, impacts, risks and opportunities.	Disclose the actual and potential impacts of nature-related dependencies, impacts, risks and opportunities on the organisation's businesses, strategy, and financial planning where such information is material.	Disclose how the organisation identifies, assesses and manages nature-related dependencies, impacts, risks and opportunities.	Disclose the metrics and targets used to assess and manage relevant nature-related dependencies, impacts, risks and opportunities where such information is material.
Recommended Disclosures	**Recommended Disclosures**	**Recommended Disclosures**	**Recommended Disclosures**
Describe the board's oversight of nature-related dependencies, impacts, risks and opportunities.	Describe the nature-related dependencies, impacts, risks and opportunities the organisation has identified over the short, medium, and long term.	(i) Describe the organisation's processes for identifying and assessing nature-related dependencies, impacts, risks and opportunities in its direct operations. (ii) Describe the organizations approach to identifying nature-related dependencies, impacts, risks and opportunities in its upstream and downstream value chain(s) and financed activities and assets for assessment.	Disclose the metrics used by the organisation to assess and manage material nature-related risks and opportunities in line with its strategy and risk management process.
Describe management's role in assessing and managing nature-related dependencies, impacts, risks and opportunities.	Describe the effect nature-related risks and opportunities have had and may have on the organisation's businesses, strategy, and financial planning.	Describe the organisation's processes for managing nature-related dependencies, impacts, risks and opportunities and actions taken in light of these processes.	Disclose the metrics used by the organisation to assess and manage dependencies and impacts on nature.
	Describe the resilience of the organisation's strategy to nature-related risks and opportunities, taking into consideration different scenarios.	Describe how processes for identifying, assessing and managing nature-related risks are integrated into the organisation's overall risk management.	Describe the targets and goals used by the organisation to manage nature-related dependencies, impacts, risks and opportunities and its performance against these.

Recommended Disclosures	Recommended Disclosures	Recommended Disclosures	Recommended Disclosures
	Disclose the locations where there are assets and/or activities in the organisation's direct operations, and upstream and/or downstream financed, where relevant, that are in: high integrity ecosystems; and/or areas of rapid decline in ecosystem integrity; and/or areas of high biodiversity importance; and/or areas of water stress; and/or areas where the organisation is likely to have significant potential dependencies and/or impacts.	Describe how affected stakeholders are engaged by the organisation in its assessment of, and in response to, nature-related dependencies, impacts, risks and opportunities.	

Source: TNFD (2023).

As with other sustainability disclosure frameworks, the expectation is that reporting will feature a combination of qualitative and quantitative disclosures. The guidance proposes a set of general and sector-specific core metrics across dependencies, impacts, risks, opportunities, and responses, with a broader list of proposed additional metrics linked to specific considerations, such as the type of business, the sector, the biome, or the location. TNFD has already published draft disclosure metrics for financial institutions, agriculture and food, and tropical forests, but is expected to publish further sector and biome guidance in 2023.

As with TCFD, TNFD proposes the use of targets to track progress. It suggests alignment with the Science-Based Targets Network target-setting approach—that is, embedding the ambition for science-based nature targets—as well as with global policy goals, particularly the Global Biodiversity Framework, with the additional guidance that entities should consider the possible trade-offs between actions and targets for climate and nature and integrate disclosures across climate and nature considerations.

However, unlike some other frameworks, it provides flexibility for the different materiality approaches of report preparers, capital providers, and market regulators. Instead, the TNFD guidance encourages reporting entities to consider and disclose the following:

▶ *"how it defines the threshold to determine which topics are material for reporting; whether it has tested its selection of material topics with investors and other stakeholders; the sources, evidence, and methods used to justify the nature-related material information to be disclosed; as well as any assumptions and subjective judgements made;*

▶ *the stakeholders and experts who have informed the materiality determination process;*

▶ *any limitations or exclusions (these could include the time periods considered to assess the effects of decisions and actions or the exclusion of some categories of business relationships from certain parts of the value chain when identifying material topics); and*

▶ *how it has prioritised the effects of its decisions and actions for reporting."*

Finally, there is a social dimension. TNFD has developed initial guidance on stakeholder engagement given the location-specific focus of nature-related assessment and response actions. Together with the *International Union for Conservation of Nature*

(IUCN), it engaged with a range of representatives of indigenous peoples and local communities "to leverage their knowledge and provide their voice and perspective to help design and develop this aspect of the TNFD framework" (TNFD 2023).

FURTHER READING

- Temperature, Alignment Tools Raynaud, Stephane Voisin Julie, Peter Tankov, Hilke Anuschka, and Alice Pauthie. 2020. "The Alignment Cookbook: A Technical Review of Methodologies Assessing a Portfolio's Alignment with Low-Carbon Trajectories or Temperature Goal." https://gsf.institutlouisbachelier.org/publication/the-alignment-cookbook-a-technical-review-of-methodologies-assessing-a-portfolios-alignment-with-low-carbon-trajectories-or-temperature-goal/.

Climate Scenario Analysis

- ETH Zurich. 2020. "Taming the Green Swan: How to Improve Climate-Related Financial Risk Assessments." www.research-collection.ethz.ch/handle/20.500.11850/428321.
- Principles for Responsible Investment 2020. "Pathways to Net Zero: Scenario Architecture for Strategic Resilience Testing and Planning." www.unpri.org/climate-change/pathways-to-net-zero-scenario-architecture-for-strategic-resilience-testing-and-planning/6006.article.
- Task Force on Climate-Related Financial Disclosures. 2020. "Guidance on Scenario Analysis for Non-Financial Companies." www.fsb.org/wp-content/uploads/P291020-3.pdf.
- United Nations. "COP 26 Together for Our Planet." www.un.org/en/climatechange/cop26.

Green and ESG-Related Products

- Climate Bonds Initiative. 2022. "Sustainable Debt Global State of the Market." www.climatebonds.net/resources/reports/global-state-market-report-2022

REFERENCES

IPCC 2022a. "Climate Change 2022: Impacts, Adaptation and Vulnerability: Summary for Policymakers." www.ipcc.ch/report/ar6/wg2/downloads/report/IPCC_AR6_WGII_SummaryForPolicymakers.pdf.

C40 Cities and AXA 2019. "Understanding Infrastructure Interdependencies in Cities" (27 November). www.axa.com/en/press/publications/understanding-infrastructure-interdependencies-in-cities.

African Development Bank Asian Development Bank Asian Infrastructure Investment Bank European Bank for Reconstruction and Development European Investment Bank Inter American Development Bank International Development Finance Club Islamic Development Bank 2019. "A Framework and Principles for Climate Resilience Metrics in Financing Operations" (December). https://publications.iadb.org/en/framework-and-principles-climate-resilience-metrics-financing-operations.

Arctic Monitoring and Assessment Programme 2021. "Arctic Climate Change Update 2021: Key Trends and Impacts: Summary for Policy-Makers." www.amap.no/documents/download/6759/inline.

BBC 2020. "Russian Arctic Oil Spill Pollutes Big Lake Near Norilsk" (9 June). www.bbc.co.uk/news/world-europe-52977740.

BHP 2020. "BHP Annual Report 2020." www.bhp.com/-/media/documents/investors/annual-reports/2020/200915_bhpannualreport2020.pdf.

BloombergNEF 2022a. "Cost of New Renewables Temporarily Rises as Inflation Starts to Bite" (30 June). https://about.bnef.com/blog/cost-of-new-renewables-temporarily-rises-as-inflation-starts-to-bite/.

Byrne, M. 2020. "Guest Post: Why Does Land Warm Up Faster Than the Oceans?" *Carbon Brief* (1 September). www.carbonbrief.org/guest-post-why-does-land-warm-up-faster-than-the-oceans.

Climate Bonds Initiative 2019. "Climate Resilience Principles." www.climatebonds.net/climate-resilience-principles.

Delevingne, Lindsay, Will Glazener, Liesbet Grégoir, Kimberly Henderson. 2020. "Climate Risk and Decarbonization: What Every Mining CEO Needs to Know." McKinsey (28 January). www.mckinsey.com/business-functions/sustainability/our-insights/climate-risk-and-decarbonization-what-every-mining-ceo-needs-to-know#.

Forster, Piers, Zeke Hausfather, Gabi Hegerl, Steven Sherwood, Kyle Armour. 2020. "Guest Post: Why Low-End 'Climate Sensitivity' Can Now Be Ruled Out." *Carbon Brief* (22 July). www.carbonbrief.org/guest-post-why-low-end-climate-sensitivity-can-now-be-ruled-out/.

Global Commission on Adaptation 2019. "Adapt Now: A Global Call for Leadership on Climate Resilience." https://gca.org/wp-content/uploads/2019/09/GlobalCommission_Report_FINAL.pdf.

Grantham, J. 2018. "The Race of Our Lives Revisited." White paper, GMO (8 August). www.gmo.com/europe/research-library/the-race-of-our-lives-revisited/.

Hausfather, Z. 2019. "Explainer: The High-Emissions 'RCP8.5' Global Warming Scenario." *Carbon Brief* (21 August). www.carbonbrief.org/explainer-the-high-emissions-rcp8-5-global-warming-scenario/.

Hausfather, Z. 2021. "Explainer: Will Global Warming 'Stop' As Soon as Net-Zero Emissions Are Reached?" Carbon Brief (29 April). www.carbonbrief.org/explainer-will-global-warming-stop-as-soon-as-net-zero-emissions-are-reached/.

Hjort, Jan, Olli Karjalainen, Juha Aalto, Sebastian Westermann, Vladimir E. Romanovsky, Frederick E. Nelson, Bernd Etzelmüller, Miska Luoto. 2018. "Degrading Permafrost Puts Arctic Infrastructure at Risk by Mid-Century." Nature Communications 9. www.nature.com/articles/s41467-018-07557-410.1038/s41467-018-07557-4

References

Institute for European Environmental Policy 2020. "More Than Half of All CO_2 Emissions since 1751 Emitted in the Last 30 Years" (29 April). https://ieep.eu/news/more-than-half-of-all-co2-emissions-since-1751-emitted-in-the-last-30-years.

International Energy Agency 2020b. "Investment Estimates for 2020 Continue to Point to a Record Slump in Spending" (23 October). www.iea.org/articles/investment-estimates-for-2020-continue-to-point-to-a-record-slump-in-spending.

International Energy Agency 2022a. "Global Methane Tracker 2022." www.iea.org/reports/global-methane-tracker-2022/methane-and-climate-change.

International Energy Agency 2022b. "World Energy Outlook 2022: Executive Summary." www.iea.org/reports/world-energy-outlook-2022/executive-summary.

IPCC 2018. "Special Report: Global Warming of 1.5°C." www.ipcc.ch/sr15/.

IPCC 2021. "Climate Change 2021: The Physical Science Basis" (6 August). www.ipcc.ch/report/ar6/wg1/downloads/report/IPCC_AR6_WGI_FullReport_small.pdf.

IPCC 2022b. "Climate Change 2022: Mitigation of Climate Change: Summary for Policymakers." https://ccli.ubc.ca/wp-content/uploads/2022/04/IPCC_AR6_WGIII_SummaryForPolicymakers.pdf.

IPCC 2023a. "Climate Change 2022: Mitigation of Climate Change Summary for Policymakers." www.ipcc.ch/report/ar6/wg3/downloads/report/IPCC_AR6_WGIII_SummaryForPolicymakers.pdf.

IPCC 2023b. "Synthesis Report of the IPCC Sixth Assessment Report (AR6)." www.ipcc.ch/report/sixth-assessment-report-cycle

Jamasmie, C. 2020. "BHP to Supply Water for Escondida Mine from Desalination Plant Only." Mining.com (4 February). www.mining.com/bhp-to-supply-water-for-escondida-mine-from-desalination-plant-only/.

Jeswani, Harish K., Andrew Chilvers, Adisa Azapagic. 2020. "Environmental Sustainability of Biofuels: A Review." Proceedings - Royal Society. Mathematical, Physical and Engineering Sciences476 (November). 10.1098/rspa.2020.0351

Jing, L. 2019. "Inside China's Leading 'Sponge City': Wuhan's War with Water." Guardian (23 January). www.theguardian.com/cities/2019/jan/23/inside-chinas-leading-sponge-city-wuhans-war-with-water.

Kalanki, Ankit, Sneha Sachar. 2018. "Revolutionizing the Air Conditioner Industry to Solve the Cooling Challenge." Rocky Mountain Institute (12 November). https://rmi.org/revolutionizing-the-air-conditioner/.

Moomaw, William R.,, G. L. Chmura,, Gillian T. Davies, C. M. Finlayson, B. A. Middleton, Susan M. Natali, J. E. Perry, N. Roulet, Ariana E. Sutton-Grier. 2018. "Wetlands in a Changing Climate: Science, Policy and Management." Wetlands 38: 183–205. https://link.springer.com/article/10.1007/s13157-018-1023-8.

Moomaw, William R., Susan A. Masino, Edward K. Faison. 2019. "Intact Forests in the United States: Proforestation Mitigates Climate Change and Serves the Greatest Good." Frontiers in Forests and Global Change (11 June). www.frontiersin.org/articles/10.3389/ffgc.2019.00027/full. 10.3389/ffgc.2019.00027

Nordhaus, W. D. 2011. "The Economics of Tail Events with an Application to Climate Change." Review of Environmental Economics and Policy5 (Summer): 240–57. www.journals.uchicago.edu/doi/10.1093/reep/rer00410.1093/reep/rer004

Norman, Joseph, Rupert Read, Yaneer Bar-Yam, Nassim Nicholas Taleb. 2015. "Climate Models and Precautionary Measures." Issues in Science and Technology (Summer). https://necsi.edu/climate-models-and-precautionary-measures.

Raworth, K. 2017. "Meet the Doughnut: The New Economic Model That Could Help End Inequality." World Economic Forum (28 April). www.weforum.org/agenda/2017/04/the-new-economic-model-that-could-end-inequality-doughnut/.

Robbins, L. 1932. An Essay on the Nature and Significance of Economic Science. London: Macmillan.

Saravanan, R. 2022. The Climate Demon. Cambridge, UK: Cambridge University Press.

Sterman, John, William Moomaw, Juliette N. Rooney-Varga, Lori Siegel. 2022. "Does Burning Wood Help or Harm the Climate?" *Bulletin of the Atomic Scientists* (10 May). https://thebulletin.org/premium/2022-05/does-wood-bioenergy-help-or-harm-the-climate/.

Stockholm Resilience Centre 2022. "Planetary Boundaries." www.stockholmresilience.org/research/planetary-boundaries.html.

Suarez, I. 2020. "5 Strategies That Achieve Climate Mitigation and Adaptation Simultaneously." World Resources Institute (10 February). www.wri.org/blog/2020/02/climate-change-mitigation-adaptation-strategies.

UNEP 2019. "Cut Global Emissions by 7.6 Percent Every Year for Next Decade to Meet 1.5°C Paris Target—UN Report." Press release (26 November). www.unep.org/news-and-stories/press-release/cut-global-emissions-76-percent-every-year-next-decade-meet-15degc.

UNEP 2021. "Emissions Gap Report 2021." www.unenvironment.org/emissions-gap-report-2021.

UNEP 2022b. "Emissions Gap Report 2022." www.unenvironment.org/emissions-gap-report-2022.

UNFCCC 1992. "Article 2: Objective." https://unfccc.int/resource/ccsites/zimbab/conven/text/art02.htm.

United Nations 1987. "Report of the World Commission on Environment and Development: Our Common Future." https://sustainabledevelopment.un.org/content/documents/5987our-common-future.pdf.

US Environmental Protection Agency 2021. "Climate Change Indicators: Greenhouse Gases." www.epa.gov/climate-indicators/greenhouse-gases.

Wang, Seaver, Adrianna Foster, Elizabeth A. Lenz, John D. Kessler, Julienne C. Stroeve, Liana O. Anderson, Merritt Turetsky. 2023. "Mechanisms and Impacts of Earth System Tipping Elements." Reviews of Geophysics61 (1). https://agupubs.onlinelibrary.wiley.com/doi/10.1029/2021RG00075710.1029/2021RG000757

Weitzman, M. L. 2011. "Fat-Tailed Uncertainty in the Economics of Catastrophic Climate Change." Review of Environmental Economics and Policy5 (Summer): 275–92. https://scholar.harvard.edu/files/weitzman/files/fattaileduncertaintyeconomics.pdf10.1093/reep/rer006

Woetzel, Jonathan, Dickon Pinner, Hamid Samandari, Hauke Engel, Mekala Krishnan, Brodie Boland, Carter Powis. 2020. "Climate Risk and Response: Physical Hazards and Socioeconomic Impacts." McKinsey Global Institute (16 January). www.mckinsey.com/business-functions/sustainability/our-insights/climate-risk-and-response-physical-hazards-and-socioeconomic-impacts?sid=3046547320.

World Bank 2018. "Turn Down the Heat: Climate Extremes, Regional Impacts, and the Case for Resilience." www.worldbank.org/en/topic/climatechange/publication/turn-down-the-heat.

World Bank 2019. "Action Plan on Climate Change Adaptation and Resilience: Managing Risks for a More Resilient Future." http://documents1.worldbank.org/curated/en/519821547481031999/The-World-Bank-Groups-Action-Plan-on-Climate-Change-Adaptation-and-Resilience-Managing-Risks-for-a-More-Resilient-Future.pdf.

World Bank 2022. "State and Trends of Carbon Pricing 2022." https://openknowledge.worldbank.org/entities/publication/a1abead2-de91-5992-bb7a-73d8aaaf767f.

BBC 2014. "Court in China Issues Record Pollution Fine" (31 December). www.bbc.co.uk/news/world-asia-china-30640385.

Bond, K. 2020. "The Future's Not in Plastics: Why Plastics Demand Won't Rescue the Oil Sector." Carbon Tracker (4 September). https://carbontracker.org/reports/the-futures-not-in-plastics/.

CDP and Global Canopy 2017. "Financial Institution Guidance: Soft Commodity Company Strategy." www.cdp.net/en/reports/downloads/2913.

Citi, G. P. S. 2021. "Biodiversity: The Ecosystem at the Heart of Business" (July). www.citifirst.com.hk/home/upload/citi_research/Biodiversity.pdf.

References

Cordell, D., J.-O. Drangerta, S. White. 2009. "The Story of Phosphorus: Global Food Security and Food for Thought." Global Environmental Change19 (May): 292–305. 10.1016/j.gloenvcha.2008.10.009

Costanza, Robert, Rudolf de Groot, Paul Sutton, Sander van der Ploeg, Sharolyn J. Anderson, Ida Kubiszewski, Stephen Farber, R. Kerry Turner. 2014. "Changes in the Value of Ecosystem Services." Global Environmental Change26 (May): 152–58. www.sciencedirect.com/science/article/pii/S095937801400068510.1016/j.gloenvcha.2014.04.002

Ellen MacArthur Foundation 2019a. "Completing the Picture: How the Circular Economy Tackles Climate Change." www.ellenmacarthurfoundation.org/assets/downloads/Completing_The_Picture_How_The_Circular_Economy-_Tackles_Climate_Change_V3_26_September.pdf.

Ellen MacArthur Foundation 2019b. "What Is a Circular Economy?" www.ellenmacarthurfoundation.org/circular-economy/concept.

European Environment Agency 2021. "Growth without Economic Growth." www.eea.europa.eu/publications/growth-without-economic-growth/growth-without-economic-growth.

Global Canopy 2021. "Time for Change: Delivering Deforestation-Free Supply Chains." https://forest500.org/publications/time-change-delivering-deforestation-free-supply-chains.

Global Carbon Project 2022. "Global Carbon Budget 2021."

Global Forest Watch 2020. "Global Deforestation Rates and Statistics by Country." www.globalforestwatch.org/dashboards/global/.

Government of the Netherlands 2017. "From a Linear to a Circular Economy." www.government.nl/topics/circular-economy/from-a-linear-to-a-circular-economy.

Green, M. 2021. "Fossil Fuel Pollution Causes One in Five Premature Deaths Globally: Study." Reuters (9 February). www.reuters.com/article/us-health-pollution-fossil/fossil-fuel-pollution-causes-one-in-five-premature-deaths-globally-study-idUSKBN2A90UB.

Haberl, H., D. Wiedenhofer, D. Virag, G. Kalt, B. Plank, P. Brockway, T. Fishman. 2020. "A Systematic Review of the Evidence on Decoupling of GDP, Resource Use and GHG Emissions, Part II: Synthesizing the Insights." Environmental Research Letters15 (6). www.researchgate.net/publication/340243504_A_systematic_review_of_the_evidence_on_decoupling_of_GDP_resource_use_and_GHG_emissions_part_II_Synthesizing_the_insights10.1088/1748-9326/ab842a

INTERPOL 2020. "Emerging Criminal Trends in the Global Plastic Waste Market since January 2018" (27 August). www.interpol.int/en/News-and-Events/News/2020/INTERPOL-report-alerts-to-sharp-rise-in-plastic-waste-crime.

IPBES 2019. "The Global Assessment Report on Biodiversity and Ecosystem Services: Summary for Policymakers." https://ipbes.net/sites/default/files/inline/files/ipbes_global_assessment_report_summary_for_policymakers.pdf.

IPCC 2019. "Special Report on the Ocean and Cryosphere in a Changing Climate." www.ipcc.ch/srocc/.

IPCC 2022a. "Climate Change 2022: Impacts, Adaptation and Vulnerability: Summary for Policymakers."www.ipcc.ch/report/ar6/wg2.

IPCC 2023a. "Climate Change 2022: Mitigation of Climate Change Summary for Policymakers." www.ipcc.ch/report/ar6/wg3/downloads/report/IPCC_AR6_WGIII_SummaryForPolicymakers.pdf.

Jack, B. Kelsey, Carolyn Kousky, Katharine R. E. Sims. 2008. "Designing Payments for Ecosystem Services: Lessons from Previous Experience with Incentive-Based Mechanisms." Proceedings of the National Academy of Sciences 105 (15 July): 9465–70. www.pnas.org/doi/10.1073/pnas.0705503104.

Juffe-Bignoli, D. 2014. "Biodiversity for Business: A Guide to Using Knowledge Products Delivered through IUCN." International Union for Conservation of Nature. https://portals.iucn.org/library/node/43361.

Landrigan, P. J. 2018. "The Lancet Commission on Pollution and Health." Lancet Commissions 391 (3 February): 462–512. .

Law, Beverly E., William R. Moomaw, Tara W. Hudiburg, William H. Schlesinger, John D. Sterman, George M. Woodwell. 2022. "Creating Strategic Reserves to Protect Forest Carbon." Land (Basel)11 (May). www.mdpi.com/2073-445X/11/5/721

Moomaw, William, Sara Blankenship. 2014. "Charting a New Course for the Oceans" (April). https://sites.tufts.edu/gdae/files/2019/10/MoomawFisheries_2014.pdf.

National Ocean Service 2021. "How Much Oxygen Comes from the Ocean?" https://oceanservice.noaa.gov/facts/ocean-oxygen.html.

New Plastics Economy 2017. "A Vision of a Circular Economy for Plastic." https://oceanfdn.org/wp-content/uploads/2010/08/npec-vision-of-a-circular-economy-for-plastic.pdf.

Nunez, C. 2019. "Deforestation Explained." National Geographic. www.nationalgeographic.com/environment/global-warming/deforestation/.

Oberle, B., S. Bringezu, S. Hatfield-Dodds, S. Hellweg. 2019. "ETH Zurich UN Global Resources Outlook 2019: Natural Resources for the Future We Want" (March). www.researchgate.net/publication/331683904_UN_Global_Resources_Outlook_2019_Natural_Resources_for_the_Future_We_Want.

OECD 2019. "Biodiversity: Finance and the Economic and Business Case for Action." www.oecd.org/environment/resources/biodiversity/G7-report-Biodiversity-Finance-and-the-Economic-and-Business-Case-for-Action.pdf.

OECD 2020. "Biodiversity and the Economic Response to COVID-19: Ensuring a Green and Resilient Recovery" (28 September). www.oecd.org/coronavirus/policy-responses/biodiversity-and-the-economic-response-to-covid-19-ensuring-a-green-and-resilient-recovery-d98b5a09/.

Paun, A. 2020. "Biodiversity in the Balance." HSBC (17 June).

PBL Netherlands Environmental Assessment Agency 2020. "Indebted to Nature. Exploring Biodiversity Risks for the Dutch Financial Sector" (19 June). www.pbl.nl/en/publications/indebted-to-nature.

Ranganathan, Janet, Richard Waite, Tim Searchinger, Craig Hanson. 2018. "How to Sustainably Feed 10 Billion People by 2050, in 21 Charts." World Resources Institute (5 December). www.wri.org/blog/2018/12/how-sustainably-feed-10-billion-people-2050-21-charts.

Ritchie, H. 2021. "Many Countries Have Decoupled Economic Growth from CO_2 Emissions, Even If We Take Offshored Production into Account." *Our World in Data* (1 December). https://ourworldindata.org/co2-gdp-decoupling.

Snowden, S. 2020. "Ground-Breaking Method to Make Graphene from Garbage Is Modern-Day Alchemy." Forbes (24 July). www.forbes.com/sites/scottsnowden/2020/07/24/ground-breaking-method-to-make-graphene-from-garbage-is-modern-day-alchemy/?sh=364742ed50d7#1d7e.

TerraCycle 2021. "Recycle Everything with TerraCycle."

Tracker, Planet. 2020b. "Investors Face Financial Risk as Salmon Industry Approaches Ecological Brink, Says Planet Tracker" (27 May). https://planet-tracker.org/investors-face-financial-risk-as-salmon-industry-approaches-ecological-brink-says-planet-tracker/.

Tracker, Planet. 2020c. "Traceability Could Double the EBIT Margin of Seafood Processors While Reducing Investor Risk, Says Planet Tracker" (13 October). https://planet-tracker.org/traceability-could-double-the-ebit-margin-of-seafood-processors-while-reducing-investor-risk-says-planet-tracker/.

Treasury, H. M. 2021. "Final Report—The Economics of Biodiversity: The Dasgupta Review" (2 February). www.gov.uk/government/publications/final-report-the-economics-of-biodiversity-the-dasgupta-review.

UN-Water 2019. "The United Nations World Water Development Report 2019: Leaving No One Behind." www.unwater.org/publications/world-water-development-report-2019/.

UNEP 2022c. "Historic Day in the Campaign to Beat Plastic Pollution: Nations Commit to Develop a Legally Binding Agreement" (2 March). www.unep.org/news-and-stories/press-release/historic-day-campaign-beat-plastic-pollution-nations-commit-develop.

References

UNESCO World Water Assessment Programme 2018. "The United Nations World Water Development Report 2018: Nature-Based Solutions for Water." https://unesdoc.unesco.org/ark:/48223/pf0000261424.

United Nations 1992. "Convention on Biological Diversity." www.cbd.int/doc/legal/cbd-en.pdf.

United Nations Department of Economic and Social Affairs 2021. "6: Ensure Availability and Sustainable Management of Water and Sanitation for All." https://sdgs.un.org/goals/goal6.

US Attorney's Office 2020. "United States Reaches Agreement to Protect New Orleans Waterways and Lake Pontchartrain." Eastern District of Louisiana (29 September). www.justice.gov/usao-edla/pr/united-states-reaches-agreement-protect-new-orleans-waterways-and-lake-pontchartrain.

Vohra, Karn, Alina Vodonos, Joel Schwartz, Eloise A. Marais, Melissa P. Sulprizio, Loretta J. Mickley. 2021. "Global Mortality from Outdoor Fine Particle Pollution Generated by Fossil Fuel Combustion: Results from GEOS-Chem." Environmental Research195 (April). www.sciencedirect.com/science/article/abs/pii/S001393512100048710.1016/j.envres.2021.110754

Waldron, A., D. C. Miller, D. Redding, A. Mooers, T. S. Kuhn, N. Nibbelink, J. T. Roberts, J. A. Tobias, J. L. Gittleman. 2017. "Reductions in Global Biodiversity Loss Predicted from Conservation Spending." *Nature* 551 (25 October): 364–67. www.nature.com/articles/nature24295. 10.1038/nature24295

WHO 2020. "Air Pollution." www.who.int/health-topics/air-pollution.

Wiedmann, T., M. Lenzen, L. T. Keyßer, J. K. Steinberger. 2020. "Scientists' Warning on Affluence." *Nature Communications* 11 (19 June). www.nature.com/articles/s41467-020-16941-y. 10.1038/s41467-020-16941-y

World Bank 2017. "What Is the Blue Economy?" (6 June). www.worldbank.org/en/news/infographic/2017/06/06/blue-economy.

World Economic Forum 2019. "Shaping the Future of Global Public Goods." www.weforum.org/system-initiatives/shaping-the-future-of-environment-and-natural-resource-security.

World Forum on Natural Capital 2021. "What Is Natural Capital?" https://naturalcapitalforum.com/about/.

WWF 2020. "Global Futures: Assessing the Global Economic Impacts of Environmental Change to Support Policy-Making." www.wwf.org.uk/sites/default/files/2020-02/GlobalFutures_SummaryReport.pdf.

WWF 2022. "The Living Planet Report 2022." www.wwf.org.uk/living-planet-report

Banerjee, Chandan, Lucia Bevere, Thierry Corti, Roman Lechner. 2023. "A Perfect Storm: Natural Catastrophes and Inflation in 2022." Swiss Re (22 March). www.swissre.com/institute/research/sigma-research/sigma-2023-01.html.

Bank of England 2021. "Climate Change: What Are the Risks to Financial Stability?" www.bankofengland.co.uk/knowledgebank/climate-change-what-are-the-risks-to-financial-stability.

Bolton, P., M. Despres, L. A. Pereira Da Silva, F. Samama, R. Svartzman. 2020. "The Green Swan: Central Banking and Financial Stability in the Age of Climate Change." Bank for International Settlements (January). www.bis.org/publ/othp31.pdf.

Breeden, S. 2019. "Avoiding the Storm: Climate Change and the Financial System." Speech, Bank of England (15 April). www.bankofengland.co.uk/-/media/boe/files/speech/2019/avoiding-the-storm-climate-change-and-the-financial-system-speech-by-sarah-breeden.pdf.

CDP 2020a. "Changing the Chain: Global Supply Chain Report 2019/20." www.cdp.net/en/research/global-reports/changing-the-chain.

CDP 2020b. "Global Supply Chain Report 2019." www.cdp.net/en/research/global-reports/global-supply-chain-report-2019.

European Commission 2019a. "Guidelines on Reporting Climate-Related Information." https://ec.europa.eu/finance/docs/policy/190618-climate-related-information-reporting-guidelines_en.pdf.

European Commission 2019b. "Report from the Commission to the European Parliament, the Council, the European Economic and Social Committee and the Committee of the Regions on the Implementation of the Circular Economy Action Plan." https://eur-lex.europa.eu/legal-content/EN/TXT/PDF/?uri=CELEX:52019DC0190&from=EN.

Finance, Trase. 2021. "The Business Case for Financial Due Diligence on Deforestation Risks" (8 March). https://insights.trase.earth/insights/the-business-case-for-financial-due-diligence-of-deforestation-risks.

Forest 500 2021. "Time for Change: Delivering Deforestation-Free Supply Chains." https://forest500.org/publications/time-change-delivering-deforestation-free-supply-chains.

Freitas, G., V. Andrade. 2020. "Brazil Ore, Power Giants Excluded from Norway's Wealth Fund." Bloomberg (13 May). www.bloomberg.com/news/articles/2020-05-13/brazil-iron-ore-power-giants-excluded-from-norway-s-wealth-fund.

Friedlingstein, Pierre. 2022. "Global Carbon Budget 2021." Earth System Science Data 14 (26 April): 1917–2005. https://essd.copernicus.org/articles/14/1917/2022/. 10.5194/essd-14-1917-2022

Global Compact, U. N. 2015. Supply Chain Sustainability: A Practical Guide for Continuous Improvement. 2nd ed., www.unglobalcompact.org/docs/issues_doc/supply_chain/SupplyChainRep_spread.pdf.

Global Reporting Initiative 2007. "Biodiversity: A GRI Reporting Resource."

Gold, R. 2019. "PG&E: The First Climate-Change Bankruptcy, Probably Not the Last." *Wall Street Journal* (18 January). www.wsj.com/articles/pg-e-wildfires-and-the-first-climate-change-bankruptcy-11547820006.

Government, H. M. 2019. "Environmental Reporting Guidelines: Including Streamlined Energy and Carbon Reporting Requirements." Department for Energy Security and Net Zero, Department for Environment, Food & Rural Affairs, and Department for Business, Energy & Industrial Strategy (29 March 2019). www.gov.uk/government/publications/environmental-reporting-natuguidelines-including-mandatory-greenhouse-gas-emissions-reporting-guidance.

Hume, N., H. Sanderson. 2019. "Global Miners Count the Cost of Their Failings." *Financial Times* (15 February). www.ft.com/content/66965d68-2bc2-11e9-88a4-c32129756dd8.

International Monetary Fund 2019. "Global Financial Stability Report: Lower for Longer" (October). www.imf.org/en/Publications/GFSR/Issues/2019/10/01/global-financial-stability-report-october-2019.

Kirakosian, Margaryta. 2020. "$4.6tn Investor Group Meets Brazilian Congress on Deforestation Concerns." CityWire Selector. https://citywireselector.com/news/4-6tn-investor-group-meets-brazilian-congress-on-deforestation-concerns/a1380621.

Laier, P. 2019. "Vale Stock Plunges after Brazil Disaster; $19 Billion in Market Value Lost." Reuters (28 January). www.reuters.com/article/us-vale-sa-disaster-stocks/vale-stock-plunges-after-brazil-disaster-19-billion-in-market-value-lost-idUSKCN1PM1JP.

Matikainen, S., E. Campiglio, D. Zenghelis. 2017. "The Climate Impact of Quantitative Easing." Grantham Research Institute (30 May). www.lse.ac.uk/granthaminstitute/publication/the-climate-impact-of-quantitative-easing/.

McGrath, M. 2020. "Climate Change: New UK Law to Curb Deforestation in Supply Chains." BBC News (25 August). www.bbc.com/news/science-environment-53891421.

Munich, R. E. 2020. "Record Hurricane Season and Major Wildfires—The Natural Disaster Figures for 2020." www.munichre.com/en/company/media-relations/media-information-and-corporate-news/media-information/2021/2020-natural-disasters-balance.html.

Prudential Regulation Authority 2015. "The Impact of Climate Change on the UK Insurance Sector" (September). www.bankofengland.co.uk/-/media/boe/files/prudential-regulation/publication/impact-of-climate-change-on-the-uk-insurance-sector.pdf.

Ratings, Fitch. 2020. "Financial Sector Confronts Deforestation as a Key ESG Risk." www.fitchratings.com/site/re/10134822.

Tracker, Planet. 2020a. "Exchange Traded Deforestation."

References

UN Global Compact and BSR.2014. "A Guide to Traceability: A Practical Approach to Advance Sustainability in the Global Supply Chains." www.unglobalcompact.org/library/791.

Amenc, N., F. Goltz, V. Liu. 2021. "Doing Good or Feeling Good? Detecting Greenwashing in Climate Investing." EDHEC Business School (August). www.edhec.edu/sites/www.edhec-portail.pprod.net/files/210921-1_doing_good_or_feeling_good.pdf.

Apparicio, S., N. Sauer. 2020. "Which Countries Have Not Ratified the Paris Climate Agreement?" Climate Home News (13 August). www.climatechangenews.com/2020/08/13/countries-yet-ratify-paris-agreement/.

ASIC 2022. "ASIC's Corporate Governance Priorities and the Year Ahead." https://asic.gov.au/about-asic/news-centre/speeches/asic-s-corporate-governance-priorities-and-the-year-ahead/.

Badlam, Justin, Jared Cox, Adi Kumar, Nehal Mehta, Sara O'Rourke, Julia Silvis McKinsey. 2022. "The Inflation Reduction Act: Here's What's in It." McKinsey (24 October). www.mckinsey.com/industries/public-and-social-sector/our-insights/the-inflation-reduction-act-heres-whats-in-it.

BloombergNEF 2020a. "China's Accelerated Decarbonization: Economic Benefits." https://assets.bbhub.io/professional/sites/24/BNEF-Chinas-Accelerated-Decarbonization-Pathways_12012020_FINAL.pdf.

BloombergNEF 2023a. "Energy Transition Investment Trends 2023." https://about.bnef.com/energy-transition-investment/.

Bond, David E., Guillermo Giralda Fustes, William De Catelle, Matt Solomon. 2022. "European Parliament and Council Reach Agreement on Carbon Border Adjustment Mechanism and EU Emissions Trading System." White & Case. www.whitecase.com/insight-alert/european-parliament-and-council-reach-agreement-carbon-border-adjustment-mechanism.

BP 2020. "Progressing Strategy Development, BP Revises Long-Term Price Assumptions, Reviews Intangible Assets and, as a Result, Expects Non-Cash Impairments and Write-Offs." Press release (15 June). www.bp.com/en/global/corporate/news-and-insights/press-releases/bp-revises-long-term-price-assumptions.html.

Brainard, L. 2021. "Financial Stability Implications of Climate Change." www.federalreserve.gov/newsevents/speech/brainard20210323a.htm.

Bullard, N. "Energy Transition's New Industrial Landscape." BloomberNEF. https://about.bnef.com/blog/energy-transitions-new-industrial-landscape/.

Carbon Pricing Leadership Coalition 2017. "Report of the High-Level Commission on Carbon Prices: Executive Summary." https://static1.squarespace.com/static/54ff9c5ce4b0a53decccfb4c/t/59b7f26b3c91f1bb0de2e41a/1505227373770/CarbonPricing_EnglishSummary.pdf.

Daramus, I. S. 2017. "Liability and Precaution." Environment: Science and Policy for Sustainable Development 59 (18 August): 48–56. .

Department for Business Energy & Industrial Strategy.2020. "Energy Trends: December 2020." www.gov.uk/government/statistics/energy-trends-december-2020.

Department of Work and Pension 2018. "Consultation Outcome: Pension Trustees: Clarifying and Strengthening Investment Duties." www.gov.uk/government/consultations/pension-trustees-clarifying-and-strengthening-investment-duties.

Di Sario, F. 2023. "Commission Releases Net-Zero Industry Act." Politico (16 March). https://www.politico.eu/article/commission-releases-net-zero-industry-act/.

ECB 2022. "ECB Economy-Wide Climate Stress Test: Methodology and Results." www.ecb.europa.eu/pub/pdf/scpops/ecb.op281~05a7735b1c.en.pdf.

EU Technical Expert Group on Sustainable Finance 2019. "TEG Final Report on Climate Benchmarks and Benchmarks' ESG Disclosures" (September). https://ec.europa.eu/info/sites/default/files/business_economy_euro/banking_and_finance/documents/190930-sustainable-finance-teg-final-report-climate-benchmarks-and-disclosures_en.pdf.

European Commission 2019a. "Guidelines on Reporting Climate-Related Information." https://ec.europa.eu/finance/docs/policy/190618-climate-related-information-reporting-guidelines_en.pdf.

European Commission 2019b. "Regulation (EU) 2019/2088 of the European Parliament and of the Council of 27 November 2019 on Sustainability-Related Disclosures in the Financial Services Sector." http://data.europa.eu/eli/reg/2019/2088/oj.

European Commission 2020. "Renewed Sustainable Finance Strategy and Implementation of the Action Plan on Financing Sustainable Growth." https://ec.europa.eu/info/publications/sustainable-finance-renewed-strategy_en.

European Commission 2021. "Questions and Answers: Corporate Sustainability Reporting Directive Proposal." https://ec.europa.eu/commission/presscorner/detail/en/qanda_21_1806.

European Commission 2023a. "A Green Deal Industrial Plan for the Net-Zero Age." https://commission.europa.eu/document/41514677-9598-4d89-a572-abe21cb037f4_en.

European Commission 2023b. "Proposal for a Regulation of the European Parliament and of the Council on Establishing a Framework of Measures for Strengthening Europe's Net-Zero Technology Products Manufacturing Ecosystem (Net Zero Industry Act)." https://eur-lex.europa.eu/legal-content/EN/TXT/?uri=CELEX%3A52023PC0161.

European Council 2022. "Council Agrees on the Carbon Border Adjustment Mechanism (CBAM)." www.consilium.europa.eu/en/press/press-releases/2022/03/15/carbon-border-adjustment-mechanism-cbam-council-agrees-its-negotiating-mandate/.

Evans, S. 2016. "Countdown to 2025: Tracking the UK Coal Phase Out." *Carbon Brief* (10 February). www.carbonbrief.org/countdown-to-2025-tracking-the-uk-coal-phase-out.

Evans, Simon, Josh Gabbatiss, Robert McSweeney, Aruna Chandrasekhar, Ayesha Tandon, Giuliana Viglione, Zeke Hausfather, Xiaoying You, Joe Goodman, Sylvia Hayes. 2021. "COP26: Key Outcomes Agreed at the UN Climate Talks in Glasgow." *Carbon Brief* (15 November). www.carbonbrief.org/cop26-key-outcomes-agreed-at-the-un-climate-talks-in-glasgow.

Fatin, L. 2020. "China's Top Regulators Announce They Will Exclude Fossil Fuels from Their Green Bonds Taxonomy. It's a Major Development!" Climate Bonds Initiative (10 June). www.climatebonds.net/2020/06/chinas-top-regulators-announce-they-will-exclude-fossil-fuels-their-green-bonds-taxonomy-it.

Financial Accounting Standards Foundation 2021. "Establishment of the Sustainability Standards Board of Japan (SSBJ) and Formation of the SSBJ Preparation Committee."

Financial Conduct Authority 2018. "FS19/6: Climate Change and Green Finance." www.fca.org.uk/publications/discussion-papers/dp18-8-climate-change-and-green-finance.

Financial Stability Board 2022. "2022 TCFD Status Report: Task Force on Climate-Related Financial Disclosures" (13 October). www.fsb.org/2022/10/2022-tcfd-status-report-task-force-on-climate-related-financial-disclosures/.

Forster, P., C. Smith, J. Rogelj. 2021. "Guest Post: The Global Methane Pledge Needs to Go Further to Help Limit Warming to 1.5C." *Carbon Brief* (2 November). www.carbonbrief.org/guest-post-the-global-methane-pledge-needs-to-go-further-to-help-limit-warming-to-1-5c.

Galer, R. 2021. "'Prudent Person Rule' Standard for the Investment of Pension Fund Assets." www.oecd.org/finance/private-pensions/2763540.pdf.

Government, H. M. 2020. "Policy Paper: The Ten Point Plan for a Green Industrial Revolution." www.gov.uk/government/publications/the-ten-point-plan-for-a-green-industrial-revolution.

Hausfather, Z., P. Forster. 2021. "Analysis: Do COP26 Promises Keep Global Warming below 2C?" *Carbon Brief* (10 November). www.carbonbrief.org/analysis-do-cop26-promises-keep-global-warming-below-2c.

International Energy Agency (IEA) 2020a. "Implementing Effective Emissions Trading Systems." www.iea.org/reports/implementing-effective-emissions-trading-systems.

References

International Energy Agency (IEA) 2020b. *Two World Energy Outlook 2020*. www.iea.org/reports/world-energy-outlook-2020.

International Maritime Organization 2020. "IMO 2020—Cutting Sulphur Oxide Emissions." www.imo.org/en/MediaCentre/HotTopics/Pages/Sulphur-2020.aspx.

IPCC 2022b. "Climate Change 2022: Mitigation of Climate Change: Summary for Policymakers." https://ccli.ubc.ca/wp-content/uploads/2022/04/IPCC_AR6_WGIII_SummaryForPolicymakers.pdf.

Kedward, K., J. Ryan-Collins, H. Chenet. 2020. "Managing Nature-Related Financial Risks: A Precautionary Policy Approach for Central Banks and Financial Supervisors." UCL Institute for Innovation and Public Purpose (18 August). www.ucl.ac.uk/bartlett/public-purpose/wp2020-09. 10.2139/ssrn.3726637

Lies, E. 2020. "Japan Aims for Zero Emissions, Carbon Neutral Society by 2050—PM." Reuters (26 October). www.reuters.com/article/uk-japan-politics-suga/japan-aims-for-zero-emissions-carbon-neutral-society-by-2050-pm-idUKKBN27B0C7?edition-redirect=ca.

Ma, J. 2017. "Ma Jun on the Importance of Environmental Risk Analysis to Financial Institutions." www.climatebonds.net/files/files/Ma_Jun_Speech_17_07_17.pdf.

Méssonier, J.-S., B. Nguyen. 2021. "Showing Off Cleaner Hands: Mandatory Climate-Related Disclosure by Financial Institutions and the Financing of Fossil Energy." www.banque-france.fr/sites/default/files/medias/documents/wp800.pdf.

Milburn, E. 2020. "Japanese Regulator Gears Up for Climate Scenario Analysis Pilot for Banks." Responsible Investor (3 September). www.responsible-investor.com/articles/japanese-regulator-gears-up-for-climate-scenario-analysis-pilot-for-banks.

Moeller, Elizabeth Vella, Sheila McCafferty Harvey, Moushami P. Joshi, Elina Teplinsky, Meghan Claire Hammond. 2021. "Hydrogen Highlights in the Bipartisan Infrastructure Bill." Pillsbury Law. www.pillsburylaw.com/en/news-and-insights/hydrogen-highlights-bipartisan-infrastructure-bill.html.

Murtaugh, J. 2021. "China Blows Past Clean Energy Record with Wind Capacity Jump." Bloomberg (20 January). www.bloomberg.com/news/articles/2021-01-20/china-blows-past-clean-energy-record-with-extra-wind-capacity.

Nachmany, M., S. Fankhauser, J. Setzer, A. Averchenkova. 2017. "Global Trends in Climate Change Legislation and Litigation: 2017 Update." Grantham Research Institute. http://eprints.lse.ac.uk/80447/.

NGFS 2022a. "NGFS Climate Scenarios for Central Banks and Supervisors." www.ngfs.net/en/ngfs-climate-scenarios-central-banks-and-supervisors-september-2022.

NGFS 2022b. "Progress Report on the Guide for Supervisors." www.ngfs.net/sites/default/files/progress_report_on_the_guide_for_supervisors_0.pdf.

Norman, Joseph, Rupert Read, Yaneer Bar-Yam, Nassim Nicholas Taleb. 2015. "Climate Models and Precautionary Measures." https://fooledbyrandomness.com/climateletter.pdf.

PRA 2019. "Enhancing Banks' and Insurers' Approaches to Managing the Financial Risks from Climate Change." www.bankofengland.co.uk/prudential-regulation/publication/2018/enhancing-banks-and-insurers-approaches-to-managing-the-financial-risks-from-climate-change.

Quinson, T. 2021. "Biden Administration Considers Reversing Trump's ESG Rule Change." Bloomberg (20 January). www.bloomberg.com/news/articles/2021-01-20/biden-administration-considers-reversing-trump-s-esg-rule-change.

SEBI 2021. "SEBI Issues Circular on 'Business Responsibility and Sustainability Reporting by Listed Entities." www.sebi.gov.in/media/press-releases/may-2021/sebi-issues-circular-on-business-responsibility-and-sustainability-reporting-by-listed-entities-_50097.html.

SEC 2022. "SEC Proposes Rules to Enhance and Standardize Climate-Related Disclosures for Investors." www.sec.gov/news/press-release/2022-46.

State Council 2021. "Full Text: Action Plan for Carbon Dioxide Peaking Before 2030." english.www.gov.cn/policies/latestreleases/202110/27/content_WS6178a47ec6d0df57f98e3dfb.html.

Taleb, Nassim Nicholas, Rupert Read, Raphael Douady, Joseph Norman, Yaneer Bar-Yam. 2014. "The Precautionary Principle (with Application to the Genetic Modification of Organisms)." https://arxiv.org/abs/1410.5787.

Tandon, S. 2020. "What Next for Sustainable Finance in India?" Grantham Research Institute. www.lse.ac.uk/granthaminstitute/news/what-next-for-sustainable-finance-in-india/.

TCFD 2017a. "Final Report: Recommendations of the Task Force on Climate-Related Financial Disclosures." https://assets.bbhub.io/company/sites/60/2020/10/FINAL-2017-TCFD-Report-11052018.pdf.

Timperley, J. 2019. "Corsia: The UN's Plan to 'Offset' Growth in Aviation Emissions." *Carbon Brief* (4 February). www.carbonbrief.org/corsia-un-plan-to-offset-growth-in-aviation-emissions-after-2020.

Treasury, H. M. 2020. "A Roadmap towards Mandatory Climate-Related Disclosures." https://assets.publishing.service.gov.uk/government/uploads/system/uploads/attachment_data/file/933783/FINAL_TCFD_ROADMAP.pdf.

UK Government 2021. "Pension Schemes Act 2021." www.legislation.gov.uk/ukpga/2021/1/section/124/enacted.

UNEP 2016. "The Kigali Amendment to the Montreal Protocol: Another Global Commitment to Stop Climate Change" (8 December). www.unenvironment.org/news-and-stories/news/kigali-amendment-montreal-protocol-another-global-commitment-stop-climate.

UNEP 2022a. "COP15 Ends with Landmark Biodiversity Agreement" (20 December). https://www.unep.org/news-and-stories/story/cop15-ends-landmark-biodiversity-agreement.

UNFCCC 2021. "Glasgow Climate Pact" (13 November). https://unfccc.int/documents/310475.

United Nations 2015. "Paris Agreement." https://unfccc.int/sites/default/files/english_paris_agreement.pdf.

White House 2021. "Fact Sheet: The Bipartisan Infrastructure Deal." www.whitehouse.gov/briefing-room/statements-releases/2021/11/06/fact-sheet-the-bipartisan-infrastructure-deal/.

World Bank 2023. "State and Trends of Carbon Pricing 2023." https://openknowledge.worldbank.org/entities/publication/58f2a409-9bb7-4ee6-899d-be47835c838f.

You, Z., E. Chiweshenga. 2022. "The Net-Zero Journey: Creating a Just Transition for Workers." abrdn. www.abrdn.com/en-my/institutional/insights-thinking-aloud/article-page/the-net-zero-journey-creating-a-just-transition-for-workers.

Climate Bonds Initiative 2019a. "ASEAN Green Financial Instruments Guide." www.climatebonds.net/resources/reports/asean-green-financial-instruments-guide.

Climate Bonds Initiative 2019b. "Latin America & Caribbean: Green Finance State of the Market 2019." www.climatebonds.net/resources/reports/latin-america-caribbean-green-finance-state-market-2019.

Coalition, Capitals. 2016. "Natural Capital Protocol." https://capitalscoalition.org/capitals-approach/natural-capital-protocol.

ESG for Investors 2022. "Counting Down Carbon: Higher Share Prices through Lower Emissions" (24 January). https://esgforinvestors.com/articles/detail/22/.

Gosden, E. 2019. "Plastic May Do Less Harm Than Alternatives, Says BP." *The Times* (7 February). www.thetimes.co.uk/article/plastic-may-do-less-harm-than-alternatives-says-bp-n7p0tt7w7.

IFC 2015. "Environmental and Social Management System Implementation Handbook."

IFRS Foundation 2021. "IFRS Foundation Announces International Sustainability Standards Board, Consolidation with CDSB and VRF, and Publication of Prototype Disclosure Requirements." www.ifrs.org/news-and-events/news/2021/11/ifrs-foundation-announces-issb-consolidation-with-cdsb-vrf-publication-of-prototypes/.

References

Macquarie, Rob, Baysa Naran, Paul Rosane, Matthew Solomon, Cooper Wetherbee. 2020. "Updated View on the Global Landscape of Climate Finance 2019." Climate Policy Initiative. www.climatepolicyinitiative.org/wp-content/uploads/2020/12/Updated-View-on-the-2019-Global-Landscape-of-Climate-Finance-1.pdf.

Naran, Baysa, Jake Connolly, Paul Rosane, Dharshan Wignarajah, Githungo Wakaba, Barbara Buchner. 2022. "Global Landscape of Climate Finance: A Decade of Data." Climate Policy Initiative (27 October). www.climatepolicyinitiative.org/publication/global-landscape-of-climate-finance-a-decade-of-data/.

Net Zero Asset Managers Initiative 2021. "Net Zero Asset Managers Initiative: Progress Report." www.netzeroassetmanagers.org/media/2021/12/NZAM-Progress-Report.pdf.

Rydge, J. 2020. "Aligning Finance with the Paris Agreement: An Overview of Concepts, Approaches, Progress and Necessary Action." Grantham Research Institute. www.lse.ac.uk/granthaminstitute/wp-content/uploads/2020/12/Aligning-finance-with-the-Paris-Agreement-3.pdf.

UNEP 2020. "Institutional Investors Transitioning Their Portfolios to Net Zero GHG Emissions by 2050." www.unepfi.org/net-zero-alliance/.

Agha, R., S. Singla. 2020. "ESG in LGIM's Active EMD Investment Process." www.lgim.com/uk/en/insights/our-thinking/esg-and-long-term-themes/esg-in-lgims-active-emd-investment-process.

Andersson, Mats, Patrick Bolton, Frédéric Samama. 2016. "Hedging Climate Risk." Financial Analysts Journal 72 (May/June): 13–32. www.tandfonline.com/doi/abs/10.2469/faj.v72.n3.410.2469/faj.v72.n3.4

Bloomberg, N. E. F. 2020b. "Scale-Up of Solar and Wind Puts Existing Coal, Gas at Risk." https://about.bnef.com/blog/scale-up-of-solar-and-wind-puts-existing-coal-gas-at-risk/.

Bolton, P., M. Kakperczyk. 2021. "Do Investors Care about Carbon Risk?" Journal of Financial Economics 142 (November): 517–49. www.sciencedirect.com/science/article/abs/pii/S0304405X21001902?via%3Dihub10.1016/j.jfineco.2021.05.008

Bolton, P., M. Despres, L. A. Pereira Da Silva, F. Samama, R. Svartzman. 2020. "The Green Swan: Central Banking and Financial Stability in the Age of Climate Change." Bank for International Settlements (January). www.bis.org/publ/othp31.pdf.

Breeden, S. 2019. "Avoiding the Storm: Climate Change and the Financial System." Speech, Bank of England (15 April). www.bankofengland.co.uk/-/media/boe/files/speech/2019/avoiding-the-storm-climate-change-and-the-financial-system-speech-by-sarah-breeden.pdf.

Cambridge Institute for Sustainability Leadership 2015. "Unhedgeable Risk: How Climate Change Sentiment Impacts Investment." www.cisl.cam.ac.uk/resources/sustainable-finance-publications/unhedgeable-risk.

Carbon Tracker Initiative 2020. "Breaking the Habit: Methodology." https://carbontransfer.wpengine.com/wp-content/uploads/2019/09/Breaking-the-Habit-Methodology-Final-1.pdf.

Ceres 2011. "Ceres Aqua Gauge: A Comprehensive Assessment Tool for Evaluating Corporate Management of Water Risk" (18 October). www.ceres.org/resources/tools/ceres-aqua-gauge-comprehensive-assessment-tool-evaluating-corporate-management.

Department for Environment Food & Rural Affairs.2020. "Enabling a Natural Capital Approach (ENCA)." www.gov.uk/guidance/enabling-a-natural-capital-approach-enca.

European Commission 2014. "Directive 2014/95/EU." https://ec.europa.eu/info/business-economy-euro/company-reporting-and-auditing/company-reporting/non-financial-reporting_en.

Gann, D. 2016. "Kodak Invented the Digital Camera—Then Killed It. Why Innovation Often Fails." World Economic Forum (23 June). www.weforum.org/agenda/2016/06/leading-innovation-through-the-chicanes/.

Garvey, Gerald T., Mohanaraman Iyer, Joanna Nash. 2018. "Carbon Footprint and Productivity: Does the 'E' in ESG Capture Efficiency as Well as Environment?" Journal of Investment Management16 (1): 59–69. https://joim.com/downloads/carbon-footprint-and-productivity-does-the-e-in-esg-capture-efficiency-as-well-as-environment/

Glasgow Financial Alliance for Net Zero 2022. "Measuring Portfolio Alignment: Driving Enhancement, Convergence, and Adoption." https://assets.bbhub.io/company/sites/63/2022/09/Measuring-Portfolio-Alignment-Enhancement-Convergence-and-Adoption-November-2022.pdf.

Görgen, Maximilian, Andrea Jacob, Martin Nerlinger, Ryan Riordan, Martin Rohleder, Marco Wilkens. 2020. "Carbon Risk." https://ssrn.com/abstract=2930897.

GPIF 2020. "Analysis of Climate Change-Related Risks and Opportunities in the GPIF Portfolio." www.gpif.go.jp/en/investment/GPIF_CLIMATE_REPORT_FY2019_2.pdf.

Greenhouse Gas Protocol 2019. "Standards."

HSBC 2020. "HSBC Climate Solutions Database." www.research.hsbc.com/C/1/1/315/KrqWFj9.

IIGCC 2021. "Paris Aligned Investment Initiative." www.iigcc.org/our-work/paris-aligned-investment-initiative/.

Legal & General 2020. "LGIM Announces Climate Solutions Capability Powered by Risk and Alignment Framework Co-Developed with Baringa Partners." https://group.legalandgeneral.com/en/newsroom/press-releases/lgim-announces-climate-solutions-capability-powered-by-risk-and-alignment-framework-co-developed-with-baringa-partners.

Natural Capital Coalition 2016. "Natural Capital Protocol". www.naturalcapitalcoalition.org/protocol This work is licensed under a Creative Commons Attribution-NonCommercial-NoDerivatives 4.0 International License © ICAEW 2016.

TCFD 2017b. "Implementing the Recommendations of the Task Force on Climate-Related Financial Disclosures." www.fsb-tcfd.org/wp-content/uploads/2017/06/FINAL-TCFD-Annex-062817.pdf.

TCFD 2021. "Guidance on Metrics, Targets, and Transition Plans." https://assets.bbhub.io/company/sites/60/2021/07/2021-Metrics_Targets_Guidance-1.pdf.

TCFD 2022. "2022 Status Report: Task Force on Climate-Related Financial Disclosures: Status Report." https://assets.bbhub.io/company/sites/60/2022/10/2022-TCFD-Status-Report.pdf.

UNEP 2017. "Enhancing Environmental Risk Assessment in Financial Decision Making."

UNEP and PRI 2023. "Target Setting Protocol Third Edition" (January). https://www.unepfi.org/industries/target-setting-protocol-third-edition/.

Zhou, X., C. Wilson, B. Caldecott. 2021. "The Energy Transition and Changing Financing Costs." University of Oxford (April). www.smithschool.ox.ac.uk/research/sustainable-finance/publications/The-energy-transition-and-changing-financing-costs.pdf.

Aviva 2022. "Biodiversity Report 2022." www.aviva.com/sustainability/COP15/.

Capitals Coalition 2016. "Natural Capital Protocol." https://capitalscoalition.org/capitals-approach/natural-capital-protocol.

Convention on Biological Diversity 2022. "COP15: Nations Adopt Four Goals, 23 Targets for 2030 in Landmark UN Biodiversity Agreement." www.cbd.int/article/cop15-cbd-press-release-final-19dec2022.

Díaz, S. 2015. "The IPBES Conceptual Framework—Connecting Nature and People." Current Opinion in Environmental Sustainability14 (June): 1–16. 10.1016/j.cosust.2014.11.002

IPBES 2019. "The Global Assessment Report on Biodiversity and Ecosystem Services: A Summary for Policymakers."

Kotzé, Petro. 2022. "Freshwater Planetary Boundary 'Considerably' Transgressed: New Research." Mongabay (27 April).

NGFS 2021. "Biodiversity and Financial Stability: Exploring the Case for Action."

References

Taskforce on Nature-related Financial Disclosures (TNFD) 2023. *Nature-related Risk and Opportunity Management and Disclosure Framework* (v0.4). https://tnfd.global. UN. 2021. "System of Environmental-Economic Accounting—Ecosystem Accounting" (29 September). https://seea.un.org/sites/seea.un.org/files/documents/EA/seea_ea_white_cover_final.pdf.

TNFD 2022a. "Societal Dimensions of Nature-Related Risk Management and Disclosure: Considerations for the TNFD Framework." Discussion paper (November). https://framework.tnfd.global/wp-content/uploads/2022/11/TNFD_Societal_Dimensions_Discussion_Paper_v0-3_C.pdf.

TNFD 2022b. *The TNFD Nature-related Risk and Opportunity Management and Disclosure Framework Beta v0.3 Summary*. https://framework.tnfd.global/introduction-to-the-framework/executive-summary/v03-beta-release.

HM Treasury, . 2021. "Final Report—The Economics of Biodiversity: The Dasgupta Review" (2 February). www.gov.uk/government/publications/final-report-the-economics-of-biodiversity-the-dasgupta-review.

UN PRI 2023. "Inevitable Policy Response: IPR Forecast Policy Scenario + Nature." www.unpri.org/inevitable-policy-response/ipr-forecast-policy-scenario--nature/10966.article.

World Bank 2020. "Mobilizing Private Finance for Nature: A World Bank Group Paper on Private Finance for Biodiversity and Ecosystem Services."

World Economic Forum and PwC 2020. "Nature Risk Rising: Why the Crisis Engulfing Nature Matters for Business and the Economy."

WWF 2022. "The Living Planet Report 2022." https://livingplanet.panda.org/en-GB/

WWF Switzerland Cadmus Group 2019. "Valuing Sustainability in Infrastructure Investments: Market Status, Barriers and Opportunities—A Landscape Analysis" (March). https://cadmusgroup.com/wp-content/uploads/2019/03/WWF_Valuing-Sustainability-in-Infrastructure-Investments.pdf?hsCtaTracking=e8f1c695-bc51-4645-b813-7d7f4de1e766%7C153dcd76-d713-4736-a2bb-66bddda2e5be

Weber, Barbara, Britta Rendlen. 2019. "Guidance Note: Integrating ESG Factors into Financial Models for Infrastructure Investments." B Capital Partners and WWF Switzerland. http://awsassets.panda.org/downloads/wwf_guidance_note_infra_.pdf.

BBP 2020. "BBP Climate Change Commitment." www.betterbuildingspartnership.co.uk/node/877.

Bennett, V. 2019. "World's First Dedicated Climate Resilience Bond, for US$ 700m, Is Issued by EBRD." European Bank for Reconstruction and Development (20 September). www.ebrd.com/news/2019/worlds-first-dedicated-climate-resilience-bond-for-us-700m-is-issued-by-ebrd-.html.

BloombergNEF 2022b. "Energy Transition Investment Trends 2022." https://assets.bbhub.io/professional/sites/24/Energy-Transition-Investment-Trends-Exec-Summary-2022.pdf.

BloombergNEF 2023b. "Global Low-Carbon Energy Technology Investment Surges Past $1 Trillion for the First Time." https://about.bnef.com/blog/global-low-carbon-energy-technology-investment-surges-past-1-trillion-for-the-first-time/.

Canalys 2022. "Global Electric Vehicle Sales up 109% in 2021, with Half in Mainland China" (14 February). www.canalys.com/newsroom/global-electric-vehicle-market-2021.

Carbon Tracker Initiative 2020. "Coal Developers Risk $600 Billion as Renewables Outcompete Worldwide." https://carbontracker.org/coal-developers-risk-600-billion-as-renewables-outcompete-worldwide/.

CICERO 2015. "CICERO Shades of Green." https://cicero.green/.

Climate Bonds Initiative 2018. "Bonds and Climate Change: The State of the Market 2018." www.climatebonds.net/resources/reports/bonds-and-climate-change-state-market-2018.

Climate Bonds Initiative 2020. "Financing Credible Transitions: How to Ensure the Transition Label Has Impact." White paper. www.climatebonds.net/resources/reports/financing-credible-transitions-white-paper.

Climate Bonds Initiative 2022a. "Climate Bonds Interactive Data Platform." www.climatebonds.net/market/data/.

Climate Bonds Initiative 2022b. "Green Bond Database Methodology." www.climatebonds.net/market/green-bond-database-methodology.

Climate Bonds Initiative 2022c. "Social & Sustainability Bond Database Methodology." www.climatebonds.net/market/social-sustainability-bond-database-methodology.

Climate Bonds Initiative 2023. "Climate Bonds Taxonomy." www.climatebonds.net/standard/taxonomy.

Collins, L. 2022. "Ukraine War: | Green Hydrogen 'Now Cheaper Than Grey in Europe, Middle East and China': BNEF." Recharge (7 March). www.rechargenews.com/energy-transition/ukraine-war-green-hydrogen-now-cheaper-than-grey-in-europe-middle-east-and-china-bnef/2-1-1180320.

Schneider Electric 2023. "Circular activities now account for 12% of its revenues and saved 100,000 metric tons of primary resources between 2018 and 2020." https://perspectives.se.com/research/circular-economy.

Ellen MacArthur Foundation 2020. "Financing the Circular Economy: Capturing the Opportunity." www.ellenmacarthurfoundation.org/assets/downloads/Financing-the-circular-economy.pdf.

Stora Enso. 2018. "About Stora Enso." www.storaenso.com/en/about-stora-enso.

European Environment Agency 2021. "Growth without Economic Growth." www.eea.europa.eu/publications/growth-without-economic-growth/growth-without-economic-growth.

European Investment Bank 2019. "A European Fund to Support the Circular Bioeconomy." www.eib.org/en/press/all/2019-328-a-european-fund-to-support-the-circular-bioeconomy.

Evans, S. 2018. "CCC: UK Should 'Move Away' from Large-Scale Biomass Burning." *Carbon Brief* (15 November). www.carbonbrief.org/ccc-uk-should-move-away-from-large-scale-biomass-burning.

Heineken 2018. "Drop the C: Reducing Our CO2 Emissions." www.theheinekencompany.com/pt-pt/node/607.

ICMA 2021. "Green Bond Principles: Voluntary Process Guidelines for Issuing Green Bonds" (June). www.icmagroup.org/green-social-and-sustainability-bonds/green-bond-principles-gbp/.

International Energy Agency 2023. "Energy Technology Perspectives 2023." www.iea.org/reports/energy-technology-perspectives-2023.

International Institute for Sustainable Development 2020. "Mexico Issues Sovereign SDG Bond for Most Vulnerable Municipalities." https://sdg.iisd.org/news/mexico-issues-sovereign-sdg-bond-for-most-vulnerable-municipalities/.

IPCC 2022b. "Climate Change 2022: Mitigation of Climate Change: Summary for Policymakers." https://ccli.ubc.ca/wp-content/uploads/2022/04/IPCC_AR6_WGIII_SummaryForPolicymakers.pdf.

ISO 2018. "Energy Management Systems—Requirements with Guidance for Use." www.iso.org/obp/ui/#iso:std:iso:50001:ed-2:v1:en.

Klesty, Victoria. 2022. "Electric Cars Hit 65% of Norway Sales as Tesla Grabs Overall Pole." Reuters (5 January). www.reuters.com/business/autos-transportation/electric-cars-take-two-thirds-norway-car-market-led-by-tesla-2022-01-03/.

Lazard 2020. "Levelized Cost of Energy, Levelized Cost of Storage, and Levelized Cost of Hydrogen 2020." www.lazard.com/perspective/levelized-cost-of-energy-and-levelized-cost-of-storage-2020/.

Liebreich Associates 2021. "The Clean Hydrogen Ladder." www.linkedin.com/pulse/clean-hydrogen-ladder-v40-michael-liebreich/.

LMA 2018. "Green Loan Principles: Supporting Environmentally Sustainable Economic Activity." www.lma.eu.com/application/files/9115/4452/5458/741_LM_Green_Loan_Principles_Booklet_V8.pdf.

LMA 2019. "Sustainability Linked Loan Principles." www.icmagroup.org/assets/documents/Regulatory/Green-Bonds/LMASustainabilityLinkedLoanPrinciples-270919.pdf.

References

Luxembourg Ministry of Finance 2020. "Luxembourg—First European Country to Lunch a Sustainability Bond Framework." Press release. https://gouvernement.lu/en/actualites/toutes_actualites/communiques/2020/09-septembre/02-cadre-obligations-durables.html.

Luxembourg Stock Exchange 2021a. "Climate Bonds—LGX Climate-Aligned Issuers." www.bourse.lu/climate-bonds-lgx-climate-aligned-issuers.

Luxembourg Stock Exchange 2021b. "LGX Expands to Welcome Climate-Aligned Issuers." www.bourse.lu/pr-lgx-welcomes-climate-aligned-issuers.

Mathis, W., R. Morison, V. Dezem. 2022. "Russia's War Supercharges Push to Make New Green Fuel." Bloomberg (10 April). www.bloomberg.com/news/articles/2022-04-10/russia-s-invasion-supercharges-push-to-make-a-new-green-fuel.

Moomaw, William, Isaac Berzin, Asaf Tzachor. 2017. "Cutting Out the Middle Fish: Marine Microalgae as the Next Sustainable Omega-3 Fatty Acids and Protein Source." Industrial Biotechnology (New Rochelle, N.Y.)13 (October). www.liebertpub.com/doi/10.1089/ind.2017.29102.wmo10.1089/ind.2017.29102.wmo

Mutua, D. C. 2023. "Sustainable Debt Issuance Fell Amid Rates Turmoil, ESG Pushback." Bloomberg (5 January). www.bloomberg.com/news/articles/2023-01-05/sustainable-debt-issuance-fell-amid-rates-turmoil-esg-pushback.

New Climate Economy 2016. "The Sustainable Infrastructure Imperative." Global Commission on the Economy and Climate. https://newclimateeconomy.report/2016/misc/downloads/.

OECD 2016. "The Ocean Economy in 2030." .10.1787/9789264251724-en

Paoli, Leonardo, Timur Gül. 2022. "Electric Cars Fend Off Supply Challenges to More Than Double Global Sales." IEA. www.iea.org/commentaries/electric-cars-fend-off-supply-challenges-to-more-than-double-global-sales.

PricewaterhouseCoopers 2020. "The State of Climate Tech 2020: The Next Frontier for Venture Capital." www.pwc.com/gx/en/services/sustainability/publications/state-of-climate-tech-2020.html.

Rizal Commercial Banking Corporation 2019. "RCBC to Issue First ASEAN Sustainability Bond in the Philippines." Press release. www.rcbc.com/Content/Web/img/about/pdf/disclosure/RCBC%20to%20issue%20First%20ASEAN%20Sustainability%20Bond%20in%20the%20Philippines.pdf.

FTSE Russell 2022. "Investing in the Green Economy 2022." https://content.ftserussell.com/sites/default/files/investing_in_the_green_economy_2022_final_8.pdf.

Singapore Ministry of the Environment and Water Resources 2019. "Zero Waste Masterplan." www.towardszerowaste.gov.sg/zero-waste-masterplan/.

Solvay 2019. "Solvay Links the Cost of €2 Bn Revolving Credit Facility to Its Ambitious Greenhouse Gas Reduction Commitments." Press release. www.solvay.com/en/press-release/solvay-links-cost-eu2-bn-revolving-credit-facility-its-ambitious-greenhouse-gas.

Sterman, John, William Moomaw, Juliette N. Rooney-Varga, Lori Siegel. 2022. "Does Wood Bioenergy Help or Harm the Environment?" (10 May). https://thebulletin.org/premium/2022-05/does-wood-bioenergy-help-or-harm-the-climate/.

World Bank 2017. "The Potential of the Blue Economy: Increasing Long-Term Benefits of the Sustainable Use of Marine Resources for Small Island Developing States and Coastal Least Developed Countries." https://openknowledge.worldbank.org/bitstream/handle/10986/26843/115545.pdf.

World Bank 2018. "Seychelles Launches World's First Sovereign Blue Bond." Press release. www.worldbank.org/en/news/press-release/2018/10/29/seychelles-launches-worlds-first-sovereign-blue-bond.

World Bank and European Commission 2019. "World Bank and European Commission Promote Blue Economy through New Tool." https://oceans-and-fisheries.ec.europa.eu/news/world-bank-and-european-commission-promote-blue-economy-through-new-tool-2019-02-14_en.

World Economic Forum 2019. "These 11 Companies Are Leading the Way to a Circular Economy." www.weforum.org/agenda/2019/02/companies-leading-way-to-circular-economy/.

World Ocean Initiative 2020. "The Wealth of Oceans: New Research Shines a Light on Ocean Accounting." https://ocean.ecoomist.com/blue-finance/articles/the-wealth-of-oceans-new-research-highlights-importance-of-ocean-accounting.

Taskforce on Nature-related Financial Disclosures (TNFD) 2023. *Nature-related Risk and Opportunity Management and Disclosure Framework* (v0.4). https://tnfd.global.

PRACTICE PROBLEMS

1. The Paris Agreement:
   a. is legally binding under the local law of each signatory country.
   b. requires every signatory to provide an annual update on its national emission commitments.
   c. aims to limit the increase in global average temperature to below 2°C above pre-industrial levels by the end of the century.

2. The first international convention to set targets for emissions of the main greenhouse gases was the:
   a. Kyoto Protocol.
   b. Paris Agreement.
   c. United Nations Sustainable Development Goals.

3. In relation to the European Green Deal, the "green supporting factor" refers to:
   a. standards and labels for green bonds.
   b. a classification system for sustainable activities.
   c. the treatment of "green" assets in the capital requirements of banks and insurers.

4. Sustainability integration is *most* effective when sustainability is embedded in the practices of:
   a. asset owners and investee companies.
   b. asset owners and financial intermediaries.
   c. asset owners, investee companies, and financial intermediaries.

5. Which of the following countries has the highest level of investments in the low-carbon energy transition?
   a. Japan
   b. China
   c. United States

6. A sustainability bond funding a climate-friendly project that may be exposed to physical and transitional climate risks yet has no strategies in place to mitigate its impact would be graded by CICERO as:
   a. brown.
   b. light green.
   c. medium green.

7. Which of the following initiatives recommends that signatories incorporate climate change effects into macroeconomic policy and fiscal planning?
   a. Helsinki Principles
   b. Equator Principles
   c. Climate Resilience Principles

8. The Network for Greening the Financial System (NGFS) comprises:
   a. multilateral institutions and agencies.
   b. asset managers and investment banks.

c. central banks and financial supervisors.

9. Which of the following carbon pricing methods is used by companies to determine the impact of climate change on the profitability of a new project?

    a. Carbon taxation
    b. Shadow carbon pricing
    c. Emission trading system (ETS)

10. In relation to ESG analysis, investors should make adjustments to the credit assessment of a company based on:

    a. solely quantitative environmental factors.
    b. the sector and geographic location of the company's assets.
    c. all environmental effects on the company, irrespective of their materiality.

11. The set of actions taken to adapt human practices to function better in a warming world is called climate change:

    a. mitigation.
    b. adaptation.
    c. resilience measures.

12. In the natural world, there is:

    a. waste.
    b. pollution.
    c. neither waste nor pollution.

13. According to the Stockholm Resilience Centre, how many of the nine planetary boundaries have already been crossed as a result of human activity?

    a. Three
    b. Six
    c. All nine

14. Compared to the rest of the world, the Arctic is warming:

    a. one-third as fast as the global average.
    b. in line with the global average.
    c. three times as fast as the global average.

15. Which of the following statements about CO_2 is *most* accurate?

    a. CO_2 levels are the highest they have been in over 800,000 years.
    b. About 10% of CO_2 emissions from the 17th century onward occurred in the last 30 years.
    c. Agriculture and land-use changes account for the highest share of CO_2 emissions.

16. In 2021, the Intergovernmental Panel on Climate Change (IPCC) estimated global warming of about 1.5°C (2.7°F) by 2040 under which emissions scenario?

    a. Very low
    b. Intermediate
    c. Very high

Practice Problems

17. The term "dismal theorem" refers to the idea that:
    a. potentially catastrophic outcomes should be valued to negative infinity.
    b. moral considerations related to future climate change warrant low discount rates.
    c. the probability of total civilizational collapse causes the discount rate to increase dramatically.

18. The Jevons paradox states that:
    a. feeding a rapidly growing population is possible without further deforestation.
    b. relative improvements in efficiency may be offset by increased consumption of a given product.
    c. the quality of remaining phosphorus reserves is expected to fall while its costs continue to rise.

19. According to the Global Reporting Initiative (GRI) framework, which of the following is most likely to have an indirect impact on biodiversity resources?
    a. The use of surface water for irrigation purposes
    b. The construction of a road to transport products from a forestry operation
    c. The disturbance of local species by the noise and light produced at a processing site

20. The basis for the carbon risk premium is that studies:
    a. definitely show that companies with higher CO_2 emissions are associated with higher returns.
    b. definitely show that companies with higher CO_2 emissions are associated with lower returns.
    c. are inconclusive in establishing a definitive link between CO_2 emissions and returns.

21. In relation to shadow carbon pricing, which of the following is incorrect?
    a. Shadow carbon pricing is used to understand the potential impact of external prices on the profitability of a project.
    b. Shadow carbon pricing is used to conceal the true cost of an entity's carbon emissions.
    c. Shadow carbon pricing is used to create a theoretical cost per ton of carbon emissions by establishing a business's internal price on carbon.

22. Which of the following would be considered a climate change adaptation strategy?
    a. Releasing sunlight-reflecting aerosols into the atmosphere to reduce temperatures
    b. Retrofitting buildings to become more energy efficient
    c. Protecting coastlines from erosion

23. Which of the following *best* describes the concept of "natural capital"?
    a. Natural resources (such as oil, gas, or timber) that can be sold for a profit in a capitalist economy
    b. The stock of natural assets, which include geology, soil, air, water, and all living things

c. The sum total of monetary benefits that are directly dependent on nature

24. Which of the following emission sources are considered Scope 3 under the GHG Protocol Standards?

   a. Company facilities
   b. Purchased electricity
   c. Purchased goods and services

25. Which of the following is *not* a Task Force on Climate-Related Financial Disclosures (TCFD) core element of climate-related disclosures?

   a. Governance
   b. Impact
   c. Risk management

26. Which of the following *best* describes a transition risk?

   a. Policy change to encourage low-carbon technologies
   b. Occurrence of extreme weather events
   c. Breakdowns in business supply chains

27. Which of the following *best* describes the principles of a circular economy?

   a. Designing out waste and pollution, keeping materials in use, and regenerating natural systems
   b. Ensuring that all products are returned to manufacturers to reuse component parts
   c. Producing goods only for consumption by customers in the manufacturer's domestic market

28. Which of the following is *not* a requirement for a bond or a loan to be considered "green" under such frameworks as the Green Bond Principles (GBP) or Green Loan Principles (GLP)?

   a. A description of the environmental benefits associated with the use of proceeds
   b. A minimum of 10 tons of certified emissions reductions per every US$1 of debt
   c. A clear process for the evaluation and selection of eligible projects

29. The long-term goal of the 2015 Paris Agreement is to limit the increase in the global average temperature above pre-industrial levels to:

   a. 1.0°C (1.8°F).
   b. 2.0°C (3.6°F).
   c. 2.5°C (4.5°F).

30. For a reasonable chance of limiting the global average temperature rise to 1.5°C (2.7°F), the Intergovernmental Panel on Climate Change (IPCC) recommends that global emissions of CO_2 must reach "net zero" around:

   a. 2050.
   b. 2030.
   c. 2100.

31. The blue economy is *best* described as:

   a. industrial activities that generate pollution of oceans and inland waterways.

Practice Problems

   b. products and processes used to clean up water-based environmental pollution.
   c. sustainable economic and social activity related to oceans and coastal areas.

32. What is the primary objective of the EU Taxonomy?
    a. To create an EU-wide classification system of sustainable activities
    b. To identify "green" activities states can finance domestically without breaching competition rules
    c. To provide classification guidance for the Scope 1, 2, and 3 emissions associated with the activities of EU companies

SOLUTIONS

1. **C is correct.** The aim of the international Paris Agreement on climate change is to pursue efforts to limit the temperature increase to 2°C (3.6°F) above pre-industrial levels by the end of the century. The Paris Agreement does not set any legally binding targets under international law. Signatories to the Paris Agreement are required to determine, plan, and report on its NDCs, with updates to commitments every five years.

2. **A is correct.** The Kyoto Protocol was adopted in 1997 and became effective in 2005. It was the first international convention to set targets for emissions of the main GHGs.

3. **C is correct.** The treatment of "green" assets in the capital requirements of banks and insurers is referred to the "green supporting factor."

4. **C is correct.** Effective ESG integration is intended to embed sustainability across the entire investment chain—from the owners of capital (asset owners) to the beneficiaries of capital (such as investee companies), as well as key intermediaries.

5. **B is correct.** China remains the country with the highest levels of investment in the low-carbon energy transition.

6. **B is correct.** In the light green grade, projects may be exposed to physical and transitional climate risks without appropriate strategies in place to protect them.

7. **A is correct.** The Helsinki Principles encourage signatories to "take climate change into account in macroeconomic policy, fiscal planning, budgeting, public investment management, and procurement practices."

8. **C is correct.** The NGFS comprises over 70 central banks and financial supervisors.

9. **B is correct.** An internal or shadow price on carbon creates a theoretical or assumed cost per ton of carbon emissions. This is used to better understand the potential impact of future climate regulation on the profitability of a project, a new business model, or an investment.

10. **B is correct.** Investors should consider quantitative and qualitative environmental factors, the company, the sector, and the geographic location. Investors should assess the material financial impacts caused by environmental risks.

11. **B is correct.** Climate change adaptation is the set of actions taken to adapt human practices to function better in a warming world with rising seas and more frequent intense droughts, precipitation and storms. Climate resilience measures are adaptation actions that are able to function even though the climate is changing. Climate change mitigation represents the multiple actions that reduce the added warming of the earth that is caused by human actions.

12. **C is correct.** In the natural world, there is neither waste nor pollution. All materials not used by any organism become either building materials, food, or energy for a different organism. The idea behind the circular economy is that it is an economy whereby all materials are used and reused multiple times.

13. **B is correct.** According to an update by the Stockholm Resilience Centre from 2022, six of nine planetary boundaries have already been crossed as a result of

Solutions

human activity: climate change; loss of biosphere integrity; land-system change; freshwater (green water boundary); novel entities (including plastic pollution); and altered biogeochemical cycles (phosphorus and nitrogen loading).

14. **C is correct.** Because the planet does not warm uniformly, the Arctic is warming more than three times faster than the global average.

15. **A is correct.** Atmospheric carbon dioxide (CO_2) is at levels not seen over the past 800,000 years. More than half the CO_2 emissions (as opposed to 10%) from the late 17th century onward have occurred in the last 30 years. It is the burning of fossil fuels rather than agriculture and land use changes that cause the highest share of CO_2 emissions.

16. **A is correct.** In 2021, the IPCC estimated that global warming is likely to reach 1.5°C (2.7°F) by 2040 even under the very low emissions scenario.

17. **A is correct.** The dismal theorem suggests that standard cost–benefit analysis is inadequate to deal with the potential downside losses from climate change. However small the probability, as long as we cannot completely rule out scenarios of climate-induced civilizational collapse, their expected value must be thought of as being equal to negative infinity.

    Economist Nicholas Stern argued that moral considerations warrant using a low discount rate when assessing future climate damages to place adequate value on the lives and welfare of future generations.

18. **B is correct.** The Jevons paradox states that relative improvements in efficiency (using fewer resources per unit of production) may be offset by increased consumption of a given product.

19. **B is correct.** A road constructed to transport products from a forestry operation can have the indirect effect of stimulating the migration of workers to an unsettled region and encouraging new commercial development along the road. This can negatively impact biodiversity resources.

    Using surface water for irrigation purposes and disturbing local species through the noise and light produced at a processing site both impact biodiversity directly.

20. **C is correct.** A carbon risk premium is said to exist when investors require higher compensation for the perceived risk from investing in high-carbon companies. Several studies have argued that that companies with higher (absolute levels of or relative increases in) CO_2 emissions are associated with higher returns. However, studies have also found evidence for the converse—a positive link between reductions in carbon footprint and improvements returns.

21. **B is correct.** Shadow carbon pricing is used in the decision-making process, particularly related to new capital projects. Its purpose is to explicitly consider the costs and risks of carbon emissions rather than to conceal them.

22. **C is correct.** Protecting coastlines from erosion is a climate change adaptation strategy because it helps reduce the anticipated adverse effects of climate change (rising seas). The other actions are climate mitigation strategies because they reduce the added warming of the Earth caused by human activities.

23. **B is correct.** Natural capital refers to the world's stock of natural assets, from which humans derive the ecosystem services that enable our survival.

24. **C is correct.** Scope 3 emissions are those produced by suppliers and customers. They exclude emissions from purchased energy, which are Scope 2 emissions.

Emissions from purchased goods and services are therefore considered Scope 3.

25. **B is correct.** The core elements of TCFD-recommended disclosures are governance, strategy, risk management, and metrics and targets. Impact is not one of the core elements.

26. **A is correct.** Transition risks stem primarily from the trade-offs associated with action on climate change, including policy changes that result in higher costs of doing business or changes in asset values. Policy changes that encourage low-carbon technologies are a good example.

27. **A is correct.** The circular economy is a broad economic model based on three principles: (1) designing out waste and pollution, (2) keeping materials in use, and (3) regenerating natural systems.

28. **B is correct.** None of the Green Bond Principles or Green Loan Principles specify a particular level of emission reductions per unit of debt.

29. **B is correct.** Signatories agreed to limit the increase by 2100 to 2.0°C (3.6°F) and to make every effort to keep the increase to 1.5°C (2.7°F).

30. **A is correct.** According to the IPCC, reaching "net zero" emissions by 2050 is required if we are to limit the global temperature rise to 1.5°C (2.7°F).

31. **C is correct.** The blue economy refers to the use of the oceans' resources for economic growth and social activities while preserving the health of the related ecosystems.

32. **A is correct.** The EU Taxonomy was established to ensure that economic activities described as environmentally sustainable meet certain minimum requirements, thereby preventing the green-washing of financial products that hold investments in these economic activities.

CHAPTER 4

Social Factors

LEARNING OUTCOMES

Mastery	The candidate should be able to:
☐	**4.1.1** explain the systemic relationships and activities between business activities and social issues, including: globalization; automation and artificial intelligence (AI); inequality and wealth creation; digital disruption, social media, and access to electronic devices; changes to work, leisure time, and education; changes to individual rights and responsibilities and family structures; changing demographics; urbanization; and religion
☐	**4.1.2** assess key megatrends influencing social change in terms of potential impact on companies and their social practices: climate change; transition risk; water scarcity; pollution; mass migration; and loss and/or degradation of natural resources and ecosystem services
☐	**4.1.3** explain key social concepts, including: human capital: development, employment standards, and health and safety; product liability/consumer protection: safety, quality, health and demographic risks, and data privacy and security; stakeholder opposition/controversial sourcing; social opportunities: access to communications, finance, and health and nutrition; social and news media; animal welfare and microbial resistance
☐	**4.1.4** assess material impacts of social issues on potential investment opportunities and the dangers of overlooking them, including: changing demographics; digitization; individual rights and responsibilities; family structures and roles; education and work; faith-based ESG investing and exercise of religion; inequality; and globalization
☐	**4.1.5** identify approaches to social analysis at country, sector, and company levels
☐	**4.1.6** apply material social factors to: risk assessment; quality of management; ratio analysis; and financial modeling

1 INTRODUCTION

Social factors are relevant from both a business and an investment perspective and are increasingly being factored into investment analysis and investment decisions. In many cases, investors expect companies to manage these issues by using a best-in-class approach, whereby a company is better than its peers on a number of material issues relevant to its sector (e.g., occupational health and safety or managing its impact on local communities). In other cases, a social issue can become the focus of an investable opportunity (e.g., gender equality funds). Companies are increasingly expected to engage with their stakeholders openly, transparently, and responsively.

This chapter first gives an overview of various social factors and their material impact on potential investment opportunities. It then outlines the most relevant **social megatrends**, highlighting their relationship with business activities and investment opportunities. Descriptions are then provided of how to identify and apply material social factors, focusing on social analysis at country, sector, and company levels in both developed and emerging economies. Finally, all the above-mentioned topics are practically applied in case studies.

2 SOCIAL AND ENVIRONMENTAL MEGATRENDS

☐ **4.1.1** explain the systemic relationships and activities between business activities and social issues, including: globalization; automation and artificial intelligence (AI); inequality and wealth creation; digital disruption, social media, and access to electronic devices; changes to work, leisure time, and education; changes to individual rights and responsibilities and family structures; changing demographics; urbanization; and religion

☐ **4.1.2** assess key megatrends influencing social change in terms of potential impact on companies and their social practices: climate change; transition risk; water scarcity; pollution; mass migration; and loss and/or degradation of natural resources and ecosystem services

Investors need to note the different social megatrends that could have an effect on the businesses of the investee companies. This section looks at the systemic relationships between these social megatrends and business activities of the investee companies, and it elaborates on the material impacts of these trends on potential investment opportunities.

What Are Social Megatrends?

Social megatrends are long-term social changes that affect governments, societies, and economies permanently over a long period of time.

The following megatrends will be described in this section:

A. Globalization

B. Automation and artificial intelligence (AI)

C. Inequality and wealth creation

Social and Environmental Megatrends

- **D.** Digital disruption, social media, and access to electronic devices
- **E.** Changes to work, leisure time, and education
- **F.** Changes to individual rights and responsibilities and family structures
- **G.** Changing demographics, including health and longevity
- **H.** Urbanization
- **I.** Religion

Some *environmental megatrends* have a significant social impact as well. These include the following:

- ▶ Climate change and transition risk
- ▶ Water scarcity
- ▶ Mass migration

All of these could, in an extreme case, result in mass migration. These social megatrends will change the way we live, work, consume, and perceive the world and, as such, will pose new risks or opportunities for investors. Next, we will look at each of these megatrends in further detail.

Globalization

One of the biggest megatrends is the integration of local and national economies into a global (and less regulated) market economy. The growth in global interactions has increased international trade and the exchange of ideas and culture. This process is also called **globalization**.

Globalization is caused by a rapid increase in cross-border movement of goods, services, technology, people, and capital. Depending on the viewpoint, it can be viewed as either a positive or a negative phenomenon. On the one hand, it is stated to have led to increased efficiency in the markets, resulting in wider availability of products at lower costs. On the other hand, it is claimed to be detrimental to social well-being due to social structural inequality.

Examples of its implications include the following:

- ▶ *Offshoring*. Due to the lower wages of workers in the garment industry in developing countries, clothes are now mainly produced in such countries as Vietnam, Bangladesh, and China. This has led to the disappearance of the textile industry in Western countries. Offshoring also takes place in other sectors.
- ▶ *Dependency*. As US-based and Asian companies dominate the industry for mobile telephones, computers, and other IT products, European countries are more dependent on these suppliers.

Automation and Artificial Intelligence (AI)

Linked to the increased economic globalization is the trend of **automation**, which is the technology by which a process or procedure is performed with minimal human assistance. Some of the biggest advantages of automation in industry are that it is:

- **a.** associated with faster production and lower labor costs; and it
- **b.** replaces hard, physical, or monotonous work.

The largest (social) disadvantage, however, is that it displaces workers due to job replacement, as technology renders their skills or experience unnecessary. It is expected that this trend will increase due to the rise of AI.

AI is expected to have a significant effect on such sectors as:

a. healthcare;
b. automotive;
c. financial services and auditing;
d. security (including military); and
e. creative (in particular, advertising and video games).

> **EXAMPLE 1**
>
> **Implications for Investors**
>
> The transportation industry is currently on the brink of becoming more automated, and it is expected that some jobs for drivers (of taxis, buses, and trucks, for example) will disappear due to self-driving vehicles. This will be beneficial for companies that develop the best self-driving cars but less so for traditional heavy goods vehicle (HGV) companies that do not innovate. One of the largest expected implications of this is that by automating the transport industry, major job losses will occur. One possible solution is to invest in upskilling staff to enable their transition to a more AI-enabled world. Investors should take this into account when assessing the risks of an investee company.

Inequality and Wealth Creation

The Organisation for Economic Co-operation and Development (OECD) analyzes trends in inequality and poverty for advanced and emerging economies. It examines the drivers of growing inequalities, such as globalization, skill-biased technological change, and changes in countries' policy approaches. It also assesses the effectiveness and efficiency of a wide range of policies, including education, labor market, and social policies, in tackling poverty and promoting more inclusive growth. According to the OECD Centre for Opportunity and Equality (COPE) 2015 report, the average income of the richest 10% of the population is about nine times that of the poorest 10% across the OECD (OECD 2015). This is also called *economic* or *income inequality*.

There is increasing evidence that growing inequality affects economies and societies. Educational opportunities and social mobility may be reduced, resulting in a less skilled and less healthy society with lower purchasing power among the lower and middle classes. This limits total economic growth.

An issue related to the topic of inequality is corporate tax strategies and whether companies are too aggressive in their tax optimization strategies. As regulators put more focus on this issue, some companies (for instance, in the technology sector) have had to pay huge fines. Others will need to adopt more conservative tax strategies in the future that will impact their bottom line.

Digital Disruption, Social Media, and Access to Electronic Devices

Another important social trend is the rise of **digital disruption**, which is the change that occurs when new digital technologies and business models affect the value proposition of existing goods and services. This trend is closely related to the increased automation and rise of AI discussed above.

Some exemplary cases of disrupting companies include Amazon, Uber, and Airbnb. They have managed to enter an existing market but with different and more digital business approaches than their competitors, effectively challenging existing business models. There are opportunities for investors who are about to invest, preferably at an early stage, in such companies, although such investments can carry a high-risk profile.

A related consequence of digital technologies is the huge amount of data that can be collected, stored, and processed (*big data*) as well as the ownership or use of the data (including data privacy, monetization of data, etc.).

Big data has many opportunities, including more personalized services, products, and (health) treatments. However, controversies have arisen because some data are being used and sold in more extreme or socially unacceptable ways. Examples include social media companies—such as Facebook, Twitter, and LinkedIn—selling data for political or marketing campaigns (e.g., the case of Cambridge Analytica allegedly using Facebook data to try to manipulate elections, or Meta agreeing to pay fines to regulators and settle class-action lawsuits relating to its data privacy and practices).

Due to these types of scandals, there is a debate around the growing need for regulating the industry. This can affect the profitability of these companies and should be considered by investors.

Finally, electronic devices are now found everywhere. Almost everyone, both in developed and emerging economies, owns a mobile phone (in many cases a smartphone) and a tablet. The *Internet of Things (IoT)* is the next frontier, where semi-intelligent appliances (called 'embedded systems') communicate directly with each other and with the internet and make autonomous decisions.

For investors, disruption represents both risks and opportunities. Analysts need to take a forward-looking approach to determine which sectors and companies will thrive and which will struggle in a digital society.

Changes to Work, Leisure Time, and Education

The way we spend our lives has changed dramatically over the last few decades. Various measures have emerged that aim to provide a broad sense of the state of our societies and of how people's lives are evolving. The OECD examines issues of well-being in its *Better Life Index*, which rates a wide range of developed and emerging economies in a number of areas, including life satisfaction.

Most countries in the developed world have seen average hours worked decrease significantly. In the UK, for example, the average annual hours actually worked per person in employment decreased from 1,775 hours in 1970 to 1,497 in 2021 (OECD.Stat 2023). This is partially caused by increases in automation and part-time employment.

New technologies increasingly enable workers to be connected to their work from remote locations. This creates an opportunity for employers and employees to adopt more flexible working patterns. However, the constant connection also makes the notion of work–life balance more elusive and can cause stress-related illnesses.

While the number of average working hours has decreased, the average level of education has increased. The percentage of employees with a higher education degree has grown over the last few decades. Yet, some sectors suffer from a lack of qualified employees and are facing an intense 'war on talent' to attract the most skilled workers.

Investors who are assessing companies that rely heavily on employees as a key asset need to pay attention to those companies' human capital management strategies, including their Diversity, Equity, and Inclusion (DEI) strategies. They should evaluate how the companies are coping with these structural changes in the labor market.

Changes to Individual Rights and Responsibilities and Family Structures

In recent decades, not only has the way we divide work and leisure time changed but also the role and importance of family (especially in developed countries). Individuals are also less reliant on the structure of the family for (economic and physical) security.

The workforce has become more diverse: More women are now entering the labor market, which has provided women with more financial independence. However, in comparison to men, women are still more likely to become and remain unemployed, have fewer chances to participate in the labor force, and often have to accept lower quality jobs when they do secure employment. Women also face wage gaps in comparison to men. To improve gender equality, a number of different initiatives have been created, and there is growing evidence that a more diverse workforce leads to better (financial) results for the company. Some best-in-class funds and impact investors take diversity (gender and other types of diversity) into account in their risk analysis and stock selection.

Changing Demographics, Including Health and Longevity

Due to improvements made in healthcare and changes in lifestyle, life expectancy is increasing. The UN reports that globally, a new baby born in 2021 could expect to live 25 years longer, on average, than a baby born in 1950 (United Nations 2023). While the recent COVID-19 pandemic disparately impaired the rate of increase in life expectancy across countries, overall, life expectancy continues to trend upward. As of 2021, life expectancy stood at 68.4 for men and 73.8 for women globally, with higher average life expectancy in developed countries (United Nations 2023).

This increased life expectancy, combined with a falling birth rate, have already caused many developed countries' populations to age. Emerging market countries are also facing ageing populations. In 2021, around 10% of the global population was above 65 years old, up from 5% in 1950. This percentage is projected to grow to 17% by 2050. China, Korea, Japan, Italy and Spain are projected to have the highest percentages of their population above 65 by 2050 (United Nations 2023). A globally aging population is likely an irreversible trend and has substantial effects on society:

1. The ratio between the active and the inactive part of the workforce drops, impacting national tax revenues and challenging pension systems, including an impact on retirement accounts that need to last longer.
2. Older people have higher accumulated savings per person than younger people but spend less on consumer goods, which is a business risk for some industries. In some categories, such as healthcare, expenditure rises sharply when populations age.

CASE STUDIES

The Impact of the Global COVID-19 Pandemic

The COVID-19 pandemic was one of the largest global health, economic, and social crises in recent history. Although it affected every population segment, it was particularly detrimental to those in the most vulnerable situations, including people living in poverty, older people, people with disabilities, and adolescents. Health and economic impacts were felt disproportionately by poor people, particularly among the unhoused, as they were unable to safely shelter and were therefore highly exposed to the dangers of the virus. People without access to running water, refugees, migrants, or displaced people also suffered disproportionately both from the pandemic and its aftermath. This could include limited movement, fewer employment opportunities, and increased xenophobia (United Nations 2020).

Other impacts include the following:

- Educational: Potential learning loss due to the widespread closures of schools and universities.
- Increased inequality: It has been found that low-income individuals were more likely to contract COVID-19 and die from it. This is likely because poorer families are more likely to live in crowded housing and work in low-skilled jobs, such as supermarkets and elderly care, which were deemed essential during the crisis. In the United States, millions of low-income people may lack access to healthcare due to being un- or underinsured.
- Psychological: There was a concern for mental health impacts, exacerbated by social isolation due to quarantining and social distancing guidelines, fear, unemployment, and financial factors.
- Reshoring: Companies and countries may decide to reduce supply chain risk by relocating production of strategic importance back to high-wage countries (United Nations Conference on Trade and Development 2020).
- Work environment: There has been a changing demand for office buildings with increased working from home (Pew Research Center 2020).

Investor Initiatives: Equitable Circulation of COVID-19 Vaccines

To ensure a more equitable global circulation of the COVID-19 vaccine, different investor initiatives were launched. The pharma group Moderna faced a shareholder proposal demanding to open up its COVID-19 vaccine technology to poorer countries and requesting an explanation regarding the high prices given the amount of government assistance it had received. Another initiative concerned vaccine manufacturers being asked to increase the availability and deployment of vaccinations around the world. A group of 65 institutional investors demanded that the global availability of vaccines be linked to the remuneration policy of managers and directors. In this way, investors have aimed to hold pharmaceutical companies accountable for their contribution to solving this problem.

Urbanization

The places where people live also change. Globally, the population has been increasingly shifting from rural to urban areas. In the 1950s, approximately 30% of the world population lived in an urban **environment**. This is expected to increase to 68% by 2050.

This shift can have different kinds of implications for societies, including the following:

- *Economic*: Dramatic increases and changes in costs can often price the local working class out of the market.
- *Environmental*: 'Urban heat islands,' where urban areas produce and retain heat, have become a growing concern.

- *Social*: There has been increased mortality from non-communicable diseases associated with lifestyle, including cancer and heart disease. Residents in poor urban areas (such as slums) also suffer "disproportionately from disease, injury, premature death, and the combination of ill-health and poverty entrenches disadvantage over time" (International Institute for Environment and Development/United Nations Population Fund 2012).

These societal implications provide business opportunities because of the growing need for infrastructure development, but they also require companies to address social and environmental issues related to urban living (for instance, pollution and waste management systems).

Religion

As a social factor, the changing religious landscape around the world has consequences for consumer preferences. Religion-based politics and conflicts can also have a profound impact on specific local economies.

All investors (faith-based or not) should therefore judge if investee companies take these changes into account from a financial perspective. A distinction should be made between exercise of religion as a social factor and faith-based investing.

Faith-based investors aim to invest their money in line with a specific named faith. These are the two most common types:

- *Christian investors*, who aim to align their investment principles to the Bible. This means that they may refrain from investing in certain companies whose activities or processes are considered to not be aligned with Christian values.
- *Islamic investors*, who look to invest in line with Shariah principles. They would not invest in companies that profit from alcohol, pornography, or gambling or companies involved in pork. They will not own investments that pay interest or invest in firms that earn a substantial part of their revenue from interest.

Norms-based exclusion has been one of the first environmental, social, and governance (ESG) investing instruments; many of these first movers were faith-based investors. The Church of England, the Church Investors Group, the Interfaith Center on Corporate Responsibility, and other faith-based investors continue to play an important role in ESG advocacy and company engagement and in submitting shareholder resolutions.

Environmental Megatrends with Social Impact

Climate change and transition risk

Climate change and the neighboring effect of **transition risk** have social implications. A widespread call is that the transition should be a 'just' transition—where the social and economic costs and benefits of transitioning to a lower-carbon economy are satisfactorily shared. In the process of adjusting to an economy that does not adversely affect the climate, sectors that employ millions of workers (such as energy, coal, manufacturing, agriculture, and forestry) must restructure. It is feared that the period of economic structural change will result in ordinary workers bearing the costs of the transition, leading to unemployment, poverty, and exclusion for the working class.

Water scarcity

Climate change has a negative impact on the availability of fresh water. Some corporations with high water usage pose a significant threat to clean and affordable water for communities. The construction of wastewater treatment plants and reduction of groundwater over-drafting appear to be obvious solutions to the worldwide problem. However, this is not as simple as it seems for the following reasons:

- Wastewater treatment is highly capital intensive, so there is restricted access to this technology in some regions.
- The rapid increase in the population of many countries makes this a race that is difficult to win.
- There are enormous costs and skillsets involved in maintaining wastewater treatment plants, even if they are successfully developed.

Mass migration

The scarcity of fresh water and desertification due to climate change in several emerging countries is believed to be one of the reasons for *mass migration* streams from developing countries to developed countries where these issues are less present. Climate change might result in an increase of 'environmental migrants,' with the most common projection being that the world will have 150 to 200 million such migrants by 2050.

Pollution and loss and/or degradation of natural resources and ecosystem services

Factors like pollution and land degradation can also result in stakeholder opposition, social unrest, and/or migration.

Conclusion

As discussed in this section, different social megatrends provide both opportunities and risks for investors and analysts. It is therefore important to be aware of these trends and take them into account when making investment decisions.

More specific information on how to apply these trends to investing can be found later in this chapter. The next sections consider key social issues and business activities.

KEY SOCIAL ISSUES AND BUSINESS ACTIVITIES   3

> 4.1.3 explain key social concepts, including: human capital: development, employment standards, and health and safety; product liability/consumer protection: safety, quality, health and demographic risks, and data privacy and security; stakeholder opposition/controversial sourcing; social opportunities: access to communications, finance, and health and nutrition; social and news media; animal welfare and microbial resistance

Where should investors start when implementing social factors in their investment decision?

1. A good starting point is to determine which social factors are most controversial or financially material in each industry.

2. As a next step, investors can assess how exposed certain companies are to these sector-specific social factors and if and how the company manages these risks. This might depend on their business models or on the nature and geographical location of their business operations.
3. Finally, where relevant, investors should assess critical social factors in the supply chain.

It should be noted that the social elements that are considered to have the largest financial materiality depend on specific aspects mostly related to their field of industry. The Sustainability Accounting Standards Board (SASB) framework gives guidance on the financially material topics within industries.

Social factors can also be categorized between those impacting external stakeholders (such as customers, local communities, and governments) and groups of internal stakeholders (such as the company's employees). See Exhibit 1 for examples of social factors that may affect these stakeholders.

Exhibit 1: Examples of Social Factors That Impact Internal and External Stakeholders

Social factors that impact *internal* stakeholders:	Social factors that impact *external* stakeholders:
Human capital development.	Stakeholder opposition and controversial sourcing.
Working conditions, health, and safety.	Product liability and consumer protection.
Human rights.	Social opportunities.
Employment standards and labor rights.	Animal welfare and antimicrobial resistance.

4 INTERNAL SOCIAL FACTORS

☐ 4.1.3 explain key social concepts, including: human capital: development, employment standards, and health and safety; product liability/consumer protection: safety, quality, health and demographic risks, and data privacy and security; stakeholder opposition/controversial sourcing; social opportunities: access to communications, finance, and health and nutrition; social and news media; animal welfare and microbial resistance

This section will provide an overview of the key **internal social factors** that can be of interest for investors.

Human Capital Development

A company's long-term strategy should take into account the development of its workforce.

This ensures that the workforce:

1. is well equipped for performing its tasks and responsibilities;

2. operates under the latest standards and regulations; and
3. remains motivated.

Good human capital management generates a culture and behaviors where the workforce is positively disposed and productive, rather than taking excessive risks or harming customer relationships. It enhances social inclusion, active citizenship, and personal development while increasing competitiveness and employability.

For an investor, the following business requirements could be assessed when analyzing a company on human capital development. Questions should include:

Does the business…

- identify required skills or competencies to deliver on its strategy as well as identify gaps within the company and areas of skill shortage in the industry ('war on talent')?
- develop an attractive value proposition to attract talent as well as ways to develop competencies of internal employees to retain talent?
- develop measures to monitor its investment in human capital development (e.g., training hours, coaching) and its return on investment (key performance indicators, or KPIs, such as employee engagement, turnover, and ability to fill vacancies with internal candidates)?

Working Conditions, Health, and Safety

One of the most widely felt social factors that has been incorporated by institutional investors is health and safety. Its focus is on protecting the workforce from accidents and fatalities. A specific subtopic is occupational health, which is about limiting workforce exposures to minimize the risk of occupational diseases (such as silicosis) or injury (for example, vibration white finger).

An example of a health and safety factor can be seen in the Rana Plaza disaster, examined in the following case study.

CASE STUDIES

Rana Plaza Disaster

On 24 April 2013, a structural failure resulted in the collapse of the Rana Plaza, an eight-story commercial building in Dhaka, Bangladesh. This resulted in a death toll of 1,134 people. Approximately 2,500 injured people were rescued from the building alive. It is considered the deadliest structural failure accident in modern human history. The building's owners ignored warnings to avoid using the building after cracks had appeared the day before. Garment workers were ordered to return the following day, and the building collapsed during the morning rush hour.

The high death toll of this disaster is at least partially caused by the managers' decision to send workers back into the factories despite knowing the risks. Managers claimed they ignored the warnings due to the pressure to complete orders for buyers on time. Some have argued that the demand for fast fashion and low-cost clothing motivated minimal oversight by clothing brands and that collectively organized trade unions could have responded to the pressure of management.

This massive tragedy drew attention to pervasive **human rights** abuses in the garment sector, as well as the failure of the Bangladesh government and corporations sourcing there to create workplaces that respect and protect the lives of workers and mitigate the risk to companies and their investors. As a

> result of the Rana Plaza disaster, over 175 brands, such as Adidas, Marks and Spencer, and H&M, have signed the Bangladesh Accord, where they pledge to commit to higher fire and health and safety standards in Bangladesh (Bangladesh Accord 2018).
>
> Led by the Interfaith Center on Corporate Responsibility, the Bangladesh Investor Initiative, an investor coalition comprising 250 institutional investors and representing over USD4.5 trillion in assets under management, was formed in May 2013 to urge a strong corporate response to Rana Plaza, including participation in the Accord (Interfaith Center on Corporate Responsibility 2023).

Health and safety performance indicators should be assessed for both permanent employees and contractors. For example, several oil and gas companies report only fatalities of their permanent employees but not of their contractors. Given the volume of contracted workers in this sector, it is critical for investors to understand if the company is providing a safe place to work. This is particularly pertinent in emerging market extractive companies.

Besides minimizing accidents and fatalities, health and safety has evolved a broader concept of working conditions that promotes employee well-being, as seen for instance through ergonomic workplaces and flexible working hours. The focus is also increasingly on mental health (such as burn out risks in the finance industry) and other employee benefits to promote their well-being outside of the workplace (including medical checks, gym membership sponsorship, and training programs on nutrition-related risks). Another example is "financial wellness," which is a fairly well-established term among US employers and HR departments. Assistance with personal financial issues like personal budgeting and retirement planning/saving leads to less distracted and less stressed workers.

Human Rights

Another important social factor for investment professionals is human rights. These are rights inherent to all human beings, regardless of:

1. race;
2. sex;
3. nationality;
4. ethnicity;
5. language;
6. religion; or
7. any other status (e.g., age, ability, socioeconomic level, or gender identity).

Human rights include the following:

1. the right to life and liberty;
2. freedom from slavery and torture;
3. freedom of opinion and expression; and
4. the right to work and education.

Everyone is entitled to these rights, without discrimination.

The most important foundation for international human rights is the *Universal Declaration of Human Rights (UDHR)*. This declaration was proclaimed by the United Nations General Assembly on 10 December 1948 by General Assembly resolution 217A and is a common standard of achievement for all peoples and all nations (United Nations 1948).

Human rights violations usually occur deep within supply chains. Companies to which major investors most often have direct exposure, and even their first and second tier suppliers, are less likely to be directly implicated in such practices. For example, in the garment industry, it is more likely that human rights violations will take place in emerging countries where clothing is produced, rather than at the stores where the clothing is being sold. However, both clients and governments expect companies to take responsibility for activities within their supply chain.

UN Guiding Principles and OECD Guidelines for Multinational Enterprises

There are many different guidelines with respect to human rights. However, two have a direct effect on companies and investors:

- The *United Nations Guiding Principles on Business and Human Rights (UNGPs)*
- The *OECD Guidelines for Multinational Enterprises (MNEs)*

United Nations Guiding Principles on Business and Human Rights

The UNGPs are a set of guidelines implementing the United Nations' "Protect, Respect and Remedy" framework for the responsibilities of transnational corporations and other business enterprises with regard to human rights (Business & Human Rights Resource Centre 2019). Developed by the Special Representative of the Secretary-General (SRSG) John Ruggie, these guiding principles provided the first global standard for preventing and addressing the risk of adverse impacts on human rights linked to business activity. They also continue to provide the internationally accepted framework for enhancing standards and practice regarding business and human rights.

The UNGPs encompass three pillars outlining how states and businesses should implement the framework:

1. The state duty to protect human rights
2. The corporate responsibility to respect human rights
3. Access to remedy for victims of business-related abuses

OECD Guidelines for Multinational Enterprises

The OECD Guidelines for MNEs are a comprehensive set of government-backed recommendations on responsible business conduct. The governments adhering to the Guidelines aim to encourage and maximize the positive impact MNEs can make to sustainable development and enduring social progress. The Guidelines are important recommendations addressed by governments to multinational enterprises operating in or from adhering countries. They provide voluntary principles and standards for responsible business conduct in such areas as:

1. employment and industrial relations;
2. human rights;
3. environment;
4. information disclosure;
5. combating bribery;
6. consumer interests;
7. science and technology;
8. competition; and
9. taxation.

The study, *Responsible Business Conduct for Institutional Investors*, helps institutional investors implement the due diligence recommendations of the OECD Guidelines for MNEs in order to prevent or address adverse impacts related to human and labor rights, the environment, and corruption in their investment portfolios (OECD 2017).

It is important to note that these guidelines do not focus on the impact social factors can have on investments (financial materiality) but rather on the responsibility investors have for the adverse impacts their investments/ companies can cause to society. Nowadays, many investors are convinced that they should take ESG factors into account, but these guidelines require governments and investors to adopt a so-called double (or dual) materiality approach and take the (positive and negative) "social return on investments" into account.

The OECD guidelines and the UNGPs are further backed by the European Union (EU) corporate social responsibility (CSR) strategy, its regulation on sustainability-related disclosures in the financial services sector, and its taxonomy for minimum social safeguards for sustainable activities.

In the Netherlands, the government, non-governmental organizations (NGOs), and institutional investors have signed a Responsible Investment Agreement in which investors agree to adopt this double materiality approach, follow the OECD guidelines, and take responsibility to try to mitigate the negative impact of their investments (International RBC/SER 2021).

Corporate Human Rights Benchmark

The *Corporate Human Rights Benchmark (CHRB)* is a collaboration led by investors and civil society organizations dedicated to creating the first open and public benchmark of corporate human rights performance (CHRB 2020).

The CHRB provides a comparative snapshot year-on-year of the largest companies on the planet, looking at the policies, processes, and practices they have in place to systematize their human rights approach and how they respond to serious allegations. Initially, only companies from three industries — agricultural products, apparel, and extractives — were chosen on the basis of their size and revenues. The measurement themes and indicators within the CHRB provide a rigorous proxy measure of corporate human rights performance, which can be used by analysts and investors. The themes consist of multiple questions that are listed in the report. These questions address:

1. governance and policy commitments;
2. embedding respect and human rights due diligence;
3. remedies and grievance mechanisms;
4. performance — company human rights practices;
5. performance — responses to serious allegations; and
6. transparency.

Human Rights 100+

Following in the footsteps of Climate Action 100+, Principles for Responsible Investment (PRI) has recently launched a new collaborative initiative for investors to address human rights and social issues through their stewardship activities: Human Rights 100+. The initiative acts as a platform that can encompass a broad range of social issues, allowing investors to prioritize the most severe human rights risks and outcomes within their stewardship activities. It includes investor collaborative engagement with companies, along with potential further escalation where needed, and also supports investor engagement with policymakers and other stakeholders to make progress on the overall goal.

Labor Rights

Assessing how companies uphold labor rights is important for investors to gain insights into the corporate culture and the level of employee satisfaction. The most important labor rights have been summarized in *International Labor Standards*. These are aimed at promoting opportunities for women and men to obtain decent and productive work with freedom, equity, security, and dignity. These standards are included in the eight fundamental conventions of the International Labour Organization (ILO 2023):

1. Freedom of Association and Protection of the Right to Organise
2. Right to Organise and Collective Bargaining
3. Forced Labour
4. Abolition of Forced Labour
5. Minimum Age
6. Worst Forms of Child Labour
7. Equal Remuneration
8. Discrimination (Employment and Occupation)

We will now explore some of these conventions in further detail.

Freedom of Association and Employee Relations

A company operates most effectively and efficiently when the workforce is positive and productive. This ensures that the costs of turnover, absenteeism, or strike actions are reduced. In order to ensure that the rights of the employees are well served, employees should have the freedom to form or join an association or a trade union that advocates for the interests of the employees.

In some countries or industries this right is limited. For example, several companies within the retail industry are renowned for their anti-union stance. Walmart has been targeted by several international institutional investors to adopt a more pro-union stance. When freedom of association is established, often other labor rights violations — such as forced labor, child labor, and discrimination — are better safeguarded.

The lack of freedom of association can occur directly at the level of the investee companies, but it is more likely to be an issue in companies' supply chains. By engaging with their investee companies on this topic, investors can press for better industrial relations within a specific sector or country.

Modern Slavery and Forced Labor

Two topics that are less frequently mentioned in responsible investment policies are modern slavery and forced labor.

Modern slavery refers to situations of exploitation that a person cannot refuse or leave because of threats, violence, coercion, deception, and/or abuse of power. This is considered to be an umbrella term encompassing such practices as forced labor, debt bondage, forced marriage, and human trafficking (United Nations 2021).

Forced labor is defined by the ILO as:

> "All work or service which is exacted from any person under the menace of any penalty and for which the said person has not offered himself voluntarily." (ILO 2022)

Modern slavery and forced labor can take place in every kind of work or service, either in the private, public, informal, or formal marketplace, but it typically occurs in industries that are poorly regulated and where the production process requires many workers. In total, no fewer than 25 million people are estimated to be in forced labor.

It is often hidden away in supply chains in the second tier and beyond. Most companies that address modern slavery and forced labor, however, both start and end their due diligence by focusing on their first-tier contractors and suppliers. Forced labor can take subtle forms, which makes detecting it very difficult.

The use or threat of physical violence is not essential to characterize a labor relationship as forced labor. Debt bondage, threatening to denounce a worker to immigration authorities, or the retention of identity papers can 'force' workers as well. The increasing complexity and international character of supply chains makes more transparency essential (Holtland and Höften 2018).

In 2015, the Parliament of the United Kingdom adopted the *Modern Slavery Act*. Further information on the UK Modern Slavery Act is provided later in this chapter.

Living Wage

In sectors that employ and rely on masses of manual labor (such as the garment and footwear, food and beverage, consumer electronics, or retail sectors), wages are often insufficient to cover workers' basic living expenses (food, clothing, housing, healthcare, and education).

The benefits of paying a **living wage** are clear. Workers who earn a living wage can meet their own basic needs and those of their families and put savings aside, thus being more likely to find their way out of poverty. They work regular working hours instead of excessive overtime to make 'ends meet' and are more likely to send their children to school instead of work.

In short, the focus on a living wage also advances the respect for a number of other fundamental human rights in global supply chains.

EXAMPLE 2

Platform Living Wage Financials

The Platform Living Wage Financials (PLWF) was established at the end of 2018 (PLWF 2020). This is a coalition of (mainly Dutch) financial institutions that encourage and monitor investee companies to address the non-payment of a living wage in their global supply chains. The investor coalition has over EUR€2.6 trillion of assets under management and uses its influence and leverage to engage with its investee companies. They:

1. measure their performance on living wage;
2. discuss the assessment results; and
3. support innovative pilots.

Finally, they make sustainable investment decisions based on (the lack of) progress subject to individual choices and policy preferences of each member of the platform.

EXTERNAL SOCIAL FACTORS

> **4.1.3** explain key social concepts, including: human capital: development, employment standards, and health and safety; product liability/consumer protection: safety, quality, health and demographic risks, and data privacy and security; stakeholder opposition/controversial sourcing; social opportunities: access to communications, finance, and health and nutrition; social and news media; animal welfare and microbial resistance

This section will provide an overview of the key **external social factors** that can be of interest for investors.

Stakeholder Opposition and Controversial Sourcing

When a company operates in a certain area, it should strive for good relationships with stakeholders, including its local communities. This ensures that the company can continue operating without political interference or informal protest and disruption. Companies should focus on local communities (located near companies' operations) and recognize how they can be involved in stakeholder engagement processes to understand their needs and concerns and how these can be addressed. A way to establish bottom-up participation is to use *Free, Prior, and Informed Consent (FPIC)*.

EXAMPLE 3

Free, Prior, and Informed Consent

A company that plans to develop on ancestral land or use resources of a territory owned by indigenous people should establish FPIC:

- *Free* simply means that there is no manipulation or coercion of the indigenous people and that the process is self-directed by those affected by the project.
- *Prior* implies that consent is sought sufficiently in advance of any activities being either commenced or authorized, and time for the consultation process to occur must be guaranteed by the relative agents.
- *Informed* suggests that the relevant indigenous people receive satisfactory information on the key points of the project, such as:

    its nature;

    its size;

    its pace;

    its reversibility;

    the scope of the project;

    the reason for it; and

    its duration.

> ▸ "Informed" is the more difficult term of the four, as different groups may find certain information more relevant. The indigenous people should also have access to the primary reports on the economic, environmental, and cultural impact that the project will have. The language used must be able to be understood by the indigenous people.
> ▸ Finally, *consent* means a process in which participation and consultation are the central pillars.(See Food and Agriculture Organization of the United Nations 2016)

Controversial sourcing is also an issue for companies with suppliers operating in emerging economies. Companies enjoy the cheap products of their suppliers, but when the cost-driven practices of many of them in these chains come to light, there is often considerable debate over the ethics of these practices.

A rather well-known example is the case of conflict minerals and blood diamonds, which are natural resources extracted in a conflict zone and sold to perpetuate the fighting. The most prominent contemporary example has been in the eastern provinces of the Democratic Republic of Congo (DRC), where various armies, rebel groups, and outside organizations have profited from mining while contributing to violence and exploitation during wars in the region.

Investors should be aware of issues around controversial sourcing and stakeholder opposition because they can become a business and reputational risk for the investee company.

Product Liability and Consumer Protection

Consumer protection refers to laws and other forms of government regulation designed to protect the rights of consumers. It is based on consumer rights, or the idea that consumers have an inherent right to basic health and safety. These are safeguarded by:

a. enforcing product safety;
b. distributing consumer-related information; and
c. preventing deceptive marketing.

Product liability is the legal responsibility imposed on a business for the manufacturing or selling of defective goods. The laws are built on the principle that manufacturers and vendors have more knowledge about the products than the consumers do. Therefore, these businesses bear the responsibility when things go wrong (even when consumers are somewhat at fault).

Product liability cases can result in civil lawsuits and lucrative monetary judgments for the plaintiffs. They can have consequences for the share price of a company if it has regular product recalls or lawsuits. Investors should take this into account in their investment analysis. There are three main types of product liability:

1. businesses being found liable to consumers when a court finds design flaws;
2. manufacturing defects; or
3. a failure to warn consumers of a possible danger. (See Dugger 2019)

Product liability is likely to lead to reputational risks since consumers can easily express their opinions via social media or boycott the product or service when it is found to be liable. Especially around consumer products, analysts should be aware of such risks.

Social Opportunities

Lack of social opportunities, especially in developing countries, is an important social issue. Many of the **Sustainable Development Goals (SDGs)** focus around this area. The most closely linked are access to basic needs and services in different areas related to health (including water), education, energy, housing, and financial inclusion.

Originally, only such specific investors as development finance institutions, NGOs, and foundations focused on these topics. For example, they invested in microfinance institutions and other impact funds to ensure that people have access to products and services related to communications, finance, and health and nutrition. However, enabling broad and affordable access to basic products and services has proved to be a good business model as well and is increasingly seen as an opportunity for both businesses and investors. This is especially true when aligning the investments with the SDG framework or trying to achieve both a financial and social return on investments.

A similar tool that can be used by investors is the *Access to Medicine Index*. The tool analyzes how 20 of the world's largest pharmaceutical companies are addressing access to medicine in 106 low- to middle-income countries for 82 diseases, conditions, and pathogens. It evaluates these companies in areas where they have the biggest potential and responsibility to make change, such as research and development (R&D) and pricing (Access to Medicine Foundation 2021).

Animal Welfare and Antimicrobial Resistance

Concerns around animal welfare have become more prevalent among consumers and investors as they increasingly recognize that it is not only ethical to minimize harm caused to animals, but it is also important to understand the negative impacts on human health resulting from intensive farming practices. As a result of antimicrobial resistance (i.e., bacteria, viruses, and some parasites becoming more resistant to antibiotics, antivirals, and antimalarials), standard treatments become increasingly ineffective and infections persist, which can result in deaths and increased spread to others.

A growing investor initiative that is focused and engaged on the risks and opportunities linked to intensive livestock production is *Farm Animal Investment Risk and Return (FAIRR)*. FAIRR focuses particularly on the increased prevalence of antimicrobial resistance due to intensive farming practices and poor antibiotic stewardship. Companies operating in these ways are more likely to face lawsuits and pressures to change their practices.

IDENTIFYING MATERIAL SOCIAL FACTORS FOR INVESTORS 6

☐ 4.1.4 assess material impacts of social issues on potential investment opportunities and the dangers of overlooking them, including: changing demographics; digitization; individual rights and responsibilities; family structures and roles; education and work; faith-based ESG investing and exercise of religion; inequality; and globalization

☐ 4.1.5 identify approaches to social analysis at country, sector, and company levels

Given the wide range of social trends and factors that could have an effect on the risks and opportunities in a portfolio, these should be considered by investors.

Until now, these factors and trends have been discussed in a general sense, as if these factors would have an impact on each country, sector, or company equally; however, this is not the case.

Analyzing which social topics are material from an investment point of view should start with an understanding of materiality at both the geographical and industry level. Once this is established, the company-level exposure can be determined by looking at the sector it operates in and which countries/regions it mostly operates in as well as by considering locations of key suppliers, plants, customers, and main tax jurisdictions.

Country

The importance or relevance of a specific social issue depends on the regional or country context, including the level of economic development, regulatory framework (e.g., when local labor laws do not fully comply with ILO principles), and cultural or historical factors. For example, population aging is an important problem in the developed world, but it is less immediate in emerging markets. Furthermore, the difference between rural and urban areas is greater in emerging markets than in developed ones.

Government legislation also plays an increasing role, as the legal duty for companies to take responsibility and check the conditions in their supply chains is becoming mandatory in certain jurisdictions. Examples include the UK Modern Slavery Act, the French Corporate Duty of Vigilance Law, the EU Conflict Minerals Regulation, and the Dutch Child Labour Due Diligence Law. Investors should look closely at how social factors and trends impact investee companies in the different countries where they operate.

CASE STUDIES

Two examples of local regulatory frameworks are the EU taxonomy for sustainable activities and the UK Modern Slavery Act.

EU Taxonomy for Sustainable Activities

The EU taxonomy sets performance thresholds for economic activities that make a substantive contribution to one of six environmental objectives:

1. climate change mitigation;
2. climate change adaptation;
3. sustainable use and protection of water and marine resources;
4. transition to a circular economy;
5. pollution prevention and control; and
6. protection and restoration of biodiversity and ecosystems.

The activity should substantially contribute to one of the objectives to become taxonomy-aligned (while doing no significant harm to the other five, where relevant) and should comply with minimum safeguards (e.g., OECD Guidelines on MNEs and the UN Guiding Principles on Business and Human Rights), as shown in the following figure.

The European Parliament and the Council established that for an economic activity to be taxonomy-aligned, the activity should be carried out "in alignment with the OECD Guidelines for Multinational Enterprises and UN Guiding Principles on Business and Human Rights, including the International Labour

Organization's ('ILO') declaration on Fundamental Rights and Principles at Work, the eight ILO core conventions and the International Bill of Human Rights" (EU Technical Expert Group on Sustainable Finance 2020, p. 17). Where applicable, more stringent requirements in EU law still apply.

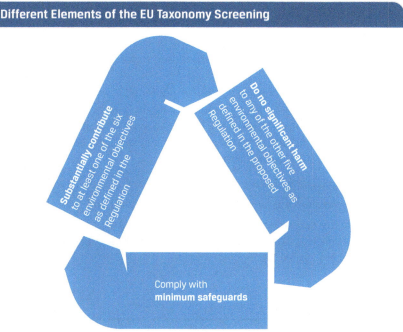

Source: EU Technical Expert Group on Sustainable Finance (2020).

UK Modern Slavery Act

The Modern Slavery Act requires both medium- and large-sized companies to provide a slavery and human trafficking statement each year, which sets out the steps taken to ensure modern slavery is not taking place in their business or supply chains. Many of these statements provide not only general information but also specific numerical data, such as the number of audits initiated for suppliers at high risk or the number of suppliers that have established corrective action plans, which can help investors assess materiality.

The regulatory pressure on companies to provide useful social data is likely to increase further. For example, in the United States, the Human Capital Management Coalition, which includes such influential investors as leading US pension funds, has petitioned the Securities and Exchange Commission to require issuers to disclose information about their human capital management policies, practices, and performance. International collaboration is also key. The International Organization of Securities Commissions (IOSCO) connects regulators over the world and provides global frameworks to support worldwide standardization, which regulators in each country can use as a basis for their own regulations.

Sector

It is important to determine what the most material social factors and trends are per sector.

Certain sectors have deeper inherent social risks, for example, due to child labor in the supply chain (clothing/cotton) or the nature of the business (mining).

Social trends also impact sectors differently. For example, automation and artificial intelligence (AI) will have a very different impact on transport (self-driving cars) compared to maintenance/servicing of vehicles (very hard to automate). Demographic change, however, will have a specific impact on the healthcare sector.

Technological developments can also help in tackling injustices in certain sectors, such as satellite imagery that can help to identify illegal deforestation.

Company Level

Companies within a sector may not all be exposed to social trends and factors in the same way.

Much will depend on a company's culture, systems, operations, and governance. For example, older, more established companies might have better systems in place to manage social risks in their supply chain, but at the same time, they may find it harder to respond when a company with a disruptive business model enters their market.

Most social issues mentioned above could:

1. impact a company's bottom line;
2. increase workforce issues (including supply chain); and
3. decrease the corporate responsibility (human rights) and its consumer expectations (e.g., animal welfare). (See EU Technical Expert Group on Sustainable Finance 2020).

7 APPLICATION OF SOCIAL FACTORS IN INVESTMENTS

☐ 4.1.6 apply material social factors to: risk assessment; quality of management; ratio analysis; and financial modeling

This section provides information on how to apply social factors in investments.

Materiality or Risk Assessment

The first step of a financial materiality or risk assessment could be to determine what the impact of social factors and trends could be on the investee companies in the different sectors, operating in the different countries (briefly described earlier. For example, some sectors, such as the mining industry and the oil and gas industry, are more susceptible to human rights violations or health and safety issues.

This financial materiality assessment should be part of a company's traditional risk assessment. Non-financial risks, such as social risks, could have a material impact on the performance of the investments and should therefore be taken into account. Besides risks, certain companies or sectors could also provide investment opportunities because they identify social trends early on and adapt their company strategy to benefit from these trends instead of being caught at a disadvantage.

Recent EU and UK regulation is asking for double materiality reporting. The concept of double materiality acknowledges that a company should report both on sustainability matters that are: 1) financially material in influencing business value and 2) 'impact material,' which is the impact of the company on the environment and people. For assessment of material negative impact, the OECD Due Diligence Guidance for Responsible Business Conduct and the UN Guiding Principles on

Business and Human Rights can be used. For a focus on positive impact and adding value for 'the organization, society, and the environment' rather than just 'financial materiality' enhancements, reference to the United Nations Sustainable Development Goals are often made.

> **CASE STUDIES**
>
> ### Amazon, Apple, and Thai Union
>
> In this case study, we will look in detail at some social issues of Apple and Amazon.
>
> ### Amazon
>
> Amazon is a multinational technology company based in Seattle, USA, that focuses on e-commerce, cloud computing, digital streaming, and AI. Amazon is known for its disruption of well-established industries through technological innovation and mass scale. Former employees, current employees, the media, and politicians have criticized Amazon for poor working conditions at the company. Some examples include the following:
>
> a. In 2011, workers had to carry out tasks in 38°C heat (100°F) at a warehouse in Breinigsville, Pennsylvania. As a result of these inhumane conditions, employees became extremely uncomfortable and suffered from dehydration; some employees collapsed. Although loading bay doors could have been opened to bring in fresh air, this was not allowed due to concerns over theft (Yarow and Kovach 2011).
>
> b. Some workers, known as 'pickers,' who travel the buildings with a trolley and a handheld scanner 'picking' customer orders, can walk up to 15 miles during their workday. If they fall behind on their targets, they can be reprimanded. The handheld scanners give real-time information to the employee on how quickly or slowly they are working; the scanners also serve to allow team leaders and area managers to track the specific locations of employees and how much 'idle time' they use when not working (O'Connor 2013).
>
> c. In March 2019, it was reported that emergency services responded to 189 calls from 46 Amazon warehouses in 17 US states between 2013 and 2018, all relating to suicidal employees. The workers attributed their mental breakdowns to employer-imposed social isolation, aggressive surveillance, and the hurried and dangerous working conditions at these fulfilment centers (Zahn and Paget 2019).
>
> d. In response to criticism that Amazon does not pay its workers a livable wage, the CEO, Jeff Bezos, announced that from 1 November 2018, all US and UK Amazon employees will earn a minimum of USD15 or GBP10.78 per hour. Amazon also announced that it would begin lobbying the US Congress to increase the federal minimum wage.
>
> e. Although it might seem that by paying lower wages or applying other strict labor conditions has a positive effect on profitability from an investor perspective, analysts should, from a financial materiality perspective, consider the possibility that legislation, social unrest, or higher than expected employee turnover/low morale will likely at some point result in disruptions and increased costs. From a double materiality perspective, the impact on employees as a stakeholder group also should be considered.

Apple/Foxconn/Inventec

Apple is an American multinational technology company based in Cupertino, California, that designs, develops, and sells consumer electronics, computer software, and online services. Apple has been criticized on the labor practices at their suppliers Foxconn and Inventec:

a. In 2006, it was reported that the working conditions in the factories where contract manufacturers Foxconn and Inventec produced the iPod were poor. One complex of factories that assembled the iPod, among other items, had over 200,000 workers living and working within it. Employees regularly worked more than 60 hours per week and made around USD100 per month. A little over half of the workers' earnings was required to pay for rent and food from the company. Apple immediately launched an investigation and worked with their manufacturers to ensure acceptable working conditions. In 2007, Apple started yearly audits of all its suppliers regarding workers' rights, slowly raising standards and removing suppliers that did not comply (Dean 2007).

b. In 2010, Apple led an investigation into the employment practices at Foxconn, the world's largest contract electronics manufacturer at the time, after the Foxconn suicides. These took place between January and November 2010, when 18 Foxconn employees attempted suicide, resulting in 14 deaths, and drew much media attention (Pomfret, Yan, and Soh 2010).

c. A 2014 BBC investigation found excessive hours and other problems persisted, despite Apple's promise to reform factory practices after the 2010 Foxconn suicides. Reporters gained access to the working conditions inside a factory through recruitment as employees. While the BBC maintained that the experiences of its reporters showed that labor violations were continuing since 2010, Apple publicly disagreed with the BBC and stated: "We are aware of no other company doing as much as Apple to ensure fair and safe working conditions (Agence France-Presse 2014)."

d. Controversies like these can impact customer loyalty, resulting in fines or employee/supplier strikes. The stock price of Apple, for example, took a 5% hit on 24 April 2012, believed to be linked to the Foxconn riots that day, which is a consequence from the high financial materiality of the topic. From a double materiality perspective, the effects or impact on the employees within the supply chain should be considered (Seeking Alpha 2012).

Thai Union

Thai Union is a Thailand-based producer of seafood-based food products with a global workforce of over 49,000 people. The company's global brand portfolio includes such international brands as Chicken of the Sea, John West, Sealect, and Petit Navire. In 2015, Greenpeace accused Thai Union of being "seriously implicated in horrendous human rights and environmental abuses" and warned shareholders and investors "of the financial risks associated with these destructive and harmful practices":

a. Such controversies led to a loss of revenue as consumers and supermarkets boycotted the products. This led to a required termination of sub-contractors and, in turn, increased transition and future costs (Seafood Source 2016).

b. In 2015, Thai Union released new codes of conduct and stated that it had terminated the relationships with 17 suppliers as a result of forced labor or human trafficking violations since the start of 2015. It also ended the use of employment brokers to source for workers for its seafood processing plants to stop debt bondage.

c. In a statement issued on 10 December 2015, Thai Union declared that it would cease working with all shrimp processing sub-contractors by the end of 2015 and bring all shrimp processing operations in-house to enable full oversight. All processing work would be directly controlled by Thai Union Group to ensure that all workers, whether migrants or Thai, would have safe, legal employment and be treated fairly and with dignity.

d. In December 2016, Thai Union and the World Tuna Purse Seine Organization (WTPO) signed a memorandum of understanding (MOU) to establish a framework to ensure fair labor practices.

e. In May 2018, Thai Union announced it had made an agreement with Greenpeace in which both parties stated that it had made substantial, positive progress on its commitment to implement measures that tackle illegal fishing and overfishing and had also improved the livelihoods of hundreds of thousands of workers throughout its supply chains. According to Greenpeace: "There is much work still to do, but it's clear the company takes its commitments seriously and is making progress to deliver them."

f. After the agreement was reached, Thai Union released a Vessel Code of Conduct, developed in collaboration with Greenpeace and the International Transport Workers' Federation.

When evaluating the financial materiality of such issues for a company investment, both social risks and the level of mitigation and management of these risks should be considered. When such issues persist, a consumer boycott or divestment by investors is possible, which could affect the share price of the company. However, improving performance can lead to the strengthening of the brand and possibly increasing or future-proofing revenues. In considering double materiality, investors should manage and take responsibility for both the actual and the potential adverse impacts of their investment decisions on people, society, and the market.

Quality of Management

Having identified which social factors are relevant for a particular company, analysts will assess the way the company manages the risks and opportunities associated with these social factors compared to its peers. This includes looking at the corporate strategy, policies in place, the processes and measures implemented, performance indicators, and public disclosure. They will look at current performance and progress over time and investigate how they compare to industry averages and key competitors. It should be noted that poor management of social factors could be an indicator of poor (stakeholder) management in general, and it could, therefore, be an effective warning for investors.

Diversity, Equity, and Inclusion

Research suggests that diversity in the management team and a strong company culture of Diversity, Equity, and Inclusion (DEI) will lead to better decision making and investment outcomes. CFA Institute has long advocated for DEI in the investment industry, and in 2022, it published its first DEI Code (USA and Canada) and Implementation Guidance (CFA Institute 2022).

Ratio Analysis and Financial Modeling

It is very useful to quantify the potential impact of social factor scenarios and include these in the ratio analysis and financial modeling of the investment.

Some scenarios that can be included in the ratio analysis are:

1. occupational health and safety issues (accident and fatalities), which can result in huge fines and liabilities;
2. human capital management issues, which can lead to greater operating costs if new employees need to be trained due to high employee turnover;
3. supply chain issues, which can impact brand reputation and revenues if consumers choose to boycott certain products;
4. local protests that lead to business disruptions at plants or factories; and
5. poor working conditions, which can result in issues with product safety.

Besides specific impacts on estimates regarding future revenues, costs, and potential liabilities in a company's financial analysis, analysts might decide to raise the discount rate to reflect a higher risk profile if a company does not manage social factors appropriately.

CASE STUDIES

Tesco Equal Pay Claim

Tesco plc is a British multinational groceries and general merchandise retailer. It is the 16th largest retailer measured by gross revenues (National Retail Federation 2020). The company reported in financial reporting period 2017/2018 total group sales of GBP51 billion and GBP1,837 million in operating profits.

However, since July 2018, the company is facing a demand for up to GBP4 billion in back pay from thousands of mainly female shopworkers in what could become the UK's largest ever equal pay claim. The retailer is claimed to have breached its duty under Section 66 of the *Equality Act 2010* by paying staff in its distribution centers more than those on the shop floor, despite the roles being of 'comparable value'. Shop floor staff — the majority of whom are female — are paid up to GBP3 less per hour than the predominantly male warehouse and distribution center workforce.

Section 66 is a 'sex equality clause' that states:

> *"If the terms of A's work do not (by whatever means) include a sex equality clause, they are to be treated as including one."*

A sex equality clause has the following effect:

- If a term of A's is less favorable to A than a corresponding term of B's is to B, A's term is modified so as not to be less favorable.
- If A does not have a term that corresponds to a term of B's that benefits B, A's terms are modified so as to include such a term.

> The employees have formed a Tesco Action Group, which is made up of around 8,000 current and former Tesco staff, to take the claim forward. The claim was formed in addition to a separate legal challenge by Leigh Day, which is representing around 1,000 current and former Tesco staff in a similar equal pay dispute.
>
> A spokesman of the company responded:
>
> > "Tesco works hard to make sure all our colleagues are paid fairly and equally for the jobs they do and are recognised for the great job they do every day serving our shoppers. There are only a very small number of claims being made, and there are strong factual and legal arguments to defend against those claims."
>
> This case is groundbreaking, financially material, and goes to the heart of social factors in labor rights. Its outcome could have significant financial consequences for the company and others in the sector.

KEY FACTS

In this chapter, an overview was given of the main social megatrends that now influence societies.

Megatrends

The social megatrends have a rather broad range and include:

- a. globalization;
- b. automation and AI in manufacturing and service sectors;
- c. inequality and wealth creation;
- d. digital disruption and social media;
- e. changes to work, leisure time, and education;
- f. changes to individual rights and responsibilities and family structures;
- g. changing demographics, including health and longevity;
- h. urbanization; and
- i. religion.

Environmental megatrends with social impact include:

- a. climate change and transition risk, including 'just' transition;
- b. water scarcity; and
- c. mass migration.

The most important internal and external factors were described earlier in the chapter. These factors are:

Internal Social Factors

- a. human capital development and DEI;
- b. health and safety;
- c. human rights;
- d. labor rights;

- e. freedom of association and employee relations;
- f. forced labor; and
- g. living wage.

External Social Factors

- a. stakeholder opposition/controversial sourcing;
- b. product liability/consumer protection;
- c. social opportunities; and
- d. animal welfare and antimicrobial resistance.

Countries, sectors, and companies are not affected equally by the different social megatrends and social factors. The analysis of which social factors are material from an investment point of view should start with an understanding of materiality at the geographical and industry levels. Once this is established, the company-level exposure can be determined by looking at the sector it operates in and which countries or regions it mostly operates in (looking at locations of key suppliers, plants, customers, and main tax jurisdictions).

Having identified which social factors are relevant for a particular company, analysts will assess the way the company manages the risks and opportunities associated with these social factors compared to its peers. This includes looking at:

- corporate strategy;
- policies in place;
- processes and measures implemented;
- performance indicators; and
- public disclosure.

This process of assessing how a company managers social factors involves looking at:

- current performance;
- progress over time; and
- how that progress compares to industry averages and key competitors.

Increasingly, investors are integrating social factors into the ratio analysis or financial models of investee companies to gain a better understanding of the potential impacts of social factors on a company's financial performance.

9 FURTHER READING

- Exclusion list of the Norges Bank Investment Management, which is used by many asset owners as guidance for their own exclusions: Norges Bank Investment Management. 2019. *Observation and Exclusion of Companies.* Available at: www.nbim.no/en/responsibility/exclusion-of-companies/
- New York University's Stern Center for Business and Human Rights' publication on the 'S' of ESG: O'Connor, C., and S. Labowitz. 2017. *Putting the 'S' in ESG: Measuring Human Rights Performance for Investors.* Available at: www.stern.nyu.edu/experience-stern/global/putting-s-esg-measuring-human-rights-performance-investors

Further Reading

- The 2018 sector takeaways and the 2018 engagement outcomes of the Platform Living Wage Financials (PLWF): PLWF. 2019. *2018 Engagement Outcomes.* Available at: www.livingwage.nl/garment-and-footwear/2018-engagement-outcomes
- PLWF. 2019. *2018 Sector Takeaways.* Available at: www.livingwage.nl/garment-and-footwear/2018-sector-takeaways/
- The Principles for Responsible Investment (PRI) supports investors' efforts to address social issues, such as human rights, working conditions, and modern slavery, with companies in their portfolio. The different human rights and labor standards publications are also recommended reading material: PRI. 2019. *Human Rights and Labor Standards.* Available at: www.unpri.org/sustainability-issues/environmental-social-and-governance-issues/social-issues/human-rights-and-labour-standards
- PRI. 2019. *Social Issues.* Available at: www.unpri.org/esg-issues/social-issues
- PRI. 2020. *Why and How Investors Should Act on Human Rights.* Available at: www.unpri.org/human-rights-and-labor-standards/why-and-how-investors-should-act-on-human-rights/6636.article
- The World Economic Forum's Global Risk Report is an authoritative publication concerning more than just social issues: World Economic Forum. 2019. *The Global Risks Report 2019.* Available at: www.weforum.org/reports/the-global-risks-report-2019

REFERENCES

International Institute for Environment and Development/United Nations Population Fund 2012. "Urbanization, Gender and Urban Poverty: Paid Work and Unpaid Carework in the City." *Urbanization and Emerging Population Issues – Working Paper 7*. https://www.unfpa.org/sites/default/files/resource-pdf/UEPI%207%20Tacoli%20Mar%202012.pdf.

OECD 2015. *OECD Insights: Income Inequality: The Gap between Rich and Poor*. www.oecd.org/publications/income-inequality-9789264246010-en.htm.

OECD Stat. 2023. "Average Annual Hours Actually Worked per Worker." OECD (data extracted 12 June 2023). https://stats.oecd.org/index.aspx?Datasetcode=ANHRS#.

Pew Research Center 2020. *How the Coronavirus Outbreak Has – and Hasn't – Changed the Way Americans Work*. www.pewresearch.org/social-trends/2020/12/09/how-the-coronavirus-outbreak-has-and-hasnt-changed-the-way-americans-work/.

United Nations 2020. *Everyone Included: Social Impact of COVID-19*. www.un.org/development/desa/dspd/everyone-included-covid-19.html.

United Nations 2023. *World Social Report 2023: Leaving No One Behind In An Ageing World*. https://www.un.org/development/desa/dspd/wp-content/uploads/sites/22/2023/01/2023wsr-fullreport.pdf.

United Nations Conference on Trade and Development (UNCTAD). 2020. *How COVID-19 Is Changing Global Value Chains*. https://unctad.org/news/how-covid-19-changing-global-value-chains.

Bangladesh Accord 2018. *The Accord on Fire and Building Safety in Bangladesh* (2013 and 2018). http://bangladeshaccord.org/.

Business & Human Rights Resource Centre 2019. *UN Guiding Principles on Business and Human Rights*. www.business-humanrights.org/en/un-guiding-principles.

CHRB 2020. *Corporate Human Rights Benchmark*. www.corporatebenchmark.org.

Holtland, H., A. Höften. 2018. *Dutch Pension Funds and Forced Labour – Speak Up*. Utrecht, Netherlands: Dutch Association of Investors for Sustainable Development (VBDO). www.vbdo.nl/wp-content/uploads/2018/12/SPEAK-UP7.pdf.

ILO 2022. *Forced Labour, Modern Slavery and Human Trafficking*. www.ilo.org/global/topics/forced-labour/lang--en/index.htm.

ILO 2023. "Conventions and Recommendations." www.ilo.org/global/standards/introduction-to-international-labour-standards/conventions-and-recommendations/lang--en/index.htm.

Interfaith Center on Corporate Responsibility 2023. *Protecting Worker Rights: ICCR's Bangladesh Initiative*. www.iccr.org/our-issues/human-rights/protecting-worker-rights-garment-workers.

International RBC/SER 2021. *Agreements on International Responsible Business Conduct*. www.imvoconvenanten.nl/en.

OECD 2017. Responsible Business Conduct for Institutional Investors: *Key Considerations for Due Diligence under the OECD Guidelines for Multinational Enterprises*. https://mneguidelines.oecd.org/RBC-for-Institutional-Investors.pdf.

PLWF 2020. *Platform Living Wage Financials*. www.livingwage.nl/platform-living-wage-financials/.

United Nations 1948. *Universal Declaration of Human Rights*.[REMOVED HYPERLINK FIELD] www.un.org/en/about-us/universal-declaration-of-human-rights.

United Nations 2021. *Slavery Is Not Merely a Historical Relic*. www.un.org/en/observances/slavery-abolition-day.

Access to Medicine Foundation 2021. 2021*Access to Medicine Index*. https://accesstomedicinefoundation.org/publications/2021-access-to-medicine-index.

References

Dugger, A. 2019. "What Is Consumer Protection? – Product Liability, Laws & Rights." CLEP Introductory Business Law Test Prep. Study.com. https://study.com/academy/lesson/what-is-consumer-protection-product-liability-laws-rights.html.

Food and Agriculture Organization of the United Nations 2016. *Free Prior and Informed Consent – Manual for Project Practitioners*. www.fao.org/3/a-i6190e.pdf.

EU Technical Expert Group on Sustainable Finance 2020. *Taxonomy: Final Report of the Technical Expert Group on Sustainable Finance* (March). https://ec.europa.eu/info/sites/info/files/business_economy_euro/banking_and_finance/documents/200309-sustainable-finance-teg-final-report-taxonomy_en.pdf.

Agence France-Presse 2014. "Apple under Fire Again for Working Conditions at Chinese Factories." *The Guardian* (19 December). www.theguardian.com/technology/2014/dec/19/apple-under-fire-again-for-working-conditions-at-chinese-factories.

CFA Institute 2022. *CFA Institute Diversity, Equity, and Inclusion Code (USA and Canada)*. www.cfainstitute.org/ethics-standards/codes/diversity-equity-inclusion.

Dean, J. 2007. "The Forbidden City of Terry Gou." *The Wall Street Journal* (11 August). www.wsj.com/articles/SB118677584137994489.

National Retail Federation 2020. *Top 50 Global Retailers 2020*.https://nrf.com/resources/top-retailers/top-50-global-retailers/top-50-global-retailers-2020.

O'Connor, S. 2013. "Amazon Unpacked." *FT Magazine* (8 February). www.ft.com/content/ed6a985c-70bd-11e2-85d0-00144feab49a.

Pomfret, J., H. Yan, K. Soh. 2010. "Foxconn Worker Plunges to Death at China Plant: Report." *Reuters* (5 November). www.reuters.com/article/us-china-foxconn-death/foxconn-worker-plunges-to-death-at-china-plant-report-idUSTRE6A41M920101105.

Seafood Source 2016. Are US Buyers Boycotting Thailand Shrimp?www.seafoodsource.com/news/supply-trade/are-u-s-buyers-boycotting-thailand-shrimp.

Seeking Alpha 2012. Did Foxconn Bring Down Apple Stock?https://seekingalpha.com/article/926801-did-foxconn-bring-down-apple-stock.

Yarow, J., C. Kovach. 2011. "10 Crazy Rules That Could Get You Fired from Amazon Warehouses." *Business Insider* (20 September). www.businessinsider.com/amazon-warehouse-rules-2011-9?international=true&r=US&IR=T.

Zahn, M., S. Paget. 2019. "'Colony of Hell': 911 Calls from Inside Amazon Warehouses." *The Daily Beast* (8 May). www.thedailybeast.com/amazon-the-shocking-911-calls-from-inside-its-warehouses.

PRACTICE PROBLEMS

1. Which of the following trends is *most* closely associated with environmental trends?

    a. Mass migration

    b. Digital disruption

    c. Increasing inequality

2. Over the last few decades, developed countries have *most likely* experienced declining:

    a. average annual working hours.

    b. levels of part-time employment.

    c. proportions of employees with higher education.

3. A developed country with an aging population is *most likely* to:

    a. achieve higher per capita savings levels.

    b. spend more per person on consumer goods.

    c. have a proportionately larger active workforce.

4. Which of the following scenarios *best* illustrates the concept of a 'just' transition?

    a. A region transitioning to renewable power prioritizes equipment installations in historically underserved areas.

    b. A government pledges a multibillion-dollar fund to employ displaced oil industry workers in safely decommissioning abandoned drill sites.

    c. A logistics company builds a new warehouse on the ancestral land of indigenous people and commits to employing a minimum number of indigenous workers.

5. An increasing focus is *most likely* placed on which of the following company health and safety performance indicators? Programs that:

    a. assist employees with personal financial issues, like budgeting.

    b. limit employee exposure to conditions that lead to occupational diseases.

    c. support employee mental health by providing free, confidential counseling.

6. In which area of a food processing company's business is forced labor *most likely* to be found?

    a. Producers of the raw agricultural ingredients processed by the company

    b. Casual laborers who work for the company only during busy seasons

    c. Purchasing agents that source the raw agricultural ingredients

7. Which of the following social issues is likely to be *most* relevant to low-to-middle income countries?

    a. An aging population

    b. Access to medicines

    c. Anti-microbial resistance

8. An investment fund scores its potential investments on a scale of one to ten based on the contributions they make to the environmental objectives under the EU taxonomy for sustainable activities. The following table shows how each

Practice Problems

company's score has changed over the past year.

	Transition to a Circular Economy	Climate Change Adaptation	Pollution Prevention and Control	Total
Company 1	+6	−2	+3	+7
Company 2	0	+7	0	+7
Company 3	+3	+2	+2	+7

Which company *most likely* complies with the EU taxonomy for sustainable activities?

a. Company 1
b. Company 2
c. Company 3

9. Within the transportation sector, advances in artificial intelligence are *most likely* to result in fewer employment opportunities for:

a. mechanics.
b. taxi drivers.
c. bulldozer operators.

10. An investment fund requires that its analysts consider an extensive list of potential social factors and trends that could affect the performance of individual investments. Which of the following steps should its analysts take first when evaluating the social suitability of a potential acquisition?

a. Carry out a materiality assessment
b. Assess the quality of investee companies' management
c. Model potential impacts of the social factors on key ratios

11. An appliance retailer is facing a consumer boycott due to reports of forced labor in its supply chain. The ratio *most likely* to be affected by the consumer action is the:

a. liabilities-to-assets ratio
b. asset turnover.
c. current ratio.

12. A portfolio analyst is modeling the potential impact of a safety incident with multiple fatalities on its mining sector holdings. Which of the following ratios is *most likely* to be affected as a result?

a. Asset turnover
b. Days of receivables
c. Liabilities-to-assets ratio

13. In 2019, the first lithium-ion battery cell gigafactory project was initiated in the European Union to reduce dependency on imports from other countries. To which social megatrend is this gigafactory *best* related?

a. Globalization
b. Inequality and wealth creation
c. Automation and artificial intelligence

14. According to the Organisation for Economic Co-operation and Development,

income inequality is:

   a. contributing to the increase in the purchasing power of the middle class.
   b. decreasing with globalization, skill-biased technological change, and changes in countries' policy approaches.
   c. determined as the ratio between the average income of the richest 10% of the population to the poorest 10% of the population.

15. Aggressive tax optimization strategies by companies is most closely related to the social megatrend of:

   a. globalization.
   b. inequality and wealth creation.
   c. changes to work, leisure time, and education.

16. Which metrics are expected to decrease as countries progress from the low- to middle-income category?

   a. Average hours worked
   b. Stress-related illnesses
   c. "War on talent" between companies

17. Which of the following *best* describes the impact of an aging population on a country's economy?

   a. Higher tax revenues for the government
   b. Lower consumer goods consumption in the country
   c. Lower accumulated savings per person for older people

18. Which of the following is *most* likely a concern for rural populations?

   a. Heat islands
   b. Job opportunities
   c. Non-communicable diseases associated with lifestyle

19. Investors following Christian faith-based investment strategies are *most likely* to avoid investments in:

   a. family-owned pork producers.
   b. companies from the gambling sector.
   c. financial instruments that pay interest revenues.

20. Which of the following standards *most likely* give industry-specific guidance on the minimal set of financially material sustainability information to be reported?

   a. Sustainability Accounting Standards Board Standards (SASB Standards)
   b. Global Reporting Initiative Standards (GRI Standards)
   c. International Labour Organisation Standards (ILO Standards)

21. Which of the following is one of the pillars of the United Nations Guiding Principles on Business and Human Rights (UNGPs)?

   a. Equal remuneration
   b. Access to remedy for victims of business-related abuses
   c. Freedom of association and protection of the right to organize

22. Which of the following statements is *most* accurate? Research supports that a

strong company culture of Diversity, Equity, and Inclusion:

   a. leads to better decision making
   b. leads to worse investment outcomes
   c. has no impact on investor decision making and investment outcomes

23. Which of the following are considered social megatrends?

   a. Human rights, health and safety, and employee relations
   b. Automation, globalization, and longevity
   c. Natural capital, biodiversity, and climate change adaptation

24. What of the following provides an example of an internal and an external social factor?

   a. Internal: biodiversity; external: product liability
   b. Internal: working conditions; external: social opportunities
   c. Internal: animal welfare; external: employee relations

25. Why is a (social) materiality assessment important?

   a. It is standard procedure in investment analysis, which makes it an important tick-box exercise.
   b. Not all countries, sectors, and companies are affected equally by the different social megatrends and social factors.
   c. A social materiality assessment is required by law in many jurisdictions.

26. Which of the following descriptions *best* illustrates the concept of a 'just' transition?

   a. A transition that is aligned with the Paris Agreement
   b. A transition that shares the financial and social burden in a fair way
   c. A transition that respects labor and human rights

27. What is the FAIRR initiative?

   a. It is a collaboration that aims to reach a just transition.
   b. It is an initiative to stimulate fair trade.
   c. It is an initiative that focuses on the increased prevalence of antimicrobial resistance.

28. The OECD Guidelines for Multinational Enterprises:

   a. state that companies should adhere to the UN Guiding Principles for Business and Human Rights.
   b. is a voluntary agreement of multinational enterprises that commits them to improving their social performance.
   c. is a comprehensive set of government-backed recommendations on responsible business conduct.

29. What does 'offshoring' refer to?

   a. Protecting coastal areas by building offshore dykes to protect cities against climate change
   b. Climate migrants moving from shore areas to more inland cities
   c. Moving company production to low-wage countries

30. Which of the following situations is *most likely* to benefit from Free, Prior, and

Informed Consent (FPIC)?

- a. Developments on the ancestral land of a territory owned by indigenous people
- b. Consumer acceptance of limitation of product liability
- c. Investments in alcohol, gambling, or tobacco

31. What does the Access to Medicine Index analyze?
    - a. How pharmaceutical companies are addressing access to medicine in low- to middle-income countries
    - b. How affordable medicines are in the major developed markets
    - c. How much time it takes to access medical assistance in developing countries

32. Which of the following is *least likely* to be associated with the automation and artificial intelligence (AI) megatrends?
    - a. Employment losses in the garment sector within developed countries
    - b. Employment gains in the IT sector
    - c. Future employment losses in the transportation sector

33. The corporate human rights benchmark (CHRB) considers:
    - a. only how corporations respond to serious human rights allegations.
    - b. only the policies, processes, and practices that systemize corporate human rights.
    - c. both the policies, process, and practices that systematize corporate human rights and how corporations respond to serious human rights allegations.

34. What is the Platform Living Wage Financials?
    - a. A platform of companies demanding their suppliers offer a living wage
    - b. A platform of financial institutions offering a living wage to their employees
    - c. A platform of investors encouraging investees to require living wages in their supply chains

35. Which of the following are considered fundamental conventions of the International Labour Organization (ILO)?
    - a. Right to organize and collective bargaining, living wage, and minimum age
    - b. Abolition of forced labor, equal remuneration, and protection against the worst forms of child labor
    - c. Collective labor agreements, healthcare, and retirement plans

36. Which of the following *best* describes income inequality trends over the last few decades?
    - a. It has been growing, which is good for the economy.
    - b. It has been growing, which has a negative effect on the economy.
    - c. It has declined, which has a negative effect on the economy.

37. Which element of the EU Taxonomy has a social aspect?
    - a. Substantially contributing to one of the six objectives
    - b. Doing no significant harm to the other five objectives
    - c. Complying with minimum safeguards

SOLUTIONS

1. **A is correct**. Some *environmental megatrends* have a severe social impact as well. These include the following: • Climate change and transition risk • Water scarcity • Mass migration.

2. **A is correct**. OECD studies indicate that most developed countries have experienced declining average working hours over the past few decades. Over the same period, part-time employment has increased as has the proportion of employees with higher education. While the number of average working hours has decreased, the average level of education has increased. The percentage of employees with a higher education degree has grown over the last few decades.

3. **A is correct.** Older populations in developed countries have higher accumulated savings per capita than younger populations. Older people are more likely to be retired, leading to proportionately smaller active workforces. Finally, older populations spend less on consumer goods compared to younger populations.

4. **B is correct**. A 'just' transition is one that avoids burdening ordinary workers with unemployment, poverty, and exclusion as part of the transition to a low carbon economy. The government's pledge to employ displaced oil industry workers provides transitional employment to workers in a vulnerable sector (oil industry) and thus best illustrates a 'just' transition.

5. **C is correct**. Health and safety has evolved a broader concept of working conditions. The focus is increasingly on mental health and other employee benefits to promote their well-being outside of the workplace. Occupational health practices, such as limiting workforce exposures to harmful conditions, are well established and widely accepted as fundamental health and safety measures. "Financial wellness" is a fairly well-established term among US employers and HR departments.

6. **A is correct**. Egregious labor rights violations, such as the use of forced labor, are often hidden deep within supply chains in the second tier and beyond. Of the options, producers of raw agricultural ingredients are deepest within the food processor's supply chain and thus the most likely to employ forced labor.

7. **B is correct**. Lack of social opportunities, including lack of access to medicines, is identified under the UN's Sustainable Development Goals as an issue in developing or low-to-middle income countries. Aging populations are more closely associated with developed countries, and anti-microbial resistance is not specifically linked to either developed or developing countries.

8. **B is correct**. Company 2 best fulfills the requirements to substantially contribute to one objective (climate change adaptation at +3 points) while doing no significant harm to the others.

9. **B is correct**. Artificial intelligence is suited to structured and repetitive tasks that can be carried out with minimal human assistance. The development of self-driving cars suggests that taxi drivers are most at risk of being displaced because of advances in artificial intelligence. Less routine work, such as troubleshooting mechanical problems and operating bulldozers in varied physical environments, is subject to lower displacement risk.

10. **A is correct**. Carrying out a materiality assessment, or determining which of the social factors and trends is likely to have a significant impact on the performance

of the investments, is the next logical step. Once the materiality assessment is complete, the potential impacts can be modeled and the quality of investee companies' management can be assessed.

11. **B is correct**. Consumer boycotts are most likely to result in lower revenues. The ratio that will be most directly affected by lower revenues is the asset turnover ratio, defined as revenues/assets.

12. **C is correct**. A safety incident is most likely to result in increased costs and liabilities for fines, lawsuits, and equipment with better safety features. The liabilities-to-assets ratio will be most directly affected by the increased liabilities. Asset turnover and days of receivables are not directly affected by either expenses or liabilities.

13. **A is correct**. The European Union is trying to reduce its dependency on imports of batteries from different countries. Dependency is one of the manifestations of the globalization megatrend.

14. **C is correct**. To measure income inequality, OECD follows throughout time the evolution of the ratio between the income received by the 10% of people with the highest income to income received by the 10% of people with the lowest income. A growing ratio shows growing income inequalities. Inequality increases according to OECD with globalization, skill-biased technological change, and changes in countries' policies. Also according to OECD, income inequality contributes to the "squeeze" of the middle classes.

15. **B is correct**. Unlike individuals earning low income, companies with higher capital can afford to have specialized tax consultants or work with tax advisory firms to find ways to avoid an important part of their tax burden. Hence, companies end up paying lower taxes than low-to-middle income individuals, further contributing to income inequality.

16. **A is correct**. Based on trends observed, average hours worked decreased in developed countries and as people's standard of living increases, people tend to put more price on leisure time. As economies develop and people start to gain more, it is expected that the level of work complexity will grow, and this leads to stress-related illnesses and a "war on talent" for companies that want to have qualified employees for more complex tasks.

17. **B is correct**. A country with an aging population experiences lower national tax revenues. Older people have higher accumulated savings per person than younger people but spend less on consumer goods.

18. **B is correct**. People in rural areas migrate to urban areas for job opportunities and improvements in the standard of living. Heat islands and non-communicable diseases are associated with the lifestyle impact of people from urban areas.

19. **B is correct**. Christian investors have investment mandates that require negative screening for companies whose activities are not aligned with Christian values and principles. Negative screening for family-owned pork producers and for instruments paying interest is specific to Islamic investors.

20. **A is correct**. SASB has developed a complete set of 77 Industry Standards. In November 2018, SASB published these Standards, providing a complete set of globally applicable industry-specific Standards that identify the minimal set of financially material sustainability topics and their associated metrics for the typical company in an industry (see https://www.sasb.org/standards/). GRI Standards cover mostly non-financial reporting, while ILO Standards promote opportu-

Solutions

nities for women and men to obtain decent and productive work, in terms of freedom, equity, security, and dignity, and are included in the fundamental conventions of the International Labour Organization.

21. **B is correct**. The UNGP framework considers three pillars: (1) the state duty to protect human rights; (2) the corporate responsibility to respect human rights; (3) access to remedy for victims of business-related abuses. Equal remuneration and freedom of association and protection of the right to organize are part of the ILO labor rights framework.

22. **A is correct**. Research suggests that diversity in the management team and a strong company culture of Diversity, Equity, and Inclusion will lead to better decision making and investment outcomes.

23. **B is correct**. Automation, globalization, and longevity are social megatrends because they refer to "long-term social changes that affect governments, societies, and economies permanently over a long period of time."

24. **B is correct**. Working conditions are considered a social factor that is internal to a company, while social opportunities (or the lack thereof, particularly in developing countries) is a social factor that is mostly outside a company's control and is thus external.

25. **B is correct**. It is important for investment analysts to assess social materiality because social factors have varying impacts at the country level, sector level, and company level.

26. **B is correct**. The 'just' transition concept focuses on fairly sharing the economic burden of the transition to a low carbon economy to avoid disproportionate impacts on ordinary workers.

27. **C is correct**. FAIRR stands for Farm Animal Investment Risk and Return. It considers the risks and opportunities linked to intensive livestock production, including the increased prevalence of antimicrobial resistance.

28. **C is correct**. The OECD Guidelines for Multinational Enterprises (MNEs) is a set of recommendations used by governments to encourage MNEs to engage in responsible business conduct that will have positive impacts on sustainable development and social progress.

29. **C is correct**. Offshoring is a feature of the globalization megatrend and refers to the movement of labor-intensive production processes to low-wage countries.

30. **A is correct**. Free, Prior, and Informed Consent (FPIC) is a stakeholder engagement process that enables companies to understand the needs and concerns of local communities. This is particularly applicable to developments on the ancestral lands of indigenous people.

31. **A is correct**. The Access to Medicine Index "analyzes how 20 of the world's largest pharmaceutical companies are addressing access to medicine in 106 low- to middle-income countries for 82 diseases, conditions, and pathogens."

32. **A is correct**. Employment losses in developed countries' garment sectors were closely related to the globalization megatrend, not automation and AI. The lower wages of developing countries' workers led to a migration of this work from developed countries to developing ones.

33. **C is correct**. "The CHRB provides a comparative snapshot year-on-year of the

34. **C is correct**. The Platform Living Wage Financials (PLWF) is a coalition of financial institutions that encourage and monitor investee companies to address the non-payment of a living wage in their global supply chains.

35. **B is correct**. Abolition of forced labor, equal remuneration, and protection against the worst forms of child labor are among the ILO's eight fundamental conventions. Living wage, healthcare, and retirement plans, while important, are not fundamental conventions.

36. **B is correct**. Income inequality has been growing over the past several decades, resulting in reduced educational opportunities and social mobility particularly for the lower and middle classes, ultimately limiting economic growth.

37. **C is correct**. The EU Taxonomy requires that activities must comply with minimum social safeguards, such as the OECD Guidelines on Multinational Enterprises and the UN Guiding Principles on Business and Human Rights, in order to qualify as sustainable. This requirement is in addition to the environmentally-focused "Substantially contribute" and "Do no significant harm" requirements.

CHAPTER 5

Governance Factors

LEARNING OUTCOMES

Mastery	The candidate should be able to:
☐	**5.1.1** explain the evolution of corporate governance frameworks: development of corporate governance; roles and responsibilities; systems and processes; shareholder engagement; minority shareholder alignment
☐	**5.1.1** explain the evolution of corporate governance frameworks: development of corporate governance; roles and responsibilities; systems and processes; shareholder engagement; minority shareholder alignment
☐	**5.1.2** assess key characteristics of effective corporate governance, and the main reasons why they may not be implemented or upheld: board structure, diversity, effectiveness, and independence; executive remuneration, performance metrics, and key performance indicators (KPIs); reporting and transparency; financial integrity and capital allocation; business ethics
☐	**5.1.3** assess and contrast the main models of corporate governance in major markets and the main variables influencing best practice: extent of variation of best practice; differences in legislation, culture, and interpretation
☐	**5.1.4** explain the role of auditors in relation to corporate governance and the challenges in effective delivery of the audit: independence of audit firms and conflicts of interest; auditor rotation; sampling of audit work and technological disruption; auditor reports; auditor liability; internal audit
☐	**5.1.5** assess material impacts of governance issues on potential investment opportunities, including the dangers of overlooking them: public finance initiatives; companies; infrastructure/private finance vehicles; societal impact
☐	**5.1.6** apply material corporate governance factors to: financial modeling; risk assessment; quality of management

1 CORPORATE GOVERNANCE: ACCOUNTABILITY AND ALIGNMENT

> **5.1.1** explain the evolution of corporate governance frameworks: development of corporate governance; roles and responsibilities; systems and processes; shareholder engagement; minority shareholder alignment

Corporate governance is the process and structure for overseeing the business and management of a company. From the Latin word for the steering of a boat, *gubernare*, governance incorporates that sense of guiding and controlling. Corporate governance has become more complex as the scale and complexity of companies have grown and as ownership has become more dispersed.

As a result, the role of the board of directors has become more important. The board is responsible for representing the owners of the company and for holding management teams accountable for running the business in the interest of its owners. The effectiveness of the board depends on whether good corporate governance practices are applied. The principles that shape these practices have been developed over the years and codified into corporate governance codes. Increasingly, investors are expecting companies to disclose their corporate governance structures and processes so that external investors and other stakeholders can understand where the company stands on the spectrum of good governance.

The types of issues that investors will address when considering a company's governance include, but are not limited to:

- shareholder rights;
- the likely success of the intended company strategy, and the effectiveness of the leadership in place to deliver it;
- executive pay;
- audit practices;
- board independence and expertise;
- transparency or accountability;
- related-party transactions; and
- dual-class share structures.

This chapter considers the *G* of environmental, social, and governance (ESG) factors, corporate governance, and gives readers insight into the core fundamentals of what the concept means, its history and development, global practices, and how governance analysis is used by investment professionals to deliver value to their clients and beneficiaries and minimize the risk of value destruction.

What Is Governance? Why Does It Matter?

Corporate governance is the process by which a company is managed and overseen. There are different rules worldwide—governance grows out of the legal system of the country in which the company is incorporated—but at its heart, governance is about people and processes. Good governance also involves developing an appropriate culture that will underpin the delivery of strong business performance without excessive risk-taking through appropriate conduct of business operations. Good corporate governance should lead to strong business performance and long-term prosperity

Corporate Governance: Accountability and Alignment

to the benefit of shareholders and the company's other stakeholders. The corporate culture needs to be supportive of that long-term business success in the interests of all stakeholders.

While at its heart corporate governance is about people (the individuals in the boardroom and how they interact with the individuals outside the boardroom), in order to exercise their responsibilities effectively, board members are supported by processes. These processes bear an increased burden in large and complex companies; at smaller companies there is greater scope for individuals at the top to have direct knowledge across a business, but at larger companies this is impossible. Companies will typically have policies and codes of conduct in place, but they will rely on processes to be confident that those policies are indeed delivered in practice. Investors will judge a company's governance based on the quality of its policies and processes and on the diligence and care with which the board oversees their implementation. Most fundamentally, they will judge governance by the quality and thoughtfulness of the people on the board.

Assessing the effectiveness of corporate governance systems within a firm gives investors insight into the accountability mechanisms and decision-making processes that support all critical decisions affecting the allocation of investors' capital and the likely delivery of long-term value. A company with sound governance is better able to address the key risks that the business faces, including environmental and social issues. Conversely, a company that is failing to manage a key long-term risk (again including environmental and social issues) may have an underlying governance failure that is blocking its ability to address the issue.

In practice, corporate governance comes down to two A's: *accountability* and *alignment.*

These concepts are reflected in many of the core elements of corporate governance standards and investor expectations.

Accountability

People need to be:

- given authority and responsibility for decision-making; and
- held accountable for the consequences of their decisions and the effectiveness of the work they deliver.

Accountability and the Board

Just as people are most effective when they are conscious of being accountable to someone—typically their manager—in the same way, senior executives need to feel accountable to the non-executive directors on their board. In turn, that board will be most effective when its non-executive members feel accountable to shareholders for effective delivery. Therefore, corporate governance has a strong focus on board structure and the independence of directors.

The mixed skill sets of directors are also important, so that discussions and debate are appropriately informed by a range of perspectives and the risk of "groupthink" is avoided. Increasing diversity and the range of perspectives in the boardroom—through gender and ethnic diversity, and also diversity in terms of professional backgrounds and experiences—has been demonstrated to deliver a more challenging culture and thus the greater accountability that is more likely to enhance long-term value.

The role of the chair of the board is vital in facilitating a balanced debate in the boardroom. Consequently, many investors prefer that the chair be an independent, non-executive director. If the chair is not independent, and especially if that individual combines the role of chair with the role of CEO, this situation can lead to an excessive concentration of powers and hamper the board's ability to:

- exercise their oversight responsibilities;
- challenge and debate performance and strategic plans;
- set the agenda, both for board meetings and for the company as a whole;
- influence succession planning; and
- debate executive remuneration.

Exhibit 1 illustrates the flow of accountability through company structures and the investment chain.

Source: Paul Lee (2020).

Accountability and Accounts

Accurate accounts are needed for accountability. The annual accounts of the company represent the formal process of the directors making themselves properly accountable to the shareholders for financial and broader business performance, which is why the first item at many annual general meetings (**AGM**s) is acceptance of the report and accounts, often through a formal vote. Hence, the central importance of transparent and honest accounting by companies, and of the independence of the audit of those accounts by the auditor. Again, it is not by chance that the auditor reports formally to shareholders each year and is reappointed annually in most countries at the AGM. The integrity of the numbers that investors look at when assessing business performance is central to their ability to hold management and boards to account. The votes to "discharge" board directors in some countries (such as Germany) effectively absolve them of liability for any actions over the year and are usually dependent on the annual report providing a full, true, and accurate disclosure of activity in the year and the position at year-end.

Increasingly, companies are also issuing Sustainability Reports to shareholders to enable a review of their performance with respect to E, S, and G issues.

Alignment and the Agency Problem

Alignment comes down to the challenge of the *agency problem*. Since the seminal publication of *The Modern Corporation and Private Property* by Adolf Berle and Gardiner Means in 1932 (seen by many as the starting point for the modern understanding of corporate governance), the agency problem has been identified as an inevitable consequence of the separation of ownership and control. The agency problem arises in that the interests of the professional managers—the agents—may not always be wholly aligned with the interests of the owners of the business, and so the company may not be run in the way the owners wish. This challenge is magnified at larger corporations, not least public companies, where ownership is fragmented among many investors owning a small fraction of the company.

Any discussion of the agency problem needs to acknowledge that the issues it raises are not so simple that they can be solved by management and the board simply doing what they are instructed to do by the shareholders. First, it will usually be difficult to discern a single message from the shareholder base of most companies, which will include multiple investors, many of whom will have conflicting views on how best to manage the company. Even where there is a single shareholder or a clear single message from the shareholders, the duty of directors under the company law of most countries is to care for the success of the company and not for the shareholders directly. There is also a risk that directors will fail in their duty if they simply abdicate their responsibilities and respond thoughtlessly to the input received from shareholders. Promoting short-term share price increases is not the same thing as promoting the long-term success of the business.

Furthermore, there can be agency problems within the investment chain itself, as a disconnect can develop between the interests of fund management firms and individual portfolio managers and those of their clients and/or ultimate beneficiaries. This agency problem is discussed in more detail in Chapter 9.

Nonetheless, the challenge of the agency problem is a risk of some divergence between the interests of shareholders, on the one hand, and the interests of company directors and management, on the other. Corporate governance attempts to ensure that there is greater alignment of the interests of the agents with the interests of the owners, through both incentives and appropriate chains of accountability, to mitigate the potential negative consequences of the agency problem.

Alignment and Executive Pay

With regard to alignment, the major focus in terms of executive pay is always on addressing the agency problem and helping to ensure that executives are not given incentives to perform in their own interests, contrary to the interests of the owners. Thus, executive pay structures aim to align the interests of management with those of the owners, usually by creating a balanced compensation package that includes performance-related remuneration based on short- and long-term goals and with a significant portion of compensation that vests over the long term. The goals ideally include a mix of key performance indicators (KPIs) related to business (both financial and non-financial) and share price performance. Many of the incentives often come with some form of equity linkage—which can, on occasion, cause the risk that management is more focused on share price development than on the performance of the business itself.

Accountability: Board Committees

The three key committees of the board, usually required by corporate governance codes, are established to respond to each of the key challenges discussed above (accountability and the board, accountability and accounts, and alignment and executive pay). These committees are:

- The *Nominations Committee* (in some markets, this is called the Corporate Governance Committee or some combination of these terms) aims to ensure that the board overall is balanced and effective, ensuring that management is accountable.
- The *Audit Committee* oversees financial reporting and the audit, delivering accountability in the accounts. The Audit Committee also oversees internal audits (where they exist) and is responsible for risk oversight unless there is a separate risk management committee.
- The *Remuneration Committee* (in some markets, this is called the Compensation Committee) seeks to deliver a proper alignment of interests through executive pay.

The roles of these committees are considered more thoroughly in the next section.

2 FORMALIZED CORPORATE GOVERNANCE FRAMEWORKS

5.1.1 explain the evolution of corporate governance frameworks: development of corporate governance; roles and responsibilities; systems and processes; shareholder engagement; minority shareholder alignment

Corporate failures and scandals have been a powerful driver for the formalization of corporate governance and the development of codes. When companies fail and investors lose money, there is often pressure for an improved approach. Examples in the United Kingdom include the Walker Review (2009), following the 2008 financial crisis, and the Kingman (2018) and Brydon (2019) reviews in the wake of Carillion's failure.

See Major Corporate Scandals (below) for further (and international) discussion.

Corporate Governance Codes

The world's first formal corporate governance code emerged in the United Kingdom in 1992. The Cadbury Committee had been brought together in May 1991 by the Financial Reporting Council, the London Stock Exchange, and the accounting profession to consider what were called "the financial aspects of corporate governance." Its creation followed the Caparo and Polly Peck scandals.

Caparo had mounted a successful takeover bid for Fidelity, only to subsequently discover that Fidelity's profits were significantly overstated. The market had pumped up the share price of Polly Peck for years based on financial reporting that later turned out to be misleading. The Cadbury Committee was created because of the perceived problems in accounting and governance. Once the committee began its work (but before the planned publication of its report), the Maxwell/Mirror Group scandal was beginning to emerge, and the Bank of Credit and Commerce International (BCCI) collapsed spectacularly in the wake of money laundering and other regulatory breaches. It was clear that much needed to change.

Much of what the Cadbury Committee recommended is still considered best practice today and has been incorporated into codes and guidelines globally. For example, the committee proposed that every public company should have an audit committee that meets at least twice a year. Notably, when the report was released, only two-thirds of the largest 250 companies in the UK had such committees at all (although nowadays they are commonplace). The report's core theme is that no individual should have "unfettered powers of decision"; so, for example, the roles of chair and CEO should not be combined, as they frequently were at the time.

A codified set of guidelines for good governance has grown from the basic concepts of accountability and alignment. Governance differs from country to country based on cultures and historical developments as well as local corporate law. At the most basic level, some countries, including Germany and the Netherlands, have *two-tier boards*, with wholly non-executive supervisory boards overseeing management boards; others have *single-tier boards*, with some dominated by executive directors (as in Japan), some having a combined CEO and chair (most commonly seen in the United States and France), and some lying in between these models (as in the UK).

The Cadbury Code model of recommendations with which companies should comply or explain any non-compliance has also been followed throughout much of the world. It is now highly unusual for any market to be without an official corporate governance code.

Since Japan adopted one in 2015, the USA is now the only major world market that does not have such a code, which is largely a consequence of corporate law being set at the individual state, rather than the federal, level. Most markets adopt the language of "comply or explain," although the Netherlands favors "apply or explain," and the Australians use the blunt "if not, why not?" The thought process, however, is the same: the code expects adherence to the relevant standard or the publication of a thoughtful and intelligent discussion of how the board delivers on the underlying principle. These discussions are gaining increased attention, not least because they offer the board an opportunity to explain how it operates to deliver value to the business on behalf of both shareholders and other stakeholders.

Companies' willingness to provide thoughtful discussions of their divergences from guidance varies. Some companies may look negatively on corporate governance, as they consider it inflexible. Indeed, there can be a risk that investors will approach corporate governance codes with inflexibility, expecting much more compliance than explanation—which is not the code's intent. Sometimes, this apparent inflexibility can arise from a failure of communication, particularly due to the reliance on proxy advisory firms (a highly concentrated group led by ISS and Glass Lewis) to mediate some of the discussions on governance and voting matters. These advisory firms tend to adhere to the details of corporate governance codes in giving recommendations on how their clients might vote. Some argue that it is the role of the proxy adviser to interpret the standards strictly, and it is for the actual shareholder to apply the flexibility that arises from a closer understanding of the specific circumstances of the individual company. Under this analysis, the problem of inflexibility may arise more from the investor client's tendency to follow the proxy adviser's recommendations, with too little independent judgment about whether those recommendations are the right ones, than from the strictness of the recommendations themselves.

These issues are discussed in more detail in Chapter 6.

Just as the Caparo and Polly Peck scandals sparked the establishment of the Cadbury Committee, and the Mirror Group and BCCI scandals provided a firm context for the publication and acceptance of its report, later scandals have continued to fuel the development of governance standards around the world:

- In the UK, shocks around pay levels at newly privatized utilities led to the *Greenbury Report*, which revised the UK's corporate governance code in 1995. It increased the visibility of remuneration structures and pressed toward transparency over the KPIs that drive performance pay and the time horizons over which pay is released (for long-term schemes, the time horizon is a minimum of three years).
- The Enron, Tyco, and WorldCom scandals in the USA led to the *Sarbanes-Oxley Act* in 2002. This law lifted expectations for greater integrity in financial reporting and created the Public Company Accounting Oversight Board (PCAOB) as the country's audit standard setter and inspector, establishing a standard for auditor independence and challenge.
- The 2003 failures at Ahold and Parmalat in the Netherlands and Italy, respectively, led to pressure for heightened standards of corporate governance and for both board and auditor independence across Europe. No longer could Europe pretend that Enron represented a problem isolated to the USA.
- The financial crisis of 2008 led to various changes around the world and to a renewed focus on corporate culture and executive pay as well as questions around audit. It also led to the creation of stewardship codes, in the UK initially and then around the world. Most notable of the legislative changes was the 2010 *Dodd-Frank Act* in the USA (formally, the Dodd-Frank Wall Street Reform and Consumer Protection Act), which, among its multiple clauses, tightened standards for, and oversight of, banks.
- In Japan, the Olympus scandal of 2011–12 revealed long-running market deceit, whereby more than US$1.5bn in losses were hidden, apparently not for personal gain but to maintain the perception of good corporate health and jobs for its workforce. When the much larger Toshiba revealed its own scandal of overstated profits in 2015, some felt that there might be something culturally wrong in Japanese companies that sought to hide the truth amid failures of governance. The combination of these shocks has helped fuel the rapid advance of Japanese governance standards and also expectations for ESG disclosures across the market.

Major Corporate Scandals: Governance Failures and Lessons Learned

CASE STUDIES

Enron (USA, 2001)

An electric utility turned energy-trading business, Enron used a range of off-balance-sheet vehicles and other aggressive accounting techniques to appear hugely profitable, even on projects that had barely begun. Its collapse led to the dismantling of its auditor, Arthur Andersen, which split apart rapidly after some of its staff in Houston were discovered to have shredded documents linked to Enron and the US Securities and Exchange Commission's (SEC) investigation.

Formalized Corporate Governance Frameworks

> Governance failings included weak oversight of the executives (reinforced by the founder, Ken Lay, remaining as executive chair) by the non-executive directors. There were also failures of commission, most clearly the decision to waive the board's own code of conduct to enable the CFO to participate personally in some of the off-balance-sheet structures whose purpose was to facilitate the removal of losses from Enron's accounts.

Enron's board of directors significantly contributed to Enron's failures through poor corporate governance and facilitated a dishonest culture that nurtured serious conflicts of interest and unethical behavior, as follows:

- The board inadequately oversaw key business and transactions in the corporation.
- The board ineffectively controlled the implementation of the company's code of conduct or policy, which enabled self-interested managers to make profits at the company's expense.
- The board did not foster an environment in which the external auditor, the internal audit function, and whistleblowers could operate effectively, and accepted the application of questionable, high-risk accounting practices and fraudulent financial reporting.

Corporate governance mitigants against failure (lessons learned):

- Required higher standards of ethical conduct
- Enhanced board independence
- Strengthening of internal control systems and provision of frameworks to identify and manage risks
- Restriction on the provision of non-audit services by external auditors

References and further reading:

- Powers, W. C., R. S. Troubh, and H. S. Winokur. 2002. *Report of Investigation by the* Special Investigative Committee of the Board of Directors of Enron Corporation (available at: http://i.cnn.net/cnn/2002/LAW/02/02/enron.report/powers.report.pdf);
- The Role of the Financial Institutions in Enron's Collapse—Volume 1: Hearings Before the Senate Permanent Subcommittee on Investigations, of the Committee on Governmental Affairs, 107th Congress. 2002. Testimony of Robert Roach, chief investigator, Permanent Subcommittee on Investigations: 14–25 (available at: https://www.govinfo.gov/content/pkg/CHRG-107shrg81313/pdf/CHRG-107shrg81313.pdf);
- Senate Permanent Subcommittee on Investigations, of the Committee on Governmental Affairs. 2002. The Role of the Board of Directors in Enron's Collapse, Senate Report 107-70 (available at: https://www.govinfo.gov/content/pkg/CPRT-107SPRT80393/pdf/CPRT-107SPRT80393.pdf);
- Nguyen, H. C. 2011. "Factors Causing Enron's Collapse: An Investigation into Corporate Governance and Company Culture." Corporate Ownership & Control 8 (3): 585–93 (available at: doi:10.22495/cocv8i3c6p2).

CASE STUDIES

Tyco International (USA/Bermuda, 2002)

When losses mounted from unsuccessful deals by this aggressive Bermuda-incorporated acquisition vehicle, questions were raised about the behavior of CEO Dennis Kozlowski. Allegations centered on inflated profits, but also on ill-gotten earnings by senior management. In the end, the trials of Kozlowski and CFO Mark Swartz centered on payments of US$150mn), which they claimed the board had authorized as their remuneration. They were convicted, but the suggested level of actual theft is believed to have exceeded US$500mn.

The culture at Tyco had long been one of lavish lifestyles for corporate leadership using corporate money and perks. Kozlowski had already grown accustomed to this culture prior to becoming CEO and extended it further. Deal-making (some 750 acquisitions in the four-year period up to 2001) became a basis for personal aggrandizement and even personal entertainment. Tyco apparently financed Kozlowski's wife's $2 million birthday party, for example. The board at best turned a blind eye to these behaviors, enabling this wasteful and unhealthy culture to persist.

Tyco International's board of directors failed in a core tenet of corporate governance, which is to protect the key interests of its stakeholders. Poor and fraudulent financial and administrative decisions contributed to the financial failure of the company, as follows:

- Tyco's CEO compromised the company's corporate governance system in positioning his close associates on the board and in prominent organizational ranks. Executives were thus able to perpetrate crimes of fraud, grand larceny and conspiracy, embezzlement, accounting conflicts of interest, commingling of assets, excessive unethical personal spending, and other questionable activities—all unchallenged.
- The board failed to safeguard the interests of key stakeholders. Tyco's CEO and board members defrauded and misled investors by keeping Tyco's share price artificially inflated, adding no lasting value to the organization for stakeholders.
- Questionable auditing practices resulted in a failure to identify the CEO's illegal financial transactions and unethical business practices (e.g., tax evasion).
- Lack of adequate monitoring and oversight
- Improper management and leadership decisions involving the inappropriate allocation of bonuses to executives
- Improper procedures in expansion and in approaches to new acquisitions

Corporate governance mitigants against failure (lessons learned):

- Ethical corporate mindset and leadership. A company's board of directors is entrusted with its shareholders' funds, such that every director has responsibility and accountability in ensuring that the company's funds are legally and properly used.
- Independent corporate governance, with a clear reputation for autonomy. Tyco's board of directors had the opportunity to examine the company's finances and identify questionable transactions.

Formalized Corporate Governance Frameworks

- Effective evaluation of the appropriateness of company remuneration, incentive programs, and KPIs
- Clear delineations between finance and operations management

References and further reading:

- Pillmore, Eric M. 2003. "How We're Fixing Up Tyco." Harvard Business Review (available at: https://hbr.org/2003/12/how-were-fixing-up-tyco).

CASE STUDIES

WorldCom (USA, 2002)

The internal audit function of this telecom business uncovered its use of one of the simplest accounting deceits—booking current expenses as capital investment, boosting profits by some US$3.8bn. A subsequent investigation concluded that, in total, assets were exaggerated by US$11bn. The fraud was undertaken to hide falling growth in a more challenging market.

At WorldCom, the board's checks and balances worked, although belatedly. An internal audit team uncovered suspicious transactions (or, rather, suspicious accounting treatments of transactions) and raised them with the chair of the audit committee. Though the chair did not immediately call a meeting of the committee, he did invite the internal audit team to discuss the issues directly with KPMG, the external auditor; in the meantime, the internal audit team persisted with its work and uncovered the full scale of the misleading accounting. When the committee finally met, it confronted the executives leading the finance function with full evidence from the internal audit and with the support of KPMG. Executive departures and public announcements—and an SEC investigation—followed. So did bankruptcy.

WorldCom's board of directors significantly contributed to WorldCom's failures through a lack of proper understanding of the company's activities and how targets were achieved. The company's cultural environment was devoid of appropriate corporate governance structures, as evidenced by the following:

- A lack of accountability and oversight
- An extremely autocratic style of management
- Senior management using fraudulent and illegal accounting methods to mislead and defraud investors and other directors
- Failure of regular and timely oversight from its internal audit function prior to whistleblowing activity

Corporate governance mitigants against failure (lessons learned):

- Establishment of robust financial controls, with proper board oversight
- Appointment of ethical, independent auditors
- Fostering a culture of legal compliance and integrity

References and further reading:

- For the SEC's litany of complaints in its 2002 enforcement action against WorldCom, go to: ttps://www.sec.gov/litigation/complaints/comp17829.htm.

CASE STUDIES

Royal Ahold (Koninklijke Ahold NV) (the Netherlands, 2002–03)

Ahold was a Dutch grocery chain that went international through acquisitions, principally in the USA, in part because management had a 15% earnings growth target. Deteriorating performance was hidden through fraud—dubious joint venture accounting, hidden costs, and vendor rebates.

While making decisions to grow internationally, the board failed to ensure that its skills and its processes also developed so that it could oversee the new broader spread of the business. Instead, the US operations faced more limited oversight and challenge than they might have, allowing frauds to develop without being uncovered until they were very substantial.

Ahold's board of directors significantly contributed to Ahold's failures through poor corporate governance, as follows:

- The absence of both internal and external oversight of international operations enabled the CEO and the CFO to improperly book sales in international subsidiaries.
- Initially, the company's owners (family) and, later, professional management exploited the intent of the law and existing regulatory structures to maintain absolute control of the company. Thus, the disciplining power of the market encouraging managers to act in the best interests of shareholders was undermined. When professional management raised capital from institutional investors, management denied them their voting rights by exploiting regulations that allow Dutch companies to issue non-voting certificates rather than voting shares. Block holders were thus unable to supplant the role of the family as a monitor of professional management.
- The family firm operated under a two-tier board structure, with a management board monitored by a separate institution, the supervisory board. The supervisory board is where the growth objective and strategy should have been debated, the strategy's implementation monitored, and oversight maintained. However, the independence of the supervisory board was compromised by the fact that former managers were a significant component of the membership of the supervisory board.
- Ahold had board members with extensive portfolios, which limited their time commitment to the firm.
- Several board members had ties with financial institutions related to Ahold (such as ABN AMRO and ING), which led to conflicts of interest with these stakeholders.
- Although board members were generally qualified based on experience and background, several politicians with little business experience served on Ahold's board.
- Incentive compensation plans that emphasized earnings growth aggravated the other shortcomings and provided a direct motivation for management's valuing earnings growth over shareholder value. Appropriately designed, option-based incentive schemes can align interests and encourage professional managers to behave in the interest of shareholders. However, executives at Ahold negated the long-term incentive effects of ownership by exercising their options and immediately selling the shares with no provision for clawback in the event of malfeasance.

- ▶ There were lax internal controls and poor financial and accounting practices on the part of Ahold in the USA, as identified and documented in the forensic audit by PricewaterhouseCoopers.
- ▶ Poor governance led to both an aggressive acquisition strategy and the use of aggressive accounting through the exploitation of the differences between Dutch and US GAAPS to disguise weak performance.

Corporate governance mitigants against failure (lessons learned):

- ▶ The management board should exercise objective judgment independent of management and devote sufficient time to the firm.
- ▶ Supervisory board members must be independent and capable and devote sufficient time to the firm.
- ▶ The management board's functions should include guiding corporate strategy; ensuring the integrity of financial reporting, disclosure, and communication; selecting an appropriate oversight standard by which other international codes are compared in instances where the business is geographically diversified; and determining framework and policy for compensating key executives.

References and further reading:

- ▶ de Jong, A. et al. 2005. "Royal Ahold: A Failure of Corporate Governance and an Accounting Scandal" Tilburg University CentER Discussion Paper (available at: https://research.tilburguniversity.edu/en/publications/royal-ahold-a-failure-of-corporate-governance-and-an-accounting-s).

CASE STUDIES

Parmalat (Italy, 2003)

False accounting spiraled from an initial 1990 decision by this Italian milk business to hide losses in its South American operations, mainly through inflating apparent revenues by double billing. In the end, in 2003, more than €4bn in cash and equivalents on the company's reported balance sheet turned out to be imaginary.

Parmalat's fraud began the way many frauds begin—accounting sleight of hand to cover up local losses. The fraud got so big because the losses persisted and the fraud was not uncovered for more than a decade, while the scale of the hole in the profits, and the efforts needed to conceal it, snowballed. Again, it appears that board oversight of international operations was less effective than it might have been. Furthermore, audit "checks and balances" seem to have failed. At the time, Italy had a rule requiring a change in audit firm every nine years. Parmalat sidestepped this rule by changing the parent company's auditor, Grant Thornton, but retaining them internationally. The market missed signals that appear obvious in retrospect, not least Parmalat's reported profit margins being far in excess of peers'.

Parmalat's board of directors presided over a weak corporate governance structure and process, in which the controlling shareholder was able to hold the positions of chair and CEO and perpetrate the following:

- Financial records filed by management were fraudulent and misleading. Members of the top management team intentionally failed to provide the correct financial information, including the status of the company's debts and losses.
- Whoever came close to learning about the accounting fraud taking place was fired, including the chief accounting officer. The cover-up, forgery, and non-disclosure were directly linked to the company's bank.
- The combined role of chair/CEO allowed the controlling shareholder to inappropriately pursue his own interests while disregarding those of the other stakeholders, including market rigging and obstructing regulators.
- The auditors failed to exercise professional due care and skill.

Corporate governance mitigants against failure (lessons learned):

- Major ethical issues touching on marketing and conflict of interest that existed between the company and its main service providers were addressed—for example, the illegal collaboration between the Bank of America and Parmalat.
- A well-conceived committee structure was established in which committees report to the full board to facilitate effective board function.
- The bylaws now require that the majority of directors be independent.
- The bylaws also mandate a separation between the chair and CEO roles.
- Independent auditors were appointed.
- The company's internal control system was redesigned to ensure the efficient management of its corporate and business affairs, to facilitate management decisions that are transparent and verifiable, to provide reliable accounting and operating information, to ensure compliance with the applicable statutes, to protect the company's integrity, and to prevent fraud against the company and the financial markets in general.

References and further reading:

- Ferrarini, G., and P. Giudici. 2005. "Financial Scandals and the Role of Private Enforcement: The Parmalat Case." Working Paper No. 40/2005, European Corporate Governance Institute (available at: https://www.ecgi.global/sites/default/files/working_papers/documents/ssrn-id730403.pdf). doi:10.2139/ssrn.730403

CASE STUDIES

Satyam (India, 2009)

The founder and chair admitted to falsifying the accounts of this IT services company. For around five years, the company had inflated revenues using thousands of false invoices; the auditor had apparently failed to check the bank statements that might have uncovered the fraud. The entire board was removed by regulators, the chair was jailed, and following a lengthy regulatory procedure, the company's auditor, PwC, was banned in 2018 from auditing any Indian public company for two years.

The founder's confession followed a proposed related-party transaction whereby Satyam would buy a real estate company from him. Though announced, the plan was retracted within a few hours after a highly negative response from shareholders—and the news that the World Bank would no longer do business with the company, barring it for eight years. The World Bank alleged that Satyam had provided improper benefits to its staff and had failed to provide proper accounts for its charges. Once problems emerged, as is so often the case, the fraud rapidly unraveled and the founder's losses in real estate ventures were revealed. The board had provided limited oversight and had perhaps believed the myth of the company's success and rapid growth. The extensive fraud was also missed by the audit process. The company was blacklisted by the World Bank over charges of bribery and was declared ineligible for contract bids for providing improper benefits to bank staff and for failing to maintain documentation to support fees.

Satyam's board of directors had problems with unethical conduct, incorrect disclosures, and transparency. The lack of transparent management dealings contributed significantly to Satyam's failures and violations of corporate governance codes, as follows:

- The board was lax and did not distinguish between its role, the role of independent directors, and the role of management, leading to inadequate and ineffective decision-making.
- The company failed to protect the rights of its shareholders and executives. For example, shareholders were denied the right to material information from the organization with respect to a merger and acquisition, and the acquisition of infrastructure and properties was announced without the consent of shareholders.
- There were also risk management issues. Cutbacks in both internal and external audit functions meant that the obligation to provide shareholders with accurate and fair financial reporting and accounting records was not fulfilled. Revenues and operating profits were falsely inflated, enabling insider trading and the payment of fraudulent gains to executives.

Corporate governance mitigants against failure (lessons learned):

- Satyam's fraud forced the government of India to re-write corporate governance rules in the areas of accountability, transparency, responsibility, and fairness and to strengthen the norms for auditors and accountants as well as independent directors appointed to the board.
- The importance of the audit function is a critical lesson for Satyam, whose founder/CEO, with a significant stake in the company, committed fraud.
- Although it is generally acknowledged that corporate governance mechanisms cannot completely prevent unethical activity by senior management, a board-established corporate governance framework implemented in both "spirit and letter of law" can help detect such activity in a relatively timely manner.
- Separation of the two roles of CEO and board chair strengthens accountability and the board oversight process.
- There should be an alignment of director and executive compensation with shareholder interests and firm performance.

References and further reading:

- Bhasin, M. 2013. "Corporate Accounting Scandal at Satyam: A Case Study of India's Enron." European Journal of Business and Social Sciences 1 (12): 25–47. available at https://www.researchgate.net/publication/271133751 _CORPORATE_ACCOUNTING_SCANDAL_AT_SATYAM_A_CASE _STUDY_OF_INDIA%27S_ENRON

CASE STUDIES

Olympus (Japan, 2011-12)

Following his appointment, new CEO Michael Woodford soon became concerned about the profitability of Olympus. He was ousted but acted as a whistleblower. Slowly, it emerged that the Japanese camera and medical instruments maker had hidden losses for many years, principally through over-priced acquisitions whereby some of the excess advisory fees paid were returned to the company to cover losses and shore up its finances.

Like many Japanese companies, Olympus was run by long-standing executives who had sought to protect the company at all costs, with remarkably few independent checks and balances. They had clearly concluded that hiding losses through convoluted schemes was preferable to honesty about the company's issues and the potential negative consequences for its workforce. Also, the supposedly independent oversight from the statutory auditors failed, because they too appear to have lacked independence from the company (or at least enough of them did).

Olympus's board of directors' collusive behavior contributed significantly to Olympus's failures amid a poor corporate governance culture, as follows:

- The company's corporate culture was rife with cronyism, which enabled the board and senior managers to turn a blind eye to falsified accounts for two decades. Following claims from a whistleblower, Olympus succumbed to pressure from investors to set up an independent committee to scrutinize a series of controversial takeover deals. This independent committee determined that the board comprised "yes-men."
- One board member openly admitted to not knowing the governance process during boardroom discussions.
- The Japanese government, regulators, and mainstream media appeared reticent to investigate questionable business practices at Olympus, such as material, unexplained payments that Olympus made to financial advisers in offshore shell companies, highlighted by the company's CEO turned whistleblower.
- The board failed in its fiduciary duty of care and did not act in the best interests of the company's shareholders. Irregular payments for acquisitions, resulting in very significant asset impairment charges in the company's accounts, went unchallenged by the board.

Corporate governance mitigants against failure (lessons learned):

- Board diversity is essential for effective decision-making, guidance, and risk management. A diverse board of directors limits the risk of undue deference and groupthink.

Formalized Corporate Governance Frameworks

- Japan's revised corporate governance code holds companies accountable to shareholders.
- Successful companies foster a culture that encourages accountable, transparent, and inclusive decision-making.
- An effective board must have competent members with an understanding of director responsibilities and duties, as well as core corporate governance skills.

References and further reading:

- Prusa, Igor. 2016. "Corporate Scandal in Japan and the Case Study of Olympus." Electronic Journal of Contemporary Japanese Studies 16 (3) (available at: https://www.japanesestudies.org.uk/ejcjs/vol16/iss3/prusa.html).

CASE STUDIES

Volkswagen (Germany, 2015)

Volkswagen was revealed to have cheated on US emissions tests on its diesel engines through software, so-called defeat devices. Although, on the face of it, this was not a governance scandal, many investors had long been concerned about the lack of accountability at the German company, where the voting shares were predominantly held by the founding families, the local government, and the government of Qatar.

The differential voting rights served to entrench these groups, enabling them to dominate the board. Management was thus able to operate in an insular and unaccountable way. Furthermore, the company's culture was driven by the view that engineers always knew best and that their actions were largely above criticism. The company needed an engineering response to the new diesel regulations, but when it failed to find one that worked on the road, it chose to seek one that at least worked during testing. The board, accustomed to not having to listen to external voices, never felt the need to ask enough questions to uncover the issue.

Volkswagen's board of directors contributed significantly to Volkswagen's emissions scandal through a weakness in corporate ethics, ownership, and governance structures, including voting rights and the makeup of its supervisory board, as follows:

- A feud among family members of the majority shareowners resulted in controversial board appointments, leading to a lack of diversity of opinion and expertise on the company's supervisory board and reduced oversight of the CEO.
- The concentration of power among the majority shareholders made the two-tier board system at the company ineffective.
- Inadequate boardroom and internal control systems fostered a culture in which problems were concealed rather than openly communicated to superiors.
- Financial incentives can be linked to compliance problems. In this case, corporate conduct that harmed the environment led to profit growth that benefited employees in the short term.

Corporate governance mitigants against failure (lessons learned):

- Appoint people to supervisory boards with relevant experience, skills, and independence. Volkswagen's deceit was perpetrated through an aggressive new sales strategy and bold claims of technological advances in software code. As the execution of corporate activity continues to shift from humans to technology, there should be an increased focus of risk management on technology innovators. In this instance, the selection, training, compensation, and oversight of programmers and software developers should probably have been a central feature of risk management, with respect to compliance with external obligations.

- Recognize that conflicts of interest between managers and shareholders are an agency cost, as are conflicts of interest between employees and shareholders—both should be managed by board directors with due care and skill and in good faith.

References and further reading:

- Jacobs, Daniel, and Lawrence P. Kalbers. 2019. "The Volkswagen Diesel Emissions Scandal and Accountability: Where Were the Auditors and Attorneys during the Sustainability Charade?" CPA Journal (available at: https://www.cpajournal.com/2019/07/22/9187/).

CASE STUDIES

Wirecard (Germany, 2020)

Wirecard, a hard-driving fintech and global payments processor, collapsed in June 2020 when long-running allegations of fraud and questionable accounting were largely confirmed by a special audit. The audit revealed that some €1.9bn of assets were missing from its accounts. It became apparent that substantial elements of Wirecard's business in the Middle East and Asia were no more than a sham and that the core payments-processing operations in Europe were barely profitable.

One of the most remarkable aspects of the scandal was the way that the media investigation—persistently pursued by the *Financial Times*—was fought at each step by the German regulator, BaFin, which was supposed to be overseeing the business. Apparently, both the regulator and the board were so taken by the opportunity for Europe to build its own fintech star that they failed to spot the red flags about the business and failed to ask enough questions as it expanded overseas. The auditor also failed to identify warning signs, especially around the overseas operations.

Wirecard's board of directors contributed significantly to Wirecard's failures through widespread corporate fraud, deception, and financial misconduct, as follows:

- There was a lack of transparency, accountability, and oversight. Due to inappropriate and ineffective internal control systems, enabling the company to violate accounting rules for many years, the supervisory board was ineffective in overseeing accounting practices.

- The supervisory board breached its duty of care in failing to conduct an independent internal investigation of the allegations concerning the company's accounting practices and in failing to prevent management's wrongdoing.

- ▶ The supervisory board failed to prevent an inherent conflict of management's interest in permitting the chair of the supervisory board to also be the chair of the audit committee. This structure limited the effectiveness of the audit committee in carrying out its fiduciary duties and responsibilities.
- ▶ BaFin, as the responsible regulatory agency, did not or could not live up to its overarching mandate to protect investors and market integrity.
- ▶ A corporate culture of always meeting earnings expectations contributed to the development of a strong incentive to manipulate earnings when financial results became unfavorable.

Corporate governance mitigants against failure (lessons learned):

- ▶ The board should execute corporate governance by developing a framework and policies within which it operates to serve the best interests of the company. The framework should ensure that all business decisions are made ethically and comply with regulations and laws. The board should establish appropriate committees for meetings with management to review significant transactions and financial information.
- ▶ External auditors should verify the existence, completeness, and accuracy of the company's financial statements.
- ▶ There must be adherence to new EU rules that strengthen corporate governance and improve the audit process.
- ▶ Early providers of information/whistleblowers must be heard by the relevant parties—regulators, auditors, and the board—and be taken seriously, and investigations must start in a timely manner.

References and further reading:

- ▶ Peters, Sandy. 2022. "Wirecard Scandal Spurs European Commission Consult to Enhance the Quality and Reliability of Corporate Reporting in Europe." Market Integrity Insights (CFA Institute) (available at: https://blogs.cfainstitute.org/marketintegrity/2022/02/23/wirecard-scandal-spurs-european-commission-consult-to-enhance-the-quality-and-reliability-of-corporate-reporting-in-europe/);
- ▶ Krahnen, J. P., K. Langenbucher, C. Leuz, and L. Pelizzon. 2020. "Wirecard Scandal: When All Lines of Defense against Corporate Fraud Fail." ProMarket (available at: https://www.promarket.org/2020/11/06/wirecard-scandal-when-all-lines-of-defense-against-corporate-fraud-fail/?mc_cid=452d0cb6fb&mc_eid=08df55fd49).

SHAREHOLDER ENGAGEMENT AND ALIGNMENT

3

☐ 5.1.1 explain the evolution of corporate governance frameworks: development of corporate governance; roles and responsibilities; systems and processes; shareholder engagement; minority shareholder alignment

Shareholder engagement is the active dialogue between companies and their investors, with the latter expressing clear views about areas of concern (which often include ESG matters). Engagement helps ensure that the board directors are accountable for their actions, which hopefully in time helps to improve the quality of their decision-making.

Engagement is discussed in depth in Chapter 6.

For minority shareholders—which institutional investors will almost always be—a crucial issue is that they not be exploited by the dominant or controlling shareholders. In many cases, protections for minority shareholders are built into company law, and they often exist in listing rules and other formal protections. These protections are usually bolstered by corporate governance codes, but the issues are so fundamental (because they relate to avoiding exploitation of minority shareholders and protection of their ownership rights) that in most countries, minority shareholders benefit from underlying legal protections.

Exploitation of minority shareholders could involve money being siphoned out of the business in ways that benefit the controlling shareholders but not the wider shareholder base, which explains why there are typically higher disclosure requirements around related-party transactions and rights for non-conflicted shareholders to approve them. Minority shareholders will also be unwilling to see the company they invested in change dramatically without their having the chance to vote on the issue. For example, in the UK listing regime, class tests are applied as follows:

- If a transaction affects more than 5% of any of a company's assets, profits, value, or capital, there must be additional disclosures (Class 2 transactions).

- If a transaction affects more than 25% of any of a company's assets, profits, value, or capital, there must be a shareholder vote to approve the deal based on detailed justifications (Class 1 transactions).

Another key area for shareholder protection is pre-emption rights. These rights ensure that an investor has the ability to maintain its position in the company. Fundamental to many markets' company laws (though not, for example, in the USA) is the idea that a company should not issue shares without giving existing shareholders the right to buy an amount sufficient to maintain their existing shareholding. Because these rights come before the prerogative of potential external investors, they are called pre-emptive, and the existence of these rights is why a large equity fundraising by companies is often called a "rights issue."

As rights issues are cumbersome, particularly if a company is issuing a relatively small number of shares, companies typically seek authority at AGMs to issue a relatively small proportion of shares (up to 5% or 10%) non-pre-emptively—that is, without having to offer them fairly to existing shareholders. Investors are usually prepared to grant such authority but with certain protections in place. Even where issues are not on a fully pre-emptive basis, there is usually an expectation that the larger institutional shareholders will be offered a so-called soft pre-emption, meaning an allocation equivalent to their existing shareholding but in a less formal, less legalistic way (which may enable the issuance to be made more swiftly). Larger issuances are more controversial, as are issues at a price possibly less than the prevailing share price. An example of a particularly unpopular model with defenders of minority shareholder rights is the "general mandate" resolutions in Hong Kong SAR, which seek to enable issuance of up to 20% of the share capital, potentially at a discount. There is a clear detriment from such transactions to the existing shareholders.

A final area in which minority shareholders can feel exploited is the mechanism of dual-class shares. Typically, one of the classes is restricted to the founders of a company (or a limited group chosen early in a company's life), who receive multiple votes compared to the class of shares that subsequent shareholders can invest in—the shares that are usually more freely traded on the stock market (and those issued freely as compensation to staff, particularly in the case of US technology businesses).

Moreover, management, which typically benefits directly from multiple voting rights and often voting control, will feel less accountable to the broader shareholder base, with whose interests management is less aligned.

Dual-class shares are often frowned upon by many investors and are rare outside the USA (though Volkswagen, as discussed in the Major Corporate Scandals section, is a European example). They are, however, becoming more visible and more common because of the current success of technology businesses, the founders of which have been keen to retain voting control. The Council of Institutional Investors (2021), the main organization for US institutions, has taken a nuanced stance on dual-class stock, recognizing that it can provide some stability in the early life of a company, but urging that it be subject to sunset clauses so the two classes are unified after, at most, seven years (the time horizon after which academic evidence suggests that dual-class stock will usually have a negative performance impact). Controversially, Snap Inc. (the parent company of Snapchat) took the dual-class stock route further and issued shares without any voting rights at all.

CHARACTERISTICS OF EFFECTIVE CORPORATE GOVERNANCE: BOARD STRUCTURE AND EXECUTIVE REMUNERATION

> 5.1.2 assess key characteristics of effective corporate governance, and the main reasons why they may not be implemented or upheld: board structure, diversity, effectiveness, and independence; executive remuneration, performance metrics, and key performance indicators (KPIs); reporting and transparency; financial integrity and capital allocation; business ethics

The current iteration of the Corporate Governance Code in the UK was published in 2018. It includes 18 principles under five themes:

- board leadership and company purpose;
- division of responsibilities;
- composition, succession, and evaluation;
- audit, risk, and internal control; and
- remuneration.

These themes are consistent across most of the world's corporate governance codes, as are (largely) the expectations and duties of the three principal board committees that almost all major companies have in place:

- the audit committee (sometimes the audit and risk committee);
- the nominations committee (sometimes the corporate governance committee or some combination of the two); and
- the remuneration committee (or the compensation committee in the USA; some companies also now incorporate into the name some reflection of a responsibility to the broader employee base).

The expectation is that the audit and remuneration committees will be populated solely by independent non-executive directors, and such directors should form a majority of the nominations committee (the chair should not lead this committee while it is seeking to appoint a successor). Some companies will establish other board committees to address issues ad hoc or on an ongoing basis, but they should use appropriate judgment in how those committees should best be populated. For example, most financial services businesses now have a separate risk committee, which is usually made up of independent non-executive directors. Other companies may have sustainability committees, or committees considering their key operational risks—such as a people committee at companies highly dependent on their workforce or a health and safety committee. Such committees assist the board in overseeing major exposures and in dealing with the workload of oversight. They are not compulsory, and certainly at smaller businesses, this workload is likely to be handled by the audit committee or by the board itself. The Code also determines appropriate disclosures to make the workings of the board transparent and to demonstrate their effectiveness to shareholders.

Published alongside the 2018 Code was a *Guide to Board Effectiveness*, which applies the same structure as the Code under the same five themes. It provides not only guidance but also questions to assist board members in considering whether they are being fully effective in their roles. The guide also provides questions that board members might choose to ask management to gain additional clarity on corporate culture. Almost half of the main body of the guide is taken up with the first theme, board leadership and company purpose—essentially, this theme focuses on culture, strategy, and maintaining appropriate relationships with key stakeholders. While this guide is a UK document that is explicitly aimed at assisting boards, the themes are useful to investors in considering the effectiveness of governance globally.

Board Structure, Diversity, Effectiveness, and Independence

As governance at its core is about people, the key to exercising effective governance is having the right people with relevant skills and experience around the boardroom table, as well as having the right board culture to enable each of them to contribute effectively to boardroom debate.

This goal is easily summarized but difficult to achieve. As can be seen from the case study sample of BHP's annual report disclosures on its board skills and diversity, there are multiple skills that boards seek to have available within the boardroom. If an issue is of high importance to the business, the usual expectation is that more than one person should have knowledge of that issue, because a board will rarely feel comfortable relying on a single perspective, particularly as that person may not always be available. Compromises need to be made, and plans need to be considered for the future to prepare for expected departures from the board—and to respond to unexpected changes (such as death or conflicts of interest). Of course, a board can have access to specialist skills through advice from experts invited to present at board meetings or to provide input in other ways. A question to consider is what skills and experience are regularly needed around the boardroom table and what skills and experience would be better accessed on an occasional, independent advisory basis.

One skill set, or at least depth of understanding, increasingly expected for every board concerns climate change—as highlighted by the specific attention to this issue in the BHP disclosures. Not every board can have a climate scientist, and indeed few boards may actually want one. But all boards need to be competent in dealing with the business complexities of the issues around climate change, so that they can appropriately consider how to adjust their business models and investment approach to reflect the increasing importance of issues surrounding climate change.. A company that fails to consider this issue is likely to misspend capital expenditures either currently or in the near future, as it invests in assets that will not have the same value in a carbon-constrained world—having a board with climate change competency could help avoid this waste. To achieve this goal, it is likely that education and training will be needed, for at least some directors. A growing number of appropriate courses are available. Boards may also increasingly have to consider skills and training in other areas, such as environmental and social risk.

As well as training for directors, boards must consider the need for refreshment of skills. The needs of the board will also change over time as its strategy evolves, and it is important to keep the skills matrix updated. The issue of director tenure and independence is discussed below.

There are many types of diversity needed for a board to be successful, though the most important is diversity of thought. The other types include diversity of gender, race, age, culture, nationality, economic background, and experience, each of which can also often help to deliver diversity of thought. The aim is to avoid groupthink in the boardroom, which may lead to a lack of questioning and challenge.

While this broad concept of diversity—diversity of thought—is well understood, most diversity initiatives focus on the most visible issues: gender and race. A number of markets now have quotas for female directors (notably Norway, which pioneered the approach, and France), and most are moving toward an expectation that at least 30% of public company directors should be women. The issue of racial diversity has been actively debated in the USA for some years, and the UK's 2017 Parker Review called for at least one non-white director on every FTSE-100 company board by 2021 and on every FTSE-250 board by 2024. A 2022 update of the review noted that 89 of the FTSE-100 companies had met the goal by the end of 2021 and that some 55% of the FTSE-250 had also already reached the goal. These initiatives gained fresh impetus from the momentum of the Black Lives Matter campaign in 2020, which could mean that more change is likely.

An effective chair brings out the contributions of each board member, which is less visible to outsiders but is a vital part of delivering board effectiveness. Investors can gain some insight into how the chair operates in the boardroom from direct dialogue with the chair and with other board members, but often the clearest indicator is the quality of the individuals on the board overall. Good directors tend not to join boards that do not allow them to contribute effectively, or if they do, they are quick to leave them. The unfortunate consequence of all this for those who invest broadly is that weak boards tend to remain weak and it is difficult to improve them without substantive changes.

Board appraisals (sometimes known as board assessments or self-assessments) are required under many corporate governance codes and can help boards to become more effective by bringing problems to the surface. Some investors are often cynical about these appraisals, as weak boards and weak chairs can relatively easily limit their impact without its being apparent to investors. It is hard to determine whether a board appraisal has been effective—though it has a better chance of succeeding if it is an external process with an independent facilitator rather than simply an internal review. In some markets, both the delivery and the findings of board appraisals are expected to be disclosed, which can help investors gain insight into a company.

CASE STUDIES

BHP Annual Report 2021, pp. 82–83: Disclosures on Board Skills, including Specifically on Climate Change Matters and Diversity

Board Skills and Experience

Total Directors	**12**
Mining	4
Senior executive who has:	
▸ deep operating or technical mining experience with a large company operating in multiple countries;	
▸ successfully optimized and led a suite of large, global, complex operating assets that have delivered consistent and sustaining levels of high performance (related to cost, returns, and throughputs);	
▸ successfully led exploration projects with proven results and performance;	
▸ delivered large capital projects that have been successful in terms of performance and returns; and	
▸ a proven record in terms of health, safety, and environmental performance and results.	
Oil and gas	2
Senior executive who has:	
▸ deep technical and operational oil and gas experience with a large company operating in multiple countries;	
▸ successfully led production operations that have delivered consistent and sustaining levels of high performance (related to cost, returns, and throughputs);	
▸ successfully led exploration projects with proven results and performance;	
▸ delivered large capital projects that have been successful in terms of performance and returns; and	
▸ a proven record in terms of health, safety, and environmental performance and results.	
Global experience	10
Global experience working in multiple geographies over an extended period of time, including a deep understanding of and experience with global markets and the macro-political and macro-economic environment.	
Strategy	11
Experience in enterprise-wide strategy development and implementation in industries with long cycles, and in developing and leading business transformation strategies.	
Risk	12
Experience and deep understanding of systemic risk and monitoring risk management frameworks and controls, and the ability to identify key emerging and existing risks to the organisation.	

Total Directors	12
Commodity value chain expertise End-to-end value or commodity chain experience—understanding of consumers, marketing demand drivers (including specific geographic markets), and other aspects of commodity chain development.	8
Financial expertise Extensive relevant experience in financial regulation and the capability to evaluate financial statements and understand key financial drivers of the business, bringing a deep understanding of corporate finance and internal financial controls and experience probing the adequacy of financial and risk controls.	12
Relevant public policy expertise Extensive experience specifically and explicitly focused on public policy or regulatory matters, including ESG (in particular, climate change) and community issues, social responsibility and transformation, and economic issues.	5
Health, safety, environment, and community Extensive experience with complex workplace health, safety, environmental, and community risks and frameworks.	10
Technology Recent experience and expertise with the development, selection, and implementation of leading and business-transforming technology and innovation, and responding to digital disruption.	5
Capital allocation and cost efficiency Extensive direct experience gained through a senior executive role in capital allocation discipline, cost efficiency, and cash flow, with proven long-term performance.	11

Twelve Directors meet the criteria of financial expertise outlined above. The Risk and Audit Committee Report contains details of how its members meet the relevant legal and regulatory requirements in relation to financial experience.

Board Skills and Experience: Climate Change

"Board members bring experience from a range of sectors, including resources, energy, finance, technology, and public policy. The Board also seeks the input of management and other independent advisers. This equips them to consider potential implications of climate change on BHP and its operational capacity, as well as understand the nature of the debate and the international policy response as it develops. In addition, there is a deep understanding of systemic risk and the potential impacts on our portfolio.

"The Board has taken measures designed to ensure its decisions are informed by climate change science and expert advisers. The Board seeks the input of management (including Dr. Fiona Wild, our Vice President of Sustainability and Climate Change) and other independent advisers. In addition, our Forum on Corporate Responsibility (which includes Don Henry, former CEO of the Australian Conservation Foundation and Changhua Wu, former Greater China Director, the Climate Group) advises operational management teams and engages with the Sustainability Committee and the Board as appropriate."

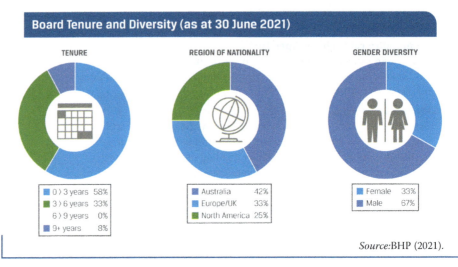

Source: BHP (2021).

Board independence is also a key concern. The aim must be to have a board that is independent of the management team and operates with independence of thought so that it can challenge both management and previous decision-making at the company (including prior board decisions).

The ICGN's Global Governance Principles set out an unusually complete investor perspective on independence criteria; these extend and elucidate some of the criteria embedded in standards in various Codes around the world. These criteria suggest that there will be questions about the independence of an individual who:

- ▶ had been an executive at the company or a subsidiary, or an adviser to the company, and there was not an appropriate gap between their employment and joining the board;
- ▶ receives, or has received, incentive pay from the company, or receives fees additional to directors' fees;
- ▶ has close family ties with any of the company's advisers, directors, or senior management;
- ▶ holds cross-directorships or has significant links with other directors through involvement in other companies or bodies;
- ▶ is a significant shareholder in the company, or is an officer of, or otherwise associated with, a significant shareholder, or is a nominee or formal representative of a shareholder or the state; and
- ▶ has been a director of the company for a long enough period that their independence may have become compromised.

The intent is not to suggest that boards should never include directors whose independence is questioned. Indeed, such individuals may provide useful skills and perspectives. However, every board needs a sufficient weight of clearly independent individuals so that it is able to operate independently and is not subject to bias or inappropriate influence. Investors recognize that independence is a state of mind, and that some individuals can be fully independent notwithstanding some of the issues raised, while others, whatever their appearance of independence, will support only a CEO or a dominant shareholder. One of the challenges for investors is being able to identify both sorts of individuals.

Most investors would prefer that a company acknowledge that an individual will not be perceived as independent (for one of the various reasons) but will nevertheless bring real value to the business, rather than assert that the individual remains fully independent notwithstanding some obvious challenge(s). As ever, the way a board approaches an issue in its disclosures will determine how shareholders consider it.

Characteristics of Effective Corporate Governance: Board Structure and Executive Remuneration

The issue of length of tenure on the board and independence is generally recognized around the world (though it is not acknowledged as an issue in some major markets, most notably the USA), though different standards are applied. As can be seen in Exhibit 2, different markets have different expectations as to how long it takes for independence to erode. Investors may often seek to apply a single global standard, while companies may expect that their local standard will be respected.

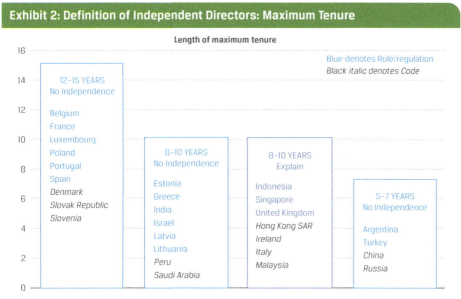

Exhibit 2: Definition of Independent Directors: Maximum Tenure

Length of maximum tenure

Blue denotes Rule/regulation
Black italic denotes Code

12–15 YEARS
No Independence

Belgium
France
Luxembourg
Poland
Portugal
Spain
Denmark
Slovak Republic
Slovenia

8–10 YEARS
No Independence

Estonia
Greece
India
Israel
Latvia
Lithuania
Peru
Saudi Arabia

8–10 YEARS
Explain

Indonesia
Singapore
United Kingdom
Hong Kong SAR
Ireland
Italy
Malaysia

5–7 YEARS
No Independence

Argentina
Turkey
China
Russia

The markets that apply an "Explain" standard are essentially asserting a rebuttable presumption that the relevant individual is not independent; if a company wishes to argue that the individual remains independent notwithstanding their tenure, an explanation is needed, which shareholders may or may not accept.

Source: OECD (2019).

Executive Remuneration

Pay is where the clearest conflict of interest between management and shareholders occurs. As (in public companies at least) it is not possible for investors to negotiate pay directly with management, shareholders need to rely on remuneration committees to do so effectively on their behalf, and they need to have confidence that the non-executive directors on those committees will negotiate well and with shareholder interests in mind.

There is a broader challenge, however: the directors' obligation is to the success of the individual company, while shareholders, in most cases, have an eye to the broader market. Therefore, while shareholders may be more concerned about a ratcheting effect of increased pay across the market as a whole (often driven by companies seeking to respond to pay benchmarks and remain competitive in terms of remuneration), directors will want to ensure the best possible candidate is appointed to their company, which may tempt them to pay up for the given individual. Often, many of the arguments about executive pay arise directly from this difference between the mindsets of the board and the shareholders.

While pay levels differ in different markets, the pay structures for top executives are broadly similar. In brief, executive pay structures in much of the world come in four categories:

- fixed salary, usually increased annually;
- benefits, including pension (typically calculated as a percentage of the salary, often at a more generous rate than is enjoyed by the wider employee base);
- annual bonus; and
- share-linked incentive (usually in the form of a long-term incentive plan, or LTIP).

While the scale of fixed salaries, and the way in which they increase (often ahead of inflation in general wages), can be controversial, most attention is focused on the variable incentives: the bonus and equity-linked portions. Bonuses are typically calculated on the basis of annual performance against metrics (often called key performance indicators, or KPIs) set at the start of a year; they are paid in cash at the end of the year—though increasingly some of the bonus is deferred for a further two or three years, often into shares that are released only at the end of the deferral period. The KPIs for bonuses will predominantly be financial metrics (usually profit-related), but often around 20% of the KPIs concern personal performance or non-financial measures, including ESG factors. Investor expectations on this matter have shifted notably in the last few years, and it is now a predominant view that at least a portion of the bonus should be driven by such ESG metrics—typically, factors that are closely aligned with the strategic aims of the business.

The longer-term equity rewards usually measure performance over at least three years and are typically paid out in shares that must be held for a further period (currently the expected minimum overall period, including the performance period and lock-up thereafter, is five or more years). Performance for these schemes is usually measured by broad-brush financial metrics, typically a combination of total shareholder return (TSR) and earnings per share (EPS).

While this brief discussion may sound complex, it is a significant simplification, as can be seen by looking at the multiple pages devoted to remuneration in an annual report.

Trust, or a lack of it, has driven much of the problem with executive reward. This issue has developed because of failures of understanding between investors who see ongoing payments for poor performance and corporations that find shareholders voting against schemes they have supported for years or have previously indicated they will support. Companies are faced with various views from investors, many of which are incompatible and so strongly held that they allow little flexibility. The fear of significant votes against a board's remuneration proposals leads many companies to produce a compromised structure, rather than something the directors fully believe will drive value in the business. This action can lead to a further escalation of quantum (the amount paid to executives, aggregated across all forms of remuneration), as a compromised structure means that executives lack confidence they can deliver what is needed to unlock the company's full potential. The higher quantum also leads to media and investor attention, and tension between the company and its shareholders is likely to escalate.

Disputes also arise from other differences in mindset. Investors tend to look for pay outcomes that match the corporate performance they enjoy as shareholders, and they are unlikely to oppose even the most generous packages when share price performance is strong (though there is increasing evidence that US companies in particular are testing the boundaries of this shareholder indifference to quantum—for instance, the 34% shareholder opposition in the say-on-pay vote at Apple's 2022 AGM, where the company's generous executive rewards raised concerns for shareholders, even given its stellar business and share price performance). Companies tend to consider performance within the business itself (seeing the share price as a function of market sentiment as much as business performance), and directors believe they need to honor contractual obligations, paying out according to the terms of the agreed incentives. This situation can sometimes lead to a disconnect in expectations: the reward that is due under the contractual incentives may seem excessive to shareholders because it does not reflect the market performance of the shares.

Overcoming these differing perspectives is necessary, but as yet no proposed alternative structure has gained sufficient traction among both investors and companies to become the universal solution to the problem.

Discussions about executive pay are also complicated by concerns about fairness and the extent to which executive pay outcomes far exceed the experience of ordinary people, as exemplified by the pay ratio disclosures now mandated by some markets (notably the UK and the USA). These disclosures compare the remuneration of the CEO with that of the firm's average-paid worker and reveal very sizable differences, often hundreds to one. While investors will often have sympathy for companies that are keen to have the best leadership, the growing tensions about income and wealth disparity make the question of fairness, as exemplified by pay ratios, an issue that is increasingly hard to ignore. These considerations are part of what is now driving the debate about the overall quantum of executive pay.

CHARACTERISTICS OF EFFECTIVE CORPORATE GOVERNANCE: TRANSPARENCY, CAPITAL ALLOCATION, AND BUSINESS ETHICS

5

5.1.2 assess key characteristics of effective corporate governance, and the main reasons why they may not be implemented or upheld: board structure, diversity, effectiveness, and independence; executive remuneration, performance metrics, and key performance indicators (KPIs); reporting and transparency; financial integrity and capital allocation; business ethics

Reporting and Transparency

Principle N of the 2018 Corporate Governance Code states:

> *"The board should present a fair, balanced and understandable assessment of the company's position and prospects."*

The starting responsibility for the oversight of company reporting sits with the audit committee, but as Principle N indicates, this responsibility is shared by the whole board. The phrase "fair, balanced and understandable" was arrived at after considerable debate and has led many companies to undertake a rigorous restructuring of their processes and reporting. Reporting and transparency are led first by the management team and then overseen by the audit committee and the board as a whole. An independent challenge then comes from the auditor.

Investors often learn much about the management team from their reporting. That is especially true where a company appears to be masking a weakening performance. One way in which this masking is sometimes done is through alternative performance metrics (APMs). These measures are adjusted forms of the accounting standard–approved measures of performance, often referred to as "adjusted" or "underlying." Their use sometimes indicates a management that is keen to flatter performance rather than admit a failure to generate better performance, as the omission of elements through these adjustments may be difficult to justify objectively. Investors are particularly wary when the APM calculations vary from one reporting period to another. A further indicator of an attempt to obscure an issue is where numbers in the narrative disclosures of the annual report do not entirely reconcile with the numbers revealed in the financial accounts in the back half of the report.

One area where there is a particular danger of inconsistency between the narrative and the financial reporting, and currently a major concern to many institutional investors, is climate change. Too often, the fine words in the narrative reporting in response to the Task Force on Climate-related Financial Disclosures (TCFD) and other reporting standards are not reflected in changes to the associated financial reporting. The International Accounting Standards Board (IASB), which sets the International Financial Reporting Standards (IFRS) for most of the world, has recently commented that material climate issues should be reflected in financial reporting, and the Principles for Responsible Investment (PRI) and other institutions have called on companies and their auditors to ensure that this reporting is delivered in practice.

The area of reporting on environmental and social factors is rapidly developing. New Zealand and the UK were the first countries to mandate that all large public companies must report according to TCFD standards, but they will not be the last.

In collaboration with the International Organization of Securities Commissions (IOSCO), the IFRS Foundation announced at COP26 the formation of a new International Sustainability Standards Board (ISSB). (IOSCO, the international body that brings together the world's securities regulators, is recognized as the global standard setter for the securities sector; COP26, held in 2021, was the 26th UN global summit to address climate change.)

The ISSB will develop a comprehensive global baseline of high-quality sustainability disclosure standards to meet investors' information needs and will consolidate the Climate Disclosure Standards Board (CDSB, an initiative of CDP) and the Value Reporting Foundation (VRF, which houses the Integrated Reporting Framework and the SASB Standards) into the IFRS Foundation.

This new body will have a multi-location structure, drawing together many of the disparate groups independently seeking to set sustainability reporting standards. It aims to ensure that the different needs of the various regions are reflected as the standards are developed.

The advent of ISSB provides the potential for unprecedented uniformity based on a consistent common standard of high-quality sustainability reporting, assessment, and analysis.

A strong audit committee should strictly oversee the reporting process to ensure fair and balanced reporting, preventing these sorts of discrepancies from occurring. A strong and challenging auditor, assisted by regulations, should also intervene to prevent any misleading of investors. Auditors also have a specific duty to highlight any apparent inconsistencies between the financial statements and other reporting by the company.

The European Securities and Markets Authority (ESMA) published a set of guidelines on the use of APMs in 2015. These guidelines require consistency, with the APMs not to be disclosed more prominently than the official measures and with a full reconciliation between the two. Unfortunately, enforcement of these standards is variable.

In a similar way, in December 2019 the IASB published an exposure draft on primary financial statements, which would allow the disclosure of a management-preferred measure of performance on the face of the income statement—but only alongside the permitted standard measures and with a full reconciliation between them. The IASB continues to consider how best to respond to the feedback it has received. It remains to be seen how effectively companies will respond to any new standard.

See the section titled "Corporate Governance and the Independent Audit Function" for a detailed discussion of audit and the challenges that arise in that area.

Financial Integrity and Capital Allocation

The key concern active shareholders usually have about a company's strategy is capital allocation (the way a company applies its financial resources to generate the most value over the long term). Key questions to be asked include how much of its cash flow does it distribute to shareholders and how much does it reinvest in existing or new business activities. It is rare for a company to have large enough resources to pursue every opportunity it identifies, and so capital allocation is as much about what a company will *not* do as about what it will. These investment decisions are crucial—whether a company can successfully deliver on them will determine the returns the company receives over future years.

Often, in part, capital allocation is a function of history: a company retains a legacy business operation, even a sizable operating business, when the opportunity for the company as a whole has in fact moved on. Shareholders can be more clear-minded than management about disposing of older businesses or operations—often, perhaps, because they may not understand the full complexities that would be involved in fully moving on from the legacy activity nor be fully aware of the consequences for stakeholders. Even where the issue is not a legacy activity, most companies have to make decisions that will see their business operations diverge over time. Conglomerates are now firmly out of favor, and most investors prefer to invest in focused businesses—with investors themselves providing diversification across their portfolio holdings. The crucial decision for the boards of such companies is how to allocate capital among the various businesses and make the most of the opportunities they have identified. Even where there is no active investor pressing for a different approach to capital allocation, the board may need to have an active dialogue with the shareholder base because different decisions about which business opportunities to pursue will appeal to different investors. In particular, some of the capital allocation options may require a change in the dividend payout to ensure that more resources can be retained for reinvestment in the business.

In a similar way, the capital structure of a company is a crucial area of debate within the boardroom and between the board and shareholders. Companies without debt on their balance sheets are often thought to be inefficient and failing to deliver the full extent of possible returns—failing to maximize return on equity. However, the 2008 financial crisis—and the more recent challenges to business resilience arising from the COVID-19 pandemic—reminded all investors that there is a danger in seeking to load companies with excess debt in order to generate greater returns on the remaining equity capital. That danger is the risk of insolvency if interest rates rise and/or if there is a downturn in the business. Having a sustainable capital structure means there must be some compromise between the extremes of maximizing returns on equity in the short term and making the company entirely robust to a downturn. Unless the company is operating in a highly volatile business (where the gearing is operational rather than financial), the board should seek to optimize the capital structure by taking on some debt.

A key financial resilience question that boards will need to answer is how they strike a balance between full resilience and maximizing short-term returns. Many shareholders will be willing to sacrifice some short-term returns so the business will be strong enough to survive a downturn. The experience of the COVID-19 pandemic has reminded investors and company boards that having such a buffer is good stewardship of a business in the long term. But the prudent balance is delicate: most shareholders would not wish businesses to be so financially secure that they could cope with any financial crisis. The multiple fundraisings by companies during the pandemic demonstrated this point in practice: good businesses with long-term futures were refinanced.

Decisions regarding share buybacks and the issuance of shares are key elements of these overall capital structure decisions and should be considered as such by both boards and shareholders. Similarly, considerations with regard to the payment of dividends to shareholders need to encompass decisions about what is a sustainable level of capital to support ongoing business success. Paying dividends beyond the cash flow from the business is clearly not sustainable and is likely to raise significant questions among shareholders, even though they may welcome the immediate cash payments. But the opposite circumstance—a low dividend payout ratio—is also likely to cause concerns, especially if the company already has significant cash on its balance sheet. This latter circumstance has proved central to disagreements between several Japanese companies and their shareholders over recent years

Business Ethics

A company needs to abide by the laws of its home country (formally known as its country of incorporation), and a multinational group must act within the laws of any country in which it operates. In some respects, such as bribery and corruption, many jurisdictions impose extraterritorial laws, meaning that a company can be guilty of an offense anywhere in the world it is involved in corruption. For example, both the USA's Foreign Corrupt Practices Act and the UK's Bribery Act have extraterritorial effect; the latter also explicitly requires every company to maintain procedures to ensure that no bribery is carried out by agents or others on its behalf.

Many companies, particularly those based in legalistic environments, tend to believe that obedience to the law is sufficient. However, many investors expect more than that, and companies aspiring to be responsible world citizens and to enjoy ownership on the public markets will need to go further. Companies need to operate while being conscious of business ethics and broader responsibilities to stakeholders and communities. By doing so, they are more likely to prosper in the long term, not least because a failure to deliver on these ethical aims may lead to a breakdown in relations with one or more key stakeholders. At its extreme, an ethical failure might lead to a loss of license to operate in a market or even as a business. An ethical approach to business will encompass such issues as:

- corporate culture and having a set of expected behavioral standards for all staff, not tolerating inappropriate behaviors;
- treating employees fairly by upholding high standards in health and safety, human rights, and avoiding modern slavery;
- offering value to customers and avoiding discriminatory or other exploitative behavior, including avoiding collusion with rivals or other anti-competitive activity;
- avoiding bribery and corruption, and fraudulent behavior;
- paying suppliers appropriately and promptly, and not seeking unfair benefit from any dominant negotiating position;

- developing appropriate relationships with local communities close to relevant business operations, and being ready to enter into dialogue on any key concerns they may have;
- approaching any regulatory or political lobbying activity honestly (including ensuring that the lobbying is not inconsistent with the company's publicly stated approach to particular issues) and without seeking unfair advantage;
- seeking to pay a fair and appropriate level of tax by approaching tax compliantly and recognizing that tax avoidance, not just tax evasion, can be inappropriate; and
- acknowledging that a company's reputation is a valuable asset that can be harmed by unethical or inappropriate behavior by the business or its staff.

Usually, the audit committee is asked to oversee business ethics as part of its broader risk remit, but different companies address these issues through different structures. A company with a robust ethical approach and culture will have robust whistleblowing procedures in place that are well publicized to staff and to which all employees (and perhaps others, such as contractors and suppliers) have access. These procedures will allow any concerned party to raise issues with people of appropriate seniority and independence, so that any apparent failure to live up to the asserted ethical standards can be identified and addressed promptly. Typically, these whistleblowing processes will be overseen by the audit committee (and sometimes by the risk committee or other appropriate board-level group), so non-executive directors can assure themselves of the independence of the process and have confidence that the company is living up to the standards that the board expects.

In practice, the approach to business ethics within a company is, like corporate culture, generally difficult for outsiders to discern, as it will always be a challenge for both non-executive directors and shareholders to have real insight into the matter.

STRUCTURAL CORPORATE GOVERNANCE DIFFERENCES IN SEVERAL MAJOR WORLD MARKETS

6

5.1.3 assess and contrast the main models of corporate governance in major markets and the main variables influencing best practice: extent of variation of best practice; differences in legislation, culture, and interpretation

The division between the supervisory board and the management board marks one of the fundamental structural differences in governance globally. The so-called two-tier boards are seen, for example, in Germany, the Netherlands, Scandinavia, and China; the single-tier (also called unitary) boards are more typical of the UK, the USA, Japan, France, and most of the rest of the world. But this structural difference covers other differences; for example, there are multiple forms of the single-tier board:

- In the USA and France, a single executive sits on the board and often bears the responsibility of both chair and CEO (though this long-held tradition of combining the two very different roles is declining in the USA, with around half of S&P 500 companies now having an independent chair). In Australia, the CEO is usually the board's single executive director (and does not usually chair the board) but is typically not subject to election by shareholders.

- In Japan, there is usually a single-tier board dominated by executive directors, with only a small handful of non-executive directors (not necessarily independent).
- In most other countries, single-tier boards have a few executive directors and a majority of non-executives (most of whom are independent), one of whom acts as chair.

By contrast, supervisory boards are all largely constituted in the same way, with all members being non-executives. In some cases, however, they are not perceived as independent, as some members may be direct representatives of major shareholders or representatives of employees, and in some cases the chair of the supervisory board is the former CEO of the company (though this tradition is slowly being abandoned).

No one model of corporate governance is better than the others. They are creatures of the legal histories and cultures of the countries in question. Best practices have been identified and incorporated into global initiatives such as the *ICGN Principles* and the *Organisation for Economic Co-operation and Development (OECD) Principles*. In the same vein, investors will often expect companies to adopt international best practices and go beyond local standards in country-specific codes. The *OECD's Corporate Governance Factbook* is a good source for details on the governance structures and approaches in 49 jurisdictions. Inevitably, the following brief survey covers a much smaller set of geographies and highlights the unusual features in corporate governance in several major world markets, including examples from developed markets and from emerging markets.

Examples from Developed Markets

Corporate Governance in Australia

Australia has a single-tier board structure, with just a single executive director (often called the managing director instead of, or as well as, CEO). This individual is typically not subject to election by shareholders, who vote on the appointment of the non-executive directors annually. Boards are also relatively small in comparison to public companies in most other major markets, with six or seven directors being typical. While some companies have moved to annual elections for all directors (other than the CEO), many still face re-election only every third year.

The Australian bluntness of their version of comply or explain—"if not, why not?"—can be reflected in a sometimes-combative relationship between companies and their shareholders. Australia was one of the first countries to make superannuation (pension) saving compulsory in order to increase that form of saving to meaningful levels, so the "super funds" are now significant. They increasingly seek to wield their influence forcefully, and a number of organizations—in particular, the Australian Council of Superannuation Investors (ACSI)—help them present shared views to companies.

Investors have a strong influence on Australian companies, as can be seen in the case of the mining company Rio Tinto in 2020. The CEO and two other senior executives were ousted following a public outcry after the company destroyed the Juukan Gorge site (caves that showed evidence of continuous human habitation for 46,000 years and were considered sacred by the local Puutu Kunti Kurrama and Pinikura peoples) to develop it for iron ore mining. Despite the company's having a license to take these actions, the public outcry and the concerns expressed by both politicians and investors made it impossible for the company not to take action against top executives.

Shareholder resolutions are relatively common in Australia, with only US companies facing more such proposals. The reason is partly because Australian law has been interpreted in a relaxed way, and partly because of the strength and organization of the shareholders. The approach can be seen in the appointment of directors, where law and regulations are deemed to mean that only a minimal shareholding is needed to make a proposal, provided the notice period for proposing a candidate has been followed. Though the thresholds for other shareholder resolutions are higher—5% of the issued capital or 100 shareholders—campaigners using social media find it relatively easy to reach the required number of shareholders.

Corporate Governance in France

While there is scope for two-tier boards in France, the vast majority of French boards are single-tier and led by a combined chair/CEO, sometimes still referred to as the Président-Directeur Général (PDG). Standards require that 40% of the directors be female and that around a third of the board be employee representatives, ensuring that the stakeholder voice is clearly heard in the boardroom. French law takes conflicts of interest particularly seriously, and shareholders are invited to vote on related-party transactions (often multiple resolutions in a single year), even those of relatively small value.

Two aspects of French governance are particularly unusual and worthy of discussion: the requirement for joint auditors and the existence of double voting rights for some shareholders. With regard to the audit, France is the only major market to require two audit firms to look at financial statements rather than the usual one firm; these firms are generally one of the Big Four (Deloitte, EY, KPMG, and PricewaterhouseCoopers, or PwC) and one from the next tier of firms. Some consider this requirement controversial, as it is seen as possible for issues to fall between the cracks between the two firms; however, the proponents of this approach suggest that there are likely to be fewer issues missed because there are more pairs of eyes considering the key concerns. The duplication of work effort (and cost) is minimized, as the only entity audited by both joint auditors is the top company and the consolidated accounts—the firms split the audit of the rest of the business units between them (with the smaller firm typically covering less than half). The staggered rotation of the audit firms provides continuity despite the requirement for regular changes of audit firm.

Under 2014's so-called Florange Act (named after a steelworks in northern France that closed and became a symbol of the risk of further industrial decline), unless there is a two-thirds shareholder vote to the contrary, French companies can award double voting rights to long-standing shareholders, defined as those who have held shares in a particular way for at least two years. The structure of this requirement means that few institutional investors qualify (certainly those outside France do not). Even a long-standing pension fund or insurance investor may find its continuity of ownership perceived as having been affected by such normal practices as a change of custodian or fund manager or by a stock-lending program. Thus, in practice, these double voting rights are perceived as a mechanism to establish management control, or control by majority shareholders, and to limit the influence of minority shareholders.

The controversial nature of the Florange Act and the potential long-term consequences of its double voting rights are illustrated in two cases.

First, at Renault: the French government was a 15% shareholder and failed to persuade the company's management and its business partner, Nissan, not to propose an opt-out from the Florange Act at its 2015 AGM. Instead, shortly before the AGM, the French government bought an additional near-5% stake in the company—enough to defeat the opt-out from the law, having given the French state double voting rights for its shareholding, which it soon reverted to the 15% level. In retrospect, this maneuver (agreed to by Emmanuel Macron, the economy minister at the time) is seen as one of the moments when the partnership between Renault and Nissan began to break down.

The second example is Vivendi, the French media conglomerate. Businessman Vincent Bolloré effectively secured his control of the company in 2015, when he was able to defeat a resolution to opt out of the Florange Act. At the time, his shareholding in Vivendi was just under 15%, and while a majority of shareholders supported the opt-out, it failed to gain the necessary two-thirds majority. As a result, Bolloré's shareholding soon gave him 20% of the votes (and more since then), which proved sufficient for him to gain full control of the company and to radically reshape its strategy.

Corporate Governance in Italy

Italy has a single-tier board structure, with typically a single executive director and an independent chair. An unusual feature of Italy's governance framework arises from its history: most company shareholder bases have been dominated by a single shareholder or group of shareholders (often led by the state, local or national, or the founding family or, in some cases, by the country's major financial institutions). The dominance of these shareholder groups could mean that the nomination and election of the boards of such companies would be entirely in their hands, leaving minority shareholders feeling unrepresented and facing wholly non-independent boards. To reassure minority shareholders that their interests would be represented, the *voto di lista* approach was developed: a designated portion of the board (typically around 30%) is reserved for minority shareholders only. Shareholders with a minimum level of shareholding (usually 1%) have the ability to propose a slate (i.e., a group) of directors, and typically there is more than one slate. The slate with the most votes is the dominant one, and the chair is appointed from it; the slate with the next most votes is considered the successful minority slate and fills the board roles designated for minority investors. The Italian investor association Assogestioni organizes minority slates for board elections each year.

At companies with a broad institutional investor base and only a limited shareholding by the "major" shareholder, there is a chance that the *voto di lista* approach could lead to the slate intended as the minority slate gaining more votes than the one intended to be dominant. In such unusual situations, the proxy agencies will recommend that their clients support the slate intended as the dominant one, so that it provides the chair and the bulk of board seats as intended. In most circumstances, the proxy agency recommendation is that clients support the Assogestioni minority slate to ensure some board participation by independent directors.

Another unusual feature of the Italian governance structure is that there are elections for statutory auditors. These auditors are not the independent auditors, who are charged with assessing the accuracy of the financial statements. Rather, the statutory auditors have a legal role to affirm the legality of certain actions by the board. Usually, one of the three to five proposed candidates is a lawyer and another is a former (financial statements) auditor. Statutory auditors are also appointed through a *voto di lista* slate process and form an additional protection for minority shareholders.

Both the boards and the statutory auditors are elected for multi-year periods, usually five years, and are not eligible for re-election in the following period. Though this approach provides a clear planning horizon, it can lead to challenges in the last year of a mandate, as there may be a sense of a weaker board that does not wish to bind its successor inappropriately. There is of course no reason why the same board should not be reappointed for a second mandate, but this happens less frequently than might be assumed.

Corporate Governance in Japan

Many companies in Japan (and also in markets such as Taiwan and South Korea) enjoy the structure of having statutory auditors (*kansayaku*), who are in addition to the independent audit firm that ensures the accuracy of the accounts. There is typically a small odd number of statutory auditors (usually three or five), each of whom is appointed individually by shareholders, typically on a four-year rotation. In theory, these auditors are independent individuals, but in many cases, this independence may be questionable as many come from family companies or the lending banks, which can have a close relationship with large companies. While in some ways these statutory auditors serve an independent challenge role somewhat equivalent to independent non-executive directors, their scope to do so is limited by their narrowly defined role and also by the questionable independence of some.

Since the changes to governance introduced by the third "arrow" of Abenomics (the moves toward economic liberalization and renewal under former Prime Minister Shinzo Abe), some companies in Japan have started moving away from the statutory auditor approach and have instead adopted the alternative structure of a "board with committees," similar to board structures seen elsewhere in the world, with non-executive directors. This move has created some challenges, as there has not been a tradition of non-executive directors in Japan, and the culture of loyal and lifetime service to single companies and of strong rivalries within industries has halted the development of a body of non-executives ready to offer advice and challenge a range of businesses. The focus in the Japanese Corporate Governance Code, introduced in 2015 and revised in mid-2018, is on the independence of non-executive directors rather than on the value they can bring to companies through their insights. This focus purely on independence has led to the appointment of some individuals whose value in a business boardroom might be doubted, but this focus is changing over time and a greater understanding of the role of the non-executive director is developing.

Although the *zaibatsu* conglomerates that dominated the Japanese economy for decades were officially dismantled after 1945, the culture of family groups of companies held together by cross-shareholdings persisted (*zaibatsu* is a Japanese term meaning "financial clique" and refers to industrial and financial business conglomerates in Japan, usually family controlled, whose influence and size allowed control over significant parts of the Japanese economy up until the end of World War II). There was a perception that these cross-shareholdings acted as deadweights on fresh strategic thinking and innovation. For this reason, the Japanese Corporate Governance Code includes provisions that discourage the maintenance of cross-shareholdings (a specific principle, 1.4, discusses cross-shareholdings and, in effect, requires the disclosure of a policy to reduce them over time). Another main focus in the code is on increasing independence on Japanese boards by requiring at least two independent non-executive directors to be in place on every board, even where the statutory auditor model is still in use.

Corporate Governance in the Netherlands

The 2017 contested takeover bid for Dutch chemicals firm AkzoNobel by US rival PPG put corporate governance in the Netherlands firmly in the spotlight. While in most countries, the bid—certainly the revised terms offered by PPG after its initial and second approaches were rebuffed—and the strong support for discussions from significant shareholders would have led to active negotiations, AkzoNobel never even came to the negotiating table. Instead, the Dutch firm successfully argued that the board owed as strong a duty to other stakeholders, particularly employees, as it did to shareholders, and further argued that the value offered to shareholders was unattractive (though the shareholders themselves largely and often publicly disagreed) and that the protections for staff were insufficient.

AkzoNobel declined to hold an extraordinary general meeting (**EGM**) proposed by several shareholders that would have considered ousting the supervisory board chair, Antony Burgmans. A May 2017 court decision by the Enterprise Chamber backed the board's understanding of Dutch corporate governance, including both its basis for not entering into discussions on a deal despite investor support and its decision not to hold the proposed EGM. Burgmans finally departed the board ahead of the 2018 AGM. In effect, the court decision backed the board's stance on the bids, and the company also benefited from significant political support—further takeover protections for all Dutch companies have since been proposed. In some ways, however, shareholders got the bulk of what they wanted in the end. Subsequently, the company sold off its specialty chemicals business, focusing instead on paints and coatings, and returned the bulk of the proceeds to shareholders.

As with other countries with supervisory board structures, shareholders in the Netherlands appoint the supervisory board and are kept at a distance from holding management accountable for performance and strategy. The AkzoNobel case demonstrates that shareholders do not necessarily come first in the Dutch corporate governance model and that other stakeholder interests must be taken into account. That is particularly true in the case of takeovers, which have long been a sensitive issue in the Netherlands and remain so—long after the dismantling of most of the so-called *stichting* structures, which were able to keep shareholders at arm's length if there was a hostile bid, securing the role of management and the supervisory board. (A *stichting* is a legal structure that can be used for any purpose. In the context of corporate governance and control, it usually refers to an organization that itself owns the shares in the underlying company and issues depositary receipts to the market. Investors would buy these instead of shares, meaning that they would not enjoy all the rights of legal shareholders.) But the AkzoNobel example also shows that, other than in the case of takeovers, the influence of shareholders is strong: the longer-term outcome of the dispute was board change and a significant streamlining of the company and return of value to shareholders.

Corporate Governance in Sweden

Governance in Sweden has been shaped by the dominance of major shareholders in the registers of many leading companies. Most prominent of these is the Wallenberg family vehicle, Investor AB. Investor AB is itself a public company but is controlled by the Wallenbergs through the mechanism of two classes of shares with differential voting rights—a feature of Swedish governance that persists at many businesses despite its controversial nature. Investor AB's ownership of other Swedish companies includes, among others:

- Atlas Copco (16.9% of the shares and 22.3% of the votes);
- ABB (12.2% of the shares and votes);
- AstraZeneca (3.9% of the shares and votes);
- SEB (20.8% of the shares and votes);
- Ericsson (7.7% of the shares and 23.6% of the votes); and
- Electrolux (16.4% of the shares and 28.4% of the votes).

Investor AB argues that its investments, and its voting influence, enable it to avoid short-term pressures and to build these businesses for the long term.

This dominance of the share capital, and particularly of the votes, could lead to Investor AB being able to appoint the bulk of corporate boards in Sweden and having even more disproportionate influence than it already does. To mitigate this dominance, Sweden has developed an unusual structure whereby a company's nominations committee is not a board committee but is instead appointed from among the shareholders—with the largest shareholders invited to participate in descending order of their shareholdings until the committee is fully populated. At the AGM, this nominations committee proposes a board (which may include no more than a single executive, with independent non-executive directors in the majority) and a chair for shareholder approval. The outcome of this procedure is reasonably positive: skilled and generally well-balanced boards. The Wallenberg family still appear in many Swedish boardrooms, frequently providing the chair. In contrast to most countries, in Sweden the proposed board is usually put forward as a single slate, meaning that shareholders have a vote on the board as a whole rather than votes on each proposed director.

Similar structures and approaches can be found in other Scandinavian markets.

Corporate Governance in the UK

The UK issued the world's first Corporate Governance Code, and the current, 2018 version—overseen by the regulator Financial Reporting Council—goes further than most others. In particular, it focuses more attention on board behaviors and corporate culture than do other Codes. Of course, it does set expectations for:

- board skills and structure;
  - the UK discourages combined chair/CEO roles and expects chairs to be independent at appointment;
  - independent non-executive directors should compose the majority of the board, though there should be at least two and preferably three or more executive directors;
- audit and risk (the board is charged with considering the company's emerging and principal risks, including ESG risks, and making a statement regarding the viability of the business over at least a three-year period from the date of the accounts);
- remuneration;
  - the UK has detailed expectations around pay, in theory linking executive pay to performance and limiting the scope of payments for failure (long-term schemes need to be genuinely long term);
  - these expectations are layered with extensive corporate law disclosure standards to apply to large UK-incorporated companies, which means that generally UK annual reports are the most coherent and informative in the world.

The UK Code's focus on board behaviors and corporate culture is much more in-depth than that of other Codes around the world and really makes the UK stand out. The second Principle of the current Code is particularly striking in this regard: "The board should establish the company's purpose, values and strategy, and satisfy itself that these and its culture are aligned. All directors must act with integrity, lead by example and promote the desired culture." The second provision reinforces this message: "The board should assess and monitor culture. Where it is not satisfied that policy, practices or behaviour throughout the business are aligned with the company's purpose, values and strategy, it should seek assurance that management has taken corrective action."

This focus on culture means that the Code places particular emphasis on a company's *workforce*, a deliberately chosen term intended to include not only those directly employed by the company but also workers more generally. Boards are expected to explain their approach to investing in and rewarding their workforce. They are also expected to stay informed about the views and attitudes of the workforce through one of three mechanisms: a director appointed from the workforce, a formal workforce advisory panel, or a non-executive director who serves as a liaison to the workforce. The last mechanism is by far the most popular; workforce directors remain highly unusual in the UK and are part of only some already fairly idiosyncratic boards (such as those at Frasers Group and JD Wetherspoon). The link to the interests of the workforce is also seen in the Code's standards on pay: the remuneration committee is expected to take account of workforce pay and culture in its consideration of executive pay, and there is a specific expectation that executive pension rates be aligned with those of the general workforce.

UK governance standards are also, in effect, set by best practice groupings, with some degree of regulatory and political backing. Most notable among these are the Hampton-Alexander Review and the Parker Review, which are pressing, respectively, for greater female representation on boards and for each board to include at least one director from a minority ethnicity. The initial goal of the former has nearly been reached (broadly, 30% female board membership); more remains to be done to reach the initial goal set by the latter.

Corporate Governance in the USA

The USA stands out in terms of governance. Now that Japan has introduced its own Corporate Governance Code, the USA is the only major market—and almost the sole country—without a Code of its own. The reason is a fundamental issue in US politics: the relationship between the federal government and the individual states. Corporate law is a matter for the states, and so there is no scope for a federal set of rules to govern corporations. Indeed, the fact that each state has its own corporate laws led to a race to the bottom for company standards among the states, competing with one another for the tax revenue from incorporating businesses. This race was comprehensively won by the small state of Delaware, which is now home to more than half of all publicly traded US corporations. The decisions of the Delaware courts are therefore of disproportionate importance to US corporate life.

In the absence of countrywide US governance standards, there have been various attempts to establish market-led best practices, of which these are the leading ones:

1. The Commonsense Corporate Governance Principles, first published in July 2016 and revised in October 2018. These principles were created by a coalition of company representatives, including the leadership of Berkshire Hathaway, BlackRock, General Electric, General Motors, JPMorgan Chase, and Verizon Communications, along with representatives of the largest US investors. These principles focus mostly on the inner workings of corporate governance, board effectiveness and accountability, and alignment through pay.

2. The Investor Stewardship Group's (ISG) Corporate Governance Principles for US Listed Companies, which came into effect at the start of 2018. As the name suggests, these principles were created by a coalition of investors (a number of whom were involved in creating the Commonsense Corporate Governance Principles). These principles are also more about the relationship between US companies and their shareholders than about their internal governance. The ISG has also produced a set of Stewardship Principles—in effect, the reciprocal responsibilities of investors in response to these corporate responsibilities.

3. The Corporate Governance Policies of the Council of Institutional Investors (CII). These policies set out in detail the approach of the CII—the pre-eminent representative of long-term investors in the USA—to the full range of corporate governance issues. These policies are less a set of principles and more an indication of the likely positions of CII members on issues that might go to a shareholder vote or be the subject of a public policy debate.

In combination, the first two initiatives represent a corporate governance code as it would be understood elsewhere in the world.

With reference to governance, what *is* regulated on a federal level in the USA is securities law: hence, the importance of the US Securities and Exchange Commission (SEC) and the rules it sets. For example, the SEC sets requirements for the independence and skills of members of the audit committees of companies listed in the USA.

These standards were set by the Sarbanes-Oxley Act. Typically, the SEC creates rules based on statutes that reflect pre-existing expectations set down as principles in other markets. Here are two examples under the Dodd-Frank legislation:

1. There is a resolution to consider executive remuneration, usually referred to as a say-on-pay vote. Under Dodd-Frank, such a resolution must be put to a shareholder vote at least every third year, though shareholders must also be offered a vote on whether they wish to have a "say on pay" more frequently; most institutional investors favor holding such votes annually.
2. The "access to the proxy" standard permits shareholders that fulfill certain criteria to add a candidate to the company's formal proxy statement, avoiding the cost and administrative complexity of mounting a full proxy fight over board membership.

In practice, the access-to-the-proxy right has rarely been used. However, the combination of these two rights has led to a positive dynamic in company-shareholder relations. More companies are now making non-executive directors—particularly an independent chair where there is a lead independent director—available for shareholder meetings. Such a dialogue would have been highly unusual just a few years ago.

Examples from Emerging Markets

Corporate Governance in Brazil

Annual corporate reporting on social, environmental, and ethical issues has been adopted among public corporations. Effective 2 January 2023, public corporations are also required to disclose ESG information in their reference form (*Formulário de Referência*) in the "comply or explain" format.

The State-Owned Enterprise Governance Program was established in September 2015 in response to scandals and political use of state-owned companies by the government. Under the Program, corporate governance rules of these companies are enhanced through:

1. clearer disclosure of the company's objectives;
2. the creation of mechanisms to remove administrators who divert company activities from the stated objective;
3. the establishment of detailed nomination criteria encompassing the qualifications and expertise of the administrators; and
4. the commitment of the public controlling shareholder to comply with corporate governance best practice.

In 2018, Brazil's first Corporate Governance Code was published. The CG Code aims to consolidate and standardize the recommendations of the main self-regulatory entities in Brazil for public corporations and is based on the "comply or explain" principle. However, adherence is required from companies whose shares are part of the IBOVESPA Index or the IBrX-100 Index.

The Brazilian Institute of Corporate Governance (IBGC) Code is considered the most established and comprehensive code of corporate governance in Brazil. Compliance with the IBGC Code is not mandatory. Based on the principle of "comply or explain," non-compliance does not trigger any penalties.

Board structure, composition, and restrictions: Companies typically have a board of directors whose members are elected by shareholders (including minority shareholders and holders of preferred shares) and a management/executive board whose members are elected by the board of directors. Although the main purpose of the two-tier governing system is to separate executives from non-executives, in many cases the board of directors includes members of the management board, such as the CEO, CFO, and Investor Relations Officer. The disclosure of material events is a duty of the company's Investor Relations Officer, who may be held personally liable for damage arising from non-disclosure. With the enactment of CVM Resolution 168, the chair and CEO positions cannot be held by the same person in public companies with annual gross income of more than BRL500mn (about USD100mn). In addition, Brazilian law allows for the establishment of a supervisory council ("fiscal board"), which should comprise entirely outside, independent members. The fiscal board's main responsibilities include overseeing the acts of the board of directors and management and reviewing the company's financial statements. It is an oversight body with an advisory role and does not participate in managing business operations. As such, neither executives nor directors (including those of the company's subsidiaries and affiliates) can serve on the supervisory council. The fiscal board is non-permanent and must be instated at the request of shareholders representing at least 10% of the voting stock or 5% of the non-voting stock. The fiscal board comprises three to five members and a like number of deputies. The conditions for election and impairment of fiscal board members, who must be Brazilian residents, are prescribed by law.

Together, the members of the board of directors, the management board, and the fiscal board are referred to as the governing entities. The CG Code states that one-third of the members of the board of directors should be independent directors. The IBGC Code does not give a specific number or proportion of independent directors but requires a "relevant" number or proportion with respect to the total number of company directors, without defining "relevant." The boards of companies listed in the Novo Mercado segment must comprise a minimum of five directors, of whom the greater of at least two or 20% must be independent.

While Brazilian legislation does not provide for any gender quota requirements, a new regulation emphasizing gender diversity and inclusion in high leadership positions is planned.

An anti-corruption law has been in place in Brazil since 29 January 2014; it has introduced administrative and civil liability of legal entities for illicit acts committed in relation to local and foreign public officials. However, there is as yet no whistleblowing legislation in Brazil.

Public companies must change independent auditors every five years and must wait at least three years before re-hiring the same auditor. Most Brazilian companies are not required to establish board committees, and therefore companies rarely form such committees. Companies may choose to establish audit committees pursuant to CVM Instruction 509 in order to, among other things, allow them to hire independent auditors for a term of up to 10 consecutive years. In addition, publicly listed financial institutions and other entities authorized to operate by the Central Bank of Brazil must establish remuneration committees.

Pursuant to changes to the Brazilian Corporation Law in 2021, it is now possible to have a class of ordinary shares with plural votes, or super-voting shares, whereby such plural votes may not exceed 10 votes per common share, which are often used by founder shareholders of start-ups and tech companies that go public. Another change removed the requirement that officers of Brazilian companies must be resident in Brazil.

Corporate Governance in India

The corporate governance framework in India is driven by a combination of mandatory statutes and regulations, voluntary guidelines, and international market best practices. In the closely held and controlled world of Indian corporates, protection of minority shareholders is a significant issue that Indian regulators must address to ensure that independent directors can fulfill their obligations.

The Companies Act 2013: This statute is administered by the Ministry of Corporate Affairs (MCA) and the Registrar of Companies (Registrar). The relevant rules apply to all companies. Through its various appointed committees and forums such as the National Foundation for Corporate Governance (NFCG), a not-for-profit trust, the MCA facilitates the exchange of experiences and ideas among corporate leaders, policymakers, regulators, law enforcement agencies, and non-governmental organizations.

Listed companies are required to have an optimum combination of executive and non-executive directors, with non-executive directors composing at least 50% of the board. The Companies Act also introduced the requirement of appointing a resident director and a female director. The focus is on accountability of the board of directors and management. The CEO and CFO of listed companies are required to (a) certify that the financial statements are fair and (b) accept responsibility for internal controls. The ownership structure in Indian companies is characterized by promoters and non-promoters, founders or controlling shareholders, and other shareholders, including minority shareholders. Transactions involving a promoter are regulated. The disclosures regime emphasizes transparency, timely reporting, and adequate disclosures to shareholders. Annual reports of listed companies must also include status reports about compliance with corporate governance norms.

India's corporate community experienced a significant shock in January 2009 from the damaging revelations about board failure and colossal financial fraud at Satyam. The Satyam scandal also served as a catalyst for the Indian government to rethink the corporate governance, disclosure, accountability, and enforcement mechanisms in place.

In response, in late 2009 the MCA released a set of voluntary guidelines for corporate governance. Viewed as a first step, the option remains open to make these guidelines mandatory. The voluntary guidelines address myriad corporate governance matters, including the independence of the board of directors; responsibilities of the board, the audit committee, auditors, and secretarial audits; and mechanisms to encourage and protect whistleblowing.

Provisions, particularly those addressing the role of insiders, include: issuance of a formal appointment letter to directors; separation of the roles of chair and CEO; institution of a nominations committee for selection of directors; limiting the number of companies in which an individual can become a director; tenure and remuneration of directors; training of board members in the company's business model and quarterly reports on business risk and risk management strategies; performance evaluation of directors; and additional provisions for statutory auditors.

In 2019, the MCA released the National Guidelines for Responsible Business Conduct (NGRBC), which sought to adopt the Gandhian principle of trusteeship, encouraging businesses to contribute toward wider development goals while seeking to maximize their profits.

The Securities and Exchange Board of India (SEBI) is the principal regulator of listed companies. SEBI monitors and regulates corporate governance of listed companies in India through Clause 49, which is incorporated in the listing agreement between stock exchanges and companies; it is compulsory for listed companies to comply with the provisions of Clause 49. Key features of Clause 49:

Board independence: Directors cannot be related to: promoters or management at the board level or one level below; an executive of the company in the preceding three years; a supplier, service provider, or customer of the company; or a shareholder owning 2% or more of the company. Nominee directors are excluded from the definition of independent director and are subject to the same responsibilities and liabilities as any other director. Where the chair is an executive or a promoter or related to a promoter or a senior official, then at least half of the board should comprise independent directors; in other cases, independent directors should constitute at least one-third of the board.

Audit committees: Listed companies must have board audit committees with a minimum of three directors, two-thirds of whom must be independent, including the chair of the committee; in addition, audit committees must comprise "financially literate" members.

Corporate social responsibility: In 2021, SEBI issued a new framework for sustainability reporting called the Business Responsibility and Sustainability Report (BRSR), applicable to the top 1,000 listed companies by market capitalization over FY2022/2023. This is a significant step toward bringing sustainability reporting up to par with financial reporting. The BRSR incorporates benchmarking industry best practices; sustainability reporting under internationally accepted disclosure parameters as set out in GRI, SASB, and TCFD, among others; assessment disclosures with a key focus on environmental and social aspects; and adaptation of key performance indicators, including reporting on leadership.

Non-regulatory bodies: Non-regulatory bodies have also published codes and guidelines on corporate governance from time to time—for example, the Desirable Corporate Governance Code published by the Confederation of Indian Industries (CII) in 2009.

Corporate Governance in South Africa

Common law and statute: South Africa modeled its company law on the English example and therefore adopted a unitary board. Much of the English common law of companies has been adopted into South African case law; however, the Companies Act 71 of 2008 was heavily influenced by the corporation legislation from Canada, Australia, and New Zealand, leading to a wider consideration of international perspectives.

The Companies Act 2011: This statute includes a statement of directors' duties. The statement is based on the common law fiduciary duties of directors and officers and on the duty to act with care, skill, and diligence; to exercise the powers and perform the functions of director in good faith, for a proper purpose, and in the best interests of the company; and to have the requisite knowledge, skill, and experience.

Directors and officers are potentially liable in accordance with the principles of the common law relating to a breach of fiduciary duties.

Due to the regulator's lack of institutional resources, enforcement is mostly left to shareholders and directors through a statutory derivative action.

The Companies Act introduced a social and ethics committee as a compulsory committee for all state-owned and publicly listed companies. Other companies may need to appoint a social and ethics committee if their public interest score is high. This committee must monitor the company's activities regarding a list of environmental and social issues and report back to the annual general meeting about these matters. Issues within the mandate of the committee include the company's standing in terms of the UN Global Compact; the OECD recommendations on corruption; the South African legislation setting out affirmative action in employment and Black economic empowerment; the environment, health, and public safety; employment relations; and consumer relationships.

King IV Report on Corporate Governance for South Africa 2016 (King IV): South Africa was one of the first countries, after the United Kingdom, to introduce a code of corporate governance, first released in 1994. South Africa's Code of Corporate Governance (King IV) has since been revised three times, leading to the current version.

King IV is intended to apply to any organization that has a governing body, extending its potential scope beyond the boards of incorporated companies to include, for instance, trustees of pension funds and councils of municipalities. Entities listed on the Johannesburg Stock Exchange (JSE) must report on their compliance with King IV's disclosure and application regime as part of their annual report.

Adoption of the Code is voluntary—compliance is based on "apply and explain." King IV proceeds from the premise that any organization claiming to practice sound governance will have applied 16 basic principles. King IV further assumes that the organization has implemented integrated reporting, without which the 16 principles cannot be fully met.

King IV includes a 17th principle that applies exclusively to institutional investors—namely, that "the governing body of an institutional shareholder should ensure that responsible investing is practiced by the organization to promote the good governance and the creation of value by the companies in which it invests."

Sustainable development is an underpinning philosophy of King IV, and it promotes a stakeholder-inclusive model of governance.

Market regulation: Certain aspects of governance as set out in King IV are mandatory as listing requirements on the JSE:

- There must be a policy evidencing a clear balance of power between directors, so that no one director has absolute powers of decision-making.
- The positions of chair and CEO must be separate. The chair must be an independent non-executive director, or otherwise a lead independent director must be appointed.
- A mandatory audit committee, remuneration committee, and social and ethics committee must be appointed in accordance with the requirements of the Companies Act.
- Unless specifically authorized by the JSE, every listed company must have an executive financial director.
- The board must have adopted a policy to promote diversity.
- The remuneration policy and implementation report must be presented at the annual general meeting for a non-binding advisory vote by shareholders. If voted against by more than 25% of the voters, the policy must indicate what measures the board will take to address the concerns raised by shareholders during the meeting. Shareholders must be invited to engage with the board on this matter and must be given the time and manner of such engagement.

7 CORPORATE GOVERNANCE AND THE INDEPENDENT AUDIT FUNCTION

☐ 5.1.4 explain the role of auditors in relation to corporate governance and the challenges in effective delivery of the audit: independence of audit firms and conflicts of interest; auditor rotation; sampling of audit work and technological disruption; auditor reports; auditor liability; internal audit

The modern concept of the auditor evolved from the financial scandals of another era.

The earliest trading businesses of the 17th century (perhaps most famously, the Dutch East India Company, or VOC) were established for a specific trade journey or a set period, after which they needed to account for their performance and share the proceeds before being allowed to renew their mandate for a further period. This procedure sometimes included an expected independent oversight of the accounts. The Industrial Revolution (circa 1760–1840) saw for the first time the creation of many more large-scale corporations that sought to raise capital from outside parties. As many of these companies were expected to have an ongoing life beyond a set period or a particular endeavor, finance providers started to insist that management account for their use of this capital at least annually, leading to requirements for both annual reports and accounts and an AGM.

The failures and downright frauds of the UK's 1840s railway boom (an early investment bubble) saw minority shareholders suffer significant losses. The law was changed in response to the inevitable outcry, requiring an audit of the annual accounts by an independent party, thus providing shareholders with assurance that the numbers presented to them were true and fair.

The concept of the audit has not changed: the auditor is there to provide an independent pair of eyes assessing the financial reports prepared by management, and to provide some assurance that those reports fairly represent the performance and position of the business. There is no absolute assurance that the numbers are correct, nor certainty that there is no fraud within the business. Auditing is a sampling process that tries to identify anomalies that can then be followed up. According to the 1896 UK Court of Appeal judgment re Kingston Cotton Mill (No. 2)—following yet another corporate failure, this time when the auditor had taken a management assertion on inventory at face value—auditors should be watchdogs, not bloodhounds. There has been an ongoing debate following every corporate failure since, as to both whether the watchdogs were asleep on the job and whether we ought to expect a little more bloodhound-like—or perhaps, to use a more modern simile, sniffer dog–like—behavior from auditors.

Reviewing Financial Statements, Annual Reports, and Wider Reporting (including Sustainability Reports)

Despite the lack of global uniformity in ESG reporting standards, companies increasingly seek to burnish their sustainability credentials by publishing detailed reports that have been independently assured by auditors.

The auditor independently examines and provides third-party assurance of the financial statements, affirming that the detailed information is free from material misstatement and inconsistencies. As a result of an audit, stakeholders may evaluate and improve the effectiveness of governance, risk management, and control over the subject matter.

This assurance work may be conducted by leading audit firms or by smaller groups of alternative assurance providers that specialize in ESG matters. Investors need to read the assurer's report carefully to understand what ESG standards have been achieved in practice and then consider what additional weight they can place on the sustainability reporting. The intention in sustainability reporting is to encourage organizations to go beyond the fundamental duty of legal compliance.

The key elements of an ESG audit that investors should consider include the scope—business strategy, policies, and operations; the timeline covering when the assessment is being carried out, and which periods are being reviewed; and how the audit is conducted, including information on checks and balances to ensure as much accuracy as possible. Although the auditor's work is often procedural, providing limited substantive assurance, a well-conducted ESG audit fosters an increase in the confidence that both current and future investors can place in reported ESG data and analysis.

Audit methods include:

- third-party certification of data and information included in the ESG report;
- provision of an independent guarantee that both data and analysis are credible and accurate; and
- attestation that published communication from management details how activities are transparently reported for ESG issues.

Examples of issues that can be evaluated in an ESG audit include:

- environmental standards, and management systems;
- energy-saving initiatives;
- facilities, water, and waste management, including recycling activities;
- product development and manufacturing processes, and efforts to reduce waste in all stages of production;
- plans for monitoring carbon emissions and mitigating or even eliminating production of toxic waste (the way the company's supply chain moves goods to customers, emissions from transportation vehicles, and fuel use can be assessed);
- use of hazardous materials in products;
- compensation for community impacts and environmental damage due to location of facilities;
- corporate transparency;
- performance on social issues related to human rights, diversity, labor standards, and working conditions; and
- remuneration policies for employees.

Assurance of ESG reporting is currently entirely voluntary and (in contrast to the financial audit) is not based on a single set of universally accepted regulatory standards. E, S, and G data are largely drawn from several organizations that expend considerable resources in developing and setting comprehensive global standards. These standards are focused on identifying and evaluating ESG risk factors that are financially important to companies.

Disclosures and frameworks can be quite detailed, yet not uniform. It is important to differentiate between management system standards and those that simply offer guidance on reporting about sustainable activities. In the case of the latter, these standards are not designed for certification purposes or for regulatory or contractual use; thus, any offer to certify, or claims of certification, would be a misrepresentation of the intent and purpose—and a misuse—of audit.

The Independence of Audit Firms and Conflicts of Interest

The independence of the audit firm is critical. Large audit firms, including the Big Four, typically offer non-audit services (consultancy work and tax advice, principally) to the companies they audit, despite the obvious risks arising from conflicts of interest. As they spend so much time within a business and interact with the finance department, auditors can build closer relationships with the management of the companies they audit than with the non-executive directors on the audit committee to whom they report, or the shareholders for whom they formally perform their work. Audit firm staff also sometimes will later work at companies they have audited. Investors often assess potential conflicts of interest by looking at how much an audit firm is being paid for its audit work versus its consultancy work and whether a company has a policy to limit this risk, though this issue is not the only sign of conflicts.

Regulators have intervened to remove the most obvious conflicts of interest, which has led to a significant decline in recent years of the scope for auditors to provide non-audit services to their clients. This trend can be seen within the EU. For example, EU law now not only provides a list of non-audit services that are the only ones an audit firm may provide to clients, but also places a monetary limit (calculated in relation to the audit fee) on their overall value. In 2019, the UK's Competition and Markets Authority proposed much more separation between the audit and non-audit arms of accountancy firms, so that audit is much less likely to be influenced by other concerns.

Another important question surrounds behavioral independence. There is a natural tendency for individuals to seek consensus and for people to want to avoid disagreement or even confrontation with those they spend time with. These natural human behaviors run counter to the very role of the auditor, which must be to question and challenge the information that the audited entity provides. Every member of the audit team must work to avoid succumbing to such tendencies, and the audit partner overseeing the whole process needs to ensure that skepticism has been maintained throughout. In particular, there must be enough time allowed for questions to be pursued fully, and enough scope for additional staffing if necessary. These ideas both run contrary to the frequent mindset that the audit firm should be efficient in its work, adhere to a timetable dictated by the company, and keep within a budget that allows the firm to generate a profit. In practice, it is not always easy for investors to be confident that the audit has been done as thoroughly as they might wish.

Auditor Rotation

The concentration of the audit market makes it more difficult to address the issues of auditor independence and effectiveness. In the EU, public companies are obliged to change auditors after 20 years at most (and to tender the audit after 10 years). With the incumbent barred from competing after 20 years and the other audit firms sometimes unwilling to give up valuable non-audit services contracts, there is a sub-optimal level of competition. Prior to the rule changes, it was frequently argued that auditor rotation might lead to issues being missed, either in the last year of a departing auditor or in the first year of a new auditor, but the reported impact has been positive: companies that have changed auditors have found the refreshed perspectives valuable yet challenging.

Sampling and Audit Work

The sampling process that underlies audit work has been mentioned previously; however, technological and AI developments may see this process change. Significant effort should go into assessing what is an appropriate level of sampling to gain a good insight into the accuracy of the underlying numbers, and also into assessing the output of that sampling. On occasion, though, it seems that the budget for the audit does more to determine the work undertaken than the need for clarity of assurance. The depth of sampling is highly dependent on the auditor's assessment of the quality of the company's own systems and financial controls (see below for a discussion of disclosures of performance materiality). In this matter, the external auditor leans on the work of the company's internal audit (the company's own process for assessing risks and the quality of reporting, also discussed below), and well-run audit committees sensibly coordinate the internal and external audits so they can get an appropriate level of assurance across the company.

Sir Donald Brydon's 2019 independent review of the quality and effectiveness of audit proposed that every audit committee produce an annual audit and assurance plan that discloses the committee's expectations for overall assurance of company reporting, including both internal and external audits, which should make this coordination more apparent and perhaps more effective. Under Sir Donald's proposals, shareholders would be invited to provide input in the development of this plan.

In theory at least, the world of big data is changing the sampling approach, and the leading audit firms are exploring methods of using technology to consider every single transaction rather than merely sampling a proportion of them. A number of independent software firms have developed packages that deliver this capability, though these firms currently seem to be more focused on the small and mid-sized end of the corporate market than on larger businesses. The challenge with any approach to assessing every transaction is spotting anomalies in this barrage of data, not just checking that the numbers add up. The technology potentially removes the need to sample—but not the need to consider intelligently the information that is delivered. This area remains a work in progress.

Enhanced Auditor Reports

Shareholders today have more insight than ever before into the work of auditors because of the new enhanced auditor reports. Originated in the UK, enhanced auditor reports have now been adopted globally. These reports include three crucial elements:

- *Scope of the audit:* This element concerns how many parts of the company the audit has covered and in what depth. Typically, an auditor will apply a full audit to the largest segments (usually geographies, but sometimes business segments) and will apply tailored audit procedures to others, but some segments may be ignored altogether.
- **Materiality**: While materiality is a qualitative concept and should vary depending on the significance of the issue and its circumstances, in practice the disclosure tends to focus on a quantitative measure of materiality: the level of transaction or valuation below which the auditor spends little time. For the biggest companies, this number can be surprisingly large (US$500m is not unusual). Of more interest to investors are the levels of materiality applied to the different segments and—where it is disclosed—the performance materiality number (the level below the materiality threshold that the auditor uses in its audit procedures to prevent problems from arising when the numbers analyzed are aggregated). The performance materiality number indicates the extent to which the auditor trusts the company's financial systems: 75% of the overall materiality threshold is typical, whereas anything around 50% to 60% suggests a low level of confidence in the company's financial controls. Such lower levels of performance materiality might indicate a highly devolved organization or one whose controls should perhaps be enhanced, which can be a useful insight for investors.

> *Key audit matters:* The third element concerns a handful of key areas of judgment in the accounts. While the areas covered will rarely come as a surprise to investors, the way in which these issues are discussed and what auditors choose to highlight in their open discussion can reveal interesting and important insights. The best auditor reports not only highlight the key areas of judgment but also indicate whether the company's reporting on them is conservative, neutral, or aggressive. This so-called graduated audit adds real value to investors' understanding of the company's reported performance.

These enhanced auditor reports upgrade prior practice, where the sole piece of insight was the auditor's opinion on whether the financial statements represented a true and fair view of the company's performance and position at the end of the financial year. When an annual report was published, it would be quick work to find out whether an auditor had given a negative opinion. Auditors' past unwillingness to provide much insight was driven by their fear of litigation in the case of a corporate failure. Investors learned that auditor reports were not worth reading—a lesson that now needs to be unlearned. Investors have much to learn from these enhanced auditor reports if they can begin to navigate the tone and specialist language used in them (or if auditors could begin to make them more accessible to the general user). These reports may be further enhanced if some of the proposals in the independent Brydon Review are adopted—indeed, Sir Donald's review proposes that auditors do a lot more to inform investors and the market as a whole. He emphasizes the importance of this role for auditors by using *inform* as one of the three key words in the title of his final report: "assess, assure and inform."

Auditor Liability

One reason that auditors give for not providing more than they are strictly required to, in terms of the audit or auditor reporting, is liability. In most markets, the auditor has unlimited liability. Indeed, the US SEC has established a rule that any company subject to its jurisdiction (which includes many foreign companies that have US listings of either their equity or their debt) may not in any way limit the liability of the auditor. Even where audit firms enjoy the benefit of a limited liability partnership (meaning that all the partners are no longer exposed to risk because of a potential failure by one of the partners), the individuals who are directly responsible for any failure, especially the partner involved, can face losing everything. This risk is seen as significant, in part, because auditors are often among the few deep-pocketed players when there is a corporate failure, and so they are regularly included in lawsuits. The extent to which the courts would attribute liability to the individuals and their firms, however, is less clear, because most of these cases are settled before they get anywhere near a judgment. Most of the settlements are private, and so it is unclear whether, in practice, the liability risk is as large as the profession tends to indicate.

Internal Audit

Internal audit should not be confused with external audit. The latter can be outsourced, but most of the time, internal audit is part of the company itself, with a formal reporting line to the executive team (though usually with a dotted line to the audit committee). It functions largely as a risk management tool, used to ensure that the company's procedures and expected behaviors are delivered in practice and to uncover misbehavior or problematic management.

Internal audit has a highly variable status in different businesses—indeed, it does not exist at all in some organizations. Where it is deployed most effectively, internal audit is a tool for both the executive team and the non-executive directors to gain confidence and comfort about the company's delivery on the ground, helping the company operate more effectively and efficiently. It can help the board feel closer to the real operations—a significant challenge for modern, large multinational businesses. There is a sea change taking place in internal audit, involving directing the work toward helping the board and senior managers protect their organization's assets, reputation, and sustainability. The Internal Audit Code of Practice, issued by the Chartered Institute of Internal Auditors in January 2020, is, in effect, a pathfinder for the profession to help it deliver fully on this promised change.

CORPORATE GOVERNANCE AND THE INVESTMENT DECISION-MAKING PROCESS

5.1.5 assess material impacts of governance issues on potential investment opportunities, including the dangers of overlooking them: public finance initiatives; companies; infrastructure/private finance vehicles; societal impact

5.1.6 apply material corporate governance factors to: financial modeling; risk assessment; quality of management

Of the three ESG factors, governance is the one most often considered by traditional investment analysts. A 2017 CFA Institute ESG survey showed that 67% of global respondents took governance into consideration in their analysis and investment decision-making (up from 64% in 2014), ahead of environmental and social factors (both at 54%). In the EMEA region, the number of analysts indicating that they took governance into account was 74%.

The primacy of governance is logical. Academic research indicates that of the three ESG factors, governance has the clearest link to financial performance. Friede, Busch, and Bassen's 2015 meta-study on ESG and financial performance notes that:

- 62% of the studies they reviewed showed a positive correlation between governance and corporate financial performance; and
- 58% of environmental studies and 55% of social studies showed the same correlation.

Similarly, in mid-2016, one UK investment manager estimated that companies with good or improving governance tended to outperform companies with poor or worsening governance by 30 basis points per month, on average, in the prior seven years. Environmental and social factors also demonstrated their ability to guide investors toward better-performing companies and away from poorly performing ones, but the dispersion in performance was about half as large.

Good governance is fundamental to a company's performance, in terms of both long-term shareholder value creation and the creation of broader prosperity for society and all stakeholders. If a company delivers good governance, it is more likely to approach environmental and social issues with the right long-term mindset and thus avoid, or effectively manage, significant risks and seize relevant opportunities. Failures can be devastating to shareholders and other capital providers. The description of the board's failings in the Enron case (where the company's market value fell from US$60bn in December 2000 to zero in October 2001) is bracing, as seen in this excerpt from the special investigation committee's report:

> *Oversight of the related-party transactions by Enron's Board of Directors and Management failed for many reasons. As a threshold matter, in our opinion the very concept of related-party transactions of this magnitude with the CFO was flawed. The Board put many controls in place, but the controls were not adequate, and they were not adequately implemented. Some senior members of Management did not exercise sufficient oversight and did not respond adequately when issues arose that required a vigorous response. The Board assigned the Audit and Compliance Committee an expanded duty to review the transactions, but the Committee carried out the reviews only in a cursory way. The Board of Directors was denied important information that might have led it to take action, but the Board also did not fully appreciate the significance of some of the specific information that came before it. Enron's outside auditors supposedly examined Enron's internal controls but did not identify or bring to the Audit Committee's attention the inadequacies in their implementation.*

Governance matters because the wrong people—or just not enough of the right people—around the boardroom table are less likely to make the best decisions, resulting in the likelihood of significant value erosion and a failure to address key risks, including environmental and social issues. And if the interests of management and shareholders are not aligned, there is also a risk of value erosion for stakeholders generally.

Thus, companies with poor governance risk destroying value—or at least adding less value than they might have done. These issues are as true of private companies as they are of public companies: governance, good or bad, is not the exclusive preserve of the public company or the exclusive concern of the public equity investor. Governance is just as much an issue in private equity investments and infrastructure vehicles (including public finance initiatives), where value can be lost as easily. The building blocks for understanding good governance—accountability and alignment, with governance being, at its heart, about people (allowing boards to get the right mix of skills and experience and an array of perspectives in the boardroom)—can be applied to any situation.

Some will say that governance is less of an issue in private equity because investors are directly represented on the board, and the same is often true in many infrastructure vehicles. Although this factor reduces the risk of misinformation and a lack of responsiveness, it does not, in itself, remove all governance risks. Indeed, given the highly indebted nature of many such investments, the margin for error is not always large, and so failure can be swift if it does occur, often overwhelming even more responsive governance structures. Certainly, as the following brief case studies (on Theranos, Uber, and WeWork) indicate, there are significant risks to consider from failures of governance within private businesses, especially start-up businesses with an iconic founder.

Corporate Governance and the Investment Decision-Making Process

> ## CASE STUDIES
>
> ### Theranos Board
>
> In 2014, around the time Theranos was raising money from private market investors at a valuation that confirmed it was—at least temporarily—a so-called unicorn (a private company valued at more than US$1bn), the company, which claimed to be reinventing blood testing with exclusive technology, had the following board of directors:
>
> - Elizabeth Holmes, 30 — founder, CEO, and chair
> - Sunny Balwani, 48 — president and COO (former software engineer)
> - Riley Bechtel, 62 — chair of the board of the construction company Bechtel Group
> - William Frist, 62 — former heart and lung transplant surgeon before becoming a US senator
> - Henry Kissinger, 90 — former US secretary of state
> - Richard Kovacevich, 70 — former CEO of Wells Fargo
> - James Mattis, 63 — retired US Marine Corps general
> - Sam Nunn, 75 — former US senator and chair of the Senate Armed Services Committee
> - William Perry, 86 — former US secretary of defense
> - Gary Roughead, 61 — retired US Navy admiral
> - George Shultz, 93 — former US secretary of state
>
> Thus, overseeing an innovative blood-testing technology company was a board where the non-executive directors were exclusively male, mostly with military or foreign service backgrounds rather than medical or scientific experience, and with an average age of 73 (excluding the two executives). There were more former secretaries of state in their 90s on the board than people with medical training. None had any expertise, or even basic experience, in blood testing.
>
> The degree of oversight offered by this board of the management and operations was always likely to be limited, and its influence was further hindered by the company's dual-class share structure that saw the founder hold 99% of the voting rights. In addition, it appears that the board met infrequently, and several directors had poor attendance rates. All this suggests that the board was not operating as effectively as it might have been. Perhaps that should not be surprising. The *Wall Street Journal* investigative reporter John Carreyrou, in his striking account of the Theranos story, *Bad Blood*, notes that Elizabeth Holmes told someone interviewing for a job at the company in 2011: "The board is just a placeholder. I make all the decisions here."
>
> In the end, all of the US$700mn invested in the business was lost (together with its largely theoretical estimated valuation of US$10bn) when the company was revealed to have falsified test results and misled investors about the nature and effectiveness of its technology.
>
> In retrospect, the Theranos board's many red flags indicated that something was amiss—at the very least, the board could have been better designed to deliver effective oversight of an early-stage, high-risk technology business with unproven leadership. The red flags at other boards may be less obvious, but the two key questions that investors will always need to ask are:

1. Is there the right mix of skills and experience, and *enough* of the right skills and experience, to properly oversee the next stage of development of this business? If there are obvious gaps, investors need to consider how those gaps might best be filled.

2. Is there the right dynamic around the boardroom table to enable the views of the appropriately skilled board members to be heard? This question is about behaviors, which are inevitably harder to identify from outside; nonetheless, there are often indications that the board dynamic is not as effective as it might be.

Theranos is not the only unicorn to experience governance challenges that affected its estimated value.

Uber, the transportation network company, felt obliged to change its governance practices in the wake of a series of damaging scandals that were affecting its growth. The founder CEO's responsibilities were reallocated, preferential voting rights were adjusted, and the board's independence was strengthened.

In 2019, WeWork was obliged to abandon its planned initial public offering (IPO)—and its valuation plummeted from the intended capitalization at listing—when investors balked at the company's approach to several governance issues, including the dominant decision-making position of the founding CEO (which would persist even after his death, when his wife was to be handed the choice of his successor) and related-party deals with the CEO. While these governance issues were addressed in the latter stages of the planned IPO process, they were enough to raise broader questions in investors' minds, including the crucial ones about business model and the absence of a clear path to profitability. In a 2020 *Financial Times* article about the company's downfall, a financial adviser who is particularly insightful on the company's governance and the CEO's management style is reported as saying, "How do you go from succeeding by not listening to succeeding by listening?"

Few governance failures are as extreme in their destruction of value as Theranos and WeWork, and few boards are as lacking in diversity and the relevant skill set as the Theranos board was. There is good evidence in the academic literature of the beneficial effect of diversity. Carter, Simkins, and Simpson's 2003 study of the *Fortune* 1000 firms found statistically significant positive relationships between the presence of women or minorities on the board and firm value, as measured by Tobin's q (a valuation measure based on the ratio between a company's market value and the replacement cost of its assets). Bernile, Bhagwat, and Yonker's 2018 study concluded that diversity in the board of directors reduces stock return volatility (consistent with diverse backgrounds working as a governance mechanism) and that firms with diverse boards tend to adopt policies that are more stable and persistent (consistent with the board decisions being less subject to idiosyncrasies). In addition, while diverse boards take less financial risk, "this behavior does not carry over onto real risk-taking activities," with diverse boards investing more in research and development (R&D). Overall, their study found that greater heterogeneity among directors leads to higher profitability and firm valuations, on average.

Governance failures lead to fines and additional liabilities, as well as litigation and other costs. Revenues fall as trust is eroded and customers boycott the company or buy from competitors, and profits fall as additional cost burdens are placed to mitigate future risks. All these effects harm security values. Governance analysis should be a core component of valuation practice.

Integrating Governance into Investment and Stewardship Processes

Different fund managers integrate governance factors into their investment decision-making in different ways. For many, it is a threshold assessment—a formal minimum criterion to consider *before* they will consider making an investment at any price. Often, it is talked about as quality of management, which, despite the name, is never simply an assessment of the CEO and CFO but, rather, of the overall team and the governance structure by which they oversee the company and (hopefully) drive the success of the business.

For others, it is a risk assessment tool, which may represent the level of confidence about future earnings or the multiple on which those earnings are placed in a valuation—or it may be reflected less in full financial models and more in a simple level of confidence in the valuation range or investment thesis.

If the analysis of corporate governance is specifically built into valuation models, this analysis is most typically done by recognizing negative governance characteristics by way of adding a risk premium to the cost of capital or raising the discount rate applied. Others regard weak governance as an engagement and investment opportunity—the logic being that governance can be improved through active dialogue with management and proxy voting, so that past underperformance, on which the company is currently valued in the market, is reversed and the valuation can be enhanced by stronger performance and an expectation of more positive performance in the future.

Many governance issues lend themselves to stewardship dialogue with companies, not least because many of these issues will be directly addressed in the AGM agenda. Investors will be obliged to take a stance on them (for many investors, that is why governance has a longer heritage than environmental and social issues—particularly because in many markets, the obligation to consider voting decisions actively is well established). In almost every market, investors will be faced annually with voting decisions on at least the following:

- accepting the report and accounts;
- board appointments;
- the appointment of the auditor, and perhaps their fees; and
- executive remuneration.

Thus, there is a natural driver, at least annually, for engagement on these issues—though investors are increasingly keen to avoid the critical points of all such discussions during the AGM season (largely April to June in the Northern Hemisphere, July in Japan, and September to November in the Southern Hemisphere). To avoid this problem, dialogue is held throughout the year, with the conclusions reached in the dialogue reflected in the voting.

Engagement is covered in depth in the next chapter.

Thus far, this chapter has considered the *G* in ESG as meaning corporate governance. While many may see corporate governance as an issue particularly for public equity investments, in fact many investments across the asset classes are in company structures in one form or another. Therefore, corporate governance concerns will have relevance for many investments, including, for example, fixed income, private equity, property, and infrastructure. The intent of this chapter is to discuss corporate governance at a level whereby its relevance across this broad range of asset classes is apparent, and the analysis can be applied and tailored as appropriate.

However, there is one asset class where the *G* of ESG will always have a very different meaning. In the sovereign debt arena, *G* means the effectiveness of the governance and robustness of the state and its institutions, the approach to the rule of law, and the general business environment (including such issues as competition and anti-corruption). In effect, the concern is about gaining assurance that the economy can prosper through good governance, so that sovereign debt obligations can continue to be covered. ESG-minded investors are increasingly integrating the analysis of these issues into their broader financial analysis of sovereign credits.

9 KEY FACTS

1. Corporate governance is the process by which a company is managed and overseen. It is framed by local law and culture, and almost all countries now have a formal but non-binding corporate governance code to set standards and expectations.

2. However, within these formal frames, governance comes down to people and how they interact; they need information and they need to be able to make the relevant people accountable for their decisions.

3. Accountability is reflected in sufficient oversight of management so that management is encouraged, pressed, and challenged to efficiently deliver for the long-term good of the business.

4. Alongside accountability sits alignment as the other core tenet of good governance. This tenet is seen most clearly in the area of pay, where the aim is an alignment of the interests of management with those of the long-term shareholder. It means that long-term value creation in the business is reflected in compensation to individual managers.

5. To deliver these two main aims of accountability and alignment, each board is expected to establish three independent and effective committees to cover the crucial areas of nominations, audit, and remuneration.

6. Corporate governance codes and guidelines, and the laws that underpin them, typically get changed in reaction to scandals in individual companies. In the UK, the Cadbury Code was the world's first governance code and was used as a model for many others.

7. The scandals frequently feature excessive, acquisitive growth and ambition, combined with overconfident management and boards that practice little challenge.

8. Effective boards need a mix of skills and experience across their membership, and a boardroom culture that enables those different perspectives to bring a diversity of thought to bear on the key issues facing the company. Independence matters—independence of thought, most of all—but knowledge and expertise also matter.

9. Good boards ensure that the company operates in an ethical and appropriate way and has a corporate culture that is conducive to long-term value creation in the interests of all stakeholders.

10. Two-tier boards are typical in Germany, the Netherlands, Scandinavia, and China; single-tier boards are typical in the USA, the UK, Japan, France, and most of the rest of the world. In the USA and France, boards generally have a single executive member, often acting as both chair and CEO. Japanese single-tier boards are dominated by executive directors, with only a handful of non-executives; most unitary boards lie somewhere in between these models.

Further Reading 339

11. Audits focus on close attention to, and assurance of, the financial statements. However, they entail only a limited requirement to read other material published alongside the financial statements and disclose inconsistencies.

12. The new enhanced auditor reports offer more valuable insights into the work of the auditor and also, potentially, into the quality of the controls and reporting at the audited company.

FURTHER READING

- Armour, T., M. Barra, E. Breen, et al. 2019. Commonsense Principles 2.0. Available at: www.governanceprinciples.org.
- Brydon, D. 2019. Assess, Assure and Inform: Improving Audit Quality and Effectiveness; Report of the Independent Review into the Quality and Effectiveness of Audit. Available at: https://assets.publishing.service.gov.uk/government/uploads/system/uploads/attachment_data/file/852960/brydon-review-final-report.pdf.
- Chartered Institute of Internal Auditors. 2020. Internal Audit Code of Practice: Guidance on Effective Internal Audit in the Private and Third Sectors. Available at: www.iia.org.uk/media/1690932/iia-internal-audit-code-report-final.pdf.
- Council of Institutional Investors. 2018. Corporate Governance Policies. Available at: www.cii.org/files/10_24_18_corp_gov_policies.pdf.
- Financial Reporting Council. 2018. Guidance on Board Effectiveness. Available at: www.frc.org.uk/getattachment/61232f60-a338-471b-ba5a-bfed25219147/2018-Guidance-on-Board-Effectiveness-FINAL.PDF.
- International Corporate Governance Network (ICGN). 2017. ICGN Global Governance Principles. Available at: www.icgn.org/policy/global-governance-principles.
- Investor Stewardship Group. 2019. Corporate Governance Principles for US Listed Companies. Available at: https://isgframework.org/corporate-governance-principles.
- Organisation for Economic Co-operation and Development (OECD). 2019. OECD Corporate Governance Factbook 2019. Available at: www.oecd.org/corporate/corporate-governance-factbook.htm.
- Recommended Books on Individual Scandals Carreyrou. J. 2019. Bad Blood: Secrets and Lies in a Silicon Valley Startup. London: Pan Macmillan.
- Woodford, M. 2012. Inside the Olympus Scandal: How I Went from CEO to Whistleblower. New York: Portfolio/Penguin.

REFERENCES

Brydon, Donald. 2019. *Assess, Assure and Inform: Improving Audit Quality and Effectiveness; Report of the Independent Review into the Quality and Effectiveness of Audit*. Available at: https://assets.publishing.service.gov.uk/government/uploads/system/uploads/attachment_data/file/852960/brydon-review-final-report.pdf.

Kingman, John. 2018. "Financial Reporting Council." RE:view2018. Available at www.gov.uk/government/publications/financial-reporting-council-review-2018

Walker, David. 2009. *A Review of Corporate Governance in UK Banks and Other Financial Industry Entities: Final Recommendations*. Available at: https://webarchive.nationalarchives.gov.uk/+/www.hm-treasury.gov.uk/d/walker_review_261109.pdf.

Council of Institutional Investors 2021. "Dual-Class Stock." Available at: www.cii.org/dualclass_stock.

BHP 2021. *Annual Report*2021. Available at: https://www.bhp.com/investors/annual-reporting/annual-report-2021.

OECD 2019. *OECD Corporate Governance Factbook*2019. Available at: https://www.oecd.org/daf/ca/OECD-Corporate-Governance-Factbook-2019.pdf.

UK Government 2017. Ethnic Diversity of UK Boards: The Parker Review. Available at: www.gov.uk/government/publications/ethnic-diversity-of-uk-boards-the-parker-review.

UK Government 2022. Improving the Ethnic Diversity of UK Boards: An update report from the Parker Review. Available at: https://assets.ey.com/content/dam/ey-sites/ey-com/en_uk/topics/diversity/ey-what-the-parker-review-tells-us-about-boardroom-diversity.pdf.

Carbon Tracker Initiative/PRI 2021. *Flying Blind: The Glaring Absence of Climate Risks in Financial Reporting*. Available at: https://www.unpri.org/download?ac=14597.

European Securities and Markets Authority (ESMA) 2015. *ESMA Guidelines on Alternative Performance Measures*. Available at: https://www.esma.europa.eu/document/esma-guidelines-alternative-performance-measures.

Financial Reporting Council 2018. *The UK Corporate Governance Code*. Available at: www.frc.org.uk/getattachment/88bd8c45-50ea-4841-95b0-d2f4f48069a2/2018-UK-Corporate-Governance-Code-FINAL.pdf.

IFRS Foundation 2019. "Exposure Draft and Comment Letters: General Presentation and Disclosures (Primary Financial Statements)." Available at: www.ifrs.org/projects/work-plan/primary-financial-statements/comment-letters-projects/ed-primary-financial-statements/.

Principles for Responsible Investment (PRI) 2021. "Accounting for Climate Change." Available at: www.unpri.org/sustainability-issues/accounting-for-climate-change.

Brydon, Donald. 2019. *Assess, Assure and Inform: Improving Audit Quality and Effectiveness; Report of the Independent Review into the Quality and Effectiveness of Audit*. Available at: https://assets.publishing.service.gov.uk/government/uploads/system/uploads/attachment_data/file/852960/brydon-review-final-report.pdf.

Chartered Institute of Internal Auditors 2020. *Internal Audit Code of Practice: Guidance on Effective Internal Audit in the Private and Third Sectors*. Available at: www.iia.org.uk/media/1691066/internal-audit-code-of-practice-report.pdf.

Competition and Markets Authority 2019. *Statutory Audit Services Market Study: Final Report*. Available at: www.gov.uk/cma-cases/statutory-audit-market-study.

Bernile, G., V. Bhagwat, S. Yonker. 2018. "Board Diversity, Firm Risk, and Corporate Policies." Journal of Financial Economics127 (3): 588–612. 10.1016/j.jfineco.2017.12.009

Carter, D. A., B. J. Simkins, W. G. Simpson. 2003. "Corporate Governance, Board Diversity, and Firm Value." Financial Review38 (1): 33–53. 10.1111/1540-6288.00034

CFA Institute 2017. *Environmental, Social and Governance (ESG) Survey*. Available at: https://www.cfainstitute.org/-/media/documents/survey/esg-survey-report-2017.ashx.

References

Friede, G., T. Busch, A. Bassen. 2015. "ESG and Financial Performance: Aggregated Evidence from More Than 2000 Empirical Studies." Journal of Sustainable Finance & Investment 5 (4): 210–33. Available at www.tandfonline.com/doi/full/10.1080/20430795.2015.111891710.1080/20430795.2015.1118917

Hermes Investment Management 2016. *ESG Investing: It Still Makes You Feel Good, It Still Makes You Money*. Available at: www.hermes-investment.com/wp-content/uploads/2018/10/hermes-esg-investing.pdf.

Platt, E., A. Edgecliffe-Johnson. 20 Feb. 2020. "WeWork: How the Ultimate Unicorn Lost Its Billions." *Financial Times*. Available at: www.ft.com/content/7938752a-52a7-11ea-90ad-25e377c0ee1f.

Powers, W. C., R. S. Troubh, H. S. Winokur. 2002. *Report of Investigation by the Special Investigative Committee of the Board of Directors of Enron Corporation*. Available at: http://i.cnn.net/cnn/2002/LAW/02/02/enron.report/powers.report.pdf.

PRACTICE PROBLEMS

1. Which element of governance *most likely* has heightened importance in larger companies as opposed to smaller ones?
   a. The effective operation of governance processes
   b. The quality and thoughtfulness of board members
   c. A culture of strong performance without excessive risk taking

2. In the evolution of corporate governance frameworks, which practice developed *most* recently?
   a. Establishment of auditor oversight regulatory bodies
   b. Decreasing prominence of combined CEO/chair roles
   c. Establishment of, and regularly scheduled meetings of, audit committees

3. The interests of institutional investors are *most likely* protected through:
   a. pre-emptive rights.
   b. related-party transactions.
   c. dual-class share structures.

4. Which of the following is considered a principal committee, in place on the boards of most major companies?
   a. Risk committee
   b. Nominations committee
   c. Social and ethics committee

5. The effectiveness of a board chair is *best* evaluated by:
   a. engaging in direct dialogue with directors.
   b. referring to a board self-assessment report.
   c. assessing the quality of the directors on the board.

6. Which executive remuneration concern is *most likely* expressed by board members?
   a. Across the market as a whole, executive pay rates continue to ratchet up.
   b. Executive pay does not reflect the market performance of the shares.
   c. The executive pay structure does not incentivize executives to deliver maximum value.

7. French and US corporate governance practices are *most likely* similar with respect to:
   a. audit requirements.
   b. institutional investor power.
   c. board structure and type of chair.

8. Which element of enhanced auditor reports *most likely* provides insight into the auditor's assessment of the company's financial controls?
   a. Key audit matters
   b. Scope of the audit
   c. Performance materiality number

Practice Problems

9. The governance analysis of a public equity investment will differ *most* significantly from that of an investment in:
   a. fixed income.
   b. sovereign debt.
   c. property and infrastructure.

10. Which of the following *best* supports board members in large, complex companies in fulfilling their responsibilities effectively?
    a. Policies
    b. Processes
    c. Codes of conduct

11. To reduce its budget deficit, the state, which is the majority shareholder in a large utility company, is requesting the full distribution of the company's annual profits to shareholders. The company is heavily indebted. Which of the following behaviors would be *most* appropriate for the independent members of the board of directors?
    a. Abstaining from voting on the matter of profits distributed to shareholders
    b. Complying with the request of the major shareholder to avoid the rise of agency problems
    c. Voting against the request of the major shareholder due to the long-term impact on the company

12. Which of the following is specific to general mandate resolutions applying to companies established in Hong Kong SAR? Without seeking shareholders' consent, a company's board of directors can decide on additional share issuances of up to:
    a. 5% of the shared capital.
    b. 10% of the shared capital.
    c. 20% of the shared capital.

13. Which of the following reflects the role of a sunset clause?
    a. Enables minority shareholders to exercise stock warrants
    b. Reduces the risk of negative company performance related to dual-class shares
    c. Protects company founders from class action lawsuits initiated by activist investors

14. A company in the oil and gas industry has 7 members on the board of directors with the following sets of skills and experience:

Skills and Experience	Number of Members with the Skill and Expertise
Oil and gas	4 members
Finance expertise	3 members
International business	3 members
Strategic planning	3 members
Audit and control	2 members
Public policy expertise	2 members

Skills and Experience	Number of Members with the Skill and Expertise
ESG issues related to oil and gas	1 member

To improve the structure of the board of directors, the company should seek to:

   a. have all members of the board knowledgeable in the oil and gas industry.
   b. have a balanced number of members of the board for each set of skills.
   c. hire another board member with expertise in ESG issues related to the oil and gas industry.

15. The responsibility for fairly reporting a company's financial position lies with the company's:

   a. external auditor.
   b. audit committee.
   c. board of directors.

16. One difference between the corporate governance practices in Japan and those in Sweden relates to the:

   a. prevalence of single-tier versus two-tier boards.
   b. requirement for appointing independent audit firms.
   c. dominance of major shareholders in leading companies.

17. In line with best global corporate governance practices, which of the following committees could consist of both independent and non-independent members?

   a. Audit committee
   b. Nominations committee
   c. Remuneration committee

18. The introduction of artificial intelligence and technological innovation into the audit process is *most likely* to reduce:

   a. the liability of the auditor.
   b. human oversight of the audit process.
   c. the number of undiscovered fraud cases resulting from the sampling approach to audit.

19. According to the ICGN's Global Governance Principles, which of the following would raise questions about the independence of a member of the board of directors? The director:

   a. has been a member of the board for the last 3 years.
   b. acted as the company's executive before joining the board of directors.
   c. has over 10 years of experience with one of the company's competitors.

20. What are the "two A's" that lie at the heart of corporate governance?

   a. Advocacy and alignment
   b. Accountability and advocacy
   c. Accountability and alignment

21. Which of the following is *least likely* to explain why the role of the chair of a company board is so important?

   a. The chair sets the agenda for board discussions.

b. The chair helps ensure that all directors make their full contribution.

c. The chair will usually also be the CEO.

22. Which of the following is *not* a board committee expected to be established at all companies?

    a. Audit
    b. Risk
    c. Remuneration

23. Which of the following scandals did *not* motivate the creation of the first corporate governance code?

    a. Polly Peck
    b. Enron
    c. Caparo

24. Which of the following phrases is commonly used to describe the model created by the Cadbury Code for adherence to its principles?

    a. If not, why not?
    b. Apply and explain.
    c. Comply or explain.

25. Which element of executive pay is *most likely* to include some metric based on ESG performance?

    a. Salary
    b. Annual bonus
    c. Long-term incentive or share scheme

26. Which of the following does *not* typically raise questions regarding an individual director's independence?

    a. A recent senior role as an adviser to the company
    b. Receiving share options in the company as part of an incentive scheme
    c. Not having been on the board long enough to fully understand the business

27. What US legislation led to the creation of the Public Company Accounting Oversight Board (PCAOB)?

    a. The Glass-Steagall Act
    b. The Sarbanes-Oxley Act
    c. The Dodd-Frank Act

28. Which European scandals in 2003 led to a reassessment of the continent's approach to corporate governance?

    a. Ahold and Parmalat
    b. WorldCom and Tyco
    c. BCCI and Caparo

29. Which area of ethical corporate behavior is *most likely* to be subject to extraterritorial legislation?

    a. Anti-corruption
    b. Supplier payments
    c. Lobbying activities

30. Which is the only major world market that does *not*, as of 2023, have a corporate governance code?

    a. Japan
    b. France
    c. USA

31. Which statement outlines the distinction between the auditor's role in relation to the financial statements and the auditor's role in relation to the rest of the annual report and accounts?

    a. Assurance on the financial statements and a report on inconsistencies in narrative reporting
    b. Guarantee of accuracy of the financial statements and a report on inconsistencies in narrative reporting
    c. Assurance on the financial statements and on narrative reporting

32. For how long can an audit firm remain in that role at an EU public company?

    a. 7 years
    b. 10 years
    c. 20 years

33. Which of the following is *not* one of the three key elements of disclosure in the new enhanced auditor reports?

    a. Scope of the audit
    b. Skepticism
    c. Key audit matters

34. Which of the following is *not* likely to be considered a G factor by a sovereign debt investor?

    a. Approach to the rule of law
    b. Regulatory effectiveness
    c. Independence of board members

35. Which of the following statements is *least* accurate? The corporate governance framework in India requires that the board of directors of listed companies must:

    a. include a female director.
    b. include a resident director.
    c. be composed entirely of non-executive directors.

36. Which of the following countries introduced a corporate governance code in 2018?

    a. India
    b. Brazil
    c. South Africa

37. Which of the following companies was blacklisted by the World Bank over charges of bribery?

    a. Satyam
    b. Olympus
    c. Parmalat

Practice Problems

38. Which of the following refers to a lesson learned from a corporate governance failure?
    a. External auditors should also provide non-audit services to a company.
    b. Clear delineations should exist between finance and operations management.
    c. A majority shareholder should serve as the company's chair and CEO to protect his interests.

39. In which of the following countries is the use of "promoters" a key characteristic of ownership structure?
    a. Sweden
    b. India
    c. Brazil

SOLUTIONS

1. **A is correct**. Board members of larger, more complex companies rely more heavily on governance processes to carry out their responsibilities. It is not possible for an individual board member to maintain sufficient direct knowledge across a complex organization, but it may be possible across smaller companies.

2. **A is correct**. Auditor oversight bodies are a relatively recent development, first established in the USA under the 2002 Sarbanes-Oxley Act. The emphasis on audit committees and the separation of the chair and CEO roles started in 1991 through the work of the Cadbury Committee in the UK.

3. **A is correct**. Pre-emptive rights ensure that investors, including institutional investors, can avoid dilution of their interest in a company by a dominant shareholder seeking to gain more control. Both related-party transactions and dual-class share structures are disadvantageous to minority shareholders such as institutional investors, as they can enable dominant shareholders to siphon resources from the company or maintain disproportionate control of voting rights, respectively.

4. **B is correct**. The nominations committee, the audit committee, and the remuneration committee are the principal committees on most public company boards.

5. **C is correct**. The quality of the directors on the board provides an indirect but otherwise clear signal of the chair's effectiveness, as strong board members are unlikely to stay on a board led by a weak chair. The other evaluation approaches can be used, but they are considered less likely to provide accurate assessments of the chair's effectiveness.

6. **C is correct**. Misunderstandings between board members and investors over executive pay have led to a lack of trust between the two parties, with board members concerned that their remuneration proposals could be voted down by investors. This situation may lead to the negotiation of a compromise executive pay structure that does not necessarily enable the executives to unlock the full potential of the company but is likely to receive voting support from investors. Broader concerns about market rates for executive pay and potential disconnects between executive pay and market performance are more often expressed by investors who are not on the board.

7. **C is correct**. Single-tier boards with combined chair and CEO roles are more common in the USA and France than in other countries. Institutional investor power is more constrained in France than in the USA because of the Florange Act of 2014. Audit requirements also differ between the two countries, as France is the only major market with a joint audit requirement.

8. **C is correct**. The auditor's assessment of the company's financial controls is implied by the magnitude of the discount from materiality used in the auditor's calculation of performance materiality. Larger discounts can signal that the company's financial controls have room for improvement.

9. **B is correct**. The assessment of governance for a sovereign debt investment includes elements not typically evaluated in assessing fixed-income or property and infrastructure issuers. Examples of sovereign-specific governance issues include corruption, competition in the economy, and adherence to the rule of law in the country's legal systems.

Solutions

10. **B is correct**. Especially in large companies where the members of the board of directors have a limited capacity of direct knowledge across the business, processes are critical for the implementation and enforcement of policies and codes of conduct.

11. **C is correct**. Members of the board of directors should not comply mindlessly with requests issued by company owners, and they should consider the long-term impact of such requests on the company's business and financial perspectives. Board members should not abdicate their responsibilities on critical matters even when there seems to be a risk of divergence between board members and shareholders.

12. **C is correct**. Companies established in Hong Kong can follow a general mandate resolution that allows them to issue up to 20% additional shared capital without seeking pre-existing shareholders' consent and without offering pre-existing shareholders pre-emptive rights (the right to participate in the issuance before external shareholders can).

13. **B is correct**. Sunset clauses allow the unification of the two classes of shares. Sunset clauses are meant to eliminate the difference in voting rights between company founders and ordinary shareholders after (at most) seven years, since the shares have been issued to prevent negative company performance.

14. **C is correct**. The board of directors should seek to have at least two individuals with expertise in a particular area. Since the company has only one board member with relevant ESG experience, it should prioritize hiring a new board member experienced in that domain. Since diversity is sought in the structure of boards of directors, not all board members need be knowledgeable in the industry where the company operates. There should be a thoughtful balancing of members' skill sets, and not all skill sets should be represented proportionally on the board.

15. **C is correct**. It is the board that is ultimately responsible for the "fair, balanced and understandable assessment of a company's position and prospects." Although financial reporting is led by the management of the company, reviewed by the audit committee, and then independently challenged by the external auditor, the responsibility remains with the entire board of directors.

16. **A is correct**. In Sweden, a Scandinavian country, most board structures are two-tier, whereby supervisory and management boards are separate and responsible for different functions. In Japan, statutory auditors and single-tier boards prevail. In both countries, there is a tendency for dominance by major shareholders in leading companies rather than having more diversified ownership of companies with many smaller shareholders. Independent audit firms are a requirement for companies in both countries.

17. **B is correct**. Audit and remuneration committees should consist of independent non-executive directors, while the nominations committee could have executive directors among its members.

18. **C is correct**. Technological innovation in audit is most likely to allow the assessment of every single transaction rather than a sample of transactions within the audit process. Technology and artificial intelligence will not eliminate human oversight or auditor liability, but they will facilitate a deep dive into companies' every transaction.

19. **B is correct**. According to the ICGN Global Governance Principles, investors might question the independence of directors who used to be executives of the

company if there "was not an appropriate gap between their employment and joining the board." Independence might be questioned if directors' tenures are too long, usually over 10 years, but some countries' codes might limit maximum tenures to as little as 5 to 7 years. A tenure of 3 years would not raise questions absent other information. There is no principle of questioning independence where the board member was recruited from competitors.

20. **C is correct**. Accountability is important because people are most effective when they are accountable for their decisions and their work. Alignment matters because without it, the company may be run in accordance with the interests of its professional managers rather than its owners.

21. **C is correct**. Corporate governance has evolved away from the practice of combining the CEO and chair roles, because it leads to an excessive concentration of power in the individual holding the position and reduces the effectiveness of the board.

22. **B is correct**. Risk committees are typically seen on the boards of financial services businesses, while audit, nominations, and remuneration/compensation committees are found on virtually all boards.

23. **B is correct**. The first formal governance code was created in the UK in 1992 in the wake of the Caparo and Polly Peck scandals. The Enron scandal emerged in the USA several years later, in 2001.

24. **C is correct**. The Cadbury Code requires that companies comply with its recommendations or explain any non-compliance with a discussion describing how the board delivers on the underlying principle.

25. **B is correct**. The key performance indicators for bonuses usually include a portion that is based on non-financial measures, including ESG factors, that align with the strategic aims of the business.

26. **C is correct**. The independence of board members may be called into question for those who have recently acted as advisers to the company, are receiving incentive pay from the company, or have had a long tenure as a director. Newer board members who have not yet fully grasped the company's business are unlikely to prompt independence concerns.

27. **B is correct**. The Sarbanes-Oxley Act of 2002 created the PCAOB to set audit standards and inspect auditors.

28. **A is correct**. The Ahold scandal in the Netherlands and the Parmalat scandal in Italy increased the pressure for stronger corporate governance standards across Europe.

29. **A is correct**. Anti-corruption behavior is most likely to be governed by extraterritorial legislation that applies regardless of the jurisdiction in which a company's involvement with corruption takes place.

30. **C is correct**. The USA is the only major world market that does not have a corporate governance code. The reason is that US corporate law is set at the state level rather than the federal level.

31. **A is correct**. Auditors provide assurance that the financial statements are fairly presented but cannot provide guarantees as to the accuracy of every number in the financial statements. Auditors also have a "specific duty to highlight any apparent inconsistencies between the financial statements and other reporting by

Solutions

the company."

32. **C is correct**. In the EU, public companies are required to change auditors after 20 years at most.

33. **B is correct**. Scope of the audit and key audit matters are critical elements of enhanced auditor reports. Skepticism is not reported on in enhanced auditor reports; rather, it is an attitude that auditors maintain throughout the audit process to ensure a critical assessment of audit evidence.

34. **C is correct**. The independence of board members relates to corporate boards and is unlikely to be considered by sovereign debt investors. They are interested in the regulatory effectiveness of the state and its institutions as well as the state's approach to the rule of law, as these factors indicate the sovereign's continued ability and willingness to cover its debt obligations.

35. **C is correct**. For listed companies, non-executive directors must compose at least 50% of the board, though the board can include executive directors. Listed companies in India are required to appoint a resident director and a female director.

36. **B is correct**. In 2018, Brazil's first Corporate Governance Code was published. India's Corporate Governance Code was issued in 2013, and South Africa's in 2011.

37. **A is correct**. Satyam was blacklisted by the World Bank over charges of bribery and declared ineligible for contract bids for providing improper benefits to bank staff and failing to maintain documentation to support fees.

38. **B is correct**. One of the lessons learned from Tyco's corporate governance failure is that there should be clear delineations between finance and operations management. A lesson learned from the Enron scandal is that there should be a restriction on the provision of non-audit services by external auditors. A lesson learned from the Parmalat failure is that there should be a provision in the bylaws for the separation of the chair and CEO roles.

39. **B is correct**. The ownership structure in Indian companies is characterized by promoters and non-promoters, founders or controlling shareholders, and other shareholders, including minority shareholders. Directors cannot be related to promoters or management at the board level or one level below.

CHAPTER 6

Engagement and Stewardship

LEARNING OUTCOMES

Mastery	The candidate should be able to:
☐	**6.1.1** explain the purpose of investor engagement and stewardship
☐	**6.1.2** explain why engagement is considered beneficial and some of the key criticisms of engagement
☐	**6.1.3** explain the main principles and requirements of stewardship codes as they apply to institutional asset management firms
☐	**6.1.4** explain how engagement is achieved in practice, including key differences in objectives, style, and tone
☐	**6.1.5** apply strategies and tactics in a goal-based engagement approach using various forms
☐	**6.1.6** explain particular forms of engagement and major escalation techniques, including: proxy voting; collective engagement; ESG investment forums
☐	**6.1.7** describe approaches of engagement across a range of asset classes

INTRODUCTION 1

This chapter delves into the critical elements of stewardship and engagement within the context of responsible investment. It starts by exploring the fundamental concepts of stewardship and engagement, elucidating their importance in contemporary investment practices. A deep dive into the practical aspects of engagement, including the various styles and the application of codes and standards, allows for a comprehensive understanding of the subject. It provides insights into code revisions, goal-setting strategies, engagement objectives, and practicalities, including the escalation and collective engagement processes.

The chapter culminates with special considerations pertinent to proxy voting and different asset classes such as corporate fixed income, sovereign debt, private equity, infrastructure, property, and fund investments. Whether you are a novice or an experienced investor, this chapter offers a holistic view of stewardship and engagement, essential components of responsible and sustainable investment strategies.

2 STEWARDSHIP AND ENGAGEMENT: WHAT'S INVOLVED AND WHY IT'S IMPORTANT

☐ **6.1.1** explain the purpose of investor engagement and stewardship

☐ **6.1.2** explain why engagement is considered beneficial and some of the key criticisms of engagement

Stewardship is typically used as an overarching term encompassing the approach that investors take as active owners of the companies and other entities in which they invest through voting and engagement. Voting is one aspect of stewardship activity and tends to focus on corporate governance matters raised at shareholders' meetings, particularly governance proposals most likely to come to a vote. A recent report indicated that the number of environmental and social proposals has been increasing, constituting 58% of shareholder proposals in 2022, with corporate governance proposals constituting 32%, versus 45% for environmental and social and 42% for governance proposals in 2018.

Engagement is the way in which investors put into effect their stewardship responsibilities in line with the Principles for Responsible Investment (PRI) Principle 2 ("We will be active owners and incorporate environmental, social and governance (ESG) issues into our ownership policies and practices"). It is often described as purposeful dialogue with a specific objective in mind; that purpose will vary from engagement to engagement but often relates to improving companies' business practices, especially in relation to the management of ESG issues.

Stewardship ought to be a consequence of investment. By contrast, activism is typically a specialist form of such engagement and stewardship, where an investment institution initiates an investment with the intent of generating investment outperformance through driving change with respect to a company's governance, capital allocation, or business practices.

This chapter considers what we mean by stewardship and engagement and covers the emergence of different styles of engagement. We consider the framework of guidelines and rules that direct the approach to stewardship and discuss how engagement can be delivered most effectively.

What Is Stewardship? What Is Engagement?

Stewardship, a term with historical roots referring to guardianship of assets, encapsulates the responsibilities of modern institutional investors to protect and grow these assets. The concept, similar to fiduciary duty, obligates the steward to act in the owner's interests, safeguarding the assets' long-term value. In today's context, this entails discouraging short-term profit taking and ensuring fair executive compensation, among other tasks, all aimed at enhancing long-term value for the asset owner.

Stewardship is the process of intervention to make sure that the value of the assets is enhanced over time, or at least does not deteriorate through neglect or mismanagement. The process can encompass the buying and selling of assets to maintain value within the fund as a whole. Engagement is one aspect of good stewardship; it is the individual interventions in specific assets to preserve and/or enhance value. In modern investment terms, this is the dialogue with the management and boards of investee companies and other assets. Voting is a particular form of engagement. It is the most visible form, because public company annual general meetings (AGMs) are public events and many institutions now make their voting actions public (some even ahead of the relevant meetings). However, by its nature, voting is formulaic, because the nature of the resolutions on which shareholders vote is restricted by law, and because the options in response to the questions asked by resolutions are essentially a binary yes or no. Engagement is much broader than just voting. The case study on Shell gives practical insight into how these distinctions can play out.

CASE STUDIES

Engagement, Communication, and Voting: Shell and Climate

At its 2021 AGM, Anglo-Dutch oil company Royal Dutch Shell (which later that year shifted to a single corporate structure as UK-based Shell plc) faced two resolutions on climate.

Resolution 20 at the May 2021 meeting, titled Shell's Energy Transition Resolution, was the company putting forward its own strategy for the process of transitioning its business from its focus on fossil fuels to a decarbonized future. This was an advisory resolution, meaning it would not be binding on the company; in effect, it was a vehicle for the company to gain shareholder endorsement of its plans.

Resolution 21 was a shareholder proposal put forward by Dutch NGO Follow This. This resolution pressed the company to do more on climate, specifically to set targets consistent with the goals of the Paris Agreement and to develop and deliver a strategy to meet those targets. As is typical of Follow This proposals, both its resolution and its supporting statement ended with the words "You have our support"; the language deliberately indicated a positive alignment with the company, as appropriate for shareholders, even if the proposal urged the company to go further and faster.

Investors were faced with an interesting set of choices. Those who were most actively engaging with the company believed that it was making strong progress in work toward transitioning its business—though many felt that even though it was moving much faster than many of its major oil peers, it was still not fast enough.

As can be seen from the votes actually cast, investors used both binary votes for and against and also registered large numbers of "votes withheld" (a formal form of abstention that must be registered and reported by companies in many markets but is not an official vote).

Resolution	Votes For	%	Votes Against	%	Votes Withheld
20 (Shell's energy transition strategy)	3,139,870,455	88.74%	398,536,568	11.26%	237,591,728
21 (shareholder resolution)	1,111,147,799	30.47%	2,535,689,229	69.53%	129,156,318

The reaction of the company to these votes is telling in a number of ways. Then CEO Ben van Beurden's formal statement on the votes reads: "This shareholder vote on our Energy Transition Strategy is a first for an energy company and we are pleased shareholders demonstrated their strong endorsement with more than 88% of votes cast in favour of our strategy. We thank shareholders for their support and look forward to our continued engagement with them. We also note the outcome of the vote on Shareholder Resolution number 21. We will seek to fully understand the reason why shareholders voted as they did, particularly those who voted both 'For' Shell's strategy and 'For' the Shareholder Resolution, and will formally report back to investors within six months."

There are a few noteworthy things in this statement:

1. Many shareholders supported both resolutions. This clearly confused the company, but from the investor perspective when faced with a series of resolutions, it is relatively easily understood. Such votes were likely (a) supportive of the company voluntarily putting forward such a resolution and expressing a positive view on the progress it was making, particularly in comparison with peers, and (b) encouraging the company to do more and act more quickly than its current plans implied.
2. Many of those shareholders had not explained their votes to the company—and given Shell's stated intention to understand those who had voted for both resolutions, it seems that a number of them were large institutional investors.
3. One source of contention was the measurement of emissions. Follow This supported a reduction in total emissions that was aligned with the Paris Agreement; Shell's proposal focused on carbon intensity, which can be misleading and can decrease even as total emissions increase.
4. Shareholders also realized that Shell continued its support of lobbying groups in Europe, the USA, and Australia who opposed measures supporting the energy transition.

Such a failure to explain voting is disappointing. Votes cast on non-binding resolutions are relatively meaningless: investors with similar views and concerns can find themselves taking marginal decisions to oppose or support the same resolution (or withhold votes). What the investor intends by its binary decision only makes sense to the company once it is explained. Failing to explain vote decisions to such a large company as Shell on such a crucial issue is a substantial omission.

In contrast to this binary nature of the vote message, engagement should be a much more complicated and nuanced dialogue. There was a good deal of engagement with Shell prior to the 2021 AGM, not least through the collective engagement vehicle Climate Action 100+. Engagement enables a richer conversation—it allows for nuance and clarification. More than that, to be effective and to have the potential to be influential, it needs to reflect a full expression of the investor's perspectives and an articulation of the reasons for those perspectives. It is a persuasive art and thus needs a more complex dialogue than can ever be possible through the narrow questions asked in resolutions for consideration at AGMs, and the even narrower answers available through the voting system.

Given its focus on preserving and enhancing long-term value on behalf of the asset owner, engagement can encompass the full range of issues that affect the long-term value of a business, including:

- strategy;
- capital structure;
- operational performance and delivery;
- risk management;
- pay;
- corporate governance;
- disclosure, including on ESG; and
- lobbying, including as part of industry groups.

ESG factors are clearly integral to these issues. Opportunities and challenges offered by ESG developments need to be reflected in the business's strategic thinking. Equally, a full assessment of operational performance must encompass not only financials but also vital areas relevant to the company's stakeholders, such as:

- highlighting the long-term health of the business, including relations with the workforce;
- establishing a culture that favors long-term value creation;
- dealing openly and fairly with suppliers and customers; and
- having proper and effective environmental controls in place.

An understanding of the complete range of key risks facing a business will always include ESG factors, and clearly remuneration and governance are integral to the G in ESG.

Stewardship and engagement are beneficial because they enhance shareholder value and support investors in the execution of their fiduciary duty—indeed, for many, stewardship is simply putting fiduciary duty into effect. When done well, stewardship and engagement encourage enhanced information flows between investors and investees as the parties discuss and debate issues. These exchanges allow them to learn from each other and to build relationships and, most importantly, to encourage change as shareholders communicate their perspectives on key issues facing the company.

As stewardship is a reflection of fiduciary duties, it needs to be actively considered by any party charged with fiduciary duties. This group will include most parties in the modern investment chain, from underlying beneficiary to asset owner (pension fund, insurer, or other fund) to fund manager and those directing the investment asset. Any of these parties could carry out stewardship functions, but in practice, the role typically rests with those having the greatest aggregated scale—usually, the fund manager. Only the very largest asset owners seek to carry out stewardship activities directly themselves (though many will actively engage with their investment managers, including about their stewardship activities). The expectations for stewardship are typically set out in the investment mandate, the contract between asset owner and fund manager (discussed in detail in Chapter 9).

In a 2018 report, Principles for Responsible Investment highlighted three ESG engagement dynamics that it believes create value (PRI 2018):

- communicative dynamics (the exchange of information);
- learning dynamics (enhancing knowledge); and
- political dynamics (building relationships).

Developing these dynamics requires investors to go beyond a superficial understanding of the company and its activities. Unless the steward strives to build communication and relationships and has a desire to learn, engagement is unlikely to be successful. To be successful in engagement, investors need to respect the individual circumstances of the company—seeking understanding and rapport—and not simply declare that things need to change. This means that good engagement is time consuming and tailored to the individual company, including the sector and geographic region in which it operates.

Different investors may have varying definitions of what successful engagement is. The usual definition of engagement—a purposeful dialogue with a specific objective in mind—presupposes something vital: that the engager sets objectives for their engagement at the start of the process, and the dialogue's purpose is to deliver those objectives over time. While various investors both set objectives and measure their delivery differently, engagement is successful only to the extent that it delivers the pre-agreed objectives. Financial success in terms of business performance or share price performance may consequently occur but will always be subsidiary to the first measurement of success. This is because much engagement is about safeguarding value rather than increasing it, and it is impossible to know what might have been in the absence of engagement.

This mindset of success being measured against the delivery of pre-agreed objectives fits well with the new thought process revealed in the UK's 2020 Stewardship Code (discussed in further detail later in this chapter). The Financial Reporting Council, in the Code, repeatedly discusses the need for signatories to disclose the outcomes of their engagement work as well as the concrete benefits from stewardship activity for clients and beneficiaries. The Code also repeatedly uses the word "outcome" to describe "delivery of objectives that benefit clients."

Just as with ESG and investment performance, there is a growing body of evidence that engagement adds value to portfolios. One of the earliest articles to provide a detailed academic analysis of engagement impact is "Returns to Shareholder Activism: Evidence from a Clinical Study of the Hermes UK Focus Fund" (Becht et al. 2006), which looked at the early years of the Hermes Focus Fund business (launched in late 1998) and considered the first 41 investments by the fund. The authors studied the internal records of Focus Fund team activities and considered their impact in terms of delivering both change at the companies in question and returns for the investors. To assess this, the authors sought to identify engagement success by analyzing the objectives that were set for each engagement at the start. They found that most of the stated objectives were achieved, with a 65% success rate overall, with the greatest success in restructuring and financial policies and slightly less success with regard to board change. Ironically perhaps, the lowest success rate was found in areas where shareholder engagement occurs more frequently, with only 25% of the desired remuneration policy changes achieved and only 44% of the sought improvements to investor relations achieved. While analyzing this success, they also found that the fund achieved positive financial returns. At the time, the overall performance of the fund was 4.9% net of fees a year more than the FTSE All-Share Performance; 90% of this excess return was attributed to activist outcomes.

Three case studies are discussed in the paper, but we will discuss just one of them briefly. Six Continents was subject to Focus Fund engagement from 2001, when it was known as Bass PLC—making clear its origins as a beer-making business. The paper notes four objectives in the engagement: (1) simplify the conglomerate structure, (2) a return of cash to shareholders, (3) a split in the roles of chair and CEO, and (4) a limit on further acquisitions, which the Focus Fund suggested had been value destroying. Over the life of the engagement, the beer business was sold and the global hotels business (including Intercontinental Hotels and Holiday Inn) was split from the UK pubs business; cash was returned through a buyback; the roles of CEO and chair were split and other governance changes were made; and acquisitions were put on hold. The engagement generated a significant return for investors in the fund and for other shareholders in the company. Ongoing shareholders have also enjoyed strong performance from Six Continents over the years since the Focus Fund engagement.

Dimson, Karakas, and Li (2015) studied a different (anonymous) fund manager's engagement record, looking at the years 1999–2009. Their study considered less activist investing and more what would now be considered standard ESG engagement and stewardship. One benefit of studying this style of engagement is that the number of cases covered in the study is substantial. Even though it considered only US activity by the fund manager, it covered more than 2,000 engagements, involving over 600 investee companies, and found an overall success rate of 18%.

The core finding of this study is clear: successful engagement activity was followed by positive abnormal financial returns. For example, for successes in climate change engagements over the study period, the excess return in the year following engagement was more than 10% and was nearly 9% for successful corporate governance engagements. Typically, the time between initial engagement and success was 1.5 years, with two or three engagements being required. On average, ESG engagements generated an abnormal return of 2.3% in the year after the initial engagement, rising to 7.1% for successful engagements and with no adverse response to unsuccessful engagements.

A more recent study (Hoepner et al. 2020) found that ESG engagement leads to a reduction in downside risk and that the effect is stronger the more successful the engagement is. In this case, the effects were strongest in relation to governance (which accounts for the majority of engagement cases) and then for social issues (so long as these are also associated with work on governance).

These studies show that engagement—if carried out well, so that it is focused on material and relevant issues and pursued with persistence—can work. Engaged companies change their behaviors against ESG factors, which leads to increased value.

Often, engagement also works to further inform investment analysis and fill out an investor's understanding of not only the potential for a business model to adapt to a changing business environment and evolving expectations but also the willingness of a particular management team and board to strategically address these challenges. Thus, engagement for many is a crucial part of active investment decision making.

Why Engagement?

Engagement helps investee companies understand their investors' (and potential investors') expectations, allowing them to shape their long-term strategies accordingly. Engagement also clearly allows investors to work closely with an investee company over time on specific governance, social, or environmental issues that the investors regard as posing a downside risk to the business. By working with companies' management—either individually or collectively—investment firms can influence companies to adopt better ESG practices, or at least to relinquish poor practices.

The Investor Forum, a UK group set up to facilitate collective dialogue between investors and investees, describes engagement as "active dialogue with a specific and targeted objective. . . . The underlying aim . . . should always be to preserve and enhance the value of assets."

In a 2019 white paper, "Defining Stewardship and Engagement," the Investor Forum provides a framework for understanding the nature and key elements of stewardship. Not least by defining stewardship in terms of assets with which an organization has been entrusted, this framework deliberately frames stewardship within the context of fiduciary duty. Trustees (of pension funds or other assets) and directors fully understand that they are fiduciaries because they are charged with caring for assets on behalf of others. Because investment institutions are also entrusted with assets, similar fiduciary duties apply to them as well. The Forum argues that stewardship is one aspect of delivering on those duties. Exhibit 1 lays out the components of stewardship.

Exhibit 1: The Components of Stewardship

Stewardship
Preserving and enhancing the value of assets with which one has been entrusted

. . . delivered through . . .

Investment approach and decision
Allocation of capital in accordance with investment purpose, mandate, and client interests, at portfolio and individual asset levels

Dialogue
Active discussions between companies and investors, of which there are two principal forms:

Monitoring	Engagement
Dialogue for investment purposes: to understand the company, its stakeholders, and its performance. Informs incremental buy/sell/hold decisions.	Purposeful dialogue with a specific and targeted objective to achieve change. Individual or collective basis, as appropriate.

... typified by ...

Detailed and specific questioning; investors seeking insights	Two-way dialogue; investors expressing opinions

... characteristics of high-quality delivery ...

- Framed by close understanding of the nature of a company and drivers of its business model and long-term opportunity to prosper.
- Appropriately resourced, so dialogue can be delivered professionally in the context of full understanding of the individual company.
- Dialogue must be consistent, direct, and honest.
- Dialogue is respectful and seeks to build mutual trust.

▸ Set in a context of mutual understanding of fund manager's investment style and approach.	▸ Set in a context of long-term ownership and focus on long-term value preservation and creation, so that engagement is aligned with investment thesis.
▸ Recognizes that change within companies is a process and sometimes takes time to be reflected in external indicators of performance.	▸ Recognizes that change is a process; while haste may at times be needed, change cannot be inappropriately rushed.
▸ Resources are used efficiently so that neither party's time is wasted.	▸ Overall resources are used efficiently, so engagement coverage is as broad as possible while also proving effective.
▸ Fuller insight leads to better-informed decisions.	▸ Clear and specific objective leads to effective change.
▸ Includes feedback so that mutual understanding can be reinforced over time.	▸ Involves reflection, so lessons are learned and taken fully into account in future.

... resulting in ...

▸ Changed investor decision making.	▸ Changed company behaviors.
▸ Efficient capital allocation by investors.	▸ Efficient capital allocation by companies.
▸ Appropriate risk-adjusted returns for clients.	▸ Appropriate risk management by companies.
▸ Preserved/enhanced value.	▸ Preserved/enhanced value.
▸ Delivery of client objectives and investment purpose.	▸ Delivery of corporate purpose and culture through effective oversight.

Source: Investor Forum 2019.

Particularly key in this analysis is the contrast that it draws between monitoring and engagement dialogues. As the paper articulates, monitoring dialogues are the conversations between investors and management to understand performance and opportunity more fully, which are typified by detailed questions from the investor and which are likely to inform buy, sell, or hold investment decisions. In contrast, engagement dialogues are conversations between investors and any level of the investee entity (including non-executive directors), featuring a two-way sharing of perspectives such that the investors express their position on key issues and highlight any concerns they may have. This two-way dialogue and expression of clear positions is necessary for engagement to deliver its intended outcomes of changed company behaviors. If engagement is to be effective in generating change outcomes, a clear objective must be set from the start.

This distinction between monitoring dialogues and genuine engagement shows the ways in which stewardship can sometimes be ineffective or inappropriate. There can be occasions where engagement activity is directed at companies that are unlikely to change and have no desire to enter into a productive dialogue with their investors. Engagement with these companies has limited benefit. Yet some clients may suspect that it is an excuse to continue to hold on to a company that is otherwise unsuitable for a portfolio because the portfolio manager wishes to keep an exposure to it for performance reasons. This is not considered real engagement and is more likely a cover for investment decision making.

The opposite can also occur: engagement as a response to poor investment decision making. Very often, a desire to engage arises from a share price fall. Active fund managers may then become concerned about issues that may have been apparent for a time but were ignored because performance was positive. Experience tends to show that such knee-jerk engagement is less likely to be effective than long-standing consistent messaging (where intensity may increase at moments of difficulty, but messaging does not just begin at those moments). Key identifiers of successful genuine engagement include clarity and consistency about objectives and ensuring that it is clear when the investor is communicating messages to the company and not just seeking information from it.

The delivery of concrete outcomes is core to the "why" of engagement. Effective engagement generates change, and if the intended engagement outcomes have been chosen well, that change will preserve and enhance long-term value at the company subject to the engagement. Thus, engagement delivers on the promise of fiduciary duty: to preserve and enhance the value of assets that the investor is overseeing on behalf of clients and beneficiaries.

In addition to the need for clear objectives focused on effecting change, the paper identifies a series of other characteristics of effective engagement. These are a gathering of the "characteristics of high-quality delivery" set out in Exhibit 1 and require that high-quality delivery:

- be set in an appropriate context of long-term ownership with a focus on long-term value preservation and creation, so that the engagement is aligned with the investment thesis;
- be framed by a close understanding of the nature of the company and the drivers of its business model and long-term opportunity to prosper;
- recognize that change is a process and that, while haste may at times be necessary, change should not be inappropriately rushed;
- use consistent, direct, and honest messaging and dialogue;
- be appropriately resourced so that it can be delivered professionally in the context of a full understanding of the individual company;
- use resources efficiently so that engagement coverage is as broad as possible while using all the tools available, including collective engagement; and
- involve reflection so that lessons are learned in order to improve future engagement activity.

These characteristics are explored through the case studies and wider discussion that follow.

Engagement in practice

Some examples of how this form of process can influence companies to adopt improved ESG practices are described in this section.

> **EXAMPLES OF ENGAGEMENT IN PRACTICE**
>
> A PRI case study (Bichta 2018) describes Boston Common Asset Management's long-term engagement with VF Corporation (VF Corp) around the water risks in its cotton and leather supply chains. This multi-year engagement—during which Boston Common submitted and then withdrew a shareholder resolution (withdrawing it in response to the company's commitment to address the issue)—saw VF Corp improve relevant reporting, undertake material risk assessment, and sign on to good practice standards in the Better Cotton Initiative.
>
> Hermes EOS's (Equity Ownership Services) engagement with Siam Cement (Chow 2018) has seen that company improve from a level one company (the lowest score) to level three as rated by the Transition Pathway Initiative (an asset owner–led initiative that assesses companies' preparation for the transition to a low-carbon economy). In early 2018, the investment firm met senior management to discuss its 2020 emissions targets. It then held a TCFD (Task Force on Climate-Related Financial Disclosures) workshop with senior executives at Siam Cement to share industry best practice and to encourage the company to improve assessment of physical risks of its assets, take part in industry collaboration, and establish a group-wide climate governance mechanism. The company has now committed to the Paris Agreement's global temperature limitation goal, extended its scenario planning, and improved its governance and business management around climate.
>
> In 2018, the Investor Forum worked with its members to address concerns around Imperial Brands' strategic direction, operational execution, and disclosures. The chair "engaged rapidly and very constructively . . . announcing a disposal programme, enhancing its communications on its approach to Next Generation Products and implementing changes to segmental reporting at the full year results." (Investor Forum 2018)

Many investment managers now produce annual reports on their stewardship activities, not least because this is a standard requirement under most of the stewardship codes that now frame the activity (as discussed in the next section). This reporting is of variable quality, and there is a tendency to report large numbers of activities rather than to focus on high-quality delivery of stewardship activity and outcomes. A recent analysis of 36 stewardship reports from leading global investment managers is titled "It's Not Just a Numbers Game" for this reason, and it identified worrying basic gaps in reported information (Redington Ltd 2022). Further, it found that only 42% of the case studies disclosed in the reports (in theory, investment managers' best stories out of their many stewardship activities) were assessed to be both proactively driven by the manager and substantive in what they were seeking to deliver. Too many managers revealed that the bulk of their stewardship activity was driven by voting concerns, which is narrow in mindset and highly reactive.

One example of better reporting on stewardship by an investment manager is the French firm AXA. This manager does not claim high numbers of activities but instead reports on a relatively high proportion of quality engagements, honestly disclosing engagement failures as well as successes. Some of these examples are fully transparent, while others are anonymized, which is sometimes necessary to maintain good relations with investments. Two small samples from AXA's stewardship report on its 2022 activity show some of the range of actions and activities that stewardship may involve, and what can be revealed in relatively short-form disclosures.

Stewardship and Engagement: What's Involved and Why It's Important

CASE STUDIES

AXA IM Stewardship Report 2022

Engagement Status: Success Milestone

We started engaging with Dublin-based cement and construction materials company CRH in 2021 to understand its plans to reduce emissions, considering the materiality of the company's business to climate change.

In our 2021 meeting held with CRH's Head of Sustainability, we communicated our desire for the company to publish an ambitious decarbonization plan. We then reengaged in 2022 to have an update on CRH targets and actions.

Since our 2021 meeting, the company has made significant progress and has now validated targets under the Science-Based Targets initiative (SBTi), backed by a bottom-up plant-by-plant industrial plant. The company also presented the main levers it intends to use to achieve its absolute emission reduction goals.

We will continue to monitor the evolution of CRH's carbon emissions. We will also look deeper at the circular economy theme, as well as the interplay between gross and net intensity.

Selected Anonymised Examples of Escalation

Sector	Geography	Nature of Issue	Escalation technique
Online retailer	US	Human rights	Targeting senior input by sending a latter, together with other investors, to the chair of the committee responsible for the oversight of diversity, equity, and inclusion issues, requesting the implementation of a shareholder resolution on freedom of association
Customer services	France	Human capital	Collaborating with other investors to send written questions to be discussed at the AGM to obtain formal and public responses to social-related questions
Food	Brazil	Deforestation	Working with a credit analyst focused on the Latin America market, with an established relationship with the company, to obtain a response to our meeting request
Banks	UK	Climate change	Voting against its climate transition plan following a lack of progress on its oil sands and coal policies. The concerns were previously shared during an engagement meeting held in 2021
Technology	US	Data privacy	Co-filling a shareholder proposal which requested more information on algorithmic systems during the 2023 AGM
Information technology	Sweden	Governance	Divestment following recurring and structural concerns of corruption

Source: AXA Investment Managers. 2023

There are also situations where engagement (or at least some form of stewardship) is *required* and an investor must take a view. These could be corporate actions, such as share issuances in which the investor can choose to participate or not, or proposed takeovers where the investor must decide whether to sell up or, if permitted, hold on to their shares. For most investors, some dialogue with the company will be needed before reaching the relevant conclusion.

Most investors now regard voting as a client asset like any other, and thus as something to be considered carefully and exercised with due thought. Voting comes around annually, at the AGM, and occasionally in between at special meetings, in most countries called extraordinary general meetings (EGMs). In addition to voting to receive the report and accounts, the issues considered at each AGM depend on local law but are often fundamental issues about the structure of the board, audit and oversight, executive pay, and the capital structure of the company. Not considering such issues with due care can clearly be seen as a failure of fiduciary duty, and due care will often require active dialogue with the company in order to understand the issues and express any concerns and perspectives.

3 CODES AND STANDARDS

6.1.3 explain the main principles and requirements of stewardship codes as they apply to institutional asset management firms

Regulators are convinced that engagement adds value, not just within investment portfolios but for markets as a whole. In his powerful 2009 report on the financial crisis, Sir David Walker stated:

> *Before the recent crisis phase there appears to have been a widespread acquiescence by institutional investors and the market in the gearing up of the balance sheets of banks . . . as a means of boosting returns on equity. The limited institutional efforts at engagement with several UK banks appear to have had little impact in restraining management before the recent crisis phase. (Walker 2009)*

Regulatory interest in stewardship has grown from the disappointment of that financial crisis. As an adjunct to the institutional investor soul-searching that followed the crisis, the Walker Report ushered in a new era of shareholder engagement. The report formally called for the Financial Reporting Council (FRC) to issue a stewardship code that provides a framework for shareholder engagement and for this code to be reinforced by a Financial Services Authority (FSA; now the Financial Conduct Authority, or FCA) requirement that any registered fund manager must make a statement as to whether and how it approached its principles.

Following consultation, in 2010 the FRC issued a stewardship code—largely unchanged from the existing *Statement of Principles on the Responsibilities of Institutional Shareholders and Agents* issued by the Institutional Shareholders Committee in 2005 (itself built upon a 1991 document, *The Responsibilities of Institutional Shareholders in the UK*). Industry best practice had not delivered in the run-up to the financial crisis, but a code with regulatory backing was thought likely to have greater force. Industry acceptance of the code was relatively rapid, particularly among fund managers.

The 2010 Stewardship Code had seven principles. Institutional investors should:

1. publicly disclose their policy on how they will discharge their stewardship responsibilities;
2. have a robust policy on managing conflicts of interest in relation to stewardship and this policy should be publicly disclosed;

3. monitor their investee companies;
4. establish clear guidelines on when and how they will escalate their activities as a method of protecting and enhancing shareholder value;
5. be willing to act collectively with other investors where appropriate;
6. have a clear policy on voting and disclosure of voting activity; and
7. report periodically on their stewardship and voting activities.

This UK Code went through a further iteration in 2012, clarifying the distinction between the roles of asset owners (pension funds and the like) and their fund managers and other agents but leaving the principles themselves almost entirely unchanged. While some of the largest pension funds may seek to carry out stewardship activities with underlying investments themselves, most delegate this role, either by a specific contract or as part of their fund management services. Thus, the role of most asset owners is to oversee, challenge, and assess the stewardship activities of their service providers.

The UK Stewardship Code model has been followed around the world, and at the time of writing, such codes are now in 20 markets, developed either by stock exchanges or regulators or by investor bodies themselves keen to advance best practice. Among these codes are the following:

- Global—*ICGN Global Stewardship Principles* (ICGN 2020)
- Europe—*EFAMA Stewardship Code* (EFAMA 2018)
- Australia—*Australian Asset Owner Stewardship Code* (ACSI 2018)
- Brazil—*AMEC Stewardship Code* (AMEC 2016)
- Hong Kong SAR—*Principles of Responsible Ownership* (Hong Kong Securities and Futures Commission 2016)
- India—*SEBI Stewardship Code* (SEBI 2019)
- Japan—*Principles for Responsible Institutional Investors* (Council of Experts on the Stewardship Code 2020)
- Singapore—*Singapore Stewardship Principles for Responsible Investors* (Stewardship Asia Centre 2022)
- South Africa—*Second Code for Responsible Investing in South Africa* (CRISA Committee 2022)
- United States—*The Stewardship Principles* (Investor Stewardship Group 2019)

The International Corporate Governance Network (ICGN) has fostered a Global Stewardship Codes Network, which brings together many of the sponsors of these and other leading codes from around the world. (Financial Reporting Council)

It is notable that while there is great consistency between the principles in each of these codes, as they all appear to be modeled closely on the seven principles of the 2012 UK Code, conflicts of interest are dealt with very differently. It has been stated that those codes drafted by the fund management industry are more likely to downplay the issue of conflicts, while those codes with greater regulatory backing place more emphasis on the issue. Perhaps most striking is the European Fund and Asset Management Association (EFAMA) Code, which is almost a direct copy of the 2012 UK Code except that it does not include a principle on conflicts—indeed, it avoids the issue almost entirely.

South Africa's Code—updated in 2022 from the 2011 original to what is now referred to as CRISA 2—is a little different. As its name implies, it covers responsible investment as a whole, not just stewardship. Principle 2 (of 5 in total) is "Diligent Stewardship" and reads: "Investment arrangements and activities should demonstrate the acceptance of ownership rights and responsibilities diligently enabling effective stewardship." Underlying this principle are implementation practices that are very similar to the elements of other stewardship codes.

Code Revisions in 2020

The UK Stewardship Code went through a more fundamental redrafting to produce the 2020 version, which came into effect on 1 January 2020 (Financial Reporting Council 2020). The new Code includes 12 principles (plus an alternate 6 for service providers), where formerly there were 7, and three times the number of pages as the 2012 code. But the biggest change isn't the growth of the document—it's the increased ambition for practical delivery by signatories. The former focus on statements of intent no longer exists. Instead, investors are now expected to report annually on activity and, most importantly, on outcomes from that activity.

Merely reporting on activity is not enough; each of the new principles has associated outcomes that must be reported on, requiring concrete examples of what has been delivered practically for clients and beneficiaries. Signatories can no longer fulfill the demands of the Code by publishing policy statements filled with ambitious assertions; instead, they must deliver practical effects from their actions.

The 12 new principles fall into four categories but cover two distinct functions.

- Principles 1 through 8 address the foundations of stewardship.
- Principles 9 through 12 focus on the practical discharge of engagement responsibilities.

The need to report on concrete outcomes applies even to the foundational Principles 1, 2, 3, 5, and 6, which cover such structural issues within the investment institution as governance, culture, and managing conflicts of interest. The outcomes that need to be disclosed in relation to these issues are evidence that those structures concretely work in practice in the clients' best interests.

Principles 7 and 8 require the integration of ESG factors into the investment process along with effective oversight of service providers. The disclosures of related outcomes need to be explanations of how these processes have been delivered effectively on behalf of clients and beneficiaries.

Principles 9 through 12 cover engagement (and voting) activities. The intended outcome of these principles (which must be part of the annual reporting) is to show substantive change at companies (or other investee assets) because of the engagement activity. The disclosure of at least some voting outcomes, not just the investor's voting activity, is also expected.

Perhaps the most challenging of the 12 is Principle 4, which charges signatories with identifying and responding to market-wide and systemic risks. Some investment institutions already recognize their obligation on behalf of beneficiaries and clients to maintain and promote well-functioning markets and social and environmental systems, but for many this may feel like a significant additional burden. The require ment to "disclose an assessment of their effectiveness in identifying and responding to" such risks imposes a new and significant burden, even for those who already recognize this as a stewardship responsibility. Only the Australian Asset Owner Stewardship Code, developed by the industry body Australian Council of Superannuation Investors (ACSI) in 2018, had a similar expectation in place, in its Principle 5:

> *Asset owners should encourage better alignment of the operation of the financial system and regulatory policy with the interests of long-term investors.*

The guidance to Principle 5 is worth setting out in full, because it makes clear the scale of the ambition, which is much broader than the typically more cautious approaches to systemic issues in other codes but accurately reflects what many asset owners consider the drivers needed to address systemic issues actively:

Asset owners' holdings are typically diversified, and their investment returns are affected by the economy as a whole.

Where asset owners have concerns regarding systemic, industry-wide policies, practices, or disclosures, they can encourage policymakers to better align the operation of the financial system and regulatory policy with the interests of long-term investors. Typical examples of industry-wide issues include advocating for Corporations Law, Listing Rule, or government policy change in relation to governance and shareholder rights, climate change, and ESG disclosures.

Examples of activities could include contributing to government, parliamentary committees, and other relevant public regulatory or policy forums.

Engagement with policymakers can be undertaken directly, or through collaborative initiatives in the interests of long-term success of companies, value creation, and investment outcomes for beneficiaries.

The ICGN's 2020 update of its 2016 Stewardship Principles also discusses the need for investors to engage with public policymakers on systemic risks, noting that these sorts of activities "can be useful to help promote public policy changes and protect shareholder rights, as well as wider systemic integrity." This may be some evidence of the new UK Code having influence internationally. But so far, it does not seem to be proving as much of a model for global stewardship codes as its predecessors. For example, when Japan updated its stewardship guidance, it followed the UK lead only in a small way. Although its new stewardship principles include a requirement to report on the outcomes of engagement activity, it is downplayed and given little prominence and so may have only a limited impact (the contrast to how central this requirement is to the new UK Code is notable). Beyond that, the 2020 changes to the Japanese Code were as follows:

- extending coverage to all asset classes, not just equity;
- incorporating sustainability and ESG;
- encouraging asset owners to become involved in stewardship and provide a little more clarity on their role in the stewardship hierarchy; and
- clarifying the position of service providers in the hierarchy and adding higher expectations of proxy advisers.

Code Provisions

Other than the new UK Stewardship Code, the principles of all the codes around the world are remarkably similar. Typically, there are six or seven principles, with the first often requiring investors to have a public policy regarding stewardship, and the last noting the need for honest and open reporting of stewardship activities. The main body of the principles between these two usually calls for:

- regular monitoring of investee companies;
- active engagement where relevant (sometimes termed "escalation," or sometimes escalation is deemed worthy of a separate principle of its own); and
- thoughtfully intelligent voting.

The two principles that are sometimes but not always present require the following:

- investors are required to manage their conflicts of interest regarding stewardship matters; and
- the escalation of stewardship activity must include a willingness to act collectively with other institutional investors.

The collective engagement issue is controversial, because there are concerns about the creation of so-called concert parties (groups of shareholders so influential that they, in effect, take control of companies without mounting a formal takeover). This is not the intention of collective engagement, as is shown by the discussion later in this chapter.

Stewardship codes now are usually expressed to apply to all asset classes, but their language tends to reveal an initial focus in practice on public equity investment. The stewardship thought process, both by regulators and by investors, and the practical delivery of stewardship actions by those investors, are most developed in public equities. There is a discussion about the application of stewardship to other asset classes later in this chapter; it is more straightforward than some practitioners may indicate.

The number of stewardship codes in Europe is likely to increase significantly following the Shareholder Rights Directive II (SRD II), which came into force in June 2019. Among other things, SRD II will raise expectations in each country about the level of stewardship carried out by local investors. This directive is likely to supersede such initiatives as the voluntary EFAMA Code (updated in 2018 from the original 2011 version) and may move European markets toward expanding expectations that have regulatory backing. While by name it is about shareholder rights, the directive is really more about shareholder responsibilities.

Expectations with regard to stewardship are set by legislation as well as by codes. Foremost among these statutes is the US ERISA legislation, the *Employee Retirement Income Security Act of 1974*. Among the Act's requirements, a number are relevant to stewardship—in particular, that advisers should act as fiduciaries in relation to the beneficiaries (under the US regime, fund management firms are deemed advisers and thus subject to this standard). Among the obligations expected under fiduciary duty (as narrowly defined in the Act; it is worth noting that elsewhere in this chapter "fiduciary duty" refers to the general common law understanding of that duty and not this US-legislated definition) is that the fund will vote at investee company general meetings and engage with companies.

In the past, the legal interpretation of the Act was thought to discourage ESG stewardship because of a bulletin statement indicating that engagement and proxy use on environmental and social issues would be rare. But fresh interpretive statements from 2018 are more supportive of stewardship. The regulator's views, set out in the US Department of Labor's *Field Assistance Bulletin No. 2018-01—Superseded by 85 FR 72846 and 85 FR 81658*, confirm that fiduciaries can vote and use proxies if there is a reasonable expectation that such activities are likely to enhance the economic value of the investment (taking costs into account). The *Bulletin* added that engagement might be prudent for indexed portfolios where ESG issues represent significant operational risks and costs. There continues to be a clear view that engagement—and indeed ESG investing—needs a firm basis in value for beneficiaries, so engaging would not be permissible to achieve purely social policy goals without making a clear link to value. (US Department of Labor 2018)

ENGAGEMENT STYLES

☐ **6.1.4** explain how engagement is achieved in practice, including key differences in objectives, style, and tone

Some asset owners will choose to engage with companies directly, through team members who act as stewards of the investment portfolios. Others expect their external fund managers to deliver this work, either through the portfolio managers who also take stewardship responsibility or through stewardship specialists (or some combination of the two). Engagement activities can also be entirely outsourced to specialist stewardship service providers.

Almost all institutional investors lean, at least in part, on one group of these service providers: the proxy voting advisory firms. These proxy advisers offer analysis and (in most cases) voting recommendations across many public companies, and almost all institutions hire them to provide the framework that ensures their voting decisions are delivered. Most also pay for their advice on those voting decisions.

Other stewardship service providers offer various degrees of engagement services by effectively stepping into the shoes of the investor to engage on their behalf. By aggregating the interests of clients, the scale that is necessary to be present and visible enough in dialogue and engagement with company management and boards can be built. Boards can offer a form of collective engagement, enabling investors to have a greater reach and influence by working alongside others and sharing precious resources. Collaborative engagement can also take place through industry initiatives and collaboration platforms (such as one offered by PRI), which are discussed in detail below.

Styles: Top-Down and Bottom-Up

To an extent, engagement styles vary depending on the heritage of stewardship teams. There is a distinction in mindset and approach between those teams with a history of governance-led engagement and those that have worked more on the environmental and social side.

The most obvious distinction is that since material E and S issues arise from the nature of a company's business activities, teams with this heritage tend to be organized by sector; since G is determined more by national law and codes, such teams are usually split according to geography. Engagement style also follows this structure to some extent. Teams tend to focus on individual environmental and social issues and to pursue those vigorously across sectors or markets as a whole. This can encompass trying to establish better practice standards and highlighting leading practice as well as targeting those perceived as laggards. The dialogue would tend to start with investor relations or sustainability teams and then be escalated upward, to both senior management and the board. Firms with a governance heritage tend to focus first on individual companies, starting with the chair (often with the assistance of the company secretary) and working through the board and down to management from there.

These are generalizations, but they illustrate the distinction between top-down and bottom-up activity. Most investment houses mix the two, though company-focused, bottom-up engagement fits most naturally with active investment approaches, particularly those with concentrated portfolios; whereas issue-based, top-down engagement tends to align more closely with passive or otherwise broadly diversified investment portfolios.

Styles: Issue-Based and Company-Focused

Passive investors, and others with broadly diversified portfolios, typically start with an issue—identified by the team from news or broader analysis or through a screening or other research provider—and seek to engage with all the companies affected by that issue (which may be a whole sector or even broader). Usually, the starting point is a letter written to all those affected, which is then followed up with dialogue. Active investors, particularly those with focused portfolios, start with the company itself and its business issues and develop a tailored engagement approach cutting across a range of issues, often with the investment teams taking a leading role. Companies selected for this approach are often identified from among investment underperformers or are firms that trigger other financial or ESG metrics. The starting point is typically to seek a direct discussion with senior management and then the board.

Larry Fink's annual letter to CEOs setting out BlackRock's engagement plans is an example of the issue-based approach taken by passive investors. In the 2019 letter, Fink wrote that their priorities for the year were

> *governance, including your company's approach to board diversity; corporate strategy and capital allocation; compensation that promotes long-termism; environmental risks and opportunities; and human capital management. These priorities reflect our commitment to engaging around issues that influence a company's prospects not over the next quarter, but over the long horizons that our clients are planning for. (Blackrock 2019)*

Issue-based approaches to engagement are often accompanied by examples of best practice in a particular area. These examples may be developed in advance of the first engagement dialogues, but they usually come out of the engagement process with those companies that are deemed to have leading practices. By expecting all companies in each sector to adopt these best practices, investors may, over time, move sector or industry practice forward. Company-focused engagement seeks to improve practice across a number of relevant ESG issues at an individual company; the aim is to enhance portfolio performance overall, in terms of both ESG and investment performance.

5 EFFECTIVE ENGAGEMENT: FORMS, GOAL SETTING

6.1.5 apply strategies and tactics in a goal-based engagement approach using various forms

Forms of Engagement

An Investor Forum white paper published in November 2019, "Collective Engagement: An Essential Stewardship Capability," identifies 12 different forms of engagement (Investor Forum 2019). Of these, 5 are types of individual engagement (engagement by a single investment institution):

1. *generic letter:* these are broad communications across a swath of investment holdings;
2. *tailored letter:* these are more targeted and can cover a range of topics at varied levels of detail;

3. *"housekeeping" engagement:* this is an annual dialogue to help maintain and enhance a relationship with a company, but with only limited objectives;
4. *active private engagement:* targeted and specific engagement; and
5. *active public engagement:* engagement deliberately made public by the institution.

The others are forms of collaborative engagement (where an institution works with one or more others):

1. *informal discussions:* institutions discuss views of particular corporate situations;
2. *collaborative campaigns:* collaborative letter-writing or market/sector-wide campaigns;
3. *follow-on dialogue:* company engagement dialogue led by one or more investors in follow-up to a broader group letter or expression of views;
4. *soliciting support:* solicitation of broader support for formal, publicly stated targets (e.g., "vote no" campaigns or support for a shareholder resolution);
5. *group meetings:* a one-off group meeting (or a series of meetings) with a company, followed up either with individual investor reflections on the discussion or with a co-signed letter;
6. *collective engagement:* a formal coalition of investors with a clear objective, typically working over time and with a coordinating body; and
7. *concert party:* a formal agreement, in any form, with concrete objectives and agreed steps (e.g., collectively proposing a shareholder resolution or agreeing on how to vote on a particular matter).

The Investor Forum paper argues that as you go through the lists, there is a greater need for formality in approach and potentially greater regulatory attention. That greater formality requires increased clarity of the engagement objective(s) and can perhaps provide greater scope for influencing the change that is sought. These are clearly generalizations but largely hold true.

Gaining greater clarity of the engagement objective is particularly important, as it forms one of the key success factors for effective engagement that the Investor Forum paper identifies (based on its own practical experience and a study of the academic literature). In full, these six success factors are as follows:

Success Factor Characteristics of Engagement Approach

SF1. Objective(s) should be specific and targeted to enable clarity around delivery.

SF2. Objectives should be strategic or governance-led or linked to material strategic and/or governance issues.

SF3. The engagement approach should be bespoke (tailored) to the target company.

Success Factor Characteristics of Investor Collaboration

SF4. The participants should have clear leadership with appropriate relationships, skills, and knowledge.

SF5. The scale of coalition gathered (both scale of shareholding and overall assets under management of the group) should be meaningful.

SF6. The coalition should have a prior relationship with and/or cultural awareness of the target company.

The Investor Forum paper continues by adding these success factors to a matrix alongside the 12 forms of engagement (listed earlier), indicating how likely each engagement is to fulfill the six stated success factors, as shown in Exhibit 2 (the darker the shading, the greater the likelihood). It also shows the conclusions that are reached (which include a number of assumptions and generalizations that are informative).

Exhibit 2: Success Factors and Styles of Institutional Investor Engagement

Success factor	CHARACTERISTICS OF ENGAGEMENT FOCUS			CHARACTERISTICS OF INVESTOR GROUPING AND APPROACH		
	SF1: Clear objective	SF2: Material and strategic	SF3: Bespoke	SF4: Effective leadership	SF5: Scale of coalition	SF6: Depth of relationship
Potential impact on effectiveness (low to high)	Express concern ↔ Specify change	Narrow ESG focus ↔ Include strategy and finance	Generic approach ↔ Close cultural awareness	Informal grouping ↔ Formal coalition	Limited ownership ↔ Broad and material share ownership	Limited relationship ↔ Top-level access
Individual institutional engagement						
Generic letter-writing				n/a	n/a	
Tailored letter-writing				n/a	n/a	
Housekeeping engagement				n/a	n/a	
Active private engagement				n/a	n/a	
Active public engagement				n/a	n/a	
Collaborative engagement						
Informal discussions						
Collaborative campaigns						
Follow-on dialogue						
Soliciting support						
Group meeting(s)						
Collective engagement						
Concert party						

Source: Investor Forum.

Strategy and Tactics: Goal Setting and Resources

Remembering our favored standard definition of engagement as a purposeful dialogue with a specific objective in mind, it is vital to the start of the engagement process to set a clear goal or objective. It may be that the scale of a problem or issue at a company isn't clear at the start of a dialogue, meaning that a clear goal cannot be set until after the dialogue has begun. But no engagement really starts at that point: it is only once a goal has been set that the engagement proper can begin. Up until that point, the investor is simply having a conversation with the company or seeking more information.

A key part of the engagement process is to keep this objective in mind throughout and to measure progress against the objective over time. Given that engagement—particularly about more complex and worthwhile goals or objectives—can take years, clarity of the process and progress toward delivery are of central importance to the quality of engagement.

There are several challenges in engagement, the most significant being the question of resources. Does the investment firm have the time, the expertise, and sufficient leverage with its investees to engage successfully?

Given the scale of most fund management firms, the number of companies in which they invest client money is large, meaning that just the monitoring element of stewardship is a significant obligation on its own. Even where individual portfolios are concentrated, the aggregate is a rather broader exposure, with many moderate-sized investment firms owning a few thousand companies and the largest fund management houses holding tens of thousands. Having enough resources to engage effectively across all the companies in a firmwide portfolio is a significant challenge. In practice, every investor is resource constrained.

Given these resource constraints, engagement strategies must be designed to deliver meaningful results in the most cost- and time-effective manner. In practice, this translates into a few operational challenges that need to be addressed in the following order:

1. Investors need to define the scope of the engagement and prioritize their engagement activities carefully to ensure that it is value-adding for their clients/beneficiaries and impactful in terms of delivering improved corporate practices.
2. Investors need to frame the engagement topic (be it climate risk or supply chain risk) into the broader discussion around strategy and long-term financial performance with the management team and the board.
3. Investors must develop a clear process that articulates realistic goals and milestones so that both investment institutions and their clients have a clear indicator to measure their expectations and the effectiveness of the engagement strategy.
4. The engagement process needs to be adapted to the local context, language, and cultural approaches to doing business. Beyond dialogue, investors also need to have clear escalation measures in case engagement fails.

In many ways, this strategy represents two different forms of necessary prioritization:

- identifying which company in a portfolio is most in need of engagement; and
- determining which engagement issues should be prioritized in the dialogue between investors and the company (if change is to be delivered effectively, investors should not raise every possible concern with the company—not least because they risk creating confusion as to what issues they believe are most in need of attention).

In recent years, several software providers have developed systems to assist in capturing the engagement process and the reporting of activity and outcomes. Over time, these systems—or internally developed alternatives—are likely to become a necessary element of the resourcing required for good engagement. Among these technology providers are Esgaia, Impactive, ResearchPool, and VerityESG.

In late 2022, PRI launched a project to develop a standard for the level of resourcing to be expected for stewardship, working with the Thinking Ahead Institute. It is exploring current best practice and aiming to produce a standard during 2023. It is assisted by a Stewardship Resourcing Working Group under the auspices of PRI.

Strategy and Tactics: Investment Context

The approach to engagement must always sit within the framework of the fund manager's investment approach, and an active manager may well find it easier to prioritize both the company and the issue since those are where most value is at risk within portfolios. The existence of risk suggests that if the manager is an active manager, selling a holding in a company (or other investment asset) may always be a possible appropriate action for a responsible fiduciary to take.

For passive investors, the same value-at-risk dynamic should be the driver, but it may come less naturally to the decision-making teams, because they are less used to identifying where the most value is at risk in the portfolio. This approach will tend to mean a focus on the largest companies and top-down on the most material issues, although there may be issues that certain clients put particular emphasis on. These issues and companies are then deemed to deserve greater attention and so move up the prioritization list.

Many fund managers are building their stewardship resources by adding to their specialist stewardship teams. Passive fund managers (who invest in the broadest range of companies) perhaps have no option but to do so, while many active investment houses are working to ensure that their active portfolio managers can deliver stewardship alongside their regular monitoring of investee companies. Even where portfolio managers take the lead, they will typically need the support and partnership of a specialist stewardship team.

Potentially, another key additional resource is external collective vehicles—commercial stewardship operations or investor groups. Many of these have staff with a different and complementary range of skills that fund managers can use. For example, engagement on a particular theme, such as palm oil or water, is likely to require knowledge and experience that may be difficult to resource internally. Collaboration with an investor with a particular skill or with a collective vehicle that can bring alternative skills to bear can enable an investor to make progress that might not be possible alone. In addition, working collectively can help those investors whose holdings might be relatively small gain traction in their discussion with management and boards. Collective vehicles are discussed in more detail later.

PRI's 2018 report on how engagement adds value for investors and companies found that individual engagement can be more strategically valuable (and might allow an investor to resolve an ambiguous or anomalous position that they might prefer to deal with alone) but also found that individual approaches can be time-consuming and costly. The report suggests that "engagement practices should be adapted to balance the trade-offs of individual and collective forms of engagement." (PRI 2018a)

In the same report, PRI identified common enablers of and barriers to successful engagement from both corporate and investor perspectives, as shown in Exhibit 3.

Exhibit 3: Contrasting Perceptions of the Enablers of and Barriers to Engagement Success

	Corporate Perspectives		Investor Perspectives	
	Enablers	**Barriers**	**Enablers**	**Barriers**
Relational Factors	▶ Existence of an actual two-way dialogue. ▶ Being honest and transparent in the dialogue, and having an "open and objective discussion."	▶ Language barriers and communication issues. ▶ Lack of continuity in interactions.	▶ Good level of commitment on both sides to meet objectives. ▶ Reciprocal understanding of the engagement process and issues on both sides. ▶ Good communication and listening capacities on both sides.	▶ Language barriers and cultural differences can hamper dialogue.

Effective Engagement: Forms, Goal Setting

	Corporate Perspectives		Investor Perspectives	
	Enablers	**Barriers**	**Enablers**	**Barriers**
Corporate Factors	▸ Responsiveness and willingness to act upon investor requests. ▸ Selecting appropriate internal experts. ▸ Knowing your investors, access to prior discussions to tailor conversations. ▸ Systematic tracking of interactions with investors.	▸ Company bureaucracy preventing changes in internal practices and/or external reporting on (new) practices. ▸ Lack of resources, insufficient knowledge to meet investor demands. ▸ Lack of actual ESG policies, practices, and/or results that can be reported externally.	▸ Corporate reactivity to requests. ▸ Board-level access in targeted companies. ▸ Access to appropriate corporate experts. ▸ Long-standing relationships with key corporate actors. ▸ Corporate proactivity to inform investors when engagement objectives/targets have been met.	▸ Refusal by top executives to be engaged on ESG issues. ▸ Functional/sustainability manager struggles to advance ESG-related issues. ▸ Too small a shareholding to attract sufficient attention. ▸ Corporate inability to meet (ongoing) objectives and targets.
Investor Factors	▸ Listening capacities of investors. ▸ Communicating in different languages. ▸ Providing questions in advance. ▸ Prior knowledge of corporate ESG practice and performance. ▸ Genuine interest in (improving) the management of ESG issues at the company. ▸ Patience and understanding regarding corporate ability to address ESG challenges.	▸ Lack of investor preparation, overly generic questions/requests. ▸ Lack of knowledge about the company (e.g., ESG policy, track record). ▸ Lack of sufficient investor tracking process to determine whether engagement requests have been met. ▸ Changing engagement objectives and targets.	▸ Client or beneficiary requests for the consideration of ESG issues. ▸ Top-management support for ESG-related investment activities. ▸ Well-resourced and experienced ESG team. ▸ Clear engagement objectives and targets. ▸ In-house tracking tools to monitor and evaluate engagement progress. ▸ Pooling of resources through collective engagement.	▸ Lack of buy-in from clients and/or top management for ESG-related investment activities. ▸ Small, under-resourced ESG team. ▸ Lack of clear engagement policies, objectives, and monitoring systems. ▸ Underdeveloped relationships with key corporate actors. ▸ Difficulty demonstrating materiality of engagement. ▸ For (interested) asset owners: insufficient mechanisms to guarantee asset managers conduct successful engagements.

Source: PRI.

Conflicts of interest can also be a behavioral barrier to engagement. The fact that many stewardship codes call for transparency around conflicts that might impinge on stewardship activities explicitly acknowledges this issue. In its 2018 report on active ownership in listed equity, PRI notes:

> *Conflicts can arise when investment managers have business relations with the same companies they engage with or whose AGMs they have to cast their votes at. A company that is selected for engagement or voting might also be related to a parent company or subsidiary of the investor. Conflicts can occur when the interests of clients or beneficiaries also diverge from each other. Finally, employees might be linked personally or professionally to a company whose securities are submitted to vote or included in the investor's engagement programme. The disclosure of actual, potential or perceived conflicts is best practice. (PRI 2018b)*

A final barrier is the emergence of competition. Historically, few people worked in this once considerably under-resourced area, and stewardship professionals were content to work together, both informally and in more formal collaborations, recognizing that working together on thematic and specific issues might be the best way to deliver change on behalf of clients. As stewardship becomes more important to clients and an increased focus for investment consultants and fund managers, there are signs that this collaborative approach may be waning. But there are exceptions, such as the Climate Action 100+ (CA 100+) collaborative engagement, to which most major institutional investors now adhere. Even there, however, various institutions are seeking to differentiate themselves by adopting different approaches (individual CA 100+ engagements are very distinct). And although each company engagement is seemingly led by a single investor, in a number of cases, other institutions are advancing their own initiatives under the CA 100+ banner.

As engagement practices evolve, a degree of competition between service providers in terms of the quality of their resources and reporting is helpful, because it enables innovative and effective services to be developed at a greater scale, lowering costs for individual fund managers. It is important that the benefits of collective activity are not forgotten, and that the investor sector continue to explore synergies in engagement priorities and amplify their collective impact.

Setting Engagement Objectives

The first key step in engagement is to set clear objectives. Given that engagement is dialogue with a clear purpose—not just dialogue for the sake of dialogue—knowing what the purpose is matters. That is why the stewardship service providers all apply some milestone measure or set of key performance indicators (KPIs) to their engagements so that their clients can hold them accountable for delivery. It also explains why PRI itself sets a KPI that its members should set objectives for the majority of their engagements. PRI's 2020 annual report confirmed that 71% of its members implement this practice, although that number is short of its 80% target. (PRI 2020)

Outcomes matter more than activity, and given the impossibility of attributing share price movements to any individual engagement success (indeed, even attributing changes in corporate practices to any individual engagement success can be a challenge), having some mechanism to test whether the objectives have been achieved is the best way for clients to have confidence about the success of engagements. Some investors also have objectives that provide a practical road map of concrete measures that the engaged company can adopt to move toward the broader objective of the engagement dialogue.

Having clear objectives helps set a clear agenda. Though successful engagement is always a conversation and thus may cover much ground, the engager needs to know the handful of issues (at most) that really need to be probed hard and brought into focus in the discussion. In many cases, the investor will share at least a version of this agenda with the company so that there are few surprises, setting a framework of honesty and openness from the start.

Clarity around objectives will also help identify the right company representatives to work with. For ESG operational matters, they will typically be the sustainability and/or investor relations teams, with escalation to the senior management and then to the board. For business strategy or operational matters, the starting point will typically be the CEO or CFO, with escalation, if need be, to the non-executive directors. For governance matters, the usual starting point will be the chair, often with the company secretary (or equivalent role) as part of the conversation, with the ability to seek further discussions with the senior independent director or lead independent director—or with other non-executives.

Practicalities of Engagement

If the matter is purely a voting issue, the first contact is normally with the company secretary (at least in those markets where such a role has prominence; in the United States and parts of continental Europe, the contact is more likely to start with the investor relations team), and then further dialogue may be with the chair of the relevant board committee (remuneration or audit) and/or the chair of the board. There are no fixed rules, and these models are often not what happens in practice. Investors need to respond according to what is appropriate at the individual company. Occasionally, it can take some effort to persuade a company that the dialogue an investor seeks is worth the relevant corporate representative's time—particularly a non-executive director's time.

Meetings can be held at the corporate head office or at the investment firm. Typically, the choice between the two is only a matter of mutual convenience, although visiting the company's office can help demonstrate the investor's interest. On rare occasions, engagement may happen on an operational or supplier site visit. Investors fully educating themselves through dedicated time on operational site visits, or through visits to one or more suppliers, can provide further standing to their engagement dialogue and reinforce the points they are seeking to make.

The engager typically has an hour with a single individual to explore a set of issues, perhaps only one of which will be the focus of the meeting. Listening is as important—often more important—than speaking. Good engagement seeks understanding and constructive dialogue as the engager explains how a proposed course of action is in the company's best interests, not purely those of the single investor. It is helpful to demonstrate knowledge of both the company and the sector to build relations, because it shows an earnest approach and helps the investor be most convincing in engagement actions (hence, the enhanced status in engagement gained from site visits).

There is also a need to identify possible reasons why the company may not want to adopt a measure that is commonly understood to be beneficial. Frequently, a company's culture, history, or employees may stand in the way of change—one reason why successful engagement is often a multi-stage, multi-year activity. Investors may find that their role has been to add weight to one side of a discussion that is already ongoing at the company, helping those who are seeking change to win that debate in the boardroom. Rarely will an issue of enough concern to an investor to bring forward as an engagement topic not have been at least raised internally within a company by someone on the board or in senior management.

To be constructive, the dialogue should initially take place privately, without media attention, not least because media interest often entrenches positions rather than allowing the fluidity that may be necessary for change to occur.

Nevertheless, over time it may become clear that greater force is required for the investor's message to be heard properly in a dialogue. That is when escalation tools may be needed.

VOTING 6

6.1.6 explain particular forms of engagement and major escalation techniques, including: proxy voting; collective engagement; ESG investment forums

Stewardship codes typically make clear that stewardship extends far beyond voting activities—for example, the Hong Kong Principles of Responsible Ownership state: "Investors' ownership responsibilities extend beyond voting." The intent is to counter the assertion still heard from some investors that delivering votes is sufficient to deliver good stewardship. The point is not that voting is irrelevant to stewardship: rather, where investors have voting rights, they have an obligation to exercise those rights with good sense and due care. Voting is a necessary but not sufficient element of good stewardship.

As mentioned earlier, shareholders—equity investors—have the right to vote at AGMs and EGMs, and in some markets, occasionally at other investor gatherings. In almost all cases, voting is proportionate to the percentage shareholding in the company, and resolutions are usually passed when more than half of those voting support them. In a few cases, special resolutions require support by 75% of those voting, and there are unusual circumstances where the number of votes cast must exceed a threshold in terms of the overall share capital (and rarer still when the number of shareholders is important). Institutions typically vote for or against, although in many markets, there is also scope for a conscious abstention (e.g., in the UK these votes are collated despite not legally being considered votes as such). Abstention is considered an active decision rather than just an absence of a vote. Abstention can sometimes be a useful tool in an engagement process where the investor does not have a fixed view on an issue yet does not want to be in the potential position later of being hampered in its criticism of an action that it has, in effect, endorsed through its vote.

Given the public nature of company general meetings, where the results are announced publicly by the company and the events themselves are often open to the media, voting decisions are often the most visible element of stewardship and engagement. Voting thus gains disproportionate media attention, and major "no" votes can earn significant media coverage. Fund managers are therefore often held to account, both in the public arena and by their clients, for their voting decisions.

Voting is often referred to as "proxy voting" because investors rarely physically attend the meetings where the voting occurs, but instead appoint an individual as proxy to cast the votes on their behalf (in most cases, this person will be the chair of the company, although anyone physically at the meeting can be appointed). Votes vest in the legal owner of the shares, which may be the custodian or a unit trust vehicle or some other intermediary, meaning that even an institutional investor will usually need formal paperwork in order to attend the meeting and vote, paperwork that clearly identifies the individual who is physically representing the investor at the meeting.

With companies' sizable portfolios and AGMs usually occurring over compressed time periods (a few months in some markets, with the extreme being Japan, where thousands of AGMs are held over just a few days), resourcing is a particular issue in the area of voting. Institutional investors typically lean on proxy firms for assistance in processing votes and in providing advice on those votes. There are two dominant proxy firms in the global market:

- ISS, with over 80% of the market; and
- Glass Lewis, with the bulk of the remainder; along with
- a few much smaller rivals, which have some market share, especially in a few localized markets.

Proxy advisers are often criticized by companies for taking what may appear to be narrow, inflexible approaches to voting and not facilitating the "explain" aspect of "comply/apply or explain." But most investors would argue that the advisers' role is not to be flexible but to focus on the general guidance and that it is up to investors to display their closer understanding of individual companies and respond appropriately to explanations. The extent to which investors use their own judgment and avoid relying on their proxy advisers—particularly in often long tails of smaller holdings outside their home market—is variable.

Voting is a key tool for the active investor, and any voting decision should be aligned with the investment thesis for the holding and any stewardship agenda that the institution has in relation to the company. That may mean voting on resolutions related to an issue but not necessarily directly considering the issue itself. Thus, for example:

- If there are concerns about the *capital structure and financial viability of the business,* investors need to pay close attention to votes in relation to dividends, share buybacks, share issuance, and scope for further debt burden.
- If there are concerns about the *effectiveness or diversity of the board*, they need to be reflected in voting decisions on director reelections (particularly in relation to the members of the nominations committee).
- Worries about the *independence or effectiveness of the audit process* should be taken into account when voting on the reappointment of the auditor, its pay, and the reappointment of members of the audit committee.

Given the level of attention on executive pay, it is perhaps not surprising that investors take a close interest in resolutions on remuneration. In many markets, there are both non-binding annual resolutions to approve pay in the year and binding votes on forward-looking policies and any new pay schemes. These are in addition to votes on the appointment of the members of the remuneration committee.

Investors will also often reflect concerns about financial or sustainability reporting in their votes on approving the report and accounts. In most markets, this resolution is symbolic, but the message sent by voting against it can still be significant. It is important to remember that even though most resolutions are seen as purely *G* issues (e.g., the approval of the accounts and the dividend, the election of directors, related-party transactions, appointment of the auditor, and such capital structure decisions as share issuance and buyback authorities), there is no reason why investor decisions on such resolutions should be driven solely by *G* considerations.

This notion can be seen, for example, in the recent debate about the incorporation of climate change issues into the financial accounts (the financial statements in the back of the annual report, rather than the narrative reporting in the front half). In September 2020, investor groups representing more than US$100 trillion in assets published an open letter calling for companies to follow International Accounting Standards Board (IASB) guidance and incorporate material climate change issues into their financials, fully disclosing their relevant assumptions (see the 2020 PRI report *Accounting for Climate Change* (PRI 2020)). The investor groups also asked that auditors play their part in ensuring this delivery and indicated their preference that the assumptions used should be compatible with the goals of the Paris Agreement. A number of investors are considering how they might vote in response to any failures to live up to this call from investors. Some are voting against reports and accounts where it is not clear that climate change has been incorporated or where the assumptions are not disclosed. Some are voting against auditors of heavily climate-exposed companies that do not include climate issues among the key matters in their auditor reports. And others are voting against key board directors of companies that do not show sufficient signs of climate awareness where they have significant risk exposures.

Any vote will rarely be meaningful in itself, because there may be a range of reasons why an investor might vote a particular way, as seen in the discussion of the votes at Royal Dutch Shell at the start of this chapter. Institutions therefore usually have active programs to communicate to companies, either in writing or in dialogue, why they have voted in particular ways. Many seek to have active discussions with companies as they work toward their voting decisions (helping them tailor decisions to companies' particular circumstances) and use those discussions as an opportunity to explain the thought process that lies behind any decision making. This dialogue is a form of low-level engagement, but it will only ever have limited impacts.

Even though institutional investors mostly do not physically attend shareholder meetings, perhaps stewards should give this opportunity more active consideration. Particularly at mid-size and smaller companies, attendance at AGMs can be negligible, and so an investor can gain unusually direct access to many directors at one time, with much scope for informal dialogue. Furthermore, because the full board typically attends most AGMs, these meetings can offer investors rare insight into board dynamics and the nature of relationships within the boardroom. Shareholder meetings usually offer opportunities for formal questioning of many board members (typically any committee chair, as well as the board chair and executive directors, will respond directly to questions; in some circumstances, the audit partner is also in attendance and may answer relevant questions, which should increase if the recommendations of the Brydon Review in this area are followed), and this formal questioning can provide scope for both insight and influence. But many will find that the informal insights gained from actually participating in general meetings are equally valuable.

Escalation of engagement

Voting against particular resolutions (notably the approval of the report and accounts, the discharge of directors, or the appointment of individual directors) is often seen as an escalation tool to reinforce engagement messaging. But there are many other ways to escalate. The Hong Kong Principles set out a list of potential escalatory actions (largely based on the list set out in the former UK Code). While the first three actions might be seen by many engagement professionals as part of a standard set of tools in normal dialogues with companies, the last four will certainly be recognized as forms of escalation:

1. holding additional meetings with management specifically to discuss concerns;
2. expressing concerns through the company's advisers;
3. meeting with the chair or other board members;
4. collaborating with other investors on particular issues;
5. making a public statement in advance of general meetings;
6. submitting resolutions and speaking at general meetings; and
7. requisitioning a general meeting and, in some cases, proposing to change board membership.

Additional methods used by some as part of their escalation models might include the following:

- writing a formal letter setting out concerns, usually following one of the previously mentioned meetings and typically to the chair; such letters are usually private but may occasionally be leaked publicly if frustrations worsen (sometimes leaks come from individuals within the company who are frustrated by a lack of progress);
- seeking dialogue with other stakeholders, including regulators, banks, creditors, customers, suppliers, the workforce, and non-governmental organizations (stakeholder dialogue is most typically a tool in European markets and is specifically noted as important in the Shareholder Rights Directive II, but it is increasingly being used elsewhere as well);

- formally requesting a special audit of the company (a right of shareholders in certain countries, most notably Germany, to consider particular areas of concern);
- taking concerns public in the media or in some other form, not only (as the principles state) at AGMs or other general meetings;
- seeking governance improvements and/or damages through litigation, other legal remedies, or arbitration; and
- formally adding the company to an exclusion list or otherwise exiting or threatening to exit the investment, though this action will amount to engagement only if it is accompanied in some way by communication with the company (as further discussed below).

The idea of escalation is that it is a ladder of additional steps to raise the stakes in an engagement. Many engagement objectives can be managed without any escalation, and investors may choose to move slower in an engagement rather than escalate to maintain positive relations with a company they wish to remain invested in for many years. But where escalation is seen as necessary, the investor must consider what additional steps might be needed to generate the change that is sought. This consideration may go through a number of stages so that the escalation goes up the ladder step by step, or it may jump up several steps at once if change is felt to be especially urgent. There is no particular ordering of the steps, although some steps are clearly more significant than others.

Given resource constraints, an investor must always be prepared to take the view that little further progress can be made at any given time and so an engagement should be paused. The investor will also need to consider whether the steps are warranted by the objective; on occasion, the right thing to do may be to withdraw and step away from the objective for a time. Typically, this action is done by a formal letter setting out the investor's concerns, which can be referred to in future years when the board may be different or in different circumstances and thus may be more responsive to engagement.

Many escalation tools need to be used wisely and not overexploited. For example, litigation must be used rarely, not least because of the expense and the staff time taken up with any legal case. The step of taking concerns public through social or other media needs to be applied with care, because investors who rarely raise issues in public are more likely to be listened to when they do than investors who are always expressing their views publicly. But often, moving an engagement from the private sphere to the public is seen as one of the most important ways to bolster influence.

One form of public engagement is putting forward a shareholder resolution—a shareholder right in most jurisdictions, although local law often restricts the nature of the resolution that can be proposed, as well as the size and period of shareholding that the proponents of the resolution must represent in order to hold the right. In many jurisdictions, the proposal of a resolution must be made public by the company; but in the United States, where they are most common, they do not typically enter the public domain until the proceedings of the relevant AGM are published. Normally, this will be after the company has tried to exclude the resolution from the AGM agenda and sought a ruling from the US Securities and Exchange Commission (SEC) as to whether this exclusion is permitted. As of the 2022 voting season, the SEC has been less restrictive, allowing significantly more shareholder proposals to appear on AGM agendas for shareholder consideration. Because of this monthslong process, proposing a shareholder resolution in the United States can be the trigger for private engagement, which may reach a sufficiently satisfactory conclusion for the investor to withdraw the resolution, thus keeping it out of the public sphere.

Collective engagement is sometimes seen as an alternative model of engagement, but we will treat it in this chapter as another form—often the most powerful form—of escalation. It is discussed in further detail in the next section.

Perhaps counterintuitively, one form of escalation that is considered by many institutions is divestment. Divestment can escalate influence only when it is done through a formal process so that the company is aware that it is approaching the point where the investor may feel obliged to sell its shares. An example of a public and influential divestment process is the one followed by the Norwegian Government Pension Fund Global. There, an independent ethics council considers whether companies should be excluded from the fund because of business activities (such as the production of indiscriminate weaponry or thermal coal) or because of breaches of behavioral norms (the UN Global Compact standards).

For example, in recent years the ethics council has recommended divestments based on a criterion adopted in 2016: behavior that leads to unacceptable carbon emission levels, including an assessment of companies' willingness and ability to change such behavior in the future. The manager running the fund (Norges Bank Investment Management, or NBIM) considers these recommendations and can exclude companies on these grounds. It has, for example, excluded four companies involved in oil sands production.

NBIM makes the full list of its exclusions public and also publicizes its decisions to exclude individual companies (as well as its occasional decisions to reverse an exclusion). This publicity forms part of an escalation process with the company in question and has a potential influence on other companies. The NBIM exclusion list is observed by a number of other investors, and some of its exclusions are adopted by others. (NBIM 2021)

Collective engagement

Collective engagement can be a very powerful tool, as building significant influence at targeted companies makes it harder for the investor perspective to be ignored. Some coalitions of investors are very large indeed. Collective engagement may be done informally, through quiet and non-specific dialogue between individual fund managers' stewardship teams, while taking care to avoid reaching agreements or even sharing concrete plans because of the constraints on acting in concert and other regulations. In addition to these informal dialogues, there are also active collective engagement vehicles of various sorts.

Collective engagement is often the most resource-efficient method of engagement; every investor is inevitably resource constrained, and pooling those limited resources should enable greater efficiency. Such efficiency also benefits the company by reducing the range of messages it receives, which in some cases can feel like a broad spectrum of conflicting opinions that are difficult to make much sense of. The pooling of resources by investors can aid their own education about an issue and also add weight and emphasis to their concerns, which may mean they are more likely to be heard.

The challenges around collective engagement are perhaps the obvious ones of coordinating a potentially disparate group of investors and trying to maintain a reasonably consistent perspective so that the company receives a clear message from its investors in key areas. A number of investors are also concerned about the rules in particular markets around anti-competitive behavior or activities that abuse or exploit the market (such as rules dealing with acting in concert, where a number of separate investors work together to use their holdings as a single bloc). Some market regulators have made clear that there is a safe harbor for institutional engagement, but such safe harbors do not exist everywhere and none have been tested robustly. Thus, unless they are careful, such investors may be seen to be acting in concert and could potentially face serious regulatory consequences, the most significant being a possible need to launch a takeover bid for the company. Hence, collective engagement must be approached with due care.

The behavioral challenges involved in being part of an investor coalition are significant. These include the challenges of reaching consensus, conflicts of interest, and competition.

Investors will often agree that there is a problem at a company or at least that they share concerns about a company. But discussions about collective action often fail because the investors are unable to reach a consensus about what might need to change at the company to address the problem. Having said that, agreement is not always possible between investors even on the nature of the problem. Companies sometimes rightly feel that they receive such a wide range of views from investors that responding to them all is impossible (although some investors often believe this is an excuse rather than a reason for inaction).

A number of asset owner organizations globally support their members in their stewardship work, such as the following:

- the Asian Corporate Governance Association (ACGA);
- Associação de Investidores no Mercado de Capitais (AMEC) in Brazil;
- Assogestioni in Italy;
- the Australian Council of Superannuation Investors (ACSI);
- the Council of Institutional Investors (CII) in the United States; and
- Eumedion in the Netherlands.

Most of these organizations have a much broader remit, with stewardship being just one element of their offerings.

In addition, investor coalitions covering ESG have been created recently, with environmental issues in particular rallying investors. Among these is Climate Action 100+ (CA 100+). There are other climate change groups, including the Asia Investor Group on Climate Change (AIGCC); the Investor Group on Climate Change (IGCC), a collaboration between Australian and New Zealand institutional investors; Europe's Institutional Investor Group on Climate Change (IIGCC); and Ceres, which coordinates US investor efforts in this area. Each of these groups has a regional remit, but all of them now seek to coordinate their actions. Although they have largely focused on lobbying and playing an effective role in the political debates on climate, they are increasingly developing company engagement, not least by performing a coordinating role on CA 100+.

CA 100+ targets the most polluting companies, appointing one institution as the lead engager and a number of small groups of institutions to work alongside it. In theory, there is a common approach and agenda, but the coordination is flexible and the lead engager is invited to respond to the specific circumstances of each company, so there can be a good deal of inconsistency between the engagements. As of June 2023, 166 companies have engaged under the banner of CA 100+, with typically two or three investors leading each engagement and a group of peers lending their support. An official benchmarking of each company's climate approach is compared with the goals of the Paris Agreement, involving 10 elements that include: whether the company has a net zero greenhouse gas emissions ambition of 2050 or sooner; short-, medium-, and long-term targets on the way to such an ambition; and whether its capital expenditure plans fit with an appropriate decarbonizing pathway.

In theory, these benchmarking elements help frame and shape every collective engagement. Nonetheless, some engagements are advancing with more vigor than others (much depends on the quality of the engagement approach of the lead engagers). While CA 100+ has had some notable successes—perhaps most clearly in relation to strategic changes by the European oil majors, such as Spain's Repsol, France's Total, Italy's ENI, UK's BP, and Shell—this progress is not universal, and all its successes are being challenged by the new context for the oil sector set by Russia's invasion of Ukraine.

PRI also has its own collective engagement service: the Collaboration Platform. Its main focus is on company engagements, occasionally targeting just a single company but more frequently identifying an issue that a number of companies face and proposing a collective approach to engaging with those companies. Usually, a single investor raises an issue on the platform and invites other PRI members to participate in the proposed engagement; typically, the engagement is then led by a small working group of investors. According to PRI's statistics, more than 2,500 groups and more than 600 engagements have used the Collaboration Platform, targeting 24,667 companies with the involvement of over 2,000 signatories.

> ### CASE STUDIES
>
> #### Slave Labor and Rainforest Charcoal in the Brazilian Pig Iron Supply Chain
>
> An early example of PRI's Collaboration Platform in action is its collective engagement regarding the use of slave labor and rainforest wood charcoal in the Brazilian pig iron supply chain, an important source of raw materials for many iron and steel producers and consumers, particularly in North America. This collaboration was formed in 2006–2007 following a *Bloomberg* cover story, "The Secret World of Modern Slavery." (Smith 2007)
>
> The collaboration identified several companies whose supply chains were affected by this issue, among them the US steel producer Nucor. The US ethical investment house Domini Social Investments performed the leadership role in the investor coalition in relation to Nucor, writing to the company in April 2007 in a letter co-signed by 10 investors from around the world. Nucor's response was inadequate in the view of the investors, and Domini and another group of (predominantly US) investors co-filed shareholder resolutions at the company on the issue at the end of 2008, 2009, and 2010.
>
> The company continued to make a weak response, leading to a 2009 shareholder resolution winning support from some 27% of shareholders voting on the issue. This set the scene for more constructive discussions in relation to the 2010 shareholder resolution. In the end, Nucor and Domini announced an agreement that led Domini to withdraw the shareholder resolution for that year. Nucor agreed to work with two key NGO initiatives in Brazil: the National Pact for the Eradication of Slave Labor and the Citizens Charcoal Institute (ICC). Specifically, it would require all its top-tier Brazilian pig iron suppliers either to join the ICC or to endorse and commit to the National Pact. Nucor also agreed to provide funding to ICC to give it the resources needed to be truly effective, and to report annually on its delivery around commitments to appropriate behavior in its supply chain.
>
> Domini later published this story, "Fighting Slavery in Brazil: Strengthening Local Solutions." (Kanzer 2011)

Formal collective stewardship vehicles take different forms. There are the commercial approaches, predominantly offered by fund managers that also offer stewardship overlay services, advancing engagement work on behalf of clients whether they invest money on the clients' behalf or not. Some of the main players in the overlay market are Columbia Threadneedle Investments' Responsible Engagement Overlay (REO) Service, Federated Hermes EOS, Robeco, and Sustainalytics (which bought the former GES International in 2019 and is now part of Morningstar).

These operations cover both voting advice and direct engagement activities. There are also non-commercial operations offering collaborative vehicles to members. Prominent among these is the UK's Investor Forum (www.investorforum.org.uk), created in 2014 as a response to the Kay Review call for such a vehicle. The Forum is being watched closely in other markets as a potential model to follow.

The Investor Forum has a detailed collective engagement framework (available in full only to its members), through which its engagements avoid running afoul of the rules on acting in concert and market abuse. Many investors see such market abuse rules as limiting their ability to carry out collective engagement effectively.

The formal structure that the Forum has developed—and its apparent effectiveness in engagement (e.g., Unilever's retreat from its plan to shift its headquarters in 2018) (Mooney 2018)—has led to international interest in the Forum as a model for other markets (e.g., in a November 2019 report, France's Club des Juristes proposed that France seek to create a similar organization). (Club des Juristes 2019)

In particular, the collective engagement framework is seen as a key mechanism to mitigate the risks that sometimes impede collective engagement; that is, the regulatory rules against seeking control of public companies except through formal takeover bids or market abuse and insider trading constraints.

ENGAGEMENT ACROSS DIFFERENT ASSET CLASSES

6.1.7 describe approaches of engagement across a range of asset classes

Although most stewardship codes assert that they are intended to apply to all asset classes, their language and approach seem very much based in the world of public equity investment. This chapter has reflected that tendency of thinking first of public equity investment, but its application is much broader. That is because the codes (and this chapter) are written in terms of principles, which can be applied with good sense and intelligence across the full range of asset classes. Many investment structures involve businesses investing in assets that in some ways look like public companies, with the immediate responsibility for managing direct property or infrastructure assets within their own boards and where directors and investors can engage. With private equity and other fund investment structures (including indirect property or infrastructure investments), investors usually interface with the fund management organization rather than the underlying assets. However, the sense of accountability and the need for alignment arise just as much in these relationships as they do in any corporate governance structure. The concepts of engagement need to be applied in a different way to respond to the circumstances and the levers of influence that are available. Because engagement is usually about influence rather than control, investors should have some scope for engagement success regardless of which formal structure they use.

Usually in these latter, more indirect investment structures, the engagement issues are related to policies and approaches regarding ESG issues rather than specific individual asset concerns. But if a concern about an individual asset demonstrates that policy approaches may not be what the investor expects, the engagement can be very specific indeed. An interesting case study on this matter is the exclusion from private equity holdings of gun manufacturers and retailers by a number of asset owners, most notably CalSTRS (the California teachers' pension scheme, which was responding in particular to the number of shootings on US school premises). For example, Cerberus enabled its investors, including CalSTRS, to exit underlying holdings in retailer Remington Outdoor in 2015.

Although, in these cases, investors will not generally have a vote and cannot formally sanction the parties, the sanction of selling a position or being unwilling to invest in future opportunities remains. That is clearly a powerful sanction in most circumstances (especially if the asset owner is a large one) and is certainly enough for the investor's counterparty to pay attention to concerns that are raised.

Corporate Fixed Income

Though fixed-income investors may ultimately be concerned with the likelihood of default, ESG factors can affect both credit ratings and spreads, leading to short-term changes in value. Companies that regularly raise capital in fixed-income markets are becoming more conscious of investors' interest in ESG as a material factor in their pricing of debt.

ESG engagement is also important for private debt, private equity, and property and infrastructure investments. These relatively long-term investments are often illiquid and involve a close partnership between investor and investee. As a consequence, there is both motive and opportunity for ESG engagement.

In relation to fixed income, PRI's guide *ESG Engagement for Fixed Income Investors: Managing Risks, Enhancing Returns* recommends that investors prioritize engagement based on the following (PRI 2018b):

- the size of a holding in the portfolio;
- issuers with lower credit quality (with less balance sheet flexibility to absorb negative ESG impacts);
- key themes that are material to sectors; and
- issuers with low ESG scores.

The greatest opportunity to push for conditions and disclosures around ESG is likely to be prior to the issuance of a particular tranche of debt. When a company needs investors to provide funds, it is more likely to be receptive to their views. In recent years, markets have been very favorable for issuers. However, in periods of rising interest rates, when money is no longer so freely available, investors will have greater leverage and should use it under those conditions. It is likely to be easier to exert influence in private debt issues, as the supply of funds is still less crowded in such markets, but investors should also be working to influence issuers in the public market.

The investor's interaction with corporate debt issuers is most commonly with their corporate treasury departments rather than more senior officials. In most cases, the parties dialogue about strategy, risk, financial structure (especially where the proposed debt sits in the debt hierarchy), and the covenants and protections for debt investors. Increasingly, however, dialogue about risk encompasses ESG matters, and debt investors are finding they can have some influence on the approach of fixed-income issuers. This scope for influence is particularly clear where debt investors engage alongside equity investors (or where investment firms bring together their engagement approaches in relation to investments in a single issuer, regardless of the asset class exposure and the portfolio in which it is held). There are instances where equity and debt investors are direct rivals over issues; for example, in the case of some transactions or capital structurings or in the case of the company nearing insolvency. In almost all cases relating to ESG matters at companies that are going concerns, however, the interests of long-term investors (whether they are exposed to equity or debt) very much align, and it will benefit all if the corporation deals effectively with an ESG concern. This overlapping of interests is shown thematically in the Venn diagram below—interests are very similar at investment-grade debt issuers and differ as the issuers become more speculative. At the point of default, there is no overlap in interests at all, and equity holders and debt investors are rivals simply trying to minimize their losses.

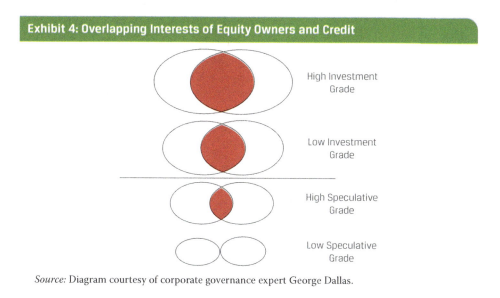

Source: Diagram courtesy of corporate governance expert George Dallas.

Sovereign Debt

Stewardship interaction with sovereign debt issuers is likely to be much more limited. Only the largest investors are likely to have any scope to influence the stance of nation-states, and even then, the influence may be minimal. Therefore, the ESG approach usually applied in this asset class is screening or an ESG tilt in the investment process rather than engagement.

Having said that, there are early signs of steps to advance investor activity in this area. In 2020, PRI produced a guide for those seeking to engage with sovereign issuers. This guide makes clear the fledgling nature of engagement in this area and focuses on learning how engagement might happen rather than on highlighting successful case studies. There is a particular focus on educating sovereign issuers about the value of green bonds and the strong market appetite for such instruments. A further area for engagement with countries is the protections they have in place for the rule of law—given how fundamental it is as a foundation for future economic growth and fair treatment of all citizens—as discussed in a recent paper from the Bingham Centre for the Rule of Law (2022).

The leading case study on sovereign debt engagement, as reported in the *Financial Times*, is the work by a group of 29 investors with assets of around US$3.7 trillion to encourage the Brazilian government to do more to limit the destruction of the Amazon rainforest. Having also had contact through the Brazilian embassies in their home nations, the group wrote to the government in June 2020, noting, among other things, that "Brazilian sovereign bonds are also likely to be deemed high risk if deforestation continues." At least some of the group are reported to be considering divesting existing holdings and excluding Brazilian debt from their sovereign portfolios to reflect these concerns. Sadly, it is unclear whether this effort has had any positive influence, as other reports suggest that Amazon rainforest destruction accelerated through 2020, reaching a 12-year high; happily, this troubling trend may be reversed under Brazilian president Lula da Silva. (Harris 2020)

Private Equity

With private equity investments, direct ESG engagement will be undertaken by the general partner (GP, the private equity house) rather than the limited partner (LP, the asset owner), although individual LPs may wish to engage with their GPs on the ways in which they are monitoring and acting on ESG issues across their portfolios. As the PRI report *ESG Monitoring, Reporting and Dialogue in Private Equity* points out:

> *The process of portfolio monitoring has value protection and enhancement potential in itself, as a systematic approach for identifying material ESG issues, setting objectives, and regularly tracking progress. It enables GPs: to identify anomalies and achievements; support regular engagement with the portfolio company on these issues; and strengthen company reporting practices that could have implications at exit. (PRI 2018c)*

Given that private equity provides a form of share ownership, the logic of extending the principles of stewardship codes to such investments may seem more natural. That's especially true when the companies are early stage and the investor has greater influence. The poor quality of the governance of a number of companies coming through the private equity system—for example, the very public failure of WeWork's initial public offering (discussed briefly in Chapter 5) was, in significant part, caused by poor corporate governance—suggests that often, less effective ESG is instilled in private equity companies than ought to be the case given the levers that private equity investors hold.

Infrastructure

Infrastructure investors are exposed to ESG across the economic lifetime of their assets. These exposures extend beyond issues related directly to a specific asset, such as health and safety, supply chains, and environment, to such factors as climate change, bribery and corruption, and the social license to operate. In applying Principle 2, PRI recommends that investors consider eight potential mechanisms to act as engaged owners in infrastructure:

1. Use ESG assessments undertaken during due diligence to prioritize attention to ESG considerations and potential for improving profitability, efficiency, and risk management.
2. Include material ESG risks and opportunities identified during due diligence in the post-acquisition plan of each asset or project company and integrate them into asset management activities.
3. Engage with and encourage the management of the business to act on the identified ESG risks and opportunities using the mechanisms available.
4. Define and communicate the expectations of ESG operations and maintenance performance to the infrastructure business managers.
5. Ensure that ESG factors identified as material during due diligence are explicitly woven into asset-level policies.
6. Advocate a governance framework that clearly articulates who has responsibility for ESG and sustainability.
7. Set performance targets for preserving or improving environmental and social impact, including regular reports to the board and investors.
8. Where possible, make ESG information and expertise available to the asset or project company to help it develop capacity.

As with private equity and property, many investors in infrastructure will work with specialist managers. In these situations, the investor's responsibility is to monitor and engage with the manager. AustralianSuper, one of Australia's largest pension schemes, has been investing in infrastructure since 1994. In a 2012 case study for PRI, AustralianSuper reported that one of its infrastructure managers had used detailed questionnaires based on the Global Reporting Initiative to analyze the impact of ESG issues for each of its 28 existing assets (PRI 2012). This analysis and benchmarking across the assets enabled the fund manager to

- improve the governance at each of the boards on which it sits;
- arrange for four Australian airports to work together to develop market best practice health and safety processes based on practices from each of the airports; and
- measure the electricity and water usage and carbon emissions of each of its assets on a regular basis, enabling the identification of energy savings for many assets.

Property

As with fixed income, there is good evidence of the positive effect of ESG on returns to real estate investments. Friede, Busch, and Bassen (2015) determined that 57% of equity studies showed a positive effect, although the positive share for bond studies was 64%, rising to 71% for real estate.

A 2014 INREV study indicated that there was a 2.8% difference in return spread between the top 10% and the bottom 10% of Global Real Estate Sustainability Benchmark (GRESB) rated properties (INREV 2014). Regulatory changes are also driving a need for greater engagement in relation to ESG in real estate.

Investors should engage indirectly by requiring their managers to report on the frameworks and metrics they use to monitor holdings. Given the significance of property as a driver of climate change (in both the construction and the operating phases), this area will be a particular focus of most investors. Property is also exposed to the physical impacts of climate change, which contributes to stranded asset risk. In addition, the UNEP Finance Initiative and others recommend that real estate investment stakeholders:

- engage, directly or indirectly, on public policy to manage risks;
- support research on ESG and climate risks; and
- support sector initiatives to develop resources to understand risks and integrate ESG.

Fund Investments

For funds of funds as an asset class, engagement with fund vehicles, covering any underlying asset class, sometimes becomes a little more complex. However, there is typically a fund board, which should represent investor interests and can be subject to engagement. Investors are often distanced from the underlying assets, but the role then is to hold to account the managers of the fund for their own investment and stewardship efforts. Closing the agency gap in these sorts of vehicles can be harder and take more effort, but so long as the investor keeps that in mind, there is certainly a role for engagement to play.

8 KEY FACTS

1. Stewardship is active, responsible ownership of companies or other assets on behalf of a long-term owner; it is a reflection of the investor's fiduciary duty to its clients and beneficiaries.

2. Engagement is active dialogue with companies for a particular purpose. Typically, it covers one or more ESG matters.

3. Voting at shareholder meetings is one element of stewardship. Often it is the most public, so it gains external attention, but it is nevertheless a limited element with limited influence on its own. Few investors attend company general meetings but could benefit from the insights and influence that come from doing so.

4. There is strong evidence that engagement, if carried out well, can positively influence corporate behavior and that the changes made can deliver long-term value.

5. Many markets have stewardship codes in place, and growing numbers are developing such codes; increasingly, these are codes with regulatory backing.

6. Generally, engagement is most successful if carried out positively and consensually, recognizing that the changes sought are in the company's interest, not in the investor's self-interest.

7. Yet sometimes engagement must be escalated in order to be effective. This can be done through a range of mechanisms, including making concerns publicly known, proposing shareholder resolutions, or working collectively with other shareholders.

8. One of the most significant constraints on investors delivering effective stewardship and engagement is inadequate resources—particularly where the investor has broad investment portfolios. Finding responses to these resource constraints is currently a major challenge, and among the answers being found are:
    - hiring new workers;
    - prioritizing with care;
    - expecting more ESG delivery from mainstream fund management teams; and
    - using collective and collaborative engagement resources.

9. Some forms of engagement start bottom-up by focusing on the specific issues faced by an individual company, while others operate top-down by applying a perspective on particular issues (e.g., climate change) across all companies in a sector or market. Typically, the approach is linked to the investor's investment approach.

10. The most effective engagement starts with clarity about the engagement objective and how delivery against that objective will be measured over time. Greater clarity in these areas will be required by the focus on outcomes in the new UK Stewardship Code and, increasingly, by clients. Engagement success often takes years to deliver in full.

11. Collective engagement is a key route to maximizing the effectiveness of limited resources, but investors must beware of regulatory constraints, such as rules against acting in concert.
12. Engagement can be carried out across the full range of investment asset classes. The principles and mindset of engagement and stewardship need to be applied with good sense and judgment to the different circumstances and the levers that the investor controls.

FURTHER READING

- Australian Council of Superannuation Investors (ACSI). 2018. *Australian Asset Owner Stewardship Code.* Available at: https://acsi.org.au/members/australian-asset-owner-stewardship-code.
- Bingham Centre for the Rule of Law. 2022. *The Rule of Law and Investor Approaches to ESG: Discussion Paper.* Available at: https://binghamcentre.biicl.org/publications/the-rule-of-law-and-investor-approaches-to-esg-discussion-paper.
- Financial Reporting Council. 2020. *UK Stewardship Code.* Available at: www.frc.org.uk/investors/uk-stewardship-code.
- International Corporate Governance Network (ICGN). 2016. *ICGN Global Stewardship Principles.* Available at: https://www.icgn.org/icgn-global-stewardship-principles.
- Investor Forum. 2019. "Defining Stewardship and Engagement." Available at: www.investorforum.org.uk/wp-content/uploads/securepdfs/2019/04/Defining-Stewardship-Engagement-April-2019.pdf.
- Principles for Responsible Investment (PRI). 2014. *Integrating ESG in Private Equity: A Guide for General Partners.* Available at: www.unpri.org/download?ac=252.
- ———. 2018. *ESG Engagement for Fixed Income Investors: Managing Risks, Enhancing Returns.* Available at: www.unpri.org/download?ac=4449.
- US Department of Labor. 2018. *Field Assistance Bulletin No. 2018-01—Superseded by 85 FR 72846 and 85 FR 81658.* Available at: www.dol.gov/agencies/ebsa/employers-and-advisers/guidance/field-assistance-bulletins/2018-01.

REFERENCES

Becht, M., J. R. Franks, C. Mayer, S. Rossi. 2006. "Returns to Shareholder Activism: Evidence from a Clinical Study of the Hermes UK Focus Fund." ECGI Finance Working Paper No. 138/2006. Available at: https://ssrn.com/abstract=934712.

Bichta, C. 2018. Growing Water Risk Resilience: An Investor Guide on Agricultural Supply Chains (engagement case study). Available at: www.unpri.org/environmental-issues/long-term-engagement-on-water-risk-management-in-the-supplychain/2811.article.

Chow, C. 2018. *Siam Cement*. Available at: www.hermes-investment.com/uki/eos-insight/eos/siam-cement/.

Dimson, E., O. Karakaş, X. Li. 2015. "Active Ownership." Review of Financial Studies 28 (12): 3225–68. Available at https://ssrn.com/abstract=215472410.1093/rfs/hhv044

Investor Forum 2018. RE:view2018. Available at www.investorforum.org.uk/wp-content/uploads/2019/01/Annual_Review_2018.pdf

Investor Forum 2019. "Defining Stewardship and Engagement." Available at: www.investorforum.org.uk/wp-content/uploads/securepdfs/2019/04/Defining-Stewardship-Engagement-April-2019.pdf.

Hoepner, A. G. F., I. Oikonomou, Z. Sautner, L. Starks, X. Zhou. 2020. "ESG Shareholder Engagement and Downside Risk." ECGI Finance Working Paper No. 671/2020. Available at: https://ssrn.com/abstract=2874252.

AXA Investment Managers 2023. AXA IM Stewardship Report 2022. Available at: https://www.axa-im.com/document/5853/view.

Principles for Responsible Investment (PRI) 2018. How ESG Engagement Creates Value for Investors and Companies (executive summary). Available at: www.unpri.org/academic-research/how-esg-engagement-creates-value-for-investors-and-companies/3054.article.

Redington Ltd 2022. "It's Not Just a Numbers Game." Available at: https://redington.co.uk/publication/stewardship-code-reporting-analysis/.

Associação de Investidores no Mercado de Capitais (AMEC) 2016. AMEC Stewardship Code. Available at: https://amecbrasil.org.br/stewardship/amec-stewardship-code/?lang=en.

Australian Council of Superannuation Investors (ACSI) 2018. *Australian Asset Owner Stewardship Code*. Available at: https://acsi.org.au/members/australian-asset-owner-stewardship-code/.

Council of Experts on the Stewardship Code 2020. *Principles for Responsible Institutional Investors: Japan's Stewardship Code*. Available at: www.fsa.go.jp/en/refer/councils/stewardship/20200324/01.pdf.

CRISA Committee 2022. Second Code for Responsible Investing in South Africa, 2022. Available at: https://www.crisa2.co.za/crisa2code/.

European Fund and Asset Management Association (EFAMA) 2018. *EFAMA Stewardship Code*. Available at: www.efama.org/newsroom/news/efama-stewardship-code-principles-asset-managers-monitoring-voting-engagement.

Financial Reporting Council 2020. *UK Stewardship Code*. Available at: www.frc.org.uk/investors/uk-stewardship-code.

Financial Reporting Council Global Stewardship Codes Network. Available at: https://www.icgn.org/networks/global-stewardship-codes-network.

Hong Kong Securities and Futures Commission 2016. *Principles of Responsible Ownership*. Available at: https://www.sfc.hk/en/Rules-and-standards/Principles-of-responsible-ownership.

International Corporate Governance Network (ICGN) 2020. *ICGN Global Stewardship Principles*. Available at: https://www.icgn.org/icgn-global-stewardship-principles.

Investor Stewardship Group 2019. *The Stewardship Principles*. Available at: https://isgframework.org/stewardship-principles/.

References

Securities and Exchange Board of India (SEBI) 2019. *SEBI Stewardship Code*. Available at: https://www.sebi.gov.in/legal/circulars/dec-2019/stewardship-code-for-all-mutual-funds-and-all-categories-of-aifs-in-relation-to-their-investment-in-listed-equities_45451.html.

Stewardship Asia Centre 2022. *Singapore Stewardship Principles for Responsible Investors*. Available at: www.stewardshipasia.com.sg/enable/investors.

US Department of Labor 2018. Field Assistance Bulletin No. 2018-01—Superseded by 85 FR 72846 and 85 FR 81658. Available at: www.dol.gov/agencies/ebsa/employers-and-advisers/guidance/field-assistance-bulletins/2018-01.

Walker, David. 2009. *A Review of Corporate Governance in UK Banks and Other Financial Industry Entities: Final Recommendations*. Available at: https://webarchive.nationalarchives.gov.uk/+/www.hm-treasury.gov.uk/d/walker_review_261109.pdf.

BlackRock 2019. "Larry Fink's 2019 Letter to CEOs." Available at: https://www.blackrock.com/corporate/investor-relations/2019-larry-fink-ceo-letter.

Investor Forum 2019. "Collective Engagement: An Essential Stewardship Capability." Available at: www.investorforum.org.uk/wp-content/uploads/securepdfs/2019/11/The-case-for-collective-engagement-211119.pdf.

Principles for Responsible Investment (PRI) 2018a. How ESG Engagement Creates Value for Investors and Companies (executive summary). Available at: www.unpri.org/academic-research/how-esg-engagement-creates-value-for-investors-and-companies/3054.article.

Principles for Responsible Investment (PRI) 2018b. A Practical Guide to Active Ownership in Listed Equity (developing an active ownership policy). Available at: www.unpri.org/listed-equity/developing-an-active-ownership-policy-/2724.article.

Principles for Responsible Investment (PRI) 2020. Annual Report 2020. Available at: https://www.unpri.org/annual-report-2020.

Club des Juristes 2019. Activisme Actionnarial (*Shareholder Activism*). Available at: www.leclubdesjuristes.com/les-commissions/activisme-actionnarial/.

Kanzer, A. (Domini Social Investments). 2011. "Fighting Slavery in Brazil: Strengthening Local Solutions." In ICCR's Social Sustainability Resource Guide: Building Sustainable Communities through Multi-party Collaboration. Available at: www.iccr.org/sites/default/files/ICCRsBuildingSustainableCommunities.pdf.

Mooney, A. 14 October 2018. "Unilever U-turn Shows How Angry Shareholders Are Securing Change." Financial Times. Available at: www.ft.com/content/d7211dba-ce21-11e8-9fe5-24ad351828ab.

Norges Bank Investment Management (NBIM) 2021. *Observation and Exclusion of Companies*. Available at: www.nbim.no/en/the-fund/responsible-investment/exclusion-of-companies/.

Principles for Responsible Investment (PRI) 2020. *Accounting for Climate Change*. Available at: www.unpri.org/sustainability-issues/accounting-for-climate-change.

Smith, M. 14 March 2007. "The Secret World of Modern Slavery." *Bloomberg*.

Bingham Centre for the Rule of Law 2022. *The Rule of Law and Investor Approaches to ESG: Discussion Paper*. Available at: https://binghamcentre.biicl.org/publications/the-rule-of-law-and-investor-approaches-to-esg-discussion-paper.

Friede, G., T. Busch, A. Bassen. 2015. "ESG and Financial Performance: Aggregated Evidence from More Than 2,000 Empirical Studies." Journal of Sustainable Finance & Investment5 (4): 210–33. Available at https://papers.ssrn.com/sol3/papers.cfm?abstract_id=269961010.1080/20430795.2015.1118917

GRESB 2021. "In Plain English: GRESB." Available at: https://www.gresb.com/nl-en/in-plain-english-gresb/.

Harris, B. 23 June 2020. "Investors Warn Brazil to Stop Amazon Destruction." *Financial Times*. Available at: www.ft.com/content/ad1d7176-ce6c-4a9b-9bbc-cbdb6691084f.

INREV 2014. *Transparency and Performance of the European Non-listed Real Estate Fund Market*. Available at: www.inrev.org/library/transparency-and-performance-european-non-listed-real-estate-fund-market.

Principles for Responsible Investment (PRI) 2012. *ESG and the Long-Term Ownership of Infrastructure Assets*. Available at: www.unpri.org/infrastructure/esg-and-the-long-term-ownership-of-infrastructure-assets/129.article.

PRI 2018a. *Applying Principle 2*. Available at: www.unpri.org/infrastructure/applying-principle-2-to-infrastructure-investing/2706.article.

PRI 2018b. *ESG Engagement for Fixed Income Investors: Managing Risks, Enhancing Returns*. Available at: www.unpri.org/download?ac=4449.

PRI 2018c. *ESG Monitoring, Reporting and Dialogue in Private Equity*. Available at: www.unpri.org/download?ac=4839.

PRI 2020. *ESG Engagement for Sovereign Debt Investors*. Available at: www.unpri.org/download?ac=12018.

UNEP Finance Initiative et al 2016. *Sustainable Real Estate Investment: Implementing the Paris Climate Agreement: An Action Framework*. Available at: www.unepfi.org/fileadmin/property/SustainableREI_DirectInvestment.pdf.

PRACTICE PROBLEMS

1. An investee company implemented an innovative methodology for tracking GHG emissions. An investor wants to understand how the methodology can lower GHG emissions for the investee. To accomplish this, the investor is most likely to engage in value-creating:

   a. political dynamics.
   b. learning dynamics.
   c. communicative dynamics.

2. Successful investor engagement tends to have the *most* positive impact:

   a. on abnormal financial returns.
   b. on changes to remuneration policies.
   c. within six months of the initial engagement contact.

3. In private equity investments, the limited partners are *most likely* to:

   a. fall outside the scope of principles of stewardship codes.
   b. initiate direct ESG engagement with the investee company.
   c. engage with the general partner, who monitors and acts on ESG issues across the portfolios.

4. The most significant change in the 2020 version of the UK Stewardship Code is the:

   a. increased emphasis on clear, robust policy statements.
   b. addition of a principle requiring management of conflicts of interest.
   c. requirement to report on the practical effects of engagement actions.

5. Collective engagement activities are *most likely* to be controversial when they:

   a. result in the creation of concert parties.
   b. are outsourced to specialist stewardship providers.
   c. are carried out through platforms such as the UK Investor Forum.

6. Which form of collaborative engagement is *most likely* to require greater formality in approach?

   a. Group meetings with the company
   b. Collaborative letter-writing campaigns
   c. Soliciting broader support for a shareholder resolution

7. Which of the following activities is *most likely* associated with the early stages of a successful engagement action?

   a. Ensuring that there is media interest
   b. Registering to speak at an annual general meeting
   c. Engaging in site visits to understand the company culture

8. A fund management entity that advances clients' engagement activities even if not investing the clients' funds is *best* described as:

   a. a proxy firm.
   b. an overlay service provider.
   c. an ESG investment consultant.

9. A portfolio has equal holdings of the following investments:

	Credit Rating	ESG Score (1 is low, 10 is high)
Bond 1	BBB+	2
Bond 2	AA–	8
Bond 3	AAA–	2

According to PRI's guide *ESG Engagement for Fixed Income Investors*, which investment is *most likely* to be the highest priority for engagement?

a. Bond 1
b. Bond 2
c. Bond 3

10. The opportunity for fixed-income investors to engage on ESG issues is *greatest* with:

a. public debt.
b. private debt.
c. sovereign debt.

11. One of the largest global investment firms holds US$1.5 trillion in AUM in over 400 actively managed mutual funds. One of the *most* challenging aspects of successful engagement with the investees is:

a. hiring external stewardship services.
b. resource constraints within the investment firm.
c. finding other asset managers to share the concerns regarding the individual investees.

12. The *best* way to assess an investor's engagement success is to consider:

a. the impact the engagement had on the investee's stock price.
b. the improvements in the investee's corporate governance policies and practices.
c. the outcome of the investor's engagement actions against engagement objectives related to the investee.

13. Which of the following is *most* accurate about stewardship in investments? Stewardship is exercised:

a. via voting and engagement.
b. by a company's stakeholders.
c. via short-term investor activism.

14. An asset manager engages with an investee company with the objective of increasing its board's gender diversity. During the engagement, two of the non-independent male board members expressed concerns regarding a forced restructuring of the board and resigned. They were replaced with two independent male members with superior skill sets. Does this outcome represent a successful form of engagement for the asset manager?

a. No
b. Yes, because the new board members are independent
c. Yes, because the new board members have superior skill sets

Practice Problems

15. According to records in the Active Ownership study, successful ESG engagement generated, on average, abnormal financial returns of approximately:
    a. 7% in the year after the initial engagement.
    b. 9% in the year after the initial engagement.
    c. 10% in the year after the initial engagement.

16. Unlike stewardship delivered through engagement, stewardship delivered through monitoring is *most likely* to:
    a. inform incremental investment decisions.
    b. seek two-way communication between investors and investees.
    c. avoid a dialogue with the investee companies to maintain the objectivity of the investor.

17. An investor with a history of governance-led engagement is *most likely* to start engagement with a company by entering into a dialogue with the:
    a. board of directors.
    b. investor relations team.
    c. senior management.

18. Which of the following forms of engagement is *most likely* to have clear engagement objectives regarding an investee company?
    a. The annual letter issued by a fund manager
    b. Informal discussions with an investee's senior management
    c. A coalition of investors established for environmental research purposes

19. Which of the following stewardship codes includes a principle stating that asset owners are encouraged to align the operation of the market-wide financial system with the long-term interests of investors?
    a. Singapore Stewardship Principles
    b. Australian Asset Owner Stewardship Code
    c. European Fund and Asset Management Association Stewardship Code

20. Which of the following forms of engagement is *most likely* seen by engagement professionals as normal engagement dialogue with companies?
    a. Requesting a general meeting
    b. Expressing concerns through the investee's advisers
    c. Making public statements in advance of general meetings

21. Investors engage in monitoring their investees to:
    a. direct investees toward adopting improved ESG practices.
    b. understand performance and business opportunities for the investees.
    c. express their position on key issues and concerns related to the investees.

22. Which of the following is *not* among the seven areas typically covered by the top-level principles of a stewardship code?
    a. Engagement and escalation
    b. Reporting and transparency
    c. Stock lending (or securities lending) policies

23. Which principle is frequently neglected in regulatory codes developed by inves-

tor groups?

   a. Voting
   b. Conflicts of interest
   c. Reporting and transparency

24. Which of the following is *not* one of the prioritization decisions that an investor must make in relation to stewardship?

   a. Which company to focus engagement attention on
   b. Which annual general meeting (AGM) resolutions to vote on
   c. What are the key engagement issues for a particular company?

25. Which of the following is a new area of focus in the 2020 version of the UK Stewardship Code?

   a. Conflicts
   b. Outcomes
   c. Collaboration

26. Which of the following is *not* among the challenges to effective engagement as part of an investor coalition?

   a. Conflicts of interest
   b. Difficulty in reaching a consensus
   c. Unwillingness to act without specific client instruction

27. Which of the following is *not* among the identified key mechanisms for the escalation of engagement?

   a. Submitting a shareholder resolution
   b. Operating collectively with other shareholders
   c. Holding additional meetings with management

28. An active investor concerned about the financial viability of a business is *most likely* to reflect that concern by voting on:

   a. dividends.
   b. auditor pay.
   c. board director re-appointment.

29. ESG engagement activities are typically:

   a. carried out by asset owners.
   b. most successful for social issues rather than environmental or governance issues.
   c. associated with abnormal positive returns in the years after successful engagement.

30. Which of the following stewardship approaches is *least likely* to be applied by small investors in sovereign debt?

   a. Exerting influence on the issuer to act on meeting the sustainable development goals
   b. Tilting the portfolios toward fixed-income holdings issued by states with achievements in meeting the sustainable development goals
   c. Screening the universe of sovereign fixed-income securities for issuers showing progress in meeting the sustainable development goals

SOLUTIONS

1. **B is correct.** The investor wants to enhance their knowledge of the innovative GHG emissions tracking methodology. The investor is most likely to engage in learning dynamics, which, according to findings by PRI, "helps to produce and diffuse new ESG knowledge amongst companies and investors, creating 'learning value.'"

2. **A is correct.** Academic studies have shown that, on average, successful engagement activities are followed by positive abnormal financial returns. The same studies showed that of the engagement objectives investigated, those related to changes in remuneration policies were least likely to be successful. The studies also showed that successful engagement is time-consuming, as the average timeframe for success was 1.5 years.

3. **C is correct.** In private equity investments, the general partner (the private equity house) typically takes responsibility for stewardship activities as part of their service agreement with the limited partner (asset owner). Since private equity investments are also equity ownerships, it is natural to extend stewardship codes to this type of investment.

4. **C is correct.** The most significant change is the requirement to report on the practical effects of engagement activities. Conflict of interest regulations and robust policy statements were in earlier versions of the Code.

5. **A is correct.** Concert parties are groups of investors acting in concert as part of a takeover bid and are subject to regulatory oversight. Even though a takeover is not the intention of collective ESG engagement activities, formalized agreements between investors to act in concert to achieve ESG objectives can raise concerns with regulators and other market participants.

6. **A is correct.** An Investor Forum white paper rated 12 forms of engagement in terms of the need for formality in approach. Of the three options listed, direct engagement between groups of investors and the company was considered most likely to require an organized, formal approach and clear engagement objectives.

7. **C is correct.** Engagement activities are most likely to be successful when an open, earnest approach is combined with a strong understanding of the company's culture and history. Site visits are particularly helpful in demonstrating investors' willingness to educate themselves and engage in constructive dialogue. Involving media or speaking at general meetings are escalation strategies that are unlikely to be helpful in the early stages of engagement.

8. **B is correct.** Overlay service providers (such as Columbia Threadneedle Investments and Sustainalytics) provide stewardship overlay services, such as voting advice and direct engagement activities, for clients regardless of whether they invest funds on the clients' behalf. Proxy advisers (such as ISS and Glass Lewis) provide voting advice and assist with processing votes but don't directly advance engagement on their clients' behalf. ESG investment consultants (such as Mercer) typically rate the ESG expertise of fund managers.

9. **A is correct.** The guide recommends prioritizing engagement with issuers with weak ESG scores and lower credit quality. Bond 1 has the lowest credit score and, along with Bond 3, the lowest ESG score. Issuers with low ESG scores are prioritized because there is greater scope for improvement; those with lower credit quality are prioritized because they are less able to absorb negative ESG impacts.

10. **B is correct**. Private debt is typically less liquid than public or sovereign debt, resulting in closer, longer-term relationships between investors and issuers of private debt. Opportunities to engage on ESG issues are enhanced because of these relationships.

11. **B is correct**. Having enough resources (time, expertise, leverage) for large asset managers to engage effectively with investee companies is a significant challenge. Firm resources are also critical in hiring external stewardship services or in engaging with other asset managers in approaching investees on problems identified.

12. **C is correct**. Setting clear objectives for engagements is critical for investors; meeting these pre-established objectives is the correct way to assess the success of engagements. PRI (Principles for Responsible Investment) recognizes the importance of the engagers applying milestone measures and KPIs (key performance indicators) in their engagement actions so they can be accountable to their clients based on meeting the KPIs. Measuring engagement success based on the stock price performance or improvements in policies at the investee level might not be as accurate as measuring engagement actions against engagement objectives.

13. **A is correct**. Stewardship responsibilities are put into effect through voting and engagement. Only the owners of a company, the investors, can act as stewards, not the general stakeholders, and they should have a long-term perspective.

14. **A is correct**. The objective of the engagement was to increase the board's gender diversity, not the number of independent directors or to improve the skill sets at the board level.

15. **A is correct**. Successful ESG engagements generated 7.1% abnormal returns in the year after the initial engagement, compared to 2.3% abnormal returns, on average, generated by ESG engagements. When ESG engagements were more targeted, the abnormal returns were even higher, with more than 10% for successful climate change engagements and more than 9% for successful corporate governance engagements.

16. **A is correct**. Both monitoring and engagement, as ways of exercising stewardship by asset managers and investors, rely on dialogue with the investee, but this dialogue seeks to inform incremental buy/sell/hold decisions in the case of monitoring, while in the case of engagement it also seeks the achievement of a targeted objective. Monitoring resorts to questioning the leadership of an investee, whereas engagement is a two-way dialogue with input from both investor and investee.

17. **A is correct**. The styles of engagement might differ depending on the heritage of the stewardship team of an investor. If an investor has a history of governance-led engagement, it will tend to engage with the board chair and the board of directors and then down to the management of the firm and the investor relations team. This approach is consistent with a top-down style of engagement. Initiating engagement with investor relations specialists or the company's management is more specific to investors with a heritage of environmental and social expertise.

18. **C is correct**. A coalition of investors with a clear purpose of engagement in research reflects a form of collective engagement with a clear objective. Clear objectives to engage with an individual investee are less likely to be expressed in an annual letter or in annual meetings with the senior management of a company.

19. **B is correct**. Only the Australian Asset Owner Stewardship Code includes a

Solutions

principle that charges signatories with identifying and responding to market-wide and systemic risks, similar to Principle 4 in the 2020 version of the UK Stewardship Code.

20. **B is correct**. Many engagement professionals see expressing concerns through the investee's advisers as a normal form of engagement with a company. Making public statements prior to general meetings and requesting general meetings represent ways to escalate engagement efforts.

21. **B is correct**. According to the Investor Forum white paper, monitoring dialogues are conversations between investors and management to understand performance and opportunity more fully. In contrast, engagement dialogues are conversations between investors and any level of the investee entity (including non-executive directors) that feature a two-way sharing of perspectives such that the investors express their position on key issues and highlight any concerns they may have.

22. **C is correct**. Unlike engagement, escalation, reporting, and transparency, stock or securities lending policies are not among the seven areas covered in most stewardship codes, which are modeled after the 2010 UK Stewardship Code.

23. **B is correct**. Codes drafted by investor groups have been observed to downplay or even disregard conflicts of interest entirely.

24. **B is correct**. Engaged investors should expect to vote on all AGM resolutions. Determining which company needs engagement attention and which issues are most important to engage on are both key prioritization decisions.

25. **B is correct**. The new code takes a more ambitious approach by requiring reporting on not just engagement activity and statements of intent but also the outcomes of engagement activities.

26. **C is correct**. Investor coalitions are challenging because of the difficulty of reaching a consensus among coalition members and the potential for conflicts of interest. Being part of an investor coalition indicates an advanced level of engagement; coalition members are unlikely to require specific client instruction before acting.

27. **A is correct**. Submitting a shareholder resolution is an escalation mechanism, whereas the others represent forms of dialogue with the investee.

28. **A is correct**. When there are concerns about a company's financial viability, investors will carefully consider their votes on dividends, as dividends would further constrain the company's cash resources.

29. **C is correct**. There is a growing body of evidence that engaged companies change their behaviors against ESG factors. Multiple studies show that successful engagements are followed by abnormal positive returns.

30. **A is correct**. Stewardship interaction with sovereign debt issuers is likely to be much more limited than that with corporate debt issuers. Only the largest investors are likely to have any scope to influence the stance of nation-states, and even then, the influence may be minimal. Therefore, the ESG approach usually applied in this asset class is ESG screening or an ESG tilt in the investment process rather than engagement.

CHAPTER 7

ESG Analysis, Valuation, and Integration

LEARNING OUTCOMES

The candidate should be able to:

- [ ] **7.1.1** describe qualitative and quantitative approaches to integrating ESG analysis into the investment process
- [ ] **7.1.2** describe the challenges of integrating ESG analysis into a firm's investment process
- [ ] **7.1.3** describe the challenges of identifying and assessing material ESG issues
- [ ] **7.1.4** describe how scorecards and other tools may be developed and constructed to assess ESG factors
- [ ] **7.1.5** interpret a company's disclosure on selected ESG topics
- [ ] **7.1.6** explain how ESG analysis complements traditional financial analysis
- [ ] **7.1.7** analyze how ESG factors may affect industry and company performance
- [ ] **7.1.8** analyze how ESG factors may affect security valuation across a range of asset classes
- [ ] **7.1.9** apply the approaches to ESG analysis and integration across a range of asset classes
- [ ] **7.1.10** explain how credit rating agencies approach ESG credit scoring
- [ ] **7.1.11** explain the approaches taken across a range of ESG integration databases and software available, and the nature of the information provided
- [ ] **7.1.12** identify the main providers of screening services or tools, similarities and differences in their methodologies, and the aims, benefits and limitations of using them
- [ ] **7.1.13** describe the limitations and constraints of information provided by ESG integration databases
- [ ] **7.1.14** describe primary and secondary sources of ESG data and information

THE DIFFERENT APPROACHES TO ESG INTEGRATION

- 7.1.1 describe qualitative and quantitative approaches to integrating ESG analysis into the investment process
- 7.1.2 describe the challenges of integrating ESG analysis into a firm's investment process

ESG analysis and integration into an investment process can be either *qualitative* (e.g., an investor's judgment on the credibility of management's net-zero commitments) or *quantitative* (e.g., an investor analyzing a company's reported carbon emissions against competitors). The line between the two is blurry and, like most techniques and tools in financial analysis, there is no single "best" approach for all investment strategies.

Qualitative ESG Analysis

Qualitative ESG analysis generally involves observations and conclusions in the form of words rather than numbers. Examples include investors analyzing the following:

- The presence and quality of issuer reporting on ESG-related topics, such as employee engagement, pay equity, accident and safety, management and board diversity, and carbon emissions. One indicator of quality is an issuer's use of a broadly accepted reporting framework, such as the standards developed by the **Sustainability Accounting Standards Board (SASB)**, which was subsumed by the **International Sustainability Standards Board (ISSB)**. Another indicator is whether the ESG reporting is audited, which is rare today but gaining traction.
- The presence and credibility of investments, policies, and commitments to ESG-related goals such as a net-zero commitment and a board-level committee on sustainability.
- Executive compensation policies linked to progress on ESG-related goals.
- Company culture, including the "tone at the top" from management and the board, and whether progress on ESG issues is a priority.
- Companies' products and services and their broad effect on society and the nonhuman world, which may be subjective but highly relevant. For example, technology companies have faced shareholder proposals from investors concerned about the potential negative impacts of social media on child development and society.

Quantitative ESG Analysis

Quantitative ESG (QESG) analysis involves numbers rather than words but still involves discretion and judgment, including the choice of which data to examine, materiality, weights relative to other data, and points of reference, such as the selection of peers for comparison. Examples of QESG analysis include the following:

- Analyzing issuer-reported and third-party ESG-related measures and metrics, such as carbon emissions, employee turnover, percentage of board members who are independent, and board and management diversity. These allow investors to assess issuers against expectations, peers, and commitments (e.g., net zero).

The Different Approaches to ESG Integration

- Aggregating ESG data into an ESG score, which is then considered as a factor in an asset allocation or security selection model (alongside other factors, such as value, size, momentum, growth, and volatility). The ESG data typically include mix of a third-party and internal proprietary data and come from large datasets of securities, rather than individual issuers, though some firms will create their own proprietary scores from individual company assessment. For instance, a global dataset might contain 2,000–4,000 companies, with 100 data points per company. Investors use application programming interfaces (APIs) to compile and assess large volumes of data efficiently.

- Using ESG data (including aggregate scores of multiple data series) for position sizing in a portfolio. For instance, a strong score on an environmental factor might be sought. Systematic approaches can attempt to derive correlations to understand how ESG factors might affect financial performance over time and then weigh those ESG factors accordingly.

- Tilting toward certain ESG factors in index-based strategies. For instance, the Japanese Government Pension Investment Fund (GPIF) and index providers have created gender-tilted versions of broad market indexes. This shows that asset owners can integrate ESG factors among different strategies and in line with their own ESG polices and philosophies.

- Thematic funds might assess alignment with priority themes that are ESG related (e.g., climate, gender). This alignment can be done with a material opportunity mapping process or by using ESG data to adjust weights accordingly.

QESG approaches can use complex mathematical modeling and data analysis, including artificial intelligence and algorithms. QESG approaches are typically used in more systematic investment strategies, including index-based strategies. Discretionary investment strategies, particularly those that focus on security selection within a concentrated portfolio, will employ both qualitative and quantitative approaches. Qualitative analysis is important for equity investors voting proxies and engaging with boards and managers on ESG issues.

Artificial Intelligence and Algorithms

Artificial intelligence (AI) and machine learning algorithms can help investors utilize more data efficiently in in QESG analysis and decision making. Examples of AI in ESG investing include the following:

- Quickly measuring companies' ESG performance and risk using incidents reported across many new sources online. ESG data providers, such as RepRisk and Truvalue Labs, use *natural language processing (NLP)* to analyze and quantify real-time company incidents and online mentions relating to child labor, corruption, and other risk areas.
  - Natural language processing is broadly defined as the automatic manipulation of natural language, such as speech and text, by software. The aim is to enable a computer to "understand" text, including contextual nuances. The technology can help investors then extract insights from large volumes of text.

- Efficiently interpreting satellite imagery with machine learning to assess issuers' carbon footprints, impact on the natural environment (e.g. deforestation), and use of proceeds from green bonds (see Burke, Driscoll, Lobell, and Ermon 2021).

- Helping to close data gaps in issuer disclosures. For example, Nguyen, Diaz-Rainey, and Kuruppuarachchi (2020) demonstrate a model that estimates issuer's Scope 3 carbon emissions from a vast number of publicly available sources.

There remain challenges in analyzing extensive datasets, especially because so many have become available in this space. Investors must define what is most material and judge the quality and relevance of data before using data in an investment process. Although improving with the passage of time, backtesting ESG data remains a challenge because the length of time series is usually less than 15 years, much shorter than most financial data series.

Bringing Qualitative and Quantitative Analyses Together

Investors often employ a hybrid approach that involves both qualitative and quantitative ESG analysis. One example is a scorecard, which turns qualitative judgments into quantitative scores. An investor may rate a company's governance from 1 to 5 by scoring it in several areas including the number of independent board members and the degree to which its compensation practices pay for performance. Another example of investors using both qualitative and quantitative approaches, which will be discussed in more detail later, is adjusting financial model inputs (e.g., revenue, profitability, capital expenditures, discount rate, valuation multiples) based on an assessment of the company's ESG risk factors. This again demonstrates that quantitative analysis can involve significant qualitative judgment.

Tools and Elements of ESG Analysis

Besides analyzing issuer-reported and third-party ESG reports and metrics, investors use several other tools in ESG analysis, including the following:

- Red flag indicators—Securities with high ESG risk are flagged and investigated further or excluded. For instance, a company with a board lacking majority independence might be flagged for deeper scrutiny on management incentives or simply be excluded from an investable universe.
- Company questionnaires and management interviews—For example, if the detail on management aspects or other material ESG information is insufficient, the investor might ask the company for specific data. Or investors might have a predefined list of standard ESG data they ask for. These questionnaires are also used in parallel with regular company meetings, where investors and companies meet to discuss the most material ESG issues.
- Checks with outside experts—For instance, an investor might interview key industry thought leaders or other stakeholders of the company, including customers, suppliers, or regulators. These checks might be complemented via interviews, surveys, or third-party sourcing, such as the use of expert networks.
- Watch lists—These lists might include securities with high ESG risk added to a watchlist for monitoring or securities with high ESG opportunities that are put on a watchlist for possible investment. For instance, once an investor has assessed ESG risks or opportunities, a news or stock price watchlist is created and monitored for stock price entry levels or for change in ESG events. For example, a highly carbon-intense company identified with high "E" risk might be monitored against changing policies on carbon taxes.

These tools—similar to ESG research broadly—can be either sourced internally by the investment manager's employees or purchased from external analysts, ESG specialists, or third-party databases.

Challenges in ESG Integration

As we will discuss throughout this chapter, there are many hurdles and challenges for investment managers in ESG integration, including those related to ESG disclosures by issuers, the inherently subjective nature of ESG analysis and decision making, and cultural challenges and biases within investment management firms.

Surveys suggest that many investors view companies' ESG disclosures as inadequate because some of the disclosures might be missing or they are incomplete, not comparable across companies, or unaudited. Investors and company management teams disagree about materiality thresholds and about what should be disclosed. Company managers argue that the vast range of possible ESG data and the conflicting demands among investors and other stakeholders, such as regulators, make disclosure demands unreasonable.

A further challenge is that there is no consensus (yet) on what constitutes complete ESG disclosure, and it probably varies by asset class. The development of issuer reporting frameworks for ESG information is nascent compared to financial reporting frameworks (e.g., IFRS and US GAAP). The number of stock exchanges and security regulators requiring ESG disclosure among listed companies is growing; Krueger, Sautner, Tang, and Zhong (2021) identified 35 countries with ESG disclosure mandates, including Australia, China, South Africa, and the United Kingdom. And there are efforts regionally and globally to create ESG reporting frameworks and disclosure standards analogous to IFRS and US GAAP in financial reporting, notably by EFRAG in the European Union and the ISSB globally.

THE ISSB

Over the first two decades of its existence, the IFRS Foundation (through its independent standard-setting board, the International Accounting Standards Board, or IASB) harmonized financial reporting standards across much of the globe through its IFRS Accounting Standards. Today, economic and investment decisions are increasingly incorporating sustainability information. Responding to the need for such information, in 2021 the IFRS Foundation established the ISSB as a sister board to the IASB, responsible for developing a truly global baseline of sustainability disclosures to further inform economic and investment decisions. There is a potential for ISSB standards to end the "alphabet soup" of fragmented, voluntary, sustainability-related standards and requirements, which would be well received by many investors and issuers who today struggle with such a complicated landscape. Of course, security regulations and laws in each jurisdiction would be required for ISSB standards to achieve the same acceptance and use as the IFRS Accounting Standards.

The ISSB's standards are built from Task Force on Climate-Related Financial Disclosures (TCFD) recommendations and the materials of the Climate Disclosure Standards Board (CDSB), SASB, and the International Integrated Reporting Council (IIRC), which were consolidated into the IFRS Foundation in 2022. Issuers and investors are encouraged to continue using the SASB Standards until they are replaced by ISSB standards.

> The ISSB is expected to finalize its first two standards, IFRS S1: General Requirements for Disclosure of Sustainability-Related Financial Information and IFRS S2: Climate-Related Disclosures, in the summer of 2023.
>
> IFRS S1 provides the basis for achieving a global baseline of sustainability disclosures. It sets out general reporting requirements for material information about sustainability-related risks and opportunities and points to other standards and frameworks in the absence of specific IFRS Standards (e.g., SASB Standards and CDSB Framework application guidance). Finally, it emphasizes the need for consistency and connections between financial statements and sustainability disclosures, requiring financial statements and sustainability disclosures to be published at the same time.
>
> IFRS S2 sets out disclosure of material information about climate-related risks and opportunities, incorporating TCFD recommendations and climate-related industry-based requirements of the SASB Standards. It requires disclosure of material information about physical risks, transition risks, and climate-related opportunities. Finally, it sets requirements for disclosures around transition planning, climate resilience, and **Scope 1, 2, and 3 emissions** in accordance with the GHG Protocol.

Comparability difficulties extend beyond companies employing different reporting frameworks to low correlation among third-party ESG ratings and varying cultural norms and expectations by geography. As we will discuss later, ESG ratings do not align to nearly the same degree as, for example, credit ratings by the major credit rating agencies; vendors use different techniques, and their objectives vary. Challenges are further magnified by cultural and regional differences. For instance, Japanese companies have historically had a far lower number of independent directors on their boards than European and US companies, which is reflected in the Corporate Governance Code of Japan. Different countries' investors and issuers also put different weights on social factors (i.e., US investors and issuers have different views of labor unions than German companies).

Given the hurdles, investment managers may not integrate ESG analysis into their investment processes. Managers may not have the resources to buy third-party ESG research or conduct it themselves. And even for firms that pursue ESG integration, there are coordination challenges; they often separate "ESG analysts" from investment analysts. Finally, they may simply disagree with the concept of ESG integration.

Criticism of ESG Integration

One of the most common criticisms of ESG investing is the difficulty for investors to correctly identify and appropriately weigh ESG factors in investment selection. Critics tend to express four primary concerns about the precision, validity, and reliability of ESG investment strategies:

1. Too inclusive of poorly performing companies—ESG funds tend to hold investments in companies that might be seen as "bad actors," such as oil and gas or packaged food companies, so it is unclear how an integrated ESG investment strategy is different from a conventional strategy. Asset owners and managers that seek to exclude such "bad actors" should pursue exclusionary strategies aligned with this goal rather than ESG integration strategies.

2. Dubious assessment criteria—The criteria used for selecting ESG factors are subjective and can reflect ideological or political viewpoints. Nonmaterial or sociopolitical factors might be overemphasized. Materiality assessments might also be considered flawed. To mitigate this concern, asset owners

should invest with asset managers that are aligned with their own assessment criteria. We also note that conventional (non-ESG) investing is not above or immune to ideology; it is simply less explicit about ideology.

3. Quality of data—The information used for selecting ESG factors often comes from the companies themselves and is not audited. This complicates the ability to verify, compare, and standardize this information. While this is generally true today, investors can mitigate this problem by corroborating data with multiple sources, and as discussed earlier, efforts are underway to harmonize reporting frameworks and for ESG information to be audited.

4. Skepticism of return benefits—Some critics argue that the evidence for the benefits of considering ESG factors in terms of financial returns is mixed or not proven (Vogel 2005). These critics suggest that the time horizon for assessing ESG factors is too short and point to time periods during which sectors that tend to be excluded (e.g., tobacco, energy, defense) outperform. Second, increased crowding into more ESG-friendly sectors (e.g., technology, health care) increases valuations, reducing those sectors' expected returns while increasing it for others, which presents a challenge for financial returns. Note that exclusions are only one type of ESG strategy, separate from ESG integration.

ESG INTEGRATION IN LISTED EQUITIES

☐ **7.1.3** describe the challenges of identifying and assessing material ESG issues

☐ **7.1.4** describe how scorecards and other tools may be developed and constructed to assess ESG factors

☐ **7.1.5** interpret a company's disclosure on selected ESG topics

ESG integration runs alongside financial analysis and occurs in different forms at various stages of the investment process (see Exhibit 1). A basic investment process and how ESG factors can be integrated for listed equities are demonstrated in this section and the next. Later sections discuss ESG integration in other asset classes.

Exhibit 1: Investment Process Stages

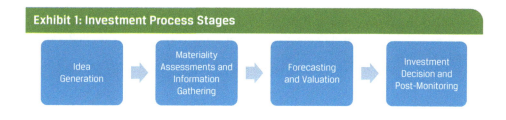

Idea Generation

Some practitioners begin the investment process by screening companies based on fundamental indicators and/or technical indicators. ESG analysis can be integrated by incorporating ESG factors as screening criteria—perhaps a mix of positive (seek high G scores), negative (avoid low G), or momentum (seek rising G or avoid declining G)—to create an attractive investment universe.

Investors may also generate ideas on a more thematic basis rather than using screens—for example, identifying companies with positive exposure to industry or megatrends (e.g., the shift toward cloud computing). ESG megatrends themselves can be used as investable themes—for instance, identifying companies that are improving access to clean water or are benefiting from the shift toward renewable energy.

At this stage, checklists—internal or externally sourced—might "red flag" companies and be used to narrow the investable universe. A threshold for corporate governance or an unacceptable ESG score or rating can include and exclude companies from the universe. This assessment may be quantitative as well (e.g., the carbon intensity of Company A is too far above an index benchmark to meet a practitioner's investment criteria).

Materiality Assessments and Gathering Information

Once an investment candidate is identified, the analyst begins the due diligence or research phase, gathering and processing a wide range of information. During this stage, the analyst conducts a materiality assessment to identify the ESG issues that are likely to have an impact on the company's financial performance and thus require further research. Material ESG issues vary by a company's industry and business model. For example, greenhouse gas (GHG) emissions are a material issue for the carbon-intensive business models of utilities, airlines, and auto manufacturers because of transition risks. GHG emissions, however, are less material for consulting companies, for which data security and privacy are greater concerns that can manifest in costly leaks of customer information.

Materiality is typically measured in terms of both the likelihood and magnitude of impact. Note that while many practitioners focus exclusively on material ESG factors, some exclusionary investing strategies must also consider factors that are not necessarily financially material (e.g., exclusion of companies that sell pork-based products by certain religious investors even if those products account for a small percentage of revenues).

Determining which ESG issues are most material involves judgment and is not an exact science. Frameworks such as the materiality maps provided by SASB (now part of the ISSB) provide guidance, but investment professionals often develop their own view on what is most material. This spectrum of opinions concerning materiality is demonstrated through the different examples of materiality maps in Exhibit 2, Exhibit 3, and Exhibit 4.

Exhibit 2: Example Materiality Map of High-Level Sectors across ESG Factors

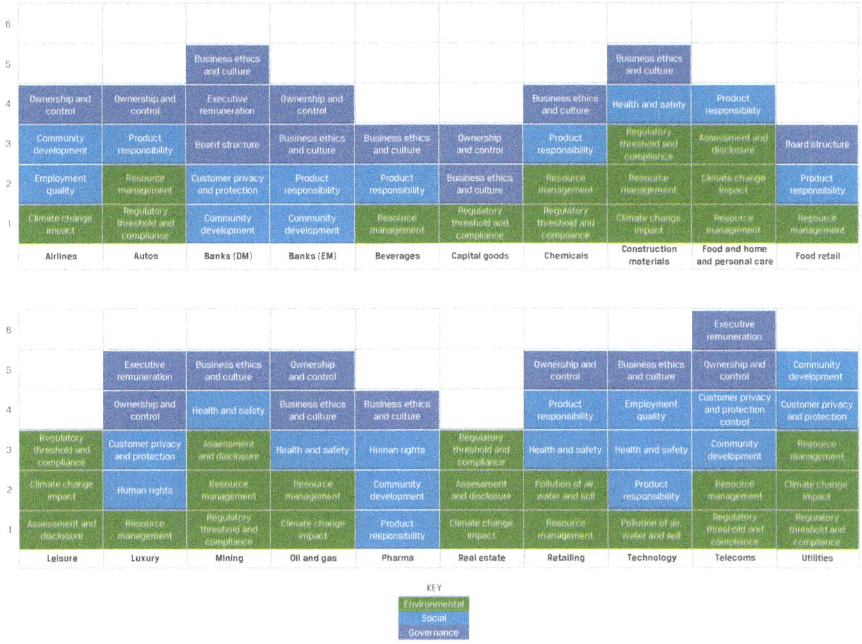

[Materiality map chart showing ESG factors across sectors including Airlines, Autos, Banks (DM), Banks (EM), Beverages, Capital goods, Chemicals, Construction materials, Food and home and personal care, Food retail, Leisure, Luxury, Mining, Oil and gas, Pharma, Real estate, Retailing, Technology, Telecoms, and Utilities. Key: Environmental, Social, Governance.]

Source: HSBC (2016).

Companies in the same sector might be judged to have different material ESG factors. For instance, in the health care industry, a medical insurer will have different material factors than a pharmaceutical company. And even in the same industry, individual companies can have different material factors. For example, while the SASB materiality map (Exhibit 4) identifies "fair marketing and advertising" as a material factor for pharmaceutical companies, this can vary by company. Taking the examples of three generic companies, A, B and C, we might have the following:

- Pharmaceutical Company A is judged to have a low risk exposure to this factor because it has up-to-date policies and training programs and has never had a regulatory warning letter.
- Pharmaceutical Company B is judged to have a high risk to this factor because it lacks a strong policy, training is minimal, and the company has received several fines and warnings from regulators.
- Pharmaceutical Company C is judged to have no risk to this factor because it currently has no commercially marketed products, only those in the research and development stage. While the factor is material to the industry, it is of limited or arguably no risk to the company in the short run.

Exhibit 3: SASB Materiality Map by Industry

Issues	Health Care	Financials	Technology and Communications	Non-renewable Resources	Transportation	Services	Resource Transformation	Consumption	Renewable Resources and Alternative Energy	Infrastructure
Environment										
Greenhouse gas (GHG) emissions			X	X	X	X	X	X	X	X
Air quality				X	X	X	X		X	X
Energy management	X		X	X	X	X	X	X	X	X
Fuel management	X			X	X	X	X	X		X
Water and wastewater management	X		X	X	X	X	X	X	X	X
Waste and hazardous materials management	X		X	X	X	X	X	X	X	X
Biodiversity impacts				X	X	X		X	X	X
Social capital										
Human rights and community relations	X			X					X	X
Access and affordability	X	X							X	X
Customer welfare	X	X			X	X	X	X		
Data security and customer privacy	X	X	X			X	X	X		
Fair disclosure and labelling	X							X		
Fair marketing and advertising	X	X				X		X		
Human capital										
Labor relations				X	X			X		X
Fair labor practices			X	X	X	X		X		
Employee health, safety and well-being	X		X	X	X	X	X	X	X	X

ESG Integration in Listed Equities

Issues	Health Care	Financials	Technology and Communications	Non-renewable Resources	Transportation	Services	Resource Transformation	Consumption	Renewable Resources and Alternative Energy	Infrastructure
Diversity and inclusion		X	X			X		X		
Compensation and benefits		X				X		X		
Recruitment, development, and retention	X		X		X	X		X		
Business model and innovation										
Lifecycle impacts of products and services	X	X	X	X	X	X	X	X	X	X
Environmental, social impacts on assets and operations	X	X		X		X		X	X	X
Product packaging	X					X	X	X		
Product quality and safety	X				X	X	X	X		
Leadership and governance										
Systemic risk management		X	X			X				X
Accident and safety management				X	X	X	X		X	X
Business ethics and transparency payments	X	X		X	X	X	X			X
Competitive behavior		X	X	X	X	X	X			X
Regulatory risk				X	X	X	X	X	X	X
Materials sourcing			X	X	X		X	X	X	
Supply chain management	X		X	X	X	X	X	X	X	

Note: As of the second quarter of 2023, these are still available, but note that SASB Standards are now the responsibility of the ISSB.
Source: SASB (2018).

Exhibit 4: Example Materiality Map of Health Care Subsectors from the SASB

Issues	Health Care					
	Biotechnology	Pharmaceuticals	Medical Equipment and Supplies	Health care Delivery	Health care Distribution	Managed Care
Environment						
GHG emissions						
Air quality						
Energy management	X	X	X			
Fuel management					X	
Water and wastewater management	X	X	X			
Waste and hazardous materials management	X	X	X	X		
Biodiversity impacts						
Social capital						
Human rights and community relations	X	X				
Access and affordability	X	X	X	X		X
Customer welfare	X	X	X	X		X
Data security and customer privacy				X		X
Fair disclosure and labelling				X		X
Fair marketing and advertising	X	X	X			
Human capital						
Labor relations						
Fair labor practices						
Employee health, safety, and well-being	X	X				
Diversity and inclusion						
Compensation and benefits						
Recruitment, development, and retention	X	X		X		
Business model and innovation						
Lifecycle impacts of products and services	X	X	X		X	
Environmental, social impacts on assets and operations				X		X
Product packaging					X	
Product quality and safety	X	X	X		X	

	Health Care					
Issues	Biotechnology	Pharmaceuticals	Medical Equipment and Supplies	Health care Delivery	Health care Distribution	Managed Care
Leadership and governance						
Systemic risk management						
Accident and safety management						
Business ethics and transparency payments	X	X	X	X	X	
Competitive behavior						
Regulatory capture and political influence						
Materials sourcing			X			
Supply chain management	X	X	X			

Note: As of the second quarter of 2023, these are still available, but note that SASB Standards are now the responsibility of the ISSB.
Source: SASB (2018).

> **EXAMPLE 1**
>
> ### Using the SASB as a Baseline Framework in a Materiality Assessment
>
> As shown in Exhibit 4, "materials sourcing" is not considered a material ESG risk in the SASB framework for biotechnology or pharmaceutical companies. However, an analyst might arrive at a different conclusion for Jazz Pharmaceuticals, which markets a cannabis-derived pharmaceutical for the treatment of certain types of seizures. It has a materials sourcing risk on two accounts:
>
> 1. Growing cannabis is a complex operation with enhanced risks compared to standard pharmaceutical and biotechnology manufacturing processes.
> 2. The regulatory oversight is more complex because two regulators are involved: the drug regulator and the pharmaceutical regulator (in the United States, the Drug Enforcement Agency and the Food and Drug Administration, respectively). For a typical pharmaceutical product, only the pharmaceutical regulator would be involved.
>
> The analyst might further judge that an ESG opportunity exists here as well because the technology needed to harvest the plants, the knowledge protection around that technology, and complying with two regulators create barriers to entry that might lead to a longer period of market exclusivity (and thus, cash flows) for the drug. In this example, the social impacts might be more complex to judge as well (certain asset owners might object to cannabis), whereas other aspects of the company's risk exposures are more typical with the industry.

As of 2023, the trend in company reporting to include more material ESG factors continues. However, various stakeholders do not agree on how to define or report materiality, so developing proprietary materiality assessments alongside standardized frameworks continues to be an important competency for investors.

Managed and Unmanaged Risks

Not all risks, ESG or otherwise, are managed or even can be managed. Manageable risks include the risk of employee safety, which can be managed through modern capital equipment and safety procedures, and data security and privacy, with security software, hardware, and employee training. *Manageable*, however, does not mean the risk can be eliminated.

Unmanaged ESG risks take two forms: (1) unmanageable risks, which are inherent in the business model and cannot be addressed by company initiatives, and (2) the management gap, which represents risks that could be managed but aren't. Potentially unmanageable risks include the carbon emissions of airlines and industrial processes in certain materials and chemical industries. An airline can manage some of the issue with new engines, sustainable aviation fuels, optimizing the number of passengers per flight, installing winglets, and minimizing the time airplanes spend idling on the runway, but it cannot eliminate all emissions. As a result, airlines may have some unmanageable risk on carbon emissions, which should contribute to its E risk score. Some airlines also look to work with credit rating agencies given the balance sheet implications arising from capex requirements associated with large purchases of energy-efficient capital equipment.

Scorecards to Assess ESG Factors

A common form of investor assessment of material ESG factors, especially when third-party research or scores are not available, is a scorecard. Scorecards translate qualitative judgments into numerical scores.

For pharmaceutical companies, fair marketing and advertising might be identified as a key ESG social risk. An investor can score companies on this risk factor from 0 to 5. High or low scores are then used in valuation or further assessment work. For example, the analyst makes the following judgments and scores after speaking with Companies X, Y, and Z:

- Company X has no policy and a history of marketing violations, so it scores a 0.
- Company Y has a brief policy and no violations, so it scores a 3.
- Company Z has a detailed policy and one minor violation, so it scores a 4.

Scores of 0 could make a company unattractive, and scores of 5 could lead to further investment work. Alternatively, aggregate scores of all material factors in the scorecard are used in further assessment or valuation work.

The scorecard technique could be used on private or public companies. Challenges to creating private company scorecards are that a rating agency score is less likely to be available and less information about it is available in the public domain. The scorecard technique can be adapted to scoring countries for sovereign bond analysis or to infrastructure and real estate. For example, environmental policies could be scored for infrastructure and commitments to a carbon net-zero plan, or corruption levels could be scored for countries.

In summary, developing a scorecard may involve the following steps:

1. Identify sector- or company-specific ESG items.
2. Break down issues into a number of indicators (e.g., policy, measures, disclosure).
3. Determine a scoring system based on what good/best practice looks like for each indicator/issue.
4. Assess a company, and give it a score.
5. Calculate aggregated scores at the issuer level, dimension level (ESG level), or total score level (depending on the relative weight of each issue).
6. Benchmark the company's performance against industry averages or its peer group.

The Challenges of Company Disclosures of ESG Information

Identifying material ESG factors and creating scorecards requires ESG information from companies. However, companies have variable disclosure policies and reporting practices, and mandatory ESG disclosure is not universal across jurisdictions. Although "material factors affecting financials" is an intuitive idea, management has wide discretion. In some cases, over disclosure of nonmaterial ESG information has been a problem. Also, companies with worsening ESG indicators sometimes decide to discontinue publication or avoid publication in the years when those indicators are poor.

Simply because a company does not disclose relevant ESG data does not necessarily mean it is managing its ESG risks or opportunities poorly. Smaller companies with fewer resources face cost constraints in reporting. There are also geographical differences in reporting, and management might assume that certain information is of limited importance to investors or is commercially sensitive. ESG information might be available to other stakeholders (e.g., supply chain information to suppliers, supply chain audit to business customers) but not publicly available to investors.

Other issues are that ESG disclosures might be unaudited, incomplete, or incomparable between companies. While poor disclosure is a challenge to market efficiency, this relative inefficiency could arguably be a source of superior risk-adjusted return for a skilled investor.

> **EXAMPLE 2**
>
> ### Assessing What an E Disclosure Might Imply
>
> A cement company discloses its carbon mitigation strategy but discloses only its carbon Scope 1 emissions, omitting Scopes 2 and 3.
>
> Some of its competitors do not disclose any carbon data, and some disclose data on all three scopes. The carbon data the company discloses would have been assured by an independent third party.
>
> An analyst might want to ask the following questions:
>
> - *What is the size of the company?* A company that is smaller with respect to employees, resources, or market capitalization might not report to the same standard as a larger company. When it comes to material risk factors, though, this might be judged as inexcusable.
> - *How well do the company's disclosures compare to those of its competitors?*
> - *Does the business model suggest Scopes 2 and 3 would be a material matter?* If most GHG emissions are associated with the production of cement rather than purchased inputs or its use by customers, the analyst may judge Scope 1 disclosures as sufficient. The fact that the Scope 1 data have third-party assurance should, with all other matters being equal, give more weight to the disclosure.
> - *How long has the company been disclosing, and has management made other commitments to future disclosure?* Answers and judgments to these types of questions will sway how analysts rate companies (e.g., in a scorecard approach) or the discount rate they might use in a discounted cash flow valuation.
> - *Does the presence of a narrative and strategy (and its strength or weakness) improve an analyst's view on disclosure?* Is this narrative reporting aligned with best practice guidance (for instance, the IASB's IFRS Practice Statement on management commentary; IFRS 2010)?
>
> As a followup, the analyst could ask the company for an explanation of the data's absence and its view on materiality and then judge its willingness to engage or commit to publishing the data. Or the analyst could estimate the data using comparable company data (e.g., a larger competitor's ratio of Scope 1 to Scope 2 and 3 GHG emissions) or find a third-party data source.

On occasion, a lack of disclosure can be enough to red flag an investment candidate completely. For example, a company hires a new CEO but will not disclose in sufficient detail what the long-term incentive plans for management are based on. This might be too strong a red flag for an investor.

> **EXAMPLE 3**
>
> ### Challenges in Emerging Markets
>
> ESG investing in emerging markets brings a different set of challenges and opportunities from investing in developed markets, including the following:
>
> - Limited data—Less disclosure and fewer available ESG ratings means benchmarking ESG performance is more challenging in emerging markets due to less data and great variability between countries and companies.
> - Potential ESG risks, such as weaker regulations, governance, and infrastructure
> - Cultural complexities—ESG integration in emerging markets may require more nuanced approaches, and principles methods from developed markets may not easily apply. This can be a particular concern for ESG ratings that take a global approach, which can disproportionately punish emerging market companies.
>
> However, emerging markets present greater opportunities for investors to engage with companies and improve ESG performance. While change takes time, investors can play a role in advancing ESG factors through capital allocation and active ownership.

3. ESG INTEGRATION IN LISTED EQUITIES: VALUATION CONSIDERATIONS

- ☐ 7.1.6 explain how ESG analysis complements traditional financial analysis
- ☐ 7.1.7 analyze how ESG factors may affect industry and company performance
- ☐ 7.1.8 analyze how ESG factors may affect security valuation across a range of asset classes

After the research stage and any relevant risk and materiality assessment, practitioners proceed to valuing the issuer and its equity. At this stage, investors integrate the impact of material ESG factors into their financial statement forecasts and/or other valuation inputs, such as multiples and discount rates.

Discounted Cash Flow Input Adjustments

If a company faces significant environmental regulations or litigation, that could hurt its future cash flows. The investor would factor in the potential costs of these risks into cash flow projections, lowering the company's valuation in a discounted cash flow (DCF) analysis. However, if a company is well positioned to benefit from ESG opportunities, such as selling products that reduce customers' electricity usage, that could boost future cash flows through higher revenue growth, increasing the value of a company's equity determined via DCF analysis. An adjustment can also be made on a more direct basis (e.g., an assessment of an environmental litigation fine of JPY5 billion), or the risk-adjusted impact of a carbon tax might be forecast to be an absolute dollar amount per year in a model.

Besides adjustments to discrete cash flow projections, analysts can adjust the discount rate (e.g., required rate of return, cost of capital) or terminal growth assumption in their DCF model to account for material ESG factors. The discount rate is the interest rate used to discount future cash flows and is typically a weighted average of the required rates of return by debt and equity investors and reflects the risk profile of the investment. The terminal growth rate is a perpetual compound annual growth rate that a company's cash flow is assumed to grow by after the discrete forecasting period (e.g., after the next 5 or 10 years of individual forecasts, an analyst assumes cash flows grow by 2% forever); it reflects the company's growth prospects. Both the discount rate and terminal growth rate have a significant impact on the value of the company resulting from the DCF model. They are unobservable inputs that inherently involve uncertainty but should be well supported and not overly optimistic or pessimistic. An investor might use a discount rate in the mid- to high-single digits and a low-single digit terminal growth rate for a stable, mature company that operates in developed markets. A higher-growth technology company operating in emerging markets would likely be valued with a higher discount rate and higher terminal growth rate.

Adjustments to the discount rate or terminal growth rate can be based on individual company factors or on a country or sector basis. For example, all coal producers and coal-powered utilities might be judged to have higher climate-related risk and thus higher discount rates. Similarly, companies with strong ESG practices could be seen as less risky, allowing for a lower discount rate. A higher (lower) discount rate leads to, all else equal, a lower (higher) estimate of intrinsic value.

The size of the discount rate or terminal growth rate adjustment depends on several judgments. The first is how significant the ESG factor is in terms of financial impact on the company. Minor risks may not warrant adjustments, while more substantial risks could justify an adjustment of 100 bps or more. The second is how well or poorly the ESG risk is managed. If the company has strong processes to address the risks and minimize impacts, a small discount rate change could be sufficient. Finally, the investor should consider typical ranges for the discount rate and terminal growth rate given the company's business model, growth, and risk profile. Looking at comparable companies' valuations can provide important context.

The analyst should be cautious about double counting ESG risk factors by, for example, reducing projected cash flows *and* increasing the discount rate in the DCF analysis for the same ESG risk factor. While this might be appropriate in a situation where the analyst judges that the expected value of future cash flows has decreased and the uncertainty around that expected value has increased, it might be punitive.

EXAMPLE 4

Discounted Cash Flow Modeling with ESG Factors

An investor is evaluating an oil and gas producer. The investor identifies climate change policy risk as significant for the company given its carbon-intensive operations and products. To incorporate this into a DCF analysis of the company, the investor may do the following:

1. Reduce revenue projections based on government policies that subsidize alternative, renewable energy sources and electric alternatives for transportation. The forecasts would factor in various scenarios for the pace and impacts of the policy.

2. Increase the discount rate to account for the risk that future cash flows could be impacted by unpredictable climate policy shifts.

While the theory and math behind the DCF analysis are beyond the scope of this curriculum, we briefly demonstrate the implementation of these adjustments in a five-year DCF analysis of the oil and gas company.

Base Case (before Adjustments)

Exhibit 5 shows the analyst's base case before making any adjustments. "Cash flow" here represents after-tax cash profits that can be distributed to investors, calculated as revenue minus cash uses for operations and reinvestment. This is a simplified model for illustrative purposes; in practice, a DCF analysis would be supported by a full financial statement model (income statement, balance sheet, statement of cash flows), in turn supported by separate models for material drivers, such as volumes, prices, and profitability.

Exhibit 5: Base Case

EUR Millions	Last 12 Months	Forecast Year 1	Forecast Year 2	Forecast Year 3	Forecast Year 4	Forecast Year 5	Thereafter (Terminal)
Revenue	28,156	29,564	31,042	32,594	34,224	35,935	
Cash operating expenses	(18,310)	(19,216)	(20,177)	(21,186)	(22,245)	(23,358)	
Income tax expense	(2,365)	(2,483)	(2,608)	(2,738)	(2,875)	(3,019)	
Capital expenditures	(4,210)	(4,435)	(4,656)	(4,889)	(5,134)	(5,390)	
Cash flow	3,271	3,429	3,601	3,781	3,970	4,168	46,779
Discounted cash flow		3,118	2,976	2,841	2,712	2,588	29,046
Sum of discounted cash flows	43,280						
Assumptions							
Revenue growth rate		5.0%	5.0%	5.0%	5.0%	5.0%	5.0%
Operating margin	35.0%	35.0%	35.0%	35.0%	35.0%	35.0%	35.0%
Tax rate	24.0%	24.0%	24.0%	24.0%	24.0%	24.0%	24.0%
CAPEX % of revenue	15.0%	15.0%	15.0%	15.0%	15.0%	15.0%	15.0%
Discount rate	10%						
Terminal growth rate	1%						

The estimated value of the company is EUR43,280 million, the sum of discounted future cash flows.

Lower Revenue (Scenario 1)

In this scenario (see Exhibit 6), the analyst assumes that growth in revenues falls from a 5% rate to −1% over the forecast period, including the terminal period. Because some of the company's operating expenses are fixed, the analyst reduces the company's operating margin as well. Since this case would likely result in the company reducing capital expenditures toward a maintenance level, the analyst also reduces the ratio of capital expenditures to revenue. The estimated value falls to EUR35,510 million.

Exhibit 6: Lower-Revenue Scenario

EUR Millions	Last 12 Months	Forecast Year 1	Forecast Year 2	Forecast Year 3	Forecast Year 4	Forecast Year 5	Thereafter (Terminal)
Revenue	28,156	29,564	30,451	31,060	31,060	30,749	
Cash operating expenses	(18,310)	(19,216)	(20,097)	(20,810)	(21,121)	(21,217)	
Income tax expense	(2,365)	(2,483)	(2,485)	(2,460)	(2,385)	(2,288)	
Capital expenditures	(4,210)	(4,435)	(4,263)	(4,038)	(3,727)	(3,382)	
Cash flow	3,271	3,429	3,605	3,752	3,827	3,862	34,759
Discounted cash flow		3,118	2,980	2,819	2,614	2,398	21,582
Sum of discounted cash flows	35,510						
Assumptions							
Revenue growth rate		5.0%	3.0%	2.0%	0.0%	-1.0%	
Operating margin	35.0%	35.0%	34.0%	33.0%	32.0%	31.0%	
Tax rate	24.0%	24.0%	24.0%	24.0%	24.0%	24.0%	
CAPEX % of revenue	15.0%	15.0%	14.0%	13.0%	12.0%	11.0%	
Discount rate	10%						
Terminal growth rate	−1%						

Higher Discount Rate (Scenario 2):

In this more straightforward scenario (see Exhibit 7), the analyst left the base-case cash flow estimates unchanged but increased the discount rate by 150 bps. The impact on the valuation is significant, although less so than for Scenario 1's adjustments (estimated DCF value is EUR3.6 billion higher than in Scenario 1).

Exhibit 7: Higher-Discount-Rate Scenario

EUR Millions	Last 12 Months	Forecast Year 1	Forecast Year 2	Forecast Year 3	Forecast Year 4	Forecast Year 5	Thereafter (Terminal)
Revenue	28,156	29,564	31,042	32,594	34,224	35,935	
Cash operating expenses	(18,310)	(19,216)	(20,177)	(21,186)	(22,245)	(23,358)	
Income tax expense	(2,365)	(2,483)	(2,608)	(2,738)	(2,875)	(3,019)	
Capital expenditures	(4,210)	(4,435)	(4,656)	(4,889)	(5,134)	(5,390)	
Cash flow	3,271	3,429	3,601	3,781	3,970	4,168	40,097
Discounted cash flow		3,118	2,976	2,841	2,712	2,588	24,897

EUR Millions	Last 12 Months	Forecast Year 1	Forecast Year 2	Forecast Year 3	Forecast Year 4	Forecast Year 5	Thereafter (Terminal)
Sum of discounted cash flows	39,131						
Assumptions							
Revenue growth rate		5.0%	5.0%	5.0%	5.0%	5.0%	
Operating margin	35.0%	35.0%	35.0%	35.0%	35.0%	35.0%	
Tax rate	24.0%	24.0%	24.0%	24.0%	24.0%	24.0%	
CAPEX % of revenue	15.0%	15.0%	15.0%	15.0%	15.0%	15.0%	
Discount rate	11.5%						
Terminal growth rate	1%						

Adjustments to Valuation Multiples

Adjustments can also be made to valuation multiples if the analyst is valuing the company on a relative basis, as shown in the following example:

- A company trades at a price-to-earnings ratio (P/E) of 15×. Its peer group has traded at a ratio between 12× and 18× over the last several years.
- An investor may judge that the company deserves to trade at a premium against peers for its ESG opportunities and/or management of material ESG risks. For example, the company has far lower employee turnover and scores highly on independent surveys of employee satisfaction and engagement, which translates to superior customer retention and revenue growth.
- Based on this and other factors, the investor assigns a fair value (price) equal to 18× next year's earnings per share estimate, finding the stock to be currently undervalued on a relative basis.

Conversely, an investor may only invest in a company with poor ESG practices or greater risks at a multiple that is *lower* than its peer average to compensate.

ESG INTEGRATION IN OTHER ASSET CLASSES: FIXED INCOME

4

- ☐ **7.1.9** apply the approaches to ESG analysis and integration across a range of asset classes
- ☐ **7.1.10** explain how credit rating agencies approach ESG credit scoring

Historically, fixed-income investors adapted the materiality and sustainability frameworks from equity investors to meet their needs. More recently, newer techniques focused specifically on bonds. Different techniques and frameworks are important because bonds differ from equities in the following ways:

- A wider range of issuers besides those that issue equity (e.g., governments, nonprofits, special-purpose entities)
- Seniority in the capital structure
- Finite maturity/term structure
- Interest and principal payments are promised on prespecified future dates
- Instruments with embedded options and/or credit enhancements, such as collateral

With a greater focus on return of capital and downside protection, fixed-income investors typically place greater emphasis on ESG factors that affect balance sheet strength (and therefore focus more on the risk of default) than equity investors, who are more concerned about growth opportunities because they own a residual claim on issuers' net profit and assets.

Proponents of the benefits of ESG investing in fixed income might point to a Barclays (2018) study looking at the performance benefits of a "high" ESG portfolio versus a "low" ESG portfolio of investment-grade bonds using two different ESG datasets (MSCI and Sustainalytics; see Exhibit 8).

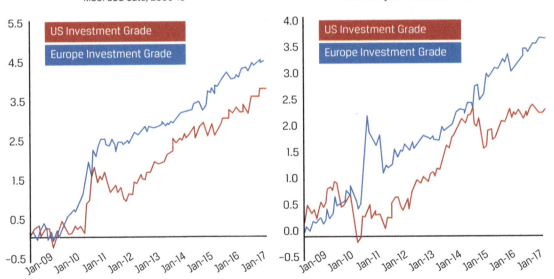

Exhibit 8: Investment-Grade Bond Portfolio Performance (High ESG over Low ESG)

Sources: Barclays (2018); Sustainalytics data based on the firm's legacy ESG ratings.

The case for sustainable bond investing strengthens, but critics would point out the flaws of correlational studies, as well as the short 2009–18 time period. Critics would further point out that ESG ratings correlate with quality and other factors, so not all the outperformance is attributable to ESG factors.

Portfolio managers are developing more sophisticated approaches beyond simple ESG tilts. Chapter 8 illustrates some of the rating distribution features developed by a fixed-income specialist asset manager in its portfolio's ESG evaluation framework. The framework uses third-party ESG data but combines the data to produce proprietary ESG metrics for that firm, including a fundamental, absolute-oriented ESG rating and a relative investment ESG score. The internal investment teams can see an ESG risk from the single-issuer level to the portfolio level, which is a value-added part of the process.

The impact of considering ESG factors in the investment decision-making process can be seen in the credit default swap (CDS) market, as well as on a single-issuer basis, such as with Volkswagen and emission testing (Griffin and Lont 2016). This would be an argument for the impact an ESG event can have on CDSs. However, the timing of subsequent CDSs does not perfectly correspond to when all the information about the emission scandal was first released. The lag in timing might suggest inefficient markets or the lagged delays that market participants have in incorporating material ESG information into CDS prices.

ESG Integration in Sovereign and Investment-Grade Fixed Income

Sovereign debt investors have started to integrate ESG factors, focusing on country-level factors, such as climate risk, freedom of expression, education levels, and corruption. Sovereign debt investors have long integrated political risk and governance factors, even if not explicitly labeled ESG issues, but such environmental factors as climate are a newer consideration. Challenges include even greater subjectivity than in the corporate sector and limited disclosures. Municipal bond instruments (debt instruments issued by government subdivisions) have ESG integration considerations similar to those of sovereign debt, as shown in Exhibit 9.

Exhibit 9: ESG Considerations: Similarities and Differences among Different Types of Issuer

	Corporate*	US Muni**	Sovereign
Issuer Structural Features that May Offset or Reduce an ESG Risk			
Taxation authority to service debt	No	Depends on security; general obligation bonds are typically full faith and credit, which can include taxing power	Yes
Monopoly over selected products or services	Occasionally	Often	Often
Debt monetization***	No	Deficit financing is rare due to balanced budget requirements	Yes
External support	Potentially from a parent company or government subsidies	Borrowers may have access to other state or federal support, depending on the jurisdiction	No, aside from bilateral or multilateral debt relief
Diversity of economic activity as a risk mitigant	Depends on size, product offering, breadth of revenue streams	Depends on issuer economic characteristics, breadth of revenue and purpose of financing	Depends on issuer economic diversification and taxable base
Managing ESG Issues			

	Corporate*	US Muni**	Sovereign
Availability of ESG data	· Disclosed by issuers · Available through CRAs and third parties · Peer comparison difficult	· Disclosed by public sources and issuers (often upon request) · Available through CRAs and third parties · Data can be patchy	· Disclosed by public sources and issuers (often upon request) · Available through CRAs and third parties · Data can be stable
Investors screening issuers for ESG reasons	Yes	Sometimes	Rarely
Degree of investor engagement with issuer	Less common than for shareholders	Less common than for corporate bondholders and more challenging	Less common for corporate bondholders and more challenging
Able to move geographic location	Yes	No****	No
Social stakeholders	Employees, customers, supply chain	Local population, taxpayers, employees and the service base	National population taxpayers
Governing body	Appointed	Depends on sector as to whether elected or appointed	May be elected

Source: PRI (2019).

On the environmental side, the inclusion of low-probability, high-impact events is analytically challenging. Nevertheless, contingent liabilities are often a driver of sovereign credit ratings, and most credit rating agencies attempt to capture such risks in their sovereign credit ratings.

> **EXAMPLE 5**
>
> ### World Bank Sovereign ESG Data Portal
>
> The World Bank relaunched its Sovereign ESG Data Portal in 2023 (the initial launch was in 2019). The portal has become an influential resource for asset managers, investment banks, rating agencies, debt management offices, and ESG data providers to inform their approach to ESG investing in the sovereign debt asset class.
>
> The portal includes 71 ESG indicators ranging from water stress, coastal protection, forest cover loss, heating and cooling degree days, precipitation anomalies, and new data on economic and social rights. It also includes additional indicators that give context to the ESG dimensions, such as the Human Capital Index, inflation, or land surface areas.
>
> As with other asset classes, there are inconsistencies across ESG rating agencies on sovereign ESG scores, even if they share the same underlying data.
>
> For example, Exhibit 10 shows correlations between Environmental scores by major ESG ratings providers.

Exhibit 10: Environmental Score Correlations

Provider	ISS	FTSE Russell/BR	MSCI	RepRisk	Robeco	Sustainalytics	V.E
ISS		0.18	0.05	0.23	0.41	0.32	0.63

Provider	ISS	FTSE Russell/BR	MSCI	RepRisk	Robeco	Sustainalytics	V.E
FTSE Russel/BR	0.18		0.38	0.49	0.68	0.63	0.34
MSCI	0.05	0.38		-0.14	0.29	0.32	0.36
RepRisk	0.23	0.49	-0.14		0.74	0.72	0.29
Robeco	0.41	0.68	0.29	0.74		0.88	0.51
Sustainalytics	0.32	0.63	0.32	0.72	0.88		0.43
V.E	0.63	0.34	0.36	0.29	0.51	0.43	

Note: BR = Beyond Ratings; VE = Vigeo Eiris.
Source: Gratcheva, Emery, and Wang (2020).

ESG Integration in Credit-Sensitive Fixed Income

ESG factors can affect credit risk at different levels:

- Issuer and company level: These are risks that affect a specific bond issue and not the whole market. They are related to such factors as the governance of an issuer, its regulatory compliance, the strength of its balance sheet, and brand reputation. For example, the yield on Volkswagen bonds rose and remained elevated for a prolonged period of time in the aftermath of its fraudulent emission scandal.
- Industry and geographic level: These risks stem from wider-ranging issues affecting the entire industry or region. They can be related to regulatory and legal factors, technological changes associated with the business activity the company is involved in, and the markets it sources from or sells to (e.g., utilities are relatively more exposed to climate change risks than media companies).

ESG Integration in Credit Ratings

Prior to 2016, credit rating agencies (CRAs) typically did not attempt to capture the environmental, ethical, or social impact of a bond issue in a credit rating (PRI 2017). When rating a carbon-intensive company, CRAs focused on other material impacts, including financial, regulatory, and legal factors that could affect the company's credit risk. Many CRAs have since began to look at a range of ESG factors, judge companies' responses to ESG risks and events, and link that to the ability to meet debt obligations. Using standard credit ratio analysis, CRAs might test the following:

- How ESG factors affect an issuer's ability to convert assets into cash (profitability and cash flow analysis)
- The impact that changing yields—due to an ESG event—could have on the cost of capital, depending on the share of debt used in the issuer's capital structure (interest coverage ratio and capital structure analysis)
- The extent to which ESG-related costs affect an issuer's ability to generate profits and add to refinancing risks
- How well an issuer's management uses the assets under its control to generate sales and profit (efficiency ratios)

Credit investors use the information provided by credit ratings to help them price, trade, and assess credit-sensitive fixed-income securities. Credit ratings are also typically used to define and limit investment mandates set by institutional investors. Many investors in investment-grade credit have limited or no ability to invest in high-yield speculative-grade credit, for example. Credit ratings are complemented by proprietary research and judgment by investors to determine the suitability of fixed-income investments.

Although ESG factors may be considered in credit ratings, they are distinct from ESG scores and ratings.

Potential Bias in Ratings

ESG ratings in credit could suffer bias as is seen in other asset classes. Three key types of bias are typically encountered:

1. Company size bias, where larger companies might obtain higher ratings because of the ability to dedicate more resources to nonfinancial disclosures.
2. Geographical bias, where a geographical bias exists toward companies in regions with high reporting requirements or some other cultural factor (e.g., higher unionization levels in Europe).
3. Industry and sector bias, where rating providers oversimplify industry weighting and company alignment.

Bias can potentially also be seen in how certain industries (e.g., technology) are assessed in comparison to other industries or through the lens of other factor labels, such as "growth" or "value."

Green Bonds

Green bonds are fixed-income instruments used to finance projects with an intended environmental benefit. Examples include projects associated with renewable energy, public transportation, energy-efficient buildings and manufacturing processes, agricultural land management, waste management, and water management. A green bond's credit risk is assessed in the same manner as a conventional bond with the exception that labeling a bond as "green" also considers the ESG or sustainability aspects of the project; that is, the use of the proceeds from the bond issuance have to lead to environmental benefits.

Often a green bond has some form of verification or assurance from a third-party organization. This organization ensures that the use of proceeds meets the criteria set out in the bond, though the covenants related to this will vary among bonds. Debate continues as to what makes a bond "green" because no global consensus exists on the types of capital projects that fit in the scope of green bonds. For example, many investors rejected Repsol's green bond issued in 2017 to finance improvements to its oil refineries. There are, however, several frameworks that may start to standardize the definition, such as the EU Green Taxonomy. As of early 2023, the EU Green Bond Standard was still undergoing EU parliamentary negotiations, although progress has been made since the proposal legislation was first published in 2021 (European Commission 2021). Note that in various countries (e.g., China) the local legislation gives the definition of green bonds and the issuance framework, while most countries have no local regulations and follow industry-derived definitions and frameworks.

Sustainability-linked bonds (SLBs) are a type of instrument similar to green bonds. Unlike a green bond, which requires the proceeds to specifically finance environmental-related projects, SLB proceeds are not "ring fenced" for a specific purpose but, rather, are issued as general obligation bonds with contractual links to the achievement of sustainability targets by the issuer. Usually, the issuer agrees to pay a higher coupon to investors if it fails to achieve a sustainability-linked target. Relative to green bonds, SLBs allow issuers more flexibility in achieving sustainability targets.

ESG INTEGRATION IN OTHER ASSET CLASSES: REAL ESTATE AND PRIVATE MARKETS

7.1.9 apply the approaches to ESG analysis and integration across a range of asset classes

ESG Integration in Real Estate Markets

Real assets (including vacant land, farmland, timber, infrastructure, intellectual property, commodities, and private real estate) carry certain advantages and challenges compared to equities and fixed income (Chambers, Black, and Lacey 2018). In many cases, investors are majority owners or own the asset outright. Majority or full ownership stakes offer investors much greater control over the definition, application, and reporting of ESG data alongside or outside existing reporting standards, such as Building Research Establishment Environmental Assessment Methodology (BREEAM) certifications or the Global Real Estate Sustainability Benchmark (GRESB). The framework has some similarities to the SASB framework discussed earlier, but the material ESG factors differ.

GRESB's full benchmark report (see Chapter 8), which does depend heavily on companies participating in the reporting process, provides the following:

- a composite of peer group information,
- overall portfolio key performance indicator (KPI) performance,
- aggregate environmental data in terms of usage and efficiency gains,
- a GRESB score that weights management, policy, and disclosure; risks and opportunities; and monitoring and environmental management systems (EMSs),
- environmental impact reduction targets, and
- data validation and assurance

Overall, material ESG factors in real estate include the following:

- Environmental factors—energy efficiency of the property, use of renewable energy, water conservation measures, waste management practices, proximity to environmental hazards, and so on
- Social factors—tenant relations, community engagement, accessibility and inclusion, local job creation, affordability, and so on

Buildings themselves also have a carbon footprint in their construction, ongoing operation and energy use, and use of land. An integrated ESG view might look at reducing a building's carbon footprint by using more efficient materials and heating, ventilation, and air-conditioning systems to lower the impact from carbon prices or deriving gains from energy efficiencies.

ESG Integration in Private Equity

ESG integration in private markets faces a number of challenges, foremost being the lack of transparency and regulatory oversight found in public markets. Current initiatives aim to address these challenges, such as the PRI's (2018) reporting frameworks. In addition, smaller, private companies are often face capacity challenges from ESG reporting requirements, with management solely focused on survival and growth. Private equity investors might have to negotiate with a founder who has a majority stake in the company.

Still, early investors can be strategic and long-term oriented, creating a powerful incentive to establish a strong set of ESG KPIs early in the company's life cycle. Some investors will perform a materiality analysis much like public equity investors do; the same SASB framework might be used or developed via the private equity industry—for example, the British Private Equity & Venture Capital Association's Responsible Investment Framework. Two case study examples of Uber and WeWork from recent years show the role governance analysis played in the IPO and valuation of Uber (Larcker and Tayan 2018) and the failed IPO of WeWork (Langevoort and Sale 2021).

A typical assessment might include the steps in Exhibit 11.

Exhibit 11: Steps in a Typical ESG Assessment

Deal Sourcing →	Investment Decision →	Ownership →	Exit →
Identifying material ESG issues during *ESG screening and due diligence*	Including material issues in the *investment memorandum* and negotiation of the *investment agreement*	Managing ESG issues during the *onboarding, engagement*, and *monitoring* of portfolio company	Adding value at *exit*

Source: PRI (2018).

Private equity investors view ESG integration through several lenses:

1. Risk management—Investors view ESG analysis as a way to identify and manage risks that could impact the financial performance of their portfolio companies. Such issues as exposure to environmental regulation and litigation risks due to poor labor practices can affect revenue, costs, and valuations if not properly managed.

2. Value creation—Some investors believe that implementing strong ESG practices can create business value by boosting employee retention, increasing customer affinity, gaining access to new markets and products, and so on. Thus, they proactively help their portfolio companies adopt ESG strategies to unlock this potential value.

3. A differentiating factor in attracting clients—Increasingly, some investors see ESG integration as a way to differentiate themselves and attract capital from the growing pool of ESG-conscious capital allocators, such as pension funds, sovereign wealth funds, and family offices. So, they include ESG factors prominently in their investment approach and reporting to appeal to these limited partners. This lens, however, raises the risk of greenwashing.

Overall, while there are philosophical similarities in identifying material ESG factors and then applying those to the analysis, the type of factors used can differ among asset classes, as can the type of integration techniques.

CASE STUDIES IN ESG INTEGRATION

☐ **7.1.9** apply the approaches to ESG analysis and integration across a range of asset classes

Several adapted case studies in equity and fixed-income investments will be highlighted in this section. Although this section does not provide detailed case studies in private equity, infrastructure, or other alternative investments, many similar techniques can be used in those asset classes. Unless otherwise mentioned, the case studies are adaptations from CFA Institute case studies (see the Further Reading section).

We will look at the following case studies:

- Case Study 1: Quantitative Systematic Approach to an Environmental Tilted Mandate in Global Equities
- Case Study 2: Fundamental ESG Integration
- Case Study 3: ESG Analysis Supporting a Premium Valuation Ratio
- Case Study 4: DCF Scenario Analysis Considering ESG Factors
- Case Study 5: Credit Analysis Integrating ESG Factors
- Case Study 6: Credit ESG Integration Practice
- Case Study 7: Sovereign Debt Analysis

CASE STUDIES

Case Study 1: Quantitative Systematic Approach to an Environmental Tilted Mandate in Global Equities

A foundation endowment with an underlying mission to fund climate science wishes to invest part of its endowment funds in a systematic global equity strategy tilted to companies that have positive environmental characteristics.

The endowment discusses a mandate with a quantitative systematic investment manager and explains that the following rules and factors are important:

- The use of at least two third-party ESG scoring systems
- A proprietary scoring system
- A publicly available environmental management policy for all invested companies
- A requirement that the average blend of the rating systems meet a minimum criterion on an E score
- Quarterly rebalancing

In practice, for specific mandates, many further detailed rules and conditions can be set on other ESG aspects or other established quantitative and fundamental factors (e.g., quality or geography).

The fund manager converts the third-party E scores through its own formula and uses the database to flag companies with no environmental management policy. The manager has an in-house team that uses a scorecard approach to score companies on material, relevant environmental risks and opportunities. This score is combined with the third-party scores and a minimum threshold set, where the bottom 20% of companies are deemed ineligible for the fund.

The remaining companies are weighted to approximately match a specified global benchmark with respect to momentum, quality, and volatility factors, as well as other nonenvironmental ESG factors, and within the bounds of other construction criteria, such as tracking error and market beta.

These calculations are performed once a quarter, and the portfolio is adjusted accordingly. The rules are examined once a year in consultation with the end client. Performance and ESG measurements are recorded and assessed. An engagement or stewardship program could be implemented for companies not meeting or in danger of not meeting the specified environmental criteria.

Case Study 2: Fundamental ESG Integration

This fund manager adjusts the most relevant financial forecasts for companies (revenue, profits or returns on capital, capital and operational expenditures, and cash flows) based on material ESG factors. It also considers the potential ESG impact on the overall security valuation by adjusting the target multiples (discount or premium and discount rate).

The chemical sector is analyzed. The following trends are assessed:

- Aging populations that will require more health and well-being products
- Regulations that influence a move toward biodegradable or bio-derived plastics
- Evolving consumer sensitivity to "green" issues

A company is considered a good target for further assessment only if it reflects positively on those trends.

Company A is well positioned to participate in these trends. Company A is one of the world's leading suppliers of specialty chemicals based on renewable raw materials that are used in personal care, life sciences, and industrial chemicals. It enjoys an industry-leading position in adopting sustainable practices, having differentiated itself from its petrochemical-based specialty chemical peers. Two-thirds of Company A's raw materials come from natural sources.

Company A has opened a new chemical plant with a renewable-source, plant-based feed stock. The fund manager judges that the new plant will allow the company to capture more of the value chain in surfactants and to charge a premium because consumers are willing to pay more for sustainable products. This will improve revenue growth through increased market share and pricing and the company is forecast to increase sales with growth 2 percentage points above the industry average for the next 10 years. These developments are embedded in a DCF forecast, and a value is calculated.

This value is then cross-checked with a P/E. The fund manager is prepared to pay a 50% premium on a current P/E basis applied to near-term earnings because of the company's strong sales and earnings growth. Company A currently trades at only a 10% P/E premium to the chemical sector. Also, the DCF model recommends a 35% target price upside in the next year.

Based on this analysis, the company is selected to go into the fund manager's portfolio.

(Note: Thanks to Hyewon Kong for the example on which this case study is based.)

Case Study 3: ESG Analysis Supporting a Premium Valuation Ratio

An investor is reviewing its portfolio and assesses Company Z, a semiconductor equipment manufacturer that has been performing well and now trades at a 50% premium to the sector on a P/E basis.

To achieve long-term value creation, in accordance with its investment philosophy, the investor needs to have a strong conviction regarding the company's ability to maintain its industry-leading products and profitability.

The investor identifies the following key operational risks for the company:

- Maintaining the company's leadership position through investment in human capital (e.g., PhD scientists and engineers), manufacturing facilities, and technology
- The potential for manufacturing delays or product defects that could affect its reputation and market share

E and S data were assessed using third-party databases. The company ranked as a top 10% performer over the relevant criteria. The following three major areas were considered strong enough to address the key operational risks raised and to recommend an even higher P/E premium, so the investor decided that the company should be kept in the portfolio:

- Attracting and retaining talent: The investor evaluated employee engagement and compensation to help gauge the risks associated with attracting and retaining talent. The company's average employee wage was significantly higher than that of its peers, and it had low employee turnover. In a highly complex R&D-intensive industry, this suggested that the company is well positioned to attract and retain top talent. This in turn should enhance the company's innovation potential.
- Sustainable business model: These elements were considered superior to those of the company's competitors:
  - Its positioning as enabling smaller, faster, and more energy-efficient electronics
  - Its customer-centric approach of providing aftermarket enhancements and refurbishments to improve customers' capital efficiency
  - Its culture of innovation and collaboration with internal and external stakeholders that have the potential to generate both new business opportunities and broader social benefits
- Asset quality and efficiency: The company had industry-leading resource (water and energy) intensity per unit of revenue, higher performance regarding water and waste recycling, and lower carbon emission intensity than its peers.

(Thanks to GS Sustain for the example on which this study is based.)

Case Study 4: DCF Scenario Analysis Considering ESG Factors

The Global Equities investment team uses an integrated approach. Rather than having separate ESG analysts, the team's portfolio managers perform and integrate ESG analysis. They believe this is a better way to value and assess stocks. The team uses multiple sources of ESG information because it represents an abundance of ESG-related opinions that require interpretation, and portfolio managers are best placed to filter this advice and ascertain how it relates to a company's business model and valuation.

The team starts with fundamental analysis to identify any material positive or negative ESG factors. The team embeds that assessment into an analysis of the competitive position and the sustainability of the business, which it then puts into valuation models. The team aims to invest only in companies that perform strongly in at least five areas:

1. business model,
2. market share opportunity,
3. end-market growth,
4. management, and
5. ESG performance.

The team identified several ESG risks (contingent liabilities) and ESG opportunities (contingent assets) for a leading health care company with businesses ranging from insurance to consulting to information technology.

ESG Risks

As custodians of the personal and medical details of millions of people, the company needs to keep the data secure: "False" savings here can have long-term consequences, including regulatory and political risks and the potential impairment of the company's social contract with customers and society at large.

The team challenged management on the risk of privacy data breaches, asking how that risk is being managed and what policies are in place to mitigate that risk. Management acknowledged that information about its data security was not available on the company's website, but several management members reassured the team about the quality of the policies, training, and general operation management of data handling and security that are in place. Nevertheless, the team modeled a DCF valuation scenario looking at the possible impact of privacy data breaches.

ESG Opportunities

The data analytics business was viewed as having strong ESG potential. The analytics business allows the company to create cheaper, better health care options for businesses, governments, and patients, creating a strong competitive advantage and an ESG contingent asset. For instance, it identified 150 diabetic patients not taking their medication properly, 123 of whom were in Texas, which enabled its client to implement location-specific measures using preventive health care techniques.

In another instance, using the company's data analytics, a state department in the United States discovered clusters of patients with asthma on certain streets and in certain buildings and found that those areas correlated with cockroach infestations, allowing the state department to successfully prosecute the landlords and ultimately raise living standards for tenants.

The team assessed the materiality of all this information and assigned a rating for the four areas critical for assessing a the company's strengths.

The team then performed DCF scenario analysis embedding the material ESG risks and opportunities. The team prefers DCF and explicit model scenarios for sales, margins, and asset turns because they are judged to be a more accurate method of modeling than an adjustment to a discount rate or terminal value for a company-specific assessment. Sum-of-the-parts and standard financial ratio assessments were also performed.

The analysis was peer reviewed within the team, and the assumptions were stress tested, challenged, and refined before the rating and valuation were confirmed. In the peer review, assumptions were flexed in real time to see how further valuation scenarios change. These include the following:

- For the upside scenario, increasing EBIT margins and sales growth
- For the downside scenario, normalizing sales to a lower growth rate (3%) and looking at the sales impact over more than one year

The core findings supported significant valuation upside and limited probability of mild downside. The stock was then added to the portfolio.

(Adapted from a Royal Bank of Canada Global Asset Management example case study [CFA Institute and PRI 2018].)

Case Study 5: Credit Analysis Integrating ESG Factors

When analyzing a corporate bond for investment, a credit investor evaluates an issuer's business profile, market position, and competitive profile, as well as fundamental credit measures (such as margins, leverage, and cash flow). The analysis then turns to an evaluation of management and sector-specific material ESG indicators, such as carbon emissions, workplace injury rates, and the composition of the board of directors.

The ESG analysis consists of a quantitative score and qualitative-based research.

The quantitative score is derived from a proprietary framework that aggregates metrics from ESG research providers and from other third-party sources.

The corporate credit analyst also performs a qualitative assessment by reviewing a company's ESG policies and targets, which might be outlined in its corporate sustainability report or on its website, and consider information learned from the engagement call.

The analyst evaluates both the score and qualitative research when assigning a sustainability rating for the company. This measure of an issuer's ESG risk profile could affect the analyst's overall internal rating. Specifically, the analyst might upgrade the internal rating to reflect a corporation's low ESG risks or downgrade the rating if the ESG risks are considered high or poorly managed.

A beverage company is examined. The research identifies several strengths and weaknesses, some of which might be material from a financial perspective. For example, because water is a key input for the ingredients used in the company's products, efforts to ensure a steady supply of water would be considered both an ESG strength and a credit strength. Furthermore, water management is a material issue for the sector because a lack of water can affect crop yields and prices and a beverage company's operations can restrict access to water by locals.

Strengths and Weaknesses of Considered Brands

	Strengths	Weaknesses
E	▸ Collaboration with suppliers to improve water efficiency by 15% in high-risk areas ▸ Its GHG emissions goal is aligned with a science-based target initiative.	▸ There is weak disclosure on progress being made to reduce packaging waste.
S	▸ It has a comprehensive human rights strategy and strong supplier code-of-conduct protocols.	▸ Certain talent retention and recruitment strategies trail best practices. ▸ Products are primarily sugary drinks, despite introduction of healthier brands.
G	▸ Robust antibribery policies govern interactions with suppliers. ▸ The board of directors formally oversees sustainability initiatives. ▸ Rigorous, year-round stakeholder engagement includes consumer groups.	▸ No significant challenges seen

The totality of material ESG information depicts a company judged to have a strong ESG profile, and a high sustainability rating is assigned, which is also incorporated into the company's final internal credit rating.

(Thanks to Robert Fernandez for the original case study on which this case study is based.)

Case Study 6: Credit ESG Integration Practice

The credit team of an asset manager uses several inputs in conducting credit risk analysis and consults a central ESG/responsibility team for firm policies, approaches, and investment tools.

At a company-specific level, the credit team reviews the proprietary measures of ESG risk—that is, its quantitative ESG (QESG) score that the firm has developed. This QESG score represents a snapshot of the company's overall ESG performance.

The QESG score is supported by the company information provided by a separate steward and engagement team (whom some practitioners consider an active ownership team) to give a sense of the potential forward trajectory.

The asset manager invested in bonds issued by a state-owned oil producer, which is now being assessed in an annual review. ESG factors emerged as recurring themes in the credit discussion. The company's labor safety track record was below the industry average, and the company had experienced frequent oil spills and leaks in the past. Spills and leaks could result in fines and production downtime, damaging the company's cash flow profile.

After this annual analysis of the credit committee, an ESG score of 4 was assigned to the company (below average on a scale of 1 to 5, with 1 being the best). Bonds already acquired were kept, but because of the low ESG score, there was no further exposure to credit.

Later that year, the ESG score was upgraded to 3 (from 4) to reflect the company's improvement in the following ESG factors:

1. Improvement in worker safety (injury frequency per million man-hours worked declined 35% year over year)

2. Progress in reducing environmental waste and emissions (water reuse increased 66% year over year, while sulfur oxide emissions declined 45% year over year)

After the score upgrade, the investors added to the bond position. The company's ability to manage ESG risks was assessed to be improving.

(Thanks to Mitch Reznick and Audra Stundziaite for the original case study on which this case study is based.)

Case Study 7: Sovereign Debt Analysis

An investor uses ESG analysis on a holistic basis in its investment framework, which prioritizes real yields and real exchange rates in the analysis of sovereign debt. The investor assigns a financial stability score (FSS) to a country based on the overall government budget strength, level of public debt, stance of the balance of payments, and ESG factors. The FSS ranges from +4 to –4 for those countries and currencies deemed to make it into the opportunity set and will lead to exclusion for those rankings below –4. However, the FSS is determined after a review of the ESG factors, and a strong sovereign financial position might be heavily penalized because of weak ESG factors. In this example, a country with a strong financial position can be significantly negatively affected by ESG factors.

The investor considered for analysis the sovereign bonds of two developed countries. It looks at the sovereign bonds of Country A because they trade at an attractive spread relative to those issued by Country B.

The structural weakness in the sovereign financial position of Country A is long-standing. Political instability has prevented successive governments from implementing lasting structural reforms, limiting the country's growth potential. While Country A compares unfavorably to most other developed world economies on most ESG indicators, weak governance underpins much of this underperformance. Such weaknesses have facilitated tax evasion and corruption, led to inefficient resource allocation, hampered productivity growth, and promoted growth in the shadow economy. An inefficient bureaucracy and a complex, slow legal system also increase transaction costs and inhibit activity.

Country A also underperforms on a number of social and environmental factors. While educational standards appear comparable with those of other OECD countries, Country A suffers skill mismatches, particularly with lower-skilled workers, which affects wage and productivity growth. This translates into very high youth unemployment and a school drop-out rate that is high compared with its peers.

In summary, while Country A has made some reform progress recently and has low private sector debt, it has high government debt, structural rigidities, unstable government, and weak levels of governance and social factors. Assessment of these ESG factors weighs on Country A's overall FSS, leaving it at the lower end of the FSS range, at –3. Given that these weaknesses have been inherent in its financial position for several years, Country A's FSS has remained unchanged over the past 10 years. Notwithstanding market volatility and credit rating agency pronouncements, the key drivers of Country A's financial stability have not materially changed over many years. Country A's potential real yield (FSS adjusted) relative to other markets, combined with risk management, kept the investor underweight position in Country A's bonds prior to the Global Financial Crisis. When valuations became more attractive in mid-2012, the investor established a gradual overweight position, despite the unchanged financial position. As yields for Country A's bonds fell in absolute and relative terms with respect to Country B's yields, the investor reduced its exposure to Country A's bonds.

(Thanks to Claudia Gollmeier for the original case study on which this case study is based.)

7 ESG INTEGRATION DATABASES AND SOFTWARE

☐ **7.1.11** explain the approaches taken across a range of ESG integration databases and software available, and the nature of the information provided

☐ **7.1.12** identify the main providers of screening services or tools, similarities and differences in their methodologies, and the aims, benefits and limitations of using them

☐ **7.1.13** describe the limitations and constraints of information provided by ESG integration databases

Typical mainstream investment research often includes an ESG or sustainability offering, and most research firms (the "sell side") will have analysts producing research in this area. One way of classifying providers is by business type:

- Large, for-profit providers that offer multiple ESG-related products and services, as well as non-ESG-related products and services (e.g., Bloomberg, FactSet, Fitch, Moody's, Morningstar, MSCI, S&P)
- Boutique, for-profit providers that offer specialty ESG products and services (e.g., RepRisk, Urgentum, Truvalue Labs, CICERO)
- Nonprofit providers that offer ESG-related products and services—for example, CDP (formerly known as Carbon Disclosure Project), IMF (economic data), the World Bank (ESG data portal), and UNEP (these services are free to the general public and in the public domain)

Another way of thinking about the services is by type of product or service; the following is a nonexhaustive list:

- ESG data—quantitative or qualitative information on the environmental, social, economic, and corporate governance practices of companies
- ESG ratings—opinions, which may be expressed as a number or letter grade, of an issuer or fund based on an assessment of a company's approach, disclosure, strategy, or performance on ESG issues (different methodologies are discussed later)
- ESG screening—tools that evaluate companies, countries, and bonds based on their exposure or involvement-specific factors, sectors, products, or services
- Voting and governance advice—typically, proxy vote advisory services, including voting guidelines on governance and other proxy voting items, such as compensation and board directorships
- ESG benchmarks and indexes—a set of securities (e.g., stocks, bonds, exchange-traded funds, or ETFs) designed to represent some aspect of the total market by including some ESG criteria in the selection

ESG Integration Databases and Software

- ESG news about and controversy alerts on a company or a country to highlight events, behaviors, and practices that might lead to reputational and business risks and opportunities
- Integrated research—typically sell-side research (investment bank or broker reports) consisting of contextualized, data-informed, analytical opinion designed to support investment decision making
- Advisory services—ESG strategy, integration, investment process, reporting, and corporate advice, within which are many specific ESG-related services, such as the following:
  - Class action litigation
  - **Sustainable Development Goals (SDGs)** reporting and alignment
  - Carbon and water analysis
  - Norms and sanctions
  - Policy development
  - Real estate assessment
  - Factor databases
  - Supply chain assessment
  - Assurance services

ESG Assessment and Ratings of Issuers

MSCI and Sustainalytics (owned by Morningstar since 2020) have large market shares in issuer ESG ratings. Both rating agencies have grown by acquiring other ESG rating providers over the past decade. However, new companies are still entering the field of ESG assessment.

The various types of assessment include the following:

- Fundamental, including risk, business model, policies, and preparedness
- Operational, including carbon impact, water stress, and human capital management
- Disclosure-based assessment
- Algorithm and news based, including controversies

Typically, a rating provider will establish a methodology to inform the rating by identifying a set of relevant ESG issues, assigning indicators to evaluate performance on those issues, and then developing a weighting and scoring process to evaluate a company.

Most established systems assign a certain level of performance on an issue based on the number of points or a grade. Points or grade assignments can be attached to a quantitative metric (e.g., the number of female directors or emissions reduced) or to qualitative assessments (e.g., a "high," "medium," or "low" assessment based on policies, procedures, or performance). Topics are also often assigned a weight, establishing different levels of influence for different topics or sets of topics on the final rating.

ESG ratings are primarily based on historical company data and alternative data sources (e.g., media sources). Rating agencies try to synthesize these data to provide investors with information to inform investment decisions. Some ESG rating providers are also developing measures of "climate risk" that attempt to assess forward-looking risk informed by the Paris Agreement and by such initiatives as the Task Force on Climate-Related Financial Disclosures.

To produce a rating, a provider will typically perform the following tasks:

- Identify indicators that determine which ESG indicators are most material to the sector in question (see the discussion of materiality mapping earlier in this chapter).
- Gather a set of data points for the identified indicators on the company in question from company public disclosures, survey responses, unstructured company data, or third-party data. Assess the data gathered for consistency, and on occasion, estimate any missing data points (not all rating providers estimate data points).
- Quantify qualitative data points through scoring or ranking methodologies; score or evaluate quantitative data points through scoring or ranking methodologies. Combine these data points with regard to the predetermined weighting system applied to the indicators to create a sector-relative score for a company that assesses its performance relative to its peer group or an absolute score—or both.

ESG factor identification is up to the rating provider; therefore, dispersal of opinions starts even before consideration of different weighting and scoring methodologies. A result of the heterogeneity in data and methodologies is that the agreement or correlation between ESG ratings of issuers by different providers is low, much lower than the >0.9 correlation between credit ratings by the three major credit rating agencies.

- A study by Chatterji, Levine, and Toffel (2009) found an approximate 0.3 correlation. However, this also included some negative correlations, meaning that what one rater found responsible another found "irresponsible." A study by Gibson, Krueger, and Schmidt (2019) shows a range of correlations.
- A study by Berg, Koelbel, and Rigobon (2021) shows a range of correlations as well; they examined at a dataset of ESG ratings from six different raters: KLD (MSCI Stats), Sustainalytics, Vigeo Eiris (Moody's), RobecoSAM (S&P Global), Asset4 (Refinitiv), and MSCI. The correlations between the ratings are on average 0.54 and range from 0.38 to 0.71.

Berg et al. (2021) noted, "This means that the information that decision makers receive from ESG rating agencies is relatively noisy." They went on to explain three major consequences:

- *"First, ESG performance is less likely to be reflected in corporate stock and bond prices, as investors face a challenge when trying to identify outperformers and laggards. Investor tastes can influence asset prices, but only when a large enough fraction of the market holds and implements a uniform nonfinancial preference. Therefore, even if a large fraction of investors has a preference for ESG performance, the divergence of the ratings disperses the effect of these preferences on asset prices.*
- *Second, the divergence hampers the ambition of companies to improve their ESG performance, because they receive mixed signals from rating agencies about which actions are expected and will be valued by the market.*
- *Third, the divergence of ratings poses a challenge for empirical research, as using one rater versus another may alter a study's results and conclusions."*

Most of the tools are available only commercially. However, the completeness of coverage varies substantially across ESG tools. The correlations might well change over time, as providers evolve the way ratings are produced. For example, Sustainalytics experienced a major change in its ESG rating system in 2019, and all main providers' processes continue to evolve.

ESG Integration Databases and Software

This evolving process also makes historic comparisons difficult. The different methodologies might also mean like-for-like comparisons are not being made in the correlations between rating agencies.

Practitioners debate how important strong correlations are:

- On the one hand, high correlations could lead to groupthink and a lack of rigorous thinking. Some believe this was one of the problems with credit rating agencies' universally positive assessment of mortgage-backed bonds before the Global Financial Crisis. To some, a low correlation is a healthy and useful outcome from ESG rating providers noting the distinction between ratings and raw data.
- On the other hand, simplicity and correlation could bring credibility to ESG ratings as a discipline and give more consistent messages to companies. As described in the quantitative investment sections, quantitative investors use these data differently than they do fundamental active investor judgments.

The sources of information used to assess ESG investments also vary among the ESG tools. Information can be collected directly (via surveys, company communication, company reports, presentations, and public documents) or indirectly (via news articles, third-party reports, and analysis). Another consideration when thinking of providers is where they have come from and which stakeholders are served. Here are some examples:

- "Traditional" ESG data and research providers, founded from the socially responsible investing industry to provide investors with sustainability data and ratings on primarily large, publicly traded companies: More recent consolidation activity has turned these providers into conglomerates with different offerings and research focuses. The level of automation is low or medium because human judgment is still used.
- "Nontraditional" ESG data and research providers: More recently, nontraditional providers, such as credit rating agencies (e.g., Fitch, Moody's, and S&P), entered the space by acquiring Trucost (in 2016) and Vigeo Eiris (in 2019). As with traditional ESG data and research providers, the level of automation is low or medium because human judgment is still used.
- AI or algorithm-driven ESG research: Launched in the past five years, these providers use new technologies, such as natural language processing, to identify ESG risks and opportunities from web-based sources. The level of automation is high.

Some of these providers might have index businesses and serve issuers as well as asset owners and asset managers. One way to think about these rating and data providers is through their broad styles and techniques:

- Raw or partially transformed data (e.g., absolute carbon emissions, or carbon intensity, which is emissions or sales)
- Rating-based on backward-looking reported data
- Ratings or information based on online, third-party, and web-reported data, aiming to be current
- Aggregators of data or ratings

The considerations that investors could take into account when choosing providers include

- the number of companies covered,
- the length of history of datasets,
- the languages used,

- the stability of methodology,
- the regularity of updates,
- asset class coverage,
- the quality of methodology,
- the range of datasets, and
- the range of tools and services offered.

Consensus on ESG ratings is currently limited among investors. In that sense, it is similar to current discussions on sell-side equity research, which is investment research typically generated by investment banks. These sell-side ratings (e.g., buy/sell/hold, overweight/underweight versus index, or target prices and credit spreads) are not expected to agree. The rating divergence in opinions can be helpful for investors in decision making because it allows both positive and negative arguments to come to light and to be assessed. However, this is somewhat different from CRAs, which typically have highly correlated credit ratings.

8. MUTUAL FUND AND FUND MANAGER ESG ASSESSMENT AND OTHER USES OF ESG DATA

7.1.14 describe primary and secondary sources of ESG data and information

Morningstar's sustainability ratings are an example of ESG fund and fund manager assessments. Mercer assesses fund managers and funds from an investment consultant viewpoint.

EXAMPLE 6

Morningstar's Sustainability Ratings

As of 2021, Morningstar covered more than 20,000 mutual funds and more than 2,000 ETFs with a score of 1 to 5 (the system was started in 2018). It uses company-level ratings from Sustainalytics (now part of Morningstar) to develop its fund ratings, and the headline rating is freely available. Morningstar takes a "holdings-based approach"—a weighted average of portfolio companies' ESG scores. No credit or assessment is given to managers' efforts on shareholder engagement and public advocacy or on their sophistication, culture, or investment strategy. One key critique of this approach is that holdings-based approaches ignore intentional ESG strategy and that the approach is necessarily backward looking.

Given that the correlation of the two major rating systems (Sustainalytics and MSCI) is low and variable and that Morningstar uses only the Sustainalytics data for its calculations, there is limited comparability between its ratings and those provided by other raters.

> **EXAMPLE 7**
>
> ### Mercer's Point System
>
> Investment consultants, such as Mercer, will also rate the ESG capabilities of fund managers, which is often done at a fund strategy level. Mercer has a 4-point score, where its highest rating of ESG = 1 is given to less than 5% of investment teams.
>
> Mercer's investment consultants might look for the following features:
>
> - ESG factors have been demonstrated as being featured in investment teams' decision-making process and corporate culture.
> - An effort has been made to build ESG factors into valuation metrics, using the investment team's own judgment about materiality and time frames.
> - There is a long-term investment horizon and low portfolio turnover.
> - Ownership policies and practices include sufficient oversight, integration with investment decision making, and transparency.
> - For alternative assets, there is evidence of pursuing best practices in transparency and evaluation, with monitoring and improvement of ESG performance as relevant for portfolio companies and sectors.
> - There is a demonstrated willingness to collaborate with other institutional investors to improve company, sector, or market performance.
> - Commitment to ESG integration can be seen across the organization.
>
> *Source:* Adapted from Mercer (2018).

The aim of these assessments is to form a view on the ESG integration practices and processes of different fund managers and strategies so asset owners, both retail and institutional, can find what best fits their needs. AS with ESG ratings of issuers, there are limitations and challenges to these ratings. These limitations include

- different methodologies (some focus on investment processes, others on portfolio holdings),
- different data sources or rating providers,
- the unaudited limited data sources,
- the time resource to make the comparisons, and
- the relatively nontransparent and noncomparable way these assessments are performed.

ESG Index Providers

Such firms as FTSE Russell and MSCI provide ESG index benchmarks. These indexes can be custom built to an investor's preferences (typically at the institutional level) and are generally commercially available in more standard versions.

The index typically relies on rule-based criteria assessed on underlying ESG scores or metrics. These criteria then go into a formula to tilt company weightings or exclude entire companies based on ESG scores and hurdles. These scores can be sourced by other ESG service providers. For instance, Sustainalytics started providing FTSE Russell with underlying data in 2019 (and had provided Morningstar with data before this).

These indexes can be used as benchmarks for fund managers to be measured against or as model funds for investors to directly invest into in a form of beta or passive management. These types of indexes have been developed into different ranges of "ESG ETFs." ETFs are made up of a basket of securities (stocks, bonds, and other assets).

These ETFs follow the underlying index or basket construction in a rule-based fashion. These can be thematic—namely, investing only in certain sectors—or tilt weightings based on ESG scores, as described earlier. These scores can be data based (e.g., carbon emissions), rating based (e.g., on a provider's ratings), or a mix of the two. Debates continue as to how well these ETFs capture potential ESG factors.

Primary and Secondary ESG Data Sources

Many ESG databases provide secondary ESG data or ratings. These are assessments transformed by a process of scoring or by a formula from a primary data source. Some providers (e.g., Bloomberg) will provide primary data sourced from company reports in an easier or consistent form to digest, along with a secondary rating (e.g., Bloomberg ESG Disclosure score).

Primary data can be sourced from companies directly via surveys, direct company communication, and company reports, presentations, and public documents.

These public documents can be sourced from nonprofit organizations, such as the UN Global Compact or the GRI, as well as the companies' own websites. A primary source might be audited or not audited, but as of 2020, many ESG performance indicators are not audited (though the number has increased since 2018 and is expected to continue to increase, verification and auditing of carbon emissions being one important data point that is increasingly audited).

Alternatively, the source may be indirect, via news articles, third-party reports and analysis, or investment and consulting research. Indirect assessment can be via a third-party source (e.g., Glassdoor for employee satisfaction data and scores, which are directly sourced from employee surveys). They could also come from government, regulatory body, or nongovernmental organization (NGO) reports into different ESG segments.

Some of these data or assessments might be used widely between organizations. For instance, CDP carbon data are used as an input by many of the major ESG rating providers, such as FTSE Russell, MSCI, and Sustainalytics.

Secondary data sources typically involve transforming the primary ESG data in some way and creating new scores, assessments, or ratings based on these transformations. These are available from commercial organizations, both financial and nonfinancial, as well as from regulators, NGOs, and other nonprofit or charitable bodies.

Conclusion

There are many techniques for ESG integration across asset classes, though most investors are aligned in seeking to maximize risk-adjusted returns in using these ESG tools. While certain tools are asset-class specific, the overall framework of identifying material ESG factors and then embedding them in valuation and assessment remains similar.

As of 2023, the field remains dynamic, as it has been over recent years, and expert techniques and tools for analysis continue to evolve.

KEY FACTS

1. Investors integrate ESG techniques to improve investment returns, lower investment risk, meet client needs, and comply with regulatory requirements.
2. A multitude of approaches can be used to integrate ESG analysis into a firm's investment process. Many approaches can be combined, and some are more suitable to specific asset classes and risks.
3. Materiality assessment is an important ESG technique because investors typically distinguish between important, material ESG factors and less important, nonmaterial ESG factors. Nonmaterial factors are viewed as not affecting investment considerations.
4. Primary ESG data come from direct sources. Secondary ESG information has been transformed or assessed. Investors can use both types of ESG sources in their analysis. ESG data, like all data, need to be interpreted in the correct contexts.
5. ESG rating agencies use a mix of ESG information and proprietary assessments to give ESG ratings to stocks and credits. Current ESG rating agencies have variable correlations between their ESG ratings because of methodological differences.
6. CRAs are increasingly using ESG factors, particularly G factors, in their credit assessments. This trend has developed and is expected to continue to develop quickly.
7. Investment consultants and asset owners will use ESG assessment to judge investment managers and as part of their decision criteria.
8. Index providers use ESG factors in establishing ESG indexes. These can be thematic or general.
9. Investors use a range of ESG ratings and techniques, both internally generated and sourced from third parties, to enhance their investment valuation and decision processes.
10. ESG tools and integration techniques continue to develop at a fast pace because of investor and end-customer demand.

FURTHER READING

- Reports and Standards Concerning ESG Practice CFA Institute. 2017. "Global Perceptions of Environmental, Social, and Governance Issues in Investing." www.cfainstitute.org/en/research/survey-reports/esg-survey-2017.
- CFA Institute and PRI. 2018. "Guidance and Case Studies for ESG Integration: Equities and Fixed Income." www.cfainstitute.org/-/media/documents/survey/guidance-case-studies-esg-integration.ashx.
- CFA Institute and the Principles for Responsible Investment. 2018. "ESG Integration in the Americas: Markets, Practices, and Data." www.cfainstitute.org/en/research/survey-reports/esg-integration-americas-survey-report.
- Financial Reporting Council. 2020. "UK Stewardship Code." www.frc.org.uk/investors/uk-stewardship-code.

- Financial Services Agency. 2017. "Principles for Responsible Institutional Investors <<Japan's Stewardship Code>>." www.fsa.go.jp/en/laws_regulations/pc_stewardship.html.
- PRI. 2016. "Credit Risk and Ratings Initiative." www.unpri.org/credit-ratings.
- Sullivan, Rory, Will Martindale, Elodie Feller, and Anna Bordon. 2019. "Fiduciary Duty in the 21st Century." United Nations Global Compact, UNEP Finance Initiative, PRI, and Inquiry. www.unepfi.org/fileadmin/documents/fiduciary_duty_21st_century.pdf.
- Tuan, M. T. 2008. "Measuring and/or Estimating Social Value Creation: Insights into Eight Integrated Cost Approaches." https://docs.gatesfoundation.org/Documents/wwl-report-measuring-estimating-social-value-creation.pdf.

Books and Articles

- Berchicci, L., and A. King. 2022. "Corporate Sustainability: A Model Uncertainty Analysis of Materiality." *Journal of Financial Reporting* 7 (2): 43–74.
- Chatterji, A., D. I. Levine, and M. W. Toffel. 2009. "How Well Do Social Ratings Actually Measure Corporate Social Responsibility?" *Journal of Economics & Management Strategy* 18 (1): 125–69.
- Edmans, A. 2011. "Does the Stock Market Fully Value Intangibles? Employee Satisfaction and Equity Prices." *Journal of Financial Economics* 101 (3): 621–40.
- Flammer, C. 2015. "Does Corporate Social Responsibility Lead to Superior Financial Performance? A Regression Discontinuity Approach." *Management Science* 61 (11): iv–vi, 2549–824.
- Haskel, J., and S. Westlake. 2017. *Capitalism without Capital: The Rise of the Intangible Economy*. Princeton, NJ: Princeton University Press.
- Khan, M., G. Serafeim, and A. Yoon. 2016. "Corporate Sustainability: First Evidence on Materiality." *Accounting Review* 91 (6): 1697–724.
- Krosinsky, C. 2018. "The Failure of Fund Sustainability Ratings." Medium.com (5 February). https://medium.com/@cary_krosinsky/the-failure-of-fund-sustainability-ratings-bea95c0b370f.
- OECD. 2017. "Responsible Business Conduct for Institutional Investors: Key Considerations for Due Diligence under the OECD Guidelines for Multinational Enterprises." https://mneguidelines.oecd.org/RBC-for-Institutional-Investors.pdf.
- PRI. 2014. "A GP's Guide to Integrating ESG Factors in Private Equity."

REFERENCES

Krueger, Philipp, Zacharias Sautner, Dragon Yongjun Tang, Rui Zhong. 2023. "The Effects of Mandatory ESG Disclosure Around the World." European Corporate Governance Institute – Finance Working Paper No. 754/2021, Swiss Finance Institute Research Paper No. 21-44. .10.2139/ssrn.3832745

Burke, Marshall, Anne Driscoll, David B. Lobell, Stefano Ermon. 2021. "Using satellite imagery to understand and promote sustainable development." Science371 (6535). 10.1126/science.abe8628

Nguyen, Quye, Ivan Diaz-Rainey, Duminda Kuruppuarachchi. 2020. "Predicting Corporate Carbon Footprints for Climate Finance Risk Analyses: A Machine Learning Approach" (June 2, 2020). USAEE Working Paper No. 20-450. 10.2139/ssrn.3617175

Vogel, D. 2005. The Market for Virtue: The Potential and Limits of Corporate Social Responsibility. Washington, DC: Brookings Institution Press.

HSBC and Equity Strategy 2016. *Global ESG Sector Playbook*.

IFRS 2010. "IFRS Practice Statement 1: Management Commentary." www.ifrs.org/issued-standards/list-of-standards/management-commentary-practice-statement/.

SASB 2028. "SASB Materiality Map." https://materiality.sasb.org/.

Barclays. 2018. "The Case for Sustainable Bond Investing Strengthens." www.investmentbank.barclays.com/content/dam/barclaysmicrosites/ibpublic/documents/our-insights/ESG2/BarclaysIB-ImpactSeries4-ESG-in-credit-5MB.pdf.

European Commission 2021. "European Green Bond Standard."

Gratcheva, Ekaterina M., Teal Emery, Dieter Wang. 2020. "Demystifying Sovereign ESG." World Bank Group, Equitable Growth, Finance and Institutions Insight. https://openknowledge.worldbank.org/entities/publication/86767582-9a12-595d-be47-71db162dca82. 10.1596/35586

Griffin, P. A., D. H. Lont. 2016. "Game Changer? The Impact of the VW Emission Cheating Scandal on the Co-Integration of Large Automakers' Securities." http://ssrn.com/abstract=2838949.

PRI 2017. "Shifting Perceptions: ESG, Credit Risk and Ratings." www.unpri.org/download?ac=5819.

PRI 2019. "A Practical Guide to ESG Integration in Sovereign Debt." www.unpri.org/fixed-income/a-practical-guide-to-esg-integration-in-sovereign-debt/4781.article.

Chambers, D. R., K. Black, N. J. Lacey. 2018. Alternative Investments: A Primer for Investment Professionals. Charlottesville, VA: CFA Institute Research Foundation; www.cfainstitute.org/en/research/foundation/2018/alternative-investments-a-primer-for-investment-professionals.

Langevoort, D. C., H. A. Sale. 2021. "Corporate Adolescence: Why Did 'We' Not Work?" (8 January). https://papers.ssrn.com/sol3/papers.cfm?abstract_id=3762718. 10.2139/ssrn.3762718

Larcker, D. F., B. Tayan. 2018. "Governance Gone Wild: Misbehavior at Uber Technologies." Harvard Law School Forum on Corporate Governance (20 January). https://corpgov.law.harvard.edu/2018/01/20/governance-gone-wild-misbehavior-at-uber-technologies/.

PRI 2018. "PRI Reporting Framework 2019: Direct—Infrastructure" (November). www.unpri.org/Uploads/l/h/o/09.inf2019_843342.pdf.

CFA Institute and PRI 2018. "Guidance and Case Studies for ESG Integration: Equities and Fixed Income." www.unpri.org/investor-tools/guidance-and-case-studies-for-esg-integration-equities-and-fixed-income/3622.article.

Berg, F., J. F. Koelbel, R. Rigobon. 2019. "Aggregate Confusion: The Divergence of ESG Ratings." Working paper. https://papers.ssrn.com/sol3/papers.cfm?abstract_id=3438533. 10.2139/ssrn.3438533

Chatterji, A., D. I. Levine, M. W. Toffel. 2009. "How Well Do Social Ratings Actually Measure Corporate Social Responsibility?" Journal of Economics & Management Strategy 18 (1): 125–69. 10.1111/j.1530-9134.2009.00210.x

Gibson, R., P. Krueger, P. S. Schmidt. 2019. "ESG Rating Disagreement and Stock Returns." Swiss Finance Institute Research Paper No. 19-67. https://papers.ssrn.com/sol3/papers.cfm?abstract_id=3433728. 10.2139/ssrn.3433728

Mercer. 2018. "Mercer ESG Ratings."

PRACTICE PROBLEMS

1. Integrating ESG factors into the investment process decreases:
   a. reputational risk.
   b. the quality of engagement activities.
   c. risk-adjusted investment returns.

2. Tools of ESG analysis include:
   a. ESG factor tilts.
   b. red flag indicators.
   c. ESG momentum tilts.

3. Which of the following represent stages of the investment process that use quantitative and qualitative approaches?
   a. Research, valuation, and portfolio construction
   b. Materiality assessment, risk mapping, and valuation
   c. Materiality assessment, risk mapping, and portfolio construction

4. An analyst noticed that an investee company's governance was worsening. To account for this, the analyst is most likely to increase:
   a. the company's equity value.
   b. the future cash flows from the company's operating activities.
   c. the discount rates in the valuation model used to value the company.

5. High carbon intensity of a project most likely leads to lower:
   a. cost of debt.
   b. risk of default on debt.
   c. fair value of a company's equity.

6. Which of the following is an example of an ESG-integrated valuation adjustment? Upward adjustment in:
   a. sales growth due to high employee engagement
   b. equity fair value due to the weak governance of a company
   c. cost of debt for new project financing with lower carbon intensity compared to similar projects

7. Which of the following is a criticism of ESG integration?
   a. Rapid advances in ESG integration techniques
   b. ESG screening emphasizes longer-term performance
   c. ESG investment strategy being too inclusive of poor companies

8. Which of the following best describes the relationship between ESG ratings and credit ratings?
   a. ESG ratings and credit ratings are positively correlated.
   b. The link between ESG ratings and credit ratings is still hotly debated among credit investors.
   c. Surveys from credit investors suggest that the S factor remains more important than E and G factors.

9. When developing a scorecard to assess ESG risks and opportunities, which of the following is most likely a challenge for assessing a private company compared to a public company?

   a. Difficulty in identifying company-specific ESG issues
   b. Inability to convert qualitative factors into quantitative scores
   c. Limited coverage of the ESG rating agencies of the private companies

10. An analyst assesses that a company's new human resources policies will lead to less hiring and lower costs to train new employees. Based on this assessment, the analyst is most likely to adjust the discounted cash flow valuation model by:

    a. increasing the cost of capital.
    b. increasing the expected operating margins.
    c. reducing future capital expenditures in balance sheet forecasts.

11. An investor is considering investing in a company that leads its industry in adopting new environmentally friendly technologies. The investor expects this competitive advantage to last for three years while the rest of the industry adopts similar technology and believes the company will continue to be an innovation leader. Compared to the industry's P/E multiple, for this company, the investor should assign a multiple that is:

    a. lower.
    b. the same.
    c. higher.

12. When compared to equity analysis, which of the following factors concerning ESG integration in fixed-income analysis is most accurate?

    a. Future growth opportunities are less important.
    b. Factors that impact balance sheet strength are less important.
    c. ESG integration for fixed-income securities implies the use of the same techniques as for equities.

13. An investment firm has decided to start integrating ESG factors into developing its investment recommendations. The firm establishes a separate team of ESG analysts made up of recruits from the business sustainability programs at several universities. Also, the firm subscribes to multiple ESG service providers for access to data and ratings. Which of the firm's actions will best help the firm overcome the challenges of ESG integration?

    a. The subscriptions for data sources
    b. The recruitment of team members
    c. The establishment of a separate team

14. During which of the three steps an ESG rating provider typically follows to produce an ESG rating does the dispersal of opinion between ESG providers start? From:

    a. gathering data points for the indicators
    b. quantifying data points via scoring or ranking
    c. identifying material ESG indicators for the sector

15. The objectives for integrating ESG factors into an investment process most likely include:

    a. meeting internal audit demands.

Practice Problems

b. increasing reputational risk at a firm and investment level.

c. improving the quality of engagement activities and increasing investment returns.

16. In relation to materiality assessment, which of the following is correct?

   a. The materiality assessment is typically conducted in the valuation stage.

   b. Evidence shows that nonmaterial factors impact financials, valuations, and company business models.

   c. Materiality is measured in terms of likelihood and magnitude of impact on a company's financial performance.

17. Which of the following best represents the order of the steps for developing an ESG scorecard?

Option A	Option B	Option C
Step 1: Determine a scoring system based on what good or best practice looks like for each indicator or issue. **Step 2:** Assess a company, and give it a score. **Step 3:** Identify sector- or company-specific ESG items. **Step 4:** Benchmark the company's performance against industry averages or peer group. **Step 5:** Calculate aggregated scores at the issue level, dimension level, or total score level. **Step 6:** Break down issues into a number of indicators.	**Step 1:** Determine a scoring system based on what good or best practice looks like for each indicator or issue. **Step 2:** Break down issues into a number of indicators. **Step 3:** Assess a company, and give it a score. **Step 4:** Identify sector- or company-specific ESG items. **Step 5:** Calculate aggregated scores at the issue level, dimension level, or total score level. **Step 6:** Benchmark the company's performance against industry averages or peer group.	**Step 1:** Identify sector- or company-specific ESG items. **Step 2:** Break down issues into a number of indicators. **Step 3:** Determine a scoring system based on what good or best practice looks like for each indicator or issue. **Step 4:** Assess a company, and give it a score. **Step 5:** Calculate aggregated scores at the issue level, dimension level, or total score level. **Step 6:** Benchmark the company's performance against industry averages or peer group.

   a. Option A
   b. Option B
   c. Option C

18. This question relates to the case study focusing on the beverage company. Which of the following are examples of material environmental factors that should be considered by an analyst?

   a. Talent retention and recruitment strategy

   b. Water efficiency and greenhouse gas (GHG) emissions

   c. Supplier code-of-conduct protocols and product mix

19. Which of the following factors are least likely to be considered by credit rating agencies (CRAs)?

   a. Environmental risk and religious or ethical risk

   b. Bankruptcy risk, litigation risk, and human capital risk

   c. Environmental risk, standard credit ratio analysis, and governance risk

20. Which of the following factors is generally considered the most important when evaluating ESG considerations around sovereign debt?

   a. Environmental factors

   b. Social factors

   c. Governance factors

21. Which of the following statements best describes a green bond?

    a. Bonds that finance green projects

    b. Bonds that are evergreen and continue for a specified duration

    c. Bonds that get the green light based on governance guidelines

22. Which of these is least likely to be an ESG-integrated valuation technique?

    a. Adjusting cash flows due to cash tax adjustments

    b. Adjusting cost of capital due to poor governance ratings

    c. Adjusting sales growth assumptions due to weak employee engagement scores

23. An analyst assesses a company as below average on ESG metrics. All other matters being equal, the analyst is most likely to:

    a. assign a P/E premium to the stock.

    b. increase the company's cost of capital.

    c. reduce company's risk of default in the forecast model.

24. Tools used by fund managers to evaluate companies based on their ESG-related exposure or ESG-specific factors are best described as:

    a. ESG data.

    b. ESG ratings.

    c. ESG screening.

25. The ratings provided by different ESG rating agencies are most likely to:

    a. be highly correlated with each other.

    b. send clear signals to companies about valued ESG actions.

    c. disperse the effect of ESG performance preferences on asset prices.

26. Research published by the Bank for International Settlements revealed that GHG emissions of borrowing firms have affected bank lending to these firms, but bank-by-bank disparities are high. Based on this information, an analyst is looking to develop a scorecard for three banks by assigning a score on a scale from 1 (poor GHG emission policies and practices) to 5 (strong GHG emission policies and practices).

    Bank A has a GHG emission policy and reports total GHG emissions/million revenue ($)

    Bank B does not have a GHG emission policy and reports Scope 1 GHG emissions/million revenue ($)

    Bank C has a GHG emission policy and reports total GHG emissions/million revenue ($) and Scope 1, 2, and 3 GHG emissions/million revenue ($)

    Which of the three banks is most likely to receive the highest score?

    a. Bank A

    b. Bank B

    c. Bank C

27. Which of the following represents a challenge for ESG integration in emerging markets compared to developed markets?

    a. Challenges in benchmarking ESG performance

    b. Fewer opportunities for investors to engage with companies and improve ESG stance

Practice Problems

   c. Limited scope for advancing ESG factors through capital allocation and active ownership

28. Company X currently trades at a P/E of 4×, and an ESG rating agency rated the company with an ESG score of A (best in class). Company Y, a peer of Company X, is rated with an ESG score of B by the same ESG rating agency. Which of the following is the most likely fair-value P/E assigned by an analyst to Company Y?

   a. 3×
   b. 4×
   c. 5×

29. A company in the technology sector contracted an ESG rating agency for an evaluation of its ESG performance. The ESG rating agency assigned the company an ESG risk rating of 24 (medium risk) on a scale from 0 (negligible risk) to 40+ (severe risk). The same company learned that it was also rated by another ESG rating agency and assigned an ESG score of 83 on a scale from 0 (defaulting ESG performance) to 100 (perfect ESG performance). This ESG score places the company among the 10 best ESG performing companies in the technology sector. The difference in methodologies and the outcomes of the rating process of the two ESG rating agencies is most likely to:

   a. inform the company's management on actions to improve ESG performance.
   b. hinder the ESG performance of the company from being reflected in the stock price.
   c. reduce the variability in findings of empirical research focusing on assessment of ESG scores.

30. After a meeting with the representatives of a pension fund, a potential new limited partner, ABC Private Equity Fund decided to divest from a profitable utility company that has a policy enforcing a mandatory 65-year-age retirement. The fund's divestment decision is most likely to seek:

   a. value creation for the managed portfolio of funds.
   b. a differentiating factor in attracting clients conscious of age discrimination.
   c. to manage risks that could impact the financial performance of its portfolio companies.

SOLUTIONS

1. **A is correct.** An investment firm might have several aims and objectives for integrating ESG factors into an investment process, such as increasing (not decreasing) investment returns, improving (not decreasing) the quality of engagement and stewardship activities and—the correct answer—lowering reputational risk at a firm level and investment level.

2. **B is correct.** Regardless of the ESG analysis classification as qualitative or quantitative, there are many types of tools used by investors. These tools may include red flag indicators, company questionnaires and management interviews, checks with outside experts, and watch lists.

3. **A is correct.** Quantitative and qualitative approaches can be used at all stages of the investment process, from idea and research generation to asset valuation and portfolio construction. Materiality assessment and risk mapping are assessment approaches, not stages of the investment process.

4. **C is correct.** Worsening governance practices identified in a company (e.g., newly elected board members might have poor skill sets, the board is left with a low number of independent members, or members of the board have long tenures leading to groupthink) lead to an increase in the discount rates used to value the company in a valuation model such as DCF analysis. The increase in discount rates leads to a reduction (not increase) in the company's equity value, and a company with poor governance practices risks a reduction in cash flows, not an increase.

5. **C is correct.** A carbon-intensive company/project might be subject to material risks, including financial, regulatory, and legal factors that could affect the company's/project's credit risk and lead to higher discount rates for the company's/project's future cash flows and lower fair value of the company/project. The risks brought by developing a high-carbon-intensity project increase the cost of debt for the company/project compared to lower-carbon-intensity companies/projects and consequentially increase the risk of default on debt.

6. **A is correct.** A high level of employee satisfaction and engagement translates to superior customer retention and revenue growth. Weak governance for a company leads to downward adjustments in equity fair values, and low-carbon-intensity projects suggest downward adjustment in cost of debt compared to other, similar projects with higher carbon intensity.

7. **C is correct.** One of the most common criticisms of ESG investing is the difficulty for investors to correctly identify and appropriately weigh ESG factors in investment selection. Critics express concerns about the precision, validity, and reliability of ESG investment strategies. One concern is that ESG mutual funds and exchange-traded funds might be holding investments in companies acknowledged as "bad actors" in one or more of the ESG dimensions.

8. **B is correct.** The link between ESG ratings and credit ratings is still hotly debated among investors. Proponents might point to a Barclays study looking at a high-ESG portfolio versus a low-ESG portfolio using two different ESG datasets (MSCI and Sustainalytics). The case for sustainable bond investing strengthens, but critics would point out the flaws of correlational studies and the short 2009–18 time period of the Barclays study. Critics further point out that the factor attributions after 2008–2009 (i.e., after the Global Financial Crisis) and some ESG ratings correlate with quality factors (though not all). The governance

factor allows for a more obvious and direct assessment. This explains why surveys suggest that G remains a more important factor for credit investors.

9. **C is correct.** Developing a scorecard to assess ESG risks and opportunities can be a technique used on private and public companies. The challenge to creating private company scorecards is that there is less likely to be a rating agency score for a private company and there is less information about a private company in the public domain. Identifying company-specific ESG factors and converting qualitative factors into quantitative scores would be challenges for all companies when developing an ESG scorecard.

10. **B is correct.** Reduction in hiring and training costs due to improved policies leads to cost savings, and the analyst would most likely increase the expected operating margins.

11. **C is correct.** The ESG analysis indicates that the company has a competitive advantage that should lead to superior returns over the next few years. The investor should assign a P/E multiple that is higher than the industry average to account for this competitive advantage.

12. **A is correct.** Future growth opportunities are less important to fixed-income investors. When considering ESG factors, equity investors are more concerned about future growth opportunities than fixed-income investors because fixed-income investors do not share in the upside potential of an investment. Fixed-income investors find that ESG impacts balance sheet strength and hence the risk of debt defaults; therefore, balance sheet strength is important. Fixed-income investments have particular characteristics (seniority in capital structure, finite maturity, etc.) that imply ESG integration techniques specific to fixed-income securities.

13. **A is correct.** Using multiple sources of information is one way to overcome the challenges of ESG integration for a firm. The low correlation between data providers and datasets in the ESG market is a challenge in the industry, but using a single source can cause a firm to not consider different opinions and lead to poor outcomes from a potentially incomplete data field. A divergence in opinions can be helpful because it allows both positive and negative arguments to be considered. Establishing a separate team can move ESG expertise away from the investment decisions and may provide a challenge to integration. Hiring team members with sustainability training is useful, but if they are all junior members, as is implied if they are hired right out of university, their opinions are often not weighed as heavily as more senior analysts.

14. **A is correct.** ESG factor identification is up to the rating provider, and thus the dispersal of opinion starts at the first step, even before consideration of different weighting and scoring methodologies.

15. **C is correct.** Improving the quality of engagement activities and increasing investment returns are among the common objectives for integrating ESG factors into the investment process.

16. **C is correct.** Typically, materiality is measured in terms of the likelihood and the magnitude of impact. The materiality assessment is usually completed at the research stage, not the valuation stage (practitioners value the issuer and its equity after the research stage and any relevant risk and materiality assessment). Nonmaterial factors are less likely to impact financials, valuations, or company business models.

17. **C is correct.** Scorecard development begins with identifying sector- or

company-specific ESG items.

18. **B is correct.** The material environmental factors in the case study's beverage company included its collaborative approach to improving water efficiency and its science-based GHG goals. The other options do not include environmental factors.

19. **A is correct.** Credit investors are typically concerned about downside risk. The G component of ESG, rather than the E or S component, is viewed as most directly related to preventing downside risk. The set of factors in option B includes E and S issues and is thus least likely to be considered by CRAs.

20. **C is correct.** Sovereign credits are usually assessed by considering their economic growth and governance. As such, the G factor is more directly relevant than the E and S factors, which are often reflected in economic growth, albeit indirectly.

21. **A is correct.** Green bonds are so named because they are typically tied to projects that create an environmental benefit—"green projects."

22. **A is correct.** The rationale for the adjustment to cash flows does not directly relate to an ESG factor. The other options do integrate ESG because the adjustment to sales growth assumptions relates to a social (S) factor (employee engagement scores), and the adjustment to cost of capital relates to a governance (G) factor (governance ratings).

23. **B is correct.** Increasing the company's cost of capital appropriately reflects the increased risk associated with the below-average ESG performance. The higher cost of capital will ultimately reduce the company's valuation. Also, a company with this ESG profile would be assigned a discount to peers' P/Es.

24. **C is correct.** ESG screening includes tools that evaluate companies, countries, and bonds based on their exposure or involvement-specific factors, sectors, products, or services.

25. **C is correct.** Investor preferences can influence asset prices when the preferences are uniformly held and implemented. Because the ESG ratings provided by different agencies are not highly correlated, there is a dispersion of the effect of investors' ESG performance preferences.

26. **C is correct.** Analysts can develop scorecards to assess materiality of different ESG factors for a company and translate qualitative judgments into numerical scores. Bank C has the strongest stance in terms of reporting GHG emissions since it has a GHG emission policy and reports GHG emissions both as total figures and broken down into Scope 1, 2, and 3 emissions.

27. **A is correct.** Although ESG integration poses general challenges regardless the domicile of the companies, for those in emerging markets, there might be additional challenges since benchmarking ESG performance is more challenging in emerging markets because of less data and high variability between countries and companies. However, emerging markets provide greater opportunities for investors to engage with companies and improve ESG performance. Also, investors can help advance ESG factors through capital allocation and active ownership.

28. **A is correct.** Company Y was rated with a lower ESG score (B) than Company X (A), showing that Company Y has weaker ESG performance. An analyst considering the ESG rating of the two companies would most likely assign a lower fair-value P/E to Company Y—that is, one of 3× compared to Company

Solutions

X's 4×. Consequentially, an investor might only invest in a company with poor ESG practices or greater risks at a multiple that is lower than its peer average to compensate.

29. **B is correct.** The difference in methodologies of ESG agency raters poses challenges for companies and investors. Since one of the ESG agency raters places the company in the medium-risk category, while another rater places the company in the ESG best-performing companies category, it might be difficult for the investors to reflect the ESG scores in the company's stock prices. Such a difference in ratings prevents the company's management from understanding whether and which actions are needed to improve ESG performance and poses challenges for empirical research efforts.

30. **B is correct.** With this decision, ABC Private Equity Fund is most likely to differentiate itself from private equity funds that are agnostic to age discrimination. Some investors see ESG integration as a way to differentiate themselves and attract capital from the growing pool of ESG-conscious capital allocators, such as pension funds, sovereign wealth funds, and family offices. So, they include ESG factors prominently in their investment approach and reporting to appeal to these limited partners.

CHAPTER 8

Integrated Portfolio Construction and Management

LEARNING OUTCOMES

Mastery | *The candidate should be able to:*

- [ ] 8.1.1 explain the impact of ESG factors on strategic asset allocation
- [ ] 8.1.2 describe approaches for ESG integration into the portfolio management process
- [ ] 8.1.3 explain approaches for how internal and external ESG research and analysis are used by portfolio managers to make investment decisions
- [ ] 8.1.4 explain the different approaches to screening and the benefits and limitations of the main approaches
- [ ] 8.1.5 explain the main indexes and benchmarking approaches applicable to sustainable and ESG investing, noting potential limitations
- [ ] 8.1.6 apply ESG screens to the main asset classes and their sub-sectors: fixed income; equities; and alternative investments
- [ ] 8.1.6 apply ESG screens to the main asset classes and their sub-sectors: fixed income, equities, and alternative investments
- [ ] 8.1.7 distinguish between ESG screening of individual companies and collective investment funds: on an absolute basis and relative to sector/peer group data
- [ ] 8.1.8 explain how ESG integration impacts the risk–return dynamic of portfolio optimization
- [ ] 8.1.9 evaluate the different types of ESG analysis/SRI in terms of key objectives, investment considerations, and risks: full ESG integration, exclusionary screening, positive alignment/best in class, active ownership, thematic investing, impact investing, other
- [ ] 8.1.10 describe approaches to managing index-based ESG portfolios

1 INTRODUCTION

Environmental, social, and governance (ESG) integration occurs at different levels of the investment process, with each level necessitating its own framework for implementation. Where previous chapters have described ESG integration at the underlying security level, this chapter examines research and methodologies for integrating ESG assessment at higher levels of the investment decision-making process, starting at strategic asset allocation (SAA) and moving on to portfolio construction and management. The more nascent stage of ESG integration at these higher levels of investment decision making makes it an exciting area, particularly as investors build more robust ESG capabilities in asset classes beyond listed equities.

This chapter draws on portfolio management theory complemented with examples of investment best practices to

- ▶ discuss research, approaches, and challenges to embedding ESG investing risk into global asset allocation models;
- ▶ examine how ESG investing can be applied to approaches across asset classes and various strategy types;
- ▶ consider how ESG investing can leverage quantitative research methods to understand risk exposure and performance return dynamics in portfolios; and
- ▶ differentiate between actively managed and index-based ESG strategies.

2 ESG INTEGRATION: STRATEGIC ASSET ALLOCATION MODELS

☐ **8.1.1** explain the impact of ESG factors on strategic asset allocation

One of the most exciting yet least developed areas in ESG integration is the degree and means to which it can inform and shape strategic asset allocation. Asset allocation is a crucial decision; differences in investors' strategic asset allocation policies may account for as much as 90% of the variability in investors' returns over time (Ibbotson and Kaplan 2000).

Traditionally, institutional investors' strategic asset allocation is driven by the strategies shown in Exhibit 1 paired with asset/liability management (ALM). While strategic asset allocation establishes ranges for asset class exposures based on return expectations and client characteristics, ALM seeks to match the cash flows of those assets with the investor's liabilities, such as a pension's fund liabilities to its beneficiaries.

A considerable misalignment can exist between strategic asset allocation and ESG integration at the individual security level, as discussed in Chapter 7. If the investor believes that ESG risk primarily resides at the underlying security-selection level, then ESG integration at that level is sensible. But if the investor believes that ESG risk represents a more top-down, material risk factor affecting portfolios—which is the case for climate change—then it may better serve the investor to integrate ESG issues at the asset allocation level.

ESG integration is most developed in listed equities and corporate bonds. Challenges clearly exist in many alternative areas, but greater ESG coverage, increasing investor awareness, and global ESG-related regulatory changes have made ESG integration at the strategic asset allocation level more relevant. In addition, research on ESG integration in strategic asset allocation has tended to focus on environmental criteria—essentially exposure and sensitivity to assumptions around both transition and physical climate risk—more than other ESG factors, based largely on current data availability, which is then used in asset allocation.

Exhibit 1: Strategic Asset Allocation Models and Their Suitability to ESG Issues

Model	Features	Potential link to ESG issues	Outputs to reflect ESG issues
Mean–variance optimization (MVO; Markowitz 1952)	MVO results in the construction of an efficient frontier that represents a mix of assets that produces the minimum standard deviation (as a proxy for risk) for the maximum level of expected return. It is based on defined asset-class buckets and long-term expected returns, risks, and correlations. The Black–Litterman Global Asset Allocation is an MVO model, using the Markowitz portfolio optimization model or modern portfolio theory (MPT).	MVO is highly sensitive to baseline assumptions, making it imperative to fully understand any revised assumptions due to ESG considerations. MVO is highly dependent on historical data as the baseline, with adjustments made to reflect future expectations. Volatility as a proxy for risk does not work well in cases of fat-tail risk and large market swings.	ESG issues could have an impact on assumptions regarding expected return, volatility, and correlation at the asset- and sub-asset-class level. ESG issues also have the potential to expand the regional and asset-class mix and to add new sub-asset classes to align with the pursuit of positive real-world impact.
Factor risk allocation (see, e.g., Idzorek and Kowara 2013)	Factor risk frameworks seek to build a diversified portfolio based on sources of risk. They typically include such factors as fundamental risks (GDP, interest rates, and inflation) and market risks (equity risk premium, illiquidity, and volatility).	The macroeconomic links to ESG issues are more difficult to quantify with precision from a purely top-down perspective. Market risk factors can be built from the bottom up using asset- and sector-level analysis.	ESG issues could require a change to baseline factor risk assumptions. Factor risk allocation offers the potential to build in new ESG-related risk factors (such as climate change) to improve diversification (particularly across market risk factors).
Total portfolio analysis (TPA; Bass, Gladstone, and Ang 2017)	Similar to factor risk allocation, TPA allows for closer review and interplay between the strategy-setting process and alignment of investment goals. Based on an agreed risk budget, asset allocations are made on expected risk exposures and are less constrained by asset class "buckets" than are traditional MVO approaches.	TPA is relevant to consider ESG issues that require the interplay between judgment about the future and quantitative analysis. TPA requires specialist knowledge to make informed judgments about future risk.	TPA's emphasis on risk budgeting and allocation of capital to opportunities within that budget (bringing alignment between top down and bottom up) would provide greater flexibility to capture the potential winners and losers in scenario analysis that also incorporates ESG-related issues.
Dynamic asset allocation (DAA; for an overview of various dynamic asset allocation techniques, see Jarvis, Lawrence, and Miao 2009)	DAA is driven by changes in risk tolerance, typically induced by cumulative performance relative to investment goals or an approaching investment horizon.	DAA could introduce an additional source of estimation errors due to the need for dynamic rebalancing.	DAA has the potential to reflect changes in baseline assumptions over different time horizons.

Model	Features	Potential link to ESG issues	Outputs to reflect ESG issues
Liability-driven asset allocation (see, e.g., Hoevenaars, Molenaar, Schotman, and Steenkamp 2008)	Liability driven investment (LDI) seeks to find the most efficient asset-class mix driven by a fund's liabilities. It is simultaneously concerned with the return of the assets, the change in value of the liabilities, and how assets and liabilities interact to determine the overall portfolio value.	LDI encounters the same limitations as MVO, with high sensitivity to baseline assumptions.	Some ESG issues could potentially impact inflation and liability assumptions.
Regime-switching models (Ang and Timmerman 2011)	Regime-switching approaches model abrupt and persistent changes in financial variables due to shifts in regulations, policies, and other secular changes. They capture fat tails, skewness, and time-varying correlations.	Regime-switching approaches are relevant for considering ESG issues where an abrupt shift is expected over time. They are also typically based more on forward-looking rather than historical data.	These approaches have the potential to capture dramatic shifts in the investment environment. These models are not yet widely used by investment practitioners.

Source: Adapted from PRI (2019a).

Despite an increasing amount of academic work (see meta-analyses such as Friede, Busch, and Bussen 2015) supporting ESG's effect on risk-adjusted returns, introducing ESG issues into the asset allocation process will undoubtedly carry exposure and weighting implications that must be considered relative to a standard, non-ESG integrated allocation (e.g., positive screening that tilts the overall asset mix to a higher-than-mean ESG rating). To be sure, this effect may well be intended. In theory, managing a mixed-asset portfolio according to a carbon constraint or desired exposure level should reduce the risk to a carbon pricing shock through lower commensurate exposure to carbon-intensive, coal-reliant utilities and potential stranded assets. There are trade-offs that investors must consider when allocating to ESG factors or "sustainability" more broadly.

Climate change—and thus climate risk—has emerged as the key material ESG factor for institutional investors to address in asset allocation strategies because it is both systemic and local. It could negatively impact the financial system and all issuers as much as it poses risk on a more localized level for specific regions, sectors, and companies. Its potential physical risks will manifest in both acute, event-driven forms (such as extreme weather) and longer-term, chronic shifts driven by the effects of elevated temperatures and rising sea levels. Exhibit 2 describes why climate risk (as one example) should be considered in a strategic asset allocation policy for different asset classes.

Exhibit 2: Macroeconomic Climate Considerations by Asset Class

Asset Classes	Subtypes	SAA/ALM Implications	Climate Change Considerations
Equities	▶ Industries or sectors ▶ Growth vs. value ▶ Large, mid-, or small cap ▶ Long vs. short positions	▶ Hedge against inflation, which can result from supply shocks and high government spending ▶ Sensitive to growth, macroeconomic performance	Sensitive to climate impacts on macroeconomic performance

Asset Classes	Subtypes	SAA/ALM Implications	Climate Change Considerations
Fixed income	▶ Sovereign, municipal, corporate ▶ Investment vs. non-investment grade (high yield)	▶ Sensitive to interest rates ▶ Typically less volatile returns	▶ Sensitive to fiscal policy related to climate challenges ▶ Sensitive to climate-related impacts on issuers' creditworthiness ▶ Many climate impacts fall within the tenor of long-term debt.
Alternative investments	▶ Real estate investment trusts (REITs) ▶ Commodities ▶ Currencies ▶ Private equity, venture capital (VC) funds ▶ Derivatives, hedge funds	▶ Attractive for diversification and for low or inverse correlation to market returns ▶ Heterogeneous and wide-ranging risk/return profiles	▶ Diversification offered by alternative assets may allow for greater hedging of climate risk. ▶ Climate risk exposure may be concentrated, opaque, or difficult to assess.

Source: Climate Finance Advisors and Ortec Finance (2019).

As shown in Exhibit 2, climate change presents different risks across asset classes. For example, carbon-intensive companies, such as coal-powered utilities, without an adaptation strategy will be at risk in the transition to a low-carbon economy. In such a scenario, the company's shareholders (who are subordinate to debt investors in the capital structure) will be disproportionately impacted. Hence, asset allocation strategies must recognize asset class sensitivity alongside systemic and company-specific risks.

As well as being one of the key recommendations of the TCFD framework, climate scenario analysis is as important in the wider asset allocation process as it is in understanding the micro-, macro-, and ESG sensitivities in a single investment portfolio. What might that look like in an asset allocation context? The asset allocator would work to optimize the portfolio for different warming scenarios using 1.5°C (2.7°F) as promoted in the Paris Agreement of 2015 as a baseline (Task Force on Climate-Related Financial Disclosures 2019). Different scenarios should stress test different asset classes across regions, sectors, time periods, and temperature assumptions.

Some ESG-motivated asset allocation choices may require near-term versus long-term trade-offs. For example, reducing (or outright divesting) positions in highly carbon-intensive investments in the energy sector will decrease exposure to long-term transition risks. However, this decision may, in turn, reduce the portfolio income yield because the energy sector is generally associated with an above-market cash flow profile and dividend income stream unless capital is redeployed in another sector with similar yield characteristics (Litterman 2015).

Mercer and Ortec Finance have both integrated climate risk into strategic asset allocation models. Mercer has continued to refine its climate scenario model, now integrating it into a long-term, strategic asset allocation methodology that extends to 2100. Mercer's report "Investing in a Time of Climate Change" also addresses the need to enlarge asset allocation models beyond equities. This report formally extends its climate-informed asset allocation process to sustainability-themed equity, private equity, and real assets, including natural resources and infrastructure. See Exhibit 3 for an approach to modeling the investment impacts of climate change.

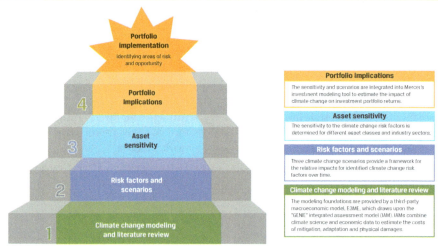

Exhibit 3: Illustrative Approach for Modeling the Investment Impacts of Climate Change

Source: Mercer (2019).

Ortec Finance's approach integrates climate risks into financial scenarios, which include transition, physical, and extreme weather impacts, and pricing dynamics to cover all asset classes. For example, Exhibit 4 illustrates the impact on a representative UK pension fund portfolio over two different investment horizons and against three simulations—orderly, disorderly, and failed—calibrated against the Paris Agreement.

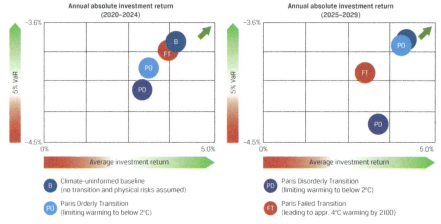

Exhibit 4: Investment Return of a Representative Pension Fund's Portfolio in Different Climate Pathways and Time Buckets (Stylized Risk-Return Projections)

Source: Climate Finance Advisors and Ortec Finance (2019).

In the nearer-term simulation, climate transition risks point to lower expected investment returns relative to the Paris-aligned pathways (orderly and disorderly). While a Paris orderly transition gradually prices in lower nearer-term earnings expectations, a Paris disorderly transition represents an earnings correction that produces a shock in 2024 and higher subsequent volatility.

In the later-term simulation (2025–2029), the portfolios' investment returns in an orderly transition are similar to the climate-uninformed baseline where transition risk and physical risks are not modeled. In contrast, both the Paris disorderly and failed transitions point to lower expected investment returns for the modeled portfolios.

- In the Paris disorderly transition pathway, the sentiment shock occurring in 2025 and the subsequent increase in volatility remain until 2026.
- The Paris failed transition pathway—characterizing a business-as-usual-scenario that brings about a 4°C (5.4°F) temperature increase by 2100—leads to diminishing investment returns as the impact of physical risk increases.[1]

ESG INTEGRATION: ASSET MANAGER SELECTION

8.1.1 explain the impact of ESG factors on strategic asset allocation

ESG factors and expectations are increasingly integrated into manager selection processes. Indeed, the PRI (2020a) has a resource guide for asset owners who allocate to ESG investment managers.

Due diligence in manager selection combines qualitative and quantitative metrics to evaluate managers' performance and investment processes. Many of the largest asset owners monitor and assess between 100 and several hundred asset managers. Asset owners (or their consultants) review this long list of tracked managers to reduce this list to a shortlist or watch list, ultimately tightening this to a final focus list of managers to allocate capital. In this respect, due diligence focuses on establishing baseline metrics to evaluate and compare managers. Metrics related to ESG integration include

- the existence of an ESG policy,
- being a party to such initiatives as the Principles for Responsible Investment (PRI),
- accountability in the form of dedicated personnel and committee oversight,
- the manner and degree in which ESG issues are integrated in the investment process,
- ownership and stewardship activities, and
- client reporting capabilities.

Exhibit 5 depicts an example of a high-level manager selection process, in this case developed by BlackRock Alternative Advisors.

---

1 Widely used models to generate the inputs for portfolio optimization (including estimates of asset returns) include the Black–Litterman model, with a range of asset return estimation techniques subsequently being developed.

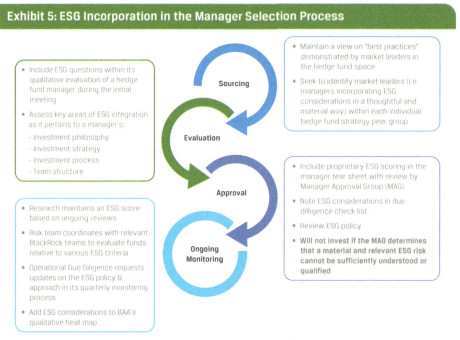

Exhibit 5: ESG Incorporation in the Manager Selection Process

Notes: Effective as of January 2020. For illustrative purposes only. Current investment process is subject to change and based on market conditions, managers' opinions, and other factors.

Source: BlackRock Alternative Advisors.

As a whole, the due diligence process scrutinizes the degree of ESG integration and the manager's investment approach. A formal monitoring and reporting framework also provides a view into the progress and evolution of a manager's ESG capabilities and resourcing. While much of this process naturally focuses on investment-facing capabilities, from ESG data integration to dedicated investment strategies, due diligence also commonly assesses operational risk of the investment manager itself. Manager due diligence may examine what organizational framework and oversight exist at the firm level to support ESG activities at the fund level, including the following:

▶ Has the manager instituted ESG and/or stewardship policies?

▶ What compliance measures are in place to ensure that exclusion-oriented and/or ESG constraint-based investment mandates and strategies are observed?

Furthermore, because of growing regulatory requirements, they may also examine the sophistication of ESG and climate risk reporting.

Asset owners are increasingly using more formal scoring frameworks for asset managers. For some, these frameworks represent a spectrum of capabilities across various strategies. Some other frameworks have gone beyond simply informing the manager selection process to now acting as a formal factor or weight in the overall manager selection and allocation process.

Exhibit 6 shows how LGT Capital Partners has tracked the development of ESG capabilities among managers it allocates capital to for nine years, with the data illustrating the progress among the hedge fund managers it monitors.

Exhibit 6: LGT Capital Partners' ESG Ratings for Its Hedge Fund Partners

Source: LGT Capital Partners (2022).

Exhibit 7 illustrates an example of another approach, assessing the ESG capabilities among alternative managers. This stylized ranking summarizes due diligence performance at the operational (firm) level and at the investment (fund) level. What enriches this exercise is that it evaluates ESG capabilities across a range of strategy types, including arbitrage, credit, long/short, and macro investing. As we will discuss later, the nature of the underlying instruments or the investment horizon or timeframe means that ESG issues are more relevant and easily applied for some strategies than others. The assessment also normalizes for investment firm size across funds, as smaller investment firms generally have fewer resources and less ability to absorb the financial costs of ESG compliance, research, data, and personnel requirements.

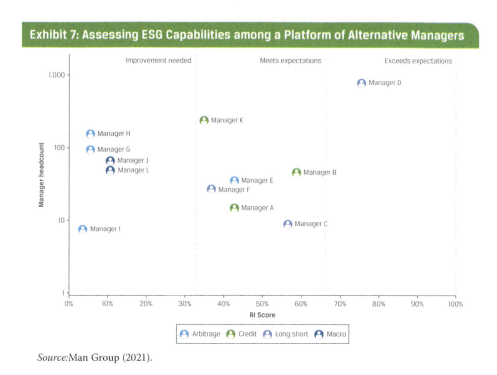

Exhibit 7: Assessing ESG Capabilities among a Platform of Alternative Managers

Source: Man Group (2021).

4. APPROACHES TO ESG INTEGRATION: PORTFOLIO-LEVEL FRAMEWORK

☐ 8.1.2 describe approaches for ESG integration into the portfolio management process

☐ 8.1.3 explain approaches for how internal and external ESG research and analysis are used by portfolio managers to make investment decisions

As earlier chapters demonstrated, there is a rich diversity of approaches for ESG integration at the individual security level. This heterogeneity is now carrying over to portfolio construction and management, where new methodologies and frameworks are leveraging ESG datasets with innovations that drive fundamental and quantitative, as well as active and passive, investment strategies.

The endgame for ESG integration at the portfolio level is the combination of top-down analytics and underlying ESG analysis to produce a more complete picture of ESG exposure and risk at the portfolio construction and management levels. In this respect, ESG integration in portfolio management requires a different manner of explanatory power than integration at the individual security level and should embed ESG considerations into

- the highest-level asset allocation decisions,
- portfolio exposure,
- risk management measures, and
- performance attribution.

Data compiled by Mercer Consulting (see Exhibit 8), one of the largest consultants to asset owners, suggests that progress in ESG integration is marked by a high degree of variation depending on asset class and investment strategy type. What is perhaps more interesting, though, is that the data show that investment managers' ESG integration efforts exceed the availability of sustainability-themed investment strategies or funds from those investment managers.

Exhibit 8: Mercer Consulting's View on ESG Integration and Availability of Strategies by Asset Class

Asset Class	Manager Progress on ESG Integration*	Availability of Sustainability-Themed Strategies**
Private equity	Medium	Low/medium
Private debt	Low/medium	Low
Real estate	Medium/high	Low
Infrastructure	High	Medium/high
Natural resources***	Medium	Medium/high

Explanatory notes:
*Refers to the percentage distribution of ESG1- and ESG2-rated strategies in the Mercer Global Investment Manager Database (GIMD), where available.
**Refers to the percentage distribution of sustainability-themed strategies compared to the asset-class universe—noting equity is a large universe, so the low relative number is not actually a low absolute

number.
***Conservative view; research updates in this asset class may result in a more favorable view than is currently held.

- ▸ *Low: below 5%*
- ▸ *Low/medium: 5%–10%*
- ▸ *Medium: 11%–20%*
- ▸ *Medium/high: 21%–40%*
- ▸ *High: above 40% (as of December 2018)*

Source: Mercer (2021). https://investment-solutions.mercer.com/content/dam/mercer-subdomains/delegated-solutions/responsible-investment/Mercer-Alternatives-Sustainability-Policy-040321.pdf

However, Exhibit 8 does not illustrate the breadth and diversity of approaches in each of these categories. Earlier chapters have discussed some of these ESG methodologies as applied to individual securities. Examining these at the portfolio level draws important distinctions and also highlights the challenges that many approaches face in the path toward a credible form of ESG integration.

APPROACHES TO ESG INTEGRATION: ROLE OF ANALYSTS, PORTFOLIO MANAGERS, AND INTERNAL AND EXTERNAL RESEARCH

8.1.2 describe approaches for ESG integration into the portfolio management process

8.1.3 explain approaches for how internal and external ESG research and analysis are used by portfolio managers to make investment decisions

As a matter of definition—to the market, clients, and stakeholders—an ESG policy should first formally outline the investment approach and degree of ESG integration in a firm. Particularly, asset managers should have ESG policies for asset classes and the approach used. The PRI provides guidance and templates to develop ESG policies.

There are well-established resources for developing a comprehensive ESG policy, though these have traditionally catered to the long-only equity and fixed-income strategies (PRI 2019b). It is worth noting that investor organizations are now addressing policy development in alternative investment areas, including hedge funds (AIMA 2021).

Further information on how ESG considerations can be embedded in investment mandates and ESG policy can be found in Chapter 9.

In an investment management firm, professionals have varying roles in ESG integration in the investment process.

Role of Analysts

Analysts (particularly fundamental analysts) present and justify investment recommendations for securities, which typically incorporate

- ▸ estimates of the security's intrinsic value,
- ▸ credit analysis,

- the potential for a re-rating or de-rating in valuation,
- potential risks,
- short-term and long-term catalysts, and
- an expectation on the security's earnings growth, credit, and cash flow profile.

ESG factors are an increasingly recognized element in security analysis; material ESG factors (which vary by sector and asset class) typically carry meaningful implications for investment theses.

Role of Portfolio Managers

The role of portfolio managers is often much broader in scope than for analysts. Using analysts' recommendations as inputs, portfolio managers often form their own views for a given security and weigh security-specific factors against

- macro- and microeconomic data,
- portfolio financial and nonfinancial exposure, and
- sensitivities to potential shocks.

ESG treatment in a portfolio context—if properly and systematically integrated, regardless of whether in active or passive portfolio management—should be considered in the same light as these other factors.

The challenge that portfolio managers face is how to widen the focus of research and datasets largely optimized for security analysis into tools that can better inform portfolio and asset allocation analysis and decision making, particularly in understanding where and how ESG factors contribute to risk-adjusted returns.

To this end, the ESG framework should illustrate a continuity from micro to macro forms of analysis, including

- the organizing principles and methodologies for ESG analysis;
- the identification and analysis of financial and nonfinancial (ESG) materiality at the individual security level,
- the approaches to build a composite picture of risks and exposure at a single portfolio level, and
- the representation of ESG risks and exposure that informs a mixed asset strategy, which may include many different underlying strategies.

In addition, recall from Chapter 7 that ESG integration will take different forms based on the types of investment strategy:

- Discretionary ESG investment strategies most commonly take the form of a fundamental portfolio approach. A portfolio manager would work to complement bottom-up financial analysis alongside the consideration of ESG factors to reinforce the investment thesis of a particular holding. The portfolio manager would then work to understand the aggregate risk at the portfolio level across all factors to understand correlation and event risks and potential shocks to the portfolio.
- Systematic investment strategies are, broadly speaking, rule-based approaches that use the statistical application of financial and/or nonfinancial factors to drive security selection. Systematic strategies generally seek to minimize the higher costs associated with discretionary active management. Where discretionary strategies often focus on depth in a portfolio,

manifested through a portfolio of few, more concentrated holdings, quantitative strategies focus on breadth, using a much larger portfolio of holdings to target risk and volatility-adjusted returns.

Historically, the most common systematic ESG strategies were index based. These involve replicating the exposures of a custom index, which have exclusion criteria. However, systematic approaches are becoming more sophisticated and rigorous with respect to ESG integration, from beta-plus funds to single- and multi-factor ESG models.

ESG integration can focus on both risks and opportunities. A bias toward either of these can lead to different return profiles at the portfolio level as the emphasis can shift from downside protection to upside participation.

Complementing Internal Research with External ESG Resources

Broadly speaking, ESG research and analysis can be categorized as external or internal. External research includes sell-side practitioner research by commercial firms (e.g., MSCI, S&P Global, Sustainalytics, investment banks), academic research, and research by governments and nonprofits (e.g., the World Bank). External research is generally available—though perhaps for a price—to all asset owners and managers. While meta-analyses surveying more than 2,000 academic studies indicate an overall positive bias in the linkage between ESG factors and investment returns (see Exhibit 9), academic studies on an individual basis often end up disconnected from practice and are not widely or generally applicable. Internal research is conducted by asset owners and managers and is proprietary to that firm.

As the ESG industry matures, institutional investors are finding an increasingly diverse universe of external research. Resources now not only include ESG-specific research content but also utilize quantitative techniques, such as natural language processing, machine learning, and artificial intelligence, to organize ESG data. Indeed, the market for ESG content and indexes surpassed US$1 billion in 2022 (up from US$300 million five years prior) and is expected to continue growing. These resources complement internal investment research and provide internal quantitative and performance analytics teams the opportunity to refine methodologies for managing ESG risk. Just as external providers are innovating ESG datasets and producing research, so too are investors developing in-house capabilities to differentiate themselves across asset classes and investment strategy types.

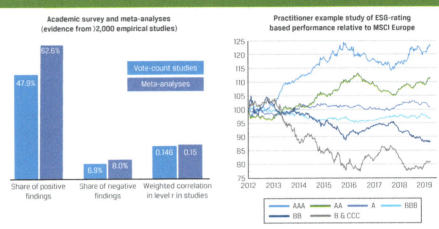

Exhibit 9: Academic vs. Practitioner Research Making ESG-Linked Performance Claims

Source: MSCI ESG Research, FactSet, and Nordea Markets (2018).

The list of external resources, which has grown significantly in breadth and depth over time, includes

- sell-side research and analysis,
- academic studies,
- investment consultant research,
- third-party ESG data provider research,
- ESG-integrated fund distribution platforms,
- asset owner and asset manager white papers,
- investor initiative research,
- nongovernmental organization (NGO) research,
- government agencies and central banks, and
- multilateral institutions and agencies.

Given the wide array of research resources available, portfolio managers should reflect on their research requirements. The profundity of research, from ESG integration at the individual security level to the portfolio level, continues to mature and provide investors with several ways to assess and report exposure.

Investors should recognize the need to differentiate themselves irrespective of their approach to ESG integration. Asset owners continue to rebase their expectations for the quality of proprietary ESG research that asset managers and consultants can provide to them. In turn, investors complement external, off-the-shelf research and data analytics with internal, proprietary ESG research.

One of the less developed areas where investors are able to both innovate and differentiate themselves is in the demonstration of how ESG considerations are embedded in their portfolio construction and management process. In this respect, the Sustainability Accounting Standards Board (SASB, now part of ISSB) has much to offer; its framework and Materiality Map span issuer-specific materiality and overall portfolio exposure. Covering equity, fixed-income, private equity, and real assets, SASB's Materiality Map[2] is capable of assessing portfolio exposure to sustainability risks and

---

2 Available at https://materiality.sasb.org/.

opportunities across each issue. However, while the SASB industry-based standards identify material issues, the SASB does not weight them for individual companies or industries. Such a determination must be made by the investor.

Another development is SASB's work on the Sustainable Industry Classification System (SICS). Modeled after the Global Industry Classification Standard (GICS), SICS offers an improved industry classification standard that speaks directly to ESG materiality. SICS organizes companies according to their sustainability attributes, such as resource intensity, sustainability risks, and innovation opportunities (Nascimento and Payal 2018).

The starting point that many portfolio managers use is to upload their portfolios onto third-party ESG data provider online platforms. While these platforms vary in sophistication, they do offer the first composite picture of a portfolio's stock-specific risks on a number of potential ESG metrics. Many of these platforms are capable of

- illustrating a portfolio's mean exposure and weighting toward low-, mid-, or high-scoring companies on ESG metrics,
- producing a picture of the portfolio's environmental and carbon exposure on an absolute value basis (for instance, expressed as weighted-average carbon intensity), and
- approximating an overall controversy or risk score for the portfolio.

Asset owners and managers increasingly recognize the limitations of third-party ESG platforms and the need to develop more sophisticated ESG analytics platforms that combine third-party and proprietary capabilities. The rationale stems from the interest not only in safeguarding portfolio holdings—particularly with regard to clients' segregated investment mandates—but also in demonstrating a differentiated approach to understanding and reporting portfolio data. Given the subjectivity and divergence among ESG rating providers, developing an approach that incorporates both third-party and proprietary ESG data lowers an overreliance on a single provider and creates greater context for discussion when reviewing the risk profile of a portfolio.

For example, a portfolio ESG analytic tool used by an asset manager may aggregate a number of different data streams from ESG providers to produce a picture of "consensus" ranking-oriented ESG scores and their variance alongside an internally produced "proprietary" ESG score, in addition to a view of absolute value–based environmental fund metrics and exposures.

These analytic tools enable investment teams to decompose both their portfolios and benchmark indexes, sort by ratings, and understand the distribution curves across a number of ESG metrics. They often provide drill-down capabilities that illustrate a more detailed picture of ESG characteristics on an underlying basis for positions.

Portfolio tools provide investors with the ability to stress test a portfolio against various ESG criteria (such as a sudden, hypothetical increase in the price of carbon emissions) to understand the sensitivity of the portfolio. This exercise is no different from how current portfolio tools provide the means to stress test portfolios against simulations, such as interest rate or oil shocks.

Measuring Portfolio Carbon Intensity

Recommendations by the TCFD provide an important model both for a move toward ESG standards convergence and in elevating risk exposure metrics to the portfolio level from the underlying asset level. Where carbon intensity was previously determined in the form of carbon footprint on a per-company or per-asset basis, for example, portfolio managers may now treat carbon exposure on a portfolio-weighted basis. Weighted-average carbon intensity measures a portfolio's exposure to carbon-intensive companies on a position-weighted carbon exposure (see Exhibit 10). It is a portfolio-level risk exposure measure, calculated as the carbon intensity (Scope 1 + 2 Emissions ÷ US$ million revenues) weighted for each position in a portfolio. This metric can be used by investors to tilt or overlay portfolios toward lower carbon exposure.

It is important to note that TCFD is a principle-based framework providing recommendations for assessing climate risk and exposure. Because TCFD is not prescriptive, different approaches to measure carbon intensity have developed. For example, while the European Union's Sustainable Finance Disclosure Regulation (SFDR) accounts for Scopes 1, 2, and 3 emissions, UK TCFD practice currently focuses on only Scope 1 and Scope 2 emissions. Scope 3 emissions, which represent indirect emissions that occur in a company's value chain, are particularly difficult to measure because of the potential lack of data, transparency, and disclosure in layers of a supply chain. As data and supply chain visibility improve, it is expected that emission analysis will normalize to cover Scopes 1, 2, and 3.

Exhibit 10: Weighted-Average Carbon Intensity at the Portfolio Level

$$\sum_n^i \left(\frac{\text{Current value of investment}_i}{\text{Current portfolio value}} \times \frac{\text{Issuer's Scope 1 and Scope 2 GHG emissions}_i}{\text{Issuer's US\$m revenue}_i} \right).$$

Source: TCFD (2017).

6. APPROACHES TO ESG INTEGRATION: QUANTITATIVE RESEARCH DEVELOPMENTS IN ESG INVESTING

- **8.1.2** describe approaches for ESG integration into the portfolio management process
- **8.1.3** explain approaches for how internal and external ESG research and analysis are used by portfolio managers to make investment decisions

One of the most exciting areas of research development in portfolio management focuses on quantitatively understanding ESG risk properties. While single-security case studies (as in Chapter 7) frame the investment process with a powerful engagement story, their anecdotal nature does not describe performance attribution from ESG exposure at a portfolio level. Portfolio analytics typically provide performance analytics that describe regional, sectoral, and stock-specific performance attribution over a given period. In the same way, the assumption or contention that ESG considerations are alpha generating must also be tested on the same attributional basis.

Describing ESG performance attribution at a portfolio level requires quantifying ESG attributes as a factor (risk premium) in their own right. Third-party data providers are developing increasingly sophisticated ESG ratings and scoring methodologies, but many fall short in describing ESG attributes as an uncorrelated, statistically independent factor. In fact, the ratings from many providers reveal a significant, underlying correlation with existing factors, such as value, quality, size, and momentum. In one respect, this should not be surprising. Transparency bias generally accrues to larger, more mature companies with higher ESG ratings. Nonetheless, the correlation with other factors effectively undermines the effort to define ESG attributes as uniquely singular enough to be included in risk factor attribution analyses.

Readers may ask what common risk factors explain ESG ratings. One means of answering this question is to examine the underlying factor exposure of the highest-rated ESG companies versus the lowest-rated companies. This exercise, shown in Exhibit 11 and 12, reveals that what is purportedly marketed as an "ESG signal" with quasi-predictive signaling power is instead driven largely by existing factors.

Exhibit 11: Underlying Factor Exposure among Existing Third-Party Data Providers (Arabesque S-Ray and RepRisk ESG)

Source: J.P. Morgan (2016).

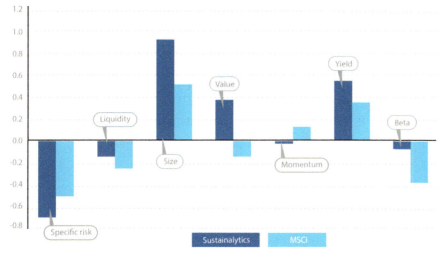

Exhibit 12: Underlying Factor Exposure among Existing Third-Party Data Providers (Sustainalytics and MSCI)

Source: Man Institute (2019).

Some practitioners view ESG ratings as a mix of size and quality factors. There is a size bias in ESG ratings in favor of large companies because large companies have the resources to disclose information and create ESG management policies. The link between quality and ESG as factors stems from the intuition that the governance of higher-ESG-rated companies overlaps with more robust decision making around capital allocation and shareholder returns.

7. THE EVOLUTION OF ESG INTEGRATION: EXCLUSIONARY PREFERENCES AND THEIR APPLICATION

8.1.4 explain the different approaches to screening and the benefits and limitations of the main approaches

8.1.5 explain the main indexes and benchmarking approaches applicable to sustainable and ESG investing, noting potential limitations

Screening represents the oldest and most straightforward approach to ESG investing. Negative screening imposes a set of exclusions on a portfolio's investable universe based on ethical preferences. The first formal use of ESG exclusions was aligned to religious values, when the Methodists avoided investing in businesses that dealt in alcohol, tobacco, and gambling. In the 18th century, the Quakers aligned their investment approach to their stance against slavery, choosing to screen out investments and boycott business interests that supported the slave trade. In a similar manner, Islamic approaches to investment apply hard or soft interpretations of shari'a principles to exclude companies that are not shari'a-compliant.[3] Exclusions today continue to typically take the form of sectors or industries commonly known as "sin" sectors that include tobacco, pornography, gaming, and alcohol. But exclusions can just as easily target specific companies or even countries.

According to statistics maintained by the Global Sustainable Investment Alliance (GSIA 2018), exclusion-based approaches remain the largest portion of dedicated ESG-screened assets under management (AUM). Their size and growth points to the expansion from traditional areas of exclusion into other areas, such as coal and nuclear weapons. ESG exclusions are not static but continue to evolve in response to new information. For example, the Russian invasion of Ukraine brought energy security into sharp focus, which had the effect of investors reconsidering blanket exclusions on fossil fuels and weapons.

Exclusions can be grouped into four basic categories:

1. universal,
2. conduct-related,
3. faith-based, and
4. idiosyncratic exclusions.

---

3 Shari'a-compliant investment funds are a type of responsible investment governed by Islamic law. Like other faith-based screening approaches, shari'a-compliant funds operate on exclusionary screening that typically excludes: conventional banking and insurance; pork and non-halal foods; alcohol; gambling; tobacco; adult entertainment; synthetic instruments, such as derivatives and swaps; and weapons. The Shariah Supervisory Board applies and arbitrates exclusionary criteria.

Universal Exclusions

Universal exclusions represent exclusions supported by global norms and conventions, such as those from the United Nations (UN) and the World Health Organization (WHO).

> **EXAMPLE 1**
>
> ### Arms and Munitions Exclusions
>
> Exclusions governing investment in controversial arms and munitions are supported by multilateral treaties, conventions, and national legislation.
>
> - The Ottawa Treaty from 1997 prohibits the use, stockpiling, production, and transfer of anti-personnel mines.
> - The UN Convention on Cluster Munitions of 2008 prohibits the use, stockpiling, production, and transfer of cluster munitions.
> - The UN Chemical Weapons Convention of 1997 prohibits the use, stockpiling, production, and transfer of chemical weapons.
> - The UN Biological Weapons Convention of 1975 prohibits the use, stockpiling, production, and transfer of biological weapons.
> - The Treaty on the Non-Proliferation of Nuclear Weapons from 1968 limits the spread of nuclear weapons to the group of so-called nuclear-weapons states (the United States, Russia, the United Kingdom, France, and China).
> - In 2009, Belgium banned investments in depleted uranium weapons.
> - The UN Global Compact announced in 2017 the decision to exclude controversial weapon sectors from participating in the initiative.
>
> ### Tobacco Exclusions
>
> Although tobacco does not exhibit the same degree of universal acceptance that the exclusion over controversial arms and munitions does, it provides another example that can be said to be supported by the following:
>
> - The WHO Framework Convention on Tobacco Control of 2003, with 181 parties committing to implementing a broad range of tobacco control measures.
> - The UN Global Compact (UNGC) announced in 2017 the decision to exclude tobacco companies from participating in the initiative because tobacco products are fundamentally misaligned with the UNGC's commitment to advancing business action toward Sustainable Development Goal (SDG) 3 and are in direct conflict with the right to public health.
> - The UN SDGs from 2015 drive a collection of 17 global goals to eradicate poverty, protect the planet, and improve prosperity; many of the goals touch on tobacco as an impediment to improved social and environmental outcomes.

Conduct-Related Exclusions

Conduct-related exclusions are generally company or country specific and are often not a statement against the nature of the business itself. Labor infractions in the form of violations against the International Labour Organization (ILO) principles are often cited.

Faith-Based Exclusions

Faith-based exclusions are specific to religious institutional or individual investors. For example, an index or portfolio may exclude companies that earn any revenue from gambling, alcohol, or adult entertainment.

For more on faith-based exclusions, see Chapter 1.

Idiosyncratic Exclusions

Idiosyncratic exclusions are exclusions that are not supported by global consensus. For example, New Zealand's pension funds are singularly bound by statutory law to exclude companies involved in the processing of whale meat products.[4]

Applying Exclusionary Preferences

Exclusionary preferences are usually adopted by asset owners rather than asset managers. While there are managers who have formally instituted some form of values-based exclusionary screens, they represent a small minority. This is because of their global reach, managing assets for many asset owners who may have conflicting exclusion preferences or none at all. Asset managers create and manage dedicated mandates for asset owners with exclusionary preferences.

Among global asset owners, Norges Bank, in its Norwegian sovereign wealth fund (SWF), implements a highly visible exclusion because of its large size. Norges Bank's exclusion list has been adopted by other Norwegian asset owners and continues to influence the construction of exclusion lists among other Nordic asset owners.[5]

It is important to highlight that some issues continue to remain difficult to implement by screening, so asset managers assume a best-efforts approach. The degree of exclusions may also carry significant implications from a portfolio management perspective. A portfolio that imposes a broad set of exclusions (particularly exclusions of entire sectors that represent a significant weight of the benchmark) will likely produce high active share and tracking error against a broad market benchmark. This magnitude of difference may lead the portfolio manager to adopt a more appropriate ESG benchmark for comparisons rather than a broad market benchmark.

---

4 Source: NZ Super Fund "Exclusions" webpage: https://nzsuperfund.nz/how-we-invest/sustainable-finance/exclusions/.
5 To see the list, go to the Norges Bank "Observation and Exclusion of Companies" webpage: www.nbim.no/en/the-fund/responsible-investment/exclusion-of-companies/.

The Evolution of ESG Integration: Exclusionary Preferences and Their Application

> **EXERCISE**
>
> Construct an equity-only portfolio that aligns with your worldview. Consult the Global Industry Classification Standard (www.msci.com/gics) to view its hierarchy of 11 sectors and underlying 25 industry groups. Discuss your construction:
>
> ▶ What sectors would you exclude? Are these normative (universally supported) or more idiosyncratic?
>
> ▶ How do your choices change the size of your investable universe?
>
> ▶ What implications would your chosen exclusions have for the overall portfolio's exposure?
>
> ▶ Would they make the portfolio more pro-cyclical or more defensive?
>
> ▶ How would they change the yield profile? What ways could you compensate for the effects of your exclusions?

Another challenge is the treatment of asset classes and securities that fall outside the traditional spectrum of responsible investment, which has generally been focused on listed equities and corporate bonds.

Indeed, the PRI itself acknowledges this limitation in the language of its signatory commitment,[6] which recognizes that ESG investing may impact the performance of portfolios to "varying degrees across companies, sectors, regions, asset classes and through time."

Equities and corporate bonds finance corporations led by boards of directors and managers who can alter ESG risk factor exposures. Other asset classes do not have this structure. For instance, currencies, derivatives, sovereign debt, asset-backed securities, real assets, and many indexes fall outside the conventional framework of ESG analysis. For some security types, it is possible to draw tenuous linkages between, for example, currency forward contracts and the ESG profile of the currency issuer, but doing so for other instruments is more difficult. For example, consider an interest rate swap that represents a derivative contract that exchanges the floating interest rate payment of a sovereign bond or loan for a fixed interest rate. Investors should certainly be aware of the underlying risks to that sovereign payment, but simply netting out the ESG risk profile of the same sovereign on both sides of the contract effectively creates a wash or cancellation.

In addition, investment strategies, particularly at the multi-asset level, commonly invest in indexes for various reasons, including for cash management to cover potential redemptions by investors. In this context, it is complicated and often can become expensive to frequently break down indexes from a screening perspective. Widely traded, liquid indexes are generally easier and less costly to decompose into their constituent or member weights, while the opposite is true for less popular, thinly traded indexes. Hence, while investors may maintain a formal exclusion list, they may also include specific language in their exclusion policy that exempts indexes in the interest of efficient portfolio management.

Exhibit 13 provides some examples of ESG indexes, benchmarks, and their methodologies.

---

6 Available at www.unpri.org/about-us/what-are-the-principles-for-responsible-investment.

Exhibit 13: ESG Indexes, Benchmarks, and Their Methodologies (January 2021)

Name	Asset class	Description
FTSE Russell	Equity	Rates above 4,000 securities in developed and emerging countries on 300 ESG indicators. Measures companies' revenue exposure and management to green and brown (fossil fuel) exposure.
FTSE4Good	Equity	Applies FTSE Russell ESG rating data to select companies with at least a 3.1 (developed) and 2.5 (emerging) rating out of 5. Companies exposed to "significant controversies" and certain business activities (tobacco, weapons, and coal) are also excluded.
MSCI ESG	Equity	Offers more than 1,000 ESG indexes. Methodology is based on ESG ratings with screening criteria available (tobacco, weapons, coal, fossil fuel, Catholic, and Islamic values). Governance factor measures UN Global Compact compliance only.
S&P (DJSI) ESG	Equity, fixed income	Best-in-class indexes based on an ESG assessment of 4,500 corporates. Rule-based selection of top 10%–30% (global or regional) of sustainable market cap based on ESG score. DJSI also offers indexes with exclusion screens (weapons, alcohol, tobacco, gambling, and pornography).
Sustainalytics	Equity	Supports partner index and passive strategies (such as STOXX, SGX, S&P, iShares, and Nifty) that employ different approaches (including negative screening, ESG ratings, low carbon, and gender diversity).
Global Real Estate Standards Board (GRESB) ESG Benchmark	Real assets-infrastructure and real estate	The GRESB ESG benchmark leverages GRESB's position as the leading investor initiative focused on real assets and infrastructure with a focus on commercial and residential real estate.

Source: Adapted from Douglas, Van Holt, and Whelan (2017).

8. ESG SCREENING WITHIN PORTFOLIOS AND ACROSS ASSET CLASSES: FIXED INCOME, CORPORATE DEBT, AND ESG BONDS

8.1.6 apply ESG screens to the main asset classes and their sub-sectors: fixed income; equities; and alternative investments

Fixed Income (Government, Sovereign, Corporate, and Other)

ESG integration in fixed income has experienced a good deal of catch-up relative to listed equities. However, ESG integration varies by fixed-income sector. In Exhibit 14, Mercer's ratings for ESG integration reveal a greater number of higher ratings—ESG1 and ESG2—in investment-grade credit, emerging market debt, and buy-and-maintain strategies, while government debt and high-yield credit have lower degrees of integration. As we will discuss, lower levels of ESG integration in such areas as sovereign debt and high-yield credit often reflect a scarcity in ESG ratings and datasets, particularly in the unlisted credit markets.

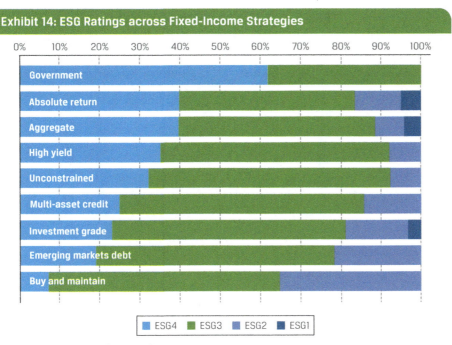

Exhibit 14: ESG Ratings across Fixed-Income Strategies

Note: All data are as of 1 December 2019.

Source: MercerInsight (2020; information on the aggregation methodology can be found in Appendix 2).

Corporate Debt

Exhibit 15 illustrates an ESG evaluation framework developed by BlueBay Asset Management, a fixed-income specialist asset manager. Based on an ESG integration approach, the framework leverages third-party ESG data to produce proprietary issuer ESG metrics:

- ▶ The fundamental ESG risk metric examines fundamental ESG risk at the issuer level.
- ▶ The investment ESG score operates at the bond security level. The ESG score takes into account varying credit risk sensitivities, which result from the exposure to ESG risk factors. These ESG risk factors are inherently present as a function of the bond's features.

The ESG score is unique in that it examines ESG considerations both as a risk and as an opportunity in the overall score. While useful at the issuer level, its value and differentiation for both internal investment teams and investors lies in elevating the picture of ESG risk from the individual bond to the single-issuer level—and ultimately understanding ESG risk in a given credit portfolio.

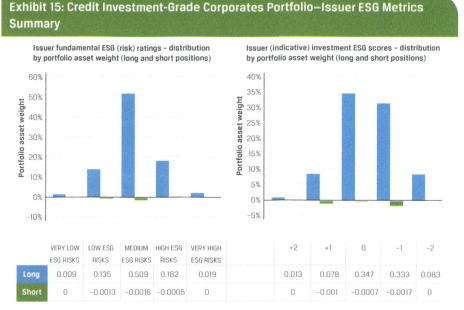

Exhibit 15: Credit Investment-Grade Corporates Portfolio—Issuer ESG Metrics Summary

	VERY LOW ESG RISKS	LOW ESG RISKS	MEDIUM ESG RISKS	HIGH ESG RISKS	VERY HIGH ESG RISKS		+2	+1	0	-1	-2
Long	0.009	0.135	0.509	0.182	0.019		0.013	0.078	0.347	0.333	0.083
Short	0	−0.0013	−0.0016	−0.0005	0		0	−0.001	−0.0007	−0.0017	0

Note: The fundamental ESG (risk) rating, assigned at the issuer level, relates to how well the borrower is managing the material ESG risks it faces, capturing current performance and trajectory of travel. The investment ESG score, assigned at the security level, relates to the extent to which the ESG risks are considered investment relevant and material and, if so, the direction and extent of that potential credit risk.

Source: BlueBay Asset Management.

ESG Bond Types

New forms of credit issuance have emerged, designed to raise funding to meet social and environmental objectives alongside a financial return. ESG bonds can be "use-of-proceeds" bonds, such as green bonds that use proceeds to finance projects with certain characteristics, or sustainability-linked bonds that link bond features, such as the coupon rate, with the issuer's overall progress on specified ESG goals.

Despite the development of ESG investing in fixed income, the absence of a universally recognized standard certification system for sustainable bonds should be acknowledged. A number of standards have emerged, notably the EU's proposal for an EU Green Bond Standard (European Commission 2019; ICMA 2018a). However, the absence of a universal standard is particularly urgent given the emergence of bond issues geared toward underlying sustainable themes, as shown in Exhibit 16. For instance, despite the green bond market emerging little more than a decade ago, labeled green bond issuance in 2022 was nearly US$600 billion, which represented 40% of total sustainable debt issuance.

Exhibit 16: Types of ESG Investing Bonds

Bond Type	Features
Green bonds	Green bonds, sometimes referred to as climate bonds, are any type of bond instrument that funds projects that provide a clear benefit to the environment, such as renewable energy projects. Originating in 2007 with the issuance of the first green bonds from the European Investment Bank and the World Bank, some green bond indexes now track the development of issuance and offer investors a passive means of investing in green bonds. More information on green bonds can be found in ICMA 2021). Benchmark indexes include • S&P Green Bond Select Index, • Bank of America Merrill Lynch Green Bond Index, and • Bloomberg Barclays MSCI Green Bond Index.
Social bonds	Social bonds fund projects that provide access to essential services, infrastructure, and social programs to underserved people and communities. Examples include projects providing • affordable housing, • microfinance lending, • health care, and • education. The Official Credit Institute (Instituto de Crédito Oficial) in Spain issued the first social bond in 2015. More information on social bonds can be found in ICMA (2020a).
Sustainability bonds	Sustainability bonds allow issuers to offer more broadly defined bonds that still create a positive social or environmental impact. In 2016, Starbucks issued the first US corporate sustainability bond (US$500 million), which directly links the company's coffee sourcing supply chain to ESG criteria. More information on sustainability bonds can be found in ICMA (2018b).
Sustainability-linked bonds	Not to be confused with sustainability bonds, sustainability-linked bonds provide financing to issuers who commit to specific improvements in sustainability outcomes. These outcomes may be defined as environmental, social, and/or governance related. More information can be found in ICMA (2020b).
Transition bonds	Transition bonds provide financing to "brown" industries with high GHG emissions (such as mining, utilities, and heavy industry). Because of this fossil fuel exposure, these sectors are generally excluded from raising capital in sustainable finance markets. Transition bonds allow companies in these sectors to raise capital designated to the transition toward greener industries.
SDG-linked bonds	Though there is common overlap with green and social bonds, SDG-linked bonds enable issuers to raise capital by specifically committing and advancing to SDG-related targets. Issuers are generally required to provide evidence and assurance for business alignment with the targeted SDGs.
Blue bonds	Blue bonds fund projects with clear marine and ocean-based benefits, such as sustainable fishing projects. The Seychelles and the World Bank jointly issued the first blue bond in 2018.

Note: For more information on green, sustainable, and social bonds, visit ICMA's "Sustainable Finance" webpage: www.icmagroup.org/sustainable-finance.

9 ESG SCREENING WITHIN PORTFOLIOS AND ACROSS ASSET CLASSES: GREEN SECURITIZATION AND SOVEREIGN DEBT GREEN SECURITIZATION

> 8.1.6 apply ESG screens to the main asset classes and their sub-sectors: fixed income, equities, and alternative investments

An emerging area in credit, driven by several central banks, including the Bank of England, leverages the momentum and research behind the green bond market to expand the conversation into green securitization. Green securitization represents the mutualization of illiquid, "green" assets or a series of assets into a security. Green collateralized loan obligations (CLOs), for which data that can be easily quantified and screened exist, constitute one such mutualized form of green securitization. This requires a common understanding of what "sustainable assets" represent in a fixed-income context.

The G20 Sustainable Finance Study Group (2018) defines sustainable assets as follows: "Sustainable loans, sustainable debt and sustainable bonds as specific financial products or debt linked to assets or investments that target environment and social sustainability; however, the more general consideration of financial sustainability is also contemplated." In the United States, agencies that securitize mortgage loans into mortgage-backed securities, such as Fannie Mae, continue to develop their green and sustainable mortgage-backed securities programs, focusing on factors for which the underlying collateral is related to social factors, such as affordable housing, or environmental factors, such as water and energy savings. Sovereign Debt ESG integration approaches that lend themselves well to equities and corporate debt run into a number of difficulties when applied to sovereign debt. While sovereign debt outstanding in money terms is exceptionally large, the number of sovereign issuers is far lower than the number of corporate issuers. Should their credit profile be strong enough, any listed corporate could issue some form of credit, from investment grade to high yield. While there is no limit to the creation of new corporate entities that issue fixed income, the pool of governments that issue debt is small by comparison and essentially finite.

By extension, the exclusion of countries (whether in the form of multilateral sanctions or economic sanctions limiting foreign direct investment) will further reduce this pool and diversification potential. Here are some examples:

- Global sanctions on Russia following its invasion of Ukraine restricted trading in Russian sovereigns.
- In 2019, the US government imposed sanctions on transactions tied to Venezuela, severely diminishing the liquidity of Venezuela's sovereign debt.[7]

Credit ratings are important for sovereign debt investors and are used at both the individual issuer and portfolio levels. Research already points to a high correlation among credit ratings, as well as between credit ratings and sovereign yields. This is quite different from the situation with ESG ratings, which have lower correlations among rating providers, reflecting varied objectives and measurement bases.

---

7 For more information, visit the US Department of the Treasury's "Venezuela-Related Sanctions" webpage: https://ofac.treasury.gov/sanctions-programs-and-country-information/venezuela-related-sanctions.

ESG Screening within Portfolios and across Asset Classes: Green Securitization and Sovereign Debt Green Securitization

Fortunately, investors benefit from a growing pool of sovereign investment research resources. Not surprisingly, many of these resources focus on governance. Many ESG-focused sovereign debt investors begin by building and integrating an ESG framework based on the World Bank's Worldwide Governance Indicators (WGI). This dataset considers:

▶ a country's governance score and
▶ its rankings on

- political stability,
- voice and accountability,
- government effectiveness,
- rule of law,
- regulatory quality, and
- control of corruption.

Although this World Bank dataset is slow moving, it offers a nearly 20-year time series and a means for investors to identify improving or deteriorating trends across these metrics. Investors can, in turn, either examine on a per-sovereign basis or, as illustrated in Exhibit 17 with four of the six World Bank indicators, reflect on the change in momentum in the context of a portfolio holding many sovereign debt positions.

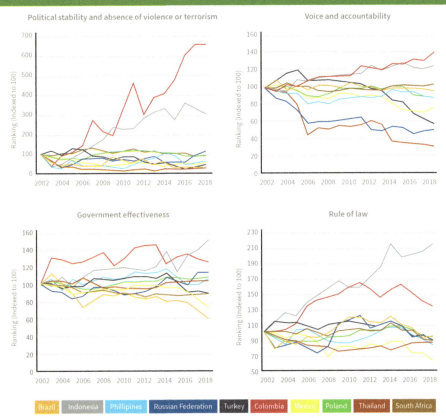

Notes: The WGI project reports aggregated and individual governance indicators for over 200 countries and territories over the period 1996–2017 for six dimensions of governance. These aggregate indicators combine the views of a large number of enterprise, citizen, and expert survey respondents in industrial and developing countries. They are based on over 30 individual data sources produced by a variety of survey institutes, think tanks, non-government organizations, international organizations, and private sector firms.

Source: World Bank (2019).

ESG tools are increasingly more sophisticated in leveraging such datasets as the World Bank's WGI to draw out correlations between economic data. Exhibit 18 shows a significant correlation between country ESG risk and credit ratings, supporting the theory that ESG may be a supporting factor for stable economies.

Exhibit 18: Correlation of Country ESG Scores and CRA Ratings

Correlating scores of each ESG pillar with the credit ratings of 115 countries reveals a strong positive correlation. Countries with better ratings also tend to have better ESG scores. This correlation is particularly true for social and governance scores and less so for environmental scores.

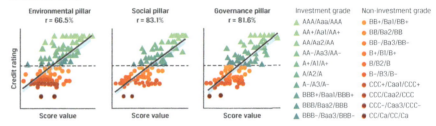

Note: The vertical axes depict the rating scale, where higher is better, and the horizontal axes measure the aggregated E, S, and G scores, averaged over six leading ESG providers. The dashed line distinguishes between investment-grade ratings above) and non-investment-grade ratings (below).

Source: Gratcheva et al (2022).

Ultimately, though, investors should aim to embed ESG considerations into their overall process, effectively normalizing it alongside other risk factor criteria. Exhibit 19 shows an example in which a *Z*-scored ESG indicator, reflecting a composite of World Bank governance data and J.P. Morgan ESG data, sits as one of the active inputs with a portfolio's sovereign scoring tool.

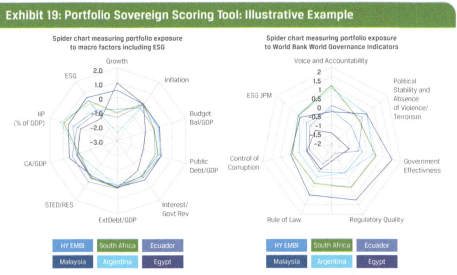

Exhibit 19: Portfolio Sovereign Scoring Tool: Illustrative Example

Notes: Z-scores measure by standard deviation the distance between a single data point and the mean. They offer a way to test a raw score result against the normal population. The J.P. Morgan ESG Index Suite (JESG) is a global fixed-income index family that integrates ESG factors in a composite benchmark. JESG applies a multi-dimensional approach to ESG investing for fixed-income investors. It incorporates ESG score integration, positive screening, and exclusions of controversial sectors and UN Global Compact violators. JESG scores are calculated daily, using data from RepRisk, Sustainalytics, and Climate Bonds Initiative as inputs.

Sources: Man Group; J.P. Morgan; World Bank; Osses and Cal (2019).

Like equities, sovereign debt is susceptible to distortion effects based on ESG ratings. These are most notable in strategies that trade in both developed and emerging economies. ESG ratings and indicators such as those of the World Bank tend to be structurally lower for emerging countries relative to developed economies, which enjoy higher standards of transparency, rule of law, regulatory authority, and anti-corruption. For instance, an emerging market debt portfolio will benefit from a higher ESG score if it is underweight with emerging markets and overweight with defensive positions, such as US Treasuries or German bunds. Hence, it is critical to understand that this developed–emerging weighting is driving the overall ESG score.

ESG SCREENING WITHIN PORTFOLIOS AND ACROSS ASSET CLASSES: LISTED AND PRIVATE EQUITY — 10

☐ 8.1.6 apply ESG screens to the main asset classes and their sub-sectors: fixed income, equities, and alternative investments

Long–Short, Hedge Fund Equity Strategies

Because of the enhanced nature of ESG disclosure among listed equities, all the responsible investment strategies discussed in this chapter lend themselves to that asset class. This ranges not only from index-based to active investment strategies but also from long-only to hedge funds. For that reason, this section will not restate the nature and mechanics of those investment strategies in a long-only context.

Hedge funds are alternative investment vehicles that use leverage to enhance returns and hedging strategies to manage net risk and produce alpha. Shorting, or short selling, involves borrowing a security generally on margin, hence the leverage component in hedge funds, and then selling it into the market to be bought later. A successful short sale means that the investor is able to cover or buy back the security at a lower price than that which was initially paid to borrow it.

Indeed, the PRI now provides resources and formally includes a hedge fund module in its Reporting Framework (PRI 2018a). In addition, organizations representing the interests of the hedge fund community—which include the Alternative Investment Managers Association (AIMA), the Managed Funds Association, and the Standards Board for Alternative Investments, as well as the PRI—now all convene working groups focused on ESG issues and regularly produce research, surveys, policy papers, and recommendations on practices.

Exhibit 20 and Exhibit 21 provide examples of an approach that a quantitative ESG long–short equity strategy might assume. As a sector-neutral portfolio, the long exposure represents the top or best decile of ESG-rated companies, while the short exposure represents the bottom or worst decile of ESG-rated stocks.[8] It uses a number of data provider scores, including a proprietary, factor-neutral one (Man Numeric); carbon intensity metrics; and even an event-driven sentiment strategy operating on ESG news using natural language processing.

Although exposure and returns vary across data and metrics, the long–short example provides empirical support for the logic that better-scoring ESG and carbon-efficient companies are capable of not only enhancing ESG exposure but also of potentially outperforming their poorer-scoring peers. In effect, the simulation finds betting against poorly rated companies has the potential to reduce risk exposure and add resilience through lower drawdown.

Note, though, that in Exhibit 20 and 21, all model spread performance shown is gross of fees and does not represent the performance of any portfolio or product. To calculate long-only model spreads, Man Numeric invests long in the top 10% ranked names in each sector and displays the gross-of-fees return. To calculate long–short model spreads, Man Numeric invests long in the top 10% ranked names in each sector and short in the bottom 10% ranked names in each sector and displays the gross-of-fees return. These spread returns are instantaneously rebalanced and do not reflect transaction costs. Rankings are based on Man Numeric's internal alpha model scores.

---

8 Market- and sector-neutral strategies are used to reduce portfolio exposure to overall risks while optimizing for investment return potential. These strategies focus on producing returns that are independent in market and sector volatility.

ESG Screening within Portfolios and across Asset Classes: Listed and Private Equity

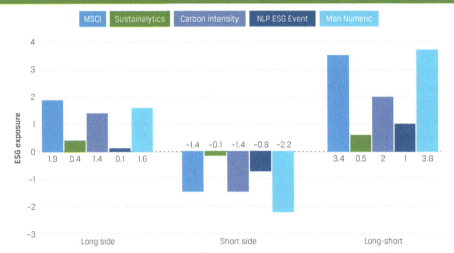

Exhibit 20: Simulative Implications of Shorting Poor-ESG Companies to Performance Exposure and Performance: Shorting Doubles Portfolio ESG Exposure

Sources: MSCI ESG score, Sustainalytics ESG score, and Man Numeric proprietary ESG score as of 31 December 2019; Furdak, Xiang, and Zheng (2020).

Exhibit 21: Simulative Implications of Shorting Poor-ESG Companies to Performance Exposure and Performance: Poor-ESG Companies Underperformed

Sources: MSCI ESG score, Sustainalytics ESG score, Trucost carbon data, and Man Numeric proprietary ESG score as of 31 December 2019; Furdak et al. (2020).

Private Equity

ESG integration in private equity faces several challenges, foremost being the lack of public transparency, established reporting standards, regulatory oversight, and public market expectations around ESG investing. The lack of compulsory nonfinancial reporting regulations, such as the EU's Non-Financial Reporting Directive (NFRD)[9] for large European companies severely limits a private equity portfolio manager's ability to leverage ESG data for relative ranking and scoring comparability.

In addition, small private companies are often capacity challenged by ESG reporting requirements. The quality, consistency, and continuity of strong integrated reports published by many public companies represent a high hurdle to achieve for smaller companies. However, earlier-stage companies may be better able to change operations and strategy to align with ESG objectives than more mature, listed companies. As a consequence, the portfolio manager will have to weigh the company's ESG trajectory (it may have established but not yet met ESG objectives) against the trajectories of more mature companies.

In some cases, private equity investors must negotiate against a strong founder or founder team, which, while a powerful internal motivator, may present long-term governance concerns. At the same time, early investors and significant shareholders are often strategic and long-term oriented, creating a powerful incentive to establish a strong set of ESG key performance indicators (KPIs) early in the company's life cycle. It may be in the interest of the general partners (GPs), investment professionals charged with investing and managing the fund's committed capital in companies, to establish specific, portfolio-wide metrics (obviously recognizing geographic and sectoral differences) as a means to support the overall portfolio strategy and communicate portfolio alignment to the fund's limited partner (LP) investors who invested in the overall private equity fund.

Exhibit 22 illustrates several ESG metrics tracked across various industries for several funds to gain a static, high-level picture of exposure.

Exhibit 22: ESG Metrics Tracked across Portfolio Companies, Apax Partners

Environmental	Social	Governance
CO_2 emissions (tonnes)	Employee sick days	Anti-corruption policy
Electricity (kwh)	Voluntary turnover	Cybersecurity function
Business air travel miles	Workers council	

Source: Adapted from the PRI.

Private equity investors may impose exclusionary screening on any number of criteria to restrict investment in certain sectors. However, private equity investors do not have the benefit of the breadth and diversity of indexes and benchmarks of the listed equity space, limiting opportunities for peer comparability analysis or portfolio optimization efforts around ESG criteria. Portfolio managers may benchmark segments of the portfolio against smaller investment universes, even including public companies, if data comparability exists.

GPs may apply some form of positive screening or thematic focus in their respective investment charter. In fact, because of the nonpublic nature of the private equity industry, LPs are increasing their expectations for GPs to integrate ESG analysis beyond screening in more robust forms. In addition, portfolio managers may establish minimum-threshold ESG scoring for portfolio inclusion. Portfolio managers may address these challenges by formally establishing an ESG program that institutes

---

9 For more information, go to the European Commission's "Non-Financial Reporting" webpage: https://ec.europa.eu/info/business-economy-euro/company-reporting-and-auditing/company-reporting/non-financial-reporting_en.

in-depth, pre-deal ESG due diligence and ESG review for portfolio companies. Since ESG data for private equity firms may be more localized or regional, quantitative and systematic capabilities applied in the listed equity space will be of much less use.

ESG SCREENING WITHIN PORTFOLIOS AND ACROSS ASSET CLASSES: REAL ASSETS—REAL ESTATE AND INFRASTRUCTURE

> **8.1.6** apply ESG screens to the main asset classes and their sub-sectors: fixed income, equities, and alternative investments

Real assets, such as real estate and infrastructure, carry certain advantages and challenges compared to the equities and corporate fixed-income investment universe. In many cases, investors are majority owners or own the asset outright. Majority or full ownership stakes offer investors much greater control over the definition, application, and reporting of ESG data alongside or outside existing reporting standards, such as that of the Global Reporting Initiative.

Much like corporate unlisted fixed income, managing a portfolio of real assets requires building a picture of what the portfolio-level risk looks like, which incorporates the correlations between the underlying assets. As discussed in Chapter 7, GRESB's full benchmark report (GRESB 2018) provides a composite of

- peer group information,
- overall portfolio KPI performance,
- aggregate environmental data in terms of usage and efficiency gains,
- a GRESB score that weights management, policy, and disclosure,
- risks and opportunities, monitoring, and environmental management systems,
- environmental impact reduction targets, and
- data validation and assurance.

Nonetheless, this report depends heavily on companies, funds, and assets participating in the GRESB reporting assessment process. For portfolios where a significant percentage of the fund's holdings do not participate in the GRESB assessment, portfolio managers will need to supplement with their own ESG scoring.

As reporting data and standards improve for real assets, investors should work toward a stronger link between ESG considerations and their financial implications. One of the counterparts to the idea of an ESG risk premium conversation discussed in this chapter for the real asset investment universe is the potential for the existence of a green risk premium in real estate. Exhibit 23 demonstrates the increasing number of studies pointing to the existence of a green building premium across regions and for both commercial and residential real estate markets. This green building premium may help investors more accurately price and understand ESG risks and implications in the real estate market.

Traditionally, residential construction had little regard for ESG factors. The primary building material was concrete based, with inefficiencies among other materials. Not surprisingly, the sector had a significant carbon footprint, largely from new builds

Exhibit 23: Real Estate Studies and the Potential for a Green Building Premium

Author/Source	Sample Period	Location	Segment	Sample Size (Number of Projects)	Scheme	Sales or Rental Yields	Price Increase/Decrease	Magnitude Sales	Magnitude Rents
Fuerst, McAllister, Nanda, and Wyatt (2013)	1995–2011	UK	Residential	325,950	EPC	Sales	Positive	6%–14%	—
Kahn and Kok (2014)	2007–2012	USA	Residential	1,604,879	Energy Star, GreenPoint Rated, LEED	Sales	Positive	9%	—
Deng, Li, and Quigley (2012)	2000–2010	Singapore	Residential	74,278	Green Mark	Sales	Positive	4%–11%	—
Yoshida and Sugiura (2015)	2002–2010	Japan	Residential	41,560	Tokyo Green Building Program	Sales	Mixed	–5%–17%	—
Fuerst and McAllister (2011)	1999–2008	USA	Office	24,479	Energy Star, LEED	Both	Positive	25%–26%	4%–5%
Kok and Jennen (2012)	2005–2010	Netherlands	Office	1,072	EPC	Rents	Positive	—	6.5%–12%
Newell, MacFarlane, and Walker (2014)	2011	Australia	Office	366	NABERS	Both	Mixed	–1%–9%	–1%–7%

Source: AllianzGI Global Solutions (2015).

and other construction activity. ESG and impact-oriented residential strategies now focus on much broader criteria, actively integrating all components—particularly social considerations—in their portfolios.

Besides reducing the carbon footprint of their housing stock through more efficient building materials, community housing strategies now make efforts to deliver affordable mixed-tenure housing solutions that provide greater social segmentation to meet the needs of the community—young people, first-time buyers, key workers, and seniors.

Investors with significant real estate exposure are increasingly leveraging the analytical modeling capabilities and historical datasets of insurance companies to understand weather risk generally and climate risk more specifically. Munich Re, one of the world's largest reinsurers, produces climate risk assessments that model potential property impact scenarios based on a broad set of natural disasters.

A climate risk profile based on over 100 years of meteorological and hazardous-event data is capable of examining the climate risk of a diversified, global property portfolio across different dimensions—from overall hazard risk factor exposure to country and city (Exhibit 24) to individual property level risk. Capabilities now enable an extremely nuanced understanding of exact longitudinal and latitudinal data.

With growing evidence of sea-level rises capable of impacting population-dense coastal areas and communities, investors may also enhance the climate rate analysis of their portfolios by profiling a portfolio's exposure to elevation and coastline proximity (Exhibit 25).

Exhibit 25: Elevation Profile of PGGM Private Real Estate Portfolio

Note: The remaining 10% of the portfolio represents elevation levels between 250 and 2,292 meters above sea level.

Source: PGGM and Munich Re (2019).

The effects of coastal erosion and flooding—ultimately leading to managed retreats—can meaningfully impact property values and insurance premiums. Indeed, a study already indicates that residential properties in the United States located in areas exposed to sea-level rises already reflect a 7% discount relative to unexposed nearby homes (Bernstein, Gustafson, and Lewis 2019).

Exhibit 24: Climate Risk Overview for the Portfolio at the City Level

City/Metropolitan Statistical Area, Country	Extratropical Storm	Flash Flood	River Flood	Storm Surge	Tornado	Tropical Cyclone	Wildfire
Marrero, USA	1.67	3.33	5.00	5.00	5.00	4.00	1.25
Savannah, USA	1.67	3.33	5.00	5.00	3.33	3.00	2.50
Palm Harbor, USA	1.67	3.33	1.00	5.00	5.00	4.00	3.75
Metairie, USA	1.49	3.33	5.00	5.00	5.00	3.11	0.00
Newark, USA	1.67	3.33	5.00	5.00	5.00	1.00	1.25
Amagasaki, Japan	1.67	3.33	5.00	5.00	1.67	4.00	1.25
Quanzhou, China	0.00	4.17	5.00	5.00	3.33	3.00	0.00
Miami, USA	1.49	3.58	0.60	3.14	5.00	4.00	0.98
Dalian Shi, China	1.67	4.91	4.43	4.43	3.33	0.00	0.00
Philadelphia, USA	1.67	3.33	0.00	5.00	5.00	1.00	2.50

Note: The numbers are based on PGGM portfolio weights of assets in each country and PGGM's rebasing of underlying hazard and risk scores.
Sources: PGGM and Munich Re (2019).

INTEGRATING ESG SCREENS IN PORTFOLIOS TO MANAGE RISK AND GENERATE RETURNS

12

☐   **8.1.6**   apply ESG screens to the main asset classes and their sub-sectors: fixed income, equities, and alternative investments

The effects and benefits of ESG integration into portfolio management are an increasingly wide area of study. Investors typically address the effects to risk-adjusted returns of ESG integration in portfolio management through two dimensions:

- Risk mitigation
- Alpha generation

ESG Integration to Manage Portfolio Risk

Risk mitigation is the exercise of assessing and minimizing the exposure of a portfolio to ESG risks. Sometimes these risks are referred to as *tail risks*. In an ESG context, tail risks are generally long term in nature and describe a significant change or move by several standard deviations in the risk profile of an asset. Depending on the position size in a portfolio, the potential volatility of such an asset may carry significant implications for the portfolio's overall risk profile and its potential risk-adjusted returns.

For example, a real estate portfolio that is heavily invested in beachfront property at risk of coastal retreat should actively assess the potential impact to the portfolio's risk-adjusted returns and consider mitigating or minimizing its exposure. Similarly, a portfolio with significant holdings in the European utility sector should routinely assess its exposure to understand its short-term risk exposure to carbon price volatility and, in the longer term, the transition risks associated with the growing demand for lower-carbon energy.

Scrutiny is required when linking the correlation between ESG integration and investment returns. Fundamentally, any strong claim regarding ESG-driven performance requires a robust means to measure ESG factors and ESG integration. While some firms have developed proprietary approaches to this problem, the ability to measure ESG performance attribution does not commercially exist.

ESG Integration to Generate Investment Returns

Although investors have traditionally used ESG analysis for **risk mitigation**, many are growing more comfortable with framing ESG analysis as a means to generate alpha. Indeed, many investors would intuitively agree with the broad assertion that a portfolio of better-managed, better-governed companies and assets would likely outperform a portfolio of poorly managed and governed peers—and potentially the market over the long term.

Yet, one of the challenges that remains is how to measure ESG-attributed performance, not just risk, at a portfolio level (which also requires some degree of consensus on what "ESG" means). Current evidence for ESG analysis as enhancing performance often comes in the form of single-security or single-asset case studies. In many respects, these are useful, such as in highlighting innovative approaches for embedding ESG factors in valuation techniques or demonstrating new stewardship tactics when engaging company management on ESG issues. However, while a case study may convincingly explain, even causally, the link between investment returns and ESG operational performance, it represents a single anecdote and is subject to selection bias. A case study does not explain ESG returns in formal attribution terms for the overall portfolio.

Generally speaking, institutional investors apply two popular approaches toward decomposing performance attribution: Brinson attribution and risk factor attribution. Brinson attribution decomposes performance returns based on a portfolio's active weights. For a given time series, this generally represents performance returns attributed to regional, sector, and stock-specific exposure.

There are efforts to embed ESG factors in risk factor analysis. A risk-based performance approach measures investment returns based on a portfolio's active factor exposures. These can be well-established Fama–French style factors or less established factors, such as liquidity, low volatility, and currency carry. Where the Brinson model emphasizes stock-specific attribution, which generally makes it popular for discretionary managers, risk factor attribution emphasizes both factor and security-specific exposures. Currently, neither model includes the capability to decompose factor risk exposure or performance attribution returns on an ESG basis.

13 QUANTITATIVE APPROACHES THAT EMBED ESG FACTORS

8.1.6 apply ESG screens to the main asset classes and their sub-sectors: fixed income, equities, and alternative investments

We have reviewed quantitative strategies that apply a tilt or overlay through a screening methodology to drive greater portfolio exposure to some ESG element. Quantitative strategies shape and direct the portfolio in aggregate or on a top-down basis rather than on an individual issuer or asset basis. A more sophisticated approach directly embeds ESG factors into the algorithmic model, driving the stock selection for the portfolio. In effect, ESG factors operate much like any other factor in a multi-factor algorithmic investment strategy.

Exhibit 26 and Exhibit 27 provide examples that depict stylized multi-factor frameworks. Exhibit 27 includes an additional ESG factor in its equal-weighted, multi-factor algorithm.

Exhibit 26: Multi-Factor Combined Framework (Stylized)

Company	Alpha Models				Rank
	Value	Momentum	Quality	Combo	
A	0.90	0.90	0.90	0.90	1
B	0.80	0.90	0.50	0.73	2
C	0.60	0.60	0.60	0.60	3
D	0.60	0.60	0.60	0.60	4
E	0.00	0.00	0.00	0.00	5

Source: Man Group (2019).

Exhibit 27: Multi-Factor Framework Integrating an ESG Factor (Stylized)

Company	Alpha Models				Combo	
	Value	Momentum	Quality	ESG	ESG Combo	Rank
C	0.60	0.60	0.60	1.00	0.70	1
A	0.90	0.90	0.90	0.00	0.68	2
B	0.80	0.90	0.50	0.10	0.58	3
D	0.60	0.60	0.60	0.00	0.45	4
E	0.00	0.00	0.00	1.00	0.25	5

Source: Man Group (2019).

Beyond the fundamental question of how to measure ESG performance and risk exposure, investors must also consider the practical and operational issues when seeking to integrate ESG screens into portfolios and mandates. More specifically, the asset class and regional exposure of a portfolio may have significant implications for the coverage and integration of the ESG screen. Equities strategies, particularly those in developed markets with a focus on mid- to large-capitalization companies, generally benefit from greater, more mature ESG research coverage by third-party data vendors. More recently, corporate fixed-income portfolios have been benefiting from more expansive ESG coverage as well as from a commitment by the CRAs to better integrate ESG factors into their credit analysis (PRI 2021a).

Exhibit 28 illustrates the ESG rating coverage gap of a high-yield credit portfolio where roughly 25% of the strategy's positions are unrated. Again, this coverage gap may be due to a number of reasons:

- The corporate bond issuer may be too small for ESG rating providers to score.
- The bond may be a new issuer that has not yet been scored.
- It may be unlisted debt.

Regardless of the reason, noting coverage gaps when reporting to the investors of a portfolio is not only informationally helpful; it also preserves the integrity of the ESG screening process.

That said, no best practice currently exists in terms of how to treat ESG coverage gaps in a portfolio. However, there are two potential approaches to address this issue:

- The simplest approach is to simply rescale the scoreable portion of the portfolio to 100% by proportionally resizing each scoreable position.
- The second approach is to apply Bayesian inference to the coverage ratio, effectively grossing it up to 100% by probabilistic inference.

Note that both approaches are reasonable with coverage gaps of up to 25%. Although no hard rule or best practice exists, normalizing for a gap in excess of 25% should be reviewed for whether it over- or underrepresents a portfolio's true ESG exposure. This potentially undermines the integrity of ESG analysis at the portfolio level for the manager and may misrepresent the ESG exposure of the portfolio to the fund's investors.

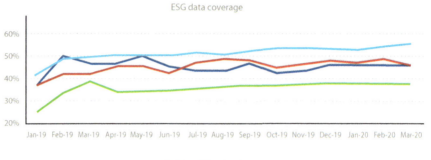
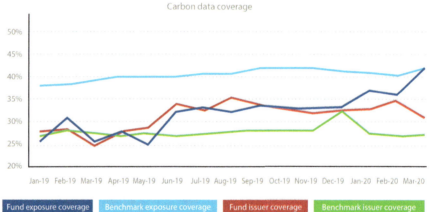

Exhibit 28: Illustrative ESG Coverage Ratio for a High-Yield Credit Portfolio

Sources: Man Group, Sustainalytics, and MSCI.

14 APPLYING ESG SCREENINGS TO INDIVIDUAL LISTED AND UNLISTED COMPANIES AND COLLECTIVE INVESTMENT FUNDS

8.1.7 distinguish between ESG screening of individual companies and collective investment funds: on an absolute basis and relative to sector/peer group data

Listed Companies and Collective Investment Funds

An asset owner or consultant screening for "ESG funds" or similar terms will yield different results depending on the methodology. While many funds may be marketed as ESG funds, the wide diversity of investment approaches makes it necessary to examine how funds differ in terms of ESG characteristics.

Broadly speaking, the PRI recognizes three main approaches to screening:

1. *Negative screening* represents the avoidance of the worst performers. Functionally speaking, an investor might apply screening toward
    - sectors,

- regions,
- individual issuers,
- business activities and practices,
- product and services, and
- even security types, such as certain commodities.

2. *Positive screening* is investment into the best ESG performers relative to industry peers across, as in Point 1, different criteria.

3. *Norms-based screening* applies existing normative frameworks in order to screen issuers against internationally recognized minimum standards of business practice. Screening generally applies globally recognized frameworks, such as treaties, protocols, declarations, and conventions, including

- the UN Global Compact,
- the UN Human Rights Declaration,
- the ILO's Declaration on Fundamental Principles and Rights at Work,
- the Kyoto Protocol, and
- the Organisation for Economic Co-operation and Development (OECD) Guidelines for Multinational Enterprises.

In addition, the PRI (2020b) has outlined a sequence of six steps for when investors implement screening as an investment approach:

1. *Identify client priorities*: Investors should clearly disclose the objectives of screening in fund documentation.
2. *Publicize clear screening criteria*: Investors should disclose screening approaches in contractual agreements, such as the investment management agreement.
3. *Introduce oversight*: Investors should establish an internal control or compliance function that
    - oversees screening,
    - conducts reviews, and
    - considers any changes in screening criteria.
4. *Adapt investment process*: Investors may want to consider refining the screening approach with greater sophistication and/or flexibility consistent with the fund documentation. Depending on the desired portfolio exposure, investors may choose to use absolute, threshold, or relative exclusion methodologies.
5. *Review portfolio implications*: Investors should regularly assess and review the implications of screening for the portfolio, including changes in exposure to volatility, tracking error, and common risk factors.
6. *Monitor, report, and audit*: Investors should implement process and data assurance control functions that are either internally or externally (third-party) assured.

Screening generally requires a quantitative lens and an ESG dataset that offers wide coverage of global securities. Morningstar, the retail fund distributor, now includes a sustainability rating for funds alongside its core fund evaluation. Its sustainability rating is based on ESG risk metrics derived from Sustainalytics company-level data, applying the scoring methodology. Indeed, several other platforms have introduced ESG analytics aimed at measuring and grading both equity and fixed-income funds based on ESG criteria for end investors (Benjamin 2019; Iacurci 2018).

For individual companies, screening on an absolute basis will automatically attribute low scores to certain industries and sectors depending on the criteria. Asset-heavy industries (and by association, companies in that industry or sector) that happen to be carbon emission intensive will likely score poorly on environmental metrics. This is useful for an investor to understand and quantify the exposure at risk in a portfolio of companies that produce high GHG emissions. For instance, if the price of carbon on the EU Emissions Trading System (ETS) suddenly appreciates, a portfolio's exposure to such companies as utilities with a high dependency on coal-fired power generation will be at risk. This approach allows an investor to run simultaneous sensitivity analyses against ESG-related shocks, such as the carbon price, to test the resilience and correlation of a portfolio.

However, this approach potentially sacrifices the benefit of a balanced portfolio relative to the market or benchmarks to which it is indexed. In other words, an absolute value approach has the potential to not provide the context necessary to manage a diversified portfolio.

In contrast, ESG screening premised on relative and peer-group datasets provides better context for building and maintaining a balanced, diversified portfolio. This approach potentially prevents wholesale exclusions of poorly rated industries, such as mining, on absolute value–based data, which may represent not only a meaningful driver of the economic cycle but also a significant weighting in main indexes. As we previously discussed, exclusions of this nature contribute to lower diversification and, consequently, higher active risk in a portfolio.

Despite the clear organizational benefits of ESG screening, whether on an absolute or a relative basis, it does carry several challenges. One common criticism is its reductive approach. In other words, its quantitative measure does not consider softer ESG forms, such as stewardship and engagement activities. In fact, an investor whose portfolio focuses on long-term stewardship opportunities in poorly rated ESG companies in order to improve performance will likely suffer from the poor optics of these companies at the portfolio level.

Exhibit 29 and Exhibit 30 depict two screens of global equities funds.

Exhibit 29 captures the top 10 performing funds on a one-year basis, which are classified as being a "sustainable investment" by Morningstar. The sustainable investment label indicates whether the fund has prospectus language that explicitly calls out its focus on

- sustainability,
- impact, or
- specific environmental, social, or governance factors in its investment process.

A sustainable investment–tagged fund may take a proactive stance by selectively stating that it invests in, for example, low-carbon or fossil fuel–free companies or firms that seek to address gender and diversity disparities in their workforce.

Despite the sustainable investment label, note the variability in the funds' respective sustainability ratings, which are based on ESG risk, as scored independently and quantitatively by Morningstar. Star ratings are a measure of a fund's risk-adjusted return against its peer group.

Exhibit 29: Morningstar-Ranked Global Equity Funds (by Sustainable Fund According to Prospectus and One-Year Performance)

Rank	Fund Standard Name	AUM US$ (millions)	Total Return Base Annualized (%)			Sustainable Fund According to Prospectus	Star Rating	Sustainability Rating
			One Year	Three Years	Five Years			
1	NEI Global Dividend	393	51.1	9.0	9.7	Yes	★★★★	Above average
2	Berenberg Sustainable World Equities	31	44.4	—	—	Yes	—	Average
3	Artisan Global Discovery	3	42.9	—	—	Yes	—	Below average
4	DNB Fund Global ESG	16	42.3	14.4	12.7	Yes	★★★	Average
5	Kames Global Sustainable Equity	130	41.0	16.3		Yes	★★★★★	Below average
6	Janus Henderson Horizon Global Sustainable Equity	199	39.6	14.1	11.3	Yes	★★★★★	High
7	Morgan Stanley INVF Global Opportunity	9,492	38.7	21.5	19.9	Yes	★★★★★	Above average
8	NN Duurzaam Aandelen Fonds	2,196	38.2	12.1	10.8	Yes	★★★	Above average
9	NN (L) Smart Connectivity	182	37.7	18.9	14.1	Yes	★★★	High
10	Öhman Global Marknad Hållbar	4,597	37.6	—	—	Yes	—	High

Note: Data are as of 31 December 2019, except for "sustainable fund according to prospectus" data, which are as of 31 March 2020. The table provides examples of fund searches in Morningstar, which is the largest platform. It is a database of funds that you can search according to different criteria, available at www.morningstar.co.uk/screener/fund.aspx.
Source: Morningstar.

Another issue that may exist is the award of a high sustainability rating for a fund that may, in fact, not have any of the essential ingredients of ESG integration—such as an ESG policy or systematic process—embedded in its process. Such a fund may be highly ranked on a coincidental basis by the fact that its portfolio reflects low exposure to carbon-intensive industries or highly ESG-rated companies purely by chance. This situation is not greenwashing, because the fund is not intentionally overrepresenting its ESG credentials. But this misalignment or mischaracterization does have the potential to confuse investors.

Exhibit 30 captures the top 10 performing funds on a one-year basis that have received a five-star rating by Morningstar. Note the coincidental ratings between several five-star funds with correspondingly high sustainability ratings, corresponding to low ESG risk.

Exhibit 30: Morningstar-Ranked Global Equity Funds (by Star Rating and One-Year Performance)

Rank	Fund Standard Name	AUM US$ (mn)	Total Return Base Annualized (%)			Sustainable Fund According to Prospectus	Star Rating	Sustainability Rating
			One Year	Three Years	Five Years			
1	Robeco QI Global Developed Conservative Equities Fund	373	17.1	10.6	12	Yes	★★★★★	Average
2	Nordea 1 – Global Portfolio Fund	160	15.3	17.1	14.9	No	★★★★★	Average
3	Nordea 1 – Global Opportunity Fund	261	15.3	15.5	13	No	★★★★★	Average
4	Double Dividend Equity Fund	—	15.2	11.4	11.2	Yes	★★★★★	High
5	SPP Global Solutions	290	15.1	15.9	14.3	Yes	★★★★★	High
6	Ethos Fund – Ethos Global Equities	177	14.9	16.6	14.5	—	★★★★★	High
7	Lindsell Train Global Equity Fund	11,043	14.7	20.1	21.9	—	★★★★★	High
8	Davy Global Brands Equity Fund	—	14.4	10.2	11	—	★★★★★	Above average
9	Mirova Global Sustainable Equity Fund	764	14.3	13.7	13.4	Yes	★★★★★	High
10	Amundi Funds Global Equity Conservative	251	14.3	10.2	10.5	No	★★★★★	Below average

Note: Data are as of 8 October 2019, except for "sustainable fund according to prospectus" data, which are as of 31 March 2020. The table provides examples of fund searches in Morningstar, which is the largest platform. It is a database of funds that you can search according to different criteria, available at www.morningstar.co.uk/uk/screener/fund.aspx.
Source: Morningstar.

Unlisted Companies and Collective Investment Funds

Despite its widespread use in listed markets, screening can also be used in the unlisted or private markets with many of the same principles and approaches applied. However, private markets and companies bring with them unique challenges. Chief among these is data: The capability to compare an investee company against cross-sectional competitor data or wider industry and sector data is often less robust because of lower degrees of disclosure and reporting.

MANAGING THE RISK AND RETURN DYNAMICS OF AN ESG-INTEGRATED PORTFOLIO

15

☐ **8.1.8** explain how ESG integration impacts the risk–return dynamic of portfolio optimization

Practitioners are increasingly benefiting from research that examines the relationship between ESG integration and its effects on risk–return dynamics. However, much of it focuses on the correlation between a particular ESG criterion and individual securities, rather than the ESG effects across an entire portfolio (Bouslah, Kryzanowski, and M'Zali 2011). Research has suggested a correlation between ESG integration and greater diversification benefits (Hoepner 2010), but this finding is largely focused on equity strategies; there is little to point at how to optimize portfolios for ESG integration and measure the risk–return compromise.

ESG integration should not be seen as detrimental to the risk–return dynamic of portfolio optimization. Rather, it should be understood as simply another factor that potentially may enhance the risk and return profile. The impact of ESG factors on portfolio outcomes ultimately rests on how much weight the investor assigns to them relative to other factors. Because of this, portfolio optimization is an increasingly important means to apply ESG criteria. Nonetheless, investors must weigh the trade-offs when quantitatively applying constraints to optimize for ESG outcomes in a portfolio. The process of portfolio optimization requires defining an upper and lower bound for a given variable and then applying it on an absolute or benchmark-relative basis.

ESG optimization via constraints distinguishes itself from exclusionary screening in that it does not apply a fixed decision to specific securities. Rather, it entails organizing the securities by their individual ESG profile to solve a specific ESG optimization at the overall portfolio level.

Exhibit 31 illustrates an example of a portfolio optimized for any given carbon emission level below the fund's benchmark (BM). Because of the absolute nature of the data and more standardized reporting metrics, environmental data are generally easier to optimize in portfolios. Applied as a linear constraint in optimization, Exhibit 31 demonstrates how the holdings overlap measured against an optimal portfolio that does not have any carbon restriction decreases as constraints become increasingly stringent across the x-axis.

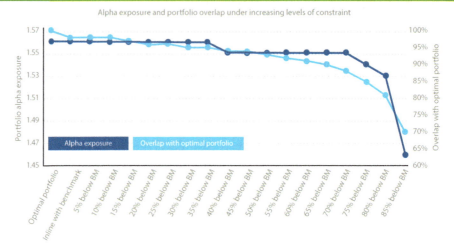

Sources: Man Numeric; Man Group (2019); Trucost.

Optimization is by no means confined to carbon data. Portfolios may seek to optimize broader ESG datasets taken from third-party vendors relative to active risk. Again, though, it is important to understand that targeted exposure that requires tighter constraints likely results in an increased deviation from the benchmark. Optimization strategies can design a fund to target either end of the distribution of a given ESG dataset. That might produce a strategy that solely invests in the top quartile of funds, or it may mean excluding the bottom quartile of companies based on ESG performance while understanding the impact of the constraint relative to portfolio optimality. Note that CFA Institute has published a report titled "Climate Change Analysis in the Investment Process," which includes a collection of case studies applying climate analysis to various asset classes and strategies (Orsagh 2020).

Index-based strategies are increasingly optimized for a given degree of ESG improvement while solving for a targeted tracking error relative to their core benchmark. Note that optimizing for broader, more subjective ESG data—which commonly operate on a sector-relative rating basis—may introduce higher active risk depending on the dataset used. For example, a company in the oil and gas sector may achieve a high environmental rating because of lower carbon emission intensity relative to its sector peers. However, environmental data alone—measured as tons of carbon emissions—will produce a greater absolute carbon exposure risk to a portfolio in the context of the market overall. Similarly, a company—for example, an asset-light company in the financial service sector—might have a poor ESG rating in its sector while simultaneously producing a low absolute carbon intensity in the context of the market.

Not surprisingly, portfolios that optimize for multiple factors—particularly, a combination of absolute data and subjective rankings—may have to accept higher active risk to achieve both targets. Under this simulation, a portfolio manager may choose to optimize the portfolio to achieve the highest MSCI ESG ratings while reducing carbon emissions (100–150 bps) with an associated increase in tracking error of 220–300 bps. A more conservative approach that seeks to minimize tracking error might instead target a tracking error of 150–200 bps, which achieves top ESG scores and a higher carbon emission reduction.

Whereas Exhibit 31 depicts a portfolio optimized solely around a carbon constraint, Exhibit 32 shows an ESG-optimized portfolio and its hypothetical effects on both ESG ratings and carbon emissions/ton against tracking error to the MSCI World

Index. The trajectory suggests some correlation between incrementally higher ESG scores and lower emissions, but this trend is more pronounced over the first 100 bps of tracking error. This correlation gradually diminishes as an ESG-optimized portfolio rebalances to underweight the tail of companies that are both lower ESG scoring and higher carbon emission intensive. While an ESG-optimized portfolio can carry early advantageous effects when taking into account a combination of absolute carbon emission data and subjective ESG rankings, investors should recognize the trade-offs against drift in tracking error.

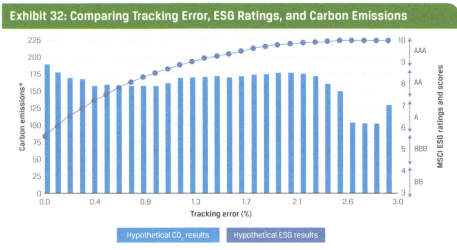

Exhibit 32: Comparing Tracking Error, ESG Ratings, and Carbon Emissions

Sources: BlackRock (2019); MSCI and BlackRock calculations as of 30 November 2017.

FULL ESG INTEGRATION, EXCLUSIONARY SCREENING, AND POSITIVE ALIGNMENT   16

8.1.9 evaluate the different types of ESG analysis/SRI in terms of key objectives, investment considerations, and risks: full ESG integration, exclusionary screening, positive alignment/best in class, active ownership, thematic investing, impact investing, other

ESG integration focuses on measurability and comparability, often applying those tools in an iterative engagement with corporate management. The PRI (2019c) defines ESG integration as "the systematic and explicit inclusion of material ESG factors into investment analysis and investment decisions."

While this ESG integration definition is most commonly applied by equity investors today, its fundamental principles are applicable to most asset classes and strategies. In other words, ESG integration should be systematic in nature in the portfolio management process rather than applied as an ad-hoc exercise. This means that ESG analysis, both as an investment framework and as an embedded process, should govern portfolio construction and management for all asset classes alongside other investment selection and risk management evaluation processes (such as financial, valuation, and factor-exposure analytics). This enables investors to better identify, assess, and quantify the materiality of ESG risks and ultimately understand the sensitivities and potential shocks in their portfolio.

The traditional argument for integrating ESG analysis has centered on its risk mitigation ability. Toward this end, negative screening seeks to avoid or minimize exposure to sectors that are more prone to risks, such as regulatory risks in the tobacco sector or such economic risks as fossil fuel–related stranded assets.

Full ESG Integration

Full ESG integration enlarges the scope of ESG analysis beyond the focus of risk mitigation. It recognizes that ESG analysis will produce a better understanding of the risk and opportunity of both losers and winners.

Full ESG integration represents the systematic process of fully embedding financial and ESG analysis into investment decision making and portfolio management. It examines the materiality of ESG information across different investment horizons in order to identify portfolio risks and investment opportunities.

Full ESG integration distinguishes itself by creating a circular process of financial and ESG analysis and iterative engagement activities with company management, concluding with these effects ultimately integrated into the valuation of a company. Specialist investors often differentiate full ESG integration from the more general practice of ESG incorporation, which encompasses varying and often less formal degrees of ESG analysis.

Fully integrated ESG strategies often combine quantitative approaches in order to exploit ESG datasets alongside fundamental tactics, such as active engagement with company management at the security level. At the portfolio level, the combination of quantitative and fundamental ESG integration provides an objective means to overlay ESG considerations with underlying, engagement-oriented interactions that help reinforce and communicate both the stock selection and portfolio management processes to end investors.

These ESG investment strategies often face fewer constraints than other ESG strategies impose. They tend not to be rule-based or box-ticking exercises. If external ESG ratings are used, they inform or complement the investment decision-making process rather than drive security selection themselves as, say, a best-in-class strategy would do. Moreover, they carry an expectation that their ESG research and integration are far more rigorous and systematic, particularly their level of active engagement with corporate management. For these reasons, their portfolios tend to be more concentrated and composed of high-conviction holdings based primarily on internal investment research.

However, full ESG integration does face its own challenges. Because it depends on deep-rooted, often proprietary ESG research, it often lacks the easily understandable optics—for instance, a high blended ESG portfolio score or low carbon exposure—that screened and best-in-class approaches provide. For these reasons, full ESG integration strategies often take greater efforts to

- evidence internal and external research resources,
- document how ESG analysis is embedded, typically in a process slide,
- track and report on engagement activities with company management,
- include portfolio exposure and weightings in sustainability themes, such as the SDGs,
- provide positive impact measurements of the portfolio against such metrics as resource efficiency, water, and energy consumption, and
- support the process with investment case studies.

> **LOW BLENDED ESG SCORE**
>
> If a full ESG integration strategy produces a low blended ESG score or higher-than-average carbon exposure, the investment team should be fully prepared to explain the logic for this circumstance. They may demonstrate, through their engagement with company management, why the market has mischaracterized a company's ESG profile or why the market has misjudged the underlying rate of improvement based on their proprietary ESG data.

Exclusionary Screening

Exclusionary screening is the oldest and simplest approach in responsible investment. Emerging under the moniker of **socially responsible investment (SRI)**, the original objective was to impose a set of values or preferences to screen through an ethical or normative framework a portfolio's exposure to specific sectors. For example, a "sin stocks" screen would typically exclude exposure in a portfolio to corporate issuers—stocks and bonds—in such sectors as tobacco, pornography, gambling, and weapons. For instance, pension plans belonging to a religious order will often exclude investment in gambling-, alcohol-, and pornography-related securities, while pension funds that represent health care workers may exclude investment in the tobacco sector.

This approach has evolved from values-based screening to increasingly sophisticated approaches that now negatively screen across a much larger set of ESG criteria. Exclusion-based approaches continue to represent the large portion of dedicated AUM. This growth in exclusions reflects an expansion from traditionally screened areas (such as controversial arms and munitions) to more recently adopted areas that include tobacco and much of the energy extraction complex (including thermal coal, oil sands, and unconventional oil and gas).

It is important to understand that the degree of exclusions may carry significant implications from a portfolio management perspective—not just in terms of higher tracking error and active share but also in unintended factor exposure. Investors (particularly asset managers) are generally more reluctant to adopt exclusions. With no beneficiaries directing a specific worldview and often a very diverse base of investors with exclusion preferences that may conflict, asset managers tend to default to as unconstrained an investment universe as possible.

Several other historical and structural drivers are behind this tendency towards sector and market neutrality. In this approach, they will often manage segregated investment mandates for asset owners that prescribe exclusions. In the alternative—specifically, hedge fund—space, managers will generally have a preference for as unconstrained an investment universe as possible in the interest of potential available alpha generation, both on the long and the short sides. The argument most often used for shorting stocks that would otherwise be on exclusion lists is a classical academic argument: that shorting securities potentially raises the cost of capital for firms in areas commonly excluded (Hvidkjær 2017).

Positive Alignment or Best in Class

Positive alignment or best in class represents, to some degree, the inverse of exclusionary screening. It uses a given ESG rating methodology to identify companies with better ESG performance relative to their industry peers. This approach is typically expressed by investing in the top decile, quintile, or quartile based on prescribed ESG criteria. The consistency of the ranking methodology and the portfolio's position-weighted exposure to higher-ranked companies are vital for this class of ESG strategies.

The diversity of ESG rating methodologies and lack of rating convergence are key challenges these strategies face. They may score highly based on the portfolio manager's methodology but poorly on another set of ESG metrics used by the fund's investor or, for instance, a fund distribution platform, such as Morningstar. Hence, best-in-class portfolios will be tested on both transparency and consistency.

Because of this rating- or score-imposed constraint, best-in-class strategies will generally have much less latitude to perform and to apply proprietary research on lower-scoring companies that happen to exhibit positive momentum or improvement in their ESG metrics. For example, recent research has demonstrated a correlation between positive momentum in ESG scores and financial returns (Dunn, Fitzgibbons, and Pomorski 2018).

Finally, a common criticism for best-in-class ESG strategies is that their focus yields diminishing ESG returns with little opportunity to demonstrate incremental gains via active ownership efforts.

17 ESG STRATEGIES, OBJECTIVES, INVESTMENT CONSIDERATIONS, AND RISKS: THEMATIC AND IMPACT INVESTING

☐ **8.1.9** evaluate the different types of ESG analysis/SRI in terms of key objectives, investment considerations, and risks: full ESG integration, exclusionary screening, positive alignment/best in class, active ownership, thematic investing, impact investing, other

Thematic Investing

Thematic investing targets sustainability-aligned themes as a means to construct a portfolio. While often designed around long-term, resource scarcity–oriented themes, such as water or clean energy, thematic funds may also focus on sustainable sectors, such as health care. This approach may be expressed both fundamentally and quantitatively through active quant strategies or more passive vehicles, such as exchange-traded funds (ETFs).

Common sustainable themes are

- clean energy,
- water,
- demographic change, and
- health care.

Addressed in the impact investing section that follows, such frameworks as the SDGs increasingly provide a way to simultaneously invest across various sustainable themes for greater diversification.

The concentrated nature of thematic investing—particularly if it is based on a single theme, such as clean energy—sacrifices the benefits of portfolio diversification. The sectoral bias of the portfolio will drive the underlying factor exposure of the fund, potentially carrying relative performance and tracking error implications. Investors in thematic funds should be aware of the potential volatility and higher or lower associated risk.

Historically, clean energy thematic funds experienced greater volatility due to a number of factors, including

- exposure to changing regulatory incentives (subsidies),
- a scarcity premium that reflected capital flows into and out of the sector, and
- poor cash flow profiles.

Hence, clean energy tends to be a pro-cyclical growth sector that underperforms when capital spending and the economic cycle contract. As an opposite example, water funds have a much more stable, regulatory outlook generally underpinned by strong cash flow and cash conversion. Often used as hedges against inflation, they will underperform during expansions in economic cycles, when investors rotate toward growth.

Impact Investing

Although **impact investing** is attracting strong AUM flows and enjoying greater visibility due to the SDGs framework, impact investment has a long legacy. As discussed in Chapter 1, impact investing describes investments made with the intention of producing positive, measurable socio-environmental impacts without sacrificing financial returns.

Impact investors represent diverse interests and expectations for financial returns. More narrowly, mission investments are made by foundations and endowment funds to fulfill charitable objectives. They have commonly employed impact strategies with the aim of improving living standards while delivering market returns or even sub-market, concessional returns.

Impact strategies may include the development of low-cost community housing or critical waste and water infrastructure. Because of the prioritization of socioeconomic objectives alongside or above financial returns, it is vital for impact strategies to build out and review reporting frameworks. The emergence of such frameworks as the SDGs has popularized and broadened impact investing beyond its historical roots to different assets, including listed securities. In this mandate, investment strategies align themselves to some portion of the SDGs' 17 themes by providing portfolio exposure to individual themes and reporting on the fund's SDG impacts and improvement in any underlying KPI, as defined by the SDG text.

Note, however, that reporting and measuring SDG methodologies vary widely among data providers. For instance, some providers measure SDG impact based on alignment to a firm's products in addition to the operational aspect, while other data measures align more broadly as a percentage of revenue exposure.

As an example, one form of portfolio analysis and reporting against the SDGs compares

- fund exposure relative to benchmark exposure,
- overall, sectoral, and thematic contribution by the SDGs,
- performance metrics by underlying security, and
- a more detailed breakdown of how the provider classifies SDG contribution.

In this case, the data provider, Vigeo Eiris (2019), an affiliate of Moody's, recognizes the individual alignment of the product and of issuer behavior alongside controversies.

Again, though, this form of reporting is generally designed for portfolio managers of investment mandates where the SDGs are either an explicit or implicit feature. Reporting in a listed context will generally lack the granularity and depth of reporting of conventional, unlisted impact portfolios. Nonetheless, it serves to support thematically consistent portfolio exposure and to signal commitment to reporting transparency. Its purpose is neither to attribute investment returns in any causal form nor to add to the portfolio's risk exposure in any quantitative manner.

Note that applied approaches of the SDGs in certain asset classes—listed equities, for example—are more challenged in evidencing the presence of additionality and intentionality. A portfolio of listed securities should take efforts to clarify how the SDGs come into play regarding fund exposure in developed markets. Investors may choose to emphasize such areas as the portfolio's exposure across various metrics that are aligned with the SDGs. This would include exposure to

- relevant product and service (revenue) exposure,
- regions, notably developing economies that the SDGs were originally designed for,
- sectors, such as water utilities, renewable energy, and health care,
- the relevance of supply chains,
- the additionality benefits of one or more of the SDGs, which may manifest in KPIs, such as job formation, renewable energy power generation, and potable water production, and
- additional sustainable forms of agriculture and aquaculture.

New analytical approaches of the SDGs are emerging because of their tremendous adoption as an investment framework. For example, the Sustainable Development Investments Asset Owner Platform (SDI AOP)—a collective of asset owners including APG, AustralianSuper, British Columbia Investment Management Corporation, and PGGM—has established an artificial intelligence–driven platform that synthesizes SDG-related contribution information for investors (see Exhibit 33). The SDI AOP dataset is unique in that it covers more than 12,000 assets from all asset classes.

Active ownership "is the use of the rights and position of ownership to influence the activities or behaviour of investee companies" (PRI 2018b). Its investment approaches use a number of different shareholder strategies aimed at driving positive change in the way a company is governed and managed. In effect, it takes an approach that is opposite to negative screening; it views the act of divestment alone as incapable of collectivizing and directing investor preferences toward change.

Active ownership may involve (1) direct engagement with company management; (2) collaborative engagement where investors collectively drive for change, filing shareholder proposals and resolutions; or (3) a proxy voting strategy that is driven by a clear agenda to

- encourage greater disclosure,
- improve transparency, and
- increase awareness of ESG issues.

Companies that trade at meaningful discounts to their peer group or whose debt is distressed often have poor ESG metrics. Through influencing companies' behavior, the strategy is based on the theory that a link exists between improvements in corporate ESG metrics and the re-rating in equity value or credit through tighter spreads.

Academic support for the efficacy of active ownership is relatively sparse. While there are numerous case studies on company-specific engagements, there is more limited data measuring prolonged engagements and their effects across dedicated active ownership strategies.

Exhibit 33: SDG Intensity Profile of Portfolio and Benchmark (SDG Active Intensity by Sector)

	No Poverty	Zero Hunger	Good Health and Well-Being	Quality Education	Clean Water and Sanitation	Affordable and Clean Energy	Industry, Innovation, and Infrastructure	Sustainable Cities and Communities	Responsible Consumption and Production	Climate Action	Life Below Water	Life on Land
Communication Services				0.09%		0.00%	0.24%					
Consumer Discretionary			0.11%	−0.01%		1.11%	0.02%	0.00%				
Consumer Staples		−0.04%	0.02%			0.00%						
Energy												
Financials						0.04%	0.04%					
Health Care		0.27%	12.80%	−0.39%	0.09%		−0.40%	−0.02%	0.16%		−0.48%	
Industrials		−0.05%	−0.23%	0.08%	−0.11%	1.44%	−0.46%	−0.01%	0.02%	−0.08%	0.08%	−0.01%
Information Technology		−0.01%	−0.06%	−0.02%	−0.01%	−0.24%	−0.01%	−1.00%			−0.03%	
Materials		−0.10%	−0.06%		0.02%	0.14%		0.02%	0.04%		0.00%	0.05%
Real Estate						−0.11%						
Utilities					0.31%	−0.06%			0.00%		0.00%	

Note: Simulation equal-weighted portfolio across all assets under coverage versus the STOXX Global 1800 as a benchmark.
Source: Entis, SDI AOP data as of 2021.

> **EXERCISE**
>
> Place yourself in the position of a large UK pension fund that is re-evaluating its pension strategy and looking to better integrate ESG investing.
>
> For UK defined contribution plans, annual manager fees are capped at 75 bps, which pays for
>
> - management,
> - performance, and
> - administration costs.
>
> This fee is often too low to attract alternative active fund managers or alternative managers in such areas as real estate, hedge funds, and infrastructure.
>
> Considering these problems, how would you begin integrating ESG analysis into the pension fund's process, given the fee limitations?
>
> - What ESG strategies discussed in this chapter will likely not be suitable?
> - What ESG analytics can be embedded in the pension fund's overall risk management process?
> - What is the best way for the pension fund to build a comprehensive understanding of manager ESG capabilities?
> - What area of ESG risk should the pension fund focus on developing?
> - What ambitions should the pension set for engagement and stewardship by its underlying managers?

18 ESG INTEGRATION IN INDEX-BASED PORTFOLIOS AND ESTABLISHED DATASETS

8.1.10 describe approaches to managing index-based ESG portfolios

The shift from active to index-based strategies represents a substantial change in the allocation and composition of overall AUM. Indeed, index-based assets have more than doubled as a percentage of total global AUM in the last decade (Sushko and Turner 2018). The shift is most pronounced in the United States, where index-based ETFs and mutual funds hold 16% of total US equity market capitalization.

Unlike more discretionary actively managed strategies, index-based strategies rely on rule-based approaches, which keep their costs low. However, the relatively nascent state of ESG analysis and its data costs potentially mean that ESG index-based strategies may run at a slightly higher fee structure relative to other index-based strategies, although still significantly lower than actively managed ESG funds (PRI 2022).

Noteworthy examples of asset owners circumventing actively-managed ESG strategies and directly investing or independently creating index-based ESG strategies include the following:

- The California State Teachers' Retirement System (CalSTRS) uses indexes to meet ESG objectives and achieve lower cost and higher efficiency for its beneficiaries, including the MSCI ACWI Low-Carbon Target Index (Mussuto 2018).
- Taiwan's Bureau of Labour Funds pension scheme selected the FTSE4Good TIP Taiwan ESG Index for a five-year index-based mandate (FTSE Russell 2018).
- Japan's Government Pension Investment Fund (GPIF), the world's largest pension fund, is well known for its use of ESG-dedicated indexes. This follows the creation of the Nikkei 400, which linked corporate governance reforms under Prime Minister Shinzo Abe to improved capital efficiency metrics, such as return on equity. GPIF's indexes include global and domestic environmental strategies, which overweight carbon-efficient companies, and a socially oriented index, the MSCI Japan Empowering Women Index. Exhibit 34 illustrates the diversity of approaches and sources that GPIF has employed within its index-based investment strategy.

Exhibit 34: Indexes Adopted by Japan's GPIF

	FTSE Blossom Japan Index	MSCI Japan ESG Select Leaders Index	MSCI Japan Empowering Women Index	S&P/JPX Carbon Efficient Index	S&P Global Ex-Japan LargeMidCap Carbon Efficient Index
Index concept	This uses the ESG assessment scheme used in the FTSE4Good Japan Index Series, which has one of the longest track records globally for ESG indexes. As a broad ESG index, it selects stocks with high absolute ESG scores and adjusts industry weights to neutral.	This is a broad ESG index that integrates various ESG risks into today's portfolio. It is based on MSCI ESG Research used globally by more than 1,000 clients The index comprises stocks with relatively high ESG scores in each industry.	MSCI calculates the gender-diversity scores based on information disclosed under the Act on Promotion of Women's Participation and Advancement in the Workplace and selects companies with higher gender-diversity scores from each sector. The first index designed to cover a broad range of factors related to gender diversity.	Based on carbon data provided by Trucost. S&P Dow Jones develops the index methodologies. The indexes are designed to increase index weights of the companies that have low carbon-to-revenue footprints (annual GHG emissions divided by annual revenues) and actively disclose carbon emission information.	
Subject of investment	Domestic equity	Domestic equity	Domestic equity	Domestic equity	Foreign equity
Parent index (number of stocks)	FTSE JAPAN INDEX (513 stocks)	MSCI JAPAN IMI TOP 700 (694 stocks)	MSCI JAPAN IMI TOP 500 (496 stocks)	TOPIX (2,124 stocks)	S&P Global ex-Japan LargeMidCap Index (2,556 stocks)
Index constituents	152	268	213	1,738	2,199

	FTSE Blossom Japan Index	MSCI Japan ESG Select Leaders Index	MSCI Japan Empowering Women Index	S&P/JPX Carbon Efficient Index	S&P Global Ex-Japan LargeMidCap Carbon Efficient Index
AUM	642.8 (USD5.9 bn)	804.3 (USD 7.3 bn)	474.6 (USD4.3 bn)	387.8 (USD3.5 bn)	1,205.2 (USD10.9 bn)

Sources: Japanese Government Pension Investment Fund (2018); based on data from each index provider.

Index-based investing approaches have evolved from the replication of established indexes, such as the S&P 500 or FTSE 100 Index, to more sophisticated strategies (see Exhibit 35). Because of the ease of use and low cost, exclusion-oriented responsible investment approaches were early adopters of index-based investing, beginning with the MSCI KLD 400 Social Index, graduating to more mainstream indexes, such as the Dow Jones Sustainability Index, and now expanding to other asset classes and strategy types.

Index-based ESG approaches now range from exclusion-oriented strategies, such as the MSCI World Ex-Tobacco, to approaches that target minimized exposure to fossil fuels either by excluding high–carbon emission and GHG-intensive industries or by applying a carbon emission cap relative to the main index. Investors' willingness to deviate from the core index based on ESG and sector or security exclusion criteria will determine the degree of differential in tracking error.

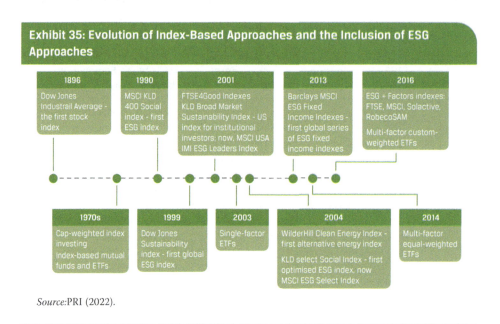

Exhibit 35: Evolution of Index-Based Approaches and the Inclusion of ESG Approaches

Source: PRI (2022).

The wider availability of ESG data and greater investor interest in responsible investment have also led to the development of new, alternative approaches in index-based investing. Single-factor ESG strategies (smart beta and beta plus) provide investors a means to weight an index toward a style factor while also screening for companies that perform better on ESG metrics. This is highly dependent on the screening methodology and the ESG dataset used. For example, the new MSCI Factor ESG Target Indexes target traditional style factors, such as value and low volatility, while weighting the portfolio toward corporates with higher MSCI ESG ratings (Skypala 2017).

Exhibit 36 illustrates the range and depth of ESG indexes developed by FTSE Russell. It addresses several investor motivations through a mix of indexes that prioritize

- ESG analysis on a holistic basis,
- subsets of ESG themes, such as climate and environmental markets,
- ethical and normative exclusions, and
- single ESG themes, such as diversity as measured by female board representation.

It also includes investment styles, such as a minimum-variance strategy with an ESG-screened overlay.

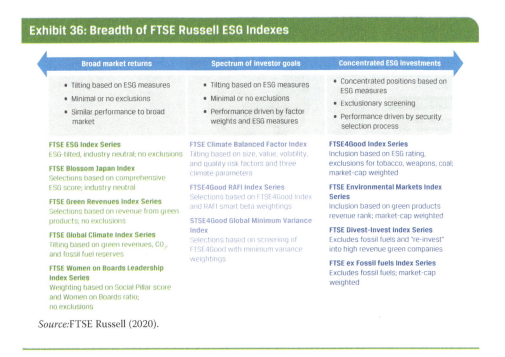

Source: FTSE Russell (2020).

Nonetheless, the inherent nature of index-based strategies presents some challenges in ESG integration.

Relying on Established Datasets

Index-based investment strategies rely on established datasets for construction. Some of these are uncontroversial, such as reconstituting indexes to apply style factors as overlays or tilts—for instance, in smart beta strategies.

Though investors develop proprietary quantitative models, these models are often both underpinned by academic theory and supported by historical data to performance backtests. As an example, more than a century of US financial market data exist to analyze business cycles and sensitivities to traditional factors, such as value and growth. And while the nuances of value continue to be debated and redefined, there is a general agreement for the fundamental identifiers of value, such as price-to-book and free cash flow multiples.

In comparison, ESG datasets lack history, comparability, and regional breadth. For example, the most extensive ESG datasets provide little more than a decade of data.

ESG disclosure also remains largely voluntary, and there is still little global convergence around ESG reporting standards. As a consequence, the methodology behind an index-based ESG strategy is highly individualistic and interpretive. The construction of an ESG index-based strategy is typically based around a third-party ESG dataset, which is premised on its own underlying selection methodology (see Exhibit 37). While the diversity of available ESG datasets has helped drive the innovation and popularity of index-based ESG strategies, it also creates the potential to confuse the market with differing and opaque integration approaches to ESG data.

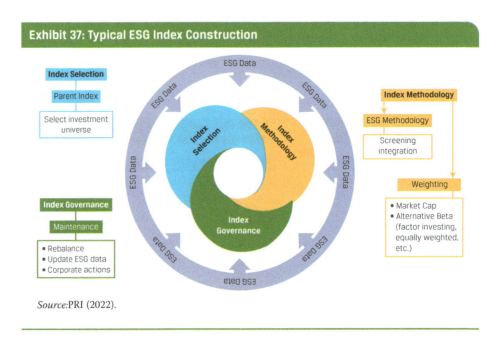

Source: PRI (2022).

Reducing or eliminating exposure to certain sectors represents a natural re-weight to the remaining sectors and index constituents. Commonly excluded sectors, such tobacco and fossil fuels, represent a specific profile. Generally speaking, companies in these sectors are more mature and value oriented. Indexes that exclude or minimize exposure to these sectors will naturally tilt portfolios toward the other sectors, such as technology and health care.

Excluding meaningful sectors or industries from an index, such as fossil fuels, will generate a higher tracking error. To be sure, targeting high tracking error is a commonly used tactic by active portfolio managers in an effort to beat their benchmark index, but this is generally carried out by deviating from the index through idiosyncratic portfolio positioning and concentration.[10] The wholesale exclusion of such sectors as fossil fuels represents an altogether different magnitude of tracking error that may dramatically alter the diversification and factor exposure of a portfolio. As discussed previously, portfolio optimization offers the means by which to mitigate these effects.

Active engagement and stewardship are key ESG ingredients. While index-based strategies are capable of proxy voting, the nature of their strategies innately limits their ability to engage with portfolio companies unless coordinated by an established stewardship team. One implication of this is that index-based investing may translate into shallower forms of stewardship activities with companies rather than more focused, often sustained, active engagement opportunities that are typical of actively managed ESG strategies. In fact, recent academic work suggests that active ESG shareholder engagement activities reduce companies' downside risks (Hoepner et al. 2022).

---

10 For more information on tracking error and active share, see Cremers and Petajisto (2009).

Despite the growth in index-based AUM, academic research examining the performance considerations and trade-offs of ESG integration into index-based portfolio management remains relatively scarce. Of the work that does exist, there is evidence of regional disparities in performance and risk-adjusted returns showing little difference in Europe and the United States.

KEY FACTS

1. Investment approaches can be characterized as discretionary and quantitative. ESG integration in discretionary approaches is process oriented, while quantitative approaches, whether active or passive, are generally rule based and factor oriented.

2. Dynamic asset allocation tactically rebalances relative to a long-term allocation target mix. Strategic asset allocation, which only intermittently rebalances relative to a target mix, is more aligned with ESG integration, but investors must consider the diversification trade-offs by allocating more to an ESG or sustainability risk budget.

3. The Task Force on Climate-related Financial Disclosures (TCFD) includes a specific recommendation for climate scenario analysis. Asset allocation strategies can stress test their overall portfolios to understand the implications of physical climate risks (operational and strategic dislocations to business) and transition climate risks (regulatory, legal, policy, technology, and market related) by simulating a number of scenarios with a baseline of 1.5°C to 2°C (2.7°F to 5.4°F).

4. Exclusionary screening can be organized into four basic categories:
   - universal,
   - conduct-related,
   - faith-based, and
   - idiosyncratic exclusions.

5. The exclusionary preferences are generally specified by the asset owners, not asset managers. As a rule-based investment approach, exclusionary screening is reductive by nature and does not generally consider softer, more qualitative forms of responsible investment, such as stewardship and engagement activities.

6. Imposing an exclusion screen or targeting an ESG score may introduce unintended factor exposure or skewness to a portfolio.

7. ESG data and rating methodologies are still nascent. With correlations among ESG data providers relatively low, at 0.35–0.40, investors should recognize the lack of convergence. One way investors can differentiate themselves is by building ESG analytics platforms that combine off-the-shelf ESG data with proprietary approaches.

8. Portfolio managers should recognize the challenges in ESG datasets and methodologies, including short historical data, lack of comparability, and coverage gaps in some asset classes and regions.

9. Simply put, index-based ESG investing describes rule-based strategies to replicate the performance and risk profile of an index/benchmark.

10. Portfolio optimization allows portfolio managers to target a specific ESG rating or environmental objective, such as carbon emission reduction, while simultaneously managing the portfolio to a tracking error range.
11. Full ESG integration involves the systematic and explicit inclusion of ESG risks and opportunities in stock selection and portfolio management.
12. Exclusionary screening imposes ethical or normative criteria to a portfolio investment universe.
13. Positive alignment introduces an inclusionary bias to a portfolio because it generally invests in better-performing companies on ESG metrics.
14. Thematic investing focuses on sustainability-related areas, such as water or renewable energy, with which to build a portfolio of companies.
15. Impact investing is unique relative to traditional ESG investing in elevating expectations of intentionality and additionality alongside (or in the case of concessional impact, below) market returns. Intentionality describes the primary motivation for investment. Additionality is the improvement in social value beyond what would have otherwise occurred without the impact investment.
16. Active ownership strategies use ownership and voting rights to drive positive change in a company, generally through direct or collaborative engagement between management and investors.

20 FURTHER READING

- G20 Sustainable Finance Study Group. 2018. "Towards a Sustainable Infrastructure Securitisation Market: The Role of Collateralised Loan Obligations." http://unepinquiry.org/wp-content/uploads/2018/12/Towards_a_sustainable_infrastructure_securitisation_market.pdf.
- AIMA. 2020. "Short Selling and Responsible Investment." www.aima.org/sound-practices/industry-guides/short-selling-and-responsible-investment.html.
- Amundi Asset Management. 2020. "ESG Investing in Recent Years: New Insights from Old Challenges."
- Andersson, M., P. Bolton, and F. Samama. 2016. "Hedging Climate Risk." Financial Analysts Journal 72 (3): 13–32. doi:10.2469/faj.v72.n3.4
- Bender, J., T. A. Bridges, C. He, A. Lester, and X. Sun. 2018. "A Blueprint for Integrating ESG into Equity Portfolios." Journal of Investment Management 16 (1).
- Benedetti, D., E. Biffis, F. Chatzimichalakis, L. L. Fedele, and I. Simm. 2019. "Climate Change Investment Risk: Optimal Portfolio Construction Ahead of the Transition to a Lower-Carbon Economy." https://link.springer.com/article/10.1007%2Fs10479-019-03458-x.
- British International Investment. 2023. "ESG Toolkit for Fund Managers." https://toolkit.cdcgroup.com/.
- Buckle, M., and S. Thomas. 2020. The Investment Environment: Official Training Manual. 18th ed. vol. 1. London: CFA Society of the United Kingdom.

Further Reading

- Buckle, M., and S. Thomas. 2020. The Investment Practice: Official Training Manual. 18th ed. vol. 2. London: CFA Society of the United Kingdom.
- CFA Institute. 2017. "Climate Change Analysis in the Investment Process." www.cfainstitute.org/-/media/documents/article/industry-research/climate-change-analyis.ashx.
- CFA Institute and Swiss Sustainable Finance. 2017. "Handbook on Sustainable Investments: Background Information and Practical Examples for Institutional Asset Owners." Research Foundation Books 2017 (5). Available at: www.cfainstitute.org/en/research/foundation/2017/handbook-on-sustainable-investments
- Chatterji, A., R. Durand, D. Levine, and S. Touboul. 2015. "Do Ratings of Firms Converge? Implications for Managers, Investors and Strategy Researchers." Strategic Management Journal 37 (8): 1597–614. doi:10.1002/smj.2407
- Climate Disclosure Standards Board and Sustainability Accounting Standards Board. 2019. "TCFD: Good Practice Handbook." www.cdsb.net/sites/default/files/tcfd_good_practice_handbook_web_a4.pdf.
- Climate Finance Advisors and Ortec Finance. 2019. "Scenario Analysis for Systemic Climate Risk: The Case for Assessing the Impacts of Climate Change on Macro-Economic Indicators Used by Institutional Investors." https://climatefinanceadvisors.com/wp-content/uploads/2019/09/310-002-Climate-Risk-Report_V5.pdf.
- Daniel, K. D., R. B. Litterman, and G. Wagner. 2019. "Applying Asset Pricing Theory to Calibrate the Price of Climate Risk." NBER Working Paper No. 22795. www.nber.org/papers/w22795.
- European Financial Reporting Advisory Group. 2020. "How to Improve Climate-Related Reporting: A Summary of Good Practices from Europe and Beyond." www.efrag.org/Assets/Download?assetUrl=/sites/webpublishing/SiteAssets/European%20Lab%20PTF-CRR%20%28Main%20Report%29.pdf.
- Friede, G., T. Busch, and A. Bassen. 2015. "ESG and Financial Performance: Aggregated Evidence from More than 2,000 Empirical Studies." REMOVED HYPERLINK FIELD Journal of Sustainable Finance & Investment 5 (4): 210–33. doi:10.1080/20430795.2015.1118917
- Furdak, R. E., E. Gao, J. Wee, and E. Wu. 2019. "ESG Data: Building a Solid Foundation." Man Group (March). www.man.com/maninstitute/esg-data-building-a-solid-foundation.
- Furdak, R. E., V. Xiang, and D. Zheng. 2020. "The Big Green Short." Man Group (June). www.man.com/maninstitute/big-green-short.
- Giglio, S., B. Kelly, and J. Stroebel. 2020. "Climate Finance." doi:10.3386/w28226
- Global Sustainable Investment Alliance. 2018. "2018 Global Sustainable Investment Review." www.gsi-alliance.org/wp-content/uploads/2019/06/GSIR_Review2018F.pdf.
- Institutional Investors Group on Climate Change. 2021. "Net Zero Investment Framework: Implementation Guide." https://www.parisalignedassetowners.org/media/2021/03/PAII-Net-Zero-Investment-Framework_Implementation-Guide.pdf.
- International Capital Market Association. 2018. "Green Bond Principles (GBP)." www.icmagroup.org/green-social-and-sustainability-bonds/green-bond-principles-gbp.

- KPMG. 2020. "Sustainable Investing: Fast-Forwarding Its Evolution." https://assets.kpmg/content/dam/kpmg/xx/pdf/2020/02/sustainable-investing.pdf.
- Lundström, E., and C. Svensson. 2014. "Including ESG Concerns in the Portfolio Selection Process: An MCDM Approach." KTH Royal Institute of Technology SCI School of Engineering Sciences. https://pdfs.semanticscholar.org/5666/0111dba181b5d3282f7f363acd08e5ea0828.pdf.
- Man Group. A Sustainable Future (podcast). www.man.com/maninstitute/a-sustainable-future-podcast.
- Mercer. 2019. "Investing in a Time of Climate Change: The Sequel 2019." https://info.mercer.com/rs/521-DEV-513/images/Climate-change-the-sequel-2019-full-report.pdf.
- Mercer. 2020. "Responsible Investment in Fixed Income." www.mercer.com/our-thinking/wealth/responsible-investment-in-fixed-income.html.
- PIMCO. 2020. "Bonds: ESG into Action." www.pimco.co.uk/en-gb/investments/esg-investing.
- Pollard, J. L., M. W. Sherwood, and R. G. Klobus. 2018. "Establishing ESG as Risk Premia." Journal of Investment Management 16 (1). www.joim.com/establishing-esg-as-risk-premia/
- PRI. 2014. "Integrating ESG in Private Equity: A Guide for General Partners." www.unpri.org/download?ac=252.
- PRI. 2016. "Asset Owner Strategy Guide: How to Craft an Investment Strategy." www.unpri.org/download?ac=4336.
- PRI. 2016. "A Practical Guide to ESG Integration for Equity Investing." https://unglobalcompact.org/library/4621.
- PRI. 2018. "ESG Monitoring, Reporting and Dialogue in Private Equity." www.unpri.org/private-equity/esg-monitoring-reporting-and-dialogue-in-private-equity/3295.article.
- PRI. 2019. "Embedding ESG Issues into Strategic Asset Allocation Frameworks." Discussion paper. www.unpri.org/embedding-esg-issues-into-strategic-asset-allocation-frameworks-discussion-paper/4815.article.
- PRI. 2019. "A Practical Guide to ESG Integration in Sovereign Debt." www.unpri.org/fixed-income/a-practical-guide-to-esg-integration-in-sovereign-debt/4781.article.
- PRI. 2020. "ESG Engagement for Sovereign Debt Investors." www.unpri.org/sovereign-debt/esg-engagement-for-sovereign-debt-investors/6687.article.
- PRI. 2020. "Reporting Framework Glossary." www.unpri.org/reporting-and-assessment/reporting-framework-glossary/6937.article.
- PRI. 2020. "Technical Guide: ESG Incorporation in Hedge Funds." www.unpri.org/hedge-funds/technical-guide-esg-incorporation-in-hedge-funds/5729.article.
- PRI. www.unpri.org. (This website contains many papers and collections of external parties' studies on ESG implementation in portfolio construction.)
- Sherwood, M. W., and J. L. Pollard. 2018. Responsible Investing: An Introduction to Environmental, Social and Governance Investments. London: Routledge. doi:10.4324/9780203712078
- van Duuren, E., A. Plantinga, and B. Scholtens. 2016. "ESG Integration and the Investment Management Process: Fundamental Investing Reinvented." Journal of Business Ethics 138:525–33. doi:10.1007/s10551-015-2610-8

Further Reading

- World Wildlife Fund and Investec Asset Management. 2019. "Sustainability & Satellites: New Frontiers in Sovereign Debt Investing." www.wwf.org.uk/sites/default/files/2019-06/Investec_Sustainability_and_satellites_June_2019.pdf.

REFERENCES

Ang, A., A. Timmerman. 2011. "Regime Changes and Financial Markets." NBER Working Paper No. 17182. www.nber.org/papers/w17182. 10.3386/w17182

Bass, R., S. Gladstone, A. Ang. 2017. "Total Portfolio Factor, Not Just Asset, Allocation." Journal of Portfolio Management Special QES Issue43 (5): 38–53. 10.3905/jpm.2017.43.5.038

Climate Finance Advisors and Ortec Finance 2019. "Scenario Analysis for Systemic Climate Risk." https://climatefinanceadvisors.com/wp-content/uploads/2019/09/310-002-Climate-Risk-Report_V5.pdf.

Friede, G., T. Busch, A. Bussen. 2015. "ESG and Financial Performance: Aggregated Evidence from More than 2,000 Empirical Studies." Journal of Sustainable Finance & Investment5 (4): 210–33. 10.1080/20430795.2015.1118917

Hoevenaars, P. M. M., R. D. J. Molenaar, P. C. Schotman, T. B. M. Steenkamp. 2008. "Strategic Asset Allocation with Liabilities: Beyond Stocks and Bonds." Journal of Economic Dynamics & Control32 (9): 2939–70. 10.1016/j.jedc.2007.11.003

Ibbotson, R. G., P. D. Kaplan. 2000. "Does Asset Allocation Policy Explain 40, 90, or 100 Percent of Performance?" Financial Analysts Journal56 (1): 26–33. 10.2469/faj.v56.n1.2327

Idzorek, T. M., M. Kowara. 2013. "Factor-Based Asset Allocation vs. Asset-Class-Based Asset Allocation." Financial Analysts Journal69 (3). www.cfainstitute.org/research/financial-analysts-journal/2013/factor-based-asset-allocation-vs-asset-class-based-asset-allocation10.2469/faj.v69.n3.7

Jarvis, S., A. Lawrence, S. Miao. 2009. "Dynamic Asset Allocation Techniques." British Actuarial Journal15 (3): 573–655. 10.1017/S1357321700005742

Litterman, R. 2015. "David Swensen on the Fossil Fuel Divestment Debate." Financial Analysts Journal71 (3): 11–12. www.cfainstitute.org/research/financial-analysts-journal/2015/david-swensen-on-the-fossil-fuel-divestment-debate10.2469/faj.v71.n3.3

Markowitz, H. 1952. "Portfolio Selection." Journal of Finance7 (1): 77–91. 10.1111/j.1540-6261.1952.tb01525.x

Mercer 2019. "Investing in a Time of Climate Change: The Sequel." https://info.mercer.com/rs/521-DEV-513/images/Climate-change-the-sequel-2019-full-report.pdf

PRI 2019a. "Embedding ESG Issues into Strategic Asset Allocation Frameworks." Discussion paper (5 September). www.unpri.org/embedding-esg-issues-into-strategic-asset-allocation-frameworks-discussion-paper/4815.article.

Task Force on Climate-Related Financial Disclosures 2019. "2019 Status Report." www.fsb-tcfd.org/wp-content/uploads/2019/06/2019-TCFD-Status-Report-FINAL-053119.pdf.

LGT Capital Partners 2020. "ESG Report 2019." www.lgtcp.com/shared/.content/publikationen/cp/esg_download/LGT-CP-ESG-Report-2019_en.pdf.

Man Group 2021. "The Wheat and the Chaff—A Guide to Rating an RI Fund Manager." www.man.com/maninstitute/wheat-and-chaff.

PRI 2020. "Asset Owner Technical Guide: Investment Manager Selection." www.unpri.org/manager-selection/asset-owner-technical-guide-investment-manager-selection-guide/6573.

Mercer 2021. Sustainable Investment Policy. Available at: https://investment-solutions.mercer.com/content/dam/mercer-subdomains/delegated-solutions/responsible-investment/Mercer-Alternatives-Sustainability-Policy-040321.pdf.

AIMA 2021. "Responsible Investment." www.aima.org/regulation/keytopics/responsible-investment.html

MSCI ESG Research FactSet Nordea Markets 2018. "Research Insights: ESG."

Nascimento, D., S. Payal. 2018. "Industry Classification & Environmental, Social and Governance (ESG) Standards" (September). www.norburypartners.com/industry-classification-esg-standards.

References

PRI 2019b. "An Introduction to Responsible Investment: Policy, Structure and Process" (15 October). www.unpri.org/introductory-guides-to-responsible-investment/an-introduction-to-responsible-investment-policy-structure-and-process/4917.article.

TCFD 2017. "Implementing the Recommendations of the Task Force on Climate-Related Financial Disclosures." www.fsb-tcfd.org/wp-content/uploads/2017/12/FINAL-TCFD-Annex-Amended-121517.pdf.

Man Institute 2019. "ESG Data: Building a Solid Foundation." www.man.com/maninstitute/esg-data-building-a-solid-foundation.

Morgan, J. P. 2016. "ESG—Environmental, Social and Governance Investing: A Quantitative Perspective of How ESG Can Enhance Your Portfolio." https://yoursri.com/media-new/download/jpm-esg-how-esg-can-enhance-your-portfolio.pdf.

Douglas, E., T. Van Holt, T. Whelan. 2017. "Responsible Investing: Guide to ESG Data Providers and Relevant Trends." Journal of Environmental Investing 9 (1): 92–114. www.thejei.com/wp-content/uploads/2017/11/Journal-of-Environmental-Investing-8-No.-1.rev_-1.pdf

GSIA 2018. "2018 Global Sustainable Investment Review." www.gsi-alliance.org/wp-content/uploads/2019/06/GSIR_Review2018F.pdf.

European Commission 2019. "EU Green Bond Standard." https://finance.ec.europa.eu/sustainable-finance/tools-and-standards/european-green-bond-standard_en.

ICMA 2018a. "Green Bond Principles (GBP)." www.icmagroup.org/green-social-and-sustainability-bonds/green-bond-principles-gbp/.

ICMA 2018b. "Sustainability Bond Guidelines." www.icmagroup.org/assets/documents/Regulatory/Green-Bonds/Sustainability-Bonds-Guidelines-June-2018-270520.pdf.

ICMA 2020a. "Social Bond Principles: Voluntary Process Guidelines for Issuing Social Bonds." www.icmagroup.org/assets/documents/Regulatory/Green-Bonds/June-2020/Social-Bond-PrinciplesJune-2020-090620.pdf.

ICMA 2020b. "Sustainability-Linked Bond Principles: Voluntary Process Guidelines." www.icmagroup.org/assets/documents/Regulatory/Green-Bonds/June-2020/Sustainability-Linked-Bond-Principles-June-2020-171120.pdf.

ICMA 2021. "Green Bond Principles: Voluntary Process Guidelines for Issuing Green Bonds." www.icmagroup.org/assets/documents/Sustainable-finance/2022-updates/Green-Bond-Principles-June-2022-060623.pdf.

MercerInsight 2020. Responsible Investment in Fixed Income.

G20 Sustainable Finance Study Group 2018. "Towards a Sustainable Infrastructure Securitisation Market: The Role of Collateralised Loan Obligations (CLO)." https://g20sfwg.org/wp-content/uploads/2021/07/Towards_a_sustainable_infrastructure_securitisation_market.pdf.

Gratcheva, Ekaterina M., Bryan Gurhy, Andrius Skarnulis, Fiona E. Stewart, Dieter Wang. 2022. "Credit Worthy: ESG Factors and Sovereign Credit Ratings." World Bank Group. https://documents1.worldbank.org/curated/en/812471642603970256/pdf/Credit-Worthy-ESG-Factors-and-Sovereign-Credit-Ratings.pdf10.1596/36866

Osses, G., M. Cal. 2019. "GEMD Strategies' Approach to Responsible Investing."

World Bank 2019. "Worldwide Governance Indicators." www.govindicators.org.

Furdak, R. E., V. Xiang, D. Zheng. 2020. "The Big Green Short." Man Group. (June). www.man.com/maninstitute/big-green-short.

PRI 2018a. "ESG Monitoring, Reporting and Dialogue in Private Equity." www.unpri.org/private-equity/esg-monitoring-reporting-and-dialogue-in-private-equity/3295.article.

AllianzGI Global Solutions 2015. "ESG in Real Estate."

Bernstein, A., M. Gustafson, R. Lewis. 2019. "Disaster on the Horizon: The Price Effect of Sea Level Rise." Journal of Financial Economics 134 (2): 253–72. 10.1016/j.jfineco.2019.03.013

Deng, Yongheng, Zhiliang Li, John M. Quigley. 2012. "Economic Returns to Energy-Efficient Investments in the Housing Market: Evidence from Singapore." Regional Science and Urban Economics 42 (3): 506–15. 10.1016/j.regsciurbeco.2011.04.004

Fuerst, Franz, Patrick M. McAllister, Anupam Nanda, Peter Wyatt. 2013. "Is Energy Efficiency Priced in the Housing Market? Some Evidence from the United Kingdom." SSRN. https://papers.ssrn.com/sol3/papers.cfm?abstract_id=2225270.

Fuerst, Franz, Patrick McAllister. 2011. "The Impact of Energy Performance Certificates on the Rental and Capital Values of Commercial Property Assets." Energy Policy 39 (10): 6608–14. 10.1016/j.enpol.2011.08.005

GRESB 2018. "GRESB Benchmark Report 2018."

Kahn, Matthew, Nils Kok. 2014. "The Capitalization of Green Labels in the California Housing Market." Regional Science and Urban Economics 47 (C): 25–34. 10.1016/j.regsciurbeco.2013.07.001

Kok, Nils, Maarten Jennen. 2012. "The Impact of Energy Labels and Accessibility on Office Rents." Energy Policy 46:489–97. 10.1016/j.enpol.2012.04.015

PGGM and Munich Re 2019. "Climate Risk Assessment in Global Real Estate Investing." www.pggm.nl/media/3ouenmff/pggm-position-paper-climate-risk-assessment-in-global-real-investing_september_2019.pdf.

Newell, Graeme, John MacFarlane, Roger Walker. 2014. "Assessing Energy Rating Premiums in the Performance of Green Office Buildings in Australia." Journal of Property Investment & Finance 32 (4): 352–370. 10.1108/JPIF-10-2013-0061

Yoshida, Jiro, Ayako Sugiura. 2015. "The Effects of Multiple Green Factors on Condominium Prices." Journal of Real Estate Finance and Economics 50:412–37. 10.1007/s11146-014-9462-3

Fama, E., K. French. 1993. "Common Risk Factors in the Returns on Stocks and Bonds." Journal of Financial Economics 33 (1): 3–56. 10.1016/0304-405X(93)90023-5

Man Group 2019. "ESG Integration—No Silver Bullet." www.man.com/maninstitute/esg-integration-no-silver-bullet.

PRI 2021a. "Statement on ESG in Credit Risk and Ratings." www.unpri.org/credit-ratings/statement-on-esg-in-credit-ratings/77.article.

Benjamin, J. 2019. "Lipper Plans ESG Scoring System for Mutual Funds." *Investment News* (12 March). www.investmentnews.com/lipper-plans-esg-scoring-system-for-mutual-funds-78547.

Iacurci, G. 2018. "UBS Global Wealth Management Will Give ESG Scores to Funds." *Investment News* (3 December). Available at: www.investmentnews.com/ubs-global-wealth-management-will-give-esg-scores-to-funds-77223.

PRI 2020b. "An Introduction to Responsible Investment: Screening" (29 May). www.unpri.org/an-introduction-to-responsible-investment/an-introduction-to-responsible-investment-screening/5834.article.

BlackRock 2019. "Creating a Sustainable Core: Balancing ESG and Risk in Index Portfolios."

Bouslah, K., L. Kryzanowski, B. M'Zali. 2011. "Relationship between Firm Risk and Individual Dimensions of Social Performance." *Proceedings of the Annual Conference of the Administrative Science Association of Canada* 32 (1): 105–22.

Hoepner, A. G. F. 2010. "Portfolio Diversification and Environmental, Social or Governance Criteria: Must Responsible Investments Really Be Poorly Diversified?" SSRN *Electronic Journal* (May). www.researchgate.net/publication/228231974_Portfolio_Diversification_and_Environmental_Social_or_Governance_Criteria_Must_Responsible_Investments_Really_Be_Poorly_Diversified. 10.2139/ssrn.1599334

Man Group 2019. "ESG Integration—No Silver Bullet." www.man.com/maninstitute/esg-integration-no-silver-bullet.

Orsagh, Matt. 2020. "Climate Change Analysis in the Investment Process." CFA Institute. www.cfainstitute.org/en/research/industry-research/climate-change-analysis.

BlackRock 2019. "Creating a Sustainable Core: Balancing ESG and Risk in Index Portfolios."

References

Dunn, J., S. Fitzgibbons, L. Pomorski. 2018. "Assessing Risk through Environmental, Social and Governance Exposures." Journal of Investment Management 16 (1). www.aqr.com/Insights/Research/Journal-Article/Assessing-Risk-through-Environmental-Social-and-Governance-Exposures

Hvidkjær, S. 2017. "ESG Investing: A Literature Review." https://dansif.dk/wp-content/uploads/2019/01/Litterature-review-UK-Sep-2017.pdf.

PRI 2019c. "A Practical Guide to ESG Integration for Equity Investing." www.unpri.org/listed-equity/a-practical-guide-to-esg-integration-for-equity-investing/10.article.

Vigeo Eiris 2019. "Portfolio Analysis: Summary Report—SDGs" (March)

PRI 2018b. "A Practical Guide to Active Ownership in Listed Equity." www.unpri.org/listed-equity/a-practical-guide-to-active-ownership-in-listed-equity/2717.article.

Cremers, K. J. M., A. Petajisto. 2009. "How Active Is Your Fund Manager? A New Measure That Predicts Performance." AFA 2007 Chicago Meetings Paper; EFA 2007 Ljubljana Meetings Paper; Yale ICF Working Paper No. 06-14.

Hoepner, Andreas G. F., Ioannis Oikonomou, Zacharias Sautner, Laura T. Starks, Xiaoyan Zhou. 2022. "ESG Shareholder Engagement and Downside Risk." European Corporate Governance Institute – Finance Working Paper No. 671/2020. 10.2139/ssrn.2874252

Japanese Government Pension Investment Fund 2018. "ESG Report 2018 for All Generations." www.gpif.go.jp/en/investment/190905_Esg_Report.pdf.

Mussuto, M. 2018. "CalSTRS Green Initiative Task Force Report Evaluates ESG Risks."

PRI 2022. "How Can a Passive Investor Be a Responsible Investor?" www.unpri.org/passive-investments/how-can-a-passive-investor-be-a-responsible-investor/4649.article.

FTSE Russell 2018. "Taiwan Bureau of Labor Funds Selects FTSE4Good TIP Taiwan ESG Index for $1.4 Billion Mandate." www.ftserussell.com/press/taiwan-bureau-labor-funds-selects-ftse4good-tip-taiwan-esg-index-14-billion-mandate.

FTSE Russell 2020. "Sustainability and ESG Indexes."

Skypala, P. 2017. "ESG Investing and Smart Beta Combination Grows in Popularity." *Financial Times* (27 November). www.ft.com/content/3f236546-c9f8-11e7-ab18-7a9fb7d6163e.

Sushko, V., G. Turner. 2018. "The Implications of Passive Investing for Securities Markets." *BIS Quarterly Review* (11 March). www.bis.org/publ/qtrpdf/r_qt1803j.htm.

PRACTICE PROBLEMS

1. Which is the most common ESG factor considered in strategic asset allocation?
   a. Climate risk
   b. Exclusionary screening
   c. Active stewardship

2. Which of the following statements *best* describes discretionary ESG investment strategies?
   a. Discretionary investment strategies impose a custom index with ESG exclusion criteria.
   b. Discretionary investment strategies complement bottom-up financial analysis with consideration of ESG factors.
   c. Discretionary investment strategies are rule-based approaches to drive security selection in ESG-integrated portfolio construction.

3. A bond that an issuer uses the proceeds from the sale of the bond to improve raw material sourcing to comply with ESG criteria is a:
   a. transition bond.
   b. sustainability bond.
   c. sustainability-linked bond.

4. Which type of bond provides financing for sustainable fishing projects?
   a. Marine bond
   b. Sustainability bond
   c. Sustainability-linked bond

5. Which of the following is a World Bank indicator for country governance?
   a. Control of corruption
   b. Affiliation with investor initiatives
   c. Length of time government has been in power

6. Investors typically address the effects to risk-adjusted returns of ESG integration in portfolio management through:
   a. risk mitigation and alpha generation.
   b. risk mitigation and dynamic asset allocation.
   c. factor risk allocation and dynamic asset allocation.

7. Which of the following is a form of idiosyncratic exclusionary screening?
   a. Exclusion of investments in firms that sell tobacco products
   b. Exclusion of companies involved in the processing of whale meat products
   c. Exclusion of firms involved in use, stockpiling, production, and transfer of cluster munitions

8. Which of the following statements about exclusionary screening is most likely to be true?
   a. Imposing an exclusion screen may introduce high tracking error against a broad market.

Practice Problems

b. Exclusionary screening imposes sustainability-related themes on a portfolio investment universe

c. Exclusionary screening considers more qualitative forms of responsible investment, such as stewardship and engagement activities

9. Which of the following about thematic investing is true?

   a. It focuses on sustainability-related areas, with which to build a portfolio of companies.

   b. It imposes normative criteria to a portfolio investment universe.

   c. It describes investments made with the intention of producing positive, measurable socio-environmental impacts without sacrificing financial returns.

10. Which of the following ESG factors is *most* often considered in strategic asset allocation?

    a. Environmental
    b. Social
    c. Governance

11. Which of the following is true about the Mean–variance optimization model for strategic asset allocation?

    a. It is relevant for considering ESG issues where an abrupt shift is expected over time.

    b. It could introduce an additional source of estimation errors due to the need for dynamic rebalancing.

    c. It is highly dependent on historical data as the baseline, with adjustments made to reflect future expectations.

12. Which of the following considers ESG risk as a bottom-up risk factor for ESG integration in strategic asset allocation?

    a. Factor risk allocation
    b. Total portfolio analysis
    c. Dynamic asset allocation

13. What is the typical role of the portfolio manager in ESG integration in the portfolio management process?

    a. Perform credit and ESG analysis of the individual security.

    b. Estimate the security's intrinsic value based on the security's earnings growth and ESG cash flow profile.

    c. Widen the focus of research for security analysis, and understand how ESG factors contribute to risk-adjusted returns in asset allocation.

14. Which of the following is one of the popular approaches institutional investors apply to appraise portfolio performance?

    a. Risk mitigation
    b. Bayesian inference
    c. Brinson attribution

15. If an investor believes ESG risk represents a top-down risk factor, then it should be integrated at the:

    a. asset allocation level.

b. security-selection level.

c. company-selection level.

16. If a portfolio includes different asset classes, which of the following statements about ESG integration is most accurate?

    a. The manager will be using a discretionary approach to portfolio construction.

    b. ESG integration is marked by a high degree of variation depending on asset class.

    c. The asset classes will be limited to public equity, fixed income, and infrastructure.

17. An asset management firm manages pooled funds and individual segregated portfolios. One of the managers proposes that the firm start evaluating the ESG composition of client portfolios by uploading the portfolios onto a third-party ESG platform. Which of the following is least likely an advantage of the proposal?

    a. It is suitable for all the firm's clients.

    b. It can produce a picture of each client's carbon exposure.

    c. It can approximate an overall controversy or risk score for the portfolio.

18. At the request of the asset owner, an asset manager has revised the equity portion of a client's portfolio to exclude companies involved in the extraction and processing of fossil fuels. The fossil fuel sector makes up a significant portion of the economy and equity markets in the client's country. In light of the revision, the manager should:

    a. create a new custom benchmark.

    b. continue to use the current equity market benchmark for consistency purposes.

    c. adopt the ESG equity benchmark from a major market data provider, such as FTSE Russell.

19. A portfolio manager is creating a bond fund with an ESG tilt. In constructing the portfolio, the manager will:

    a. be limited to short-term maturities to avoid climate risk.

    b. be able to select green bonds based on a universally accepted ranking system.

    c. have a smaller investable universe to select from for sovereign bonds compared to corporate bonds.

20. A hedge fund manager wanting to offer a sector-neutral portfolio has decided to adopt a quantitative ESG long–short equity strategy. To implement this strategy, her exposures will include going:

    a. long the top decile of ESG-rated stocks.

    b. short the top decile of ESG-rated stocks.

    c. long the bottom decile of ESG-rated stocks.

21. Which of the following statements concerning full ESG integration in a portfolio is most accurate?

    a. It can be accomplished using negative screening.

    b. It is based on internally developed research and data.

    c. It may combine quantitative approaches and active engagement.

Practice Problems 529

22. Compared to a traditional index-based portfolio, an index-based portfolio constructed by excluding meaningful sectors or industries in an index will most likely have a lower:
    a. fee structure.
    b. tracking error.
    c. level of diversification.

23. Which of these does *not* describe an approach to ESG integration in a portfolio?
    a. Impact investing
    b. Green securitization
    c. Negative screening

24. Which of these topics is *not* generally expected to be addressed by the portfolio management–related section of a fund's ESG policy?
    a. Stewardship and active engagement efforts
    b. Corporate social responsibility activities, such as community volunteering
    c. ESG risk in the risk management function

25. Which of the following is *not* a reason for an asset owner to implement an exclusionary screening approach?
    a. It reflects fundamental values of the asset owner's beneficiaries.
    b. It improves the portfolio's diversification benefits.
    c. It is the simplest approach to responsible investment.

26. Which of the following is *most likely* an active systematic approach to embedding ESG analysis in a portfolio?
    a. Weighting ESG as an idiosyncratic factor in a proprietary multi-factor stock selection algorithm
    b. Consideration of ESG scoring and relevant metrics in security-specific investment decisions
    c. Minimizing tracking error against ESG benchmark indexes

27. What ESG feature is often overlooked in screening approaches for collective investment funds?
    a. Exclusions, such as those that are "socially conscious"
    b. Position-weighted ESG portfolio score
    c. Stewardship

28. Why have ESG index funds been criticized as being more active than they are made out to be?
    a. They have lower costs than traditional index-based strategies.
    b. The opaque methodology and construction of ESG indexes may include space for human judgment and bias.
    c. Index inclusion may create crowding and overvaluation in specific securities.

29. Which of the following is *most likely* to develop an investment recommendation for a security that may be suitable for an ESG-integrated portfolio?
    a. A portfolio manager
    b. A fundamental analyst

c. An asset owner

30. An ESG integration approach that focuses on more concentrated holdings of fewer securities is *best* described as:

   a. a discretionary strategy.
   b. an index-based strategy.
   c. a quantitative multi-factor strategy.

31. A pension fund whose beneficiaries prohibit holdings of investments involved with controversial arms and nuclear weapons is *best* described as applying:

   a. universal exclusions.
   b. conduct-related exclusions.
   c. faith-based exclusions.

SOLUTIONS

1. **A is correct.** Climate risk is the most common ESG factor considered in asset allocation because it is both systemic and local. It could negatively impact the financial system and all issuers as much as it poses risk on a more localized level for specific regions, sectors, and companies. Its potential physical risks will manifest in both acute, event-driven forms (such as extreme weather) and longer-term, chronic shifts driven by the effects of elevated temperatures and rising sea levels.

2. **B is correct.** Discretionary ESG investment strategies most commonly take the form of a fundamental portfolio approach. A portfolio manager would work to complement bottom-up financial analysis alongside the consideration of ESG factors to reinforce the investment thesis of a particular holding.

3. **B is correct.** Sustainability bonds allow issuers to offer more broadly defined bonds that still create a positive social or environmental impact. In 2016, Starbucks issued the first US corporate sustainability bond, of US$500 million, which directly links the company's coffee sourcing supply chain to ESG criteria.

4. **C is correct.** New forms of credit issuance have emerged, designed to raise funding to meet social and environmental objectives alongside a financial return. Sustainability-linked bonds can be used by an issuer to fund projects that contribute to meeting marine and ocean-based sustainability measures, such as sustainable fishing projects.

5. **A is correct.** The Worldwide Governance Indicators project reports aggregated and individual governance indicators for over 200 countries for six dimensions of governance: political stability, voice and accountability, government effectiveness, rule of law, regulatory quality, and control of corruption.

6. **A is correct.** The effects and benefits of ESG integration into portfolio management are an increasingly wide area of study. Investors typically address the effects to risk-adjusted returns of ESG integration in portfolio management through risk mitigation and alpha generation. Although investors have traditionally used ESG analysis for risk mitigation, many are growing more comfortable with framing ESG analysis as a means to generate alpha.

7. **B is correct.** Idiosyncratic exclusions are exclusions that are not supported by global consensus. For example, New Zealand's pension funds are singularly bound by statutory law to exclude companies involved in the processing of whale meat products.1.2.

8. **A is correct.** The degree of exclusions may carry significant implications from a portfolio management perspective. A portfolio that imposes a broad set of exclusions (particularly sector exclusions, which represent a significant weight of their benchmark), will likely produce high active share and tracking error against a broad market index.

9. **A is correct.** Thematic investing focuses on sustainability-related areas, such as water or renewable energy, with which to build a portfolio of companies. Thematic investing targets sustainability-aligned themes as a means to construct a portfolio.

10. **A is correct.** Climate risk (in the "E" category) is the most common ESG factor considered in asset allocation because it is both systemic and local. Research on

ESG integration in strategic asset allocation has tended to focus on environmental criteria, essentially exposure and sensitivity to assumptions around climate risk, more than other ESG factors.

11. **C is correct.** Mean–variance optimization is highly sensitive to baseline assumptions, making it imperative to fully understand any revised assumptions due to ESG considerations. The method is also highly dependent on historical data as the baseline, with adjustments made to reflect future expectations.

12. **A is correct.** If the investor believes that ESG risk primarily resides at the underlying security-selection level, then ESG integration at that level is sensible. But if the investor believes that ESG risk represents a more top-down risk factor affecting most or all securities—which may be the case with climate change—then it may better serve the investor to integrate ESG analysis at the asset allocation level. The macroeconomic links to ESG issues are more difficult to quantify with precision from a purely top-down perspective. Market risk factors can be built from the bottom up using asset- and sector-level analysis under the factor risk allocation model.

13. **C is correct.** The role of portfolio managers is often much broader in scope than that of analysts. Using analysts' recommendations as inputs, portfolio managers often form their own views for a given security and weigh security-specific factors against macro- and microeconomic data, portfolio financial and nonfinancial exposure, and sensitivities to potential shocks. The challenge that portfolio managers face is how to widen the focus of research and datasets largely optimized for security analysis into tools that can better inform portfolio and asset allocation analysis and decision making, particularly in understanding where and how ESG factors contribute to risk-adjusted returns.

14. **C is correct.** Institutional investors generally apply two popular approaches to decomposing performance attribution: Brinson attribution and risk factor attribution. Brinson attribution decomposes performance returns based on a portfolio's active weights. For a given time series, this generally represents performance returns attributed to regional, sector, and stock-specific exposure.

15. **A is correct.** If the investor believes that ESG risk primarily resides at the underlying security-selection level, then ESG integration at that level is sensible. But if the investor believes that ESG risk represents a more top-down risk factor affecting most or all securities—which may be the case with climate change—then ESG integration at the asset allocation level may better serve the investor.

16. **B is correct.** ESG integration is marked by a high degree of variation by asset class, which means there can be a wide range of diverse approaches (strategies) within and between asset classes in the same portfolio. Although the level of ESG integration available varies by asset class, it is available in more asset classes than just listed equities, fixed income, and infrastructure. ESG integration can be accomplished using either a discretionary or systematic investment strategy.

17. **A is correct.** The proposal is not suitable for all clients. Uploading portfolios to a third-party platform can have many advantages, including illustrating a portfolio's mean exposure and weighting toward low-, mid-, or high-scoring companies on ESG metrics; producing a picture of the portfolio's environmental and carbon exposure on an absolute-value basis, for instance, expressed as weighted-average carbon intensity; and approximating an overall controversy or risk score for the portfolio. However, third-party platforms are not suitable if there are concerns around privacy issues. A client may also not be concerned about ESG integration in their portfolio and hence not interested in the potential information that can

Solutions

be gained from such a platform.

18. **A is correct.** The manager should create a new custom benchmark reflecting the asset allocation of the revised equity portion of the portfolio. If a portfolio applies exclusionary screening to one sector of the economy and that sector is significant, there will be tracking error and active share relative to a broad market benchmark and, therefore, the current market benchmark is likely no longer suitable. An ESG benchmark from a major market provider may also not be suitable unless it is specifically constructed to exclude the same sector. It might be based on other ESG factors.

19. **C is correct.** An ESG-tilted portfolio could hold both corporate and sovereign debt, but the investable universe for sovereign debt is much smaller than the number of corporates that issue corporate debt. While sovereign debt outstanding in money terms is exceptionally large, the number of sovereign issuers is far lower than the number of corporate issuers. There is not currently a universally accepted ranking system for green bonds. If the manager is concerned about a particular issuer's ability to manage climate risk, the manager might limit the investment in that issuer's debt to shorter maturities, but that would not apply to all bonds in the portfolio.

20. **A is correct.** A sector-neutral ESG long–short strategy would be structured with long exposure representing the top decile of ESG-rated companies while the short exposure represents the bottom or worst decile of ESG-rated stocks.

21. **C is correct.** Full ESG integration often combines quantitative approaches, in order to exploit ESG datasets, alongside fundamental tactics, such as active engagement, to produce a better understanding of both risks and opportunities. Negative screening is more focused on risk mitigation and does not represent full ESG integration. Although full ESG integration may be based on internally developed research, it likely also makes use of external datasets and ratings.

22. **C is correct.** Indexed-based ESG portfolios constructed by excluding meaningful sectors or industries in an index will generate a higher tracking error and will normally have a lower level of diversification than a traditional portfolio. The exclusion usually results in slightly higher fees and higher tracking error vis-à-vis an index-based portfolio.

23. **B is correct.** Green securitization is not an approach to ESG integration in a portfolio. Rather, it represents the mutualization of illiquid "green" assets into a security.

24. **B is correct.** Corporate social responsibility activities, such as community volunteering, typically fall outside the portfolio management–related section of a fund's ESG policies. Policies related to stewardship and ESG risk apply across the portfolio and are much more likely to be included in the portfolio management–related section.

25. **B is correct.** Exclusionary screening can result in unintended factor exposure that decreases the portfolio's diversification. Asset managers are accordingly reluctant to adopt exclusions. Despite this, asset owners often seek out an exclusionary screening approach because it is a simple way of investing responsibly. The sectors that are excluded (e.g., "sin stocks") often reflect the asset owner's ethical preferences.

26. **A is correct.** Using a multi-factor stock selection algorithm is a systematic ESG strategy because it directs the portfolio on a top-down basis, unlike a security-specific investment decision. Minimizing tracking error suggests an

index-based, rather than active, approach.

27. **C is correct.** ESG screening for collective funds is usually carried out in a quantitative way by applying specific ESG criteria (e.g., ESG ratings) to a dataset with significant coverage. It does not typically consider softer ESG forms, such as stewardship and engagement activities.

28. **B is correct.** The methodology behind ESG indexes is developed based on ESG datasets that lack history, comparability, and completeness. Judgment and interpretation are therefore required to construct the indexes, which may introduce bias.

29. **B is correct.** Analysts (particularly fundamental analysts) present and justify investment recommendations for securities. Portfolio managers have a much broader scope. A portfolio manager would work to complement bottom-up financial analysis alongside the consideration of ESG factors to reinforce the investment thesis of a particular holding. The portfolio manager would then work to understand the aggregate risk at the portfolio level across all factors to understand correlation and event risks and potential shocks to the portfolio.

30. **A is correct.** Discretionary strategies focus on depth in a portfolio, manifested as fewer, more concentrated holdings. Quantitative and index-based strategies focus on breadth and use a much larger portfolio of holdings.

31. **A is correct.** Universal exclusions are those supported by global norms and conventions. Exclusions governing investment in controversial arms and munitions are supported by multilateral treaties, conventions, and national legislation. Excluding them is consistent with global norms.

CHAPTER 9

Investment Mandates, Portfolio Analytics, and Client Reporting

LEARNING OUTCOMES

Mastery	The candidate should be able to:
☐	**9.1.1** explain why mandate construction is of particular relevance and importance to the effective delivery of ESG investing: linking sustainable investing to the mandate; defining the sustainable investment strategy
☐	**9.1.2** explain how ESG screens can be embedded within investment mandates/portfolio guidelines to generate investment returns and manage portfolio risk
☐	**9.1.3** explain the most common features of ESG investing that asset owners and intermediaries, including pension consultants and fund selectors, are seeking to identify through request for proposal (RFP) and selection processes: voting, engagement, examples of decision making, and screening process
☐	**9.1.4** explain examples of greenwashing by financial market participants and the regulatory and reputational consequences of making misrepresentations
☐	**9.1.5** explain the different client types and their objectives which influence the type of ESG investing strategy selected
☐	**9.1.6** explain the key mechanisms for reporting on and monitoring performance and mandate alignment with client objectives
☐	**9.1.7** explain the key challenges in measuring and reporting ESG-related investment performance: active, passive, and smart beta approaches; performance attribution; sensitivity analysis; risk measurement; engagement activity/impact; and integrated reporting and investment review

INTRODUCTION

This chapter aims to consolidate the discussions from the previous sections by demonstrating how these subjects are implemented in real-world scenarios:

- through mandates, regulations, and expectations set by clients and

- how fund managers communicate their environmental, social, and governance (ESG) work to their clients.

We will discuss how the challenges of the agency problem can occur within the investment chain and between investors and corporate management, as well as how the core corporate governance precepts of accountability and alignment can also be used to derive appropriate answers to these challenges. Designing mandates to deliver investment processes focused on the long-term horizons typically sought by asset owners is key, though delivering this in practice is complex.

The chapter also discusses requests for proposals (RFPs), which are evaluation documents for consultants and asset allocators to conduct initial due diligence on prospective asset managers and an important mechanism for identifying potential providers of fund management services. If done well, the RFP process enables asset managers to provide useful information to consultants, asset owners, and asset allocators by which they can be compared and evaluated. More broadly, the chapter considers the assessments that clients and their advisers use to identify appropriate fund managers and gain assurance that they are continuing to deliver the agreed investment processes.

Finally, this chapter covers the screening and portfolio analytics tools that are emerging to assist asset owners and their advisers to assess ESG factors or to provide them with an appropriate basis for raising questions about fund manager approaches to ESG investing.

Accountability to Clients and Alignment with Them

The veteran founder of Vanguard, John Bogle, called our society a "double-agency" one—namely, a society in which corporate agents (as a practical matter, corporate CEOs) "who are duty-bound to represent their shareholders face money manager/agents, who are themselves duty-bound to represent their mutual fund shareholders and their other clients, often pension funds" (Bogle 2018, p. 9).

According to Bogle, there is a similarity between the agency problem that corporate governance is designed to address and the agency problems that occur in the investment chain. As with corporate governance, these investment chain agency problems can be addressed (though not completely solved) by careful alignment and accountability:

- Alignment should be designed such that the time frames and structures of portfolio manager assessment and remuneration closely reflect both the performance experienced by the clients they serve and the time frames over which they need performance to be delivered.
- Accountability requires that portfolio managers respond to the clearly expressed intentions of their clients and report as fully as required.

Client mandates can deliver these two elements if they are designed well. There are a number of steps in properly designing mandates and in the oversight and monitoring processes that assess whether the mandates have, in fact, been delivered in practice. These steps can be characterized as shown in the following subsections.

Clarifying Client Needs: Defining the ESG Investment Strategy

The first step in the effective design of a mandate is that clients should be clear about their needs and set them out in a clear statement of ESG investment beliefs. Doing so will require them to define their investment goals and beliefs. Institutional clients will typically be keenly aware of the goals that they are trying to achieve (their risk-adjusted return target over the appropriate time horizon) but may find it harder to define their investment beliefs. Nevertheless, it is these beliefs that will help them to define how they believe they will create value and to set their investment approach. The investment

Introduction

beliefs—which might be expressed in a statement of investment principles—ought to guide the overall approach toward ESG investment (and investment more generally) and will help frame any mandate agreed with an investment manager.

Fully Aligning Investment with Client ESG Beliefs

Once the client's investment beliefs are clarified, the next challenge is to ensure that they are reflected operationally in the fund manager's investment approach. Doing so can require a clear framing of basic expectations, such as sustainability approaches, guidelines, and clarifying to the client the implications of these on the investment universe and risk–return characteristics.

As suggested by a Principles for Responsible Investment (PRI) report, asset owners should ensure that mandates align investment across asset classes with their beliefs and strategies (while the text implies an equity mandate, the intent of its ambition is to expect integration and engagement, as appropriate, across all asset classes):

> *Attention should be paid to aligning timeframes through fees and pay structures, ensuring that ESG issues are fully integrated into investment decision-making, and ensuring that the investment manager engages with companies and issuers, and votes shareholdings. (PRI 2016a, p. 18)*

Developing Client-Relevant ESG-Aware Investment Mandates

Ensuring that the mandate is fully operational is typically done through a detailed RFP process and subsequent investment management agreement (IMA) discussions. Typically, this takes the form of a detailed questionnaire sent to a long list of potential managers. For those asset owners with a more focused approach to ESG investing, the questions will be detailed and challenging and form a significant element of the RFP decision-making process. Asset owners use the questionnaire to sift providers to develop a shortlist of potential managers, and then there is usually a so-called beauty-parade series of meetings between appropriate representatives of the asset owner (sometimes the investment committee of the board, executive team members, or just an investment consultant, depending on the scale of the mandate or the asset owner and its internal resources) and a number of potential fund managers (typically there are around three managers included at this stage of the process).

Tailoring ESG Investment Approach to Client Expectations

Different types of clients have very different expectations regarding ESG issues in comparison to the rest of their other investment approaches. Responding to those different expectations may require entirely different investment approaches and, indeed, different fund types. It is vital that the fund manager ensures that the investment approach is aligned to client beliefs and expectations. This may be done outside the legal mandate as well as within it.

Holding Managers to Account

Once the mandate is agreed upon, the client will wish to ensure that the fund manager is indeed delivering in accordance with the mandate. While focus should not be limited to assessing delivery of financial performance in line with expectations, equal attention should be paid to reasons behind both striking outperformance and notable underperformance versus expectations. Additionally, for ESG mandates in particular, the assessment is likely to be across a broader range of issues, including financial performance. There are two forms that this work will take:

- monitoring meetings between the client and the fund manager and
- the manager's measurement and reporting of its ESG performance.

- Each of these areas is explored in more depth later in this chapter.

2. CLARIFYING CLIENT NEEDS: DEFINING THE ESG INVESTMENT STRATEGY

☐ 9.1.1 explain why mandate construction is of particular relevance and importance to the effective delivery of ESG investing: linking sustainable investing to the mandate; defining the sustainable investment strategy

In order to incorporate the longer-term perspective discussed in Chapter 1 and an ESG mindset into the mandates that asset owners give fund managers, asset owners need to have a clear understanding of their own views on ESG investment and investment more generally. Today, it is common for asset owners to set out their investment beliefs—namely, a philosophy of what the institution believes will drive returns and deliver value over the relevant time horizon. Most asset owners these days also incorporate a perspective on ESG factors.

The UK Pensions and Lifetime Savings Association (PLSA) produces a Stewardship Checklist for its members, which encourages just such a development of a broader philosophical approach (PLSA 2020).

EXAMPLE 1

PLSA Stewardship Checklist

In this checklist (which is useful not just to pension schemes but for all asset owners), there are three key requirements. To ensure an effective and meaningful stewardship strategy, investors should do the following:

- Be clear about how stewardship fits in their investment strategy and policy and how it helps meet their investment objectives. This should include
  - a clear and agreed understanding of the trustee board and relevant organizations' (e.g., the employer's) overall mission, purpose, and objectives;
  - a defined set of agreed investment beliefs—including on ESG issues—at a level that ensures everyone is comfortable but that is also sufficiently granular to meaningfully inform and guide the investment strategy and objectives;
  - a robust framework for deciding and monitoring a scheme's investment policies—including on ESG issues—and the role that acting as an engaged steward of members' assets plays in this (this can be either a stand-alone policy or fully integrated into a scheme's investment policies); and
  - a strategy for how stewardship fits into the manager selection process and ongoing relationship monitoring.

Clarifying Client Needs: Defining the ESG Investment Strategy

> ▶ Seek to ensure that fund managers and other service providers deliver effective integration of long-term ESG factors into their investment approach. Using due diligence and the fund manager appointment process, pension schemes will gain a clear understanding of the ESG integration and stewardship approaches of prospective fund managers. Schemes should ensure that these approaches are fully consistent with the scheme's investment strategy, policy, and objectives over the appropriate time horizon.
>
> ▶ Work with their advisers to consider the level of resources available for stewardship activities, which assets are covered, and what the appropriate structure is. Some schemes will have the resources for an in-house stewardship team. Others will need to outsource stewardship to either their existing asset manager or a specialist stewardship "overlay" provider. Note that delegating stewardship activities does not absolve schemes of responsibility. Instead, they should take ownership of the stewardship approach and ensure they have a clear understanding of work carried out on their behalf.

As the PLSA indicates, the investment philosophy is often shaped by the overall purpose of the organization, set by its founding documents. For many asset owners today, it is vital that ESG factors are integrated into that purpose—not least because, since October 2019, changes to the United Kingdom's Occupational Pension Scheme (Investment) Regulations 2005 have required pension schemes to set out in their statement of investment principles (SIPs) their policies on how they consider financially material ESG factors in their investment approach, as well as the extent to which they undertake stewardship, including engagement and voting. New reporting requirements, in line with the European Union's Shareholder Rights Directive II, will reinforce the same sort of approach across the EU. Many other markets around the world have established similar expectations. The typical starting point for the investment process is how ESG factors are viewed in the context of an overall investment philosophy or purpose.

The following are two representative examples of how such purposes are articulated by major global asset owners.

Paraphrased from CPP Investments (2020):

> *CPP Investments invests the assets of the CPP with a singular objective—to maximize returns without undue risk of loss taking into account the factors that may affect the funding of the CPP. Our investment strategy is designed to capitalize on our comparative advantages while ensuring we maintain our commitment to responsible investing.*

Paraphrased from AustralianSuper (2020):

> *We work hard to maximize investment returns over the long term, so members can enjoy a better future. As long-term investors, we focus on investing in a mix of quality assets that can grow members' savings over time. We balance this with an understanding of the risks we need to take to achieve this objective and deliver competitive returns against our peers.*
>
> *Our four core investment beliefs are the foundation of our investment approach. A rigorous governance framework and disciplined investment process help us allocate and manage members' savings and maintain our position as one of Australia's leading super funds.*
>
> "Our four investment beliefs:
>
> 1. *We aim to enhance member returns.*

2. *We believe in active management – both asset allocation and stock selection.*

3. *We use our scale to reduce costs and better structure investments.*

4. *We're aware of our responsibility to the broader community, consistent with our obligations to maximise benefits to members." (AustralianSuper 2020)*

How the purpose and investment beliefs and philosophy see ESG factors impacting investment performance—whether as risk factors or value creators—will shape how ESG investing is integrated into mandates and what the asset owner will expect of its fund managers. This is well articulated in a McKinsey article from October 2017 (Bernow, Klempner, and Magnin 2017). The article provides a framework for considering how to develop a policy and philosophy and then how it can practically be implemented. The authors state that "a sustainable investment strategy consists of building blocks familiar to institutional investors: a balance between risk and return and a thesis about which factors strongly influence corporate financial performance" (Bernow, Klempner, and Magnin 2017).

Responding to these two building blocks, the authors suggest that there are two fundamental questions that asset owners need to ask in developing their ESG investment philosophy. The first question is,

> *"Are ESG factors more important for risk management or value creation?" . . . If the mandate focuses on risk management, then the strategy might be designed to exclude companies, sectors, or geographies that investors see as particularly risky with respect to ESG factors, or to engage in dialogue with corporate managers about how to mitigate ESG risks. If value creation is the focus, on the other hand, investors might overweight their portfolios with companies or sectors that exhibit strong performance on ESG-related factors they believe are linked to value creation." (Bernow, Klempner, and Magnin 2017)*

The second question is, "What ESG factors are material?" The authors note that this is much less straightforward than the simple statement of the issue might make it seem and that there are substantial reporting projects dedicated to identifying what is material at a sector level, let alone at an individual company level. The nature of the investment portfolio also adds a layer of complexity. The authors argue that "the selection of material factors is often influenced to some extent by exposure to asset classes, geographies, and specific companies. For example, governance factors tend to be especially important for private equity investments, since these investments are typically characterized by large ownership shares and limited regulatory oversight" (Bernow, Klempner, and Magnin 2017).

3 FULLY ALIGNING INVESTMENT WITH CLIENT ESG BELIEFS

☐ 9.1.2 explain how ESG screens can be embedded within investment mandates/portfolio guidelines to generate investment returns and manage portfolio risk

Once the asset owner client has developed its investment philosophy and beliefs, these need to be translated into the specifics of the mandates that it awards to its fund managers. As a report from McKinsey indicates, there are two key questions that will frame how this is delivered in practice:

- Is ESG a risk management tool or a source of investment advantage?
- Which aspects of ESG most matter from the perspective of the asset owner? (Bernow, Klempner, and Magnin 2017)

Determining the answers to these questions will be the starting point for shaping the mandates awarded. Furthermore, in shaping the detailed expectations, the answers will need to be reflected in the terms of the individual mandates themselves.

The answers will also help shape the overall *strategic asset allocation (SAA)* of the asset owner—the long-term exposures that it chooses to have in terms of asset classes and geographies. They may also inform decisions around the asset owner's *tactical asset allocation (TAA)*, or the short-term variations around the SAA to respond to nearer-term market and other circumstances.

EXAMPLE 2

Pension Fund Concerned about Climate Change

A pension fund has strong beliefs regarding the impending impacts of climate change, whereby:

- The fund might establish multiple mandates investing in new technologies, including renewable energy generation.
- The fund's mainstream equity and debt mandates may well include screens that exclude fossil fuel investments.
- The fund may require that any sovereign bond mandate include an active ESG overlay that seeks to limit exposure in countries where the physical impacts of climate change are likely to be most acute.
- The fund may have decarbonization targets for the mandates that may have an impact on sector allocation and security selection.

EXAMPLE 3

Foundation Investment Portfolio Concerned about Human Rights Abuses

A foundation investment portfolio, where the investment beliefs feature major concerns regarding human rights abuses, might be more likely to:

- apply a screening approach across portfolios requiring the exclusion of any investment facing significant allegations and
- screen out exposures to certain countries where human rights abuses are perceived to be a frequent occurrence or where human rights standards are deteriorating at a rapid rate.

Naturally, in practice, the investment beliefs and the mandates that are created to reflect them are rarely as one dimensional as the two previous examples might imply. Furthermore, the client will always have an expectation of investment returns being generated alongside delivery of whatever broader expectations it places on the investment approach.

The report from McKinsey also provides a helpful framework for understanding the different ways in which ESG considerations can be reflected in an asset owner's investment approach and thus be fully operationalized in the work of its fund managers. This is shown in Exhibit 1.

Exhibit 1: Leading Institutions Apply Sustainable Investing Practices across Six Dimensions of Their Investment Process and Operations

Dimension of Investing	Elements of Sustainable Investing
Investment mandate	▸ Consideration of ESG factors, including prioritization
	▸ Targets
Investment beliefs and strategy	▸ Rationale for ESG integration
	▸ Material ESG factors
Investment operations enablers:	
✓ Tools and processes	▸ Negative screening
	▸ Positive screening
	▸ Proactive engagement
✓ Resources and organization	▸ ESG expertise and capabilities
	▸ Integration with investment teams
	▸ Collaborations and partnerships
✓ Performance management	▸ Review of external managers (screening and follow-up)
	▸ Follow-up on internal managers (including incentives)
✓ Public reporting	▸ Accountability
	▸ Transparency

Source: Bernow, Klempner, and Magnin (2017).

Fund managers hoping to win mandates that reflect ESG considerations will seek to develop their own policies that fully integrate ESG approaches into their portfolio management. There is an element of both marketing their approach and differentiating themselves in a crowded investment marketplace. An overarching policy also helps train and shape the mindset of the investment teams. An ESG policy should formally outline the investment approach and degree of ESG integration within a firm.

Such an ESG policy is an opportunity for a fund manager to highlight the relevance or, in some cases, the lack of relevance of responsible investment norms and principles (such as those issued by the PRI) to a firm's investment strategy or strategies. A number of investment strategies face inherent challenges, some of which may be due to

- the lack of ESG data within their scope or
- a relative scarcity of methodologies and best practices to apply ESG integration in an asset class.

In each case, it is worth noting that the ESG market is developing very rapidly and new offerings are being brought to the market all the time, meaning that there are increasingly fewer gaps in supply. Whether these new offerings meet their needs will be for the asset owners to decide.

> **CASE STUDIES**
>
> The following are two examples of ESG philosophies from leading fund management firms.
>
> ### RBC Global Asset Management:
>
> We invest in sustainable, great companies at attractive valuations and steward them for the long-term, using intangible, ESG and business assessment combined with strong risk analysis. Financial analysis and ESG assessment are intertwined in judging businesses, and businesses thrive over the long term when they invest in ESG intangible factors that lead to stronger, more sustainable financials.
>
> ESG is a non-traditional source of risk and opportunity but it should form part of every fundamental assessment. The relevance of these issues varies from industry to industry, so we believe it is important to integrate ESG into the company assessment rather than as a pre-screen or overlay. It eases engagement and ensures ESG risks and opportunities are incorporated into the fundamental valuation analysis driving financials. (RBC Global Asset Management 2019)
>
> ### Generation Investment Management:
>
> We undertake in-depth research to apply our investment strategy. We construct portfolios of sustainable companies with the confidence derived from our deep research and analysis.
>
> A sustainable company is:
>
> 1. one whose current earnings do not borrow from its future earnings;
> 2. one whose sustainability practices drive performance and competitive positioning; and
> 3. one that provides goods and services consistent with a net-zero, prosperous, equitable, healthy and safe society. (Generation Investment Management 2023)

These philosophical statements then need to be operationalized into ESG policies that cover a range of practical issues. Regardless of the investment strategy or asset class, such an ESG policy needs to address the manner in which the portfolio manager

- addresses ESG issues at portfolio reviews,
- establishes the rationale and methodology for ESG portfolio-level assessment,
- assesses exposure to ESG risk within the risk management function,
- determines ESG impacts to the portfolio,
- responds in the investment decision-making process to ESG implications, and
- discloses ESG exposure to the fund's investors.

Portfolio managers should also find ways to embed ESG information in annual or interim reports alongside financial information and manager commentary to fund investors. Annual reports may include

- ESG activities across the portfolio,
- the frequency of engagement, and
- highlighted activities and their outcomes.

Portfolios with private or unlisted security exposure may choose to report portfolio performance against key performance indicators (KPIs) over a given investment period and relative to peers.

4 DEVELOPING CLIENT-RELEVANT ESG-AWARE INVESTMENT MANDATES

> **9.1.3** explain the most common features of ESG investing that asset owners and intermediaries, including pension consultants and fund selectors, are seeking to identify through request for proposal (RFP) and selection processes: voting, engagement, examples of decision making, and screening process

The International Corporate Governance Network's (ICGN's) "ICGN Model Contract Terms between Asset Owners and Managers" provides a helpful framework and proposes best practices for ESG-aware investment mandates around

- the monitoring and use of ESG factors,
- the integration of ESG factors into investment decision making,
- adherence to good practice around stewardship, and
- voting and reporting requirements.

The document states, "As important as setting standards within fund management contracts is how clients can effectively call their fund managers to account in respect of these mandates. The intended standards will most effectively be delivered where managers are made accountable on a regular basis for their delivery against them" (ICGN 2012, p. 13).

Holding Fund Managers Accountable

According to a 2016 PRI report, "How Asset Owners Can Drive Responsible Investment," investment mandates should require investment managers to do the following:

- *"implement the asset owner's investment beliefs and relevant investment policies;*
- *integrate ESG issues into their investment research, analysis and decision-making processes.*
- *invest in a manner consistent with the asset owner's time horizons, understanding the key risks that must be managed to achieve the asset owner's portfolio goals;*

- *implement effective stewardship processes, including engagement with companies and issuers on ESG issues and, for listed equities, voting all shareholdings—this engagement should align with the asset owner's responsible investment and related policies;*
- *engage constructively and proactively with policymakers on responsible investment and ESG-related issues—this engagement should align with the asset owner's responsible investment and related policies;*
- *report on the actions taken and outcomes achieved—the reporting should enable the asset owner to assess the manner in which the investment manager has implemented the asset owner's investment beliefs and policies, and to understand how this has affected investment performance and ESG outcomes and impacts." (PRI 2016a, p. 19)*

Evaluating Managers' Investment Strategies

Different asset managers adopt different responsible investment strategies because their investment philosophy and investment processes may fundamentally differ. For instance,

- some active investors focus on fundamental company-specific research, while others may emphasize quant models;
- some will be more event driven, while others will be more focused on identifying companies with a long-term track record of delivering superior financial performance; and
- passive investment approaches need to build ESG priorities into the design of the mandate and the way in which investment assets are selected; typically, this is by either
  - excluding certain investments (e.g., the fossil fuel sector or particularly carbon-intensive aspects of it) or
  - applying a "tilt" to a broad index (so that, to pursue the climate change example, the least carbon-intensive companies are chosen in each sector meaning that the overall portfolio has a reduced intensity).

As a result, different managers will integrate ESG factors in different ways:

- as a threshold requirement before investment can be considered,
- as factors that inform the valuation or provide a quant basis for adjusting (or tilting) exposures,
- as a risk assessment that offers a level of confidence in the valuation,
- as a basis for stewardship engagement, or
- as a combination of two or more of these methods, which is very often the case.

An alternative form of classification has been developed by CFA Institute, in its "ESG Disclosure Standards for Investment Products" issued on 1 November 2021 (CFA Institute 2021). Please see the appendix of this chapter for more information.

The usual way that consultants and clients seek to understand and test fund managers' capabilities and approaches is through an RFP process (an invitation to pitch for potential business; see the following section for more details), usually followed by interviews of short-listed candidates. Naturally, the client wants to gain confidence that the fund manager can deliver satisfactory financial returns while staying within relevant risk parameters. In addition, with regard to ESG considerations, the client wants to know

- whether the approach to integration is sufficiently robust to deliver an appropriate portfolio structure,
- that the fund manager can deliver with certainty any hard constraints on the portfolio (such as negative screens),
- that the manager can deliver appropriately effective engagement to preserve and enhance value, and
- that the manager delivers in practice what it sets out as its approach in these respects in its policy documents and other assertions.

There is often an overarching concern that the client is seeking confidence that the fund management firm genuinely has a solid ESG philosophy underpinning its actions, because that gives the greatest confidence that the ESG activity is genuine and robust and will be delivered consistently over time.

Unless the fund manager can deliver all these necessary requirements, it is unlikely to make it through the due diligence process.

The RFP Process

The RFP process is a formalized one and partly formulaic in most cases. The questions asked are generally high level, and although they sometimes ask for examples of delivery to ensure that the fund manager can demonstrate the truth behind its assertions, the resulting information will rarely reveal much of the substance of what is going on. The questioning now typically goes deeper than the basic question of whether the fund manager is a signatory to PRI (which for a period of time in many RFPs was the sole ESG question), but this is often still the starting point.

Exhibit 2 shows an example of a questionnaire an institutional asset owner might use in determining what investment approach a fund manager uses:

Exhibit 2: Sample RFP Checklist of ESG Approaches

- ☐ Systematically considers financially material ESG information in investment decisions.
- ☐ Tracks an ESG index and/or uses an ESG index as an investment universe.
- ☐ Systematically applies ESG criteria to exclude certain investments and/or to determine if an investment is eligible for inclusion in the fund's portfolio.
- ☐ Sets allocation targets and/or constraints based on the ESG characteristics of investments.
- ☐ Sets targets and/or constraints for fund-level ESG characteristics.
- ☐ Considers ESG issues when exercising the rights and position associated with the ownership, management, and oversight of the fund's assets.
- ☐ Has an explicit objective to generate a positive, measurable ESG outcome alongside a financial return.

The larger fund managers have RFP teams that deal with the flow of questions and hold a bank of answers, which builds and extends over time with input from practitioners, but this may occasionally come at the detriment of tailoring of responses. The result is that clients will be able to ask only the second- and third-level questions that get closer to the truth of the underlying processes in the face-to-face interviews of the

Developing Client-Relevant ESG-Aware Investment Mandates

short-listed candidates, which are typically the second part of a manager due diligence process. The RFP questioning process does at least have the benefit of narrowing the field to a shortlist of potential providers.

Exhibit 3 (marginally adapted from the original from PLSA) sets out what might be the major ESG considerations for a pension fund or other asset owner when seeking to allocate a new mandate across the full range of potential asset classes. These are elements that may need to be reflected in the RFP process to ensure that ESG issues are appropriately considered by the relevant mandate.

Exhibit 3: Possible Routes to Incorporating ESG Factors by Asset Class

	Mandate Choice	Investment Integration	Engagement
Passive/index tracking	Trustees should consider the index benchmark and any ESG tilts.	No or limited manager discretion in stock selection	Managers can exert influence on companies through engagement and voting. There is also scope for influence on market- and system-wide issues.
Active equity	Trustees could invest in ESG-oriented mandates, such as sustainable equity.	Managers should consider financially material ESG factors and their impact on future profitability in company evaluation. Traditionally, data availability and quality have limited the ability to do this in quantitative analysis, though this is changing.	Managers can exert influence on companies through engagement and voting.
Active fixed income	Some assets (such as green bonds) could be considered by trustees, but probably only as part of a broader fixed-income mandate.	Managers should consider the potential for ESG risks to impact credit ratings and borrowers' future ability to make repayments.	It is possible for managers to have engagement with borrowers on material ESG risks, particularly at the time of initial issuance.
Real estate	Some real estate strategies could have E and/or S objectives, and appropriate assets may be targeted to achieve these.	Managers should consider material environmental and social risks during acquisition and development and manage resource use during occupation.	Managers can engage with tenants and the local community to address potential issues and drive change.
Infrastructure	Trustees can consider portfolios biased toward infrastructure that supports a sustainable future.	Managers should assess the physical and societal risks arising from infrastructure assets. Longevity of investment means that systemic issues need to be considered.	Managers can exert influence on underlying companies or asset management through governance arrangements (e.g., board seats).
Private debt	Trustees could consider mandates that target lending at certain sustainable activities.	Managers should identify and seek mitigation of potential ESG risks during due diligence on loans.	Managers should have ongoing dialogue with borrowers to ensure that emerging and identified ESG risks are managed.
Private equity	Trustees can assess which companies the manager may target and the potential for unwanted or desired ESG exposures to arise.	The longevity of the investment means that systemic risks need to be considered. Managers should assess potential ESG risks during due diligence and ongoing ownership.	Managers would be expected to have a high level of influence over company management and ensure that governance structures are effective.

Source: Based on PLSA and Investor Forum (2020).

Assessing Stewardship and Engagement

As the PLSA and Investor Forum explain in their "Engaging the Engagers" report (the text refers just to pension schemes, but the same is true for all asset owners; similarly, the focus of the report is on engagement but the thinking extends to ESG issues more generally),

> *The appointment process for a new asset manager offers a key opportunity for pension schemes to thoroughly assess the market for a manager whose approach to stewardship, engagement and (where relevant) voting aligns with the scheme's own. Where a pension scheme is looking to hire a new asset manager through a tender and due diligence process, the statement of expectations with regard to stewardship should form a part of the contractual relationship with the manager. The due diligence process is likely to include some assessment of whether the manager can fulfil the pension scheme's expectations in the asset classes and geographies in question. (PLSA and Investor Forum 2020, p. 14)*

The document goes on to offer a series of potential questions to ask a fund manager as part of the due diligence process before appointment of a manager. As it states, not all questions will be suitable to every situation (for example, different asset classes or natures of mandate will demand different assessment criteria), and all will need to be tailored to the circumstances of the specific mandate. Nonetheless, the following list from the "Engaging the Engagers" report provides a good basis for asset owners to seek to test potential service providers and for fund managers to demonstrate the value that they can bring through their ESG work:

- *"Understanding how the manager sees stewardship and engagement and what its main drivers for action are. This includes how consistently that philosophy is applied across asset classes and geographies.*
- *How long term is the fund management firm's investment mindset? Is this reflected in the portfolio exposures, turnover and approach to engagement? How do these approaches vary across different teams and portfolios?*
- *How does the manager decide on the resourcing given to stewardship? How is this overall resource shared across the firm's portfolios, asset classes and geographies? What plans are there for changing the resourcing of stewardship?*
- *For which portfolios and asset classes does the manager believe it most needs to improve its approach to stewardship and engagement currently? What is being done to bring those up to the standards in the wider organisation ?*
- *Seeking confidence in the processes by which the manager's objectives are set and progress against them is monitored.*
- *What systems does the fund manager have in place to capture engagement objectives systematically and to measure progress against those objectives?*
- *What differences do those systems reveal about the nature and effectiveness of engagement between different asset classes, portfolios or geographies?*
- *If different teams within the fund management firm have investment exposure to the same company or asset, how does the firm seek to have a concerted approach to stewardship and engagement? How does it leverage different perspectives and understandings of a business from those different teams?*
- *Understanding how the manager allocates its engagement efforts between the different forms of engagement.*
- *What form of engagement takes the majority of the manager's engagement resource? Why?*

- *Are different forms of engagement more relevant in different asset classes, portfolios or geographies? Explain how.*
- *What is the process for agreeing to escalate an engagement? What are the range of escalation tools available?*
- *How does the application of escalation vary between different asset classes, portfolios or geographies? Are these differences appropriate?" (PLSA and Investor Forum 2020, p. 19)*

The aim of these questions is to provide a basis for assessing how robust each fund manager's approach to the area of stewardship and engagement is and, thus, a framework for effective differentiation between providers. The focus of the PLSA and Investor Forum report is largely on engagement, and so the focus of these questions is also. It is, however, relatively straightforward to broaden the coverage of the questions to encompass ESG integration as well (or instead).

Investment Integration

Asset owners have their own investment philosophies and preferred investment styles, so as clients, they will seek to test whether the responsible investment strategy adopted by the fund manager is coherent with their broader investment strategy and aligned with their preferences.

Therefore, clients' key questions in this regard will always be around the investment decision-making process. Typically, this operates on two levels:

- An analysis of the formal process and, in particular, how ESG factors are integrated. This will usually also incorporate an assessment of the portfolio as it stands (perhaps using some of the available analytical tools) to take a view as to whether it is consistent with the assertions regarding ESG integration.
- A discussion of the process as it has been applied to individual assets, usually framed by the client identifying one or more assets that are questionable from an ESG perspective and testing how it was that the assets in question were deemed to be appropriate to be included in the portfolio.

It is this systematic approach of assessing the overall portfolio that usually reveals whether there is any real substance to the ESG element of the investment process.

The client is attempting to get under the surface of the fund manager's decision-making processes, to understand what actually determines whether an asset will be included in a portfolio or not and the decisions that lead to different weightings in the portfolio. It is only through highlighting the factors that may lead to these concrete investment decisions that the fund manager can genuinely demonstrate that its ESG integration approach

- is real and robust and
- can be replicated effectively over time.

Furthermore, it is only through understanding how these factors drive concrete investment decisions that the client will begin to have confidence in the robustness of the way ESG factors are integrated in practice. If the fund manager is appointed, future dialogue (the regular review meetings, typically annual, though sometimes more frequent) will again focus on assessing the overall portfolio for consistency with the asserted ESG integration and testing individual investment decisions to assess whether the investment process remains as promised and continues to robustly integrate ESG factors into decision making. It is consistency of investment approach that an asset owner tends to be seeking.

Later in this chapter, we present sample questions that a client might ask a fund manager as part of ongoing monitoring; some of these might also be useful or could be adapted for due diligence discussions.

As well as testing the investment process with hard cases, clients will usually look at metrics—notably portfolio turnover and Sharpe and other ratios—to see if these are consistent with what they understand of the investment process.

Increasingly, there are now also ESG portfolio assessment tools to facilitate the assessment of the portfolio as a whole. These look at the overall ESG assessment of the portfolio constituents (typically an overview of the portfolio assessed against each category of E, S, and G) and identify outliers in the portfolio, comparing these to the benchmark. While these assessments are subject to the challenges around ESG analysis (most notably, they are typically highly dependent on the disclosures made by individual companies, which are of variable quality and detail), they at least offer a basis for clients to test and challenge the effectiveness of ESG integration.

For further detail on challenges in ESG analysis, see Chapter 7.

Clients might also request that the fund manager provide them with an ESG performance attribution analysis, providing some insights into the value added by ESG factors on stock selection.

Clients can use these insights to test and challenge whether portfolio managers continue to invest in line with the method that they were hired to deliver.

This topic is discussed in more depth later in this chapter.

Engagement and Voting

The other key area of client expectation is effective stewardship delivery. Clients will probe and test the effectiveness of fund manager voting and engagement approaches—both policy and delivery.

There are two crucial bases of assessment for any asset owner:

1. Who does the stewardship work? Specifically, is it outsourced—delivered by a specialist stewardship team—or is it conducted by portfolio managers (or how do these distinct groups – external and internal, successfully work together)?

2. How are resources assigned to stewardship? Specifically, what is the magnitude of dedicated resources.

It should be no surprise that resourcing poses a real challenge to the effectiveness of engagement. As a recent study by the Institute of Chartered Secretaries & Administrators (ICSA, now the Chartered Governance Institute) states, "One factor mentioned by both issuers and investors [was] investors' resource constraints. With many major investors often holding thousands of firms in their portfolios[,] it is only natural that their resources are stretched to engage meaningfully with all companies" (ICSA 2018, p. 33).

While teams are being expanded, this challenge remains; certainly, company chairpersons believe that limited investor resources are a major limitation for effective engagement, and it is a repeated frustration for them. The ICSA study findings might cause some issuers to perceive that "increases in the quantity of engagement are not always accompanied by an increase in the quality of engagement" (ICSA 2018, p. 33).

As discussed in depth in Chapter 6, prioritization of engagements is a key way for fund managers to respond to resource constraints. Asset owners will want to understand how the fund manager prioritizes engagements, both in terms of focusing on individual assets and in terms of prioritization of particular issues for engagement. Part of a responsive fund manager's approach to prioritization will be to understand what clients' key priorities are and how these might best be reflected in the fund manager's program of activity. An asset owner will seek to understand through the due diligence process how they can best influence their fund manager and how responsive to their priorities the chosen fund manager is likely to be.

Concentrated portfolios are more easily resourced from a stewardship perspective, and those investment management firms that most pride themselves on being active stewards tend to be genuinely concentrated and so can commit significant resources to these activities. This leads to one way of addressing the resourcing issue: portfolio managers themselves becoming more actively involved in stewardship. This is more natural for fundamental active equity managers who hold concentrated portfolios of stocks and would typically maintain a constant dialogue with management. This is particularly true in markets with low liquidity (such as small caps or emerging markets), where the option for larger investors to exit is less available, but stewardship becomes challenging with larger portfolios of many stocks where managers may not have a direct dialogue with all the companies. Fund management firms with more diversified portfolios are more likely to develop larger, more stand-alone stewardship teams.

The alternatives to building specialist stewardship resources internally are outsourcing and collective action.

Assessing the Quality of Engagement and Voting

Since resources can be limited, clients should always ask how the fund manager ensures that the use of its resources is most effective. Fund managers should be able to set out a thought-through, structured approach to targeting engagement and delivering change for the benefit of clients.

Voting is also considered by clients as a key aspect of stewardship. Voting often gets more attention in client assessments because the datapoints on voting are clearer. For example:

- How does the fund manager vote in general?
- By what process does the manager reach its decisions?
- How did the manager vote on specific controversial matters?

The most sophisticated clients seek to discuss specific votes for individual companies as the basis for testing whether the policy and process actually lead to justifiable results in practice. This enables more granular discussion, which reveals more of the substance of the fund manager's approach and prevents the fund manager from selecting individual cases that put its work in the best light.

Assessing engagement is harder. Because engagement is nuanced and long term, it is hard to have a clear view of its effectiveness. It occurs in private meetings, so the visibility of even the activity itself is low, and the difficulty goes further: Effectiveness is largely invisible even for the engager. Any investor that asserts with certainty that he has made a change happen at a company is most likely overstating his case: In almost every case, this simply cannot be known. There may be a correlation between what an investor sought and what happened, but correlation is different from causation. After all, it is not shareholders who make decisions about the strategies of companies but company boards; shareholders can influence and persuade, but it will always be the board that actually decides.

This reality in assessing engagement is reflected in the performance measurements that investors place around engagement. Mostly developed by the stewardship overlay providers, these tend to be schemes that reflect the changes made by companies as engagement progresses. Expressed as either milestones or objectives, the engagers measure progress toward concrete change or better practice over the three or more years typical of the engagement process. It is these metrics that clients can assess and challenge, in addition to having direct dialogue with the engagement team, to gain some confidence in the robustness and sensitivities that lie behind the measurements.

5 GREENWASHING AND ITS CONSEQUENCE

9.1.4 explain examples of greenwashing by financial market participants and the regulatory and reputational consequences of making misrepresentations

Greenwashing is a term first coined in the 1980s by prominent environmentalist Jay Westerveld. According to the International Organization of Securities Commissions (IOSCO), it refers to the practice by asset managers of misrepresenting their sustainability-related practices or the sustainability-related features of their investment products (IOSCO 2022). Such practices may vary in scope and severity—from the inappropriate use of specific sustainability-related terms used in an offering document to misrepresentations about an entity's sustainability-related commitments (IOSCO 2022). It may involve deceptive marketing practices that deliberately misrepresent a product's sustainable impact or the practice of gaining an unfair competitive advantage by marketing a financial product as environmentally friendly, when in fact basic environmental standards have not been met.

More generally, greenwashing describes where a company makes false statements about its ESG practices to appeal to customers interested in environmentally friendly and sustainable practices. In most cases, greenwashing is used to convince the customer that a company has a positive ethical or environmental impact in order to appeal to them.

The issue of greenwashing partly stems partly from the fact that it can arise in different forms. Those of greatest concern are cases where there is a deliberate intention to deceive, but it can also arise where genuine green ambition has failed to be realized and/or where there is simply a lack of knowledge or understanding of what constitutes authentic, accurate, and identifiable green credentials. As efforts towards sustainability and decarbonization increase, more firms seek to showcase their green credentials and identify commercial opportunities.

Categories of Misrepresentation

Greenwashing can take many forms including making commitments without follow-up, misrepresenting product attributes, and making false or misleading disclosures.

- *Commitments without any guarantees of action:* A growing number of asset managers have set high-level ambitions with regard to decarbonization targets, but many have struggled to follow through on those pledges and to align their commitments with their fiduciary duties. For example, net zero pledges made by members of the Glasgow Financial Alliance for Net Zero (GFANZ) at the COP26 climate summit in 2021 remain unfulfilled.

    The GFANZ also clarified its criteria giving financial firms scope to set weaker fossil fuel finance targets, ostensibly easing tensions among members threatening to leave. While the International Energy Agency's (IEA's)

Greenwashing and Its Consequence

"Net Zero" scenario rules out any new fossil fuel projects, members of GFANZ warned that a complete moratorium could hasten a disorderly and unjust transition.

- ▸ *Product attributes:* A securities class action suit was filed against a food and beverage company, whereby shareholders claimed that the company had misrepresented the environmental benefits of its production methods in its regulatory filings. The company claimed that its techniques were environmentally friendly, but the claimants argued that, in actual fact, the company's production processes exhibited about the same amount of greenhouse gas emissions, required similar land usage, and utilized suppliers that produced dangerously high volumes of wastewater as other industry participants (Nestlé Waters North America Securities Litigation 2021).

- ▸ *Disclosures:* This category of misrepresentation involves disclosures that are particularly about social factors and related material financial risks. For example, enforcement action was brought against one of the world's largest iron ore producers in relation to alleged false and misleading claims about the safety of its dams. For example, enforcement action was brought against one of the world's largest iron ore producers, Vale S.A, in relation to alleged false and misleading claims about the safety of its dams (US SEC 2022c).

Reputational Consequences

Greenwashing is not just a minor reputational issue but rather a longer term, more systemic risk that undermines trust and confidence in a company, its brand, and its ability to do what it needs to do: attract customers, talent, finance, partners, etc. Marketing claims could, unless wholly accurate, result in greenwashing litigation that can cost significant time and money and cause serious reputational damage.

At the first annual forum of the UK Centre for Greening Finance and Investment (CGFI) on 4 July 2022, Emma Howard Boyd, Chair of the UK Environment Agency, and interim Chair of the Green Finance Institute, said the following in her keynote speech:

> *Companies that believe their own greenwash are embedding liability and storing up risk. Organizations have been warned; greenwashing their sustainability credentials will jeopardize the interests of shareholders and increase costs to their business. If we fail to identify and address greenwashing, we allow ourselves false confidence that we are already addressing the causes and treating the symptoms of the climate crisis. (Boyd 2022)*

The following examples show how greenwashing can lead to serious consequences. In 2022, German authorities raided the offices of both parent company Deutsche Bank and its asset management unit DWS due to allegations of greenwashing DWS, in which it had exaggerated the sustainability of investments. Amid plans to tighten its internal controls following the scandal, FY2022 net profits dropped by 23%, driven partially by a planned increase in transformation costs and legal expenses. The firm's new CEO has stated that he cannot rule out DWS having to pay fines for its infraction (Arons, Matussek, and Comfort 2022).

InfluenceMap, a London-based non-profit, found in 2021 that 55% of funds marketed as either low-carbon, fossil-fuel free or green energy exaggerated their environmental claims. The group also estimated that more than 70% of funds promising ESG goals fell short of their targets. Investors and customers are becoming more knowledgeable in assessing claims and will punish companies accordingly if they think they are being misled. Companies can also become the focus of activist groups (Influence Map 2021).

Using Data to Combat Greenwashing

As sustainability reporting continues to evolve within an expanding scope, claims are being subjected to a higher level of scrutiny. Greenwashing becomes an issue when labels are derived from a single definitive element that cannot be adequately tested. Metrics vary by industry; a single metric is likely not enough to facilitate meaningful comparison between companies nor provide a comprehensive picture of ESG practices.

Researchers at Chicago Booth conducted an interesting study on ESG disclosures and found that the weights and assumptions underlying many ESG scoring systems are opaque. Whether a company disclosed information about its environmental impact was more predictive of a high environmental ESG score, rather than actually better environmental performance, as measured by the researchers' performance ratings. It is therefore critical that ESG ratings and data providers improve the reliability, comparability, and interpretability of their ESG ratings and data products (Dey, Bushee, and Hall 2023).

Investors and issuers of financial products should be intensively dedicated to the traceability and credibility of the sustainability features they have to consider in investment advice and financial portfolio management. The challenge is in ensuring that ESG scoring systems used in ESG investing give companies credit based on performance, and not simply for disclosing information. Data transparency is critical in assessing exactly what ESG considerations are being incorporated, accurate measurement of data and its analysis, as well as determining how impactful that analysis is. In essence, continued strides being made in defining the most reputable methodology to use and robust data to capture will help avoid accusations of greenwashing.

Around the world, countries have distinct strategic priorities that hinder the harmonization of ESG standards. While some are focused on slowing down climate change or addressing its consequences, others primarily seek to grow their economies in a sustainable manner. China, for instance, only has reporting requirements for certain high-polluting firms. The United States and the EU have significant differences on ESG standards, which are all evolving at their own speeds and aim at different moving targets. For US investors, there is now a focus on social issues, whereas in Europe, the focus has been more on environmental issues. This variety fuels inconsistency in how ESG data are measured and reported by companies, investors, rating agencies, and data providers.

Regulations and the threat of fines are not enough on their own to combat greenwashing. The accuracy of claims must be substantiated with hard corroborating evidence. Greater data transparency, clarity, and consistency about green claims ultimately brings confidence about the reliability of sustainable disclosures. Firms should include activities of their supply chain(s) and/or third-party service provider(s) in their data collection, verification, validation, and assurance processes. Information available from media reports, whistleblower notifications, and adverse findings reported by internal control functions, external auditors, or depositaries may be used. Adoption of standardized methods of reporting and the use of independent third-party certification from established data providers can help mitigate against genuine errors and enhance credibility. Firms should also be encouraged to be open and share reliable data sources, calculation methodologies used in analytics, and their experiences regarding the impact of green products, both in terms of use and production.

Clear communication is vital: Sustainability information must be communicated in a manner that is comprehensible and adequate. Information on websites, in prospectuses, and anywhere sustainability claims are made must be kept updated and fit for purpose.

Assessing Indirect and Direct Impacts of Greenwashing

The biggest impact greenwashing has is on the consumer's trust. If a company is found to have been lying, it hurts their brand reputation and could see them lose customers. However, it also risks damaging the public's trust around genuine ESG-related initiatives and products. A report from cloud banking platform Mambu (2022) found that 67% of global consumers believe their current financial institution is guilty of greenwashing. Greenwashing can undermine confidence in the claims behind sustainable products, ultimately putting customers off supporting supposedly greener options, which cannot be a good outcome for those offering genuinely positive impact. It is important that the investors receive truthful information, which they are entitled to, as this contributes to maintaining the confidence in financial products and sustainability disclosures.

Although any effort is good, the difference between a truly sustainable company and a greenwashed one has real implications for investors. Legitimate ESG investments perform well and are less volatile because the companies are more effectively managing the following market risks:

- Environmental risks: Companies with low environmental impact are less likely to suffer from pollution regulation or business disruption due to water dependence or climate shifts.

- Social risks: Companies committed to social welfare are less likely to face strikes, factory shutdowns, labor lawsuits, or poor public perception for unfair or unsafe labor practices.

- Governance risks: The least "green" of the three, companies with poor governance can face issues from business ethics to shareholder disputes, unexpected leadership changes, unethical accounting practices, or tax issues.

- Conscious quitting risks: Where sustainability professionals leave their jobs because it is perceived that the values of their employer are not aligned with their own. Sustainability professionals need to fully comprehend the commerciality of what the business is trying to do and why sustainability is important, either from a risk management perspective or a value creation perspective.

In essence, greenwashed companies have all the risks without the advantages.

Greenhushing: Uncertainty over what does or doesn't qualify as green creates a phenomenon of 'greenhushing,' where those making good strides towards more sustainable practices are unwilling to reveal as much for fear of retribution or misinterpretation.

To avoid greenwashing accusations, some brands and businesses may feel compelled not to communicate as much about their environmental plans, instead sitting quietly on the information they have or do not have (i.e., greenhushing). For example, there were reports that after the CMA launched its work in the fashion industry, some brands quietly scaled back their product labeling and filtering options relating to the environment (George 2023).

Scopewashing: Many companies hide their harmful practices behind more positive ones—for example, providing an incomplete picture of environmental impact by focusing too much on carbon emissions and ignoring other factors such as recyclability and toxicity. Companies stating that they are taking positive action in one area while negatively contributing to another is a practice called scopewashing. This may include, for example, manufacturing fast chargers in a high emissions factory. Companies must avoid reporting the extent of their emissions in a misleading way, for example, by sharing direct emissions from the factory, but not reporting indirect emission from energy transport and materials.

Competence greenwashing: In the face of growing regulatory and market pressure, companies are contending with ensuring their ESG credentials are fit for purpose. Some boards, executives, and employees use hyperbole to highlight their knowledge, skills, and experience in sustainability—a practice coined by sustainable finance academic Kim Schumacher as "competence greenwashing." According to a 2022 study by Reuters, the number of Chief Sustainability Officers (CSOs) has more than tripled globally since 2021. Demand for green skills is growing too. In Asia Pacific, where the energy transition has been relatively slow, hiring for green jobs has grown by 30% over the past five years (Urso 2022). The proportion of executives with ESG in their job titles has proliferated, and professionals with limited experience find they are responsible for "green funds" asset allocation.

Addressing Greenwashing

Regulators have only recently begun to address greenwashing, evidenced by the growing number of consultations with industry stakeholders. The aim is to develop the same level of resources and competence as is available for assessing misleading financial claims. It is challenging to assess whether an ESG claim is true or not without fully understanding what ESG means and what industry standards on this sort of data are. Increased transparency in data collection, verification, validation, and assurance processes will help industry stakeholders close the knowledge and skills gap. Literacy in sustainability has also increased significantly through sustainability conversion courses and training programs to build that capacity and expertise.

The role of the CSO is not defined by any regulation; there are multiple functions that person should be fulfilling. The CSO function is a C-suite role typically reporting to a CEO. Based on interviews with well over 100 CSOs, the valued qualities required to consider the many and wide variety of issues that factor in sustainability strategic decision-making are business insight, change management, executive influence, leadership, and innovation.

> - "If you start from scratch, then creating more awareness in the entire organization is never wrong as a first step.
> - If you are a large organization and you have the resources, start building a team with genuine ESG experts. Take somebody internally who knows the organization[,] but also be aware that you need people with actual non-financial subject matter expertise and material ESG expertise.
> - Do not hire somebody solely based on ESG self-labeling or ESG-related certificate acronyms in their CV. Look at their actual education and track records in ESG.
> - Try to build a diverse team, comprising for example finance and natural science experts, because that leads to [a] mutually beneficial cross-pollination effect. Different people with different backgrounds can learn from each other.
> - If you are a small organization and do not have the resources, then try to start collaborating with the research sector. They often have non-financial specialists—maybe not with a business orientation, but they can provide you with the material technical knowledge."
>
> *Source:* Schumacher (2021)

Misleading statements

Most examples of greenwashing occur as a result of poor choices in statements and language used. Firms may use certain words or phrases that are broad and vague to appeal to eco-conscious customers; these words imply sustainability even though their products or practices are not sustainable or are not sustainable to the degree asserted by these companies. As a result, impressions are created of a more environmentally sustainable product than in actual reality (e.g., "packaging made of 35% recycled plastic"). Further examples of exaggerated claims about carbon neutrality include "company's environmental footprint reduced by 20% since 2018" or "CO_2 emissions linked to this product halved as compared to 2022." Misleading advertising tactics that use green color schemes and images are unfair to companies that are genuinely working to improve their environmental performance.

A European Commission study published in 2020 found that 53% of the environmental claims examined were "vague, misleading, or unfounded" and 40% of green claims were "completely unsubstantiated." The study also found that there were 230 sustainability labels and 100 green energy labels in the EU with vastly different levels of transparency, and half of all green labels offered weak or non-existent verification (European Commission 2023).

The European Commission does an annual "sweep" of websites to screen for potential breaches. In 2020, for the first time the European Commission focused their sweep on greenwashing. When assessing 344 sustainability claims made online, it found that in almost half of the cases, these claims were false or deceptive, and in about 42% of cases, the claims made by the companies that were screened could amount to greenwashing. Additionally, in 57.5% of cases, the trader did not provide enough information to assess the claim's accuracy (European Commission 2021).

The huge variety of "green" labels has undermined consumer confidence, as labels differ widely in robustness and reliability, leading to widespread skepticism. Criteria used by some companies may be lower than what customers might reasonably expect from their descriptions and overall presentation (e.g., a false % presentation of 'green' content). Some items can be included that do not meet the criteria used by the business. In other instances, misleading statements are caused by a lack of information provided to customers in the form of missing data. Statements made by the companies about false accreditation schemes and standards can also potentially mislead.

In many cases, companies will spend more money on marketing the sustainability of their products than actually making the environmentally friendly and sustainable changes to their business that they profess to be implementing. Consumers should be able to choose sustainable products based on reliable and verifiable information.

Core Greenwashing Characteristics

The European Supervisory Agencies (ESAs)—consisting of the European Banking Authority (EBA), the European Insurance and Occupational Pensions Authority (EIOPA), and the European Securities and Markets Authority (ESMA)—set out a number of core greenwashing characteristics:

1. Similarly with the communication of other misleading claims there are several ways in which sustainability-related statements, declarations, actions, omissions or communications may be misleading. On the one hand, communications can be misleading due to the omission of information that consumers or investors would need to take an informed transactional or investment decision (including but not limited to partial, selective, unclear, unintelligible, inconsistent, vague, oversimplistic, ambiguous or untimely information, unsubstantiated statements). On the other hand, communications can be misleading due to the actual provision of information, relevant

to an informed transactional or investment decision, that is false, deceives or is likely to deceive consumers or investors (including but not limited to mislabelling, misclassification, mis-targeted marketing);

2. Greenwashing can occur either at entity level (e.g. in relation to an entity's sustainability strategy or performance), at product level (e.g. in relation to products' sustainability characteristics or performance) or at service level including advice and payment services (e.g. in relation to the integration of sustainability-related preferences to the provision of financial advice).

3. Greenwashing can be either intentional or unintentional (e.g. resulting from negligence or from misinterpretation of the sustainable finance regulatory framework requirement).

4. Greenwashing can occur at any point where sustainability-related statements, declarations or communications are made, including at different stages of the cycle of financial products/services (e.g. manufacturing, delivery, marketing, sales, monitoring) or of the investment value chain (e.g. issuer, benchmark/rating provider, investment firms, etc.).

5. Greenwashing may occur in specific disclosures required by the EU sustainable finance regulatory framework (e.g. SFDR Article 9 product-level disclosure requirements). Greenwashing may also occur as a result of non-compliance with general principles – as featured either in general EU financial legislation or more specifically in EU sustainable finance legislation (e.g. the requirement to provide information that is fair, clear and not misleading). In that context, greenwashing may occur in relation to entities that are currently outside of the remit of the EU sustainable finance legislation as it currently stands (e.g. ESG ratings).

6. Greenwashing can be triggered by the entity to which the sustainability communications relate or by the entity responsible for the product, or it can be triggered by third parties (e.g., ESG rating providers or third-party verifiers).

7. If not addressed, greenwashing will undermine trust in sustainable finance markets and policies, regardless of whether immediate damage to individual consumers or investors (in particular through mis-selling) or the gain of an unfair competitive advantage has been ascertained (European Securities and Markets Authority 2021).

Regulation, Code, Guidelines

Regulators around the world are making moves to tackle greenwashing claims. 'Green claims,' sometimes called 'environmental claims' or 'eco-friendly claims,' are claims that show how a product, service, brand, or business provides a benefit or is less harmful to the environment. Many businesses use green claims to help market their products or services, and they often make voluntary environmental statements without any or little evidence and proof to back up those claims. They do this through a range of methods, such as statements, symbols, emblems, logos, graphics, colors, and product brand names.

EU

Green Claims Directive (GCD)
In March 2023, the European Commission adopted a proposal for a directive on the substantiation and communication of explicit environmental claims. The GCD targets explicit claims made on a voluntary basis by businesses towards consumers. It aims

to make green claims reliable, comparable, and verifiable across the EU; protect consumers from greenwashing; contribute to creating a circular and green EU economy by enabling consumers to make informed purchasing decisions; and help establish a level playing field when it comes to environmental impacts, aspects, or performance of products or the trader itself.

The GCD provides minimum requirements for valid, comparable, and verifiable information about the environmental impacts of products that make green claims and sets clear criteria for companies to prove their environmental claims. Evidence must be credible, supported by scientific evidence, and take into account international standards and life cycle analyses. The new rule will require verification by independent auditors before claims can be made and marketed. Furthermore, the Commission proposes to strengthen control and certification by independent verifiers. The GCD will also regulate environmental labels in order to avoid their proliferation and reinforce trust in existing ones.

Enforcement of the GCD will take place at the member state level, subject to the condition that penalties must be "effective, proportionate and dissuasive." Penalties for violation range from imposed fines, which deprive companies of the benefits of infringements (these can be up to 4% of turnover in cross border cases), to confiscation of revenues and temporary exclusion from public procurement processes for up to 12 months and public funding.

It is envisaged that adoption of the proposal will boost the competitiveness of businesses that are striving to increase the environmental sustainability of their products and activities.

The EU Ecolabel

Established in 1992, the EU Ecolabel is the official EU voluntary label for environmental excellence. Globally recognized, it certifies products that have a guaranteed, independently verified, low environmental impact. Certification is awarded to goods and services that meet high environmental standards throughout their entire life cycle—from raw material extraction through manufacturing and production to distribution operations to waste disposal. The Ecolabel also encourages companies to develop innovative products that are durable, easy to repair, and recyclable. The Ecolabel is exempt from the GCD since it already adheres to a third-party verification standard.

Stricter rules on ecolabeling

New public labeling schemes will not be allowed after the GCD kicks in, except under EU law. Should a member state require a new certification, it can turn to the EU to develop it. For private schemes, new ones will be allowed but only if added value can be demonstrated to the national authorities in charge of approving them. Public and private schemes from countries in developing markets will need to be submitted for an approval procedure before being admitted to the EU market. Additionally, labels with aggregated scores will no longer be allowed. These are considered misleading as the consumer does not see the full picture when several environmental impacts are accumulated.

Beyond the EU, other national regulators and supervisory bodies have taken action or introduced new policies to counter greenwashing, including the US SEC, the UK FCA, and IOSCO.

UK

Green Claims Code

The Competition and Markets Authority (CMA) first published the 'Green Claims Code' in September 2021. The code, a list of six key principles, is designed to prevent businesses from making misleading environmental claims about their products and services, as defined by British consumer law. The code applies in the United Kingdom only and covers issues including inaccurate claims, overstated claims, and claims that don't enable 'fair and meaningful' comparisons. The principles state that claims must:

- be truthful and accurate;
- be clear and unambiguous;
- not omit or hide important/relevant information;
- be fair and meaningful, if they include comparisons;
- consider the full life cycle; and
- be substantiated.

To investigate a particular business's claims and assess compliance with the Code, the CMA will first need to issue a letter of consultation. Once the business responds, the CMA announces the investigation publicly. As the investigation concludes, the CMA has the power to order the business to make recommended changes to its messaging on a voluntary basis. Should the business fail to do so, the CMA can begin litigation. The CMA is currently unable to fine companies for greenwashing; however, there is the ultimate risk of ending up in court and, by extension, fines and reputational damages.[1]

Financial Conduct Authority (FCA)

The FCA has consulted on its own package of measures to "clamp down on greenwashing" (FCA 2022). From mid-2023, the FCA will introduce its anti-greenwashing rule that will apply to all firms. As part of this, the use of ESG-related terminology, such as "green" and "sustainable," will be limited to ensure alignment with their proposed sustainable strategies and objectives. The aim is to combat "exaggerated, misleading or unsubstantiated claims about ESG credentials," which damage confidence in the investment products that are actually green and sustainable (FCA 2022). The FCA also proposes to introduce sustainable investment product labels that will give consumers confidence to choose the right product for them.

Any serious offences of greenwashing would be breaches of the *Consumer Protection from Unfair Trading regulations 2008*. Under proposed laws, the CMA will be able to impose civil monetary penalties for breaches of "core" consumer laws.

IOSCO

In November 2021, IOSCO published two reports addressing greenwashing in two areas of critical importance in sustainable finance. The *Final Report on Recommendations on Sustainability-Related Practices, Policies, Procedures and Disclosure in Asset Management* lays down a series of recommendations for asset managers covering regulatory and supervisory expectations for asset managers; related disclosure both at the firm and product levels; terminology; and financial and investor education (IOSCO 2021b).

The *Final Report on Environmental, Social and Governance (ESG) Ratings and Data Products Providers* explores the developments and challenges related to the use of ESG ratings and data products and seeks to better understand the implications of the increasingly important role of these products for financial markets. As most jurisdictions do not currently have regulatory oversight frameworks in place for such providers, the report recommends that regulators could consider focusing more attention on ESG ratings and data providers that may be subject to their jurisdiction and could consider whether there is sufficient oversight of ESG ratings and data products providers (IOSCO 2021a). Underpinning this high-level recommendation is a set of specific recommendations about the type of issues that regulators and ESG ratings and data providers could both consider in developing their regulatory frameworks and internal processes, respectively. These recommendations have a focus on the governance and processes implemented by ESG ratings and data providers and call for transparency surrounding the methodologies that underpin ratings (IOSCO 2021a).

Improving sustainability-related practices, policies, procedures, and disclosures in the asset management industry and ensuring transparency and good governance of ESG ratings and data providers would together provide investors with internationally consistent and comparable sustainability-related information, which would help prevent greenwashing and foster investor confidence in sustainable finance.

France

France introduced laws in January 2023 requiring firms claiming a product is carbon-neutral to report on all the greenhouse emissions of that product for its entire lifecycle.

United States

Greenwashing regulation has been ramping up in the United States. In May 2022, the Securities and Exchange Commission (SEC) issued the proposed Names Rule and ESG Disclosure Rule targeting greenwashing in the naming and purpose of claimed ESG funds. Final action is expected in 2023. The proposed rule covers regulating ESG-related practices of registered investment companies, business development companies, and private funds managed by registered investment advisers (US SEC 2022b).

The proposed ESG rule accompanies the Corporate Climate Disclosure regulations proposed in March 2022 (US SEC 2022a) and recommends additional disclosure requirements related to any greenhouse gas (GHG) emissions components of ESG-related statements and disclosures. These will include specific information about calculations and estimations. Three tiers of increased disclosure requirements will be imposed on funds and advisers with corresponding ESG information, data, metrics, and strategies based on the distinction between a fund or adviser; considering ESG as integrated into an overall investment strategy; focusing more specifically on an ESG investment strategy; or seeking to achieve an ESG objective via investments made.

Japan

In response to greenwashing concerns, in January 2023, the Financial Services Agency (FSA) of Japan proposed new guidelines that define the scope of ESG Public Funds subject to the guidelines. The guidelines also address checkpoints for disclosures and management of ESG Public Funds, when Investment Trust Managers (ITMs) registered under the Financial Instruments and Exchange Act of Japan create Funds as ESG Public Funds (Japanese FSA 2023).

IDENTIFICATION OF MATERIAL BREACHES AND PENALTIES

HSBC – Global financial services

Claim: In the lead-up to the COP26 climate change conference, HSBC published a series of two out-of-home advertisements. The first highlighted how HSBC had provided up to USD1trillion in financing and investments globally to help its clients transition to net zero. This advertisement was set against a backdrop of waves crashing on a shore. The second stated that HSBC was helping to plant 2 million trees, which would lock in 1.25 million tons of carbon over their lifetime. This advertisement was set against a backdrop of tree growth rings with the tagline "Climate change doesn't do borders."

Issue with claim: The UK advertising watchdog Advertising Standards Authority banned the series of HSBC adverts on the grounds of "misleading advertising and environmental claims," citing HSBC's failure to acknowledge its own contribution to emissions, and said any future campaigns must disclose the bank's contribution to the climate crisis. Despite the initiatives highlighted in the adverts, HSBC was continuing to significantly finance investments in businesses and industries that emitted notable levels of carbon dioxide and other greenhouse gases. Thereby, the watchdog concluded that the adverts omitted material information about environmental claims.

Claim: A senior banker referred to climate crisis warnings as "unsubstantiated and shrill." In its 2021 annual report, HSBC stated its financed emissions—clients and projects it provided loans and services to—were linked to the release of 65.3 million tons of carbon dioxide per year (HSBC 2022).

Issue with claim: The figure only accounted for its oil and gas clients and would likely be much higher if other carbon-heavy industries, such as utilities, construction, transport, and coalmining, were included. HSBC is believed to have provided USD87 billion in financing to fossil fuel companies between the start of 2015 and the end of 2021 (Rainforest Action Network 2022).

The UK advertising watchdog stipulated that HSBC must ensure that any future environmental claims are "adequately qualified" and that they do not omit material information about its contribution to carbon dioxide and greenhouse gas emissions (BBC 2022).

Nestle – Global food and beverages company

Claim: The company made claims in 2018 about achieving 100% recyclable or reusable packaging by 2025. Four years later, Nestle noted that 66% of its total packaging was already recyclable or reusable.

Issue with claim: The claim failed to consider Nestle's dependency on governments to create recycling centers and on consumers to recycle. Both these activities are outside of Nestle's remit, and as a result, Nestle packaging can be found littering beaches, oceans, and fields.

Claim: Nestle committed to reducing virgin plastic usage by one-third by 2025.

Issue with claim: In the same report, the company quoted a study from Pew Charitable Trusts and SYSTEMIQ that the annual flow of plastic into oceans will almost triple by 2040 (Wanner 2021). Nestle's actions are too little to stem the critical issue of global plastic waste.

Claim: Nestle has set out a clear roadmap for achieving net zero emissions by 2050, at the latest.

Issue with claim: According to a 2021 World Economic Forum report, only about 5% of Nestle's emission footprint is generated through direct operations. Emissions by its suppliers are 10% higher and are generally not counted in reporting.

Claim: Leading ESG ratings providers Sustainalytics and MSCI rate Nestle as a sustainability leader.

Issue with claim: In 2020, Nestle had been named among the world's top plastic polluters for the third year in a row (Eonnet 2020). ESG scoring systems from leading ESG ratings providers have limitations as their rating systems often do not consider supply chain emissions.

Coca-Cola – Global beverages company

Claim: Coca-Cola has made claims that it is committed to collecting and recycling a bottle or can for everyone it sells by 2030.

Issue with claim: Coca-Cola holds the disturbing title of 2021's largest corporate plastic polluter worldwide for the fourth year in a row, according to a global brand audit from the non-profit #BreakFreeFromPlastic (2021). In June 2021, the environmental organization Earth Island Institute filed a lawsuit against Coca-Cola for greenwashing its contribution to global plastic pollution.

Claim: Coca-Cola has reported that its bottles are 25% marine plastic and that bottles with 100% recycled plastic are available in 18 markets.

Issue with claim: The Changing Markets Foundation (2022) cites claims that companies are intercepting and using "ocean-bound" or "recyclable" plastic to tackle the plastic pollution crisis as some of the most common examples of greenwashing.

Claim: Leading ESG ratings providers Sustainalytics and MSCI rate Coca-Cola as a sustainability leader.

Issue with claim: ESG scoring systems from leading ESG ratings providers have limitations as their rating systems often do not consider supply chain emissions. According to a 2017 study, up to 91% of all the plastic waste ever generated has not been recycled and ended up being incinerated in landfills or in the natural environment (Geyer, Jambeck, and Law 2017).

ExxonMobil

Claim: The CEO of ExxonMobil made statements in 2020 about focusing on solving climate change for society as a whole—without reducing its emissions.

Issue with claim: Including all emissions, Exxon Mobil's carbon footprint is roughly equivalent to emissions from Canada.

ExxonMobil was ordered to pay a USD14.25 million fine over air pollution at its Texas crude oil refinery. This was reported to be the largest penalty ever assessed in a citizen enforcement suit over air pollution.

Claim: The company plans to maintain USD20 billion to USD25 billion in capital and fossil fuel expenditures through 2025.

Issue with claim: Between 2010 and 2018, Exxon devoted just 0.2% of capital expenditures to low-carbon energy, such as wind and solar (ClientEarth 2021).

BP

Claim: Exxon competitor BP officially changed its name to Beyond Petroleum in 2001 and installed solar panels on the roofs of many gas stations. The green revamp was supposed to project an eco-friendly and climate-forward company image.

Issue with claim: Although solar is a good step, putting solar panels on gas station roofs won't come remotely close to offsetting carbon emissions produced from the company's oil and gas production.

Claim: In 2019, the company ran ad campaigns focusing on BP's low carbon energy products: "Keep Advancing" and "Possibilities Everywhere."

Issue with claim: In 2019, an OECD complaint was filed by ClientEarth, alleging BP's adverts misled the public given that over 96% of the oil giant's annual expenditures are still on oil and gas (ClientEarth 2019).

Walmart

Claim: Walmart has declared a shift to a low-carbon operating model to keep up with competitors.

Issue with claim: The low-carbon operating model ignores the fact that the bulk of Walmart's emissions come from its supply chain. While its emissions-reducing initiative Project Gigaton is a positive move, the company does not take responsibility for indirect emissions.

In terms of the social parameters of ESG, Walmart has long faced criticism for employee treatment, including offering only part-time positions without insurance. A low-carbon footprint should not detract from improving working conditions.

Claim: Walmart wrongfully marketed at least two dozen textile items as made from bamboo and produced using eco-friendly processes when the items were in fact made from rayon.

Issue with claim: Converting bamboo to rayon "requires the use of toxic chemicals and results in hazardous pollutants" the Federal Trade Commission (FTC) stated. In 2022, the FTC filed a suit against the retailer for "deceptive green claims" that Walmart had made about its textile products. Walmart was ordered to pay USD3 million in civil penalties (US Department of Justice 2022).

Volkswagen

Claim: Volkswagen marketed "low-emissions and eco-friendly" vehicles.

Issue with claim: Volkswagen developed and installed proprietary software into many of its diesel vehicles to detect when a vehicle was undergoing an emissions test and temporarily reduce emissions. In normal driving scenarios, the engines emitted up to 40 times the allowed EPA limit for pollutants.

Volkswagen faced a series of fines and settlements from regulatory agencies and government bodies, totaling billions of dollars, for "rigging diesel-powered vehicles to cheat on government emissions tests" (Rogers and Spector 2017). One of the most significant was the USD4.3 billion criminal fine imposed by the US Department of Justice, which represented a major blow to Volkswagen's financial stability.

Fast Fashion

According to the World Economic Forum's 2021 report, the fashion industry contributes about 5% of global emissions. Fast fashion encourages the repeated turnover of synthetic fibers and petroleum-based products that end up in landfills or incinerators. Uniqlo (owned by Central China New Life Limited), Hennes & Mauritz (H&M), Lululemon, ASOS, and Adidas are just a few of the companies that have been called out for projecting an eco-friendly image while contributing to the pollution problem through fast fashion.

Including specific details, such as specific units of measurement (e.g., "70% organic cotton" rather than "made with organic cotton," could help mitigate risks of misleading statements. Furthermore, in comparing a product's sustainability to that of a competitor's, a like-for-like comparison should be made regarding the type of product to avoid misleading customers.

The Danish Financial Supervisory Authority (the Danish FSA)

The Danish Financial Supervisory Authority (the Danish FSA) conducted a thematic review of sustainability disclosures in prospectuses and key investor information documents (KIIDs) for eight funds that have sustainable investments as an objective (also known as "fully sustainable" funds). The review shows that the management companies (MCs) for the eight funds have not ensured that the funds disclose information on sustainability in a clear, adequate, and comprehensive manner. The sustainability disclosures are, therefore, insufficient on several material areas.

Outcome of the review: The thematic review conducted by the Danish FSA (2023) showed that, in general, the Management Companies of the eight funds had provided too-generic disclosures on sustainability issues in the prospectuses for several of the funds. Moreover, in several material areas the information is insufficient, as the information is either unclear, inconsistent, or incomplete.

The Danish FSA also found that the key investor information document (KIID) for several funds included neither a description of the sustainable investment objectives of the funds nor a description of the objectives, which is inconsistent with the objective stated in the prospectus.

The identified deficiencies related to material issues and constituted a clear violation of the requirements under SFDR and the EU Taxonomy regulation. Hence, the Danish FSA made use of its normal supervisory tools in the form of orders.

In June 2022, ESMA's Supervisory Briefing confirmed that national regulators should take enforcement action for breaches of SFDR in relation to greenwashing. This includes where disclosures are severely misleading, such as a significant discrepancy between what a financial product actually invests in and what has been disclosed to investors in pre-contractual disclosure documentation.

TAILORING THE ESG INVESTMENT APPROACH TO CLIENT EXPECTATIONS

6

> 9.1.5 explain the different client types and their objectives which influence the type of ESG investing strategy selected

Different client types (institutional, retail, or private) have different investment objectives, risk/return profiles, time horizons, and drivers. These will influence the type of ESG investing strategies they will consider most attractive.

Exhibit 4 provides (highly) simplified and generalized insights into the likely primary drivers toward ESG investing and thus the relevant risk/return profiles and implied favored ESG approach for broad groupings of investors. As with all generalizations, there will be many individual exceptions to these indicative and broad-brush characteristics.

Exhibit 4: Overview of Investor Drivers

Investor	Defined benefit (DB) pension scheme	Defined contribution (DC) pension scheme	General insurer	Life insurer	Sovereign wealth fund	Foundation	Individual investor
Investment time horizon	10–70 years	10–70 years	1–2 years	10–50 years	30–150+ years	50–250+ years	1–50 years

Investor	Defined benefit (DB) pension scheme	Defined contribution (DC) pension scheme	General insurer	Life insurer	Sovereign wealth fund	Foundation	Individual investor
Primary driver for ESG investment	Fiduciary duty	Fiduciary duty, personal perspectives of beneficiaries	Awareness of financial impacts of climate change	Recognition of implications of lengthy investment time horizons	Reputational risk	Reputational risk, investment consistent with founding or charitable aims	Personal ethics and perspectives
Risk mindset	Long-term perspective should permit higher risk tolerance	Where individual beneficiaries are permitted to switch providers, greater risk aversion than time horizon might otherwise imply	Loss aversion	Long-term perspective typically permits higher risk tolerance	High tolerance for illiquidity and short-term underperformance	High tolerance for illiquidity and short-term underperformance	Loss aversion
Implied favored ESG approach	ESG integration	Some exclusions, ESG integration	ESG integration	ESG integration	Some exclusions, ESG engagement approach often most important	Exclusions likely, to ensure investment is consistent with founding or charitable aims	Screened funds, strong ESG integration

In the institutional investment community, clients generally expect that ESG principles will be genuinely applied across the approach so that the asset owner can invest in diverse asset classes and benefit across each from the integration of ESG factors and effective stewardship engagement. This expectation is increasingly true whatever asset class the asset owner is investing in (the scale of the membership of PRI emphasizes the scale of the commitment to ESG investing overall), and questions about the overall ESG philosophy and approach of the investment firm are usually built into RFP discussions.

As discussed earlier, often these expectations are written into the mandate—the contract between the fund manager and the client. On occasion, however, the specific ESG (or other) requirements of a client are not included in the contractual mandate itself but rather in a side letter, which also has contractual obligations. An insight into this model is provided by the Brunel Asset Management Accord (Brunel Pension Partnership 2018). This document sets out a pension manager's approach to long-term investment and ESG factors but in language that Brunel Pension Partnership believes is less suited to the hard legal language of a specific contract but more to a softer form of agreement, whereby the fund managers are enabled to more clearly understand the client's perspective and thus align to it. For the purposes of this chapter, we discuss mandates in a way that encompasses side letters or any other legal documents that frame the agreement between a client and a fund manager.

The issue of time horizons of the asset owner and the overall investment philosophy—incorporating the institution's understanding of ESG factors and their impact on value over those time horizons—goes to the core of delivering mandates that actually encourage fund managers to respond appropriately to ESG risks and opportunities. As the ICGN's Model Mandate puts it,

> *The time horizon of most asset owners is considerably longer than that of fund managers. Thus, for long-term portfolios, the factors and risks which matter to the asset owner are somewhat different from those typically considered within fund management processes. But as these factors and risks will impact their long-term returns, many asset owners are keen to see more effective integration of these longer-term factors into investment processes.* (ICGN 2012, p. 9)

Even where an asset owner is seeking to invest in a particular ESG fund (for example, a bond fund tilted away from CO_2-intensive industries and toward businesses less likely to be disrupted by carbon taxes and constraints), asset owners are unlikely to simply ask about the approach in that specific fund. Rather, the overall mindset and philosophy of the fund manager are important because they provide a context of confidence that the specific fund has backing and will be resourced long term. Engagement is often an integrated activity across the investment firm, meaning that there may be an opportunity to leverage off activity on behalf of other portfolios and asset classes.

To take the example of a carbon-tilted bond fund, there might be direct stewardship in relation to the fixed-income investments, but the fund could also benefit from the investor's broader engagement approach. This means that the fund could be informed by engagement on equity portfolios. Thus, the bond fund also could benefit from the changes that equity engagement can deliver for holdings in the bond portfolio.

Fund managers that integrate ESG factors across their funds and genuinely join up their activities find that engaging with firms with the perspective of equity and bond investment (and potentially other exposures—for example, through property portfolios) is often the most productive route. The investment house's overall approach to ESG investing thus matters to large asset owners, which will tend to probe whether this collaboration across the investment firm happens effectively.

The same is true for retail investors as well, but often these investors are looking more for a product. Inevitably, they are constrained by the investment vehicles that they can invest in; however, they are also more likely to be seeking out an investment fund that suits their personal ethics and perspective on the world. Therefore, they may seek out funds that exclude "sin stocks" or avoid particularly carbon-intensive businesses. In fact, this approach is often mirrored by some institutional investors, such as foundations or religion-linked asset owners, if they have a moral constraint on their freedom to invest. For these investors, the ability to deliver exclusions and effectively screened portfolios is often more important than the broader philosophical approach of the investment firm. Stewardship engagement is typically important to these investors but may also get less challenge and focus in discussions.

Growing fields such as impact investing have developed from offerings to high-net-worth individuals and from foundations into more mainstream investment vehicles. These are at times offered to mainstream asset owners, although there are issues around the scalability of such investments. In many cases, it is difficult for large asset owners to take an interest in such opportunities because they may not be available in large enough pools for it to be worth the attention of the asset owner.

Liquidity is also an issue for this form of investment: Traditionally a private market form of investing, money is often locked up for lengthy periods, and exiting a position may be difficult for an institutional or retail investor in need of liquidity. One response from the investment community may be rebranding broader investment approaches as "impact"; the wise client will never buy on the basis of the brand but will always look to understand what the underlying investment philosophy and process is for any product and select accordingly. Nonetheless, fund managers' consideration of their portfolios' broader real-world impacts—and reporting on them—conceptualizes investment as part of the real world rather than in some way divorced from it.

7 HOLDING MANAGERS TO ACCOUNT: MONITORING DELIVERY

☐ **9.1.6** explain the key mechanisms for reporting on and monitoring performance and mandate alignment with client objectives

There will typically be annual performance discussions with fund managers once appointed. However, some clients may

- insist on more frequent dialogue (particularly the case if financial or other performance has given rise to concerns) or
- choose to send a message that they care only about the longer term by waiting longer for any such discussions.

Performance (at least for assets that are freely traded or otherwise regularly valued) is likely to be assessed or at least seen more frequently than once a year. One of the challenges for clients is always to ensure that their fund managers do not become short term in their approach because they are aware the client is considering performance on a regular basis.

The Brunel Asset Management Accord highlights one way in which clients can monitor long-term focus. The document emphasizes that short-term underperformance is not in itself likely to give rise to undue concern for the client: "Investment performance, particularly in the short term, will be of limited significance in evaluating the manager" (Brunel Pension Partnership 2018, p. 2). Rather, the Accord highlights the following factors that may cause concern:

- *"Persistent failure to adhere to Brunel's investment principles and the spirit of the accord.*
- *A change in investment style, or investments that do not fit into the expected style.*
- *Lack of understanding of reasons for any underperformance, and/or a reluctance to learn lessons from mistakes. Conversely, complacency after good performance should be avoided.*
- *Failure to follow the investment restrictions or manage risk appropriately, including taking too little risk.*
- *Organisation instability or the loss of key personnel." (Brunel Pension Partnership 2018, pp. 1, 2)*

This focus on culture and conflicts—and an investment approach that is not consistent with the expected investment style—is consistent with the thinking of the ICGN Model Mandate. Among other things, it asks for early reporting of the following:

- *"the turnover in the portfolio for the reporting period and an explanation if the turnover is outside the expected turnover range for that period; . . .*
- *any changes to governance, ownership or structure of the manager, or in its investment approach or risk appetite; . . .*
- *any regulatory investigation or legal proceedings against the manager, any key staff or the fund; . . .*
- *any changes in staff ownership in the fund or any equivalent vehicle managed by the manager or changes in staff ownership in the manager itself; . . .*
- *regular financial accounts of the manager; . . .*
- *any changes in or waivers of the manager's conflicts of interest policy; and*

> *any additional conflicts that have arisen over the reporting period."* (ICGN 2012)

Moving away from market benchmarking helps change the mindset about performance and the particular focus on any underperformance. For example, for a client to seek absolute returns or performance of a certain number of percentage points above base rates is very different from seeking performance ahead of the standard equity benchmarks. Nonetheless, fund managers may be easily tempted to act in a more short-term way if they perform poorly against a general market performance, and clients who are concerned for long-term performance need to guard against this temptation.

As both Brunel Pension Partnership and the ICGN have shown, the crucial assessment in terms of ESG factors is whether the investment approach has been consistent with the process promised in the mandate and witnessed through the due diligence process. In many ways, the annual or other performance assessment is likely in practice to reflect the style of a due diligence process, seeking to confirm that the approach has remained consistent or to assess what may have changed.

To provide insights into what these processes are likely to involve, the following case study includes a sample set of probing questions of the sort that an asset owner might ask in discussions with a fund manager in ongoing regular conversations to assess whether the manager is performing in accordance with expectations. These are indicative only and are intended to provide an idea of the nature of insight and discussion that an actively engaged asset owner will be seeking (note that a few of these questions are developed from examples published in PLSA and Investor Forum 2020).

CASE STUDIES

Assessing a Fund's ESG Approach

There are several categories of questions an asset owner might ask to gauge a fund manager's ESG approach

Structural and Cultural

You place great emphasis on the size and experience of your firm's investment team.

- How do you ensure that you get a consistent level of quality in terms of ESG analysis from such a disparate group of analysts?
- Are there sectors or geographies where you currently worry that the analysis may be weaker?
- What do you do to address any weaknesses?

You highlight your interaction with other investment teams.

- What does this amount to in practice?
- Please provide concrete examples of how this has worked in the recent past, one with your ESG team and one with one of the other teams.
- How has interaction changed in recent years?

How are your holdings in XX and YY consistent with your stated approach to stewardship and long-term investment? Aren't there clear risks associated with these businesses? How have your investment teams factored those risks into their decision making?

You have carried out a lengthy dialogue and engagement with ZZ.

- What impact has that had on the investment decision and the relative weighting in portfolios?

Property/Infrastructure Investments, Direct and Indirect

- In your estimate, which of your various property and infrastructure business holdings is best positioned in terms of preparedness for climate change and physical disruptions, which seem increasingly frequent from extreme weather events?
- Which of your holdings is the least ready given the differences in geographical exposure to disruption?
- What does that mean for your portfolio positioning?

Financial Sector Investments

Bank X has recently made a commitment on coal project financing.

- Do you believe that undertaking is strong enough to ensure its risk profile on carbon-intensive assets?
- Not least given the bank's ongoing lending to oil- and gas-related projects, do you believe that it has a clear understanding of climate risk and potentially stranded assets in its lending portfolio?
- How have you assessed the lending practices of non-bank lenders in your portfolio relative to their peers? Please describe how you have analyzed their risk management in light of the significant failures in the sector and tightening regulatory environment.

You are interested in Insurance Company AA.

- Have you discussed with Insurance Company AA its approach to the risk of exposure to disruptions arising from climate change?
- How have you assessed its overall transition risk exposure?
- Are you confident that the company understands its exposures fully and is equipped and skilled enough to manage them appropriately?

Industrial Sector Investments

You are liaising with Industrial Business Y.

- Are you concerned by the allegations regarding worker treatment at Industrial Business Y?
- Have you built into your model any expectation of fines or substantial damage claims, and are you confident that the dividend remains secure in most realistic scenarios?
- Can you be sure that the business is sustainable when it relies on such employment practices to maintain profitability?
- Do you have concerns about the costs of any changes in facilities or working practices to avoid such exposures in the future?
- Do you believe the company will retain staff and continue to be able to recruit appropriately skilled individuals?

Holding Managers to Account: Monitoring Delivery

You have a sizable aggregate position in Company GG. The governance of the company is particularly weak.

- What makes you comfortable that the business is run and overseen effectively and will appropriately address emerging challenges?
- Is the complexity of the corporate structure more about financial structuring and tax minimization than anything else?
- In which case, is there a risk that the management and board (which suffers from poor independence and weak governance) may miss signals from the underlying businesses because information flow is weak through the complex corporate structure?
- How are you engaging with the company on these issues, and what progress have you made so far?

You are liaising with Company BB.

- What do you think about Company BB's exposure to corruption risks?
- Does it have satisfactory management structures to mitigate and manage such exposures?
- Are you confident in the company's approach to money laundering protections and in knowing the full backgrounds of its business partners?

Extractives Sector Investments

You have some significant holdings in oil and gas businesses.

- What is your reflection on the risks that they face in terms of stranded assets?
- Which of these companies best understands the risks of climate change for their business models?
- How are they considering transitioning their businesses to a more carbon-constrained world?

State-linked extractives company Z is also highly politicized.

- Are you content that its investments are commercial and will give economic returns, rather than more based in geopolitics on behalf of the government?

You hold a number of mining businesses. Their business models are inherently unsustainable.

- Which of these companies manages its environmental and social (E&S) risks best, and which retains the greatest downside exposures?
- Which has a better handle on health and safety issues, and which better considers the implications of climate change (including the physical risks of extreme weather events) for their business?
- What has that analysis meant for your investment allocations?

Debt Investments

The fund has a number of sovereign debt holdings, in particular exposures to the CC and DD governments.

- Do you believe those countries have appropriate and effective national responses to the challenge of climate change?
- Aren't their nations and economies particularly exposed to extreme weather events and also to water shortages already—factors that will only intensify as climate change progresses over the time horizon of your bond holdings?
- Will they be able to respond robustly and effectively to these challenges, without affecting economic activity and their ability to finance existing debt?
- What is your exposure to green bonds in the portfolio? Why is there only minimal exposure?

Engagement

- Is there clear disclosure of the processes by which objectives are set and progress against them monitored?
- Who on the team sets engagement objectives? What is the oversight process to ensure that these objectives are robust and material and remain consistently so across the organization?
- How is progress against objectives assessed and captured for reporting? How do you gain confidence that material change has indeed been delivered?
- How do you decide to escalate an engagement if it has not been effective initially? What is the decision-making process, and how do teams decide between different forms of escalation (such as collaborative engagement or going public with concerns)?
- Can you give examples of cases where you have chosen to exit investments rather than continue to pursue engagement?

Test the quality, materiality, and bespoke nature of the objectives for an appropriate sample of engagements.

- Asset EE is a significant holding and faces some key risks. Can you demonstrate objectives that are in place for engagement with the investment, what actions have been taken to deliver those objectives, and what progress has been made in delivery?
- You have sold out of Asset FF over the period. Can you outline the engagement experience with its management over the last two years? What would have needed to change for you to be comfortable continuing to hold the asset?
- Are headline market-wide announcements reinforced by robust and tailored asset-specific activity?
- You have made substantial public statements in the last period. How do these get translated to concrete actions on the ground? How have the dialogues with individual assets changed as a result? Please give examples, including of the relevant objectives set for engagement.

Portfolio-Wide Assessment

The other form of ongoing assessment of ESG delivery that clients are likely to perform is some form of portfolio-wide assessment. Inevitably, because this covers portfolios as a whole, it is on a more statistical basis as opposed to the more anecdotal basis of the questions in the previous case study. The main ESG research firms (example MSCI and Morningstar Sustainalytics) now provide standard tools for asset owners to assess the ESG factors in their portfolios and also ESG-linked performance attribution. Typically, an asset owner that signs up for these tools will receive an analysis of all its portfolios; alternatively, a fund manager might choose to use the service in order to test its own approach and prepare for client questioning.

Inevitably, because some of these tools are based on the research firms' data, they will be subject to the issues that arise around the quality and consistency of that data; as a result, some fund managers may raise concerns that these are not fair representations of the portfolios that they construct and of the quality of their ESG integration. Such a fund manager should be prepared to demonstrate how its own analysis of the ESG exposure of assets in the portfolio is a more accurate representation than those provided by external research firms. Even though there are limits to the quality of the external research, these analyses offer a basis for a conversation. If all parties take into account the limitations of the third-party approach (rather than assuming that the analysis provides perfect insight), the conversation can be challenging yet meaningful. In particular, the questioning can help the fund manager reveal once again the quality of its ESG integration and the depth of thought that goes into its investment decision making.

The following case study provides insight into the sort of data and analysis that might be provided in one of these standard ESG portfolio analysis tools. It also discusses ways in which a client might use that information to probe the quality of delivery by a fund manager.

CASE STUDIES

ESG Attribution

This case study highlights the style of reporting that a client might receive from a fund manager or a third-party ESG research provider about the portfolio and the questions that might arise as a result. Of course, some fund managers carry out this form of research themselves, so they can, at least in part, pre-empt these questions or at least be ready for them when they do arise. It would be possible, of course, for the client to look at the data and comparisons for aggregate ESG figures, but the use of individual E, S, and G factors seems most common.

Portfolio New Deal: Overall Portfolio Analysis

	Portfolio New Deal (%)	Benchmark (%)	Positioning above or below Benchmark (%)
E score	79.2	83.4	−4.2
S score	81.7	80.3	1.4
G score	84.2	84.6	−0.4

This analysis suggests that the portfolio is placed

- better than the benchmark on S factors,
- almost at benchmark on G factors, and
- significantly below benchmark on E factors.

Client interest is therefore likely to focus particularly on E exposures in the portfolio.

Naturally, there would be scope for a discussion about whether the benchmark is an appropriate comparison for the portfolio (in the same way that this is frequently a discussion in relation to investment performance analysis). There is also scope for debate and discussion about the ESG research provider's analysis, although this is probably best done on an individual company basis. Most clients recognize that there are flaws in any firm's ESG analysis and are likely to view discussions on individual ratings as an opportunity to test and understand the quality of the fund manager's own ESG analysis and integration.

Individual Company Analysis from an ESG Research Provider

There are usually separate tables for each E, S, and G score in these forms of analysis; we provide a sample of only one here. For the purposes of this case study, the table below focuses on the E score in the context of the overall portfolio positioning.

Bottom Five E Detractors

Company	E Score (%)	Portfolio E Score (%)	Benchmark E Score (%)	Detraction Level (%)
Digger Mining		79.2	83.4	50.2
Smoky Power Generation	39.7	79.2	83.4	43.7
Flaring Oil Producer	48.1	79.2	83.4	35.3
Leaky Manufacturing	56.7	79.2	83.4	26.7
Sullen Motors	62.1	79.2	83.4	21.3

Very often the client will also see a group of outperformers for each of the ESG categories but naturally will tend to focus on the detractors. They will concentrate on the individual cases and the investment decisions that have led to their inclusion in the portfolio (taking particular interest in whether their inclusion is consistent with the agreed mandate) and are likely to also use these specific cases to seek to understand

- what the relevant investment decisions reveal about the investment process overall,
- whether that overall process is consistent with their understanding of what the fund manager had undertaken to do in the due diligence discussions and in the agreed mandate, and
- whether they remain comfortable with the investment process given their clearer understanding of it.

It is likely, therefore, that an asset owner will ask some of the sorts of probing questions highlighted in the previous case study to assess whether

- the companies are indeed a sensible part of the portfolio or
- they are evidence that the manager is not in fact delivering the investment process (integrating ESG factors) that has been contracted for.

Very often a fund manager will explain that the rating provided by the agency is based on historical data and that the fund manager's own engagement with the company indicates that it has already changed or is in the process of change. The client is likely then to explore

1. what engagement the fund manager has carried out,
2. its level of confidence in the company's approach as a result of that engagement, and
3. over what time horizon that change is likely to be more visible to external parties.

Prudent clients return to these cases after an appropriate amount of time has passed to see what has indeed changed over that period. Changes that reflect the fund manager's explanation will clearly reinforce client confidence; a lack of concrete change and no real prospect of such change may undermine it. Time often enables clearer determination of superior analysis.

Frequently, analyses include the carbon intensity of companies in the portfolio, often in comparison to a suitable index. We do not provide an example of this in this chapter, but for many clients, it will be an issue for close attention. It is also likely to be an area for close questioning, particularly if a fund manager's purported focus on climate change issues does not seem to be reflected in a less carbon-intensive portfolio. Again, if the fund manager asserts that this is a timing issue with the service provider's analysis, the client is likely to want to explore that further at future meetings once the manager's alternative analysis has had a chance to be delivered in practice.

HOLDING MANAGERS TO ACCOUNT: MEASUREMENT AND REPORTING   8

9.1.7 explain the key challenges in measuring and reporting ESG-related investment performance: active, passive, and smart beta approaches; performance attribution; sensitivity analysis; risk measurement; engagement activity/impact; and integrated reporting and investment review

ESG reporting by investment managers is widespread but varies in the quality of disclosure. It ranges from

- general discussions of current debates and themes with no clear linkage to the work of the fund manager, sometimes associated with generalized aspirations or assertions, to
- much more concrete discussions of the work actually done by fund managers and delivered in practice, to

- the shape of portfolios and change through engagement.

As discussed in detail in Chapter 6, the new UK Stewardship Code calls for more reporting on outcomes from stewardship and ESG activity, rather than just discussions about broader events or the policies and activities of signatories. This pressure for discussion of what has concretely been delivered to the benefit of clients (which some managers call "impact") should improve the quality of fund manager reporting, reducing generalized reporting and increasing the focus on concrete activity.

Annual Reports

Investment firms typically produce annual (and often quarterly) reports describing

- their investment processes,
- the themes that they have worked on, and
- case studies on ESG investing or stewardship (or both).

Investment firms that are signatories to the PRI are also required to submit an annual report (PRI Transparency Report) on their activities. According to the PRI, the reporting process allows signatories to

- evaluate their responsible investment progress against an industry-standard framework,
- receive ongoing feedback and tools for improvement,
- benchmark their performance against peers,
- see the big picture by understanding the state of the market,
- strengthen internal processes and build ESG capacity, and
- summarize activities for staff, clients, shareholders, and regulators. (PRI 2020b)

A public version of the PRI Transparency Report, as well as the headline scores, is made available to others. Naturally, those fund managers that perform particularly well on the PRI assessment will tend to highlight and publicize this—emphasizing in particular those asset classes where the fund manager performs best.

Alongside these reports, there are now multiple tools available to deliver information on the ESG characteristics of a portfolio and to measure those relative to relevant benchmarks. As a 2016 report by the Pensions and Lifetime Savings Association (PLSA) pointed out,

> *By applying ESG data to existing standard benchmarks, the pension fund can measure its portfolios against the same standard market benchmarks currently used to measure performance. For example, if the pension fund measures equity performance against the MSCI World, it can continue to use this same benchmark, but this time containing an ESG data set, to facilitate a comparison of the portfolio's ESG score with the MSCI World. Conversely, a pension fund could choose customised ESG indices for a more effective comparison. For example, if a pension fund has excluded fossil fuel stocks from its portfolio, it may wish to measure ESG performance against an index that has been optimised to exclude fossil fuel stocks. (PLSA 2016, p. 17)*

Real World Impacts

Another form of reporting that some fund managers provide on the ESG characteristics of their portfolios is to report on real-world impacts, or at least on the equivalent real-world impacts. Such measures as the tree-planting equivalent of a carbon-tilted fund (or the equivalent of the number of cars taken off the road) are somewhat theoretical and clearly rely on multiple assumptions; nonetheless, they relate the investment process to the real world and may prove especially powerful for retail investors, in particular. Such reporting is still in its early stages and may well need further assurance and consistency to have real power.

There are also numerous performance attribution service providers, disaggregating the drivers of investment performance and identifying where performance comes from. Investors will be used to identifying the five leading stock performers and detractors from performance over their client's defined reporting period. This is usually accompanied by factor analysis and measurement of risk exposures as well.

The attribution of returns to ESG factors is challenging, not least because of the significant range of investment approaches that are included in the broad realm of ESG investing. It is relatively easy to assess the performance drag or enhancement that comes from excluding an industrial sector (such as tobacco), but it is hard to demonstrate the value added by a program of engagement, particularly given the timescales usually required for engagement programs to reach positive outcomes. Furthermore, the more fully integrated ESG factors become in the investment process, the harder it is to disaggregate a particular ESG driver from the broader investment decision.

Disclosures

In 2015, the PLSA published a disclosure guide for public equities developed by a group of pension schemes, setting out some pared-down expectations for manager-reporting on both ESG integration and stewardship activities. The disclosure on ESG integration asks for separate disclosure on both

- identification of ESG risk and
- the management and monitoring of ESG risks and opportunities, with suggested possible disclosures in respect of each (PLSA 2015).

The following are the first three possible points offered as ways to demonstrate the identification of ESG risk and opportunity:

- "Examples of where and why the manager is prepared to take either stock or sector ESG risks or where it sees opportunities.
- Quantitative or qualitative examples of material ESG factors identified in fundamental analysis and stock valuation.
- Identification of long-term ESG secular trends and themes (as potential determinants of future growth or valuation, etc.) and the extent to which they have influenced portfolio construction decisions" (PLSA 2015).

The proposed possible disclosures to demonstrate the management and monitoring of ESG risks and opportunities include the following:

> *"Stock level ESG analysis for top risk and performance detractors/contributors in the reporting period.*
> *Any material changes to portfolio companies' ESG performance. Examples may include where the manager's view of ESG risk and opportunity differs from the market/rating agencies"* (PLSA 2015).

Similarly, the ICGN Model Mandate requests two areas of disclosure that are ESG-specific (ICGN 2012):

- *The manager's assessment of ESG risks that are embedded in the portfolio.* This should include both what these risks are and what the manager has done to identify, monitor, and manage them. This can readily be compared against the external tools used to assess ESG risk in the portfolio or the ESG element of the performance factorial analysis. This should prove to be a core element of the portfolio manager demonstrating genuine ESG investment credentials.
- *A detailed disclosure of stewardship engagement and voting activity.* The mandate is clear that these need to be two separate disclosures—that is, mere disclosure of voting activity is not sufficient to satisfy the requirement for engagement disclosure.

The PRI's 2016 "Practical Guide to ESG Integration for Equity Investing," which builds on the PRI 2013 publication on aligning expectations, includes multiple case studies from fund managers outlining their approach to ESG integration and highlighting their assessments of how their ESG work has added value (PRI 2016b). Similarly, for government debt investors, the PRI offers "ESG Engagement for Sovereign Debt Investors" (PRI 2020a).

It is apparent that there are as many approaches to the integration of ESG factors as there are underlying investment approaches themselves. What the asset owner will want to know is whether the ESG approach is

- genuinely aligned with the fund manager's investment style,
- delivered effectively in practice, and
- aligned with her own investment needs and beliefs.

To guard against fund managers selecting individual cases that put their work in the best light, some clients seek to identify outliers so that they can test whether the asserted method for ESG integration is genuinely delivered in practice, consistently across the portfolio as a whole.

There is no set or agreed format for engagement disclosure, so each fund manager has its own model. Typically, this includes statistics on activity at a greater or lesser level of granularity. It is no longer acceptable to provide statistics at the organization level that are not specifically tailored to the fund in question. In addition, the typical disclosure includes a sample of written descriptions of individual engagement meetings; again, these should be tailored to the fund, but many fund managers reveal more about the focus of their activities than they intend by the imbalance in their reporting toward their home market and region.

Many fund managers and, particularly, the specialist stewardship providers, disclose their form of analysis of what has been delivered in the period through their engagement activities. Most use some measure of either milestones or progress against KPIs to provide their assessment of progress. These are proprietary models and inevitably are somewhat prone to some bias in the analysis; however, clients are able to test these in detail. At a minimum, these disclosures provide some transparency into deliverables from engagement.

KEY FACTS

1. Agency problems exist in the investment chain just as they exist between companies and their owners. This agency problem also extends to aligning ESG beliefs.
2. Accountability and alignment can be delivered in large part through aligning the time horizons of fund managers with their clients. This helps ensure that fund managers will work to accomplish their fiduciary duties.
3. This can be reinforced through a focus on longer-term factors rather than short-term performance assessment.
4. ESG integration will vary between different fund management firms and individual portfolio managers, tailored to the established investment style and approach.
5. Increasing numbers of advisory services are available to help clients assess the ESG delivery of their fund managers and attribute performance and E, S, and G characteristics of the portfolio. These are perhaps best used in dialogue with managers to test whether they are delivering their expected investment style in practice.
6. Asset owners will seek to challenge and debate hard cases of individual assets in portfolios so that they can understand how effective ESG integration is in practice and how well the portfolio reflects that integration.
7. Inadequate resourcing of ESG work is always a constraint on effectiveness and the application of the integration and engagement approach across portfolios. Collective engagement is one key way to bolster resources.
8. The ESG expectations of clients have a range of drivers and therefore manifest in different forms.

APPENDIX: CFA INSTITUTE DISCLOSURE STANDARDS AND SFDR DISCLOSURES

The following sections provide some background information on CFA Institute Disclosure Standards and SFDR disclosures.

Global ESG Disclosure Standards for Investment Products

On 1 November 2021, CFA Institute issued the Global ESG Disclosure Standards for Investment Products, the first global voluntary standards for disclosing how an investment product considers ESG issues in its objectives, investment process, and stewardship activities.

The purpose of the Global ESG Disclosure Standards for Investment Products is to facilitate fair representation and full disclosure of an investment product's consideration of ESG issues in its objectives, investment process, or stewardship activities. When investment products' ESG approaches are fairly represented and fully disclosed, investors, consultants, advisers, and distributors can better understand, evaluate, and compare investment products, and the potential for greenwashing diminishes.

The Global ESG Disclosure Standards for Investment Products are compatible with

- all types of investment vehicles, including but not limited to pooled funds, exchange-traded funds (ETFs), strategies for separately managed accounts, limited partnerships, and insurance-based investment products;
- all asset classes, including but not limited to listed equities, fixed income, private equity, private debt, infrastructure, and real estate;
- all ESG approaches, including but not limited to ESG integration, exclusion, screening, best-in-class, thematic and sustainability-themed investing, impact investing, and stewardship;
- active and passive strategies; and
- national and regional investment product ESG disclosure regulations.

Compliance with the Global ESG Disclosure Standards for Investment Products is voluntary. An investment manager may choose the investment products to which it applies the standards. An investment manager may also choose to have an independent third party provide assurance for one or more of its ESG disclosure statements. All requirements and recommendations for both investment managers and firms conducting assurance engagements are contained in the Examination Procedures for the Global ESG Disclosure Standards for Investment Products, issued on 7 February 2023.

The Global ESG Disclosure Standards for Investment Products were developed and are maintained with extensive input from the volunteer investment professionals who have served and continue to serve on the CFA Institute ESG Technical Committee, ESG Examination Subcommittee, and ESG Working Group.

ESG Disclosure Statement Template. www.cfainstitute.org/-/media/documents/ESG-standards/eds-template.docx

Examination Procedures for the Global ESG Disclosure Standards for Investment Products. www.cfainstitute.org/-/media/documents/ESG-standards/Examination-Procedures-Global_ESG-Disclsosure-Standards-for-Investment-Products.pdf

Global ESG Disclosure Standards for Investment Products. www.cfainstitute.org/-/media/documents/ESG-standards/Global-ESG-Disclosure-Standards-for-Investment-Products.pdf

Global ESG Disclosure Standards for Investment Products Handbook. www.cfainstitute.org/-/media/documents/ESG-standards/Global-ESG-Disclosure-Standards-for-Investment-Products-Handbook.pdf

SFDR Disclosures

On 6 April 2022, the European Commission adopted a set of technical standards to be used by financial market participants when disclosing sustainability-related information under the SFDR. The derived Delegated Regulation specifies the exact content, methodology, and presentation of the information to be disclosed, thereby improving its quality and comparability. Under these rules, financial market participants will provide detailed information about how they tackle and reduce any possible negative impacts that their investments may have on the environment and society in general.

These new requirements are expected to help assess the sustainability performance of financial products. Compliance with sustainability-related disclosures will contribute to strengthening investor protection and reduce greenwashing. This will ultimately support the financial system's transition toward a more sustainable economy.

Appendix: CFA Institute Disclosure Standards and SFDR Disclosures

Following the launch of Level 1 requirements going into effect in March 2021, Level 2 requirements also came into effect in January 2023. Firms will have until 30 June 2023 to make their SFDR disclosures, with the requirement then recurring on an annual basis.

ESMA Supervisory Briefing on Sustainability

On 31 May 2022, ESMA published a Supervisory Briefing titled "Sustainability Risks and Disclosures in the Area of Investment Management" ["Briefing"]. This Briefing promotes common supervisory approaches and practices across EU Member States in order to minimize the risk of different levels of investor protection depending on where the relevant fund is domiciled or marketed on a cross-border basis. ESMA's expectation is that having a common approach will help increase transparency for investors as well as avoid the practice of greenwashing This Briefing also provides a summary of ESMA's views on compliance with the various obligations under the SFDR and Taxonomy Regulation, as follows.

- **Fund documentation and marketing material**: Information provided to investors to evaluate proposed funds must be accurate, fair, clear, not misleading, simple, and concise. An important aspect of this information is the proportion of the non-financial characteristics. For example, with respect to Article 8 funds, Recital 11 of the proposed SFDR RTS (Regulatory Technical Standards) notes that disclosure criteria for the selection of underlying assets should be limited to those criteria that are binding on the fund manager in the investment decision-making process. Recital 16 of the SFDR RTS warns against greenwashing risks where funds apply "non-binding" exclusion strategies.
- **Verifying compliance with pre-contractual disclosures**: ESMA suggests using a checklist of information to be provided to help assess compliance of funds.
- **Verifying the consistency of information in fund documentation and marketing material**:
  - Presentation of disclosures – avoid using boilerplate language and technical jargon that may not be understood by the average investor; limit cross-references and hyperlinks, and hyperlinks should link to [the] precise place where the relevant information may be found and be maintained over time.
  - Principles-based guidance on fund names – ESG-related terms should be used only when materially supported by evidence of sustainability characteristics that are reflected in the fund's investment objectives, policy, and strategy.
  - Sustainable investment policy and objectives – Should be clearly identified. Expressions such as "the fund pursues ESG objectives in general" must be avoided.
  - Investment strategy – Should be clearly identified and should clearly state how it is linked to the sustainable objectives or characteristics and how it helps achieve this.
- **Verifying compliance with website disclosure obligations**: Managers should clearly identify the financial product to which the information in the sustainability-related disclosure section relates and display the fund's environmental or social characteristics or its sustainable investment objective prominently.

- **Verifying compliance with periodic disclosure obligations**: A checklist of the information to be provided in periodic reports could help assess whether disclosing funds are complying with their obligations. At a minimum, the main body of the annual report should contain a prominent statement referring to the information to be found in the annex and the periodic report should be properly completed in full.
  - Commission Delegated Regulation (EU) 2022/1288 of 6 April 2022 Supplementing Regulation (EU) 2019/2088 of the European Parliament and of the Council. www.afec.es/documentos/english/delegated-regulation-2022-1288.pdf.
  - ANNEX I. Template Principal Adverse Sustainability Impacts Statement. https://ec.europa.eu/finance/docs/level-2-measures/C_2022_1931_1_EN_annexe_acte_autonome_part1_v6.pdf.
  - ANNEX II. Template Pre-Contractual Disclosure for the Financial Products Referred to in Article 8, Paragraphs 1, 2, and 2a, of Regulation (EU) 2019/2088 and Article 6, First Paragraph, of Regulation (EU) 2020/852. https://iif-reit_sustainability.disclosure.site/data/themes_93/IIF_SFDR_Disclosure_Article_8.pdf.
  - ANNEX III. Template Pre-Contractual Disclosure for the Financial Products Referred to in Article 9, Paragraphs 1 to 4a, of Regulation (EU) 2019/2088 and Article 5, First Paragraph, of Regulation (EU) 2020/852. https://ec.europa.eu/finance/docs/level-2-measures/C_2022_1931_3_EN_annexe_acte_autonome_cp_part1_v5.pdf.
  - ANNEX IV. Template Periodic Disclosure for the Financial Products Referred to in Article 8, Paragraphs 1, 2, and 2a, of Regulation (EU) 2019/2088 and Article 6, First Paragraph, of Regulation (EU) 2020/852. https://lexparency.org/eu/32022R1288/ANX_IV/.
  - ANNEX V. Template Periodic Disclosure for the Financial Products Referred to in Article 9, Paragraphs 1 to 4a, of Regulation (EU) 2019/2088 and Article 5, First Paragraph, of Regulation (EU) 2020/852. https://lexparency.org/eu/32022R1288/ANX_V/.
- **Alternatives:** To date, SFDR disclosures have been silent on how to deal with short positions. In the context of taxonomy alignment, the RTS states that the calculation of taxonomy alignment should be netted by applying the methodology used to calculate net short positions in the EU short-selling regulation. Although this only explicitly refers to the calculation of taxonomy alignments, firms using short positions in their products may find this useful in determining how to approach shorting techniques/strategies in the context of the SFDR disclosures more broadly.

11 FURTHER READING

- Investor Forum. 2017. "The Investor Forum Review 2017." www.investorforum.org.uk/wp-content/uploads/2018/07/Annual-review-2017.pdf.
- Lee, P. 2008. "Long-Term Low Friction: An Investment Framework Which Works for the Beneficiaries Rather Than Their Agents." Tomorrow's Investor (September). www.thersa.org/globalassets/pdfs/blogs/rsa-paul-lee.pdf.

Further Reading

- PRI. 2016. "Attributing Performance to ESG Factors" (4 September). www.unpri.org/listed-equity/attributing-performance-to-esg-factors/742.article.

REFERENCES

Bogle, J. C. 2018. "The Modern Corporation and the Public Interest." Financial Analysts Journal 74 (3): 8–17. 10.2469/faj.v74.n3.1

PRI 2016a. "How Asset Owners Can Drive Responsible Investment: Beliefs, Strategies and Mandates." www.unpri.org/download?ac=1398.

AustralianSuper 2020. "How We Invest Members' Super: Our Long-Term Vision." www.australiansuper.com/investments/how-we-invest.

Bernow, S., B. Klempner, C. Magnin. 2017. "From 'Why' to 'Why Not': Sustainable Investing as the New Normal." McKinsey & Company (25 October). www.mckinsey.com/industries/private-equity-and-principal-investors/our-insights/from-why-to-why-not-sustainable-investing-as-the-new-normal.

CPP Investments 2020. "How We Invest." www.cppib.com/en/how-we-invest.

PLSA 2020. "PLSA Stewardship Guide and Voting Guidelines 2020." https://hsfnotes.com/corporate/2020/03/06/plsa-stewardship-guide-and-voting-guidelines-2020/.

Bernow, S., B. Klempner, C. Magnin. 2017. "From 'Why' to 'Why Not': Sustainable Investing as the New Normal." McKinsey & Company (25 October). www.mckinsey.com/industries/private-equity-and-principal-investors/our-insights/from-why-to-why-not-sustainable-investing-as-the-new-normal.

Generation Investment Management 2023. "Our Investment Process." https://www.generationim.com/our-strategies/global-equity/.

RBC Global Asset Management 2019. "RBC Global Equity." http://global.rbcgam.com/global-equities/default.fs.

CFA Institute 2021. "Global ESG Disclosure Standards for Investment Products." www.cfainstitute.org/-/media/documents/ESG-standards/Global-ESG-Disclosure-Standards-for-Investment-Products.pdf.

ICGN 2012. "ICGN Model Mandate Initiative: Model Contract Terms between Asset Owners and Managers." www.icgn.org/sites/default/files/2021-06/ICGN_Model-Contract-Terms_2015_0.pdf.

ICSA 2018. "Shareholder Engagement: The State of Play" (July). www.amecbrasil.org.br/wp-content/uploads/2018/07/ICSA_Shareholder_Engagement_July_2018.pdf.

PLSA and Investor Forum 2020. "Engaging the Engagers: A Practical Toolkit for Schemes to Achieve Effective Stewardship through Their Managers"(July). www.investorforum.org.uk/wp-content/uploads/securepdfs/2020/07/Engaging-the-Engagers-stewardship-toolkit.pdf.

PRI 2016a. "How Asset Owners Can Drive Responsible Investment: Beliefs, Strategies and Mandates." www.unpri.org/download?ac=1398.

Arons, Steven, Karin Matussek, Nicholas Comfort. 2022. "Deutsche Bank, DWS Raided Over Allegations of Greenwashing." *Bloomberg* (31 May). www.bloomberg.com/news/articles/2022-05-31/deutsche-bank-s-dws-unit-raided-amid-allegations-of-greenwashing.

BBC 2022. "HSBC Climate Change Adverts Banned by UK Watchdog" (19 October). www.bbc.com/news/business-63309878.

Boyd, Emma Howard. 2022. "Plenary Keynote" given at the UK CGFI Annual Forum (4 July). www.youtube.com/watch?v=nnVw3Lmj0T4. #BreakFreeFromPlastic. 2021. "Brand Audit 2021." https://brandaudit.breakfreefromplastic.org/wp-content/uploads/2022/11/BRAND-AUDIT-REPORT-2021.pdf.

Changing Markets Foundation 2022. "Brands Exposed for 'Misleading and Mendacious' Packaging Claims" (30 June). changingmarkets.org/wp-content/uploads/2022/06/Greenwash.com-packaging-press-release.pdf.

ClientEarth 2019. "Our OECD Complaint Against BP Explained" (19 December). www.clientearth.org/latest/latest-updates/stories/our-oecd-complaint-against-bp-explained.

ClientEarth 2021. "Greenwashing Files: ExxonMobil." www.clientearth.org/projects/the-greenwashing-files/exxonmobil.

References

Danish FSA 2023. "Thematic Review of Sustainability Disclosures for Funds Having Sustainable Investments as an Objective" (3 February). www.dfsa.dk/News/Press-releases/2023/Thematicreview_sustainabilityInvestments_030223.

Dey, Monica, Brian Bushee, Brian Hall. 2023. "The Weight of ESG Disclosures." Journal of Finance78 (2): 937–72.

Eonnet, Estelle. 2020. "The Coca-Cola Company, PepsiCo and Nestlé named top plastic polluters for the third year in a row" (2 December). www.breakfreefromplastic.org/2020/12/02/top-plastic-polluters-of-2020.

EU 2020. "Regulation (EU) 2020/852 of the European Parliament and of the Council" (18 June). https://eur-lex.europa.eu/legal-content/EN/TXT/?uri=celex%3A32020R0852.

European Commission 2021. "Screening of Websites for 'Greenwashing': Half Eof Green Claims Lack Evidence" (28 January). https://ec.europa.eu/commission/presscorner/detail/en/ip_21_269.

European Commission 2023. "Consumer Protection: Enabling Sustainable Choices and Ending Greenwashing" (22 March). https://ec.europa.eu/commission/presscorner/detail/en/IP_23_1692.

European Securities and Markets Authority (ESMA) 2021, November 15). Technical Advice on the Scope of the Sustainable Finance Disclosure Regulation (SFDR). [PDF]https://maples.com/en/knowledge-centre/2022/6/guide-to-the-eu-sustainable-finance-disclosure-regulation.

FCA 2022. "FCA Proposes New Rules to Tackle Greenwashing" (25 October). www.fca.org.uk/news/press-releases/fca-proposes-new-rules-tackle-greenwashing.

George, Sarah. 2023. "Avoiding greenwash: How can UK businesses avoid falling foul of the Green Claims Code?" *Edie* (27 January). www.edie.net/how-can-uk-businesses-avoid-falling-foul-of-the-green-claims-code/.

Geyer, Roland, Jenna R. Jambeck, Kara Lavender Law. 2017. "Production, Use, and Fate of All Plastics Ever Made." Science Advances3 (7). www.science.org/doi/10.1126/sciadv.1700782. 10.1126/sciadv.1700782

HSBC 2022. *Annual Report and Accounts 2021*.www.hsbc.com/-/files/hsbc/investors/hsbc-results/2021/annual/pdfs/hsbc-holdings-plc/220222-annual-report-and-accounts-2021.pdf.

IOSCO 2021a. "Environmental, Social and Governance (ESG) Ratings and Data Products Providers: Final Report" (November). www.iosco.org/library/pubdocs/pdf/IOSCOPD690.pdf.

IOSCO 2021b. "Recommendations on Sustainability-Related Practices, Policies, Procedures and Disclosure in Asset Management: Final Report" (November). www.iosco.org/library/pubdocs/pdf/IOSCOPD688.pdf.

IOSCO 2022. "IOSCO Good Sustainable Finance Practices for Financial Markets Voluntary Standard Setting Bodies and Industry Associations: Call for Action" (7 November). www.iosco.org/library/pubdocs/pdf/IOSCOPD717.pdf.

Japanese FSA 2023. "Proposed Partial Amendment to the 'Comprehensive Supervisory Guidelines for Financial Instruments Business Operators, etc.'" www.fsa.go.jp/news/r4/shouken/20221219/02.pdf.

Mambu 2022. "Over Two Thirds of Global Consumers Want Their Bank or Financial Institution to Become More Sustainable in Future" (31 May). mambu.com/insights/press/over-two-thirds-of-global-consumers-want-their-bank-or-financial-institution-to-become-more.

Influence Map 2021. "Climate Funds: Are They Paris Aligned?" (August). influencemap.org/report/Climate-Funds-Are-They-Paris-Aligned-3eb83347267949847084306dae01c7b0.

Nestlé Waters North America Securities Litigation 2021. WL 3426030 (N.D. Cal. May 20, 2021).

Rainforest Action Network 2022. *HSBC: Fossil Fuel Finance 2015-2021*. www.ran.org/publications/banking-on-climate-chaos-2022.

Rogers, Christina, Mike Spector. 2017. "Judge Slaps VW with $2.8 Billion Criminal Fine in Emissions Fraud." *The Wall Street Journal* (21 April). www.wsj.com/articles/judge-slaps-vw-with-2-8-billion-criminal-fine-in-emissions-fraud-1492789096.

Schumacher, Kim. 2021. "Dr. Kim Schumacher on ESG competence greenwashing: 'We should not equate awareness or passion with subject matter expertise'" (31 May). Sustainability and ESG News Central Europe; sustainabilitynews.eu/dr-kim-schumacher-on-esg-competence-greenwashing-we-should-not-equate-awareness-or-passion-with-subject-matter-expertise.

Urso, Federica. 2022. "Number of Company Sustainability Officers Triples in 2021 – Study." Reuters (4 May). www.reuters.com/business/sustainable-business/number-company-sustainability-officers-triples-2021-study-2022-05-04.

US Department of Justice 2022." Kohl's and Walmart Agree to Pay $5.5 Million in Combined Penalties for Alleged Deceptive Violations of the Textile Act and Rules and FTC Act Around the Use of Bamboo" (May 5). www.justice.gov/opa/pr/kohl-s-and-walmart-agree-pay-55-million-combined-penalties-alleged-deceptive-violations.

US SEC 2022a. "The Enhancement and Standardization of Climate-Related Disclosures for Investors: Proposed Rule" (21 March). www.sec.gov/rules/proposed/2022/33-11042.pdf.

US SEC 2022b. "Investment Company Names: Proposed Rule" (25 May). www.sec.gov/rules/proposed/2022/ic-34593.pdf.

US SEC 2022c. "SEC Charges Brazilian Mining Company with Misleading Investors about Safety Prior to Deadly Dam Collapse." www.sec.gov/news/press-release/2022-72.

Wanner, Antonia. 2021. "Reimagining, Rethinking, and Recycling Our Packaging." Nestle Our Stories (March). www.nestle.com/stories/reimagining-rethinking-recycling-our-packaging.

Brunel Pension Partnership 2018. "Brunel Asset Management Accord." www.brunelpensionpartnership.org/wp-content/uploads/2018/11/Brunel-Asset-Management-Accord-2018.pdf.

ICGN 2012. "ICGN Model Mandate Initiative: Model Contract Terms between Asset Owners and Managers." www.icgn.org/sites/default/files/2021-06/ICGN_Model-Contract-Terms_2015_0.pdf.

Brunel Pension Partnership 2018. "Brunel Asset Management Accord." www.brunelpensionpartnership.org/wp-content/uploads/2018/11/Brunel-Asset-Management-Accord-2018.pdf.

ICGN 2012. "ICGN Model Mandate Initiative: Model Contract Terms between Asset Owners and Managers." www.icgn.org/sites/default/files/2021-06/ICGN_Model-Contract-Terms_2015_0.pdf.

PLSA and Investor Forum 2020. "Engaging the Engagers: A Practical Toolkit for Schemes to Achieve Effective Stewardship through Their Managers" (July). www.investorforum.org.uk/wp-content/uploads/securepdfs/2020/07/Engaging-the-Engagers-stewardship-toolkit.pdf.

ICGN 2012. "ICGN Model Mandate Initiative: Model Contract Terms between Asset Owners and Managers." www.icgn.org/sites/default/files/2021-06/ICGN_Model-Contract-Terms_2015_0.pdf.

PLSA 2015. "A Guide to Responsible Investment Reporting in Public Equity" (January). www.sustainablefinance.ch/upload/cms/user/2015_01_26_guide_to_responsible_investment_reporting_in_public_equity_published_NAPF1.pdf.

PLSA 2016. "Environmental, Social and Corporate Governance (ESG) Made Simple Guide"(May). www.plsa.co.uk/portals/0/Documents/0585-Environmental-Social-and-Corporate-Governance-ESG-Made-Simple.pdf.

PRI 2013. "Aligning Expectations: Guidance for Asset Owners on Incorporating ESG Factors into Manager Selection, Appointment and Monitoring" (February). www.unpri.org/download?ac=1614.

PRI 2016b. "Practical Guide to ESG Integration for Equity Investing: Executive Summary." www.unpri.org/listed-equity/a-practical-guide-to-esg-integration-for-equity-investing/10.article.

PRI 2020a. "ESG Engagement for Sovereign Debt Investors." www.unpri.org/download?ac=12018.

References

PRI 2020b. "The Reporting Process." www.unpri.org/reporting-and-assessment-resources/reporting-for-signatories/3057.article.

PRACTICE PROBLEMS

1. What is the first step in the effective design of a client ESG investment mandate?
   a. Tailor ESG investment approach to client expectations.
   b. Develop client-relevant ESG-aware investment mandates.
   c. Clarify client needs and set them out in a clear statement of ESG investment beliefs.

2. An ESG policy of a fund management firm needs to address the manner in which the portfolio manager establishes:
   a. engagement with companies and issuers on ESG issues.
   b. rationale and methodology for ESG portfolio-level assessment.
   c. engagement with policymakers on responsible investment and ESG-related issues.

3. Which of the following best describes an ESG-related thematic focus? It:
   a. seeks to generate a positive, measurable social or environmental impact alongside a financial return.
   b. aims to invest in sectors, industries, or companies that are expected to benefit from long-term macro or structural ESG-related trends.
   c. excludes securities, issuers, or companies from the investment product based on certain ESG-related activities, business practices, or business segments.

4. To incorporate ESG factors in index tracking, managers can exert influence on companies through:
   a. engagement and voting.
   b. governance arrangements.
   c. representation on board seats.

5. Which of the following is the *most likely* primary driver of ESG investment for a sovereign wealth fund?
   a. Fiduciary duty
   b. Reputational risk
   c. Awareness of financial impacts of climate change

6. Which of the following describes the risk mindset of a general insurer?
   a. Loss aversion
   b. High risk tolerance
   c. High tolerance for illiquidity

7. Exclusions is the *most likely* implied favored ESG approach of a:
   a. general insurer.
   b. charitable foundation.
   c. defined benefit pension scheme.

8. The Brunel Asset Management Accord:
   a. emphasizes that short-term underperformance is not in itself likely to give rise to undue concern.

Practice Problems

    b. provides a helpful framework and proposes best practices for ESG-aware investment mandates.

    c. produces a Stewardship Checklist for asset owners to ensure an effective and meaningful stewardship strategy.

9. The PLSA's guide on ESG integration requires disclosure on:

    a. elimination of ESG risks.

    b. short-term ESG secular trends.

    c. management and monitoring of ESG risks and opportunities.

10. The ICGN Model Mandate requires ESG-specific disclosure on:

    a. an ESG risk materiality map.

    b. ESG-aware investment mandates.

    c. stewardship engagement and voting activity.

11. Greenwashing refers to companies:

    a. hiding their harmful practices behind more positive ones.

    b. engaging constructively and proactively with policymakers on responsible investment and ESG-related issues.

    c. making false statements about its ESG practices to appeal to customers interested in environmentally friendly and sustainable practices hiding their harmful practices behind more positive ones.

12. Which of the following is a core greenwashing characteristic set out by the European Supervisory Agencies?

    a. Greenwashing can only be triggered by third party ESG rating providers.

    b. Greenwashing must be an intentional misinterpretation of the sustainable finance regulatory framework requirement.

    c. Greenwashing will undermine trust in sustainable finance markets and policies, regardless of whether immediate damage to individual consumers or investors or the gain of an unfair competitive advantage has been ascertained.

13. Which of the following is *not* an example of greenwashing?

    a. A company makes accurate representations of the environmental benefits of its production methods in its regulatory filings.

    b. A company represented that its techniques were environmentally friendly and utilized suppliers that produced high volumes of wastewater.

    c. A bank advertised its global financing extended to help its clients transition to net zero and continued to significantly finance investments in businesses and industries that emitted notable levels of carbon dioxide and other greenhouse gases.

14. An asset owner seeking to hire an investment manager believes that ESG factors are most important for risk management. To implement that belief, the asset manager will *most likely* suggest a strategy that:

    a. structures the portfolio to replicate an ESG benchmark fund.

    b. excludes some companies, sectors, or geographies based on ESG-related factors.

    c. overweights the portfolio with companies that exhibit strong performance on related ESG factors.

15. When determining the materiality of ESG factors in portfolio construction, the consideration of governance factors tends to be especially important for which asset class?

    a. Public equity
    b. Fixed income
    c. Private equity

16. A multi-strategy investment firm that manages both fundamental and quantitative strategy portfolios *most likely* applies:

    a. ESG integration to all asset classes in a portfolio.
    b. a consistent ESG approach to both types of portfolios.
    c. a policy of active engagement in its concentrated fundamental portfolios.

17. If an investor wants to make investments that they believe have relatively fewer negative effects and more positive effects, which of the following ESG-related approaches would be *least* effective?

    a. Impact investing
    b. Thematic investing
    c. Best-in-class investing

18. When searching for an asset manager, what is the *most* important information, with respect to ESG considerations, a client wants to understand from the RFP (Request for Proposal)?

    a. The source of ESG data the manager uses in their investment process
    b. That the manager can deliver in practice what is set out in the policy documents
    c. The number of engagement activities the manger has undertaken and the outcomes of those activities

19. When seeking to implement ESG factors into an investment mandate, which of the following statements regarding the investment time horizon is *most* accurate?

    a. Asset owners and asset managers have similar time horizons.
    b. Asset managers have a longer time horizon than asset owners.
    c. Asset owners have a longer time horizon than asset managers.

20. An asset owner is having a regular meeting with their fund manager about the fund's performance and the integration of the asset owner's ESG beliefs. The asset owner notes that the fund has a significant holding in Beta Company (Beta) and is concerned that the governance of Beta is weak. Which is the *most* appropriate question the asset owner could ask the fund manager about their concern?

    a. What makes you comfortable that Beta is run and overseen effectively and is addressing ESG challenges?
    b. Do you believe Beta will retain staff and continue to be able to recruit appropriately skilled individuals?
    c. Have you discussed with Beta its approach to the risk of exposure to disruptions arising from climate change?

21. What is the *least likely* reason a fund manager will use an ESG research firm, like MSCI, to evaluate the portfolios it manages?

    a. To test its own approach to ESG against a database
    b. To prepare for clients' questions about their ESG integration

Practice Problems

c. To have access to the high quality of data from the research firm

22. For which type of ESG activity would it be easiest to evaluate the impact on a portfolio's performance?
    a. Excluding an industrial sector (e.g., tobacco)
    b. Implementing a program of active engagement
    c. Screening of companies for exploitive labor practices in their supply chain

23. Which of the following statements concerning the reporting of engagement activities by fund managers is *most* accurate?
    a. There is an agreed format for disclosing engagement activities
    b. Disclosing voting activities satisfies the reporting requirement for engagement activities
    c. Typical disclosures include a sample of written descriptions of individual engagement meetings

24. Which of the following, according to the Brunel Asset Management Accord, is *not* in itself a likely cause for concern?
    a. A change in the expected investment style
    b. Short-term underperformance
    c. Lack of understanding of reasons for underperformance

25. What behavioral step should clients take to ensure that fund managers invest in alignment with the investment horizons as agreed in ESG-focused client mandates?
    a. Clients assess investment performance predictably but *less* frequently
    b. Clients raise questions about the ESG characteristics of each company newly purchased by a fund manager
    c. Clients raise questions about the ESG characteristics of each company that is sold by a fund manager

26. Which of the following is *not* a typical way in which asset managers integrate ESG factors?
    a. Use ESG as a threshold requirement before investment can be considered
    b. Use ESG as a risk assessment that offers a level of confidence in the valuation
    c. Use ESG as a basis for explaining investment holdings to clients

27. Which of the following are expected to be reported under the Pensions and Lifetime Savings Association (PLSA) disclosure guide for public equities?
    a. ESG integration and stewardship activities
    b. Social impact and stakeholder engagement
    c. ESG risk and carbon footprint

28. Which of the following is *not* one of McKinsey's proposed dimensions of investing for the purposes of applying sustainable investing practices?
    a. Investment beliefs and strategy
    b. Regulatory and policy environment
    c. Performance management

29. Which of these forms of asset owner is *most likely* to apply an exclusion policy

barring investment in all assets exposed to a particular business area?

- a. Defined benefit pension scheme
- b. Charitable foundation
- c. Sovereign wealth fund

30. Which of the following is *least likely* a driver for clients to seek ESG investment?

- a. Fiduciary duty
- b. Reputational risk
- c. A belief that social issues are unimportant

31. Which of the following is *least likely* a way for a fund manager to demonstrate identification of ESG risk and opportunity, according to the Pensions and Lifetime Savings Association (PLSA)?

- a. Evaluation of how much financial return is directly attributable to ESG factors
- b. Quantitative or qualitative examples of material ESG factors identified in fundamental analysis and stock valuation
- c. Identification of long-term ESG secular trends and themes and the extent to which they have influenced portfolio construction decisions

32. Which of the following is likely to be a primary ESG driver for a defined benefit pension scheme?

- a. Reputational risk
- b. Fiduciary duty
- c. Personal ethics

33. Which two ESG-specific areas of disclosure are requested by the International Corporate Governance Network (ICGN) Model Mandate?

- a. A breakdown of the return on investment for each stakeholder group and details of how each form of ESG risk has been hedged by the portfolio manager
- b. A materiality map identifying the ESG impact of all investments and a detailed disclosure of the voting record of all executive and non-executive directors
- c. A detailed disclosure of stewardship engagement and voting activity and the manager's assessment of ESG risks embedded in the portfolio.

34. A document that sets out an asset owner's risk-adjusted return target, time horizon, and ESG investment beliefs for a fund manager is *best* described as an investment:

- a. recommendation.
- b. mandate.
- c. approach.

35. In responding to a request for proposal, a fund manager proposes selecting the least carbon-intensive of the acceptable investments in each sector. The assets owner's investment mandate is *most likely* aligned with integrating ESG factors:

- a. as a threshold requirement.
- b. as a basis for stewardship engagement.
- c. by applying a tilt to the portfolio's exposures.

SOLUTIONS

1. **C is correct**. The first step in the effective design of a mandate is that clients should be clear about their needs and set them out in a clear statement of ESG investment beliefs. Doing so will require them to define their investment goals and beliefs, which will help them define how they plan to create value and how they will orient their investment approach. The investment beliefs—which might be expressed in a statement of investment principles—ought to guide the overall approach toward ESG investment (and investment more generally) and will help frame any mandate agreed with an investment manager.

2. **B is correct**. An ESG policy should formally outline the investment approach and degree of ESG integration in a firm. An ESG policy needs to address the manner in which the portfolio manager
   - addresses ESG issues at portfolio reviews,
   - establishes the rationale and methodology for ESG portfolio-level assessment,
   - assesses exposure to ESG risk in the risk management function,
   - determines ESG impacts to the portfolio,
   - responds in the investment decision-making process to ESG implications, and
   - discloses ESG exposure to the fund's investors.

3. **B is correct**. The ESG Disclosure Standards for Investment Products proposed by CFA Institute highlight six ESG investment approaches. An ESG-related thematic focus aims to invest in sectors, industries, or companies that are expected to benefit from long-term macro or structural ESG-related trends.

4. **A is correct**. There are major ESG considerations for a pension fund or other asset owner when seeking to allocate a new mandate across the full range of potential asset classes. The elements to ensure that ESG issues are appropriately delivered by the relevant mandate include mandate choice, investment integration, and engagement. In the case of passive/index tracking, managers can exert influence on companies through engagement and voting. There is also scope for influence on market- and system-wide issues.

5. **B is correct**. Different client types (institutional, retail, or private) have different investment objectives, risk/return profiles, and drivers. These will influence the type of ESG investing strategies they will consider most attractive. In the case of a sovereign wealth fund, the primary driver for ESG investment is reputational risk.

6. **A is correct**. Different client types (institutional, retail, or private) have different investment objectives, risk/return profiles, and drivers. The risk mindset of a general insurer is loss aversion, compared to a defined benefit pension scheme, which has a higher risk tolerance, and a sovereign wealth fund, which has high tolerance for illiquidity.

7. **B is correct**. Different client types (institutional, retail, or private) have different investment objectives, risk/return profiles, and drivers. These will influence the type of ESG investing strategies they will consider most attractive. The *most likely* implied favored ESG approach of a charitable foundation is exclusions, to ensure investment is consistent with founding or charitable aims.

8. **A is correct**. The Brunel Asset Management Accord sets out a pension manager's approach to long-term investment and ESG factors. It emphasizes that short-term underperformance is not in itself likely to give rise to undue concern

for the client: "Investment performance, particularly in the short term, will be of limited significance in evaluating the manager."

9. **C is correct**. The PLSA published a disclosure guide for public equities developed by a group of pension schemes, setting out some pared-down expectations for manager reporting on both ESG integration and stewardship activities. The disclosure on ESG integration asks for separate disclosure on both identification of ESG risk and the management and monitoring of ESG risks and opportunities.

10. **C is correct**. The ICGN Model Mandate requests two areas of disclosure that are ESG specific:

    the manager's assessment of ESG risks that are embedded in the portfolio

    a detailed disclosure of stewardship engagement and voting activity

11. **C is correct**. Greenwashing describes where a company makes false statements about its ESG practices to appeal to customers interested in environmentally friendly and sustainable practices. Scopewashing refers to companies hiding their harmful practices behind more positive ones.

12. **C is correct**. Greenwashing will undermine trust in sustainable finance markets and policies, regardless of whether immediate damage to individual consumers or investors (in particular through mis-selling) or the gain of an unfair competitive advantage has been ascertained. Greenwashing can be either intentional or unintentional. Greenwashing can be triggered by the entity to which the sustainability communications relate or by the entity responsible for the product, or it can be triggered by third parties (e.g., ESG rating providers or third-party verifiers).

13. **A is correct**. The possible categories of misrepresentation include commitments without any guarantees of action, misstatements on product attributes, or misleading disclosures.

    Misstatements on product attributes: A securities class action was filed against a food and beverage company, whereby shareholders claimed that the company had misrepresented the environmental benefits of its production methods in its regulatory filings. The company claimed that its techniques were environmentally friendly, but the claimants argued that, in actual fact, the company's production processes exhibited almost equivalent greenhouse gas emissions, required similar land usage, and utilized suppliers that produced dangerously high volumes of wastewater.

    Misleading disclosures: The UK advertising watchdog banned the series of HSBC adverts on the grounds of "misleading advertising and environmental claims", citing HSBC's failure to acknowledge its own contribution to emissions and said any future campaigns must disclose the bank's contribution to the climate crisis. Despite the initiatives highlighted in the adverts, HSBC was continuing to significantly finance investments in businesses and industries that emitted notable levels of carbon dioxide and other greenhouse gases.

14. **B is correct**. If an ESG mandate is to focus on risk management, then a possible strategy would be to exclude companies, sectors, or geographies that the investor sees as particularly risky with respect to ESG factors. If value creation were the focus, then the manager might overweight the portfolio with companies or sectors that exhibit strong performance on ESG-related factors they believe are linked to value creation. (Although companies that have good corporate governance often have good ratings for E&S factors as well, that is not always the case, so focusing on only one of the ESG factors would not necessarily reduce the portfolio's risk.)

15. **C is correct.** Governance factors tend to be especially important for private

Solutions

investments, since they are typically characterized by large ownership shares and limited regulatory oversight.

16. **C is correct.** Active engagement is more relevant and easier to apply in portfolios following a concentrated fundamental strategy than more diverse quantitative portfolios. The ESG strategies could vary by portfolio as the firm tries to target investors with different ESG beliefs. Some asset classes, like money market funds and commodities, have limited ESG integration currently available making it difficult to apply ESG integration to all asset classes.

17. **B is correct.** Thematic investing would not be the most effective way to achieve the investment objective of selecting investments with relatively fewer negative effects and more positive effects. Impact investing and best-in-class investing could be more effective ways to achieve that objective.

18. **B is correct.** The most important information a client wants to understand from the RFP is that the manager actually delivers in practice what is set out as the approach in policy documents. The source of ESG data and the results of engagement activities are things a client might be seeking to understand, but they are not the most important as in isolation they will not provide information on if the manager can deliver what the client is seeking.

19. **C is correct.** Per the *ICGN Model Mandate*, "The time horizon of most asset owners is considerably longer than that of fund managers." The different horizons make it important for the asset owner to ensure ESG integration of the factors that concerned them.

20. **A is correct.** If the asset owner is concerned about weak governance at Beta, the question about how Beta is run and overseen would be the most appropriate question. The question about recruiting staff would be more useful in assessing social issues and not directly weak governance. The question about disruption arising from climate change addresses environmental issues, not necessarily weak governance.

21. **C is correct.** The least likely reason to use an ESG research firm is to have access to high quality data. The data in a research firm's database are subject to issues arising from the quality and consistency of the data. Fund managers may not believe the outside data are a fair representation of the firm's portfolios and ESG integration. A fund manager might choose to use a service like MSCI to test its own approach to ESG integration and to prepare for client questioning.

22. **A is correct.** It is relatively easy to assess the performance drag or enhancement that comes from excluding an industrial sector. There may even be benchmarks available reflecting the same restrictions. It is more difficult to demonstrate the value added by a program of engagement. It would be difficult to monitor the labor practices in the supply chains of all companies in a benchmark.

23. **C is correct.** Typical disclosures include a sample of written descriptions of individual engagement meetings. For engagement activities, it is not sufficient to disclose only voting activities; a detailed disclosure of stewardship engagement is also required under the *ICGN Model Mandate*. There is no agreed format for disclosing engagement activities.

24. **B is correct.** The Brunel Asset Management Accord emphasizes a long-term commitment to the agreed investment process and specifically states that short-term investment performance will be of limited significance in evaluating the asset manager.

25. **A is correct**. By assessing investment performance on a predictable but less frequent basis, clients implicitly signal their interest in the long-term performance of the assets under the agreed investment mandate.

26. **C is correct**. Explaining investment holdings to clients is not a way of integrating ESG factors. The explanation may be provided after the ESG factor integration process has enabled the construction of the portfolio.

27. **A is correct**. The Pensions and Lifetime Savings Association's 2015 disclosure guide set out expectations for manager reporting on both ESG integration and stewardship activities.

28. **B is correct**. McKinsey's proposed dimensions include the investment mandate, investment beliefs and strategy, and investment operations enablers, including performance management. The regulatory and policy environment is not included amongst the dimensions.

29. **B is correct**. Charitable foundations are most likely to favor an exclusion policy to ensure the investments are consistent with its founding or charitable aims.

30. **C is correct**. A belief that social issues are unimportant is at least partly inconsistent with ESG investing. Common drivers of ESG investing include fiduciary duty (e.g., for pension funds) and reputational risk (e.g., for sovereign wealth funds and foundations).

31. **A is correct**. Attribution of the financial return to ESG factors provides information on the consequences of the manager's portfolio construction decisions. The other options describe more direct ways to demonstrate identification of ESG risk and opportunity.

32. **B is correct**. The most likely primary driver for ESG investing by a defined benefit pension scheme is fiduciary duty.

33. **C is correct**. The ICGN Model Mandate requests ESG-specific disclosures on stewardship engagement and voting activity and on the manager's assessment of ESG risks embedded in the portfolio.

34. **B is correct**. A document that sets out an asset owner's investment goals and beliefs for use by a fund manager in understanding the asset owner's needs is called an investment mandate. Using the investment mandate, fund managers develop suitable investment approaches. Investment recommendations are usually developed by analysts to explain why a particular security is suitable for a portfolio.

35. **C is correct**. The approach describes a quantitative basis for adjusting or 'tilting' the exposures to be more climate-sensitive than they otherwise would be.

Glossary

AGM Annual general meeting, a formal gathering of shareholders to conduct official business of a company. The shareholders have the right to make some decisions about the future of the company, and these meetings are the occasions when those decisions are made. The agendas very much depend on the law of the state or country of the company's incorporation (see also EGM).

Automation Technology by which a process or procedure is performed with minimum human assistance. It is associated with faster production and cheaper labor costs, replacing hard, physical, or monotonous work.

Best-in-class investment Best-in-class investment involves selecting only the companies that overcome a defined ranking hurdle, established using ESG criteria within each sector or industry.

Carbon footprint The annual amount of greenhouse gas emissions, mainly carbon dioxide (CO_2), that result from the activities of an individual or a group of people, especially their use of energy and transport and consumption of goods and services. It is measured as the mass, in kilograms or tons per year, either of carbon dioxide emissions alone or of the carbon dioxide equivalent effect of other greenhouse gas emissions.

CDP CDP (formerly known as the Carbon Disclosure Project) is a non-governmental organization that supports companies, financial institutions, and cities to disclose and manage their environmental impact. It runs a global environmental disclosure system in which nearly 10,000 companies, as well as cities, states, and regions, report on their risks and opportunities on climate change, water security, and deforestation.

Circular economy An economic model based inter alia on sharing, leasing, reuse, repair, refurbishment, and recycling, in an (almost) closed loop, that aims to retain the highest utility and value of products, components, and materials at all times.

Climate change Climate change is defined as a change of climate, directly or indirectly attributed to human activity, that alters the composition of the global atmosphere and that is in addition to natural climate variability observed over comparable time periods.

Climate change adaptation Climate change adaptation is about adapting to a changing climate—involving adjusting to actual or expected future climate events—thereby increasing society's resilience to climate change and reducing vulnerabilities to its harmful effects.

Climate change mitigation Human intervention that involves reducing the sources of greenhouse gas emissions (for example, the burning of fossil fuels for electricity, heat, or transport), slowing down the process, or enhancing the "sink" that stores these gases, such as forests, oceans, and soil.

Climate Disclosure Standards Board (CDSB) The Climate Disclosure Standards Board (CDSB) is an international consortium of business and environmental non-governmental organizations with the mission to create the enabling conditions for material climate change and natural capital information to be integrated into mainstream reporting.

Consumer protection Laws and other forms of government regulation designed to protect the rights of consumers.

Digital disruption The change that occurs when new digital technologies and business models affect the value proposition of existing goods and services.

EGM Extraordinary general meeting, a formal gathering of shareholders to conduct official business of a company. The shareholders have the right to make some decisions about the future of the company, and these meetings are the occasions when those decisions are made. The agendas very much depend on the law of the state or country of the company's incorporation (see also AGM).

Engagement The active process of dialogue with a company where the investor is seeking specific change. Engagement is often a lengthy process involving many iterations of contact with senior representatives of the company.

Environment The sum of all external conditions affecting the life, development, and survival of an organism.

ESG integration The inclusion of ESG considerations within financial analysis and investment decisions. This may be done in various ways, tailored to the investment style and approach of the fund manager.

ESG investing ESG investing is an approach to managing assets where investors explicitly acknowledge the relevance of environmental, social, and governance (ESG) factors in their investment decisions, as well as their own role as owners and creditors, with the long-term return of an investment portfolio in mind. It aims to correctly price social, environmental, and economic risks and opportunities.

Ethical and faith-based investment Ethical (also known as values-driven) and faith-based investment refers to investing in line with certain principles, usually using negative screening to avoid investing in companies whose products and services are deemed morally objectionable by the investor or certain religions, international declarations, conventions, or voluntary agreements.

External social factors Social factors related to how the product impacts society, such as payment of taxes, social media, and tobacco.

Externalities This term refers to situations where the production or consumption of goods and services creates costs or benefits for others that are not reflected in the prices charged for them. In other words, externalities include the consumption, production, and investment decisions of firms (and individuals) that affect people not directly involved in the transactions. Externalities can be either negative or positive.

Forest Stewardship Council (FSC) An international non-profit organization that promotes responsible forest management worldwide.

Global Impact Investing Network (GIIN) The GIIN focuses on reducing barriers to impact investment by building critical infrastructure and developing activities, education, and research that help accelerate the development of a coherent impact investing industry.

Global Reporting Initiative (GRI) The GRI publishes the GRI Standards, which provide guidance on disclosure across environmental, social, and economic factors for all stakeholders, including investors. Used by organizations worldwide, the GRI framework is among the most well known.

Global Sustainable Investment Alliance (GSIA) Many countries have a national forum for responsible investment. The GSIA is an international collaboration of these membership-based sustainable investment organizations. It is a forum itself for advancing ESG investing across all regions and asset classes.

Globalization The process of interaction and integration among people, companies, and governments worldwide. It is marked by the spread of products, information, jobs, and culture across borders.

Green bonds Bonds used in green finance whereby the proceeds are earmarked toward environmental-related products.

Green investment Green investment refers to allocating capital to assets that mitigate climate change, biodiversity loss, resource inefficiency, and other environmental problems.

Greenhouse gases (GHGs) Gases including carbon dioxide (CO_2), water vapor, methane, and nitrous oxide that interact with infrared radiation and, when present in the atmosphere, have the effect of warming the global climate. Without naturally occurring greenhouse gases, the earth's temperature would be several tens of degrees Celsius colder than it is now (and life would not have evolved in its current form).

Human rights Rights inherent to all human beings regardless of race, sex, nationality, ethnicity, language, religion, or any other status. Human rights include the right to life and liberty, freedom from slavery and torture, freedom of opinion and expression, and the right to work and receive an education. Everyone is entitled to these rights without discrimination.

Impact investing Impact investing refers to investments made with the specific intent of generating positive, measurable social and environmental impact alongside a financial return (which differentiates it from philanthropy).

Institutional Investors Group on Climate Change (IIGCC) IIGCC is the European membership body for investor collaboration on climate change. With over 240 members, IIGCC works to support and help define the public policies, investment practices, and corporate behaviors that address the long-term risks and opportunities associated with climate change.

Integrated Reporting Framework (IRF) The IRF, put forward by the IIRC, encourages companies to integrate sustainability into their strategy and risk assessment by integrating it into the traditional annual report. The integrated report aims to make it easier for investors to review such information as part of normal research processes and thus increase the likelihood that sustainability information is material to investment decisions.

Internal social factors Social factors within a company, such as fatalities, employee treatment, gender balance, and pay ratios.

International Corporate Governance Network (ICGN) The ICGN is an investor-led organization established in 1995 to promote effective standards of corporate governance and investor stewardship to advance efficient markets.

International Integrated Reporting Council (IIRC) An organization encouraging companies to produce integrated reports, which unite financial and ESG considerations in a single document.

International Sustainability Standards Board (ISSB) Formed in November 2021, the ISSB is one of IFRS Foundation's two standard-setting boards (the other being the IASB, which develops IFRS financial reporting standards). ISSB develops—in the public interest—a global baseline of high-quality sustainability disclosure standards to meet investors' information needs. ISSB standards are embedded in SASB's standards and its industry-based approach.

Investment managers refers to people or organizations that invest on behalf of their clients under an investment mandate that those clients have agreed to.

Investors is a very generic term that refers to parties—both retail investors and institutional investors—that hold a financial stake in an asset. Investors can invest in any type of asset class, be it debt or equity, and an investor can be an asset owner or an asset manager.

Living wage A wage that is sufficient to cover workers' basic living expenses, such as food, clothing, housing, healthcare, and education.

Materiality A core consideration in ESG investing; a factor is material if it will drive long-term financial value in a particular business. Not every ESG factor is material at every company all the time. A core challenge for ESG investors is to identify the factors that are material to a business at a particular time.

Principles for Responsible Investment (PRI) The PRI comprises an international network of investors—signatories—working together toward a common goal to understand the implications of ESG considerations for investment and ownership decisions and practices.

Product liability The legal responsibility imposed on a business for the manufacturing or selling of defective goods.

Responsible investment Responsible investment is a strategy and practice to incorporate ESG factors into investment decisions and active ownership. It considers both how ESG factors might influence the risk-adjusted return of an asset and the stability of an economy and how investment in and engagement with assets and investees can impact society and the environment.

Risk mitigation Risk mitigation describes a strategy or effort to manage and minimize a portfolio's exposure to ESG risks. Risk mitigation extends from embedding robust review processes into risk management to actively minimizing the portfolio's exposure to ESG risks. These risks are typically tail or long-term risks—for instance, in carbon-heavy or stranded assets.

Roundtable on Sustainable Palm Oil (RSPO) An international non-profit organization that promotes the production and use of sustainable palm oil and the end of deforestation and social conflict associated with palm oil production.

Scope 1, 2, and 3 emissions A categorization of the sources of greenhouse gas emissions from companies. Direct emissions from a company's core operations are Scope 1. Indirect emissions from purchased energy are Scope 2. Indirect emissions from the broader value chain (e.g., those produced by suppliers and customers) are Scope 3.

Shareholder engagement Shareholder engagement reflects active ownership by investors in which the investor seeks to influence a corporation's decisions on ESG matters, either through dialogue with corporate officers or votes at a shareholder assembly (in the case of equity).

Shareholder Rights Directive (SRD) An EU law implemented in June 2019 into the local laws of each member country. It sets standards for the treatment of shareholders by EU companies. The second Shareholder Rights Directive (often abbreviated as SRD II) relates more to shareholder responsibilities than rights and covers mandates and stewardship obligations.

Shareholders hold a direct equity position in a firm, and both individual persons and financial institutions can be shareholders. The term comes from the individual or investment firm literally having a share of the company. It is most commonly used when talking about the rights and responsibilities that come with being an "owner" of a company, such as stewardship, voting, and engagement. This differentiates it from a situation where an individual or an investment firm lends money or invests in a bond (in other words, they are not an equityholder of a company). Because bond investors do not have a share and are not owners of a company, they cannot vote. Nonetheless, expectations around engagement are increasing for those who invest in loans and bonds as well, making the difference between the two terms more subtle.

Social investment Social investment refers to allocating capital to assets that address social challenges.

Social megatrends Long-term social changes that affect governments, societies, and economies permanently over a long period of time, such as increased globalization; changes in work, family, and leisure time; and the rise of automation and artificial intelligence (AI) in manufacturing and service sectors.

Socially responsible investment (SRI) One of the subsets of ESG investing; generally used as a catch-all term for investments made with a conscious desire for lower exposure to assets deemed to be less sustainable or responsible and/or increased exposure to those displaying greater sustainability or responsibility.

Stewardship The broad term for an investor operating as a good long-term owner of assets, standing in the shoes of the underlying clients to ensure that value is added or preserved over time.

Strategic asset allocation (SAA) Strategic asset allocation is an investment strategy premised on long-term asset allocation. This strategy rebalances its portfolio only when the asset mix represents significant deviation from the

Sustainability Accounting Standards Board (SASB) The SASB issues standards that are focused on the key material sustainability issues that affect 70-plus industry categories. These, along with the SASB materiality maps, are particularly helpful for investors determining what is material for reporting, and aids more standardized benchmarking.

Sustainability-linked bonds (SLBs) Bonds used to finance a broad range of sustainability-related projects. Bond proceeds are not specifically ring-fenced but, rather, have such features as the coupon rate linked to the achievement of issuer-wide sustainability targets or goals.

Sustainable Development Goals (SDGs) A set of 17 interconnected global goals set in 2015 by the UN General Assembly (UNGA), succeeding the Millennium Development goals. The SDGs seek to address key global challenges, including those related to poverty, inequality, climate change, environmental degradation, peace, and justice.

Sustainable investment Sustainable investment refers to the selection of assets that contribute in some way to a sustainable economy—that is, an asset that minimizes natural and social resource depletion. It is a broad term that may be used for the consideration of typical ESG issues and may include best-in-class. It can also include ESG integration, which considers how ESG issues impact a security's risk and return profile.

Task Force on Climate-Related Financial Disclosures (TCFD) The Financial Stability Board's TCFD is a market-driven initiative developed to establish and recommend a general framework for identifying, assessing, and reporting climate-related financial disclosure. TCFD focuses on four key areas: (1) Governance: the organization's governance around climate-related risk and opportunities; (2) Strategy: the actual and potential impacts of climate-related risk and opportunities on the organization's businesses, strategy, and financial planning; (3) Risk management: the processes used by the organization to identify, assess, and manage climate-related risks; (4) Metrics and targets: the metrics and targets used to assess and manage relevant climate-related risks and opportunities.

Thematic investment refers to selecting companies that fall under a sustainability-related theme, such as clean technology, sustainable agriculture, health care, or climate change mitigation.

Transition risk Transition risk relates to risks that result from changes in climate and energy policies, a shift to low-carbon technologies, and liability issues.

Triple bottom line The triple bottom line (TBL or 3BL) is an accounting framework with three parts: social, environmental (or ecological), and financial (people, planet, and profit).

United Nations Environment Programme Finance Initiative (UNEP FI) UNEP FI is a partnership between UNEP and the global financial sector to mobilize private sector finance for sustainable development.

United Nations Framework Convention on Climate Change (UNFCCC) An international treaty adopted in 1992 to stabilize greenhouse gas emissions in the atmosphere that would prevent dangerous man-made interference with the climate system. The UNFCCC is also the name of the UN Secretariat, based in Bonn, Germany, that has the responsibility to support the operation of the treaty.

United Nations Global Compact (UNGC) Launched in 2000, the UNGC is a collaboration between leading companies and the United Nations. With over 8,000 corporate signatories globally, signatories agree to adhere to the 10 principles, derived from broader global standards, such as the Universal Declaration of Human Rights and the International Labour Organization's Declaration on Fundamental Principles and Rights at Work. The UNGC has provided investors with a helpful set of principles to assess and engage with companies, as well as directly aided companies in becoming more sustainable.

Made in the USA
Las Vegas, NV
11 April 2025

20783745R00328